The IFPUG Guide
to IT and Software Measurement

The **IFPUG** Guide
to IT and Software Measurement

Edited by IFPUG

CRC Press
Taylor & Francis Group
Boca Raton London New York

CRC Press is an imprint of the
Taylor & Francis Group, an **informa** business

AN AUERBACH BOOK

CRC Press
Taylor & Francis Group
6000 Broken Sound Parkway NW, Suite 300
Boca Raton, FL 33487-2742

First issued in paperback 2019

© 2012 by Taylor & Francis Group, LLC
CRC Press is an imprint of Taylor & Francis Group, an Informa business

No claim to original U.S. Government works

ISBN-13: 978-1-4398-6930-7 (hbk)
ISBN-13: 978-0-367-38147-9 (pbk)

Visit the Taylor & Francis Web site at
http://www.taylorandfrancis.com

and the CRC Press Web site at
http://www.crcpress.com

Contents

SECTION III ESTIMATION: INTRODUCTION
LUIGI BUGLIONE

SECTION IV FUNCTION POINTS: INTRODUCTION
SIVASUBRAMANYAM BALASUBRAMANYAM

SECTION V MEASUREMENT PROGRAMS: INTRODUCTION
DAWN COLEY

Foreword

Perhaps we are too hard on ourselves in the software industry. When I attend conferences, I constantly hear tales of woe about how poorly we perform; how we fail to deliver systems on time, or on budget, or even at all. Indeed, I have prefaced my own presentations with depressing reports of our failings to add strength to my message that we should learn from history. We mostly concentrate on the negatives and worry ourselves with what has to be done to fix them.

Then something positive happens. A book like this is created, and as I read down the list of 52 contributors, I am amazed and heartened that so many well-qualified, experienced doyens of the industry, from 13 countries, are giving their time and working selflessly to improve its performance. But the contributors only did part of the work; Janet Russac and her colleagues at IFPUG climbed a mountain to attract the contributors and then compiled and edited what it is you hold in your hand.

If the software industry wants to be embraced as an engineering discipline, then it must engage engineering practices and deliver acceptable outputs that provide its customers with the expected returns on their investments. Good engineers measure things. Software engineers must do likewise and employ measurement and metrics. Why is a large part of our industry still loath to do this? Without statistical evidence, we cannot make claims of the use of best practices. We must measure, we must apply appropriate and useful metrics, we must collect and analyze what we measure, and we must learn from the results of that analysis. This book is an important contributor to the promotion and application of software measurement.

When Allan Albrecht developed the idea of Function Points in the late 1970s, he probably did not envisage their use across the world thirty-plus years later. Sadly, we cannot ask him, and the world is a sadder place for his passing. But the International Function Point Users Group (IFPUG), formed to administer and grow what he started, continues to find new ways to educate people about the importance and use of software measurement, metrics, and management. This book, IFPUG's second, is a vital component in their education offensive.

Although the themes running through the chapters in this book are measurement and metrics, the application of these themes is to the practical issues faced by project managers, CIOs, sales people, testers, QA personnel, outsourcers, bid evaluators, and IT managers. This volume should be a close-at-hand reference for all these people.

Peter R Hill, CEO
International Software Benchmarking Standards Group (ISBSG) Limited

Introduction

In 2002, as Vice Chair of the Management Reporting Committee (MRC) of the International Function Point Users Group (IFPUG), I had the very special and unique opportunity to help bring about the publication of IFPUG's first book, *IT Measurement: Practical Advice from the Experts* (Addison-Wesley, April 2002). The book, a compilation of chapters from 43 experts as well as practitioners and service providers in the field of IT measurement, was a huge success. Covering a range of topics including benchmarking, estimation, outsourcing, balanced scorecards, and many other areas of interest, there was something for everyone involved or interested in managing information technology projects.

Ten years later, that first book is still selling and now, as an IFPUG board member and Director of Applied Programs as liaison to the MRC, I have had the privilege of spearheading IFPUG's second book, *The IFPUG Guide to IT and Software Measurement*. In the last ten years, the IT world has continued to expand and rapidly change. We now hear terms like agile development and cloud computing, topics that were not around or at least not prevalent ten years ago. Estimation, benchmarking and such are still as noteworthy as ever, and as in all other IT areas, continually evolving. Hence, we felt the need for this second book that will cover new topics but also give fresh perspectives on some of the topics covered in the first book.

We were fortunate to have many of the authors who contributed to the first book return to contribute to this second book, as well as having several new authors. As with the first book, the authors receive no compensation other than the opportunity to include their biography and, if desired, a company profile. They have contributed their time, talents, and knowledge for the betterment of the IT industry as a whole. We are very grateful to them.

I personally would like to thank the members of the MRC. Their dedication, hard work, and tireless efforts made this second book possible. As a published author, I know how difficult it is to get a book from the idea stage to a printed work. When you are a volunteer group, working with over 40 international authors and a deadline, it is a monumental task. These men and women spent hundreds of hours of personal time over the last two years to produce this book, with no compensation other than a thank you for a job well done. On behalf of IFPUG and the IT community, thanks to the following committee members:

Heidi Malkiewicz, Committee Chair
Dawn Coley, Vice Chair
Pierre Almén
Sivasubramanyam Balasubramanyam
Luigi Buglione

I would also like to offer special thanks to Bonnie Brown, Joe Schofield, and Kriste Lawrence. All three are IFPUG members who helped in the editing of this book. Your contributions and support were invaluable.

And last, a thanks to the IFPUG community as a whole, from the board of directors who approved this project to individual members who contributed to some of the writings in the book to all of the corporations and individuals who support IFPUG on a daily basis.

The International Function Point Users' Group (IFPUG) is a non-profit, member-governed organization. The mission of IFPUG is to be a recognized leader in promoting and encouraging the effective management of application software development and maintenance activities through the use of Function Point Analysis (FPA) and other software measurement techniques. IFPUG endorses FPA as its standard methodology for software sizing. In support of this, IFPUG maintains the Function Point Counting Practices Manual, the recognized industry standard for FPA. In 2011, the Assessment Practices Manual (APM) was released by IFPUG. The APM provides a quantifiable measure for the non-functional size of software development by means of documented guidance, definitions, and practices about non-functional software features and related sizing criteria. The chapter within this book titled "Software Non-functional Assessment Process (SNAP)" introduces the concept.

IFPUG also provides a forum for networking and information exchange that promotes and encourages the use of software product and process metrics. IFPUG members benefit from a variety of services, including the following:

- Annual conference: IFPUG's annual conference, International Software Measurement and Analysis (ISMA) Conference, brings together leading industry experts, practitioners, and technology vendors for a two-day exchange of experiences and presentations on the latest happenings in the field of software metrics. The Vendor Showcase provides conference attendees the opportunity to compare state-of-the-art products and services in support of the IT measurement discipline.
- Educational seminars and workshops: In addition to its conferences, IFPUG offers a variety of training opportunities designed to complement sound software management practices. Workshops cover a range of topics including

Function Point counting practices, project management techniques, and process improvement strategies. Workshops are held in September immediately preceding the annual conference.

■ Professional certification: Through its Certified Function Point Specialist (CFPS) program, IFPUG offers professional certification for practitioners of FPA. The certification program also covers Function Point training materials and software tools designed to perform FPA tasks.

■ Working committees and task groups: IFPUG working committees and task groups support the advancement of software metrics disciplines and are at the center of the activities that contribute value to an IFPUG Member. They create and/or manage the many useful materials that are available to members. They participate in selected international efforts to ensure that Function Points are fully considered by such bodies and to bring useful information and materials to IFPUG members. They offer opportunities to network with other members about subjects of mutual interest, which can aid both professional and personal growth. They provide a way to contribute to the industry that supports us.

■ Data collection, analysis, and dissemination: IFPUG supports the collection, analysis and dissemination of data about software projects through several activities. In cooperation with other metrics organizations from around the world, IFPUG participates as a lead member in the International Software Benchmarking Standards Group Ltd. (ISBSG). Through this effort, IFPUG is supporting the collection and maintenance of three independent databases of project/application information from around the world, and the preparation and dissemination of reports and electronic media containing information about the projects/applications in the databases. Also, through industry and academic relationships, IFPUG sponsors and supports projects for applied research on software measurement issues and conducts studies in support of advancing the Function Point counting standards.

■ Industry publications: IFPUG produces and maintains a suite of timely publications on software measurement standards and guidelines. *MetricViews*, the official newsletter of IFPUG, is a leading source of current information, ideas, and success stories in the field of software measurement.

For further information on IFPUG, please visit www.ifpug.org.

Janet Harris Russac, CFPS, CSMS
IFPUG Director of Applied Programs

INSIGHTS FROM THE EXPERTS

INTRODUCTION

Janet Russac

When embarking on the journey of producing a book that would become known as *The IFPUG Guide to IT and Software Measurement* and thinking about potential contributors, a couple of names immediately came to mind: Capers Jones and David Garmus. These two men not only are considered experts in the field of Function Point Analysis but also in software measurement as a whole. Between them, they have contributed enormously to both fields, and the International Function Point Users Group (IFPUG) and software measurement community have been the benefactors of their work and knowledge.

Capers Jones is currently the president of Capers Jones & Associates LLC and is the founder and former chair of Software Productivity Research LLC (SPR) holding the title of Chief Scientist Emeritus at SPR. Capers is a well-known author and international public speaker. In his chapter of this book, Capers proposes a suite of 13 functional metrics for economic analysis.

Noting that Function Point metrics are the most accurate and effective metrics yet developed for performing software economic studies, quality studies, and value analysis, he proposes that the logic of Function Point metrics should be applied to a linked suite of similar metrics that can size other business and technical topics. This would enable large-scale economic analysis of complex systems that involve software, data, hardware, websites, and other business topics that need concurrent sizing, planning, estimating, and economic analysis.

David Garmus is the cofounder of the David Consulting Group and he serves as a Past President of IFPUG, a past member of the IFPUG Counting Practices

Committee and a current member of the Software Non-functional Assessment Process (SNAP) Working Group. David is an acknowledged authority in the sizing, measurement, and estimation of software application development and maintenance, and he is the author of many books and a highly sought-after speaker. In his chapter, "A Guide to Sizing and Estimating Projects Using International Function Point Users Group Function Points," David discusses the three aspects of size, complexity, and risk factors, which when factored together will result in an accurate estimate. He notes that the software problem domain must be accurately assessed for its size and complexity and that experience tells us that at the point in time when we need an initial estimate (early in the system's life cycle), we cannot presume to have all the necessary information at our disposal. David then goes on to explain the IFPUG Function Point methodology and its value to the estimating process. David also discusses IFPUG's Framework for Non-Functional Sizing (named SNAP), a realistic and practical methodology for establishing a link between non-functional size and the effort to provide the non-functional requirements.

Chapter 1

A Proposed Suite of Thirteen Functional Metrics for Economic Analysis

Capers Jones

Contents

Economic Analysis Using a Suite of Functional Metrics

Introduction

From their first publication in 1978, Function Point metrics have proven their value for software application sizing, cost estimation, quality predictions, benchmarks, and overall economic studies.

The International Function Point Users Group (IFPUG) has become the largest software measurement association in the world. There are also other Function Point variants that are growing rapidly too, including COSMIC Function Points, NESMA Function Points, FISMA Function Points, and a number of others.

Yet software does not exist in a vacuum. There are many related business topics that lack effective size metrics. One critical example is that of the data used by software applications.

Most large companies own more data than they do software. The costs of acquiring data and maintaining it are at least as high as software development and maintenance costs. Data migration from legacy applications to new applications can take more than three calendar years. Data quality is suspected to be worse than software quality, but no one really knows because there is no effective size metric for quantifying database volumes or measuring data quality.

It would seem to be useful to apply the logic of Function Point metrics to other critical business topics and create an integrated suite of functional metrics that could encompass not only software, but the related areas of data, websites, hardware devices, and also risk and value.

Software and online data are among the most widely utilized commodities in human history. If you consider the total usage of various commodities, the approximate global rank in terms of overall usage would be:

1. Water
2. Salt
3. Rice
4. Wheat
5. Bread
6. Corn
7. Fish
8. Clothing
9. Shoes

10. Software
11. Online data
12. Alcoholic beverages
13. Electricity
14. Gasoline and oil
15. Aluminum

(The sources of data for this table include a number of websites and government tables. The importance is not actual rankings, but the fact that software and online data in 2011 are used so widely that they can be included in the list.)

The expansion of software (and online data) to join the world's most widely used commodities means that there is an urgent need for better metrics and better economic analysis.

Because of the widespread deployment of software and the millions of software applications already developed or to be developed in the future, software economic studies are among the most critical of any form of business analysis. Unfortunately, lack of an integrated suite of metrics makes software economic analysis extremely difficult.

This article proposes a suite of related metrics that are based on the logic of Function Points, but expanding that logic to other business and technical areas. The metrics are hypothetical and additional research would be needed to actually develop such a metrics suite.

Potential Expansion of Functional Metrics to Other Topics

In spite of the considerable success of Function Point metrics in improving software quality and economic research, there are a number of important topics that still cannot be measured well or even measured at all in some cases. Here are some areas where there is a need for related metrics within a broad family of functional metrics:

1. Application Function Point metrics
2. Component feature point metrics
3. Hardware Function Point metrics
4. COTS application point metrics
5. Micro Function Point metrics
6. Data point metrics
7. Website point metrics
8. Software usage point metrics
9. Service point metrics

10. Risk point metrics
11. Value point metrics
12. Security point metrics
13. Configuration point metrics (developed by IBM)

This combination of a related family of functional metrics would expand the ability to perform economic studies of modern businesses and government operations that use software, websites, data, and other business artifacts at the same time for the same ultimate goals. Let us now consider each of these metrics in turn.

The Need for Application Function Point Metrics

From their first external publication outside of IBM in 1978, Function Point metrics have become the de facto standard for quantifying software applications. As of 2011, the usage of Function Points encompasses international benchmark studies, outsource agreements, economic analysis, quality analysis, and many other important business topics. The governments of South Korea and Brazil now require Function Point metrics for software contracts. The major topics found within Function Points as originally defined by Allan Albrecht include:

- Inputs
- Outputs
- Inquiries
- Logical files
- Interfaces
- Complexity adjustments

There are a number of tools available for counting Function Points, but human judgment is also needed. Both IFPUG and the other major Function Point user groups provide training and also examinations that lead to the position of "Certified Function Point Analysts."

Function Points are now the most widely used metric for quantifying software application size, for quantifying productivity and quality, and for quantifying application development costs. There is only sparse data on application maintenance costs, but that situation is improving. The International Software Benchmark Standards Group (ISBSG) now includes software maintenance data. Several companies such as the Software Improvement Group (SIG), Relativity Technologies, CAST Software, Optimyth, and Computer Aid measure and evaluate maintainability.

It should be noted that software is treated as a taxable asset by the Internal Revenue Service (IRS) in the United States and by most other international tax organizations. Function Point metrics are now widely used in determining the taxable value of software when companies are bought or sold.

The Need for Component Feature Point Metrics

Although Function Points are the dominant metric for software applications, in today's world of 2011, applications are often created from libraries of reusable components, objects, and other existing software segments. While some of these may have been counted via normal Function Point Analysis, most are of unknown size.

There is a need to extend normal Function Point Analysis down at least one level to be able to size reusable modules, objects, and the contents of class libraries. To avoid confusion with the term Function Points, which normally apply to entire applications, it might be better to use a different term such as "component feature points."

Component feature points:

- Inputs
- Outputs
- Inquiries
- Logical files
- Interfaces
- Complexity adjustments

Examples of the kinds of specific features that might be sized using component feature points would include, but not be limited to:

1. Input validation	(25 to 50 component feature points)
2. Output formatting	(10 to 30 component feature points)
3. Query processing	(3 to 15 component feature points)
4. Currency exchange rate calculation	(5 to 15 component feature points)
5. Inflation rate calculation	(5 to 10 component feature points)
6. Compound interest calculation	(5 to 25 component feature points)
7. Sensor-based input monitoring	(10 to 35 component feature points)
8. Earned-value calculations	(30 to 75 component feature points)
9. Internal rate of return (IRR)	(5 to 15 component feature points)
10. Accounting rate of return (ARR)	(5 to 15 component feature points)

The basic idea is to assemble a taxonomy of standard components that are likely to be acquired from reusable sources rather than custom developed. In other words, component feature points shift the logic of functional analysis from the external applications themselves to the inner structure and anatomy of applications.

As of 2011, the total number of possible reusable components is unknown, but probably is in the range of about 500–2500. There is also a lack of a standard taxonomy for identifying the specific features of software components. These are problems that need additional research.

The best way to develop an effective taxonomy of application features would probably be a forensic analysis of a sample of current software applications, with the intent of establishing a solid taxonomy of specific features including those inserted from reusable materials.

Component feature points would adhere to the same general counting rules as standard Function Points, but would be aimed at individual modules and features that are intended to be reused in multiple applications. Because some of the smaller components may be below the boundary line for normal Function Point Analyses, see the section on "Micro Function Points" later in this paper.

The Need for Hardware Function Point Metrics

The U.S. Navy, the U.S. Air Force, the U.S. Army, and the other military services have a significant number of complex projects that involve hardware, software, and microcode. Several years ago, the Navy posed an interesting question: "Is it possible to develop a metric like Function Points for hardware projects so that we can do integrated cost analysis across the hardware/software barrier?"

In addition to military equipment there are thousands of products that feature embedded software: medical devices, smart phones, GPS units, cochlear implants, hearing aids, pacemakers, MRI devices, automobile antilock brakes, aircraft control systems, and countless others. All of these hybrid devices require sizing and estimating both the software and hardware components at the same time.

The ability to perform integrated sizing, cost, and quality studies that could deal with software, hardware, databases, and human service and support activities would be a notable advance indeed. A hypothetical engineering point metric might include the following factors.

Hardware Function Points:

- Inputs
- Outputs
- Constraints
- Innovations
- Algorithms
- Subcomponents

Integrated cost estimates across the hardware/software boundary would be very welcome in many manufacturing and military domains. These hardware Function Points would be utilized for embedded applications such as medical devices, digital cameras, and smart appliances. They would also be used for weapons systems and avionics packages. They would also be used for all complex devices such as automobile engines that use software and hardware concurrently. Hardware Function Points would be a useful addition to an overall metrics suite.

The Need for COTS Function Point Metrics

Many small corporations and some large ones buy or acquire more software than they build. The generic name for packaged applications is "commercial off-the-shelf software," which is usually abbreviated to COTS.

COTS packages could be sized using conventional Function Point Analysis if vendors wished to do this, but most do not. As of 2011, it is technically possible to size COTS packages using pattern matching. The same is true for sizing open-source applications. The open-source business sector is growing rapidly, and many open-source applications are now included in corporate portfolios.

The concept of pattern matching uses a formal taxonomy of types of applications that includes the class of the application (internal or external), the type (embedded software, information technology, systems or middleware, etc.), and several other parameters. An application to be sized is placed on the taxonomy. Applications that have the same "pattern" on the taxonomy are usually of almost the same size in Function Points. The pattern-matching approach uses a combination of a standard taxonomy and mathematical algorithms to provide a synthetic Function Point total, based on historical applications whose sizes already exist. While normal Function Points are in the public domain, the pattern-matching approach is covered by a patent application. Some of the other metrics in this paper may also include patentable algorithms.

The pattern-matching approach substitutes historical data for manual counting, and to be effective the patterns must be based on a formal taxonomy. Pattern matching applies some of the principles of biological classification to software classification.

A study performed by the author of the corporate portfolio of a major Fortune 500 corporation noted that the company owned software in the following volumes:

Application Types	Ownership
Information systems	1360
COTS packages	1190
Systems software	850
Embedded applications	510
Tools (software development)	340
Manufacturing and robotics	310
End user developed	200

Application Types	Ownership
Open source	115
SaaS applications	5
Total	4880

As can be seen, COTS packages ranked number two in the corporation's overall portfolio and comprised 24.4% of the total portfolio. This is far too important a topic to be excluded from sizing and economic analysis. For one thing, effective "make or buy" analysis or determining whether to build software or acquire software packages needs the sizes of both the COTS packages and the internal packages to ensure that features sets are comparable. In fact, both Function Points and component feature points would be valuable for COTS analysis.

Note that the pattern-matching method can also size "Software as a Service" or SaaS applications such as Google Docs. Essentially any software application can be sized using this method so long as it can be placed on the basic taxonomy of application types. Of course, the complexity questions will have to be approximated by the person using the sizing method, but most can be assumed to center on "average" values.

Examples of various COTS, SaaS, and open-source applications sized via pattern matching include:

Application	Size in Function Points
SAP	296,704
Windows 7	165,245
Office 2010	93,498
Skype	21,202
Apple iPhone	19,366
Linux	17,505
Google Docs	47,668
Google search engine	18,640
GPS navigation	1,508
Laser printer driver	1,248
Cochlear implant	1,041
Atomic watch	933

Right now, COTS packages and SaaS packages (and most open-source applications) are outside the boundaries of normal Function Point metrics primarily because the essential inputs for Function Point Analysis are not provided by the vendors.

It would be useful to include COTS packages in economic studies if vendors published the Function Point sizes of commercial software applications. This is unlikely to happen in the near future. A COTS, SaaS, and open-source pattern-matching metric might include the following factors:

- Taxonomy
- Scope
- Class
- Type
- Problem complexity
- Code complexity
- Data complexity

The inclusion of COTS points is desirable for dealing with "make or buy" decisions in which possible in-house development of software is contrasted with possible acquisition of a commercial package.

In today's world, many large and important applications are combinations of custom code, COTS packages, open-source packages, reusable components, and objects. There is a strong business need to be able to size these hybrid applications.

There is also a strong business need to be able to size 100% of the contents of corporate portfolios, and almost 50% of the contents of portfolios are in the form of COTS packages, open-source packages, SaaS services, and other kinds of applications whose developers have not commissioned normal Function Point Analysis.

The Need for Micro Function Point Metrics

A surprising amount of software work takes place in the form of very small enhancements and bug repairs that are below about 15 Function Points in size. In fact, almost 20% of the total effort devoted to software enhancements and about 90% of the effort devoted to software bug repairs deal with small segments below 15 Function Points in size.

The original Function Point metric had mathematical limits associated with the complexity adjustment factors that made small applications difficult to size. Also, the large volume of small enhancements and the even larger volume of software defect repairs would be time consuming and expensive for normal Function Point Analysis.

The same method of pattern matching can easily be applied to small updates and bug repairs, and this form of sizing takes only a few minutes.

There are three possibilities for micro Function Points: (1) normal Function Point Analysis with changes to eliminate the lower boundaries of adjustment factors; (2) pattern matching; and (3) backfiring or mathematical conversion from counts of logical code statements.

1. Micro Function Points using normal counts
   Inputs
   Outputs
   Inquiries
   Logical files
   Interfaces
   Revised complexity adjustments
2. Micro Function Points using pattern matching
   Taxonomy
   Scope
   Class
   Type
   Problem complexity
   Code complexity
   Data complexity
3. Backfiring
   Basic assembly = 320 statements per Function Point
   C = 128 statements per Function Point
   (2,600 other languages with varying ratios)

Backfiring or mathematical conversion from logical code statements is as old as Function Point Analysis. The first backfire results were published by Allan Albrecht in the 1970s based on simultaneous measurements of logical code statements and Function Points within IBM.

Surprisingly, none of the Function Point organizations have ever analyzed backfire data. Backfiring is not as accurate as normal Function Point Analysis due to variations in programming styles, but it remains a popular method due to the high speed and low cost of backfiring compared to normal Function Point Analysis.

There are published tables of ratios between logical code statements and Function Points available for about 800 programming languages. In fact, the number of companies and projects that use backfiring circa 2011 is probably larger than the number of companies that use normal Function Point Analysis.

As an example of why micro Function Points are needed, a typical software bug report when examined in situ in the software itself is usually between about 0.1 and 4.0 Function Points in size—much too small for normal Function Point Analysis.

Individually each of these bugs might be ignored, but large systems such as Windows 7 or SAP can receive more than 50,000 bug reports per year. Thus, the total volume of these tiny objects can top 100,000 Function Points and the costs associated with processing them can top $50,000,000 per year. There is a definite need for a rapid and inexpensive method for including thousands of small changes into overall software cost and economic analyses.

Since normal Function Point Analysis tends to operate at a rate of about 400 Function Points per day or 50 Function Points per hour, counting a typical small enhancement of 10 Function Points would require perhaps 12 minutes.

The pattern-matching method operates more or less at a fixed speed of about 1.5 minutes per size calculation, regardless of whether an enterprise resource planning (ERP) package of 300,000 Function Points or an enhancement of 10 Function Points is being sized. Therefore, pattern matching would take about 1.5 minutes.

What would probably be a suitable solution would be to size a statistically valid sample of several hundred small bug repairs and small enhancements, and then simply use those values for sizing purposes. For example, if an analysis of 1000 bugs finds the mean average size to be 0.75 Function Points, then that value might be used for including small repairs in overall economic studies.

The Need for Data Point Metrics

In addition to software, companies own huge and growing volumes of data and information. As topics such as repositories, data warehouses, data quality, data mining, and online analytical processing (OLAP) become more common, it is obvious that there are no good metrics for sizing the volumes of information that companies own. Neither are there good metrics for exploring data quality, the costs of creating data, migrating data, or eventually retiring aging legacy data.

A metric similar to Function Points in structure but aimed at data and information rather than software would be a valuable addition to the software domain. A hypothetical data point metric might include the following factors:

- Logical files
- Entities
- Relationships
- Attributes
- Inquiries
- Interfaces

Surprisingly, database and data warehouse vendors have performed no research on data metrics. Each year more and more data is collected and stored, but there are no economic studies of data costs, data quality, data life expectancy, and other important business topics involving data.

If you look at the entire portfolio of a major corporation such as a large bank, they probably own about 3,000 software applications with an aggregate size of perhaps 7,500,000 Function Points. But the volume of data owned by the same bank would probably be 50,000,000 data points if there were an effective data point metric in existence.

It is a known fact that the average number of software defects released to customers is about 0.75 per Function Point. No one knows the average number of data errors, but from analysis of data problems within several large companies, it is probable that data errors in currently active databases approach 2.5 defects per "data point" or almost three times as many errors as software itself.

There is a very strong economic need to include data acquisition costs, data repair costs, and data quality in corporate financial analyses. The data point metric would probably be as useful and as widely utilized as the Function Point metric itself. Lack of quantification of data size, data acquisition costs, data migration costs, and data quality are critical gaps in corporate asset economic analysis. A data point is important enough so that it might well be protected by a patent.

Data is already a marketable product and hundreds of companies sell data in the form of mailing lists, financial data, tax information, and the like. If data is treated as a taxable asset by the IRS, then the need for a data point metric will be critical for tax calculations and for use in determining the asset value of data when companies are bought or sold.

Since the theft of valuable data is now one of the most common crimes in the world, an effective data point metric could also be used in ascertaining the value of lost or stolen data.

The Need for Website Point Metrics

In today's business world of 2011, every significant company has a website, and an ever-growing amount of business is transacted using these websites.

While Function Points can handle the software that lies behind the surface of websites, Function Points do not deal with website content in the forms of graphical images, animation, and other surface features. There is a strong business need to develop "website points" that would be able to show website development costs, maintenance costs, and website quality.

Some of the topics that would be included in "website points" are the following:

- Transactions
- Inquiries
- Images
- Text
- Audio
- Animation

An examination of any of today's large and complex websites such as Amazon, Google, state governments, and even small companies immediately demonstrates that sizing and quantification are needed for many more topics than just the software that controls these websites.

From a rudimentary analysis of website economics, it appears that the cost of the content of websites exceeds the cost of the software controlling the website by somewhere between 10 to 1 and 100 to 1. Massive websites such as Amazon are at the high end of this spectrum. But the essential point is that websites need formal sizing methods and reliable economic methods.

The software that controls the Amazon website is probably about 18,000 Function Points in size. But the total web content displayed on the Amazon site would probably top 25,000,000 website points if such a metric existed.

The Need for Software Usage Point Metrics

Function Point metrics in all of their various flavors have been used primarily to measure software development. But these same metrics can also be used to measure software usage and consumption.

In order to come to grips with software usage patterns, some additional information is needed:

- Is the software used by knowledge workers such as physicians and lawyers?
- Is the software used for business transactions such as sales?
- Is the software used to control physical devices such as navigational instruments?
- Is the software used to control military weapons systems?

Table 1.1 illustrates the approximate usage patterns noted for 30 different occupation groups in 2010.

Software usage points are identical to normal Function Points, except that they are aimed at consumption of software rather than production of software. Software usage patterns play a major role in quantifying the value of many software applications. Software usage can be calculated using either normal Function Point Analysis or pattern matching.

Usage points using normal Function Point counts:

- Inputs
- Outputs
- Inquiries
- Logical files
- Interfaces
- Revised complexity adjustments
- Knowledge usage
- Operational usage
- Transactional usage
- Indirect usage (in embedded devices)

Usage points using pattern matching:

- Taxonomy
- Scope
- Class

Table 1.1 Daily Software Usage by 30 Occupation Groups (Size Expressed in Terms of IFPUG Function Points, Version 4.2)

	Occupation Groups	Size in Function Points	Number of Packages	Hours Used per Day	Value to Users
1	NSA analysts	7,500,000	60	24.00	10.00
2	Military planners	5,000,000	50	7.50	9.00
3	Astronaut (Space Shuttle)	3,750,000	50	24.00	10.00
4	Physicians	3,500,000	25	3.00	9.00
5	Ship captains (naval)	2,500,000	60	24.00	8.00
6	Aircraft pilots (military)	2,000,000	50	24.00	10.00
7	FBI agents	1,250,000	15	3.00	7.00
8	Ship captains (civilian)	1,000,000	35	24.00	7.00
9	Biotech researchers	1,000,000	20	4.50	6.00
10	Airline pilots (civilian)	750,000	25	12.00	7.00
11	Movie special effects engineer	750,000	15	6.00	9.00
12	Air-traffic controllers	550,000	5	24.00	9.00
13	Attorneys	325,000	12	2.50	5.00
14	Combat officers	250,000	12	10.00	6.00

15	Accountants	175,000	10	3.00	4.00
16	Pharmacists	150,000	6	3.50	4.00
17	U.S. Congress staff	125,000	15	6.00	4.00
18	Electrical engineers	100,000	25	2.50	5.00
19	Combat troops	75,000	7	18.00	6.00
20	Software engineers	50,000	20	6.50	8.00
21	Police officers	50,000	6	8.00	4.00
22	Corporate officers	50,000	10	1.50	3.00
23	Stock brokers	50,000	15	10.00	5.00
24	Project managers	35,000	15	2.00	5.00
25	IRS tax agents	35,000	12	8.00	6.00
26	Civil engineers	25,000	10	2.00	6.00
27	Airline travel reservations	20,000	3	12.00	9.00
28	Railroad routing and control	15,000	3	24.00	9.00
29	Customer support (software)	10,000	3	8.00	4.00
30	Supermarket clerks	3,000	2	7.00	4.00
	Averages	1,036,433	20	10.88	6.60

■ Type
■ Problem complexity
■ Code complexity
■ Data complexity
■ Knowledge usage
■ Operational usage
■ Transactional usage
■ Indirect usage (in embedded devices)

Usage points are not really a brand new metric but rather Function Points augmented by additional information and aimed in a different direction.

Incidentally, it is the examining of software usage patterns that led to placing software as number 10 on the list of widely used commodities at the beginning of this chapter.

The Need for Service Point Metrics

The utility of Function Points for software studies has raised the question as to whether or not something similar can be done for service groups such as customer support, human resources, sales personnel, and even health and legal professionals.

Once software is deployed, a substantial amount of effort is devoted to responding to customer requests for support. This service effort consists of answering basic questions, dealing with reported bugs, and making new information available to clients as it is created.

The cost drivers of software service are based on five primary factors:

1. The size of the application in Function Points
2. The number of latent bugs in the application at release
3. The number of clients using the application
4. The number of translations into other national languages
5. The planned response interval for customer support contacts

What would be useful would be a metric similar in structure to Function Points, only aimed at service functions within large corporations. Right now, there is no easy way to explore the lifetime costs of systems that include extensive human service components and software components. A hypothetical service point metric might include the following factors:

■ Customers (entities)
■ Countries where the application is used
■ Latent defects at deployment
■ Desired response time for customer contacts
■ Inquiries
■ Reference sources
■ Rules and regulations (constraints)

Experiments with variations on the Function Point metric have been carried out for software customer support groups. The results have been encouraging, but are not yet at a point for formal publication.

The United States is now largely a service-oriented economy. Software has a significant amount of total cost of ownership (TCO) tied up in service-related activities.

The Need for Value Point Metrics

One of the major weaknesses of the software industry has been in the area of value analysis and the quantification of value. All too often, what passes for "value" is essentially nothing more than cost reductions or perhaps revenue increases. While these are certainly important topics, there are a host of other aspects of value that also need to be examined and measured: customer satisfaction, employee morale, national security, safety, medical value, and a host of other topics. A hypothetical value point metric might include the following factors:

- Safety improvements
- National security improvements
- Health and medical improvements
- Patents and intellectual property
- Risk reduction
- Synergy (compound values)
- Cost reduction
- Revenue increases
- Market share increases
- Schedule improvements
- Competitive advantages
- Customer satisfaction improvements
- Employee morale improvements
- Mandates or statutes

Note that although cost reduction and revenue increases are both tangible value factors, a host of other less tangible factors also need to be examined, weighted, and included in a value point metric.

Intangible value is the current major lack of today's methods of value analysis. There is no good way to quantify topics such as medical value, security value, or military value.

A value point metric would assign points for the following: (1) direct revenues; (2) indirect revenues; (3) transaction rate improvements; (4) operational cost reduction; (5) secondary cost reduction; (6) patents and intellectual property; (7) enterprise prestige; (8) market share improvements, (9) customer satisfaction improvements; and (10) employee morale improvements. In other words, both financial and nonfinancial value would be assigned value points. The sum total of value points would include both financial and nonfinancial value such as medical and military value.

The Need for Risk Point Metrics

Software projects are nothing if not risky. Indeed, the observed failure rate of software projects is higher than almost any other manufactured product. While software risk analysis is a maturing discipline, there are still no metrics that can indicate the magnitude of risks. Ideally, both risks and value could be analyzed together. A hypothetical risk point metric might include the following factors:

- Risks of death or injury
- Risks to national security
- Risks of property destruction
- Risks of theft or pilferage
- Risks of litigation
- Risks of business interruption
- Risks of business slowdown
- Risks of market share loss
- Risks of schedule delays
- Risks of cost overruns
- Risks of competitive actions
- Risks of customer dissatisfaction
- Risks of staff dissatisfaction

Large software projects fail almost as often as they succeed, which is a distressing observation that has been independently confirmed.

It is interesting that project management failures in the form of optimistic estimates and poor quality control tend to be the dominant reasons for software project failures.

The bottom line is that risk analysis supported by some form of risk point quantification might reduce the excessive number of software project failures that are endemic to the production of large software applications.

As it happens, there is extensive data available on software risks. A number of risks correlate strongly to application size measured in Function Points. The larger the application, the greater the number of risks will occur and the more urgent the need for risk abatement solutions.

Risk points could be combined with value points, Function Points, and data points for determining whether or not to fund large and complex software projects that might not succeed. While Function Points are useful in funding decisions, the costs of data migration and data acquisition need to be considered too, as do risk factors.

The Need for Security Points

Software and the data processed by software now control most of the major assets of the industrialized world. All citizens now have proprietary information stored in dozens of databases: birth dates, social security numbers, bank account numbers, mortgages, debts, credit ratings, and dozens of other confidential topics are stored in numerous government and commercial databases.

Hacking, worms, denial-of-service attacks, and identity theft are daily occurrences, and there is no sign that they will be reduced in numbers in the future.

These facts indicate a strong need for a "security point" metric that will provide quantification of the probable risks of both planned new applications and also legacy applications that process vital information.

Security points:

- Value of the information processed
- Volume of valuable information (using data points)
- Consequences of information theft or loss
- Consequences of disruption or denial of service
- Security flaw prevention methods
- Security attack monitoring methods
- Immediate responses for security attacks

Security as of 2011 is not as thorough as it should be. Hopefully the development of a security point metric will encourage software developers, executives, and clients to be more proactive in avoiding security risks and more effective in dealing with security attacks.

The purpose of security points is twofold: one is to identify all of the security risk topics in a formal manner; the second is to identify all of the known security solutions in a formal manner. It is obvious that security cannot be fully effective by using only firewalls and external software to intercept viruses, worms, and other malware. Software needs to have a stronger immune system that can fight off invading malware due to better internal controls and eliminating today's practice of transferring control and exposing confidential information.

The Need for Configuration Points

This thirteenth metric was not developed by the author but was provided by George Stark of the IBM Global Technology Center in Austin, TX. IBM has been a pioneer in metrics research since the original Function Point metrics were developed at IBM White Plains in the mid-1970s.

The configuration point metric is used to predict the work effort for deploying complex suites of software and hardware that need to operate together. Unlike some of the prior metrics in this report, configuration points have been used on a number of actual installations since their creation in 2006 and seem to generate useful information.

Configuration points:

■ Cabling
■ Software assets and configurations
■ Computing assets
■ Communication assets
■ External interfaces

Value-added adjustments:

■ Security
■ Installation ease
■ Common components
■ Environment complexity
■ Customizations
■ External services
■ Staff experience

When used for deploying large and complex combinations of software and devices, the range of component points to date has been between about 30,000 and 70,000. When comparing component points to standard Function Points, it can be seen that this metric is clearly aimed at the problems of deploying fairly massive combinations of features.

Example of a Multimetric Economic Analysis

Because this proposed suite of metrics is hypothetical and does not actually exist as of 2011, it might be of interest to show how some of these metrics might be used. (In this small example, some of the metrics aimed at large applications such as configuration points are not shown.) Let us consider an example of a small embedded device such as a smart phone or a handheld GPS that utilizes a combination of hardware, software, and data in order to operate as shown in Table 1.2.

As can be seen, normal Function Points are used for the software portion of this product. But since it also has a hardware component and uses data, hardware points and data points are part of the cost of the application.

While smart phones are security risks, GPS devices are not usually subject to hacking in a civilian context. Therefore, the risk and security totals are not high.

Value points would be based on a combination of direct revenues and indirect revenues for training and peripherals. There might also be drag-along revenues for additional services such as applications.

Table 1.2   Example of a Multimetric Economic Analysis

	Number	Cost	Total
Development metrics			
Function Points	1,000	$1,000	$1,000,000
Data points	1,500	$500	$750,000
Hardware Function Points	750	$2,500	$1,875,000
Subtotal	3,250	$1,115	$3,625,000
Annual maintenance metrics			
Enhancements (micro Function Points)	150	$750	$112,500
Defects (micro Function Points)	750	$500	$375,000
Service points	5,000	$125	$625,000
Data maintenance	125	$250	$31,250
Hardware maintenance	200	$750	$150,000
Annual subtotal	6,225	$179	$1,112,500
Total cost of ownership (TCO)			
(Development + 5 years of usage)			
Development	3,250	$1,115	$3,625,000
Maintenance, enhancement, and service	29,500	$189	$5,562,500
Data maintenance	625	$250	$156,250
Hardware maintenance	1,000	$750	$750,000
Application total TCO	34,375	$294	$10,093,750
Risk and value metrics			
Risk points	2,000	$1,250	$2,500,000
Security points	1,000	$2,000	$2,000,000
Subtotal	3,000	$3,250	$4,500,000
Value points	45,000	$2,000	$90,000,000
Net value	10,625	$7,521	$79,906,250
Return on investment (ROI)			$8.92

Note that software development itself is less than one tenth of the TCO. Note also that economic value should be based on TCO for the entire product, and not just the software component.

The Probable Effort and Skill Sets for Creating a Suite of Functional Metrics

Allan Albrecht, John Gaffney, and other IBM colleagues worked on the development of Function Point metrics for several years before reaching a final version that achieved consistently good results.

Each of the proposed metrics in this chapter would probably require a team that includes both Function Point experts and domain experts in topics such as data structures, hardware engineering, accounting, and other relevant topics. A single inventor might be able to derive some of these metrics, but probably a multidisciplinary team would have more success.

Because Function Points already exist, creating a family of metrics that utilize similar logic would not be trivial, but would probably not be quite as difficult as the original development of Function Points at IBM in the 1970s. Following are the probable team sizes, skill sets, and schedules for creating a family of functional metrics:

Metric and Skills	Team Size	Schedule (Months)
1. Application Function Point metrics* Software engineering Accounting and finance Statistical analysis	6	24
2. Component feature point metrics** Function Point Analysis Software engineering Taxonomy construction	4	12
3. Hardware Function Point metrics Function Points Electrical engineering Mechanical engineering Aeronautical engineering Accounting and finance	6	18

Metric and Skills	Team Size	Schedule (Months)
4. COTS application point metrics*** Function Point Analysis Taxonomy construction Software engineering	1	6
5. Micro Function Points** Function Point Analysis Maintenance of software	3	3
6. Data point metrics Function Point Analysis Data structure analysis Data normalization methods Accounting and finance	6	18
7. Website point metrics Function Point Analysis Website design Web content sources Graphical design Accounting and finance	6	18
8. Software usage point metrics* Function Point Analysis Accounting and finance	1	3
9. Service point metrics Function Point Analysis Info. Tech. Infrastructure Library	4	9
10. Risk point metrics Function Point Analysis Software risks Software risk abatement Accounting and finance	4	6

Metric and Skills	Team Size	Schedule (Months)
11. Value point metrics Function Point Analysis Accounting and finance Software engineering Economic modeling Multivariate analysis	6	9
12. Security point metrics Software security principles Costs of security breaches Function Point Analysis	6	6
13. Configuration points* (Developed by IBM)	NA	NA
Total	53	132

*   Metric currently exists
**   Metric exists in prototype form
***   Metric is covered by a patent application

As can be seen, the set of possible functional metrics discussed in this chapter requires substantial research. This kind of research would normally be performed either by a university or by the research division of a major company such as IBM, Microsoft, Google, Oracle, and the like. Indeed configuration points are a recent metric developed by IBM.

For example, as a database company, Oracle should certainly be interested in data point metrics and should already have data about migration costs, data quality, and the like. But as of 2011, database and ERP installation routinely cost more than expected, while data migration efforts routinely run late and encounter data quality problems. Data economics remains a critical unknown in corporate economic studies.

The purpose of this chapter is to illustrate that while Function Points are valuable metrics for software economic analysis, software does not exist in a vacuum and many other business and technical topics would benefit from the logic of functional metrics.

The most critical gaps in metrics as of 2011 are the lack of effective metrics for dealing with data size and data quality and the lack of effective metrics that can integrate tangible and intangible value.

It goes without saying that the suite of metrics cannot be developed in isolation. They need to be considered as a set, and they also need to be commensurate with standard Function Points so that the various functional metrics can be dealt with mathematically and be used for statistical analysis as a combined set of related metrics.

The 13 proposed metrics discussed in this chapter are not necessarily the only additional metrics that might be useful. The fundamental point is that the Function Point community should expand their vision from software alone and begin to address other critical business problems that lack effective metrics and measurement techniques.

Summary and Conclusions

The value of Function Point metrics for economic analysis of software applications is good enough to suggest that the same logic might usefully be applied to other business topics that are difficult to measure.

The two most difficult measurement topics as of 2011 are data and value. Data lacks any metrics whatsoever, and there is no reliable information on data costs or data quality. Value has metrics for revenues and cost reduction, but no effective metrics for handling nonfinancial values such as medical value, military value, and many others.

Further Readings

DeMarco, T. 1995. *Why Does Software Cost So Much?* New York: Dorset House.

Fleming, Q. W., and J. M. Koppelman. 2000. *Earned Value Project Management.* 2nd ed. New York: Project Management Institute.

Gack, G. 2010. *Managing the Black Hole: The Executive's Guide to Managing Risk.* Thomason, GA: The Business Expert Publisher.

Galorath, D. D., and M. W. Evans. 2006. *Software Sizing, Estimation, and Risk Management: When Performance Is Measured Performance Improves.* Philadelphia, AP: Auerbach.

Garmus, D., and D. Herron. 1995. *Measuring the Software Process: A Practical Guide to Functional Measurement.* Englewood Cliffs, NJ: Prentice Hall.

Garmus, D., and D. Herron. 2001. *Function Point Analysis.* Boston, MA: Addison Wesley.

Harris, M., D. Herron, and S. Iwanicki. 2008. *The Business Value of IT.* Boca Raton, FL: CRC Press.

Hill, P., ed. 2011. *Practical Software Estimation.* New York: McGraw Hill

Jones, C. 1998. *Sizing Up Software.* Vol. 279(6), 104–9. New York: Scientific American Magazine.

Jones, C. 2000. *Software Assessments, Benchmarks, and Best Practices.* Boston, MA: Addison Wesley Longman.

Jones, C. 2006. *Conflict and Litigation between Software Clients and Developers.* Version 6. Burlington, MA: Software Productivity Research.

Jones, C. 2007. *Estimating Software Costs.* 2nd ed. New York: McGraw Hill.

Jones, C. 2008. *Applied Software Measurement.* 3rd ed. New York: McGraw Hill.

Jones, C. 2010. *A New Business Model for Function Point Metrics.* Version 9.0. Narragansett, RI: Capers Jones & Associates LLC.

Jones, C. 2011. Provisional Patent Application 126203 00002. In *A Method of Rapid Early Sizing for Software Applications*. Narragansett, RI: Capers Jones & Associates LLC.

Kan, S. H. 2003. *Metrics and Models in Software Quality Engineering*. 2nd ed. Boston, MA: Addison Wesley Longman.

Kaplan, R. S., and D. B. Norton. 2004. *The Balanced Scorecard*. Boston, MA: Harvard University Press.

McConnell, S. 2006. *Software Estimation – Demystifying the Black Art*. Redmond, WA: Microsoft Press.

Parthasarathy, M. A. 2007. *Practical Software Estimation – Function Point Methods for Insourced and Outsourced Projects*. Boston, MA: Addison Wesley.

Stark, G. 2006. *Personal Communication on Configuration Points*. Austin, TX: IBM Global Technology Center.

Strassmann, P. 1997. *The Squandered Computer*. Stamford, CT: Information Economics Press.

Stutzke, R. D. 2005. *Estimating Software-Intensive Systems – Projects, Products, and Processes*. Boston, MA: Addison Wesley.

About the Author

Capers Jones is currently the president of Capers Jones & Associates LLC. He is also the founder and former chairman of Software Productivity Research (SPR) LLC. He holds the title of Chief Scientist Emeritus at SPR. Capers Jones founded SPR in 1984.

Before founding SPR, Capers was assistant director of programming technology for the ITT Corporation at the Programming Technology Center in Stratford, Connecticut. He was also a manager and software researcher at IBM in California where he designed IBM's first software cost estimating tool in 1973.

Capers Jones is a well-known author and international public speaker. Some of his books have been translated into five languages. His two most recent books are *Software Engineering Best Practices*, McGraw Hill, 2010 and *The Economics of Software Quality*, Addison Wesley, summer of 2011 with Olivier Bonsignour as coauthor.

Among his other book titles are *Patterns of Software Systems Failure and Success* (Prentice Hall 1994), *Applied Software Measurement, third edition* (McGraw Hill 2008), *Software Quality: Analysis and Guidelines for Success* (International Thomson 1997), *Software Cost Estimation, second edition* (McGraw Hill 2007), and *Software Assessments, Benchmarks, and Best Practices* (Addison Wesley Longman 2000).

Capers and his colleagues have collected historical data from hundreds of corporations and more than 30 government organizations. This historical data is a key resource for judging the effectiveness of software process improvement methods.

This data is also widely cited in software litigation in cases where quality, productivity, and schedules are part of the proceedings.

Chapter 2

A Guide to Sizing and Estimating Projects Using International Function Point Users Group Function Points

David Garmus

Contents

Introduction

Stakeholders involved with the development of software are frequently challenged to provide early and accurate software project estimates. It speaks poorly of the software community that accurate estimation practices, early in the lifecycle, have not been adequately resolved and standardized.

Three significant issues play a role in the estimating challenge:

1. The need to identify and express, as early as possible in the project, the application software functional requirements requested by the user.
2. The need to identify and express the application software non-functional requirements taking into account all of the technical and quality issues for the project.
3. The need to understand the software development team's capability to deliver the required software solution within a specified environment taking into account all of the risk factors relating to the environment and people's skills and motivation.

Once these issues are resolved, the effort required to deliver the product can be more accurately predicted.

The software requirement can be defined as the scope of the required software functionality impacted (to be built or customized) by the project activities as well as the technical and quality issues. The software requirement must be accurately identified by users or those individuals who have requested the software to be built, and then assessed for its size and complexity. To complicate the situation, experience tells us that at the point in time when we need an initial estimate (early in the system's life cycle), we typically do not have all of the necessary information available. Therefore, we must follow a relatively rigorous process that enables a further determination of the requirements.

Functional size can be measured using the International Function Point Users Group (IFPUG) functional size measurement method discussed in the IFPUG Counting Practices Manual [1], based on the functional user requirements. Function Point Analysis measures the functionality requested and received by the user independent of the technical and quality details involved. Function Points provide a more precise measurement of software size and are designed to remove the ambiguity from consideration of the software being examined. Instead of an abstract notion of size, we derive a more accurate estimate of a project's size. Function Point Analysis conforms to the ISO/IEC 14143-1:2007 standard for functional measurement.

IFPUG has recently developed a sizing measure that can be used to size nonfunctional requirements for the development and delivery of a software product known as Software Non-functional Assessment Process (SNAP), which is presented as a separate chapter in this book. The main objective of IFPUG's Framework for Non-Functional Sizing (2008) project was to provide a non-functional framework that could be used to establish a link between non-functional size and the effort to provide the non-functional requirements. The non-functional assessment provides information that can identify requirements that impact quality and productivity by quantifying the size of non-functional requirements of the software that the user requests and receives. The resulting framework has been released by IFPUG as the SNAP Assessment Practices Manual [2].

Having both Function Point data and non-functional requirements provides a more complete and accurate picture of software development. However, the SNAP scope will always be limited to the "product" non-functional requirements assessment, rather than including "external" requirements related to the organization delivering the project/product. Organizational, personnel, and support requirements for the project certainly have an impact on the overall project effort estimation, but they are not included in the SNAP point calculation.

Risk factors relating to the environment and people's skills and motivation influence the organization's capability to deliver. The identification and assessment of these project risks should also be completed at the beginning of each project when a project manager is better positioned to develop a plan that works. The resulting plan should focus on the project team's capability and capacity to deliver requested functionality in accordance with customer requirements. In the world of continually evolving technologies, project managers face ever-increasing challenges in managing software development projects. Is your organization building software with new technologies in new environments? Client/Server platforms, multitiered architectures, object-oriented design, web-based users, and e-business customers are the norm today. If you are facing the technology revolution, your project managers may need new skills to succeed in today's complex software development environments. A project manager should not commence a project without evaluating the team's capabilities, before committing to an estimate of time and effort. An effective project manager focuses on the successful delivery of quality software within time and budget constraints. Once the project manager understands the delivery capability of the team's current resources, he or she is better positioned to quantify the size (scope) of each project and develop project plans with remarkable precision, plans that work!

It is recommended that project managers follow an ISO standard for sizing software that has the flexibility to modify estimates as the project progresses. Experience tells us that although a project manager needs an estimate early in the development process, the estimate is rarely based on complete information. Therefore, the project manager should follow a rigorous estimating process that permits further clarification of the requirements as the project proceeds through the development cycle. The methodology should enable an estimate to be quickly revised and subsequent changes to be captured while maintaining the basis of the original estimate.

Effective estimation requires that a historical baseline of performance including size, resources, and schedule be maintained. An organization should develop

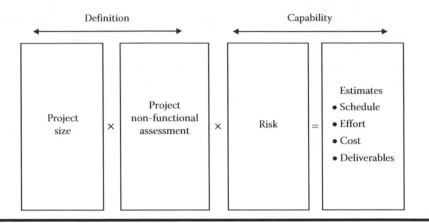

Figure 2.1   Estimation model.

profiles that reflect rates of delivery for projects of a given functional size, non-functional assessment, and risk. In turn, this information can be used to predict and explore "what-if" scenarios for future projects.

An effective estimating model, as shown in Figure 2.1, considers three elements: size, non-functional assessment, and risk to determine an estimate.

Project Size

By far, the project-sizing technique that delivers the greatest accuracy and flexibility is the IFPUG Function Point methodology. Based on logical user-defined requirements, IFPUG Function Points permit the early sizing of the software requirement. In addition, the IFPUG Function Point methodology presents the opportunity to size a user requirement regardless of the level of detail available. An accurate Function Point size can be determined from the detailed information included in a thorough user requirements document or a functional specification. An adequate Function Point size can even be derived from the limited information available in an early proposal.

The IFPUG Function Point methodology is dependent upon identification of five elements: inputs, outputs, inquiries, internal stores of data, and external references to data. Within the IFPUG methodology, these are known as external inputs, external outputs, external inquiries, internal logical files, and external interface files. During the early stages of development, these elements are exposed at a functional level (e.g., an output report will be required although the detailed characteristics of that report might not be known). The Function Point counting methodology identifies these five elements. As more information becomes available regarding the characteristics of these elements (that is, data attributes, file types referenced, and so on), the more detailed the Function Point count becomes. During the early phases of a count, it may be necessary to assume levels of complexity within the system (e.g., is the report going to be simple or complex). Point values are assigned to each transactional and data function using tables contained in the IFPUG Counting Practices Manual. The value in the concept of using IFPUG Function Points is that it allows for accurate functional sizing, and in fact requires it early in the process.

Function Point Analysis permits us to estimate the size of a planned application and measure the size of an existing application. It can also be used to measure the size of changes to an existing application, whether those changes are in the detailed design phase or have already been completed. Knowing the functional size allows many other useful metrics to be determined.

Alternative sizing methods, such as counting lines of code, are dependent upon information that is not available until later in the development life cycle. Other functional measurement methods require detailed knowledge about system processing that is not available early enough for accurate counting, for example, states and transitions.

IFPUG Function Points accurately size the stated requirement. If the requirement is not clearly or fully defined, the project will not be properly sized. When there are missing, brief, or vague requirements, a simple interview process with the requesting user can be conducted to more fully define the requirements. Function Points can be utilized to better identify stated external inputs, external outputs, external inquiries, internal logical files, and external interface files. For an average size project, hours, not days, are required to complete the diagramming and sizing task.

Non-Functional Assessment

In addition to the project size, a non-functional assessment must be performed for the project. Before IFPUG's Framework for Non-Functional Sizing was developed, earlier versions of the IFPUG Counting Practices Manual acknowledged the existence of 14 general system characteristics (GSCs):

1. Data communications
2. Distributed data processing
3. Performance
4. Heavily used configuration
5. Transaction rate
6. Online data entry
7. End-user efficiency
8. Online update
9. Complex processing
10. Reusability
11. Installation ease
12. Operational ease
13. Multiple sites
14. Facilitate change

Each of these 14 characteristics was assigned a degree of influence between 0 and 5; consequently, the total degree of influence ranged between 0 and 70, which then was applied in a formula to become a value adjustment factor to the Function Point count. Although this was part of the Function Point methodology for many years, IFPUG embarked upon the effort to replace these GSCs through the use of SNAP, a more realistic and practical methodology to establish a link between the non-functional size and the effort to provide the non-functional requirements.

The SNAP assessment provides information that can identify items impacting quality and productivity by quantifying the size of non-functional requirements of the software that the user requests and receives. ISO has defined technical requirements as those requirements that relate to the technology and environment for the development, maintenance, support, and execution of the software. ISO has defined quality requirements as those characteristics that form part of the quality model: functionality, reliability, usability, efficiency, maintainability, and portability. SNAP offers a project assessment method that uses a series of questions grouped by category to measure the impact of non-functional requirements on the development and delivery (size) of the software product. The result will be the size of the non-functional requirements, just as the functional size is the size of the functional requirements.

Categories focus on those non-functional requirements that impact the development and delivery (size) of the software product but exclude on-site specific organizational factors that impact development effort and project duration but do not affect the delivered product size. Categories are generic enough to allow for future technologies. Each category includes subcategories or individual components, which are evaluated using assessment questions in order to produce an estimated impact of the category on product size.

Categories and subcategories include the following:

- Data operations
  - Data entry validations
  - Logical and mathematical operations
  - Data formatting
  - Internal data movement
- Interface design
  - UI changes
  - Help methods
  - Multiple input methods
  - Multiple output formats
- Technical environment
  - Multiple platforms
  - Database technology
  - Configuration

- Batch processing system
- Multiple technologies
■ Architecture
- Mission critical (real-time system)
- Component-based software development (CBSD)
- Design complexity

Assessment questions for each subcategory are related to specific attribute(s) that allows for the non-functional assessment of the given subcategory. Ratings will be ranges, qualitative values, ordinal values, and so on, depending upon the particular subcategory. Ratings are converted into SNAP counting units (SCUs); the SCU can be a component, a process, or an activity identified according to the nature of the subcategory. The complexity level of an assessment rating or the value of the SCU within each subcategory is mapped to a size, which is the arithmetic sum of the sizes of all SCUs identified in each subcategory. SNAP points are the final non-functional size obtained by combining all category values.

The reader is directed to Chapter 26 in this book for an overall outline of this non-functional sizing measure. Complete guidelines are contained in the IFPUG SNAP Assessment Practices Manual.

Factors That Impact Delivery

Over and above the SNAP assessment, the delivery of a project must evaluate risk factors relating to the environment in which the project will be delivered and the skill sets and motivation of the stakeholders involved. The capability to deliver software is based upon a variety of negative risk factors and positive influencing factors that influence a development organization's ability to deliver software in a timely and economical fashion. These factors include such things as the software processes that will be used, the skill levels of the development staff and user personnel who will be involved, the methodology and automation that will be utilized for development, and the influences of the physical environment. In fact, there are numerous factors that influence our ability to deliver software in a timely process with high quality.

In order to get an accurate, balanced picture of a project team, an assessment should be conducted for the risk influencing factors in each of the key phases of a development project: requirements, definition, design, development, and testing. Examples of site-specific organizational factors that impact development effort, quality, and project duration include the following:

■ Are the team size and the number of managers involved appropriate?
■ Do multiple managers manage the same project team members?
■ What are the team dynamics (how well the project team will work together)?

- Do all team members understand their individual roles?
- How is morale of the team members (are members happy to be assigned to this project)?
- Is the project manager experienced (especially for the type of project and business area)?
- Is the project management methodology to be followed familiar and practical?
- Do all stakeholders agree on schedules, deliverables, and so on?
- Are requirements documents complete, clear, and stable?
- Are there project and development supporting tools?
- Do the users have experience with the application and business knowledge?
- Is this a functional repeat of a well-understood application or a new application?
- Is the project introducing new technology?
- Does the project team have all training needed?
- Do the users have experience with software development projects?
- Does the development team have experience with the type of software being developed?
- Does the development team have experience with the business line of the software?
- Does the development team have experience for each development phase of the project (requirements, design, reviews and inspections, code, and test)?
- Does the development team have experience with the languages/code to be used?
- Has the project team been trained in code reviews and inspections?
- What amount and types of testing are to be accomplished for the project?
- Has the project team been trained in system testing (process and automation)?
- Is there outside development testing planned plus development and user testing?
- Will test plans be written and formally reviewed?
- Is the work area satisfactory or will it hinder productivity?
- Are there huddle and breakout rooms for meetings?
- Are there multiple development sites (are they in different physical locations)?
- Are offshore development personnel planned?
- What is the computer support environment for the team?
- Are there adequate case tools, PCs, and development software for each team member?
- What reuse of requirements, design, code, inspection, and test cases is planned?
- What review and inspection process will be followed?
- How familiar and practical is the technology to be used in the project?

The key to effectively managing these negative risk factors and positive influencing factors is centered on the development of an historical baseline of performance. An organization should develop profiles that reflect rate of delivery for a project

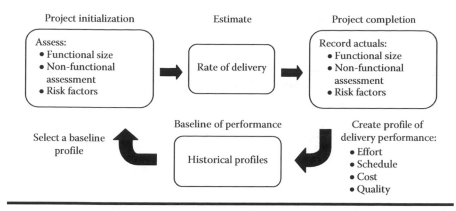

Figure 2.2   Project profiles.

of a given size, non-functional assessment, and negative risk factors and positive influencing factors as reflected in Figure 2.2. As indicated, this information should be used to predict and explore "what-if" scenarios on future projects. Virtually all of the project estimation tools in the marketplace today follow this same process.

Industry Data

Organizations have not typically invested the resources necessary to develop internal rate of delivery performance baselines that can be used to derive estimating templates. Consequently, industry data baselines of performance delivery rates initially may provide significant value. Industry data points allow organizations to use generic delivery rates as a means to "ballpark" their estimates. As organizations continue to develop an experience base of their own, they should transition from the use of industry data to use of their own data.

The desire for industry data is so great that many companies are willing to accept publicly available industry data at face value. Of growing concern is the fact that many providers and publishers of industry data have collected information that has not been validated, is not current, or is incomplete. To avoid any such pitfalls, the following criteria should be applied when obtaining industry data:

■ Does it separately report your industry and business area?
■ What is the mix of data; for example, platform, source code language, application type, and so on?
■ Does it reflect the same functional and non-functional size measurement methodology as you are using?
■ When were the projects completed?
■ Is the data useful?

- Is the source reliable?
- What is the cost versus value of the data?

It is highly recommended that you consider the use of data from the International Software Benchmark Standards Group (ISBSG) benchmark repository.

What Steps Should an Organization Take to Better Size and Estimate?

Before the Project

The project manager should determine the goals and expectations of all stakeholders including all levels of IT management and the customer, identify the desired project outcome in detail in order to determine the resources required, and efficiently manage the development project.

An effective manager will simulate various scenarios before meeting with the customer in order to consider all of the possible options. Then, meet with the customer and decide together the scenario that will best serve the organization's business needs. Validate that it is realistic and achievable.

The customer's expectations now reflect the project's most likely outcome. Having participated in selecting the development strategy, the customer is no longer an outsider, simply levying tasks on your team. He has become a part of the team itself, recognizing the same real-world constraints.

During the Project

As the project proceeds, events occur that were not anticipated in the initial planning phase. Each could have an impact on the project's outcome. Meet with the customer to clarify all factors that have changed. Then use the estimating process to generate a new set of alternative scenarios for consideration. Together, just as with the initial forecast, decide which scenario will best achieve the organization's business objectives, and get buy-in. Then, manage the customer's expectations.

Once all negative risk factors and positive influencing factors have been identified, the project size has been estimated, and the project plan and work breakdown structure have been created, the project manager is positioned to successfully manage to the revised plan.

Manage with a quality focus that includes effective reviews and inspections. Inspecting and approving the requirements, design documents, and code will provide assurance to the customer, project manager, and development team that the software will meet requirements, satisfy or exceed expectations, and be usable. The Software Engineering Institute (SEI) highly recommends this process, which when properly implemented will result in software delivery at a reduced cost, improved quality, and a shorter delivery schedule.

After the Project

After a project is successfully completed, key information should be collected, continuing the process identified as in Figure 2.2. It is important to collect this data during and immediately after a project, because it will soon be forgotten. All data about the processes and activities performed by the team during the project should be collected. The qualitative and quantitative results should be consolidated into a report for a post-implementation review and to update the baseline of performance as a historical profile. The quantitative results will then be available for the next project. Always promote best practices and provide recommendations for the next project managers. Do not allow busy schedules, organization size, or past failures in process improvement initiatives to prevent your organization from utilizing a successful approach.

Summary

Accurate and early estimation requires that:

- All requirements must be identified.
- Both functional and non-functional size must be calculated.
- An assessment of the organization's capacity to deliver based upon all known negative risk factors and positive influencing factors must be completed.
- Historical data or industry data points should be utilized to estimate delivery rates or to enable comparison between projects.
- Project managers must be equipped with the proper tools and techniques necessary to accurately estimate projects. The return on that investment will be obvious to any organization that has previously failed to deliver quality software on time because of inaccurate estimation and project planning.

References

1. The International Function Point Users Group. 2010. *Function Point Counting Practices Manual, Release 4.3. Princeton Junction.* New Jersey: IFPUG Standards.
2. The International Function Point Users Group. 2011. *SNAP Assessment Practices Manual. Princeton Junction.* New Jersey: IFPUG Standards.

About the Author

David is an acknowledged authority in the sizing, measurement, and estimation of software application development and maintenance. As a cofounder of the David Consulting Group, he supports software development organizations in achieving software excellence with a metric-centered approach.

He serves as a past president of the International Function Point Users Group (IFPUG), a past member of the IFPUG Counting Practices Committee and a current member of the Software Non-functional Assessment Process Working Group. Mr. Garmus is a Certified Function Point Specialist, having fulfilled all IFPUG requirements for this title under all releases of the IFPUG Counting Practices Manual, and a past Certified Software Measurement specialist.

He has a BS from the University of California at Los Angeles and an MBA from Harvard University Graduate School of Business Administration. He has been a frequent speaker at ITMPI, IFPUG, QAI, PMI, SEI, and IEEE Conferences, and he has authored numerous articles and four books including:

> *Measuring the Software Process: A Practical Guide to Functional Measurements,* Prentice Hall, 1996 with David Herron.
>
> *Function Point Analysis: Measurement Practices for Successful Software Projects,* Addison-Wesley, 2001 with David Herron.
>
> *IT Measurement: Practical Advice from the Experts,* Addison-Wesley, April 2002 as a Contributor.
>
> *The Certified Function Point Specialist Examination Guide,* Auerbach Publications/ CRC Press, 2011 with Janet Russac and Royce Edwards.
>
> "IT Metrics and Benchmarking," *Cutter IT Journal,* Guest Editor, June 2003.
>
> "IT Metrics and Benchmarking," *Cutter IT Journal,* Guest Editor, November 2003.
>
> "Identifying Your Organization's Best Practices," *CrossTalk, The Journal of Defense Software Engineering,* June 2005 with David Herron.
>
> "The Principles of Sizing and Estimating Projects Using IFPUG Function Points," *Software Tech News,* June 2006.
>
> "On Time and On Budget, How Did You Do It," *IT Metrics and Productivity Institute e-Newsletter,* November 4, 2008.
>
> "Software Non-functional Assessment Framework," *IT Metrics and Productivity Institute e-Newsletter,* September 1, 2009.

Please refer to the website of The David Consulting Group at www .davidconsultinggroup.com to obtain other articles written by David Garmus on software sizing and project management and measurement.

BENCHMARKING INTRODUCTION

Pierre Almén

When we measure performance, performance increases—the Hawthorn effect

Benchmarking within IT has been done for over 25 years. It started with benchmarking of IT operations, followed by benchmarking of networks, help desks, and PCs. About 10 years later, the first benchmarking was done with application development and maintenance. When benchmarking, a normalized measure of output is needed and IFPUG Function Points have, from the beginning, been seen as the primary method for normalizing the size of development projects and applications. I have been benchmarking IT organizations since late 1990, primarily Application Development and Maintenance. As a Function Point practitioner since 1984 and one of the first to be a Certified Function Point Specialist, it was obvious that IFPUG Function Points could and should be used. Many Application Development and Maintenance managers have seen their organization as a "black box" without knowing if improvement initiatives have given a positive result, if a project's estimate is in the right order of magnitude, if the application quality is market comparable, if the outsourced price is competitive, etc. By normalizing the work done within Application Development and Maintenance, together with adequate and suitable comparison data, benchmarking can help the CIOs and IT managers make more fact-based decisions.

In the first chapter of this section, Heidi Malkiewicz and Lori Mayer from Accenture in the United States discuss the benchmarking process. Based on their own field experience, they provide guidance about how to use Function Points for forecasting maintenance costs and how to establish proper Service Level Agreement (SLA) targets. In order to do this, they stress the need and urgency for having a proper and regular data gathering process for establishing project repositories that represent the real value and logical baseline for any organization. Final thoughts are about benchmarking criteria for vendor selection using well-known TQM techniques.

Pam Morris from Australia is the CEO of Total Metrics, has over 20 years of experience of software measurement, and is Vice President of the International Software Benchmarking Group (ISBGS). In her chapter, she shows how the sponsor should work with the benchmark supplier, internal or external, and the stakeholders to establish "Terms of Reference" for the benchmarking activity. Through performing that activity, comparative benchmarking is achievable, and the benchmarking data can be aligned with market data from similar environments.

Nishant Pandey, a Lead Consultant within Capgemini Canada, with a Certificate in IT Benchmarking from Stanford University, describes benchmarking techniques in his chapter. He demonstrates with case studies how benchmarking of IT is done. Nishant describes in his chapter a simple but effective tool—the box whisker technique.

Chapter 3

Acquiring External Benchmark Data

Heidi Malkiewicz and Lori Mayer

Contents

Introduction

External benchmark data can be a useful part of any software measurement program as it provides an objective way to analyze existing data or to establish a starting point for future measurement. While purchasing and utilizing external benchmark data may appear to be a straightforward process, there are a fair number of nuances to consider to ensure that the resulting data is both meaningful and relevant to your organization. This chapter will provide guidance on the process of defining data requirements, using the data, and selecting a vendor for benchmarking.

43

Defining Data Requirements

Before setting out in search of benchmark data, you should consider both how the data will be used and what data is needed. Defining your data requirements up front will help to ensure that the data will meet your needs and add long-term benefit to your organization.

Data Usage

Benchmarking data can be used in a variety of ways depending on the objectives of your organization. Assessing your data usage requirements upfront ensures that you have a clear vision of the data that is required and how it may be used to achieve the greatest benefit. It is important to consider both immediate needs and potential longer-term use to ensure the data acquired will best suit the needs of your organization over time. There are many potential uses for external benchmark data and these will vary from organization to organization depending on the type of business and the role of the organization in the software measurement process. Some of the most typical applications of benchmark data include the following:

- Assess current performance
- Establish a baseline from which to measure future improvement
- Provide guidance on budgeting
- Assist in defining service-level agreement (SLA) targets

Benchmarking provides a quantitative method for understanding how an enterprise compares to itself, to its peers, or to the industry. The type of benchmark needed depends on the overall objectives of the benchmark and is driven by the requirements of the organization being examined. An external benchmark can help to facilitate a more objective discussion within your company and can also act as a confirmation of whether your organization is leading, in alignment with, or lagging the industry. This helps to set the stage for ongoing, sustainable improvement. Now let us examine how external benchmark data may be used under each of the applications outlined above.

To Assess Current Performance

External benchmark data can be effective in analyzing the performance of an IT group and provides a gauge on whether that organization is improving over time. To enable this type of assessment, a comparison of the group to itself at one point in time versus another is all that is required. If your organization has already established a formal baseline and has been measuring performance against that baseline on a periodic basis, then the external benchmark will not provide any additional value for assessing current performance, but can still serve as a confirmation that you are on par with industry. However, if your organization is not performing formal software measurement today, then the external benchmark can be used to derive this measurement. To understand if your performance is getting better over time, two benchmarks are required. The first benchmark will establish your baseline or starting point and is used as a comparison point in conjunction with the second benchmark to analyze your improvement. The second benchmark will measure your performance against those same baseline measures, but at a later point in time. The baseline results from the two benchmarks are used to analyze whether your organization has improved, remained consistent, or declined between the two measurement periods. This information is useful for understanding whether changes or improvements made within your organization between the two points in time have had a positive or negative impact on your performance. If your organization is already measuring periodic performance, but you want to understand how your organization's performance compares to your peers or to others in the software industry, then the external benchmark will provide some additional context.

To facilitate a benchmark that provides a comparison to industry, you will need performance data to compare against the benchmark data. This data must represent your performance over a sustained period of time. Most organizations will have peaks and valleys in their performance from one reporting period to the next due to cyclic or seasonal variations, changes in number of occurrences, etc. Therefore, it is important to compare against an extended data set to gain the most complete understanding of the "typical" performance of the organization and to further minimize the highs and lows in the comparison data set. When examining an extended data set, it is useful to collect certain project attributes in order to assess whether the data represents typical performance and for use in filtering project data to create clusters of similar projects. The data demographics section in this chapter explores this concept in more detail. Furthermore, the external benchmark data must be similar in scope, scale, and demographics to the data being measured within your business to provide a meaningful comparison. The process of confirming and ensuring this alignment is called "normalization" and will be discussed in more detail later within this chapter.

Additionally, a benchmark can provide valuable guidance on where current performance issues exist and where investments may be required to improve performance. Careful consideration should be given when defining your benchmarking requirements to ensure the data is at a low enough level to conduct a detailed analysis to support this level of decision making. Benchmark data can be a powerful tool for objective decisions that have a long-term impact. Let us examine further how benchmark data may be used to gain additional insight into where improvements are required.

Suppose a recent benchmark indicates your application development productivity is lagging industry for web enhancements. You know from the benchmark what the productivity is of each individual web enhancement over the last 6 months.

Through the benchmark, you are able to determine that web enhancements for front office systems have better quality than back office systems. This allows your organization to launch a deeper investigation into what is driving down the quality in the back office systems and what is being done to deliver good quality on front office systems. Utilizing benchmark data in this fashion can be a powerful tool for objective and fact-based decision making.

To Establish a Baseline from Which to Measure Future Improvement

Having a formal measurement process in place to measure the overall health and improvement in an organization over time can be an important decision-making tool. It provides a view into what is working well within the company and where improvement is needed. A measurement program is also useful to understand whether investments in and changes to the organization are having the desired impact. The information can further be used to drive improvement decisions through quantitative analysis of problem areas and a more thorough understanding of the levers that are impacting your organization's performance over time. Empowering your business in this way requires an understanding of your current performance through a formal baseline.

For organizations without a formal measurement process in place today, a baseline serves as the starting point for measuring future improvement. There are two methods for obtaining a baseline of your current performance:

1. Create your own baseline using internal data.
2. Leverage an external benchmark vendor to establish the baseline.

While creating your own internal baseline will provide the most relevant understanding of your performance, it can be both costly and time consuming. A typical baseline can range between 6 and 12 months and should be comprised of at least 30 data points depending on the availability and accuracy of representative historical data. Additionally, your organization may not have the expertise or experience required to build an accurate baseline. Another alternative is to utilize an external benchmark provider to conduct the benchmark in conjunction with your department. An external benchmark provider should be able to provide the expertise needed to conduct a benchmark effectively and efficiently through the use of a formal, robust and well-tested methodology. This initial benchmark will provide an understanding of your current performance and will be used in conjunction with a second benchmark to measure your improvement over time. Regardless of which method you choose to establish your baseline, subsequent measurement or benchmarks must be conducted in the same manner using consistent definition and selection criteria to ensure an apples-to-apples comparison.

To Provide Guidance on Budgeting and Pricing

Benchmark data can be leveraged for both internal budget decisions and external pricing decisions due to its objective and quantitative nature. Either internal or external benchmark data can be used for this purpose as long as it represents the current performance of the organization. An understanding of the current performance is important as it best describes the capability of the organization in its current state.

When using benchmark data as input into budget decisions, the component you are trying to estimate must be comparable in size, scope, scale, etc., to ensure the estimate is most representative. To help facilitate this, you must predict and account for any changes in these factors when preparing the future estimate and use them to adjust your benchmark accordingly. Let us look at an example of how this would work.

Suppose you are trying to estimate your application maintenance costs for the upcoming year. You have a recent benchmark that indicates that your maintenance costs for the current year are $10M for a portfolio of 35,000 Function Points, which equates to an average cost of approximately $286 per Function Point. (Note that the median value could also be evaluated in conjunction with the average.) You do not expect any significant changes to your application portfolio in the upcoming year in terms of changes to the technologies utilized, enhancements to the applications, retirements of applications, changes in the number or level of expertise of your labor resources, etc. However, you are expecting the addition of three large-scale applications from a company acquisition that amounts to roughly 9,000 Function Points (you do not have an understanding of the cost associated with these additional Function Points). The benchmark data can be used to adjust your current year's maintenance cost in order to understand the cost of this acquisition and to predict your budget for your upcoming year as follows.

1. Calculate maintenance cost per Function Point for current application portfolio: ($10M/35,000) = $286 per Function Point
2. Calculate additional maintenance cost for acquired applications: $286 per Function Point * 9,000 additional Function Points = $2.6M additional maintenance cost
3. Calculate estimated cost for the upcoming year = $10M + $2.6M = $12.6M

This example demonstrates how benchmark data can be utilized as a data point to help predict the additional cost of significant organizational changes in an objective and quantitative manner. However, it is important to note that only the labor and seat costs can be reasonably predicted year over year using past actuals as described above. Other nonlabor costs (e.g., travel, software license maintenance fees, new hardware costs, etc.) and costs associated with work that does not generate Function Points (e.g., hardware upgrades, cosmetic or regulatory changes, etc.) may vary from year to year and cannot be forecasted in this manner.

Furthermore, while this example demonstrates how benchmark data can be used in a predictive fashion at a portfolio level, it is advisable to perform this analysis at a lower level (i.e., application level) to best predict the impact of these types of changes. For example, you should consider the impacts to your portfolio based on technology, platform, size, age, business importance, and level of support as these factors can have a major impact on future cost approximations. These factors are discussed further in the data demographics section of this chapter.

To Assist in Defining Service-Level Agreement Targets

Both service providers and organizations looking to outsource can benefit from using benchmark data to guide decisions about service level agreement (SLA) targets. It is essential to analyze internal performance through an internal benchmark to set reasonable expectations of what the current level of performance is and how much that can be improved. To compliment the internal benchmark, external benchmarks exist for many of the common metrics seen as part of contractual SLAs or key performance indicators (KPIs) in outsourcing agreements including budget and schedule adherence, quality, response/resolution time, application availability, etc., and can be used to further validate expected levels of performance. It is important to distinguish between SLAs and KPIs since these metric sets typically serve different and distinct purposes. Both SLAs and KPIs serve to highlight the performance of an organization and both have associated targets from which to measure ongoing improvement. SLAs are typically written to hold a service provider contractually or commercially accountable for the results while KPIs typically serve as supporting metrics to the SLAs and do not have associated contractual penalties. External benchmarking data can be used in conjunction with both SLAs and KPIs, but the use of external benchmarking data can vary depending on your perspective as a service provider or organization.

As a service provider, external benchmark data acts as an indicator of market performance that can be useful in evaluating whether your proposed SLA/KPI targets are in alignment with industry and therefore, your competitors. When using external benchmark data for this purpose, it is advisable to obtain benchmark data from multiple vendors as the data can vary (sometimes significantly) across vendors based on a number of factors. Some of the factors that can influence benchmark data include the source of the data, the demographics of the organizations and projects/applications within the data, the volume and age of the data, etc. These differences are typically accounted for through a process called normalization. Normalization helps to ensure that the data is comparable between two data sets and is a critical step before utilizing an external benchmark to establish performance expectations or set SLA/KPI targets. The concept of normalization is discussed in detail later within this chapter.

As a company considering outsourcing, external benchmark data can serve as an indication of your organization's current performance and confirm whether your performance is in alignment with industry. This information can further act to validate outsourcing decisions by giving objective proof of where your organization is performing well and where improvement opportunities may exist. Furthermore, the results of a recent benchmark performed on your organization can be used as input into setting SLA targets since it provides the basis for the minimum performance you would expect for the same work performed by a vendor or service provider.

Regardless of the business driver for acquiring external benchmark data, it is important to spend time upfront to define your data requirements when acquiring external benchmark data. Next, we will take a closer look at how to effectively define your data requirements.

Data Demographics

It is important when benchmarking to understand the attributes and demographics that describe the data you are looking to compare. Analyzing this information upfront will help to ensure that the benchmark most closely aligns with your comparison data set and will provide greater confidence in the results. It is not very useful to compare your internal software development and maintenance to external benchmark data made up of remarkably different attributes. For example, if your portfolio was made up solely of web-based applications supported in India, you would not want to compare yourself to benchmark data primarily made up of data warehouse applications supported in the United States. External data should be further segmented into similar groups to get the most useful comparison.

It is essential to define your data demographics and data segments upfront to ensure the external benchmark will meet both your short-term and long-term needs. The data demographics required in the benchmark may vary by metric based on what is unique within your organization and what factors tend to influence your performance.

Unfortunately, it is sometimes difficult to ascertain which factors are truly impacting your performance without detailed data to analyze your performance. To assist you with this analysis, you should consider these common demographics that are often found to drive software metric results for application maintenance and development work. These demographics should be evaluated at a high level to provide an understanding of your portfolio and the work performed within your organization:

- Technology (SAP, Java, .NET, C, COBOL, etc.)
- Platform (web, client–server, mainframe, package software)
- Size (based on effort or Function Points)
- Industry (telecom, financial services, automotive, etc.)
- Location where software development and maintenance work is performed

Some demographics specific to applications should also be considered for any application maintenance related metrics, including the following:

- Application maturity/age
- Business importance
- Level of support required (e.g., 24 × 7)
- Degree of application change

To properly define the demographics required to be represented in the benchmark data, you must first understand the demographics of the data set against which you intend to compare. Not only is it important to understand the overall categories of work represented in your data set, but you will also want to understand the mix of data within these categories. For example, you should understand the volume of web versus client–server applications in your portfolio and ensure the benchmark data has a consistent ratio of web to client–server. It is also important to understand that as the mix of your portfolio changes over time, so should subsequent benchmarks to accurately account for this as well. A complete understanding of the demographics of your data will ensure the benchmark best represents the type of work being performed and will be most predictive of your organization's performance. The demographics will drive the data segments or categories to delineate further the benchmark data required. For example, if the benchmark includes application maintenance productivity, you would want to consider having the data segmented by application maturity as industry data suggests this has a direct influence on the productivity of an application. A reputable benchmark vendor should be able to suggest some reasonable data segments for your consideration. Keep in mind, however, that having the data segment is only meaningful if similar attributes are captured to segment the data you will be comparing against in the benchmark.

Volume is another important factor when evaluating the applicability of external benchmark data. You should carefully examine the volume of data in the comparison data set(s), which include both the data being compared internally and the data being compared from an external source. Data sets that include only a few data points should raise suspicion regarding the ability of the data to either represent (for internal data sets) or predict (for external data sets) performance. Data sets with higher volumes provide a greater confidence that the results were sustained over a large number of occurrences. Unfortunately, there is no hard and fast industry rule regarding volumes, but experience has demonstrated that as many as 30 (or more) data points may be required to provide a statistically valid sample set for comparison purposes. Understanding both the volume and demographics represented in an external benchmark data set is an important consideration when selecting a benchmarking vendor.

Normalization is another critical component of any benchmark. It is the process of aligning multiple data sets to ensure the data is stated on a consistent basis and therefore reasonably comparable. Normalization should be performed for every data set that you plan to compare and for each individual metric you intend to benchmark. Without proper normalization, you cannot be confident that the comparison is valid. Furthermore, improperly normalized data sets can result in incorrect conclusions and drive the wrong behaviors. For example, suppose you purchased an external benchmark that suggests that your application maintenance productivity is worse than industry. At first glance, that sounds like concerning news. However, upon further investigation you find that the data is not properly normalized and that the level of support required is quite different between your organization and the other companies in the benchmark. In fact you have found that your organization has significantly more priority 1 tickets (requiring 4 hour resolution time) than some of your industry peers (which allow for 8-hour resolution time). After working with the benchmark provider to properly normalize the data, you learn that your productivity performance is actually slightly above industry.

Understanding how "size" is defined is another important consideration during normalization as not all benchmark providers define size in the same way. It is crucial to understand further how the size was derived within the benchmark data. For example, if size is defined as functional size measured in Function Points, were the Function Points derived through traditional, manual Function Point counting methods? Were they counted using an automated technique or tool? Were they calculated from lines of code or use cases? It is important to understand how the values used in the external benchmark are derived and to ensure consistency between the data sets being analyzed.

As we have seen, it is important to define thoroughly your data demographics and to ensure the data is properly normalized upfront to support a valid like-to-like comparison. This is a crucial step when conducting a formal benchmark.

Benchmark Frequency

The true value of benchmarking is in understanding how the performance of the organization being benchmarked changes and ideally improves over time. This drives the need for an initial benchmark followed by a periodic and ongoing benchmark to understand whether improvement is being realized over time. However, the frequency of benchmarking depends on a number of factors. These factors should be carefully considered when evaluating whether a benchmark should be performed. The factors that typically drive the frequency of a benchmark can include the following:

■ Cost
■ Availability of dedicated and knowledgeable resources to participate in the benchmark
■ Scale and scope of changes within the organization

- Readiness of the organization
- Contractual commitments requiring benchmarking

Each of these factors should be understood and considered when evaluating the need for a benchmark.

Cost is typically one of the primary considerations. Since benchmarks can be costly due to the time and effort required to execute the benchmark, you should seek to understand the benefit that is expected to be gained by performing the benchmark. A simple cost-benefit analysis can be performed to analyze this. You will also need one or more internal resources to engage and manage the external benchmark vendor(s) and to gather the internal data required as mentioned above. Due to the cost and effort typically associated with performing a benchmark, benchmarks are typically only recommended every 2–3 years.

A benchmark may also be useful to measure the impact of significant changes within the organization. Benchmarking both before and after a change provides a perspective on how the change impacts your company over time. The second measurement should be performed when the change has been fully implemented and the organization has returned to a "steady state." Some examples of significant changes that can be useful to benchmark include the following:

- Large merger or acquisition
- Noteworthy changes in technologies utilized
- Integration of a large pool of vendors, contractors, or outsourcing providers
- Significant methodology changes (e.g., move from waterfall to agile, CMMI achievement, ITIL alignment, etc.)
- Significant changes in the organizational model (pyramid, roles/responsibilities, etc.)

You should further consider the readiness of the organization for the benchmark. Readiness is an indication of whether the business is at a point to understand, evaluate, and take action on the results of the benchmark. You should consider whether the results of the benchmark would be meaningful. The results will not be meaningful, for example, if the organization is in the midst of a significant change or transition such as those outlined above. In this case, perhaps the current time is not appropriate for a benchmark and would be more valuable at another point in time. Another consideration is whether the organization is able to make changes and improvements within the organization based on the results and suggested areas of improvement from the benchmark. Is the funding available to make the improvements desired? Are the appropriate resources available to drive the changes? These are important considerations when assessing the organization's readiness for a benchmark.

A contractual commitment may also drive the need for a benchmark. Organizations that have vendors or outsourcing providers performing a portion of their work may perform a benchmark to ensure they are getting a "fair" price for the work and to confirm the vendor is improving their performance over time. Such contractual commitments are established and agreed to upfront and should specify the frequency and scope of the benchmark, which vendors must be utilized to conduct the benchmark, and how the results will be used.

If benchmarking will be a reoccurring event, you should consider purchasing a subscription to a benchmarking service. Committing to purchase multiple benchmarks over a specified period of time may allow you to negotiate a lower price than if the benchmarks are purchased individually. Additionally, utilizing the same vendor over time has advantages as it ensures the benchmarks are performed consistently, and could reduce the overall benchmark effort and duration.

Regardless of the driver for the benchmark, having dedicated, experienced professionals directing the benchmark activities ensures it is performed as efficiently and effectively as possible. Experienced benchmarkers can guide your organization on what to benchmark, how to interpret the results and offer suggestions on improvement opportunities.

Vendor Selection

There are several considerations when selecting a vendor to perform a software measurement benchmark. Clearly and thoroughly evaluating vendors at the outset will help to drive a benchmark that aligns closely with your organization's objectives. The first step in benchmarking is to define a list of potential vendors. Your list of potential vendors may include companies you have utilized in the past, companies with a good reputation, familiar companies that you have seen at industry events such as IFPUG, recommendations from trusted colleagues, or vendors that you are contractually bound to use. Once you have defined your list of potential vendors, the next step is to understand supplier viability.

It is important to properly investigate the company you are acquiring data from to verify whether they are a viable and trustworthy provider. This will ensure that the benchmark data has the credibility necessary to support the actions you intend to take as a result of the benchmark. Additionally, you will want a supplier with which you can build a long-term relationship, and who understands your company and your business. Supplier viability can be assessed by interviewing each vendor independently using an objective and consistent method. You should consider the following factors for each vendor:

■ How long have they been in business? How many clients have they served? What types of services have they performed?
■ What experience do they have with benchmarking? How many and what kinds of benchmarks have they performed before? Can they provide credentials to support their work for other companies?

- Can they provide the data required?
- Is the data recent (e.g., within the last 12 months) enough to be meaningful? Does it include the relevant time periods?
- Are they able to properly normalize the data? Does their data contain the attributes necessary to perform the normalization?
- Does the vendor utilize a reputable source for the data? Is it self-reported or gathered through former benchmarks they have conducted?
- Can they supply adequate volumes of data that meet data demographic and segmentation to match your organization?
- Are they able to meet defined timeline and cost requirements?
- For metrics that use Function Points, were the Function Points counted using Certified Function Point Specialists (CFPS)? Does the Counting Practices Manual (CPM) version align with your internal data (if applicable)?
- Do they have restrictions regarding the use of the data (consider internal and external usage requirements)?
- Will they provide ongoing Q&A support for questions after the benchmark is delivered?

Using a structured approach to select a benchmarking vendor is recommended as it provides a more objective approach for selecting a vendor that best meets your needs.

Pair-wise comparison is one method for evaluating among alternatives, in this case benchmarking vendors. For those familiar with Quality Function Deployment (QFD),* the pair-wise comparison method is based upon the principles of QFD that were first defined by Mizuno and Akao in the late 1960s to inject quality control and customer satisfaction into the requirements process. Pair-wise comparison provides a simple and mathematical approach to evaluating alternatives and assessing them against the criteria that are most important to your organization. The primary steps involved in a pair-wise comparison include the following:

- Define selection criteria
- Define rating scale
- Rank selection criteria
- Assess each vendor against the selection criteria
- Calculate and evaluate results

The first step in conducting a pair-wise comparison is to define the selection criteria. The selection criteria will include the factors that are most important in your decision for selecting a vendor. They can be built from the list of interview factors above or you may have other factors that need consideration. It is important

---

* QFD was developed in Japan in the late 1960s by Professors Shigeru Mizuno and Yoji Akao. See Mazur (1991) for the history of the QFD technique.

Table 3.1   Rating Scale

Rating Scale	
5	High ability to meet criteria
3	Moderate ability to meet criteria
1	Low ability to meet criteria
0	Alternative does not meet criteria

to put a clear and succinct definition around each selection criteria to minimize interpretation during the rating process. Once the selection criteria are defined, the rating scale should be defined.

As shown in Table 3.1, the rating scale is typically defined with four or more layers and is used to assess each alternative's ability to meet the individual selection criteria.

The numeric values represent each alternative's (the vendor is this case) ability to meet the selection criteria. The numeric values are used as a point-value multiplier in step 5. This rating scale should be used consistently across all selection criteria and when evaluating each individual vendor against the criteria. Once the rating scale is defined, the selection criteria should be ranked.

Ranking the selection criteria provides a mechanism for identifying which of the selection criteria are most important, which are least important, and which ones are more important when compared to one another. Ample time should be spent upfront discussing both the selection criteria and the ranking with the stakeholders to ensure all user viewpoints are considered. The ranking should be done in a pair-wise fashion until all selection criteria are ranked from 1 (least important) to X (most important), where X is the total number of selection criteria. Once the ranking is finalized, each vendor will need to be evaluated against the selection criteria.

Each vendor is evaluated against the selection criteria and a numeric value is assigned that represents the vendor's ability to meet that selection criteria. Based on the four-layer approach described above, each vendor would be assessed a value of 0–5. Any value within this range may be used to delineate further the vendors or if you believe a vendors' ability to meet the criteria falls between two values. For example, if you feel that a vendor's ability to meet a selection criteria is somewhere between moderate (3) and high (5), then you could assign a value of 4. Additionally, it is useful to evaluate each vendor in a pair-wise fashion against single-selection criterion before moving on to the next criteria. This allows for a comparative assignment of each vendor's ability to meet the selection criteria relative to the other vendors. Once the vendor assessment against the selection criteria is complete, the results are calculated.

The pair-wise results are calculated individually for each vendor. The numeric value assigned to each selection criteria is multiplied by the ranking value of that selection criterion and the results are summed together for that vendor. This will produce a single numeric value that represents the strength of each vendor's ability to meet the criteria (as a whole) that are most important to your organization. A similar process is performed for each of the vendors being assessed and the overall numeric values are compared. A higher numeric value for a vendor indicates that the vendor is better able to meet the needs of your organization based on the selection criteria defined. Let us look at a basic example.

Suppose you are evaluating four vendors to perform a benchmark of your internal performance. Let us call them vendors A, B, C, and D. Next, let us suppose you have defined the selection criteria that are most important to your organization and ranked them in a pair-wise fashion. The result of your ranking can be seen in the Ranking row in Table 3.2. As you can see, Vendor Viability is most important (denoted with a ranking of 8), whereas Data Usage Limitations are least important (denoted with a ranking of 1). You have also evaluated the ability of each vendor to meet the selection criteria and to what degree by assigning a value between 0 and 5 to each. You will note that overlapping values are allowed where more than one vendor can be assigned the same value for single-selection criteria. The results are calculated by vendor and documented in the Total column. (Table 3.2 shows the results of the assessment.) Based on this assessment, Vendor B is best able to meet the selection criteria with an overall total of 153. Vendor A is second with a score of 144 and followed by Vendors C and D with 135 and 115, respectively. Based on the scores, both Vendors A and B should be considered since these vendors are most able to meet the benchmarking needs of the organization. However, Vendors C and D should probably not be considered since based on the scoring they are least likely to meet the requirements that were identified as most important to the organization.

As the example demonstrates, performing a pair-wise comparison can provide an objective and mathematical way of selecting a vendor. This technique can provide assurance that your choice is directionally correct and may further help you to rule out a vendor from consideration or narrow down your choices to a few select vendors. Once the vendor has been selected, you can move forward with formal procurement of the benchmark data.

When arranging for procurement of external benchmark data, it is important to document exactly what (metrics, definitions, demographics, data segmentation, volume requirements, etc.) you expect to be delivered, in what format, when, and at what cost in a formal agreement. It may also be helpful to provide the vendor with a sample layout of how you expect the data to be formatted as this provides additional clarity on what you expect to receive from the vendor and can help to avoid any surprises when the benchmark is delivered. Finally, the agreement should specify any restrictions around usage of the data for both internal and external purposes.

Table 3.2 Results of Assessment

Vendor	Required Data Is Available	High Degree of Normalization	Annual Refresh Rate	Data Coverage Time Period	Reputable Data Source	Data Usage Limitations	Vendor Viability	Low-Benchmark Cost	Total
Ranking	7	6	2	3	5	1	8	4	
A	5	4	4	5	5	1	4	1	144
B	4	5	5	5	3	3	5	3	153
C	3	5	2	2	3	3	5	4	135
D	2	2	5	5	3	5	4	3	115

Conclusion

Navigating the acquisition of benchmarking data can be confusing and cumbersome at times. This chapter has provided guidance and considerations for acquiring external benchmarking data built on many years of experience and some trial and error. External benchmarks should be driven by first defining the intended usage of the data, the demographics required, and the frequency in which benchmarking should be conducted. Once these basic parameters are understood, an objective method, such as the pair-wise comparison approach discussed in this chapter, should be utilized to select a vendor. Following a methodical approach to performing a benchmark will help to ensure that the resulting information best describes the current health and performance of your organization and will establish the basis for assessing ongoing improvement.

Reference

1. Mazur, G. 1991. *History of QFD*. QFD Institute. http://www.qfdi.org/what_is_qfd/history_of_qfd.html (December 12, 2011).

About the Authors

Heidi Malkiewicz currently works for Accenture managing benchmarks and supporting large-scale global clients that use Function Points. Heidi has been an employee of Accenture for the past 14 years. Heidi has been a Certified Function Point Specialist for over 10 years and actively utilizes her certification through Function Point counting and analysis, teaching and mentoring others on Function Points, and managing productivity programs.

Lori Mayer is a senior manager with Accenture with deep expertise in Function Point Analysis, productivity measurement, broad-scale metrics and balanced scorecard reporting, and establishing SLAs. She has spent the last 15 years focused on implementing and managing productivity measurement programs for several large-scale global clients and continues to guide prospective and current clients on proven practices. Lori is the founder of Accenture's global productivity and Function Point community of practice and has previously presented at the ISMA conference.

Chapter 4

Effective Applications Development and Maintenance and Support Benchmarking

Pam Morris

Contents

Overview

Benchmarking the Applications Development and Maintenance and Support (AD/M) environment can potentially provide significant insights into the performance of IT processes and identify how and where they can be most effectively improved. However, many organizations initiate a benchmarking activity without first fully determining the objective of the benchmark or the benefits they hope to achieve, or establishing the criteria by which projects and applications will be selected and compared. This chapter explores the reasons why organizations choose to benchmark, identifies the potential benefits of benchmarking, and highlights the pitfalls of failing to appropriately plan the benchmarking activity or introduce rigor into the benchmarking process to ensure its success.

Why Benchmark?

Benchmarking involves the measurement and comparison of the performance and outcomes (products) from selected IT processes for the purpose of improvement, establishing a competitive position, and/or to provide input into management decision making. Although many IT organizations routinely collect cost, effort, defect, and in some cases functional size data, they rarely go the extra step of turning this raw "data" into "information" that would facilitate change. Benchmarking is the activity that turns data into information by measuring current practices, comparing current performance with past performance or peer performance, and interpreting the results. Usually, organizations start by focusing on *internal* benchmarking to target areas for improvement before going the next step of comparing themselves with *external* business units or wider industry performance. However, this is not always the case; it often takes the results of an industry comparison to identify the high cost of poor IT practices, which then motivates management to rethink their AD/M strategy and start some internal measurement. As a result of a benchmark report, management may choose to reduce costs by outsourcing their IT development and support or alternatively by targeting internal processes for improvement. Benchmarking also enables organizations to assess their performance against their competitors and evaluate the benefits and cost savings of investing in new tools, techniques, or technologies.

Benchmarking Risks

In more recent years, benchmarking has been progressively used as a means to assess and compare the cost-effectiveness of IT suppliers. Most large fixed-term outsourcing contracts include clauses that financially reward or penalize the supplier, based on the supplier's performance against an industry benchmark or an established client performance baseline. These bonus/penalty incentives are often priced as a percentage of the total worth of the contract and can result in payments of millions of dollars flowing either way. In some cases, as the contract expiry approaches, the contract requires an "independent" organization to benchmark the supplier's performance prior to renewal. If the outcome of the performance comparison is positive, then both client and supplier are encouraged to continue; but if the outcome is negative, then it may result in contract cancellation. Given the ongoing cost of a benchmarking activity, and the potentially high risk of incurring large payouts and/or contract cancellation, it is surprising how few organizations define a rigorous process around the benchmarking activity and develop an agreed "Terms of Reference" for the benchmarking activity prior to starting.

Terms of Reference

It is our recommendation that before engaging a benchmark supplier or funding an in-house benchmarking program, the sponsors work with the benchmarker and stakeholders to establish the Terms of Reference for the benchmarking activity. These terms should include the agreed position for each of the following:

1. Strategic intent of the benchmark
   - How will the results be used?
2. Type of benchmark
   - Internal and/or external?
3. Benchmark performance metrics
   - What are the processes or products required to be assessed to satisfy the goals of the benchmark and how will they be measured?
4. Standards for measures
   - What are the agreed units of measurement, data accuracy, and validation requirements?
5. Scope of the benchmark
   - What are the inclusion and exclusion criteria for projects and applications?
6. Frequency of benchmark
   - When and how often should measures be collected and reported?
7. Benchmark peers
   - What are the criteria by which equivalent sample data will be selected for comparison?
8. Benchmarking report
   - Who will be the audience and what will be the report's structure, content, and level of detail provided to support the results?
9. Dispute resolution process
   - What is the process that will be followed should disagreement arise about the validity of the benchmarking results?

Strategic Intent of the Benchmark

Sponsors of the benchmark need to work with IT management to establish the following:

- The objectives of the benchmarking activity, that is, what are the results required to demonstrate, within what period, and for what purpose. In addition, what are the criteria by which the benchmark will be judged successful? Common reasons for benchmarking include monitoring the following:
  - Process improvement initiatives
  - Outsourcing contract performance against targets
  - Consistency in performance across organizational units
  - Benefits achieved from new investments or decisions compared to benefits claimed
  - Performance compared to competitors or industry as a whole
- The stakeholders, that is, who will be responsible for the benchmark's design, data collection, analysis, review, approval, sign off, and funding.

Type of Benchmark

Establish whether the organization will benchmark as follows:

- *Internally* to demonstrate improvement trends over time for the organization's internal processes, or
- *Externally* to compare internal results with external independent organizational units or industry as a whole

Organizations that are aware of their own limitations will recognize their need to improve without first being compared externally to demonstrate how much improvement is required. As a first step, it is recommended that organizations start with internal benchmarking, and then when their own measurement and benchmarking processes are established, do some external benchmarking to establish their industry competitiveness. However, prior to determining standards for the collection, analysis, and reporting of their benchmark metrics, they should first identify their proposed strategy for external benchmarking. This enables their internal benchmarking framework to be aligned to that of the external benchmark data set, thereby facilitating the next step of external benchmarking without any rework to realign the data.

Benchmark Performance Metrics

Benchmarking AD/M should ideally monitor the performance of all the four perspectives identified in the Balanced Scorecard approach—Financial, Customer,

Business Processes, and Learning and Growth. Although this is the ideal approach, in our experience, IT organizations focus their initial IT benchmarking activities on the areas that directly impact their IT costs. They measure the cost-effectiveness and quality of their IT processes and products by optimizing the following key result areas (KRAs):

- Cost-effectiveness of the process—Are they getting "value" for money invested?
- Efficiency of the process—How "productively" is their software being developed or maintained?
- Speed of delivery—How "quickly" can they deliver software product or "solve a problem"?
- Quality of the product—How "good" is the software product or service they deliver?
- Quality of the process—How much time and money is wasted in "rework"?
- Customer satisfaction—How often does their delivery of software products and related services meet or exceed their customer's expectations?

Benchmarking is not a "one size fits all activity." Many "Benchmarking Service Providers" offer turnkey solutions that fail to take into account the individual needs of their clients. By clearly defining the strategic intent of the benchmark before engaging a benchmark provider, an organization ensures that client organizational goals are met and the solution being offered provides a good "fit." Once this is decided, they can then focus on benchmarking key performance indicators (KPIs) that demonstrate achievement of those goals. For example, for many telecommunications and financial sector companies, maintaining competitive advantage is the key to their success, and so they need their IT department to constantly deliver new and innovative products to their market. In this case, "speed of delivery" becomes their highest priority to optimize their competitive position. In comparison, recent budget cuts for government agencies may focus their improvement needs on maximizing their IT cost-effectiveness. Before starting a benchmarking activity, identify the key organizational goals and their corresponding KRAs and then one or two KPIs within that area that will demonstrate the achievement of the identified goals. When conducting an external benchmark, some compromise may need to be made in the selection of KPIs as these must align to performance measures for which industry/peer data is available.

Standards for Measures

When comparing between projects, business units, and/or organizations, you need to ensure that the measurement units collected are equivalent. This is not merely a matter of stating that cost will be measured in US dollars, size will be measured in Function Points, and effort will be measured in days. Although the "cost" of software projects is probably the most carefully collected project metric and the most important for the organization to monitor, it is a very difficult unit of measure to benchmark over time. This is becoming increasingly the case in a world of offshore multi-country development, where currency conversion rates fluctuate daily and salary rates rise with different rates of inflation across countries and time. Comparing dollars spent per Function Point this year with previous years requires multiple adjustments, and each adjustment has the potential to introduce errors. Instead, most organizations choose to measure cost effectiveness by measuring the effort input instead of cost input. Although it may seem straight forward to measure the *Project Productivity Rate* as the number of Function Points delivered per person day, to really compare "apples to apples," the benchmarking analysis needs to ensure that for each of the participating organizational units, the following characteristics of the size and effort measures are consistent:

- *Type of Function Points* recorded—IFPUG, COSMIC, or NESMA Function Points. Has the size reported been actually measured or is it an approximation derived by converting lines of source code to Function Points? Which version of the Functional Size Methodology (IFPUG 4.0 to 4.3) has been used and has all data in the sample set being measured using this same version?
- *Type of day* recorded—Not all organizations work the same number of hours in a day. If days were calculated by dividing time sheet hours by 8, then how was the number of hours collected? Did they include all the hours "worked" including overtime (10 hours = 1.25 days), or only the hours "paid" thereby excluding 2 hours unpaid overtime (8 hours = 1 day)? Did they collect hours from project codes on time sheets and include only productive working hours dedicated to the project, that is, excluding breaks, non-project meetings, e-mail (6 hours = 0.75 days)?
- *Accuracy of the measures*—Did they accurately *measure* the Function Points and extract *exact* effort hours from time sheets or did they roughly estimate size using approximation techniques or multiply the team size by the months allocated to the projects to get hours and days [1]?
- *Scope of the effort measures*—Did they include all the effort of all the people who contributed to the project including the steering group, administration staff, business users, operational staff, or did they just include the time of the project manager, analysts, programmers, and testing team?
- *Scope of the size measures*—When measuring functional size, did they measure all the software delivered to the users, including package functionality delivered unchanged or did they just measure the functionality built and/or configured by the project team?
- *Scope of the project life cycle activities* included in the effort data—Did the project team work on the whole life cycle from planning through to implementation, or did the business area complete the planning and requirements

before handing the project to the development team? Did the project effort figures include or exclude all the activities included in the project budget such as the extensive research into project technology choices during the planning stage, the data loading activity for all the data files, and the extensive world-wide training of thousands of end users?

Every organization has different ways of measuring and recording their metrics. The resulting productivity rate may vary up to tenfold depending on which of the various combinations of the above choices are made for measuring effort and size. To avoid basing decisions on invalid comparisons, agreed standards need to be established at the beginning of the benchmarking activity for each of the measures supporting the selected KPIs for each contributing organizational unit. Each measure needs to be clearly defined and communicated to all participants involved in the collection, recording, and analysis of the data. If some data are inconsistent with the standards, then it should be either excluded from the benchmark or transformed to be consistent and appropriate error margins noted and applied to the results.

To simplify this process and facilitate external industry benchmarking, it is recommended that organizations adopt the de facto data collection standards and definitions for measuring AD/M developed by the International Software Benchmarking Standards Group (ISBSG) [2, 3].

The ISBSG community recognized the need for formal standardization of AD/M measurement and, in 2004, developed the first working draft of a benchmarking standard that became the basis for the new ISO/IEC framework of benchmarking standards. The first part of a five-part framework for Benchmarking Information Technology was approved in May 2011 to become an ISO International standard (*ISO/IEC 29155-1. Systems and software engineering—Information technology project performance benchmarking framework—Part 1: Concepts and definitions*). Seventeen countries participated in the review of the interim drafts and the final approval vote for the standard. This international collaborative process ensures the result is robust and the outcome is accepted across the IT industry. The ISBSG is already a recognized industry leader in setting standards for data collection. A number of software metrics–related tool vendors and benchmarking providers have adopted the ISBSG data collection and reporting standards and have integrated the ISBSG data set in their tools.

Scope of Benchmark

Not all the software implementation projects or software applications supported are suitable candidates for inclusion in the benchmarking activity or can be grouped into a homogeneous set for comparison. All candidate projects and applications should be investigated and categorized on the following types of characteristics to make a decision about their acceptability into the benchmarking set or if they need to be grouped and compared separately:

- *Different delivery options*—Different types of projects include different development activities as a part of their delivery. For example, a package implementation with little customization has significantly reduced effort expended on design and coding activities, and care would need to be taken to determine if it is appropriate to include these types of projects in a benchmarking set of bespoke software projects.
- *Different types of requirements*—Although most projects require delivery of both non-functional and functional requirements, some focus primarily on enhancing the non-functional (technical and/or quality) characteristics of the software or fixing defects. Examples of technical projects are a platform upgrade, reorganizing the database structure to optimize performance, refactoring code to optimize flexibility, or upgrading the look and feel of the user interface to enhance usability. Although these projects may consume large amounts of development team effort, they deliver few, if any, Function Points. It is, therefore, inappropriate to include technical or "defect fixing" projects into productivity comparisons that include projects that primarily deliver user functionality.
- *Different resourcing profiles*—Projects that include only the planning, requirements specification, and acceptance testing effort, with all other life cycle processes being outsourced, should not be grouped into a data set that includes projects where effort has been recorded for all phases of the project life cycle.
- *Different technology profiles*—The ISBSG have identified several technology-based attributes that significantly affect the rate of delivery of a project including the coding language, the development platform (environment), and the database technology. Be aware that it is difficult to establish and compare trends over time if there is a wide variation in the mix of the technology profiles within a single project or of the projects in the benchmarking set.
- *Different size profiles*—As a risk mitigation strategy, very large-scale projects (>3000 fps) often require more formal administrative governance processes, more rigorous development processes, more complete project documentation, and utilization of specialty resources, compared with average sized projects (300–1500 fps). All these add additional overhead effort to the project that negatively impacts productivity. Interestingly, very small projects (<50 fps) that follow the same formal development process as larger projects also tend to show low productivity rates (up to fivefold lower than medium-sized projects [4]) due to the disproportionate overhead of administration, management, and documentation efforts. These small projects (<50 fps) also show wide variations (up to tenfold) in productivity and therefore should be excluded

from benchmarking data sets. When aggregating projects in the benchmarking set, ensure that there is an even mix of project sizes, or group projects into benchmarking sets of comparable size bands [5].

■ *Diverse and/or large user base*—Projects that have a very diverse set of business user stakeholders with significantly different functional and cultural requirements consume more effort to develop, maintain, and support than projects with a single set of homogenous users.

■ *Different functional domains*—The ISO/IEC framework standards for functional size measurement (ISO/IEC 14143 parts 1 to 6) recognize that software functionality can be classified into different functional domains, for example, "process-rich," real-time, and process control software compared with "data-rich" information management software. Although the IFPUG method measures in all domains, the characteristics of the domain will influence the size result. For example, in data-rich domains, the stored data will contribute more significantly to the final result than in process-rich or strongly algorithmic domains. The differing contribution of the data to the final size will impact the measured productivity and quality metrics. Care should be taken to ensure that benchmarking data sets comprise software from similar domains.

■ *Different project classifications*—Different organizations have different definitions for what constitutes an IT project. Some define a project as the implementation of a business initiative (e.g., implement a new government goods and services tax), and others regard a project as a work package implemented by a project team. A business initiative project may have requirements to modify many applications and will comprise multiple subprojects, where a subproject is equivalent to a change request or work package with discrete requirements for each application. The project will have its own overhead activities required to manage and integrate all work packages. These overhead activities cannot be attributed to a particular work package but to the project as a whole. The subprojects will have their own effort, cost, and size profiles. Often the subprojects are implemented in different technologies because they impact different applications, further compounding issues of aggregating metrics and profiling the project. Similar issues arise with definitions of a project when treating a new release of an application as a project to be benchmarked. Typically, the release is made up of multiple change requests, and each change request is implemented by its own project team. Release overheads are incurred in a number of activities such as release management, planning, system testing, integration, and acceptance testing. These activities are usually not recorded at the change request level. When benchmarking against industry projects, you need to ensure that you are comparing against a "project/release" or a "subproject/work package" because the productivity rates of the project/release type project will be decreased by the overhead effort and cost.

It is recommended that before selecting the projects or applications to be benchmarked, they are first grouped into like projects and then classified using the above categories, to either ensure that each of the benchmarking sets consists of an even mix of all types, or if this is not able to be achieved, that they are grouped into "like" categories for comparison exclusively within those categories.

Frequency of Benchmark

The frequency in which data are collected, analyzed, and reported will be determined by the goals of the benchmarking activity. However, when determining how often these activities need to be done, the following need to be considered:

■ *Project durations and demonstrating trends*—If the benchmarking objective is to demonstrate the benefits of implementing new tools or technologies, it may take several cycles before these benefits become evident. The learning curve experienced when adopting new practices often shows a negative effect on productivity for anything up to 18 months after implementation. In addition, if project durations are more than 1–2 years, then it may take several years to demonstrate any benefits. In this case, it may be best to baseline the metrics, then benchmark again after 2 years to observe a result. Benchmarking trends in a KPI assumes that "everything else" stays the same, and any improvements observed are due to the changes implemented, or any failure to see improvement is due to failure of the change to be effective. Unfortunately, the IT world does not "stand still" while you benchmark. IT technology, tools, and techniques tend to be in a continual state of evolution. Over successive benchmarking periods, external forces of change will be introduced and will have an impact. The challenge to the benchmarker is to capture these variables and identify their influence on the results. It is, therefore, imperative that the benchmarker is fully apprised of all the "soft" factors that are likely to impact the "hard" benchmark metrics.
■ *Allocating projects to benchmarking periods*—Projects with long durations may span several benchmarking periods. Some benchmarkers implement "macro" benchmarking, whereby they collect all the effort and costs consumed for a 12-month period from the financial and time sheeting systems and then divide by the Function Points delivered in that period. Issues arise when projects span several periods and so their inputs (effort and cost) are included in all the periods but their outputs (Function Points delivered) are included only in the final period. This phenomenon skews the productivity to be very low for initial periods and very high for the last period. A workaround can be achieved by proportioning the Function Points across the periods based on an "earned-value" type approach.

■ *Usefulness of the result*—If the benchmark periods are set too widely apart, by the time the data are analyzed and reported, the usefulness of the information may have diminished, as often the course of time has changed the relevance of the results to current practices. The late delivery of results may identify an issue that, for maximum effectiveness, should have been identified and addressed at the point it occurred. For example, in the referenced case study [6], the organization only reported their benchmark results annually. By the time they identified that their new strategy, to implement small projects in response to stakeholder demands, was costing them five times as much as aggregating requirements into larger projects, it had already cost them millions of dollars. When benchmarking is used for process improvement and there are long delays in reporting, it is difficult to do a root cause analysis on why a project is an exception, if the project team has since disbanded and the history is lost. However, if benchmarks are reported at intervals that are too short, normal deviations from the median, or "noise" in the results, can be incorrectly interpreted as a trend and responded to inappropriately. Select a benchmarking period that is aligned with the organization's decision-making processes, so that the recommendations in the benchmarking report can be actioned promptly. For example, results should be reported before decisions on budget allocations or timed to be presented before steering group strategy meetings.

■ *Statistical validity of the result*—Before deciding on a benchmark period, you need to assess how many projects will be implemented in that period that satisfy the inclusion criteria for the benchmark, and you need to have collected sufficient data to support the benchmark. For the result to be statistically significant, you need a valid sample size and a valid methodology for selecting the sample. The rule of thumb is to sample at least 10% of the total instances and have a sample set of not less than 30. Ideally, the margin of error for the result is less than 10%, with a confidence level of 95%. However, this is difficult to achieve if you are benchmarking retrospectively and you need to rely on data that have been collected prior to the benchmarking Terms of Reference being established. Prior to starting the benchmarking activity, the stakeholders should agree on what is an acceptable margin of error and desired confidence level in the result. This is important because large outsourcing contracts are known to impose year-on-year performance improvement targets for suppliers of 10%. If the sample set is small and the margin of error is greater than 10%, then the benchmarking activity will not be sensitive enough to demonstrate any productivity gains achieved.

Benchmarking Peers

Previous discussions have highlighted the factors to categorize individual projects and applications to ensure that sample sets of data for internal benchmarking are comparable. However, when an external data benchmarking set is derived from industry or selected from one or more external organizations, then additional factors need to be considered.

- *Organizational type of the benchmarking partner*—This needs to be comparable, for example, care should be taken comparing the results from a large IT development shop with those from a small boutique developer, as they will have significantly different development environments. Large government and banking and financial institutions stand out as having productivity rates that are generally lower than other types of organizations. These organizations typically have projects that impact very large, monolithic, multilayered legacy systems. The productivity of their enhancement projects is negatively impacted by their applications' inherently complex internal structure, multiple interfaces, out-of-date systems documentation, and inaccessibility to developers who are familiar with all the underlying functionality. Compounding the technical issues, any major project decision is required to be approved by multiple levels of bureaucracy, adding further delays and consuming additional effort and costs.
- *Different user priorities*—The end use of the software (e.g., military, medical, financial) may dictate the rigor applied to the software development process. A requirement for high-quality bug-free software will focus development activities and priorities on prevention of defect injection and maximum defect clearance rates rather than project cost-effectiveness and efficiency. Different end-user priorities need to be considered when selecting appropriate benchmarking partners.
- *Quality of the external data set*—Because of the reticence of organizations to make their performance data publicly accessible, the most common way for organizations to externally benchmark against industry data is either by engaging an external benchmark provider organization that has their own data repository or by purchasing industry data from the ISBSG [7]. Benchmarking clients need to investigate fully the provenance of the data set they are going to be compared against (based on the criteria outlined in the Terms of Reference above) before deciding on their approach. The ISBSG's data set has the advantage of being a very cost-effective solution and an "open repository." That is, ISBSG provides detailed demographics of its industry sourced benchmark data, and its data includes all attributes of the projects, while maintaining the anonymity of submitters. Most benchmark provider organizations have a more "black box" approach and only disclose the aggregated summarized results of their benchmark data set, making it more difficult for a client to assess independently the relevance and validity of comparing it with their own data. The ISBSG also discloses the age of its data, which is important in a fast-changing IT environment. More than 70% of the Maintenance and Support data and more than 30% of the Development

and Enhancement data are less than 4 years old. It is also very widely representative in that it is voluntarily submitted by IT organizations from more than 20 countries. Each project set is independently validated by ISBSG for its integrity and assigned a quality rating, and so the user can decide on whether to include or exclude a particular project or application from the benchmark set. However, the client organization should also be realistic in their expectations of the external benchmark data set. The normal process of submission, validation, and analysis of external benchmark data means that the data can be up to 18 months old before it is formally "published" as a part of the benchmark set. A client who is undertaking leading edge developments may have difficulty finding comparable data sets.

■ *Filtering of submission data in an external data set*—If a data set has been contributed voluntarily, then the submitters typically select their "best" projects for inclusion. The resultant mean KPIs derived from the data set tend to represent the "best in class" rather than industry norms. In our experience with the ISBSG data, the industry norm is closer to the 25 percentile of performance than the mean. In contrast, benchmarking data sets that have been derived from ad hoc sampling methods have median and mean values that align more closely to the median and mean values found in industry. The submission profile of the industry data set needs to be known and understood when comparing and reporting the data and determining where an organization is positioned compared with industry.

Benchmarking Report

Before commencing the benchmarking process, it is recommended that the sponsors and key stakeholders agree on how the information will be reported. They need to decide on the reports:

■ *Structure and content*—That is, what will be included in the table of contents and how will the results be formatted?

■ *Level of granularity*—That is, will the data reported be aggregated by project, application, or organizational unit?

■ *Presentation technology*—That is, will the data be embedded as graphs in a document or provided online via a business analytics portal allowing interactive drill-down capability?

■ *Confidentiality and audience*—Who will have access to the report results and how will it be distributed?

■ *Review process and acceptance criteria*—That is, who will establish the reasonableness of the data prior to draft publication and who is responsible for approving the final report and actioning its recommendations?

■ *Feedback process*—For improvement of benchmarking activity, that is, what is the process for continual improvement of the benchmarking process?

Dispute Resolution Process

If the Terms of Reference are established prior to the benchmarking activity and agreed by all parties, then any areas of contention should be resolved prior to the results being published. However, as mentioned earlier, in some circumstances, there are significant financial risks for an organization that believes that it has been unfairly compared. It is recommended that if benchmarking is incorporated into contractual performance requirements, then a formal dispute resolution process also be included as part of the contract.

Summary

Although the above warnings appear to indicate that comparative benchmarking is difficult to achieve, in our experience, this is not the case. It is surprising in reality to see the results of pooling data into a benchmarking set and how well they align with results from external data sets from a similar environment. In our experience, the rules of thumb derived from industry data are able to predict accurately the scale of effort or the cost of a project, indicating that the measures from one data set can be used to predict the results of another.

However, as consultants who have worked for more than 20 years in the benchmarking industry, we are constantly confronted with contracts that require performance targets based on a single number to be derived from a large heterogeneous data set. Such benchmarks are unlikely to deliver useful results, and client expectations need to be managed from the outset. The Terms of Reference described above are provided as guidance for consideration when embarking on a benchmarking activity. Only some variables will apply to your unique situation. If they do apply, consider their impact and choose to accommodate or ignore them from an informed position; fail to consider them at your own risk.

References

1. Morris, P. 2004. Levels of Function Point Counting. http://www.totalmetrics .com/function-point-resources/downloads/Levels-of-Function-Point-Counting.pdf (accessed December 2011).
2. ISBSG Data Collection Questionnaire (DCQ). 2011. http://www.isbsg.org/ISBSG new.nsf/WebPages/286528C58F55415BCA257474001C7B48?open Select IFPUG/ NESMA DCQ (accessed December 2011).
3. ISBSG. 2010. http://www.isbsg.org/ISBSGnew.nsf/WebPages/286528C58F55415BC A257474001C7B48?open Select M&S DCQ (MS Word doc). (accessed December 2011).
4. Morris, P. 2010. The Cost of Speed. IFPUG Metrics Views. Vol. 4(1): 14–18. http:// www.ifpug.org/newsletterArchives/newsletters/July%202010%20MetricViews.pdf (accessed December 2011).

5. Rules, G. 2005. Rules Relative Size Scale. http://www.smsexemplar.com/wp-content/uploads/RulesRelativeSizeScale-v1b.pdf (accessed December 2011).
6. Morris, P. 2010. Cost of Speed. IFPUG Metrics Views. Vol. 4(1): 14–18. International Software Benchmarking Standards Group (ISBSG). http://www.isbsg.org/ (accessed December 2011).
7. International Software Benchmarking Standards Group (ISBSG). http://www.isbsg.org/.

About the Author

Pam Morris (BSc. GradDipCom. DipEd) founded Total Metrics in 1994 in response to the software industry's need to better manage and control their software development processes. Total Metrics' mission is to increase the awareness on the importance of measurement in all IT process improvement initiatives. As the software development industry advances, Morris works with the Total Metrics team of internationally certified consultants to constantly adapt their tools, services, and training courses to meet the changing needs.

Morris has over 20 years experience in software development and since 1989 has specialized in the area of software measurement and process improvement. Morris is the managing director of Total Metrics and past president of the Australian Software Metrics Association (ASMA), where she currently holds a position on their Executive and Benchmarking Database Special Interest groups. In 2007, she was elected as vice president of the International Software Benchmarking Standards Group (ISBSG) and is on the ISO/IEC Study Group for the NWI Benchmarking Standard. She represents Standards Australia as the international project editor of ISO standards 14143-1 and 2 for functional size measurement (FSM). She was the international convenor of ISO/IEC/WG12 group developing FSM standards from 1997 to 2004. She plays an active role internationally in the development of measurement standards, was a member of the International Function Point Users Group (IFPUG) Counting Practices Committee in the United States from 1993 to 2000, and is a reviewer of IFPUG documents. She is a member of the COSMIC-FFP Core Group that is responsible for the development of the COSMIC-FFP FSM method. She has been an IFPUG Certified Function Point Specialist (CFPS) since 1994 and a COSMIC certified practitioner and a certified software measurement specialist (CSMS Level 3) since 2006. In 2006, Morris was awarded the Australian ITP Lifetime Achievement Award for her services to the IT industry. In 2007, Morris was invited to be an international expert partner of the Chinese Software Benchmarking Standards Group.

Morris is a regular guest speaker on the topic of software metrics at numerous international conferences in the United States, China, Japan, India, South Korea, New Zealand, Germany, South Africa, Spain, Italy, Switzerland, Brazil, and the United Kingdom.

Chapter 5

Benchmarking Techniques and Their Applications in IT and Software Measurement

Nishant Pandey

Contents

Over the past decade, benchmarking techniques have emerged as an important tool for performance measurement and process improvements. The IT industry has used benchmarking effectively to improve its processes and enhance the value IT delivers to the business. Benchmarking has evolved into a preferred technique that many organizations are using to set high goals based on global standards. A well-directed and efficiently performed benchmarking study can lead to an increased understanding of the current state of an organization's performance. Additionally, benchmarking can help determine promising practices that can lead to improvement in performance and increased chances of success when adapted judiciously.

This chapter aims at discussing core concepts related to benchmarking specifically focusing on how the IT industry is using benchmarking methods to improve performance.

Defining Benchmarking

The term "benchmark" can be described as a "best in class performance measure" that can be used as a standard. The term "benchmarking," as it applies to the IT and business world, can be defined as the process of comparing an organization's performance against that of the best performers in a particular field, with the intention of observing, learning, and adapting to improve performance over time by bridging the performance gap.

History and Evolution of Benchmarking and Benchmarking Techniques

Early usage of benchmarking can be found in measurement of geodetic points for elevation reference used by surveyors. With increased focus on quality improvement by the 1950s, more and more organizations understood the importance of being a front-runner in their chosen field of operation. This attention to quality measurement and improvement in turn led to increased interest in quality management discipline. In the early 1980s, Xerox corporation conducted a benchmarking project to learn and improve its warehouse management and distribution by comparing its performance to that of L. L. Bean, a clothing store catalog retailer—an entirely different type of organization, but a front-runner in distribution and warehousing. This study was widely discussed by industry experts and quality improvement professionals and helped spark an interest in the field. Over the past few years, benchmarking has evolved into an advanced quality concept that involves a diligent and methodical approach for achieving performance improvements. The positive impact that benchmarking techniques have had in providing organizations with competitive advantages has led to benchmarking being used as a strategic management tool.

Benefits of Benchmarking

Before dwelling deeper into benchmarking techniques, it might be a good idea to discuss the benefits of a well-focused benchmarking study. The following direct benefits can be realized by utilizing sound benchmarking practices:

- Increased awareness about current state and current challenges
- Catalyst for initiating brainstorming on possible reasons for observed trends
- Increased knowledge and understanding of good practices followed by the benchmark
- Action plans for adapting a few or most of the good practices used by the benchmark

One indirect but very important benefit that can come from a benchmarking study is increased quality orientation in the organization. With an enhanced vision for quality and measurement of metrics and analysis of trends, there comes increased accountability and responsibility in those involved in managing the process.

Types of Benchmarking

Though benchmarking exercises are performed by various organizations to meet specific goals, the underlying fundamentals of all benchmarking studies remain similar. The main focus of a benchmarking study is comparative measurement of performance and analysis around how exceptional performance can be attained. One might ask that if underlying principles are very similar, from where does the distinction between various types of benchmarking studies arise? The distinction between various types of benchmarking studies is based on the data collection methodology and relation between the involved parties.

The following types of benchmarking studies are commonly performed.

Internal Benchmarking

An internal benchmarking exercise involves participants and benchmarks internal to the organization. The performance of various internal departments can be analyzed to determine better practices that have led to better performance in specific areas. Analysis can then be performed for implementing the better practices to other departments after appropriately tailoring these to meet the specific needs of these departments. One of the advantages of internal benchmarking is that there is relatively lesser cost involved. Internal benchmarking also ensures that confidential data about a company's performance and internal affairs is not shared with anyone outside the organization. Although this type of benchmarking exercise forms a good training ground for training employees in management by measurement in general and benchmarking techniques in particular, it might not be able to provide much insight into performance with respect to competitors.

External Benchmarking

External benchmarking is a benchmarking exercise that focuses on looking outside an organization to observe how other organizations that are working toward similar goals have achieved their goals in more efficient or less expensive ways. External benchmarking can prove to be costlier than internal benchmarking because of the effort required to gather performance data on the competition. It is much more difficult to obtain correct and reliable information with regard to external organizations. Often these exercises are conducted by third parties, usually specialized consulting firms that have extensive industry knowledge and access to industry data and trends.

Collaborative Benchmarking

Collaborative benchmarking generally involves an exchange of metric and performance data among a group of organizations that agree to collaborate and share best practices and performance data in order to learn from each other's experience. Collaborative benchmarking is a form of external benchmarking.

Product Benchmarking

In more recent times, the concepts of benchmarking and benchmarking techniques have been applied to benchmark attributes related to the performance of commercially available off-the-shelf (COTS) products that are built to match precise user expectations. An example of product benchmarking might be a benchmarking study that compares the transaction processing time for various credit card authorizations processing products available for a credit card company to use for its new credit card launch. Selection of the best available product or software system might be an output of such a benchmarking study.

Conducting a Benchmarking Study

A well-planned benchmarking study has a commonly used sequence of events that can be termed as phases of any benchmarking project. There may be slight variations in terminology used in various organizations and industries, but for the most part, benchmarking activities can be broadly categorized into the following phases:

- Planning and preparation
- Data collection and research
- Data and trend analysis
- Identifying performance gap and best practices
- Communicating and reporting results
- Initiating a program for continuous improvement

Planning and Preparation

The first and foremost step toward performing any useful benchmarking study involves preparation and planning related to the study. The effort and resources spent in performing the study can be directed toward specific aims of the benchmarking organization if proper and detailed planning is performed (Figure 5.1). It is very important to address the following three fundamental questions with respect to the benchmarking exercise at hand:

- What is to be benchmarked as a part of this benchmarking exercise?
- What is the chosen benchmark?
- What strategic objective does the benchmarking exercise ultimately seek to address?

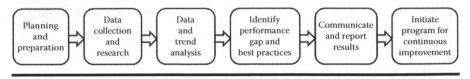

Figure 5.1 Phases of a benchmarking study.

Significant preparation and groundwork is necessary before a benchmarking study can be started. One of the main tasks in the planning and preparation phase is to build consensus amongst the participating parties (internal or external) regarding the strategic goals of the benchmarking exercise. Obtaining support from senior management and ensuring proper communication channels are also crucial to the success of the benchmarking exercise. Initial analysis around what sources exist for gathering data and verifying accessibility of these sources is also an important step that usually starts in the planning and preparation phase.

Data Collection and Research

After initial planning and preparation have been performed to the satisfaction of the team responsible for the benchmarking study, suitable research needs to be carried out to collect data on metrics and trends that are most relevant to the needs of the particular benchmarking study in focus. This is a very time consuming and crucial phase for the benchmarking study. The results and recommendations of any benchmarking study are only as good as the accuracy of the data collected and suitability of the data sample used for analyzing the trends. Data needs to be collected to satisfy two distinct aspects:

1. Current state of the benchmarking organization
2. Performance of the chosen benchmark

Current State of the Benchmarking Organization

Organizations that maintain a database of performance metrics can find the organizational baseline to be an important tool for performing the benchmarking exercise. In case no or little data is available regarding certain aspects of performance that are important for the benchmarking study, it might be a good idea to start collection of this data in the initial planning and preparation phase itself. In cases where a direct metric is not available, it might be a good idea to use indirect but connected metrics to quantify one's current performance level.

Performance of the Chosen Benchmark

Collecting data regarding the benchmark usually begins with analysis of publicly known and published information. It might be more difficult and time consuming to obtain data related to benchmark performance in cases where a competitor has been chosen as a benchmark. Other techniques to obtain such data might include participation in customer surveys, written questionnaires, site visits, and requests for collaboration. At times, there is no single organization chosen as a benchmark; instead the chosen point of reference is taken as the emerging industry trend data. There exist many "for profit" and "not for profit" organizations that publish sanitized data on such industry trends periodically. One way to gain access to such averages and trends is to participate in surveys hosted by organizations and groups of repute. The results of such surveys are usually shared with all participants after ensuring data is sanitized to ensure no confidential or inappropriate information (as governed by the agreement with the participating organization) is shared. Performance data shared in such forums is usually masked to protect the interests of the participating organizations.

Data and Trend Analysis

After data has been collected for key areas that are in the scope of the benchmarking study, it is important to ensure that it is properly analyzed to obtain relevant information. As a part of this phase, data analysis techniques are applied to the collected data sets, with the aim of highlighting useful and pertinent information and deriving performance trends. Quantitative and qualitative aspects of data are categorically analyzed as a part of the data and trend analysis phase.

The data analysis exercise should include cleansing of collected data to inspect and correct any erroneous data elements. The quality of collected data is representative of the sample selected for obtaining the data. It might be a good idea to assess the quality of data by applying techniques to determine any "extreme observations" or outliers. These outliers must be analyzed separately to ensure that these are correct data points and from a representative sample set. Commonly used tools for analysis of data include correlation and scatter plots, frequency counts, histograms, probability distribution trends, standard deviation, and data distribution analysis.

When considering relative performance with respect to benchmarks, it might be a good idea to measure the current level of performance in terms of *percentiles* (value of a variable below which a certain percent of observations fall). For instance, the strategic goal of a telecom company might be to be within the top 10% of telecom service providers (or 90 percentile mark) in the arena of customer satisfaction. In such a case, representing the output of the data analysis phase in a format that quantifies customer satisfaction on a point-based index and measuring current performance relatively in the form of percentiles might help gain a clear perspective on the current state (Figure 5.2).

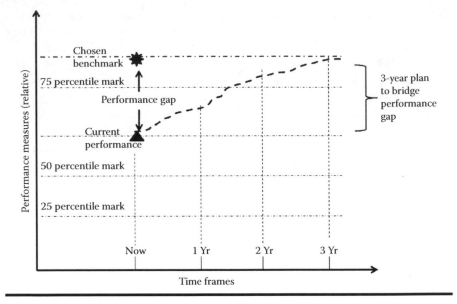

Figure 5.2 Setting goals using benchmarking techniques.

Identifying Performance Gaps and Best Practices

The benchmarking team works toward understanding the performance gap that exists between the benchmarking organization and the benchmark. It is important to identify the practices being followed by the chosen benchmark and how these translate to superior performance. It is important to note that best practices are context dependent and not all of these might lead to similar results for the benchmarking organization. It is a good idea to consider a broader set of best practices and then choose a smaller subset based on recommendations of various stakeholders.

Communicating and Reporting Results

It is important to record and report the results of a benchmarking exercise properly. In most instances, the benchmarking study is a project in itself, with a defined objective and an agreed upon end date. It is thus important to ensure that the results of benchmarking analysis are recorded appropriately and shared with concerned parties on a timely basis. Both the content and representation of the results play an important role in determining the usefulness of the benchmarking report. Any good benchmarking report should contain information pertaining to the strategic goals of the benchmarking exercise, approach considerations, involved participants, data collection methodology, data analysis details, best practices, and details on how these can be adapted to lead to superior performance for the benchmarking organization.

Initiating Program for Continuous Improvement

Armed with facts and findings from the benchmarking study, organizations can capitalize on the drive and momentum received by conducting the benchmarking study by embarking on a journey of continuous improvement. It is important to reassess performance against benchmarks periodically. Benchmarking, like any other pursuit of quality, is related to a continuous journey toward better products, services, and processes.

Benchmarking in the Context of IT and Software Measurement

With the increased focus on maximizing returns on IT investment and increased need for prudent spending decisions, improving an organization's processes to provide better, more reliable, and more efficient products and services has become increasingly important. This section discusses applications of benchmarking in the context of the IT and software industry.

Over the past few years, application of quality management techniques has increased in the IT industry. Armed with increased awareness on quality processes, the IT industry has successfully adapted quality practices and principles that were used by the manufacturing industry in the past. The propagation of Six Sigma methods, Lean principles, and other quality management philosophies has ensured that the IT industry has been able to better itself to meet the new challenges and pressures it faces. An emerging trend in the IT and software management field is the increasing use of benchmarking studies to gain competitive advantage. Benchmarking techniques have been utilized by some IT organizations to gauge their performance relative to a chosen benchmark. Analysis of software project metrics using benchmarking techniques has also become a more popular tool in the past few years.

What Can Be Benchmarked in the IT Context?

Almost any important metric can become a candidate to be evaluated using benchmarking if it is linked to an organization's quality goals. Below is a list of metrics that are generally chosen as candidates for benchmarking in the IT and software measurement industry.

- Total cost of ownership of IT services
- Blended rate of IT services provided by various vendors
- Project financials like contribution margins
- Return on IT investment
- Effort variance
- Schedule variance

- Review comment density
- Number and types of defects in artifacts
- Defect turnaround times
- Defect age
- Product and software performance metrics

The above list is indicative and is not exhaustive by any means. The choice of a metric or a combination of metrics needs to be made based on the needs of the organization performing the benchmarking study. It is possible to benchmark the performance of products, processes, and teams using metrics benchmarking. The exercise of benchmarking metrics with data collected from past releases is a useful tool for comparing, understanding, and analyzing performance trends.

The Box and Whisker Technique

There are many tools and techniques available for benchmarking software products, processes, and performances. One simple yet effective method for benchmarking a project's performance is related to the concept of descriptive statistics. A *box-and-whisker diagram* can serve as a simple and effective tool for graphically depicting groups of numerical data.

Let us assume that we plan on benchmarking defects classified as "operator errors" for a recently completed testing project against that of similar past projects. It is known that the operator errors metric of the current project (defined as defects that were due to operator mistakes measured as a percentage of total defects logged by the testing team) is 10%. It is not known however how this project metric compares with the past projects delivered in the organization. Benchmarking can help provide some answers.

It is important to collect information on sample size, sample maximum and minimum, and upper and lower quartiles as shown below to be able to plot a box-and-whisker plot.

- Sample size = 25 (data from 25 such projects was considered)
- Sample range = 1% to 20%
- Sample maximum = 20%
- Sample minimum = 1%
- Current level = 10%
- Mean (average) = 7.64%

Analysis on the above data needs to be performed to gauge how the various data points perform compared to one another. This can be found by using percentile numbers instead of actual data values. The top quartile (75 percentile mark) and bottom quartile (25 percentile mark) are of particular interest in most benchmarking studies. Continuing on the above discussion of operator errors, let us further assume the following values of the metric mark the top and bottom quartile:

- Top quartile (Q1) = 3%
- Bottom quartile (Q3) = 11%

Including the median or mean values can lead to additional insights related to any skew in the collected data sample. Including this in the equation can help obtain a more precise analysis of current performance level with respect to the metric being benchmarked (Figure 5.3).

- Median = 7%
- Mean = 7.64%

	Operator error (%)	
Project 3	1%	
Project 4	1%	
Project 5	2%	
Project 21	2%	75 percentile mark
Project 22	3%	
Project 6	4%	
Project 7	4%	
Project 8	4%	
Project 9	5%	
Project 18	5%	
Project 19	5%	
Project 20	6%	
Project 25	7%	
Project 23	8%	
Project 24	8%	
Project 2	10%	
Project 12	10%	
Project 13	10%	
Project 14	11%	25 percentile mark
Project 16	11%	
Project 17	11%	
Project 1	12%	
Project 15	13%	
Project 11	18%	
Project 10	20%	

- Data sorted in ascending order for percentile analysis

Figure 5.3   Percentile analysis.

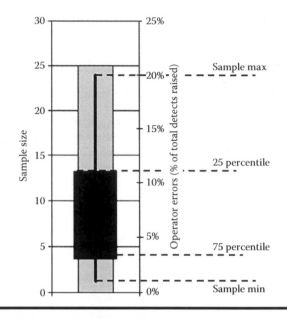

Figure 5.4 Sample box-and-whisker plot.

The graphical representation of the metric data of the sample discussed above using the box-and-whisker plot is given in Figure 5.4.

The following inferences can be made from the above metric benchmarking analysis:

■ In past projects, operator errors have varied from 1% to 20% (range).
■ Values greater than 11% and less than 3% are rare occurrences.
■ The current metric falls under the majority range and is not an outlier.
■ The current metric is greater than the mean and median value.
■ The metric under observation for this project has a greater value than many past projects.
■ The whisker depicts the spread of the data and the box depicts its dispersion.

If the current metric falls in the outliers (outside the 25 percentile to 75 percentile range), then it might make sense to investigate the reasons behind the fact. Sometimes the outliers may be because of exceptional performance (exceptionally good or exceptionally bad, depending upon the metric under review). Most of the times, however, there might be other reasons that lead to outliers (unrelated to performance and related to exceptional circumstances).

Benchmarking Case Studies

In this section, we discuss practical usage of benchmarking techniques using case studies. These case studies have been included to provide readers with examples of real-life scenarios where benchmarking techniques can be employed in IT and software measurement. Readers are encouraged to use these examples as catalysts to think of specific problems at their workplace that they can attempt to resolve using benchmarking techniques.

Case Study 1—The Test Manager's Dilemma

Case Description

Zara is a Test Manager for a crucial system testing effort. She and her team of 10 testers have been involved in testing various new releases of software in the past. The testing team is currently in the process of executing test cases and reporting the defects that are found in the process. The testing phase was 2 months in duration of which 1 month has already passed. The progress has been slow, partly due to the time it is taking to fix the defects. The defect support team members, who are responsible for fixing the defects, are working simultaneously on two projects. It has been Zara's experience that because of the lack of much-needed timely attention on fixing the defects, poor quality code has had to be delivered in the past. Zara plans to work with Gerry, the manager of the defect support team, to find a solution to this problem of defect turnaround times that has persisted for a long time in the organization. Zara has access to testing metrics data from past releases and decides to turn to this metric database and benchmarking techniques to look for a solution.

Commentary on the Benchmarking Solution

Zara worked with her team members to analyze data from past releases. She also referred to international journals to research industry averages related to software metrics. After she had done an initial analysis and had some data with her, she had a meeting with Gerry and tried to gain his support in this initiative. Although Gerry was slightly hesitant at first, he agreed to participate in this "experiment" because of the possible advantages that Zara was confident of achieving. Zara proceeded to collect more data and started applying benchmarking techniques to the collected data. An extract on the important observations and findings on the benchmarking study has been included below.

Defect Age

Zara and Gerry agreed that the defects were open for a long time, and this led to the execution of test cases being delayed. Zara looked at the defect management tool to extract defect age (defined as the total days elapsed between the dates a defect was opened and closed). It was found that the average defect age was 10 days for the releases that had been tested over the past 2 years. Zara tried to compare

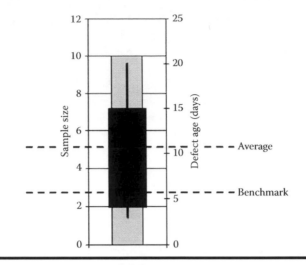

Figure 5.5 Case study 1 (box-and-whisker plot for defect age metric).

the existing release's numbers with the cumulative data from past releases. She also worked with Gerry to determine a benchmark value for defect age in the particular release-based environment. Both of them agreed that most of the defects could have been fixed in an average of 4 days, provided someone had been working on these. Taking a cautious approach, they chose 6 days as a benchmark and performed the current state analysis using the box-and-whisker technique on the defect age metric.

Gerry and Zara presented the analysis to their team members and asked them about ways to reduce the defect age (Figure 5.5).

Best Practices from Research and Brainstorming

Changes in Defect Log Template

The defect support team came forward with ideas for including additional information to the defect log template. When this additional information was included in the defect reports, the developers had to spend less time researching this information. This in turn led to faster resolution of defects.

Changes in Defect Assignment Process

The testing team raised a point that all defects were currently being raised by the 10 test team members and assigned to Charles, who was the team lead of the defect support team. It was Charles who assigned the defects to the support team members. Sometimes when Charles was busy in meetings or out of the office, this process had led to defects not being assigned to the defect support team on time. The team decided to start assigning critical defects directly to the concerned support

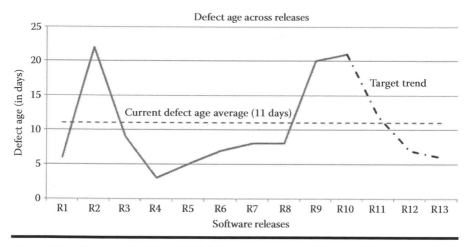

Figure 5.6   Case study 1 (trend of defect age across software releases).

team members and update Charles in the daily status meeting on such defects. This led to further reduction in the defect age (Figure 5.6).

Case for Additional Resources

Gerry and Zara decided to use these metrics to build a case for requesting additional temporary resources to assist during the system testing phase of the releases. They were able to convince the resource management team for some additional team members who were temporarily allocated to reduce quality risks highlighted by Gerry and Zara.

Targets for Continual Improvement

Zara, Gerry, and team came up with a time bound target and detailed plan to achieve their target of reducing the average defect age to 5 days in the course of the next 6 months. In a period of 2 months, with their second release after the implementation of the benchmarking program, they have been able to beat their interim target by a small margin. Whether they will be able to reach their goals in time now depends upon how well their team follows the improvement plan and how the team looks for better ways to ensure reduction in defect age.

Case Study 2—A Case for Vendor Management

Case Description

Joanne has recently joined the vendor management group. In her new role in the bank's IT division, she has been entrusted with the task of making recommendations about choosing a strategic vendor partner from the current vendor pool. During her initial analysis, Joanne has found that there are more than 10 vendor companies that are providing software development and testing services to the bank. She also found that there is little uniformity in terms of the quality, nature, and rate of services offered by these vendor organizations. It is one of the goals of the senior management to reduce the overhead effort currently required to manage vendor delivery and transition to a service-level agreement (SLA) based, managed services mode of operation. Based on her discussions with senior management, Joanne understood that the chosen vendor organization will be responsible for end-to-end delivery of software development and testing services.

In addition to recommending vendors most suitable for the planned transition to the managed services mode, Joanne is expected to suggest service levels that should be used to ensure that the quality of deliverables is not affected adversely by this transition.

Commentary on the Benchmarking Solution

Joanne started on this task by gathering metric data available for projects completed by the vendor organizations. Where metric data was not readily available, Joanne relied on surveys and interviews with various department leads and project managers to get a fair idea of current performance levels and satisfaction levels for the services provided by each of the vendor organizations. Over a period of 2 weeks, Joanne was able to get sufficient data to start the benchmarking exercise. She used the data from these 10 vendor organizations to form the data sample for the benchmarking exercise. Although she would be able to use the data from all the 10 vendor organizations to build up the sample set, she planned to benchmark the performance of 5 of these 10 vendor organizations because she was able to eliminate 5 of the choices based on other mandatory criteria set by management.

Joanne analyzed customer satisfaction (calculated on a 10-point scale based on surveys), average cost of services provided in dollars per hour, quality of deliverables, schedule variance, and effort variance metrics. Joanne found that customer satisfaction and average cost of services were the two most important aspects of senior management. A snapshot of the results of the benchmarking exercise performed by Joanne is given in Figure 5.7.

Best Practices from Research and Brainstorming

Narrowing Down to Two Best Choices

Instead of looking at performance attributes independently, Joanne looked at combinations of performance attributes and compared these for the five chosen vendors. This analysis gave the management a perspective on the relative performance of the vendor organizations. This data, when taken in conjunction with the strategic aims of the organization, helped choose the strategic partner for outsourcing of IT services (Figure 5.8).

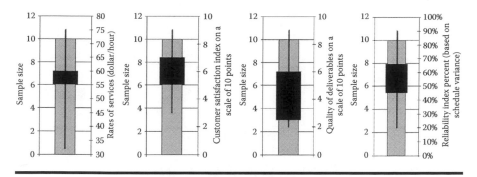

Figure 5.7 Case study 2 (box-and-whisker plots for various metrics).

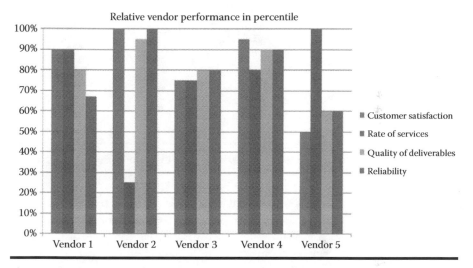

Figure 5.8 Case study 2 (vendor evaluation based on performance metrics).

Determining Service Levels

Joanne used the data she had meticulously collected for vendor selection to determine service levels that were realistically achievable and yet challenging at the same time. Using benchmarking techniques, she was able to use past performance trends and determine SLAs that could be taken as benchmarks for chosen performance attributes (Figure 5.9).

Case Study 3—Increased Accountability and Responsibility, a By-Product of Benchmarking

Linda is a program manager in a major IT consulting organization. She manages a program in the credit card technology domain. The program that Linda manages

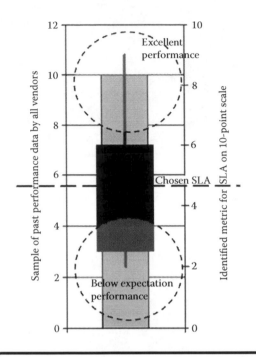

Figure 5.9 Case study 2 (using benchmarking for determining service levels).

has around 8 to 10 concurrent and overlapping projects being executed at a time. Overall, Linda is happy with the way these projects have been managed in the past. However, she sometimes feels that though the project managers are ensuring proper quality and timely deliverables, more work could be done in the area of reducing costs and achieving greater return on investments. She is particularly pleased with the work of one of the project managers, Henry, who has maintained a detailed log of project financials, estimated and actual costs of various projects managed by him, cumulative margin tracking, and other project financials. Linda wishes to inculcate similar accountability and financial responsibility in all her project managers.

Commentary on the Benchmarking Solution

When Linda started asking all her project managers to maintain metrics related to project finance, they were initially resistant to change. Many of them questioned the actual need for these numbers and were not very keen on adding new activities to their already busy schedules. Linda worked with them to explain to them the importance of having detailed project financials and related information. She assigned Henry the task of mentoring the other team members and motivating them to maintain records of such metrics in a uniform format. Over the next 6 months, the team was able to build a database of such financial metrics for the projects they managed during that time. Linda and her team decided to benchmark their project financials against the industry averages that Linda and Henry had researched. After performing a benchmarking exercise, the team found that although they were performing well as a team there were still a few challenges that they needed to address.

Best Practices from Research and Brainstorming

Linda and her team set up a 2-year goal and are working toward achieving it with the cooperation and support of the organization's senior management team. They are currently looking at outsourcing certain type of projects in order to ensure one of their aims of reducing total IT spend is met. Linda is happy to see that the project managers are working hard to meet these goals. She has observed a spirit of healthy competition between the project managers as they find innovative ways to better their performance and the program's financial health.

Conclusion

Benchmarking has become an essential tool in the IT industry's quality toolbox. Benchmarking techniques will continue to be a strategic tool for performance measurement in the IT industry. Aided by increased awareness and increased opportunities for sharing of industry knowledge, benchmarking has evolved into a commonly used technique for relative performance measurement and setting of realistic, achievable, and challenging targets. The already strong bond between strategy and benchmarking will continue to grow stronger in the years to come. Benchmarking techniques will continue to help IT companies measure their performance and challenge them to better their performance by observing, learning, and adapting from the best in class.

Bibliography

Keehley, P., and Abercrombie N. N. *Benchmarking in the Public and Nonprofit Sectors: Best Practices for Achieving Performance Breakthroughs.* 2nd ed. San Francisco, CA: Wiley, 2008.

Black, R. *Managing the Testing Process.* 2nd ed. Wiley, 2002.

Watson, G. H. *Strategic Benchmarking: How to Rate Your Company's Performance against the World's Best.* John Wiley & Sons, 1993.

About the Author

Nishant Pandey, lead consultant with Capgemini Canada, is currently working in the business process management domain. Prior to moving to this role, Nishant was working as the program test manager for a prestigious client of Capgemini

Financial Services in the USA. Nishant has 9 years of work experience in the field of software engineering and quality assurance. He is a certified project manager and test manager. Additionally, Mr. Pandey holds a Bachelor of Engineering Degree in Electronics and Telecommunications from the University of Pune (India) and has completed the Certificate in IT Benchmarking from Stanford University (USA). Many of his articles on software metric benchmarking, software quality assurance, process improvements, and software testing have been featured in publications of international repute.

ESTIMATION
INTRODUCTION

Luigi Buglione

The best we can do is size up the chances, calculate the risks involved, estimate our ability to deal with them, and then make our plans with confidence

Henry Ford

One interesting thing to observe from real life compared to the way many IT projects are managed is that in real life we store plenty of historical, qualitative, and quantitative data that can be used for doing estimates. This is different from IT projects, where often estimates are still done by experience and analogy. A doctor needs to have a plenty of input measures in order to initially produce a diagnosis and later a prognosis. A car driver (or a GPS system) needs at least to know the distance from the arrival point, the traffic situation, the possible speed for that path, and the general conditions about his/her car in order to determine the time of arrival.

On the other hand, an IT project manager often does not have a large amount of input measures (or very few, in comparison) in order to produce a reliable estimate for time and costs. Thus, the first open question could be: Are we measuring the right phenomenon in our organization? If not, why?

The other interesting issue from the above quote from Henry Ford involves the term "confidence"; another value that should be historically tracked (but rarely is) is the difference between an estimate and its actual value. The root-cause analysis (RCA) from historical data is the most valuable source of information to an organization for improving its performance and achieving results over time. As James Joyce said, "A man's errors are his portals of discovery." We should learn from experience, but experience should be kept inside the organization and not shared externally. Another misconception is that a proper, structured estimation process should calculate the overall project time and cost values to be reflected within each project phase but with less detail and effort. But shouldn't an estimate for how much time, cost, and resources are needed for the Testing phase result from testing-related measures (with a bottom–up approach) and not simply be derived as a percentage from the overall project estimates? Estimation is hard work, but not a "black art," as in the title of a well-known book by Steve McConnell.

In this section, there are seven chapters, each one involving a different facet of estimation. Murali Chemuturi proposes an overview of the most typical techniques and approaches to determine project effort, while also applying functional size measures such as Function Points and related information from historical data, then applying Project Delivery Rates (PDR) typical for a certain domain/environment. Emilia Mendes faced the estimation of web projects through a predictive and diagnostic reasoning approach. The analysis of 22 projects using Bayesian networks (BNs) shows how it is possible to focus on the few, core vital parameters for improving estimates after starting with a larger set of parameters. Luiz Flávio Santos Ribeiro proposes a method for estimating software testing effort using a customized version of Test Point Analysis (TPA) called Adapted TPA (ATPA). This method was used experimentally with some public Brazilian organizations. Ricardo Valerdi discusses the role of optimism in judgment and in the decision-making process, arguing the reasons for eventual bias and why it could lead to a better cost estimation. Last but not least, Luca Santillo discusses how to produce reliable estimates dealing with uncertainty by reducing the so-called Cone of Uncertainty.

Chapter 6

Effort Estimation for Software Projects

Murali Chemuturi

Contents

Introduction

Is it mandatory to carry out software functional size estimation? If I am asked, it would be difficult for me to answer affirmatively without any hesitation. It definitely is advantageous to carry out software functional size estimation but it certainly is not mandatory to do so. However, if I were asked if it is mandatory to carry out software development effort estimation, I would neither have hesitation nor lose a minute to answer in a resounding "Yes!" Estimating software functional size would allow us to form an idea about the effort, cost, and duration it takes to develop the specified software product, as well as derive the productivity of software development activity, which in turn facilitates benchmarking the organization with other similar organizations or the project with other projects in the same organization. Effort estimation facilitates estimation of the resources (namely, human resources, equipment resources, monetary resources, and time resources) required to execute the project successfully. This chapter discusses the methodologies for arriving at the effort required for development of a software product. This chapter also discusses briefly the concept of software productivity to aid in arriving at software development effort from software functional size.

Techniques for Estimating the Software Development Effort

We have the following techniques for arriving at the estimated effort for a software development project:

- Deriving the effort estimate from the software functional size estimate:
  - Directly converting software functional size into effort
  - Using parametric models like Constructive Cost Model (COCOMO) [1] to derive effort from software functional size estimate
- Estimating the software development effort directly:
  - Task-based estimation
  - Delphi technique
  - Analogy-based estimation
  - Ballparking

We will discuss each of these techniques in greater detail in the ensuing sections.

Deriving Effort Estimate from Software Functional Size

This is perhaps the most popular method of carrying out effort estimation for software development projects. In this method, a conversion factor, usually referred to as the Project Delivery Rate (PDR), is applied to the software functional size to obtain the effort estimate for the software project. Now, there are two ways of applying PDR to software functional size to obtain software development effort. They are the following:

1. Applying a single PDR to the software functional size
2. Applying multiple PDRs to the software functional size

Let us discuss each of these methods in greater detail.

Deriving Effort by Applying a Single PDR

In this method, we convert software functional size into software development effort applying only one PDR. This PDR is assumed to include all the activities necessary for developing the software product including requirements analysis, software design, construction, and quality assurance. This PDR is often referred to as "Macro PDR."

There are two ways of expressing the PDR:

1. As the number of person hours (PH) per unit of software functional size, say, one Function Point (FP)
2. As the amount of software functional size (say, FP) per unit of time, say, person day (PD)

Using the first notation, for example, a PDR of 10 PH per FP means, it takes 10 PH on average to develop software of functional size of one FP. We use the below formula to obtain the effort for the project applying the PDR:

$$\text{Effort} = \text{Software functional size} \times \text{PDR}$$

Now, assume that we have estimated the software functional size for a given software development project as 1000 FP, and the PDR is 10 PH per FP. Substituting these values in the above formula, we get:

$$\text{Effort} = 1000 \times 10$$

That is—10,000 PH.

It is also common to express the PDR as software functional size that can be developed in a unit time. In this instance, the PDR is mentioned as the number of FP per PD (person day), say, 0.7 FP per PD, which means that in one person day a software of functional size 0.7 FP can be developed. When we use this form of notation, we derive the effort from software functional size using the below formula:

$$\text{Effort} = \text{Software functional size}/\text{PDR}$$

Let us assume a software development product of functional size 1000 FP and a PDR of 0.7 FP per PD. Substituting these values in the above formula, we get:

$$\text{Effort} = 1000/0.7$$

$$\text{That is—}1428.57 \text{ PD.}$$

We can use either notation of PDR, that is, either PH per FP or FP per PD depending on our organizational standard practice. The first notation (PH per FP) is more prevalent in the United States and the second notation is more common in India.

Merits of Using a Single PDR (Macro PDR)

The following are the merits of using a single PDR to convert software functional size into software development effort:

- It is very easy to derive the PDR from organizational data.
- Most of the existing timesheets would be adequate for deriving the PDR and there would be no need to use more elaborate time booking systems.
- It is easy to understand and apply. There is just one figure to use, either to multiply or divide, to obtain software development effort.
- This method would average out over a number of projects and would give satisfactory results, on the whole.
- This is the most common method adopted across the industry facilitating easy benchmarking of project data across the industry.

Demerits of Using a Single PDR (Macro PDR)

The following are the demerits of using a single PDR:

- This can be used only for a full life-cycle project. Alternatively, we need to have a different PDR for full life-cycle projects and for each type of partial life-cycle project. As we do not have a standard software development life cycle across the industry or an organization, we need to have a different PDR figure for each different life cycle. Deriving so many productivity figures, for each of the life cycles or partial life cycles, is cumbersome.

■ In reality, software development is not one single specialty. It consists of a number of disparate activities needing differently skilled personnel, each having different rates of productivity (pace of achievement). It is not right to view a heterogeneous set of activities as a homogenous set of activities and apply one PDR.

■ When we apply one single PDR, we are implying that different activities (say software design and construction or requirements analysis and testing) have the same PDR, which is not true.

■ While this method may give satisfactory results on average over a large number of projects, it would not be accurate for any single given project.

■ The probability of the effort estimate being reliable is low for any given project.

Deriving Effort by Applying Multiple PDRs

Recognizing that software development is composed of multiple disparate and heterogeneous activities is the idea behind using multiple productivity figures. That is, a different PDR is used for a different class of software development activity. When we use a different PDR for each of the different activities, it is often referred to as "Micro PDR."

For example, requirements analysis is normally carried out by business analysts, software design is carried out by software architects, database design is carried out by database administrators (DBAs), user interface (UI) design is carried out by UI specialists, construction is carried out by programmers, and testing is carried out by testers. Each of these activities has a different pace of achievement. Therefore, the software functional size is converted into software development effort activity-by-activity using a different PDR for each of the activities.

For example, we may classify software development activities into:

■ Requirements analysis
■ Software design
■ Database design
■ UI design
■ Construction
■ Testing
■ And so on...

The phases enumerated above are only an example. It is common for each software development organization to have a specific software development life cycle and the reader is advised to use the phases according to his/her organizational standard. One guiding principle, however, is to classify the activities by the specialty needed to perform the activity. For example, we may combine all activities performed by business analysts as one set and all activities performed by programmers as one set and so on.

We can assign a different PDR for each of these activities. An example of this is shown in Table 6.1.

Using the PDRs given in Table 6.1, we can convert software functional size into software development effort. Let us assume a product of functional size 1000 FP. This is depicted in Table 6.2.

Table 6.1   Assignment of PDRs for Each of the Software Development Activities

Software Development Activity	PDR—PH per FP
Requirements analysis	2
Software design	3
Database design	1
UI design	1
Construction	3
Testing	2

Table 6.2   Conversion of Software Functional Size (1000 FP) into Software Development Effort (PDR—PH per FP)

Software Development Activity	PDR—PH per FP	Software Development Effort in PH
Requirements analysis	2	2,000
Software design	3	3,000
Database design	1	1,000
UI design	1	1,000
Construction	3	3,000
Testing	2	2,000
Total software development effort		12,000

Table 6.3 Conversion of Software Functional Size (1000 FP) into Software Development Effort (PDR—FP per PD)

Software Development Activity	PDR—FP per PD	Software Development Effort in PD
Requirements analysis	4	250
Software design	3	333.33
Database design	8	125
UI design	8	125
Construction	3	333.33
Testing	4	250
Total software development effort		1,416.66

Derivation of software development effort using the second notation of PDR (FP per PD) is depicted, assuming a product of functional size 1000 FP, in Table 6.3. Please note that Table 6.3 is an example and not a comprehensive depiction of all possible phases that may be used. The reader is advised to follow his/her organizational standard in this regard. We may adopt either method conforming to the organizational standard practice.

Merits of Using Multiple PDRs (Micro PDR) to Convert Software Functional Size into Effort

The merits of using multiple PDRs (Micro PDR) to convert software functional size into software development effort are the following:

■ Dividing the software development activity into the constituent tasks allows us to convert software functional size into effort for either full life-cycle projects or partial life-cycle projects, or any software development life-cycle projects. This is especially useful, as we do not have a standard software development life cycle.
■ Since we apply PDR at the activity level (micro PDR), we get more reliable effort estimates.
■ As we have PDR for all the activities, there is a better schedule to monitor project execution as well as to analyze effort variances between estimated effort and actual effort, allowing us to pinpoint the origins of and reasons for variance and to effect process improvements.

Demerits of Using Multiple PDRs (Micro PDR) to Convert Software Functional Size into Effort

The demerits of using multiple PDRs (micro PDR) to convert software functional size into software development effort are the following:

- In order to use this method, we need to derive multiple PDRs for different software development activities. This may necessitate more detailed time sheets and data collection mechanisms in the organization. It would also require more computations and effort to maintain the PDRs.
- This method may require specialist personnel to derive and maintain different PDRs.

Handling Uncertainty Inherent in Converting Software Functional Size into Effort

The term "estimation" itself indicates that it precedes actual performance, and hence, there is inherent uncertainty. It becomes more prominent especially when we use averages that by definition are valid over large numbers but may not be accurate in any one given case.

Almost always, there is a difference between the estimated value and the actual value. When a software project is completed, it is customary to carry out "variance analysis" and compute the absolute variance and the relative variance between the actual values (of both size and effort). The formulas for absolute variance and relative variance are given as follows:

$$\text{Absolute variance} = \text{Actual value} - \text{Estimated value}$$

$$\text{Relative variance} = [(\text{Actual value} - \text{Estimated value})/\text{Actual value}] \times 100$$

Absolute variance does not facilitate comparison between different project performances as their size/effort would vary. Relative variance, as it is expressed as percentage, allows us to compare between project performances. Therefore, it is common to use relative variance in the software development industry. Relative variance is normally referred to as "variance" and is usually expressed as a percentage. Variance, when applied at the stage of estimation to predict the probability of meeting the estimated value during the project execution, is referred to as the "relative error." Each organization would derive a relative error (RE) over a number of projects. This RE would be used as a measure of uncertainty inherent in the estimate. However, the RE is likely to vary from project to project and is dependent on a number of factors including the information (in terms of both quality and quantity) used during estimation, the methodology used, the expertise available, the duration available for estimation, and so on. It is not rare for the actual variance to be as much as 100% or more in the software development industry.

Therefore, we need to understand that there is uncertainty in the effort estimate derived from software functional size, applying either one PDR or multiple productivity figures. It is not possible to do away with uncertainty in software estimation completely, but we can either reduce the uncertainty or reduce the impact of uncertainty.

We have three methods for handling this uncertainty in software development effort estimation:

1. We assume uncertainty in software functional size. Therefore, we use one PDR but three software functional sizes for the software product to handle uncertainty:
   a. Best-case software functional size—when every component is built to its minimum functional size.
   b. Worst-case software functional size—when every component is built to its maximum functional size.
   c. Normal-case software functional size—when components are built in varying degrees of functional size with some at the maximum functional size, some at the minimum functional size, and some at the in-between functional sizes.
2. We assume uncertainty in the PDR. Therefore, we use one software functional size but three PDRs to handle uncertainty:
   a. Best-case PDR—when the highest pace of output is achieved and the PDR is at its highest.
   b. Worst-case PDR— when the lowest pace of output is achieved and the PDR is at its lowest.
   c. Normal-case PDR—when the pace of output is neither the highest nor the lowest; it is an in-between value.
3. We may also assume uncertainty in both software functional size and PDR. Here we use the minimum and maximum effort estimates considering both the above derivations.

Some people may argue that we need not consider uncertainty in software functional size as it is arrived at conforming to a validated methodology and that each component has but one functional size. The uncertainty is not in the methodology of arriving at the software functional size, but it is in the ability of predicting all the components that form part of the proposed software product. It is possible that some of the components are forgotten/missed. Therefore, there is, even if limited, uncertainty in software functional size too.

When the functional domain of the project being estimated is new but the software development platform is familiar to the organization, there would be higher uncertainty in software functional size. When the software development platform is new but the domain is familiar to the organization, there would be higher uncertainty in the PDR. If both the domain and the platform were new to the organization, there would be higher uncertainty in both software functional size and the PDR. We need to assess uncertainty case-by-case to determine if we need to handle it in either software functional size or PDR or both.

Table 6.4 depicts an example of handling uncertainty in software functional size applying the same PDR assuming a normal-case product functional size of 1000 FP and a PDR of 10 PH per FP.

We present the estimated effort saying that the project could be completed with a minimum of 9,000 PH and a maximum of 11,000 PH, but we expect it to finish within 10,000 PH. Thus, we are not only giving the nominal value, but we are also giving the limits of variance the project could be subjected to in terms of software development effort. This would improve the predictability of project performance at the software estimation stage.

The best-case and worst-case figures in Table 6.4 are assumed figures. In reality, we need to estimate these figures along with normal-case functional size while carrying out software functional size estimation if we expect that there would be higher uncertainty in software functional size.

Table 6.5 depicts an example of the method to handle uncertainty in PDR assuming a product functional size of 1000 FP and a normal-case PDR of 10 PH per FP.

We present the estimated effort saying that the project could be completed with a minimum of 9,500 PH and a maximum of 12,000 PH, but we expect it to finish with 10,000 PH. Thus we are not only giving the nominal value, but we are also giving the limits of variance the project could be subjected to in terms of software development effort. This would improve the predictability of project performance at the software estimation stage.

Table 6.4   Handling Uncertainty in Software Functional Size

Software Functional Size	Functional Size in FP	Effort in PH
Best case	900	9,000
Worst case	1,100	11,000
Normal case	1,000	10,000

Table 6.5   Handling Uncertainty in the PDR

Productivity	PDR in PH per FP	Effort in PH
Best case	9.5	9,500
Worst case	12	12,000
Normal case	10	10,000

Normally, handling either the software functional size or the productivity would suffice for most projects. If we need to handle uncertainty in both software functional size and productivity, we need to use both the methodologies depicted in Tables 6.4 and 6.5 but give the minimum effort and the maximum effort from the combined set of values arrived at. In the above examples, the minimum effort is 9,000 PH (from Table 6.4), maximum value is 12,000 PH (from Table 6.5), and we present these figures as the range.

Table 6.6 depicts an example of handling uncertainty in software functional size using multiple PDRs and Table 6.7 depicts handling uncertainty in PDR using multiple PDRs. Please note that all the figures in Table 6.7 are assumed figures and are used for illustrative purposes only. They are not to be misunderstood to be validated values.

It is always better to give a set of figures for an estimation request. That way, we provide better insight to the decision makers as well as providing them elasticity in their decision making. We need to remember that pricing is a commercial decision and by giving them a range of estimated values, the decision makers would understand the rock-bottom cost below which they should not price and the maximum cost that needs to be expended if the worst set of conditions prevail during the execution of the project. We also need to remember that the estimate is not the same as commitment. Commitment is made to the customer by the decision makers keeping the competition in mind. When the estimate undershoots the

Table 6.6   Handling Uncertainty in Software Functional Size Using Multiple PDRs

Activity	PDR in PH per FP	Effort with Best-Case Functional Size in PH (900 FP)	Effort with Worst-Case Functional Size in PH in FP (1100 FP)	Effort with Normal-Case Functional Size in PH in FP (1000 FP)
Requirements analysis	2	1,800	2,200	2,000
Software design	3	2,700	3,300	3,000
Database design	1	900	1,100	1,000
UI design	1	900	1,100	1,000
Construction	3	2,700	3,300	3,000
Testing	2	1,800	2,200	2,000
Total effort		10,800	13,200	12,000

Table 6.7   Handling Uncertainty in PDR Using Multiple PDRs Assuming Software Functional Size of 1000 FP

Activity	Effort with Best-Case PDR		Effort with Worst-Case PDR		Effort with Normal-Case PDR	
	PDR	Effort	PDR	Effort	PDR	Effort
Requirements analysis	1.5	1,500	3	3,000	2	2,000
Software design	1	1,000	4	4,000	3	3,000
Database design	0.5	500	2	2,000	1	1,000
UI design	0.5	500	2	2,000	1	1,000
Construction	1	1,000	4	4,000	3	3,000
Testing	1	1,000	3	3,000	2	2,000
Total effort		5,5000		18,000		12,000

commitment (that is, estimated effort is more than the committed effort), there are alternatives available for project executors, which include using better tools, methods, resources, or subcontracting to meet the commitment. It pays to remember that an estimate is made with assumed values and commitments are made to win the order. These two could be divergent. Making the right commitments is a subject for marketers and senior management, and how to make the correct commitment is a subject beyond this chapter. How to meet the commitments is a subject for project executors. Estimators need to provide the best possible estimate and leave the rest to marketers, senior management, and project executors.

Productivity

One crucial aspect of deriving the software development effort from software functional size is the conversion factor that converts software functional size into software development effort. If the figure is erroneous, the resultant effort will also be erroneous. The more important question, however, is how do we obtain the conversion figure? It is an organizational responsibility to make the conversion figures available to the estimators. Normally, the project management office (PMO), the organizational metrics council (OMC), the standards group (or the process group), or the quality assurance department in the organization own the responsibility to provide the conversion figures to the estimators. The plural term is used because it is probable that organizations use multiple software development platforms, and therefore, each platform would have a different pace of achievement.

Now it is appropriate to understand the term "productivity" itself before we set out on explaining how to obtain the productivity figures. One definition of productivity is that it is output divided by input. It sounds just like the definition of the term "efficiency." The term "efficiency," however, is used in the context of machines and the term "productivity" is used in the context of human beings. Another definition of the term "productivity" is the set of inputs needed to produce a unit of output. Since the main input is the human effort in the case of software development, productivity is the amount of human effort, measured in PH, required to produce a unit of software measured in FP. Thus, productivity in the case of software development is to be understood as the PH per FP. We may state thus:

■ Productivity of requirements analysis is 3 PH per FP
■ Productivity of software design is 5 PH per FP
■ Productivity of construction is 4 PH per FP
■ Productivity of testing is 2 PH per FP
■ And so on…

IFPUG's "Guidelines for Software Measurement" [2] states the above method of specifying the productivity (so many PH per FP) as PDR.

The Institute of Industrial Engineering, USA (www.iienet.org) has a more comprehensive definition for productivity, defining it as follows: "*Standard time* (productivity) *is the amount of time required to accomplish a unit of work* (say, one FP) *in a defined environment using defined methods, by a qualified worker after adjustment, at a pace that can be maintained day after day without any harmful physical effects.*" This definition also takes into consideration the environment, methods of working, the qualification and adjustment of the worker, and the pace at which the work is carried out. We ought to note the emphasis placed on the word "pace," which should be sustainable for the entire day but is not the peak speed. It is not a 100-meter dash in Olympics; it is more like a marathon (26 miles or 42 km). It is the optimum pace where the pace of achievement and safety of the individual are balanced. The pace is such that it earns more than the expenditure. In addition, it is such that it exerts the person but not to the extent of damaging the person's health in any manner. We need to understand that we estimate software development effort at this optimum pace. However, the actual pace of working during the project execution could be different, either slower or faster. It is for the project execution team to ensure that every member of the project team maintains this optimum pace. If the actual pace of working is slower, the actual effort is likely to be more than the estimated effort, and if the pace is faster than the optimum pace, then the actual effort is likely to be less than the estimated effort.

Another common confusion prevalent among the estimators is the difference in skill levels. People in an organization have different levels of skill. People with more experience are more skilled than a new entrant. Generally, skill level is classified into five levels, namely super skill, very good skill, good skill, fair skill, and poor skill. A poorly skilled person could be a trainee and a super skilled person could have more than seven years of experience. When we estimate, we take into consideration "good" level skill—that is, an average skilled person. When we execute the project, we may get a mix of skills. Then there would be variance between the estimated effort and actual effort, and this variance is due to an assignable reason. It is for the agency allocating resources to the project team to ensure that equivalence is achieved between the estimated and allocated number of persons when the skill levels are normalized to good level skill, if variance between the estimated and actual effort needs to be minimized. It is not adequate to say, "Ten persons are estimated and we gave ten people." The ten given might be equivalent to twelve or eight people of good skill. The given number must be equivalent to ten people of good skill level.

In essence, we assume people with good skill level are putting in a good level of effort at the time of estimating the effort and duration necessary for completing the project. It is for the project execution team to obtain an equivalent number of people in terms of skill level and ensure that they put in a good level of effort to have a fair assessment of variance between the estimated values and actual values.

Now that we have a better understanding of productivity, let us now discuss how to obtain the PDRs.

Deriving PDR from Past Records

The most common method in the software development industry is to derive the PDRs from the past records of the organization. This is based on the premise that the actual values obtained during past projects within the organization are better indicators of future performance than figures obtained from elsewhere. We need to have executed a significant number of projects in the same development platform to be able to use this method. Here are the steps in deriving PDR from past records:

- Sift the past project records into different development platforms for which we are deriving the PDRs.
- For each project carry out a variance analysis contrasting the actual effort values with the estimated effort values. All variances in the actual values due to assignable causes need to be normalized to arrive at the normalized actual effort for the project.
- We derive the actual functional size of the software product in FP.
- We divide the normalized actual effort by the actual software functional size to obtain the PDR for the development platform.
- If we are deriving multiple PDRs for different software development activities, we need to repeat the above steps for each of the development activities.
- We need to repeat the above steps for all the projects with the same development platform so that we have a set of PDRs collated from a number of projects.

■ We derive an average PDR from the above projects for the organization. It is better to use the "statistical mode" to derive the average if the number of projects considered is small. The "statistical mean" would give better result if we have a large number of projects.

Table 6.8 depicts the derivation of PDR for a development platform, say programming in Java.

We cannot obtain the statistical mode from this data directly. We need to form them into groups and then derive the mode. We can also round off each of the values to the nearest integer as shown in Table 6.9 to derive the mode.

Table 6.8   Derivation of PDR

Project	Functional Size in FP	Normalized Effort in PH	PDR in PH per FP
A	1,000	4,000	4
B	1,500	5,625	3.75
C	600	3,300	5.55
D	6,500	24,115	3.71
E	8,250	32,340	3.92
Average productivity			4.23

Table 6.9   Deriving PDR Using the Mode by Rounding Off to the Nearest Integer

Project	Functional Size in FP	Normalized Effort in PH	PDR in PH per FP	PDR Rounded Off to the Nearest Integer in PH per FP
A	1,000	4,000	4	4
B	1,500	5,624	3.75	4
C	600	3,300	5.55	6
D	6,500	24,115	3.71	4
E	8,250	32,340	3.92	4
Average productivity			4.23 (mean)	4 (mode)

Now it is clear that the modal value is 4 PH per FP. It is better to use the mode for a smaller number of projects, as unlike statistical mean, it is not influenced by extreme values.

Merits of Deriving PDR from Past Records

The following are the merits of deriving PDR from past records of the organization:

- Actual achievement within the organization is a better indicator of future performance than any other value.
- It is reliable and free from any bias.
- It is easy to derive and maintain.
- It is easy to convince people because it is based on actual performance and not on perceived performance.

Demerits of Deriving PDR from Past Records

The following are the demerits of deriving PDR from past records of the organization:

- Past records tell us what *has been* achieved but not what *should have been* achieved.
- When a new software development platform is to be used, past data would not be available, and hence, this method cannot be used to derive PDR.
- It is possible that conditions in the future would be different (especially use of tools and methods) from the past, rendering the PDR erroneous.
- If we do not normalize the actual effort before deriving the PDR, it would be in error. It is not easy to normalize the actual effort spent in an earlier project. It calls for significant skill and effort to be spent in normalization and rarely do organizations spend that effort.
- While it is common to estimate the software functional size, it is the exception rather than the rule to measure the functional size of a completed software product. If we use the estimated functional size and actual effort values that are not normalized, the derived PDR is anything but credible.

In some cases, the organization may not have past records to rely upon. New and young organizations would not have past project records owing to their recent incorporation. Some organizations might not have maintained their project records in a way that is useful for subjecting them to statistical analysis. For such organizations that are desirous of using this approach, there are a few alternatives to obtain project data, namely the following:

- International professional organizations such as IFPUG and ISBSG provide relevant project data for a little attribution.

- Local professional organizations such as Software Process Improvement Network (SPIN) and Software Project Managers Network (SPMN) may provide this data with or without any attribution to their members.
- Professional associations such as IEEE Computer Society, Computer Society of India, Australian Computer Society, UK Software Metrics Association (UKSMA), and NESMA (Netherlands Software Metrics Association) may provide such data with or without any attribution to their members.

Deriving PDR Using Industrial Engineering Studies

All other industries except the software development industry use industrial engineering (IE) studies to derive productivity and set work norms. They have a set of techniques like time study, motion study, synthesis, work sampling, analytical estimation, and so on to set work standards (productivity) based on the principle of "a fair day's work for a fair day's pay." There are many advantages in using this method to derive a productivity figure:

- This method gives us what should be achieved in the present set of conditions, rather than what was achieved.
- With this method, we can derive PDR even for newer technologies and software development platforms.
- The values derived using this method are fair to both the organization and the individual.
- The values derived using this method are free from any influences like extreme values or biases.
- These values allow us to identify super performers and poor performers and facilitate better rewards in the organization.

The work sampling method is best suited to study software development activities. One precaution while using this method is to employ well-trained IE professionals. Trying to do it in-house by software professionals untrained in IE techniques would be counterproductive.

Deriving Effort from Software Functional Size Using Parametric Models

There are some parametric models such as COCOMO by Dr. Barry Boehm [1] and SEER by Galorath (www.galorath.com). They have derived formulas and methodologies by studying a large number of software development projects. These formulas and methodologies use software functional size as the primary input and certain other factors that affect the project to arrive at the software development effort for the project.

COCOMO is a very popular parametric model in the software development industry. The original COCOMO uses kilo lines of code (KLOC) as the software functional size and derives software development effort. COCOMO II is an improved version of COCOMO and uses object points as the software functional size.

There are other parametric models like SLIM, COSTAR, SEER, etc. Detailed discussion of all these methods is beyond the scope of this chapter. These are cited here only to have a complete discussion of the derivation of software development effort from software functional size.

Arriving at Software Development Effort Directly

The following techniques are available for arriving at the software development effort directly without estimating the software functional size.

- Task-based estimation
- Delphi estimation technique
- Analogy-based estimation
- Ballparking

While detailed explanation of each of these techniques is out of the scope of this chapter, let us discuss these techniques in a little more detail. Interested readers who wish to make use of these techniques are advised to refer to published material on these techniques to gain a complete understanding.

Task-Based Estimation

In this technique, we enumerate all the tasks that must be completed to execute the project. Then we assign the effort required to complete each of the tasks. We sum up the individual task efforts to arrive at the total effort required to complete the project. It is also common to divide the project into its constituent modules and enumerate the tasks for each module or to classify the tasks under software development phases. One other variant is to assign three effort estimates for each task and derive the average effort estimate using the statistical beta distribution. This average is normally referred to as the "most likely time" for the task. Table 6.10 shows a brief example of a software development estimate using the task-based estimation technique. Expected effort is computed using the following formula:

Expected effort = [(4 × normal-case effort) + best-case effort + worst-case effort]/6

The advantage with this technique is that we automatically obtain a range of values for the effort estimate, including the best case, worst case, normal case, and the expected effort. We can also subject the values to the beta probability distribution and derive the probability of meeting a given project completion date. Project management tools such as MS Project and Primavera facilitate usage of this technique. Many variants can be found to this technique in different organizations.

Table 6.10 Task-Based Estimation

Project—TBE Example					
Software Development Phase	*Software Development Task*	*Best-Case Effort in PH*	*Worst-Case Effort in PH*	*Normal-Case Effort in PH*	*Expected Effort in PH*
Requirements analysis	Preparation	2	4	3	3.00
-- do --	Conduct interviews	4	6	5	5.00
-- do --	Prepare requirements specification	3	6	4	4.17
Software design	Database design	5	8	6	6.17
-- do --	UI design	8	12	10	10.00
-- do --	Report design	6	8	7	7.00
-- do --	Program design	12	16	14	14.00
And so on...					
Total effort		40	60	49	49.34

One advantage of this technique is that we have a list of all activities for the project, which can be used to work out the project schedule in detail. Another advantage of this list is that we can track the project progress effectively.

Delphi Estimation Technique

Delphi is a place in Greece where in ancient times virgin girls were appointed as "Oracles" in the temple. These Oracles made predictions about various topics, and people approached them when they were faced with any issue. The predictions of the Oracles were considered as "wise counsel." Taking a cue from the Oracles, the Delphi software estimation technique uses senior and experienced software developers to make predictions about the software functional size and software development effort required for the proposed project. When only one expert is used, this technique is referred to as Delphi technique, and when multiple experts are used, it is referred to as "wideband Delphi" technique.

In this technique, the following are the steps to derive the software development effort:

- Select the expert/experts—normally multiple experts (in odd number) are selected to reduce the uncertainty.
- The experts are briefed about the project, including the risks, opportunities, assumptions, and so on by the estimate coordinator, who is normally a marketing person or a software project manager.
- The experts consider the project information and give their best guesses to the coordinator.
- The divergence in the estimates is converged by the coordinator either in a meeting or discussions with individual experts.
- The resultant estimate is then used by the project team.

One advantage with this technique is that we can obtain both software functional size as well as the software development effort. It is also very quick to arrive at the estimate and if the right experts are carefully selected and briefed properly, this technique is capable of giving surprisingly reliable estimates.

Analogy-Based Estimation

The idea behind analogy-based estimation is the premise that it is easier and quicker to develop a new estimate extrapolating the estimate of a past project than to do it from scratch. In this technique, a similar project completed earlier in the organization is taken as the basis for the proposed project estimate. The differences between both the past project and present project are considered item-by-item and adjustments are made to the estimate of the past project to arrive at the estimate of the new project. Here are the steps in carrying out estimation using this technique:

1. Create a short listing of candidate projects from the organizational repository. We consider the following aspects while short listing past projects:
   a. Similarity in the functional domains—this is the most important aspect. There would be no point in selecting a customer relationship management (CRM) project when considering estimation for a financial accounting project.
   b. Similarity in organizational size—it is also futile to select a project executed in a single location small/medium organization when estimating for a multilocation large organization.
   c. Similarity in application development platform—again, it would serve no purpose if we select a project that was developed on a mainframe computer while estimating for a personal computer (PC) and web-based project.

    d. Similarity in programming languages—it would be similar if the languages belong to a family like C, C++, and Java. The difference would be beyond reconciliation if the past project was developed in COBOL and the present project is expected to be developed in Java.

    e. Similarity in the number of application tiers—again, it would be of little help if the past project was on a batch processing system and the present project is on a multitiered online, Internet-based project.

2. Select the project whose estimate is going to be used from the short-listed projects. We need to select one project that is closest to the present project in terms of functional domain, development platform, programming language, and number of application tiers. We need to recognize that we will not get a 100% match and need to select a project that is as close as possible to the present project realizing fully well that we need to make adjustments for the differences between the selected past project and the project for which we are carrying out estimation.

3. Enumerate the differences between the selected past project and the current project. Having selected a past project as the basis for carrying out estimation for the present project, the next step is to compare and contrast both the projects and enumerate all the differences between them. The differences could be in the functionality, development platform, programming language, or any other aspect. This list would then be used to make adjustments to arrive at the estimate of the new project.

4. Make adjustments in the estimate to bridge the differences uncovered in step 3. Using the gaps list arrived at in step 3, we make adjustments in the estimate of the new project. If a feature is missing in the old project, we add that feature along with its estimate. If a feature is present in the past project but absent in the new project, we eliminate it from the new estimate. If a feature is present in both projects but in a different degree, we modify the earlier estimate to reflect the current degree of the feature. These alterations are made using best judgment or using data from the organizational knowledge repository. Now we are ready with the estimate for the new project.

5. Arrange for peer review and implement the feedback. Peer review is carried out by a peer of the estimator. Peer review is based on the principle that "two heads are better than one" to make something comprehensive and defect free. A peer review uncovers defects that crept in due to oversight, wrong computations, wrong inferences, etc., and allows us an opportunity to correct the defects before it reaches the decision makers. Arrange a peer review for the estimate of the current project and implement the feedback, so that the estimate is as reliable as it can be.

6. Present the estimate. Now present the estimate using the organizational template for estimates. List out all the assumptions, exclusions, and any special notes.

The advantages of analogy-based estimation are that it facilitates estimation of both software functional size and software development effort, besides making it quicker and easier to arrive at the new estimate.

Ballparking

Ballparking is akin to Delphi estimation except that the project team itself makes the estimate. It is the best hunch of the person carrying out the estimation that is reflected in the estimate. The reliability of the estimate depends on the experience and knowledge of the person carrying out the estimate. When the person carrying out the estimate is a person who has executed projects in the same functional domain and development platform, this technique does give very reliable estimates. It may be surprising but this technique is used very widely in the software development industry especially when there is little or no time for preparing an elaborate software estimate. There is no formal methodology or process for using this technique. However, usually some rules of thumb are used, such as 3 days for a screen, 2 days for a report, 4 days for a third generation language (3GL) routine, 1 day for a graphic, and so on.

Impact of Scheduling on Effort Estimation

Scheduling is assigning calendar dates and resources to planned activities. It is during the scheduling process that estimated effort is distributed among personnel of different specialities who will be working on the project. Two types of scheduling are performed usually, namely, "forward-pass" scheduling and "backward-pass" scheduling. In forward-pass scheduling, we start at the date on which the project can begin and assign dates from the first activity proceeding progressively toward the project ending activity. In doing so, we may find, in some cases, the schedule may not meet the committed project end date. In backward-pass scheduling, we begin at the last activity in the project and assign it the project end date specified by the customer and regress toward the project start activity. In this method of scheduling, we may find that we have to start the project earlier than the possible project start date. How to reconcile these aberrations is beyond the scope of this chapter. Interested readers are advised to read a detailed book on scheduling or PERT/CPM.

Once we have worked out the schedule, we allocate resources to each of the activities. When we do so, we may find that some resources, especially the shared resources such as the database specialists, architects, testers, specialist programmers, etc., may be allocated to multiple activities in multiple projects concurrently resulting in having to postpone some activities due to overallocation of the shared resource. When we postpone activities due to nonavailability of shared resources, the dependent resources are idle for some periods in the project life cycle even though their time is still booked against the project itself. It is not uncommon that most projects have some idle time for its resources. Similarly, work fragmentation stretches the effort of the allocated resources. For example, let us say a specific task allocated to a resource finishes 1 hour before the end of the day. Ideally, the resource must immediately start the next activity but in reality it would just be wishful thinking to expect the resource to do so. Therefore, the effort estimate arrived at (either by converting the software functional size into software development effort or using other effort estimation techniques) needs to be adjusted for the wasted effort uncovered in the scheduling before committing the effort estimate to decision makers.

Final Words and Conclusions about Software Development Effort Estimation

In summary, we can derive software development effort by the following:

- Converting software functional size into effort
  - Using a single PDR
  - Using multiple PDRs
  - Using a parametric estimation model
- Deriving software development effort directly by
  - Task-based estimation
  - Delphi estimation technique
  - Analogy-based estimation
  - Ballparking
- Scheduling has an impact on the estimated effort in terms of wasted effort either due to nonavailability of shared resources or work fragmentation, and hence, it is advocated to commit the software development effort only after preparing the schedule for the project.
- Uncertainty is inherent to software development estimation, which can be handled either by using multiple software functional sizes or multiple PDRs.
- Presentation is equally important and a software estimate needs to be presented in the organizational template, which should include all assumptions, exclusions, and any special notes along with the estimate.

Having thus summarized the discussion about effort estimation in this chapter, I would like to recommend the following:

- It is advantageous to estimate the functional size of the proposed software product and then derive the development effort from the software functional size. This, as already discussed earlier, allows us to ascertain the efficiency with which the software would be developed.

- We should not resort to other methods of effort estimation unless it is determined that functional size estimation is not feasible. We should always try to use functional size estimation.
- We should handle uncertainty in effort estimation either in the size or in the conversion factor.
- Do not commit the effort estimate until scheduling is carried out.
- It is better to derive PDRs using IE studies, as they are fair to both the organization as well as the individual. IE studies give us PDRs unsullied by either biases or errors in data or derivation.

References

1. Boehm B. W., E. Horowitz, R. Madachy, D. Reifer, B. K. Clark, B. Steece, A. W. Brown, S. Chulani, and C. Abts. 2000. *Software Cost Estimation with COCOMO II.* Upper Saddle River, NJ: Prentice Hall.
2. IFPUG. 2004. *Guidelines to Software Measurement.* 2nd ed. International Function Point User Group. http://www.ifpug.org (accessed December, 2011).

Bibliography

Murali Chemuturi. *Software Estimation: Best Practices, Tools and Techniques for Software Project Estimators.* Fort Lauderdale, FL: J. Ross Publishing, Inc, 2009.

About the Author

Murali Chemuturi is a fellow of Industrial Engineering and has obtained an MBA along with a PG Diploma in Computers. He has over 40 years of experience in various facets of manufacturing and IT industries. He has authored two books titled *Software Estimation: Best Practices, Tools, and Techniques for Software Project Estimators* and *Mastering Software Quality Assurance: Best Practices, Tools, and Techniques for Software Developers,* and coauthored a third book titled *Mastering Software Project Management: Best Practices, Tools, and Techniques* with Thomas M. Cagley, Jr. All three books were published by J. Ross Publishing Inc. Murali Chemuturi also developed and markets the software estimation tool EstimatorPal and the software project management tool PMPal. He currently leads Chemuturi Consultants providing consultancy and training in software engineering and process to IT organizations. He can be reached through email—murali@chemuturi.com.

Chapter 7

Software and Web Effort Estimation via Predictive and Diagnostic Reasoning

Emilia Mendes

Contents

Introduction

Information technology projects involving the development of either web or software applications need to be managed effectively, so that their associated applications can be delivered on time and within budget. One of the main aspects of effective project management is the use of sound effort estimates. A sound effort estimate represents a realistic estimate of the amount of effort (in person hours) needed to develop a web or software application. Once obtained, this estimate is used as a basis to predict project costs and to allocate resources (e.g., developers) to a project. An effort estimate is generally derived taking into account the following input: (1) the characteristics of the new project and the corresponding application to be developed; and (2) the characteristics of previous "similar" projects and corresponding applications, for which actual effort is known. Note that the project and application characteristics employed herein are only those assumed to be relevant in determining effort.

The process that is generally used when deriving an effort estimate is presented in Figure 7.1. The input to this process is the following:

1. Data and/or knowledge on past finished projects, for which actual effort is known, represented by project and application characteristics believed to have an effect on the amount of effort needed to accomplish a task/activity/process. Whenever a company does not have either data or experience on similar projects and their corresponding applications, these tend to be replaced by an "educated guess" based on prior experience with dissimilar projects.
2. Data relating to the new project for which effort is to be estimated (estimated size and other factors), which are estimated based on the new application's requirements (e.g., what functionality the application should offer to users).

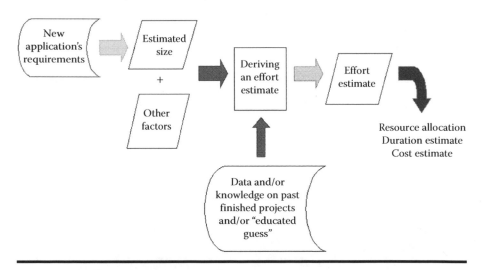

Figure 7.1   Effort estimation process.

Such data also use the same project characteristics employed in step 1. There are currently several measures that can be used to estimate an application's size, such as Function Points [1] (applicable to conventional software applications) or the Tukutuku measures [2] (applicable to web applications).

The output of this process is an effort estimate, which is then used to allocate resources and to estimate project duration and costs.

To date, expert-based effort estimation is the technique most commonly used when estimating effort for web and software projects. However, the issue with this technique is that it relies on tacit knowledge, which is intrinsically subjective, and therefore, whenever the effort estimates are good, the mechanism that was used to obtain those estimates cannot be repeated given that the factors that were taken into account by the experts are not explicitly known. Given this situation, the research in this field started to investigate the use of techniques and corresponding models to represent explicitly the relationship between effort and project and application characteristics. Numerous techniques have been used to build such models, such as statistical multivariate regression, case-based reasoning, classification and regression trees, neural networks, and Bayesian networks (BNs). Further details on each of these techniques are given in the study by Mendes and Mosley [3]. The building of explicit effort models is shown in Figure 7.2, where the estimation process itself includes two subprocesses, which are as follows:

1. Effort model building: This subprocess represents the use of techniques to help with the construction of a tangible representation of the association between project and application characteristics and effort using data/knowledge from

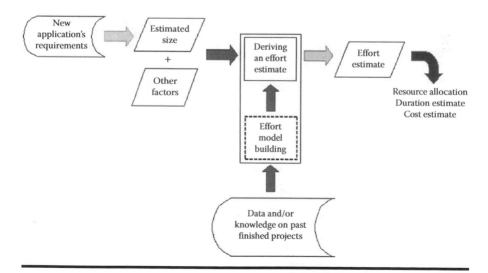

Figure 7.2   Effort estimation process with explicit modeling.

past finished projects for which actual effort is known. Such representation can take several forms, for example, an equation, a binary tree, or an acyclic graph. This subprocess is shown using a dashed line because in some instances no concrete model representation exists, for example, when employing a technique such as case-based reasoning.

2. Deriving an effort estimate: This subprocess represents either the use of the estimated characteristics of a new project and application as input to a concrete effort model that provides an effort estimate or the use of the estimated characteristics of a new project as input to the subprocess (from step 1) that derives an effort estimate using previous knowledge from past projects.

The effort estimation of web and software applications is a very complex domain where the relationships between the factors believed to affect effort, and effort itself, are nondeterministic and are also inherently uncertain. In most cases, effort estimation is based on experts' experience, where knowledge or data from past finished projects are used to estimate effort for new projects not yet initiated. The assumption here is that previous applications have similar characteristics to the new applications to be developed, and therefore, prior knowledge and/or data can be useful in estimating effort for future applications. We would also like to point out that in our view, web and software development differ in a number of areas such as application characteristics; primary technologies used; approach to quality delivered; development process drivers; availability of the application; customers (stakeholders); update rate (maintenance cycles); people involved in development, architecture and network; disciplines involved; legal, social, and ethical issues; and information structuring and design. A detailed discussion on this issue is provided in the study by Mendes, Mosley, and Counsell [4].

The objective of this chapter is twofold: first, to detail a methodology that enables the representation of tacit knowledge and which was employed to build software effort estimation models for several web and software companies in Auckland (New Zealand) and Rio de Janeiro (Brazil); second, to describe a case study where a web effort estimation model was created for a web company in Auckland (New Zealand). It took 11 weeks to construct the model (3-hour weekly meetings) with the participation of an experienced project manager as domain expert (DE); it contained 36 factors identified by the project manager as influential to software effort and risk management and also 48 relationships associating those factors. Once built, the model was validated using data from 22 past finished projects and, from that point onward, was used as a basis for the predictions presented to clients. The predictions provided by the model were considered by the company to be more accurate than their previous expert-based predictions.

The two following sections: "Introduction to Bayesian Networks," and "General Process Used to Build Bayesian Networks," will introduce the technique we used to build the web effort prediction model, followed by a general description of the methodology used, and the specific details on how the company-specific model was created. Finally, conclusions and comments on future work are given in the Conclusion.

Introduction to Bayesian Networks

A BN is a model that supports reasoning with uncertainty due to the way in which it incorporates existing knowledge of a complex domain [5]. This knowledge is represented using two parts. The first, the qualitative part, represents the structure of a BN as depicted by a directed acyclic graph (digraph) (see Figure 7.3). The digraph's nodes represent the relevant variables (factors) in the domain being modeled, which can be of different types (e.g., observable or latent, categorical). The digraph's arcs represent the causal relationships between variables, where relationships are quantified probabilistically [5]. Figure 7.3 shows three factors—"Pages Complexity," "Functionality Complexity," and "Total Effort"—and two causal relationships—from Pages Complexity to Total Effort, and from Functionality Complexity to Total Effort. Within the context of this chapter, Pages Complexity represents the amount of effort (person/hours) needed to implement the web pages (create the content, graphics, and design) that are part of a web application; Functionality Complexity represents the amount of effort (person/hours) needed to implement the server and client-side scripts (e.g., JavaScript) being used by the web application; Total Effort corresponds to the total effort (person/hours) needed to develop a web application.

The second, the quantitative part, associates a conditional probability table (CPT) to each node, its probability distribution. A parent node's CPT describes the relative probability of each state (value) (Figure 7.3, nodes Pages Complexity and Functionality Complexity); a child node's CPT describes the relative probability of each state conditional on every combination of states of its parents (Figure 7.3, node Total Effort). Therefore, for example, the relative probability of Total Effort being Low conditional on Pages Complexity and Functionality Complexity being both Low is 0.7. Each row in a CPT represents a conditional probability distribution, and therefore, its values sum up to one [5]. Formally, the posterior distribution of the BN is based on Bayes' rule [5]:

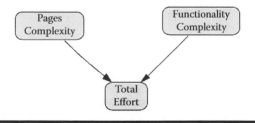

Figure 7.3   A small Bayesian network and three conditional probability tables.

$$p(X \mid E) = \frac{p(E \mid X)p(X)}{p(E)},$$ (7.1)

where

- $p(X \mid E)$ is called the *posterior* distribution and represents the probability of X given evidence E
- $p(X)$ is called the *prior* distribution and represents the probability of X before evidence E is given
- $p(E \mid X)$ is called the *likelihood* function and denotes the probability of E assuming X is true

Once a BN is specified, evidence (e.g., values) can be entered into any node and probabilities for the remaining nodes automatically calculated using Bayes' rule [5]. Therefore, BNs can be used for different types of reasoning, such as predictive, diagnostic, and "what-if" analyses to investigate the impact that changes on some nodes have on others.

General Process Used to Build Bayesian Networks

The BN presented in this chapter was built and validated using an adaptation of the Knowledge Engineering of Bayesian Networks (KEBN) process proposed in the study by Woodberry et al. [6] (see Figure 7.4). The arrows in Figure 7.4 represent flows through the different processes, depicted by rectangles. Such processes are executed either by people—the knowledge engineer (KE) and the DEs (white rectangles)—or by automatic algorithms (dark grey rectangles). Within the context of this chapter, the author was the KE, and one web project manager from a well-established web company in Auckland was the DE.

The three main subprocesses comprising the adapted KEBN process are (1) structural development; (2) parameter estimation; and (3) model validation. The adapted KEBN process iterates over these three subprocesses until a complete BN is built and validated. Each of these three subprocesses is detailed in the following subsections.

Structural Development

The structural development subprocess represents the qualitative component of a BN, which results in a graphical structure comprised of, in our case, the factors (nodes and variables) and causal relationships identified as fundamental for effort estimation of web projects. In addition to identifying variables, their types (e.g., query variable, evidence variable), and causal relationships, this subprocess

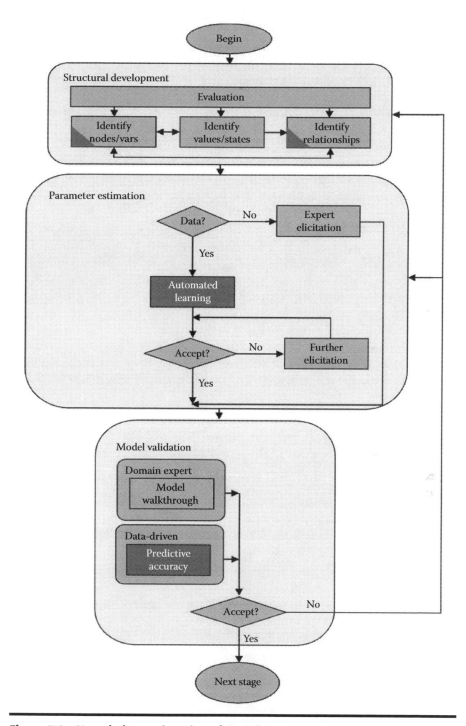

Figure 7.4 Knowledge Engineering of Bayesian Networks process.

also includes the identification of the states (values) that each variable should take, and if they are discrete or continuous. In practice, currently available BN tools require that continuous variables be discretized by converting them into multi-nomial variables [6]; this was also the case with the BN software used in the case study described in this chapter. The structure of the BN is refined through an itera-tive process. This structure construction process has been validated in the previous studies [7] and uses the principles of problem solving employed in data modeling and software development [8]. As will be detailed later, existing literature in web effort estimation and knowledge from a DE were used to elicit the web effort BN's structure. Throughout this subprocess, the KE(s) also evaluate(s) the structure of the BN, which is done in two stages. The first entails checking whether variables and their values have a clear meaning, all relevant variables have been included, variables are named conveniently, and all states are appropriate (exhaustive and exclusive), and a check for any states that can be combined. The second stage entails reviewing the BN's graph structure (causal structure) to ensure that any identified d-separation dependencies comply with the types of variables used and causality assumptions. D-seperation dependencies are used to identify variables influenced by evidence coming from other variables in the BN [9]. Once the BN structure is assumed to be close to final, KEs may still need to optimize this structure to reduce the number of probabilities that need to be elicited or learnt for the network. If optimization is needed, then techniques that change the causal structure (e.g., divorcing [9]) and the use of parametric probability distributions (e.g., noisy-OR gates [7]) are used.

Parameter Estimation

The parameter estimation subprocess represents the quantitative component of a BN, where conditional probabilities corresponding to the quantification of the relationships between variables [9] are obtained. Such probabilities can be attained via expert elicitation, automatically from data, from existing literature, or using a combination of these. When probabilities are elicited from scratch, or even if they only need to be revisited, this step can be very time consuming. To minimize the number of probabilities to be elicited, some techniques have been proposed in the literature [1,10]; however, as far as we are aware, there is no empirical evidence to date comparing their effectiveness for prediction with probabilities elicited from scratch, using large and realistic BNs. This is one of the topics of our future work.

Model Validation

The model validation subprocess validates the BN that results from the two pre-vious subprocesses and determines whether it is necessary to revisit any of those subprocesses. Two different validation methods are generally used—model walk-through and predictive accuracy. Each is described below:

1. Model walkthrough represents the use of real-case scenarios that are pre-pared and used by DEs to assess whether the predictions provided by a BN correspond to the predictions that experts would have chosen based on their own expertise. Success is measured as the frequency with which the BN's predicted value for a target variable (e.g., quality, effort) that has the highest probability corresponds to the experts' own assessment.

2. Predictive accuracy uses past data (e.g., past project data), rather than scenarios, to obtain predictions. Data (evidence) is entered on the BN model, and success is measured as the frequency with which the BN's predicted value for a target variable (e.g. quality, effort) that has the highest probability corresponds to the actual past data. However, previous literature also documents a different measure of success, proposed by Pendharkar, Subramanian, and Rodger [11] and later used by Mendes [12,13] and Mendes and Mosley [3]. Herein, an effort point forecast for each past project being used for validation is obtained by computing estimated effort as the sum of the probability (ρ) of a given effort scale point multiplied by its related mean effort (μ), after normalizing the prob-abilities such that their sum equals one. Therefore, assuming that estimated effort is measured using a five-point scale (very low to very high), we have

$$\text{Estimated(effort)} = \rho_{\text{very low}}\mu_{\text{very low}} + \rho_{\text{low}}\mu_{\text{low}} + \rho_{\text{medium}}\mu_{\text{medium}}$$
$$+ \rho_{\text{high}}\mu_{\text{high}} + \rho_{\text{very high}}\mu_{\text{very high}} \tag{7.2}$$

Process Used to Build the Web Effort Bayesian Network Model

Introduction

This section revisits the adapted KEBN process (see Figure 7.4), detailing the tasks carried out for each of the three main subprocesses of that process. Before starting the elicitation of the web effort prediction BN model, the DE, who participated in all subprocesses, was presented with an overview of BN models and examples of "what-if" scenarios using a made-up BN. This, we believe, facilitated the entire process as the use of an example, and the brief explanation of each of the steps in the KEBN process, provided a concrete understanding of what to expect. We also made it clear that the KE was solely a facilitator of the process and that the web company's commitment was paramount for the success of the entire process.

The whole process took 66 person hours to be completed, with two people par-ticipating at 11 3-hour slots.

The DE who took part in this case study was the project manager of a well-established web company in Auckland (New Zealand). At the time the model was built, the company had ~20 employees. The project manager had worked in multimedia and web development for more than 15 years. In addition, this company also developed a wide range of kiosk software applications, using different types of technology.

Detailed Structural Development and Parameter Estimation

As a starting point, to aid the DE in identifying the fundamental factors that the DE took into account when preparing a quote for a new web project, we used the set of variables from the Tukutuku dataset* [2], detailed in Table 7.1. We first sketched them out on a white board, each one inside an oval shape, and then explained what each one meant within the context of the Tukutuku project. Our previous experience eliciting BNs in other domains (e.g., ecology) suggested that it was best to start with a few factors (even if they were not to be reused by the DE), rather than to use a "blank canvas" as a starting point.

Once the Tukutuku variables had been sketched out and explained, the next step was to remove all those that the DE did not find relevant, or to modify existing variables to suit the DE's experience, followed by adding to the white board any new additional variables (factors) suggested by the DE. We also documented descriptions for each of the factors suggested and modified. Next, we identified the states that each factor would take. All states were discrete. Whenever a factor represented a measure of effort (e.g., Total Effort), we also documented the effort range corresponding to each state, to avoid any future ambiguity. For example, "very low" Total Effort corresponded to 4+ to 10 person hours, etc. Once all states were identified and documented, it was time to elicit the cause and effect relationships.

As a starting point to this task, we used a simple medical example from the study by Jensen [9] (see Figure 7.5).

This example clearly introduces one of the most important points to consider when identifying cause and effect relationships—the timeline of events. If smoking is to be a cause of lung cancer, it is important that the cause precede the effect. This may sound obvious with regard to the example used; however, it is our view that the use of this simple example significantly helped the DE understand the notion of cause and effect, and how this related to web effort estimation and the BN being elicited.

Once the cause and effect relationships were identified the web effort causal structure was as follows (see Figure 7.6). Note that Figure 7.6 is not a BN based directly on Table 7.1. During this process, the nodes "Final effort estimate" and "Total effort estimate" were each reached by a large number of relationships;

---

* http://www.metriq.biz/tukutuku

Table 7.1   Tukutuku Variables

Variable Name	Description
Project data	
TypeProj	Type of project (new or enhancement)
nLang	Number of different development languages used
DocProc	If project followed defined and documented process
ProImpr	If project team involved in a process improvement program
Metrics	If project team part of a software metrics program
DevTeam	Size of a project's development team
TeamExp	Average team experience with the development language(s) employed
Web application	
TotWP	Total number of web pages (new and reused)
NewWP	Total number of new web pages
TotImg	Total number of images (new and reused)
NewImg	Total number of new images created
Num_Fots	Number of features reused without any adaptation
HFotsA	Number of reused high-effort features/functions adapted
Hnew	Number of new high-effort features/functions
TotHigh	Total number of high-effort features/functions
Num_FotsA	Number of reused low-effort features adapted
New	Number of new low-effort features/functions
TotNHigh	Total number of low-effort features/functions

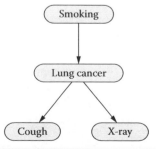

Figure 7.5   A small Bayesian network model and two conditional probability tables.

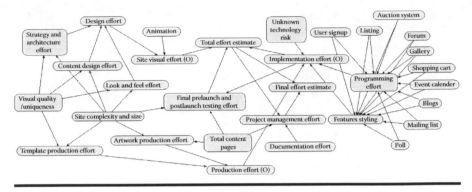

Figure 7.6   Expert-based web effort causal structure.

therefore, this structure needed to be simplified to reduce the number of probabilities to be elicited. New nodes were suggested by the KE (names ending in "(O)," see Figure 7.6) and validated by the DE. This is the final structure presented in Figure 7.6.

Each of the factors used in the web effort estimation BN model is presented in Table 7.2. Whenever a description is missing, this is because the factor's name is already self-explanatory.

At this point, the DE seemed happy with the BN's causal structure, and the work on eliciting the probabilities was initiated. Most of the probabilities were created from scratch; however, some were also obtained from existing data on past finished web projects. The probabilities elicitation subprocess took 36 hours (one DE and one KE). The complete BN, including its probabilities, is shown in Figure 7.7. Figure 7.5 shows the BN using belief bars rather than labeled factors, so readers can see the probabilities that were elicited.

Detailed Model Validation

Both model walkthrough and predictive accuracy were used to validate the web effort estimation BN model, where the former was the first type of validation to be employed. The DE used 10 different scenarios to check whether the node "Final effort estimate" would provide the highest probability to the effort state that corresponded to the DE's own suggestions. All scenarios were run successfully; however, it was also necessary to use data from past projects, for which total effort was known, to check the model's calibration. A validation set containing data on 22 projects was used. The DE selected a range of projects presenting different sizes and levels of complexity, where all 22 projects were representative of the types and sizes of projects developed by the web company.

Table 7.2 Description of All the Factors Elicited from the DE

Factor	Categories	Description, Observation
Template production effort	Very low (8+ to 16 phrs)	Effort making (producing) all the different templates for all the different pages.
	Low (16+ to 24 phrs)	
	Medium (24+ to 40 phrs)	
	Medium-high (40+ to 60 phrs)	
	High (60+ to 90 phrs)	
	Very high (90+ to 120 phrs)	
	Super high (120+ phrs)	
Artwork production effort	Very low (0+ to 8 phrs)	Effort making (producing) all the artwork for all the different pages.
	Low (8+ to 16 phrs)	
	Medium (16+ to 24 phrs)	
	Medium-high (24+ to 40 phrs)	
	High (40+ to 60 phrs)	
	Very high (60+ to 80 phrs)	
	Super high (80+ phrs)	

(Continued)

Table 7.2 Description of All the Factors Elicited from the DE (*Continued*)

Factor	Categories	Description, Observation
Team experience	25%	Percentage of team members with optimal experience.
	50%	
	75%	
	100%	
Tight deadline	Yes, no	
Unknown technology risk	Yes, no	
External hosting	Yes, no	
Overall risk	Low, medium, high	
Content design effort	Very low (0+ to 8 phrs)	
	Low (8+ to 24 phrs)	
	Medium (24+ to 40 phrs)	
	Medium-high (40+ to 60 phrs)	
	High (60+ phrs)	
Visual quality/ uniqueness	Template standard, template high, custom-medium, custom-high	Uniqueness of the application's visual quality.

Site complexity and size	Small (1 audience group/topic)	Number of different types of sections (content areas/types of functionality; different audience groups). The greater the number of different types of users, the greater the care with providing functionality and content areas that are suitable to each type of user. It involves identifying how each part of the site will suit its audience, but making it all cohesive.
	Medium (2 audience groups/topics)	
	Medium-large (3 audience groups/topics)	
	Large (4 audience groups/topics)	
	Very large (5+ audience groups/topics)	
Strategy and architecture effort	Very low (0+ to 8 phrs)	How to make sure a user does not get lost; how to make sure you give your audience what they want, that they will find what they need. The architecture represents the navigation (providing landscape points to enable people to navigate without getting lost). The strategy represents deciding on the best mechanisms to enable users to find what they need quickly.
	Low (8+ to 16 phrs)	
	Medium (16+ to 24 phrs)	
	High (24+ to 40 phrs)	
	Very high (40+ to 60 phrs)	
	Super high (60+ phrs)	
Look and feel effort	Very low (0+ to 8 phrs)	Web branding design and art direction.
	Low (8+ to 24 phrs)	
	Medium-low (24+ to 40 phrs)	
	Medium (40+ to 60 phrs)	
	High (60+ phrs)	

(Continued)

Table 7.2   Description of All the Factors Elicited from the DE (*Continued*)

Factor	Categories	Description, Observation
Design effort	Very low (0+ to 16 phrs)	
	Low (16+ to 40 phrs)	
	Medium (40+ to 80 phrs)	
	Medium-high (80+ to 124 phrs)	
	High (124+ to 160 phrs)	
	Very high (160+ phrs)	
Site visual effort	Very low (0+ to 24 phrs)	
	Low (24+ to 56 phrs)	
	Medium (56+ to 104 phrs)	
	Medium-high (104+ to 164 phrs)	
	High (164+ to 220 phrs)	
	Very high (220+ phrs)	
Total content pages (assumes that the client has provided the content and images)	(1–10 pages)	
	(11–20 pages)	
	(20–35 pages)	
	(35–50 pages)	
	(51–75 pages)	
	(76–100 pages)	
	(101–125 pages)	
	(126–250+ pages)	

Programming effort	Very very low (1.5 to 4 phrs)	Represents the effort used to implement or adapt the features that will be part of a web application (e.g., forum, gallery, shopping cart).
	Very low (4+ to 12 phrs)	
	Low (12+ to 20 phrs)	
	Medium-low (20+ to 40 phrs)	
	Medium (40+ to 80 phrs)	
	Medium-high (80+ to 120 phrs)	
	High (120+ to 200 phrs)	
	Very high (200+ to 400 phrs)	
	Very very high (400+ to 600 phrs)	
Production effort	Super very low (8+ to 24 phrs)	
	Low (24+ to 40 phrs)	
	Medium (40+ to 64 phrs)	
	Medium-high (64+ to 100 phrs)	
	High (100+ to 150 phrs)	
	Very high (150+ to 200 phrs)	
	Super high (200+ phrs)	

(Continued)

Table 7.2 Description of All the Factors Elicited from the DE (*Continued*)

Factor	Categories	Description, Observation
Documentation effort	None	Applies when some documentation needs to be created for the client.
	Little customization (0+ to 10 phrs)	
	Medium customized (10+ to 20 phrs)	
	Highly customized (20 to 60 phrs)	
	Entirely new document (60+ phrs)	
Animation effort	None	
	Very low (0+ to 8 phrs)	
	Low (8+ to 16 phrs)	
	Medium (16+ to 24 phrs)	
	Medium-high (24+ to 40 phrs)	
	High (40+ to 60 phrs)	
	Very high (60+ to 100 phrs)	
	Super high (100+ phrs)	
Final prelaunch and postlaunch testing effort	Low (0+ to 12 phrs)	
	Medium-low (12+ to 20 phrs)	
	Medium (20+ to 80 phrs)	
	High (80+ to 140 phrs)	
	Extremely high (140+ phrs)	

Client approvals and communications	Yes	Client difficulty.
	No	
Features styling (additional effort styling the features)	Very low (0+ to 4 phrs)	This represents the effort needed to adapt, for example, style sheets to take all the widgets of a particular feature (e.g., shopping cart) into account. A simplistic example would be if the site is to be pink, then styling represents the effort to ensure that all the features added to the site comply with this requirement—being pink.
	Low (4+ to 12 phrs)	
	Medium (12+ to 30 phrs)	
	High (30+ to 64 phrs)	
	Very high (64+ to 120 phrs)	
	Very very high (120+ to 160 phrs)	
Implementation effort	Very low (11+ to 48 phrs)	Represents the effort to adapt features. If a given feature needs to be developed from scratch, they will estimate it outside this model.
	Low (48+ to 80 phrs)	
	Medium-low (80+ to 130 phrs)	
	Medium (130+ to 224 phrs)	
	Medium-high (224+ to 340 phrs)	
	High (340+ to 550 phrs)	
	Very high (550+ to 1000 phrs)	
	Very very high (1000+ to 1400 phrs)	
	Super high (1400+ phrs)	

(Continued)

Table 7.2 Description of All the Factors Elicited from the DE (Continued)

Factor	Categories	Description, Observation
Project management effort	Very low (0+ to 10 phrs)	
	Low (10+ to 15 phrs)	
	Medium-low (15+ to 30 phrs)	
	Medium (30+ to 40 phrs)	
	Medium-high (40+ to 50 phrs)	
	High (50+ to 70 phrs)	
	Very high (70+ phrs)	
Final effort estimate	Low level 1 (18+ to 40 phrs)	
	Low level 2 (40+ to 80 phrs)	
	Medium level 1 (80+ to 140 phrs)	
	Medium level 2 (140+ to 200 phrs)	
	Medium level 3 (200+ to 300 phrs)	
	Medium-high level 1 (300+ to 500 phrs)	
	Medium-high level 2 (500+ to 800 phrs)	
	High level 1 (800+ to 1000 phrs)	
	High level 2 (1000+ to 1300 phrs)	
	High level 3 (1300+ to 1500 phrs)	
	High level 4 (1500+ to 1700 phrs)	
	High level 5 (1700+ phrs)	

Total effort estimate	Low level 1 (18+ to 40 phrs)
	Low level 2 (40+ to 80 phrs)
	Medium level 1 (80+ to 140 phrs)
	Medium level 2 (140+ to 200 phrs)
	Medium level 3 (200+ to 300 phrs)
	Medium-high level 1 (300+ to 500 phrs)
	Medium-high level 2 (500+ to 800 phrs)
	High level 1 (800+ to 1000 phrs)
	High level 2 (1000+ to 1300 phrs)
	High level 3 (1300+ to 1500 phrs)
	High level 4 (1500+ to 1700 phrs)
	High level 5 (1700+ phrs)

(Continued)

Table 7.2 Description of All the Factors Elicited from the DE (*Continued*)

Factor	Categories	Description, Observation
Final effort estimate with risk	Low level 1 (18+ to 43 phrs)	
	Low level 2 (43+ to 87 phrs)	
	Medium level 1 (87+ to 150 phrs)	
	Medium level 2 (150+ to 215 phrs)	
	Medium level 3 (215+ to 320 phrs)	
	Medium-high level 1 (320+ to 530 phrs)	
	Medium-high level 2 (530+ to 840 phrs)	
	High level 1 (840+ to 1040 phrs)	
	High level 2 (1040+ to 1350 phrs)	
	High level 3 (1350+ to 1570 phrs)	
	High level 4 (1570+ to 2000 phrs)	
	High level 5 (2000+ phrs)	
User signup	Yes	Users can sign up to the website and create their own accounts.
	No	

Forum	Yes			
	No			
Auction system	Yes			
	No			
Listing (classified ads, property listings, etc.)	None			
	One			
	Two			
	Three			
Gallery	None			
	One			
	Two			
	Three			

(Continued)

Table 7.2 Description of All the Factors Elicited from the DE (*Continued*)

Factor	Categories	Description, Observation
Shopping cart	Yes	
	No	
Event calendar	Yes	Displays a calendar control on the website; events can be added to it.
	No	
Blogs (same as news)	None	
	One	
	Two	
	Three	
Poll	None	
	One	
	Two	
Mailing list	Yes	
	No	

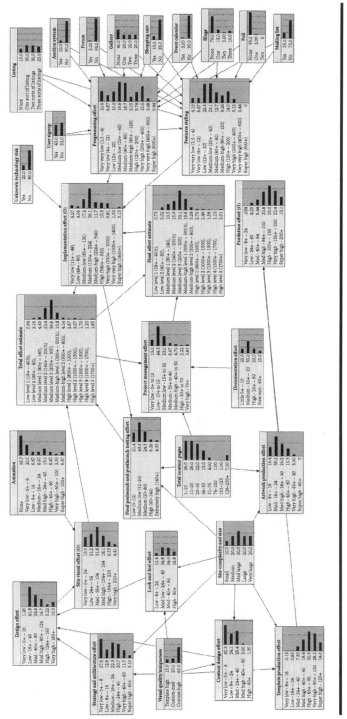

Figure 7.7 Expert-based web effort estimation Bayesian network.

For each project, evidence was entered in the BN model (an example is given in Figure 7.8, where evidence is characterized by dark grey nodes with probabilities equal to 100% [1...]), and the effort range corresponding to the highest probability provided for Final effort estimate was compared with that project's actual effort. For example, in Figure 7.8, this would correspond to Final effort estimate = medium level 3. The company had also defined the range of effort values associated with each of the categories used to measure Final effort estimate. In the case of the company described herein, medium level 3 corresponded to 200+ to 300 person hours. Whenever actual effort did not fall within the effort range associated with the category with the highest probability, there was a mismatch; this meant that some probabilities needed to be adjusted. To know which nodes to target first, we used a sensitivity analysis report, which provided the effect of each parent node on a given query node. Within our context, the query node was Final effort estimate. Within the context of this work, hardly any calibration was needed.

Whenever probabilities were adjusted, we reentered the evidence for each of the projects in the validation set that had already been used in the validation step to ensure that the calibration already carried out had not been affected. This was done to ensure that each calibration would always be an improvement on the previous one. Within the scope of the model presented herein, of the 22 projects used for validation, only one required the model to be recalibrated. This means that for all the 21 projects remaining, the BN model presented the highest probability to the effort range that contained the actual effort for the project being used for validation. Once all 22 projects were used to validate the model, the DE assumed that the validation step was complete.

In terms of the use of this BN model, it can also be employed for diagnostic reasoning and to run numerous "what-if" scenarios. Figure 7.9 shows an example of a model being used for diagnostic reasoning, where the evidence was entered for Final effort estimate and used to assess the highest probabilities for each of the other factors.

The BN model was completed in March 2010 and has been successfully used to estimate effort for new web projects developed by the company. Prior to using the model, the company that is focused on in this chapter did not even know what set of factors they considered fundamental when estimating effort for their new projects; therefore, the elicitation of factors and their causal relationships alone was already considered very helpful to them. In addition, they found it extremely useful to be able to run numerous "what-if" scenarios to help with their decision making, and in addition, to be able to obtain a range of possible effort values and their associated uncertainty. These were very useful to negotiate project costs with clients, given that the effort estimates were based on much more solid knowledge than simply their tacit knowledge.

The factors that were identified by the DE did not include any of the factors used when applying a Function Points methodology for measuring size, because this company did not measure size using Function Points. However, the methodology that has been presented herein would equally apply to companies that employ Function Points.

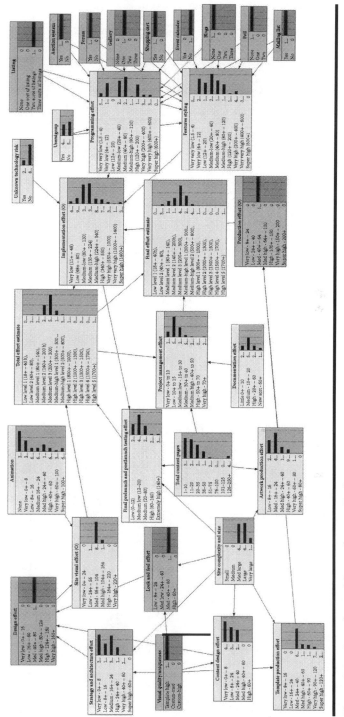

Figure 7.8 Entering evidence for prediction.

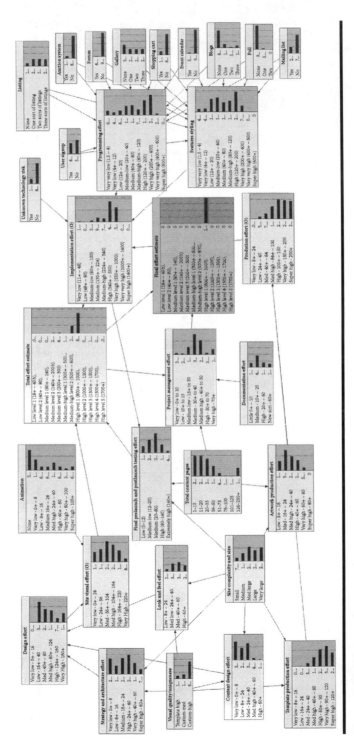

Figure 7.9 Diagnostic reasoning.

We believe that the successful development of this web effort estimation BN model was greatly influenced by the commitment of the company and by the DE's experience estimating effort.

Future Research Directions

The same way as the web company discussed in this chapter has done, we believe that other companies could benefit greatly from using models that enable the representation of domain knowledge and the uncertainty that is inherent to that domain. One possible avenue for future work is to conduct a workshop with several companies to elicit a generic model to be used for effort and risk estimation of web projects (or any other domain judged important for the participating companies). This is something that is in common practice in other fields, such as ecology.

Conclusion

This chapter has presented a case study where a Bayesian model for web effort estimation was built using knowledge from a DE and data on past finished web projects developed by the company. This model was developed using the KEBN process (see Figure 7.4). Each session with the DE lasted for no longer than 3 hours. The final BN model was calibrated using data on 22 past projects. These projects represented typical web projects developed by the company and believed by the expert to provide enough data for model calibration. Since the model's adoption, it has been successfully used to provide effort quotes for new web projects managed by the company.

We have developed other BN models that were validated using data ranging from 8 to 12 past projects only. According to our experience with building BNs for effort estimation, the most important aspect to obtain a sound model relates to the DE's knowledge of the effort estimation domain. Experienced experts will build models that require very little validation.

The entire process used to build and validate the BN model took 66 person hours as follows: 24 person hours for the first 4 weeks (1 DE + 1 KE) and 42 hours for the last 7 weeks (1 DE + 1 KE).

The elicitation process enables experts to think deeply about their effort estimation process and the factors taken into account during that process, which in itself is already advantageous to a company. This has been pointed out to us not only by the DE whose model is presented herein but also by other companies with which we worked on model elicitations.

To date, we have completed the elicitation of 10 expert-driven Bayesian models for web and software effort estimation with the collaboration of NZ companies. Currently, other models are being developed for the Brazilian ICT.

References

1. Druzdzel, M. J., and L. C. van der Gaag. 2000. Building probabilistic networks: Where do the numbers come from? *IEEE Trans Knowl Data Eng* 12(4):481–6.
2. IFPUG. 1999. *Function Point Counting Practices Manual, Release 4.1.* Westerville, Ohio: International Function Point Users Group.
3. Jensen, F. V. 1996. *An Introduction to Bayesian Networks.* London: UCL Press.
4. Mendes, E. 2007. Predicting web development effort using a Bayesian network. In *Proceedings of the Evaluation and Assessment in Software Engineering Conference*, 83–93 London: British Computing Society.
5. Mendes, E. 2008. The use of Bayesian networks for web effort estimation: further investigation, In *Proceedings of the International Conference on Web Engineering*, 203–16 New York: The Institute of Electrical and Electronic Engineers.
6. Mendes, E., and N. Mosley. 2008. Bayesian network models for web effort prediction: A comparative study. *IEEE Trans SoftwEng* 34(6):723–37.
7. Mendes, E., N. Mosley, and S. Counsell. 2005a. Investigating web size metrics for early web cost estimation. *J Syst Softw* 77(2):157–72.
8. Mendes, E., N. Mosley, and S. Counsell. 2005b. The need for web engineering: An introduction. In *Web Engineering*, ed. E. Mendes and N. Mosley, 1–28. Heidelberg: Springer-Verlag.
9. Pearl J. 1988. *Probabilistic Reasoning in Intelligent Systems.* San Mateo, CA: Morgan Kaufmann.
10. Pendharkar, P.C., G. H. Subramanian, and J. A. Rodger. 2005. A probabilistic model for predicting software development effort. *IEEE Trans SoftwEng* 31(7), 615–24.
11. Studer, R., V. R. Benjamins, and D. Fensel. 1998. Knowledge engineering: Principles and methods. *Data Knowl Eng* 25:161–97.
12. Tang, Z., and B. McCabe. 2007. Developing complete conditional probability tables from fractional data for Bayesian belief networks. *J Comput Civ Eng* 21(4), 265–76.
13. Woodberry, O., A. Nicholson, K. Korb, and C. Pollino. 2004. Parameterising Bayesian networks. In *Proceedings of the Australian Conference on Artificial Intelligence*, 1101–07 Heidelberg: Lecture Notes in Computer Science, Springer.

About the Author

Emilia Mendes has active research interests in web and software measurement and metrics. She has authored/coauthored more than 150 refereed publications, which include two books, one edited (2005—*Web Engineering*) and one authored (2007—*Cost Estimation Techniques for Web Projects*). She is on the editorial board of seven international journals and has been invited for numerous talks and keynotes on web/software metrics and measurement. She worked in the software industry for 10 years before obtaining her PhD in 1999 in Computer Science from the University of Southampton (United Kingdom) and collaborates actively with the ICT industry worldwide.

Chapter 8

An Experience in Estimating Software Testing Effort

Luiz Flávio Santos Ribeiro

Contents

Introduction

Working out a software budget in the IT world is always a challenging task—it has been so ever since the early days of the mainframe. This is all the more so today, when we are faced with new technologies on a daily basis. It would be just great if these technologies would carry on their labels such data as performance, productivity, and cost per hour, and if, when plugged in, we could rest assured of the accuracy and reliability of the data. However, we know it is not that way. It is when we need to estimate the cost of a software item that problems start. One most common problem is that the label of the technology to build it unfortunately fails to provide information on the data required for that estimate. On the other hand, even when information is provided, it might not be reliable.

Software testing has been gaining an ever-increasing importance in the life cycle of systems, attaining from 30% to 50% of the total software development costs, as attested by a number of recent research and essays [1]. Standing out from among other software test estimate techniques is Test Point Analysis (TPA) [2]. TPA owes its unique position to its offering a good level of accuracy, providing a wider range of test coverage and the necessary effort for test planning and execution.

The problem with this technique though is that, when estimating function complexity it is necessary to open the code, an expensive and error-susceptible procedure. In addition, when carrying out an estimate, during, say, the design stage or even a requirement definition stage, the code is often not yet ready for an estimation of its complexity. A new technique, Adapted Test Point Analysis (ATPA) [3], suggests that the estimate of function complexity should be made by counting the transaction Function Points [4] of said function. It would make things a lot easier since the Function Point count worksheet would be available as soon as the system's functional requirements were defined. This technique has shown satisfactory results on three projects previously measured as shown in Table 8.1.

This is why ATPA has aroused the interest of Prodemge, an IT-solutions company providing services for the State of Minas Gerais, Brazil (http://www .prodemge.gov.br/), which has used this technique on a few proof of concept projects to estimate the planning and execution of the software testing. Four systems have been chosen for the experience: one enhancement and three development projects. The programming language used is Java, coupled with a JCompany framework and Oracle 10g database. All applications are web based.

In this chapter, all mentions of Function Points have the same reference [4].

Table 8.1 Comparative Results from Three Projects

	Function Points (FPA) [1]	Estimated Test Hours (Project Manager) [2]	Estimated Test Hours (ATPA) [3]	Performed Test Hours [4]	Margin of Error (Project Manager) (%) [5 = (3 − 4)/4]	Margin of Error (ATPA) (%) [6 = (3 − 4)/4]
Project A	45	30.00	58.96	54.00	−44.44	+9.19
Project B	19	89.40	153.12	209.00	−57.24	−26.74
Project C	79	260.70	85.71	63.30	+311.85	+35.40

A Base for Experience

The first of these systems, termed PREVI, is being implemented for one security institute. The major benefits currently offered in the area of health care are purchase of medicine, medical consultation, hospitalization, dental treatment, and lab tests.

The health service makes intensive use of several different systems, on different platforms, for the management and control of health-care activities with a view to both the grant of benefits and the payment for the services provided. The project's overall goal was not to downsize, but rather to create a management system that would contemplate leveraging existing functionalities, provide for online audit, facilitate its utilization and upkeep, and promote improved attendance reliability. The modules tested encompass the entire process of attendance (medical, hospital, dental) for the health plan beneficiaries, totaling some 510 Function Points.

The second system tested was the Infoscip (the Fire and Panic Safety Service Information System for the Minas Gerais Military Police Fire Department). Pursuant to the state's legislation, all buildings destined for collective use must obtain a fire inspection certificate issued by the Fire Department attesting to compliance with the fire and panic safety.

The Infoscip is a pioneering project in the country, assisting all units of the Military Police Fire Department across the entire state in providing support to the process of issuance of fire safety certificates and building inspection. This process consists of an assessment by a duly qualified engineer of the panic and fire safety project, which, following approval by the Fire Department, must be fully implemented. After completion of the project, an inspection visit is requested, and, if compliance is confirmed, a fire safety certificate is issued.

The building inspection project allows for any person, entity, or public agency to report building irregularities. Once an irregularity is confirmed, the owner or the person in charge of the building is given a period of time to rectify the offending work. Noncompliance with panic and fire safety regulations may result in fines or even in the building being interdicted. The modules tested concern the development project (158 Function Points) and enhancement (278 Function Points) to the inspection and fine enforcement controls.

The technique as applied to the government network system has come as an answer to the state demand for unified telecommunication service management. The project is aimed to implement, operate, maintain, and manage the integration of entities and agencies statewide through the Multiservice IP network, with a view to centralize monitoring of events relating to communication service providers. This system is expected to bring about a significant leap in quality in monitoring compliance with service level indicators, as in the event a contract provision fails to be duly fulfilled by the telecommunication provider, the client can be promptly informed thereof.

Agency or entity managers across the state may request access to the Internet, alter, or otherwise terminate the service, as well as apply for registration of connection-related support calls. Access will be done through a portal that furnishes managers with consultations and reports, so they can follow up on open calls and requests (relating solely to the respective agency or entity). By availing themselves of the portal, managers can also request changes in speed or in modality or canceling of access, among other services. They may also obtain consultations and reports, thus assisting other analysts in monitoring their own access, this way furthering the assessment of compliance with such service level indicators as agreed to with the provider. The modules tested amounted to 353 Function Points.

Technique Used

For the purpose of carrying out estimates of the test activities for the above-mentioned systems use was made of the ATPA technique [3], an adaptation of the TPA technique [2], which covers the functional tests (black box) preceding the structural tests (white box). TPA helps to identify all risks involved in performing the tests and also to evaluate the relative importance of the various functions with a view to use the available time as efficiently as possible.

As per TPA, there are three relevant elements: (1) the size of the system in question, in Function Points; (2) the test strategy; and (3) the productivity, which is expressed by the number of hours taken to perform a task measured by Function Points. Together, the first two elements determine the volume of work in test points:

$$V = S + T \tag{8.1}$$

where V = volume (in test points), S = size (in Function Points), and T = test strategy (selection of components, quality characteristics to be tested, and test coverage).

To calculate the test estimate:

$$E = V \times P \tag{8.2}$$

where E = test estimate (in hours), and P = productivity (time required for a test work).

The first element, size, is determined mainly by the number of Function Points assigned to it. Other factors have an influence on size, such as complexity (which relates to the number of conditions in a function), interface (number of files maintained by a function and the number of other functions using those files), and uniformity (which provides a measure of the extent of reuse of test tools). The second element, test strategy, relates to the various quality characteristics, the importance of the various system functions, and the degree of coverage relevance.

The third element, productivity, relates to the time taken to realize one test point, as determined by the size of the information system and the testing strategy. It has two components: (1) a productivity figure, based on the test team's knowledge and skills specific to a given organization and (2) an environmental factor, which indicates the extent to which the environment influences the test activities to which the productivity is related.

Calculation of the number of total test hours is as follows:

$$TP = \sum TPf + (FP \times Qi)/500 \qquad (8.3)$$

where TP = total number of test points assigned to the system as a whole; $\sum TPf$ = sum of points assigned the individual functions (dynamic test points); FP = total number of Function Points assigned to the system as a whole (minimum value 500); and Qi = weighting factor for the indirectly measurable quality characteristics.

TPA sums together the number of dynamic and static test points, and then multiplies the result by the environmental factor and the productivity factor, thereby obtaining the number of primary test hours. The total number of test hours can be obtained by adding to this value an allowance for secondary test activities, represented by planning and control.

When using TPA to calculate the number of dynamic test points, function-dependent factors and the quality requirements regarding the dynamic quality characteristics to be tested should be taken into account.

The following function-dependent factors should be evaluated:

- User importance
- Usage intensity
- Interface
- Complexity
- Uniformity

The following explicitly measurable quality characteristics are recognized:

- Suitability
- Security
- Usability
- Efficiency

The static test point count depends on the Function Point count for the system as a whole; the static measurable quality characteristics should be analyzed for their relevance for test purposes.

Adapted Test Point Analysis Technique

Since TPA fails to indicate explicitly where and how to find the information necessary to calculate an estimate, and further does not address important facts of the test process or clarify how calculations and classifications are made, a few adjustments to the technique were required as follows:

■ The technique demands that a system's functionalities be classified according to its usage intensity and complexity. In this process, it has been proposed to include in the "Requirements Specification" artifact a list of the system functionalities with classifications for the degree of importance for the user, its intensity of use, and complexity.

■ According to the technique, the complexity of the functionality is defined by the algorithm of the function or part of the program that performs the functionality and is measured by the number of commands provided in the existing algorithm. Since the technique is used to perform effort estimates and these are usually carried out during project planning, when the source code is not ready yet, it is necessary to define an alternative way of classifying every functionality according to its complexity. It has been then proposed that the classification of the complexity of each function be performed based on the Complexity column contained in the Function Points count sheet. Thus, if the feature has low complexity in the Function Point count, it is assigned the weight of 3. If it has average complexity, its weight is equal to 6, and if the complexity is high, the weight is equal to 12 (the value of the weights was maintained as described in the original technique).

■ Regarding the classification of the interface complexity, the technique aims to identify the degree of coupling among functionalities. The technique suggests that features be classified according to the interface based on the number of files affected by the function being measured and the number of functions that affect the logical file. To measure a function in Function Points, it is necessary to define the number of files or data sets that it accesses. If the function does not modify any files, the technique recommends that it be given the weight of a low interface. However, the technique does not specify how the test analyst must get this information to produce the estimates. Thus, it has been defined in this process that this classification is obtained from the Function Point count in which a new field called "ILFs Changed" has been included. This field must be filled in for each elementary process stating the number of which groups of data it alters. Given the number of changed files, it is possible to determine the interface among functions. It has been proposed that the calculation should be performed as follows: one should check how many files an elementary process changes and multiply this by the number of times this file is changed in the whole system. For example, an elementary process called "Insert Project" changes only one file ("Project"), and this file is changed by five other processes in the Function Point count. Thus, the complexity of this interface would be low ($1 \times 5 = 5$), according to the original technique. To assign the interface complexity classification, only the elementary processes classified as External Inputs (EI) have been considered because the External Queries (EQ) processes should always receive a low complexity value.

■ Regarding the uniformity classification, which measures the level of reuse of testing materials, the technique always applies the values 0.6 and 1.0. The 0.6 value is applied if there is complete reuse of the test material, that is, the material used is of a similar or identical function to be validated. The 1.0 value is used when there is no reuse of the material. This item of the technique is also adapted by applying the value of 0.8 if only part of the material is reused.

■ The technique requires that the test team be classified as to their qualifications. For this, the technique takes into account the experience and productivity of the team. The technique suggests that this classification should range between 0.7 and 2.0, considering that the more qualified the team is, the lower its classification should be. Since the technique does not specify where this information can be obtained, in the proposed process such information is obtained from the Project Plan, which contains a description of the team's characteristics and requirements. It has been proposed that this classification should be done by setting the weight of 0.7 if the productivity is low, 1.3 for medium, and 2.0 for high. This classification should be made for each testing project analyzing only the people who are involved in it, and it should not consider the average skills of the whole test team.

■ Another field has also been included in the Project Plan to describe the characteristics of the management tools that are used in the process, since the technique does not describe how this information is obtained. This information is important to calculate the Control and Planning Index (CPI).

■ It is not explicitly clear where general information on test environment and test materials can be found. It has been determined that in the proposed process such information be identified in the "Test Plan." This information is required to yield the estimates and should include the following:
  - If there is a previous test plan
  - What the characteristics of the test environment are and if the team is familiar with it
  - If test material is available (database, tables, etc.)
  - If automation tools are used

■ According to the technique, dynamic quality characteristics measure how requirements quality may affect the test quality. The technique does not mention where this classification should be obtained nor does it makes it clear how it should be performed or whether it refers to every functionality or the system as a whole. In the proposed process, it has been considered that it refers to the system as a whole. This information is registered in the quality plan.

■ According to the technique, the calculation of static test points should be performed only if the team adopts procedures for documentation and code review using checklists, otherwise it must be null. It has been proposed that this information be obtained from the quality plan as well as any information related to indicators and documentation standards in the process.

■ In order to classify the size of the test team, the technique considers only the existence of teams with over three members. However, it is common to have just one person responsible for planning and executing the tests. Thus, the technique was adapted to consider teams of one to four members. These teams should be assigned a weight equal to 0.03.

Results

Although Prodemge regards the results as being very good, it does not expect the margin of error for the test estimates to be the same as obtained on those tests (Table 8.2). This is because Prodemge knows that, on tests carried out previously with the ATPA technique, the margin of error reached slightly higher levels (Table 8.1).

Due to difficulty in setting an exact value for calculation of the estimates, the weights for the dynamic quality were assumed to be average. The productivity factor used was 0.7, considering that the Prodemge test team is well organized, well prepared, and run by highly qualified professionals. The environmental factor weight calculation yielded a result of 0.95.

Table 8.2 Proof of Concept Results

	Function Points (FPA) [1]	Calculated Test Points (ATPA) [2]	Estimated Test Hours (ATPA) [3]	Performed Test Hours [4]	Margin of Error (%) [5 = (3 − 4)/4]
State Government Network System	353	269	179	152	+17.76
INFOSCIP Development	158	146	97	88	+10.22
INFOSCIP Enhancement	278	167	111	100	+11.00
PREVI	510	631	420	440	−4.55

In view of the results obtained by applying the Veenendal and Dekkers technique, with the use of the adaptations by Souza and Barbosa, Prodemge will come to adopt this resource for the evaluation of software test statistics. The investment necessary for training and development of the test team is low when measured against the advantages of obtaining more realistic budgets and schedules as far as software testing is concerned. Current estimates of software testing make use of the Capers Jones exponential formula [5]:

$$TC = (FP)^{1.2} \tag{8.4}$$

where TC = number of test cases, and FP = Function Points.

The Estimate for Test Cases specifications is calculated as follows:

$$E^1 = TC \times A^1P \tag{8.5}$$

where E^1 = estimate (in hours) for test cases specifications, and A^1P = average (in hours) of the duration to specify the test cases obtained from Prodemge's historical data.

The Estimate for Effort for Functional Tests is given as follows:

$$E^2 = PF \times A^2P$$

where E^2 = estimate (in hours) for Effort for Functional Tests, and A^2P = average (in hours) of the durations to run the executions of the functional tests per Function Points from Prodemge's historical data.

This estimate gives goods results in terms of effort; however, it does not provide a test coverage. This was the reason why Prodemge wanted to change its internal software testing methodology, adopting the ATPA technique.

References

1. RUP (Rational Unified Process). http://www.wthreex.com/rup/portuguese/index.htm (accessed March, 2011). Path: Disciplinas/Teste/Introdução.
2. Veenendaal, E. V., and T. Dekkers. 2011. *Test Point Analysis: A Method for Test Estimation.* http://pt.scribd.com/doc/51734428/Test-Point-Analysis-dekkers. (accessed March, 2011).
3. Souza, P. P., and Barbosa, M. W. 2010. Tailoring the test point analysis estimation technique in a software testing process. In *IV Encontro Brasileiro de Testes (EBTS)*. Recife.
4. IFPUG, 2010. *Function Point Counting Practices Manual Release 4.3.1 (CPM)*. The International Function Point Users Group. http://www.ifpug.org (accessed March, 2011). Electronic document available for IFPUG's members only.
5. Capers, J., 2007. *Estimating Software Costs: Bringing Realism to Estimating.* New York: McGraw-Hill.

About the Author

Luiz Flávio Santos Ribeiro is a civil engineer (PUC-MG), a postgraduate at information systems (UNA-MG) and is a Certified Function Point Specialist (CFPS-IFPUG). He has over 20 years of experience as an analyst in application development and maintenance, a DBA and a data administrator. He is currently working in software process management as an artifact reviewer and a metrics analysis consultant. Email: lflavio.ribeiro@hotmail.com

Chapter 9

Producing Reliable Estimates through Quantitative Uncertainty Assessment

Luca Santillo

Contents

> *When you can measure what you are speaking about, and express it in numbers, you know something about it; otherwise your knowledge is of a meager and unsatisfactory kind.*
>
> **Lord Kelvin**
> *physicist, 1889*

Introduction

This chapter addresses the topic of producing reliable estimates—by means of a quantitative assessment of the uncertainty that is implicit in any measure and that inevitably propagates from input variables to outcomes in any estimation model. We might extend the scope of Lord Kelvin's well-known original statement to the fact that achieving numbers without assessing their uncertainties means "knowing (facts) without knowing (their applicability)," thus being still unsatisfactory.

In the so-called hard science field, for example, physics, a precise method for assessing such uncertainty propagation has been developed and is being used constantly in practical cases. This sound approach to uncertainty assessment can be shifted with no need of tailoring to software measurement, regardless of the specific model, formula, or algorithm being applied, provided that input variables to such models are "quantifiable" (read: clearly defined and collected, and finally measured, according to standard measurement methods). For instance, input variables might be specifications and functional requirements and output variable(s) might be the functional size of the software being measured, or input variables might be functional and non-functional requirements, such as those measured by FPA and the forthcoming SNAP approach, respectively, and the output variable(s) might be costs, efforts, and/or duration of a software project.

What Is Uncertainty?

Uncertainty is "[a] non-negative parameter characterizing the dispersion of the quantity values being attributed to a measure and, based on the information used" [1, p. 39]. (The "measurand" is the conceptual or physical subject being measured.)

Uncertainty is unavoidable. Decision making in the ICT and software industry is more and more applied to relevant issues (read: economically crucial and often related to human safety and security). The true message is that decision making, based on software measurement, should rigorously address the uncertainty assessment, rather than approximating with any sort of facile rule of thumb (such as "take 10% of the size as a confidence interval") or, even worse, neglecting it with a sort of "feel good" approach such as "it worked yesterday, it'll work tomorrow." In other words, the risks associated with the uncertainty in any measurement or estimation model should be assessed quantitatively *prior* to their prioritization and possible minimization.

Uncertainty is unavoidable, but it can be assessed, quantified, and therefore managed. Rather than avoiding (mentioning) uncertainty, we should embrace it and put ourselves in a position of controlling it as much as possible [2].

To keep the treated topic as simple as possible, only the case with continuous quantities is treated—a generalization to discrete variables should, however, not be very difficult for use in real cases. In addition, the assumption of independent input variables in our examples is important. Any possibility of cross-relationships among input variables can only worsen the final uncertainty (technically, this would result from covariance analysis and the fact that while errors "sometimes" compensate each other, uncertainties unfortunately do not). Finally, the uncertainty type we will deal with is assumed to be "random," that is related to the precision carried by the estimated or measured variables, and with a normal distribution. If any systematic uncertainty is ever found, it should be dealt with by removing it and/or refining the estimation model to take it into account systematically, as well as for skewed or peculiar probability distributions of the input uncertainties. (For an interesting set of hints for evaluating an estimation model, derived from the discussion in this chapter and the previous assumptions, see the end of the chapter.)

The uncertainty issue and the way to tackle it in software measurement were introduced in previous publications and further developed through research in the field by the author [3,4]. This chapter summarizes those results, discusses them along with the Cone of Uncertainty, and includes a list of recommendations to practitioners in software estimation.

How Certain Is Your Uncertainty?

Producing estimate values without any indicator of the reliability (confidence) of the estimates is just a "guess" with no quality index. Any model might produce an estimate such as "ten person-months" or "one billion dollars," but decision makers will make completely different decisions depending on being it "ten person-months within a 10% confidence interval" versus "ten person-months within a 50% confidence interval," or "one billion ± 5%" versus "one billion ± 30%." Besides not providing any expression for the uncertainty or associated error, most estimation models suggest rules of thumb for confidence ranges, which are often proven to be unrealistic or too large for any practical usage. A common concept related to uncertainty in software estimation is the Cone of Uncertainty, originally proposed within the framework of the Constructive Cost Model (COCOMO) by Barry Bohem as the "Funnel Curve" [5]. Figure 9.1 depicts a recent version of the Cone of Uncertainty, where the order of magnitudes of uncertainty over the progress of a project are shown [6]. In fact, the real values of such uncertainty a priori can only be obtained by the hereby proposed approach for uncertainty propagation, or analogous rigorous approaches, while extensive data collection over a large amount of projects would be necessary to draw a real-world version of the Cone of Uncertainty a posteriori.

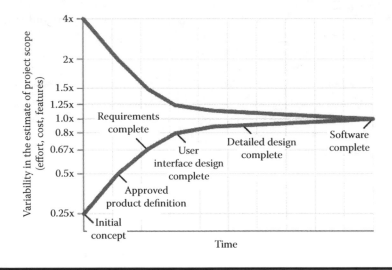

Figure 9.1   The Cone of Uncertainty based on common project milestones (and their approximate positioning over time).

Generic Uncertainty Propagation Theory

The brief description of uncertainty propagation theory in this section is based on one of many textbooks available in science and engineering [7]. Math details are avoided for the sake of simplicity—the interested reader can find further information in previous publications [4]. When the quantity to be determined is derived from several measured quantities, and if the measured quantities are independent of each other (i.e., contributions are not correlated), the uncertainty Δ ("delta") of each contribution may be considered separately. A typical method by which one may calculate the contributions of direct measured independent variables in the dependent variable being derived is the "derivative method." The basic idea is to determine by how much the derived quantity would change if any of the independent variables were changed by its uncertainty. This method makes use of derivatives derived from the formula that expresses the model being considered. However, for most typical operations in formulas, simple expressions can be used instead of derivatives, thus providing a quick way to express the uncertainty for the model being considered.

Table 9.1 shows these simple expressions for uncertainties related to generic formulas, where A and B are the input variables, X is the output variable, and c is a constant. When the square of ΔX is shown, the value for ΔX can be obtained by taking the square root. When $\Delta X/X$ is computable, or $\Delta A/A$ and $\Delta B/B$ are shown, it is denoted as "relative error (uncertainty)," and it is usually expressed as a percentage.

When a constant is included, it is assumed that its uncertainty is negligible (otherwise, it should be treated as a variable, with a given uncertainty itself); in software measurement, we rarely observe real constants. This remark applies also

Table 9.1 Common Expressions in Uncertainty Propagation ($\sqrt{}$ is for "Square Root" and $|...|$ for "Absolute Value")

Operation	Formula	Uncertainty
Addition	$X = A + B$	$\Delta X = \sqrt{[(\Delta A)^2 + (\Delta B)^2]}$
Subtraction	$X = A - B$	$\Delta X = \sqrt{[(\Delta A)^2 + (\Delta B)^2]}$
Multiplication	$X = A \times B$	$\Delta X = X\sqrt{[(\Delta A/A)^2 + (\Delta B/B)^2]}$
Division	$X = A/B$	$\Delta X = X\sqrt{[(\Delta A/A)^2 + (\Delta B/B)^2]}$
Product by constant	$X = c \times A$	$\Delta X = c\Delta A$
Exponentiation	$X = c \times A^n$	$\Delta X = X\,|n|\,(\Delta A/A)$
Logarithm	$X = \ln(c \times A)$	$\Delta X = \Delta A/A$
Exponential function	$X = e^A$	$\Delta X = X \times \Delta A$

to exponentiation: the uncertainty is "simple" if the exponent is a known constant, otherwise its uncertainty must be considered as well, in a more complex way (this is the case for several COCOMO formulas or the ISBSG regression formula for effort or duration, where the value of the exponent is derived by some further calculation, or statistics average, which by definition is not exact and depends on the validity and the dimension of the sample being considered).

When a formula involves more than two input variables or more than one operation, the final uncertainty can be achieved additively by combining the uncertainty expressions from Table 9.1 (e.g., if $X = A + B + C$, consider first $A + B$, then the result $+ C$).

It is worthwhile noting that because uncertainty is absolute (i.e., the random error considered on both input and output variables can be above or below the true value), the uncertainty expression for opposite operations, such as addition versus subtraction or multiplication versus division, is unchanged.

Applications and Examples

Any estimation formula can be considered to provide an example for uncertainty propagation. This section provides some examples. By all means, this is not a comprehensive set of estimation models; we neither suggest nor recommend the models hereby considered over any other example in the literature or the industry.

Functional Size

This example applies to any functional size measurement method, as well as to any approximation technique such as early and quick simple approaches, where the measurer, the requirements being measured, or the approximation technique itself might inject uncertainty in the amount or the values associated with input variables, and the input variables are the functions being identified. (Functional size is not an estimation model per se, but its results are often taken as an input variable to other models—it is, therefore, worthwhile understanding how uncertainty on input variables arises, before further models are applied on such variables.)

In the IFPUG method [8], we identify logical files (ILF and EIF) and elementary processes (EI, EO, and EQ) and we assess them on a low/average/high complexity scale. The (unadjusted) functional size formula for IFPUG can be expressed as

$$
\begin{aligned}
\text{Size}_{(UFP)} = \; & 7 \times N_{\text{ILF-LOW}} + 10 \times N_{\text{ILF-AVERAGE}} + 15 \times N_{\text{ILF-HIGH}} + \\
& 5 \times N_{\text{EIF-LOW}} + 7 \times N_{\text{EIF-AVERAGE}} + 10 \times N_{\text{EIF-HIGH}} + \\
& 3 \times N_{\text{EI-LOW}} + 4 \times N_{\text{EI-AVERAGE}} + 6 \times N_{\text{EI-HIGH}} + \\
& 4 \times N_{\text{EO-LOW}} + 5 \times N_{\text{EO-AVERAGE}} + 7 \times N_{\text{EO-HIGH}} + \\
& 3 \times N_{\text{EQ-LOW}} + 4 \times N_{\text{EQ-AVERAGE}} + 6 \times N_{\text{EQ-HIGH}}
\end{aligned}
\tag{9.1}
$$

With respect to this formula, if the measurer fails in identifying a function (file or process) and/or counts a function that should not be counted according to the measurement rules, then the measurer is introducing an error in a single value for N_{A-B}, where "A" denotes the type of the function and "B" denotes the complexity rating. If the measurer is correct in identifying a function but assigns the wrong complexity value to it, then the person is introducing a double error, because the function is not counted under the correct figure and it is wrongly counted under another figure.

For sake of readability, we rewrite the formula in abbreviated form as

$$
\begin{aligned}
\text{Size} = \text{Size}\big(N_{11}, N_{12}, \; \dots \; , N_{52}, N_{53}\big) = \\
7N_{11} + 10N_{12} + 15N_{13} + \\
5N_{21} + 7N_{22} + 10N_{23} + \\
3N_{31} + 4N_{32} + 6N_{33} + \\
4N_{41} + 5N_{42} + 7N_{43} + \\
3N_{51} + 4N_{52} + 6N_{53}
\end{aligned}
\tag{9.2}
$$

Although long, this formula is easily recognized as a combination of additions and multiplications, where the multiplication coefficients are fixed by definition in the measurement method (constants) and the measurer has to determine 15 quantities of N_{AB}. By combining the expressions of addition uncertainty from

Table 9.1, we easily obtain the uncertainty expression for the functional size in the IFPUG method:

$$\Delta Size = \sqrt{(7\Delta N_{11})^2 + (10\Delta N_{12})^2 + L + (4\Delta N_{52})^2 + (6\Delta N_{53})^2} \qquad (9.3)$$

Again, although long, this expression has a simple form and confirms us with any experienced measure know, that is, "an error in identifying (amounts of) logical files is more impacting than an error in identifying (amounts of) elementary processes."

In approximation techniques, such as "indicative" or "estimated" or "early and quick" approaches, we should consider also the uncertainty derived by using average values for logical files and elementary processes, instead of the exact complexity values. Therefore, the uncertainty in the outcome of any approximation technique should be carefully considered, and such approaches should not be used when exact values are required, such as in relevant project estimates or contractual environments, where economical values are associated with functional sizes.

If adjustment is provided, further uncertainty should be evaluated. For instance, for the uncertainty associated with the value adjustment factor, it can be shown that for an average relative uncertainty of less than 5% on the General System Characteristics assessment, a relative error larger than 5% is obtained [4]. In fact, this is a general result: the more the sources of uncertainty, the larger the uncertainty on the outcomes.

ISBSG Regression Formulas

The International Software Benchmarking Standards Group provides useful data and information regarding software benchmarking and estimation [9]. Besides suggesting several alternatives to software estimation, the ISBSG proposes several regression equations for effort estimation, as well as duration and speed of delivery, as a technique to produce indicative or ballpark project estimates. We consider here just one of these equations as an example:

$$PWE = A \times Size^B \times Team\ Size^C \qquad (9.4)$$

where PWE is Project Work Effort (in person hours), Size is the estimated functional size (in Function Points), and Team Size is the average size of the project team, that is the (estimated) amount of human resources involved. It is crucial to note that the regression coefficients *A*, *B*, and *C* in this equation are in fact not constants, and they vary for both the sample being considered and the specific set of factors of the environment being considered (the environment and the sample are to be considered independent features). As a "simple" example of the uncertainty propagation, let us consider the regression coefficients as being constant, as if only the Size and the Team Size could vary in practice. This would lead to the uncertainty expression for the estimated effort:

$$\frac{\Delta \text{PWE}}{\text{PWE}} = \sqrt{\left(B \frac{\Delta \text{Size}}{\text{Size}} \right)^2 + \left(C \frac{\Delta \text{Team Size}}{\text{Team Size}} \right)^2} \tag{9.5}$$

where each factor in the uncertainty formula has been considered as if the other is constant (i.e., first the uncertainty deriving from variations in Size has been taken into account with fixed values of Team Size, then the opposite). If we take some (example) values for a given environment from ISBSG, such as $A = 38.97$, $B = 0.434$, $C = 0.951$, with Size = 256 FP, and Team Size = 4 people, we obtain an effort estimate of PWE = 1627 person hours.

Assuming an average uncertainty of 10% on both the Size and the Team Size, we would then obtain a relative error on effort of 10% or approximately 160 person hours. This first example might suggest that the uncertainties average rather than sum up, but this single calculation is a "fake friend" and a misleading one. The previous uncertainty formula is to be considered highly "optimistic" for several reasons:

■ The regression coefficients are considered as being fixed.
■ The covariance between Size and Team Size has been ignored.
■ The values for fixed values are less than 1.

More complex cases would arise in practice and we would be led to higher values of uncertainty for the estimated value of the Project Work Effort, especially for the latter assumption—relative uncertainties associated with coefficient A and especially with exponents B and C would be added in absolute values, and in some cases multiplied with the relative uncertainties of other variables, thus easily yielding realistic uncertainties that could easily double the average relative uncertainty on the input variables. Rather than experimenting further with the ISBSG example, we can switch to a similar case, in the next section.

COCOMO Estimation Model

The COCOMO case [10] has been addressed in detail in a previous publication [4]. We recall only the final results here, derived by exact derivatives (the reader might try to achieve similar results, although approximated, by means of the uncertainty expressions from Table 9.1). The generic estimation equation of the Constructive

Cost Model assumes a relationship between effort and size, in a two-step process. First, nominal effort is derived from size:

$$\text{Nominal Effort} = A \times \text{Size}^B \qquad (9.6)$$

where Size is expressed in lines of code or Function Points (obviously, different values of the coefficients A and B would apply for different software sizing units, which is beyond the scope of the discussion of the current topic) and the nominal effort is expressed in person hours (or multiples) and represents an average or ballpark estimate. The nominal effort equation recalls the ISBSG example in the previous section. Hereby, we consider instead that coefficients in the formula (A and B) may also vary, and therefore, they carry their own uncertainties. The full uncertainty expression on Nominal Effort [4] is given by

$$\Delta\text{Nominal Effort} = \sqrt{(\text{Size}^B \Delta A)^2 + \left(AB \frac{\text{Size}^B}{\text{Size}} \Delta\text{Size} \right)^2 + (A\,\text{Size}^B \ln(\text{Size})\Delta B)^2} \quad (9.7)$$

As an example, let us consider values of Size = (1000 FP ± 200) (this would represent an approximated size at the very beginning of the project, with no details, 20% relative uncertainty), A = (10 ± 1) person hours (10% relative uncertainty) and B = (1.10 ± 0.01) dimensionless (just 1% relative uncertainty on the exponent). We would then obtain (rounded values)

Nominal Effort = $(20{,}000 \pm 5{,}000)$ person hours, or a relative error of 25%

One might argue that reducing the highest of the relative uncertainties in the input variables, that is the approximation on the size in Function Points in our example, we would achieve a reduced level of uncertainty in the estimate of the effort. Unfortunately, this is not always the case. Even with the best approximation techniques, or even when the size of the project can be measured with high precision, we remain with two major uncertainty sources:

- No early technique in the beginning of the project can ensure that the true value will stay as approximated in the beginning.
- The impact of other factors are as important as the size in the uncertainty expression, if not more relevant.

While the former factor (i.e., change request) might be taken into account by providing better approximation techniques, or by forcing the project not to vary its scope beyond a given threshold (controlled change requests), the latter (e.g., non-functional requirements if size is expressed in Function Points, or other non-sizeable aspects) depends solely on the quality of the calibration of the estimation model and is not under the control of the specific project.

Let us consider a set of different conditions for this first level of the example. Table 9.2 shows the result of the uncertainty over the nominal effort when uncertainty is varying over the input variables (the first row is the example previously calculated; highlighted cells are those whose values are varied with respect to the first row).

What we can derive from this experiment is that when a nonlinear relationship exists between variables in the estimation model, the impact of some variables in the uncertainty propagation is higher than the impact of other variables (the exponent *B* in this case), eventually leading to catastrophic situations with final relative uncertainties well over 50%. More specifically, the previous case pushes us to avoid approximation techniques, such as "early and dirty" sizes for the input variables, such as the Function Point size—again, the more accurate we get the input variables, the less uncertainty we inherit in the output estimation. By the way, it is worthwhile noting that by using approximation techniques instead of standard measurement practices also keeps allowing the "user" to avoid eliciting detailed requirements to feed the project and its estimation. In other words, approximating in the beginning and continuing to approximate during the project keeps bad habits in the requirements management alive. What a measurement method should

Table 9.2   Uncertainty Variations per Separate Input Variables in a Simple COCOMO-Like Formula

Size (Function Points)	A (Person Hours)	B	Nominal Effort (Person Hours)
1,000 ± 200 (20%)	10 ± 1 (10%)	1.10 ± 0.01 (1%)	20,000 ± 5,000 (25%)
1,000 ± 100 (10%)	10 ± 1 (10%)	1.10 ± 0.01 (1%)	20,000 ± 3,300 (16%)
1,000 ± 200 (20%)	*10.0 ± 0.5 (5%)*	1.10 ± 0.01 (1%)	20,000 ± 4,700 (23.5%)
1,000 ± 200 (20%)	10 ± 1 (10%)	*1,100 ± 0.005 (0.5%)*	20,000 ± 4,800 (24%)
1,000 ± 200 (20%)	10 ± 1 (10%)	*1.1 ± 0.1 (10%)*	20,000 ± 14,600 (73%)
1,000 ± 10 (1%)	10 ± 1 (10%)	*1.1 ± 0.1 (10%)*	20,000 ± 13,900 (70%)
1,000 ± 10 (1%)	*10.0 ± 0.1 (1%)*	*1.1 ± 0.1 (10%)*	20,000 ± 13,800 (69%)

allow, if standardized and based on sound practices, is for a bounded uncertainty range of about ±5% in any result. This would correspond to a detailed level of description of the requirements being measured. Any value beyond that interval is not a measure but rather a guess. (And any value much below that interval, at the current maturity level of the industry, would be unfeasible in most practical cases—again, uncertainty can be reduced, but not down to null value.)

In fact, the COCOMO model is not complete with the nominal effort. The impact of non-functional requirements, as well as the impact of project or process-related factors, team capabilities, and so on, typically makes any project different from any other project in the past, regardless of having the same "size." The adjusted effort estimate is therefore obtained by taking into account the product of several factors (cost drivers) over the nominal effort:

$$\text{Adjusted Effort} = \left(\prod \text{Cost Drivers} \right) \times \text{Nominal Effort} \tag{9.8}$$

The amount of cost drivers ranges from less than 10 to about 20, based on the version of the COCOMO model and the stage and type of the software project being considered. Each cost driver is dimensionless, may generically have values between 0.75 and 1.25, and is considered to be independent from all other cost drivers (hence, the multiplication of overall cost drivers in the formula). For sake of simplicity, we will consider "only" a set of seven cost drivers, with an estimated value of 0.95 per each, and an average relative error of 5% per each (real cases might vary significantly with respect to this simple example; while cost drivers might assume continuous values, the COCOMO standard model considers a scale of fixed values for practical purposes). With a relative uncertainty of 25% on the nominal effort, the adjusted effort in our example would be [4]

$$\text{Adjusted Effort} = \left(14,000 \pm 5,000 \right) \text{ person hours, or a relative error of 36\%}$$

Apparently, using cost drivers has allowed us to adjust the estimate (from 20,000 person hours to 14,000 person hours in our example), while keeping an approximated uncertainty of "only" 5,000 person hours. Unfortunately, the relative error is increased. This is an unavoidable effect of having added some variables in the model. While the aim was to refine the estimate, the uncertainty is now larger than on the nominal effort estimate.

Also, we note here that only a small number of (fake) cost drivers was considered—the choice of which factors have priority over the others might be a smart action for good estimation, rather than adding factors over factors to the estimation model in an attempt at improving the estimates—this would create higher uncertainties in the end, whereas the general estimate might not improve significantly (as a set of suggestions for the list of the factors, see GUFPI-ISMA [11]).

It is up to the project stakeholders to investigate by how much uncertainty should be reduced (or equivalently, to what extent uncertainty is acceptable), project by project, and therefore which actions should be taken, and on which of the variables, to do so. For instance, in a contractual environment, uncertainties above 10% are usually not acceptable and should be dealt with through specific actions (e.g., postponing to a future project changes that would not be measured with through sufficient accuracy in the current project).

Many other examples might be explored (for instance, in the study by Santillo [4] the case of the Jensen-Putnam model, or so-called software equation, is addressed). The reader is challenged to derive his/her own uncertainty expressions for most available (or local) estimation models—the outcomes might be unexpected and possibly surprising.

Advice for the Young at Estimation

We conclude this discussion with a list of recommendations on how to address the uncertainty issue. Beyond any numerical exploration of estimation models, some hints can be generalized and are highly recommended for consideration before you put your "numbers" into "models," regardless of being a brand new model built from scratch or a preexisting one in the industry or from the literature. While experienced project managers and estimators might find this list somehow trivial, novices might get some valuable advice on how to avoid unwanted mistakes in their first estimates.

- **Prefer structured models,** where input and output variables are clearly distinguished (separated) and no significant dependence among any two of the input variables is present. In other words, do not double-count risks (ensure a given factor is considered only once, in one variable, within the model), otherwise, the final uncertainty would be over-assessed.
- **Do not miss important factors**—even when not easily measured, important factors should always be considered; in other words, do not choose a model solely based on what you "can" measure, but rather try to find a way—as standardized as possible—to measure any factor you consider relevant for the estimated case(s).
- **Consider rare events and related risks.** These might be excluded from your estimate, as long as you mention them separately, or you can perform parallel estimates with and without such factors, to be aware of unlikely, still catastrophic eventualities. In other words, unimportant factors might be excluded from the explicit estimation model, but they should not be neglected from the model assumptions and statements.
- **Build what-if scenarios** out of the model, to compare different options for the input variables, to represent what the real extent of possible outcomes is.

Do not trust the model forecast as is, and do not neglect the possibility of having all factors against the estimated case (or in favor of it)—unlikely does not mean impossible.

■ **Keep it simple and straightforward** (not stupid)—trying to capture any single factor that might influence the software process is a never-ending attempt and would not necessarily lead to better and better results; try whenever possible to restrict the number of variables while catching the most important ones, for example, by defining a "boundary" to the problem and/or aggregating variables with shared characteristics.

■ **Keep it simple and safe** (but again, not stupid)—at the same time, do not oversimplify and be aware of what you are neglecting from the model. Relevant factors should not be removed, even if they cause a given uncertainty to propagate. Try controlling their input values, instead, to reduce the resulting uncertainty. In other words, avoid facile models and simple approximations just because of lesser uncertainty, or you will end with fake results—they might "feel good," but they likely would not reflect reality.

■ **Limit the uncertainty you put in** the input variables as much as possible—early and quick approaches are dangerous, they allow for a "feel good" statement, until you discover the real uncertainty in them was actually intolerable for any practical purpose. In other words, standard measurement methods for input variables (such as certified FPA for the functional size) are to be preferred over any easy approximation for reliable estimation.

■ When unable to assess the uncertainty of a variable, **consider the range and the frequency of errors** for that variable in previous cases. How often and by what amount has that variable been found to be incorrectly reported in the past? Build your own statistics, until you will be able to assess a realistic uncertainty range for it.

■ **Perform benchmarking** against similar or external cases—a single product line, company environment, or local measurement process would fail sooner or later, because new cases will always carry new features and therefore new uncertainty sources.

■ **Prioritize variables**—those whose impact on the outcome uncertainty is higher are the most relevant to be considered, refined, measured, and controlled as the project progresses.

■ **Do not trust simple statements,** such as "the confidence is [whatever value] %" (where "whatever value might seem truly optimistic as 1%, desired as 10%, realistic as 25%, or catastrophic as 50% or higher)—always inquire about the model being applied and explore what the uncertainty propagation expression tells you about the real uncertainty. (This is regardless of "the model says so" or "the expert says so".)

■ While **"errors (often) balance," uncertainties do not**—expecting that the worst case will not happen is a matter of hope, if not simply hazardous, and certainly not a practice of aware project management and decision making.

Back to the Cone of Uncertainty and Conclusions

Looking at Figure 9.1 again, we can now consider a new perspective of the figures stating that in the beginning of a project our initial estimate might be, on average, one fourth smaller as well as four times larger than the final value. In addition, McConnell [6] states that the Cone of Uncertainty represents the "best-case accuracy that is possible to have in software estimates at different points in a project," (p. 37) that it is "easily possible to do worse." Is beating the Cone impossible?

Uncertainty propagation as discussed in this chapter clearly adds a new perspective on software measurement and estimation. Because uncertainty is unavoidable and models' sensitivity on input variables is often relevant, uncertainty propagation is a feature that cannot be ignored in risk-aware project management and business. Moreover, dealing with quantitative assessment (of both variables and their associated uncertainties) allows for transparency in estimation to avoid biases and cognitive illusions. Uncertainty propagation, when correctly applied, allows us to locate the acceptable trade-off between expressing the software process in quantitative formulas and predefined models and accepting the fact that processes in reality are always more complex and uncertain than any model will be able to catch. We cannot annihilate the (Cone of) Uncertainty but reducing it by means of accurate measurement and a careful selection of models, their factors, and their assessment—yes, we can!

References

1. ISO. 2007. *International Vocabulary of Metrology—Basic and General Concepts and Associated Terms (VIM)*. ISO/IEC GUIDE 99:2007. Geneva, Switzerland: International Organization for Standardization. www.iso.org (accessed June 30, 2011).
2. Clampitt, P. G. and R. J. DeKoch. 2001. *Embracing Uncertainty: The Essence of Leadership*. Armonk, NY: M.E. Sharpe.
3. Santillo, L. 2002. ESE: Enhanced software estimation. In *IT Measurement: Practical Advice from the Experts*, ed. IFPUG, 391–406. Indianapolis, IN: Pearson Education.
4. Santillo, L. 2006. Error propagation in software measurement and estimation. In *Procs 12th Intl Workshop on Software Measurement (IWSM)*, 371–82. Aachen, Germany: Shaker Verlag.
5. Boehm, B. 1981. *Software Engineering Economics*. Englewood Cliffs, NJ: Prentice-Hall.
6. McConnell, S. 2006. *Software Estimation: Demystifying the Black Art*. Redmond, Washington: Microsoft Press.
7. Taylor, R. 1997. *Introduction to Error Analysis: The Study of Uncertainties in Physical Measurements*. 2nd ed. Herndon, VA: University Science Books.
8. IFPUG. 2010. Function Point Counting Practices Manual, Release 4.3.1 (CPM). In *The International Function Point Users Group*. Princeton Junction, NJ: IFPUG. www.ifpug.org/ (accessed June 30, 2011).
9. ISBSG. 2011. *Practical Software Project Estimation: A Toolkit for Estimating Software Development Effort & Duration*. New York, NJ: McGraw-Hill. www.isbsg.org/ (accessed June 30, 2011).

10. Boehm, B., C. Abts, and A. Winsor Brown, et al. 2000. *Software Cost Estimation with Cocomo II.* Prentice Hall. Upper Saddle River, New Jersey 07458.
11. GUFPI-ISMA. 2011. *Tassonomia dei Fattori d'Impatto della Produttività dei Progetti Software. (Taxonomy of Productivity Impacting Factors for Software Porjects.), Release 1.0.* Italy: GUFPI-ISMA. www.gufpi-isma.org/sbc/tassonomia/ (accessed June 30, 2011).

About the Author

Luca Santillo (Agile Metrics, CEO) is a recognized software measurement expert, holding certifications, publications, and valuable results since the mid-1990s at national as well as international levels. He is a Certified Function Point Specialist in both IFPUG and COSMIC methods and he publishes guidelines and innovative applications of FPA in fields such as data warehousing, web-based systems, ERP packages, middleware applications, service-oriented architectures, a development, Early & Quick sizing & Smart Function Point approximation. His M.Sc. in Physics allows him to apply exact methods to the emerging field of software measurement, with innovative insights and measurement culture divulgation towards practitioners. He chairs several working groups in national and international bodies, related to Function Points and benchmarking. He is a contributing member of the Core Team of the SNAP (Software Non-functional Assessment Process) project by IFPUG. To date, he is president of the Italian Function Point Users Group & Software Metrics Association (GUFPI-ISMA), one of the directors and honorary treasurer of the International Software Benchmarking Standards Group (ISBSG), and Italian member of the International Advisory Council of the Common Software Measurement Consortium (COSMIC). He has been appointed president of COSMIC for the 2012–2014 period. As a consultant and trainer, he helped several medium-to-large companies to apply FPA, productivity assessment, and quantitative project management, to software development. So far, he has managed the measurement of over 500 software projects or applications and trained over 1000 people in Function Point Analysis and software estimation models. Luca Santillo can be reached globally at: luca.santillo@gmail.com.

About Agile Metrics

Agile Metrics provides specialized services and products to promote measurement, benchmarking and process improvement, worldwide. Agile Metrics also holds an active role in the research field, through certified expertise and collaboration with acknowledged professionals, standardization bodies and business partners in Europe, North and South America, Asia and Oceania. Please refer to Agile Metrics' website at www.agilemetrics.it to obtain products evaluation copies and free articles on software measurement, estimation and benchmarking.

Chapter 10

Optimism in Cost Estimation

Ricardo Valerdi

Contents

Introduction

Biases continue to be an important aspect of software cost estimation because they often occur subconsciously and can frequently lead to unfavorable outcomes. Optimism bias is one type of cognitive illusion that is often overlooked because of its association with good health and positive outcomes. However, the existence of optimism bias in cost estimation can be very damaging especially when it distorts a person's ability to forecast events.

Building from foundations in behavioral economics, we seek to understand better optimism bias by exploring the benefits and downsides of optimism and their empirically based origins. This provides a backdrop for a methodology for quantifying optimism and pessimism followed by a discussion about certain professions that make well-calibrated decisions. Unfortunately, we find that cost estimators are overly optimistic in their decisions compared to other professions.

Results are explored from a survey given to a cohort of 80 engineers, which ultimately portray the degree to which optimism bias influences decision making in the estimation of cost and schedule of large projects. A calibration exercise is designed to calibrate optimism in engineers with the ultimate goal of helping cost estimation realism. Finally, advice is provided to help individual decision makers better optimize their optimism.

The implications of this work are twofold. First, the mechanism for quantifying optimism in engineers provides useful insight into the degree of optimism that exists in cost estimation tasks. This can influence a number of decision-making processes that may traditionally be seen as immune from biases due to their routine nature. Second, the process for calibrating optimism provides a way to validate the effectiveness of optimism reduction techniques on different types of decision makers. It also helps to distinguish between certain people who are more receptive to bias corrections and are therefore more likely to be better estimators in real life.

Calibrating Optimism in Decision Makers

The motivation behind this work stems from the strong influence that human decision making has in product development, specifically cost estimation. Engineers often develop very sophisticated, well calibrated, and accurate algorithmic cost models based on historical data of technical nature. These models provide estimates of cost and duration of projects based on well-understood technical parameters. However, the human element involved in estimating the inputs to these models as well as the use and interpretation of these models is poorly understood.

Equally important in the area of judgment and decision making are the limits of human performance. It is known that humans cannot run 1 mile (1.6 kilometers) in less than 3 minutes and cannot jump over 9 feet (3 meters) because of the limitations of their physical abilities. There are equivalent limits of the mental abilities of humans in terms of our ability to remember a certain number of digits or to perform certain mathematical computations [1]. There are also influences from our experiences and training that have a direct impact on the way we make judgments and decisions. In particular, these experiences shape the way we see the world and determine whether we are optimistic or pessimistic in certain circumstances.

The Role of Optimism in Judgment and Decision Making

It is important to distinguish between judgment and decision making since these terms are often used interchangeably. A judgment is when the knowledge of the values and relations of things are determined [2]. A decision is the cognitive process of selecting among available options [2]. In this chapter, the focus will be on judgments only because the decision-making aspect involves an entirely different mechanism. It is important to consider how people make judgments about, in this case, the cost of a product they want to develop in the future. The focus on optimism is because it represents a class of biases that is often ignored and can lead to unfavorable long-term outcomes despite its more visible short-term benefits.

Engineers are sometimes too optimistic of their own abilities and claim, "one half of the glass is a hundred percent full." To correct optimism, it must first be measured. An important concept presented in this chapter is a methodology for quantifying a decision maker's optimism level based on the field of meteorology [3]. This example provides a framework for measuring the potential effectiveness of training mechanisms to reduce optimism and supports the hypothesis that *optimism can be reduced through training.*

This chapter provides an overview of optimism, its advantages and disadvantages, its empirically based origins, a method to quantify it, results of an optimism survey given to a group of engineers, and a discussion of optimism across professions. We conclude with a discussion of techniques that can help individuals better manage optimism and an investigation regarding the feasibility of estimation calibration, by performing an exercise on a small group of estimators, to infer if similar practices and techniques can be used to calibrate engineers. One important implication of this work is that it demonstrates how experience can be substituted by training. The calibration process can accelerate the ability of a decision maker to be less optimistic and more realistic.

The Double-Edged Sword of Optimism

This investigation into optimism is driven by the following question: *If being an optimist is good, then why can it sometimes be so bad?* In other words, why is something that is so good in life potentially so problematic in the workplace?

Optimism is truly a double-edged sword with its range of advantages and disadvantages. We will first focus on comparing optimism and pessimism and then focus on optimism itself, how it can be better controlled, and how it differs across professions.

Optimism Defined

An optimist is a person who is unrealistic about the short term but realistic about the long term, while a pessimist is a person who is realistic in both their short term and long term thinking [4]. There are other aspects of being a pessimist, for example, whenever a bad experience takes place, a pessimist considers the experience permanent and pervasive across other similar experiences. On the other hand, an optimist can have a bad experience and perceive it as a temporal and specific one that can end whenever one chooses.

Indirect Benefits of Optimism

Happiness is all around us. Aristotle [5] refers to a "golden mean" where we can reach a balance of happiness. In Zen Buddhism, the goal is to be happy [6]. The words "life, liberty, and the pursuit of happiness" are in the US Declaration of Independence and the Japanese constitution. There is even an organization called Optimist International dedicated to helping youth. The direct benefits of optimism are obvious; it helps people cope with negative events and carry a positive outlook on life that is very often transferred to others.

There are several indirect benefits of being an optimist, the most recognized of which are improved physical health [7] and success in life [8]. Conversely, it has been shown scientifically that pessimistic people are more likely to have health problems later in life [9]. One study focused on religious nuns found that those who wrote more positive things about their lives tended to live longer and the ones that wrote less positive things died earlier [10]. Optimistic people have also been found to be more creative and productive [11], better at performing cognitive tasks [12], and less likely to get divorced [13]. More importantly, those who are optimistic believe that things can be accomplished—even if they are unrealistic—which results in being seen as competent and entrepreneurial in the workplace [14]. These are the attractive aspects of being an optimistic person. Research also shows that being an optimist does not translate to being wealthier [15], which complements the notion that being wealthier does not necessarily make you happier. The conclusion is that people across all socioeconomic levels can be happy for different reasons.

Downsides of Optimism in the Workplace

There are several disadvantages of being too optimistic in work-related situations. Some common examples are being too optimistic about the output of a particular factory and being unable to meet demand, estimating real estate prices without regard to market fluctuations, and deciding to drill for oil in a location that does not show promise from geological analysis. Each example has penalties in the billions of dollars because if the estimate is too narrow (i.e., with low variation) or too confident it can result in unrealistic business expectations and poor financial outcomes [14].

It is common for optimists to be seen as detached from reality [16]. This is where the "half of the glass is one hundred percent full" is commonly cited, also known as the Pollyanna principle [17]. Optimists are seen as Pollyannaish because they see the silver lining in every dark cloud. Being too optimistic often causes others to perceive you as naïve.

Empirically Based Origins

The question that follows is *why are certain people pessimistic or optimistic?* There are many studies that provide predictors of optimism, the most interesting of which is age [18]. The theory behind this is that, the older you are, the happier and more optimistic you tend to be. There are several explanations for this; one of them is that people learn how to optimize their life over time. Individuals learn what they like and dislike and do not bother with the useless tasks and instead focus on playing golf or playing with grandkids and—as a result—enjoy life more. However, this is a selective data set because it is based on the people who are still alive. Those nuns who were pessimistic tended to die earlier and may have affected the results of the study by biasing the sample analyzed.

One of the sources of pessimism is a person's *set point* that is defined by their genetic makeup [19]. A person's default mood is often what defines them. Some people are generally pessimistic because the way they were raised influences the way they look at life. These are crucial perspectives for understanding why people are pessimistic or optimistic.

Presence of Optimism

There is ample evidence that individuals are optimistic most of the time as evidenced by their misestimation of project costs [20], the length of future tasks [21], their personal abilities [14], their knowledge about history [22], whether they will complete their academic thesis on time [23], their favorite sports team [24], and their sense of humor [25]. The German author Johann Wolfgang von Goethe said "For a man to achieve all that is demanded of him he must regard himself as greater than he is." Society rewards those who are optimistic and frowns upon those who are pessimistic. If people always underestimate themselves, then it will be difficult for them to achieve the extraordinary. This demonstrates a contrast that involves the benefits and drawbacks of being optimistic. In the next section, we provide a methodology for quantifying optimism bias to measure its frequency among different professions.

Quantifying Optimism Bias

Considering the disadvantages of optimism in a variety of situations, it is important to understand when it is present so that it can be managed. To identify the presence of optimism, we provide a two-dimensional scale that can be used to compare a person's confidence about a certain estimate versus the accuracy of an actual estimate. It was originally developed for assessing the accuracy of weather reporters in the 1950s [3] and is shown in Figure 10.1.

A perfectly calibrated person is someone who consistently falls along the diagonal ($f_i = d_i$). This means that if their confidence about a quantity is 50%, they are actually correct 50% of the time. Whenever their confidence (f_i) is greater than their accuracy (d_i), that person is considered to be optimistic. If the opposite is true, that person is considered to be pessimistic. A Brier score can be calculated for each individual as represented in Figure 10.2.

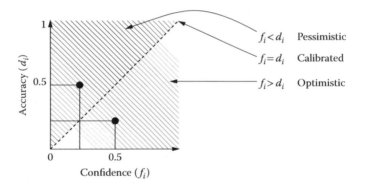

Figure 10.1 Confidence versus accuracy dimensions.

$$Brier\_score = \left(\frac{1}{N}\right) \sum_{i=1}^{N} (f_i - d_i)^2$$

f_i = respondent's probability that their judgment is correct
d_i = outcome of the respondent's accuracy
N = total number of judgments

Where
f_i is a subjective probability
d_i is an objective (empirical) probability

Figure 10.2 Equation for Brier score.

A higher Brier score indicates a greater distance from the diagonal, which may indicate optimism or pessimism. The judgments of a well-calibrated person would consistently fall along the diagonal, that is, their subjective probabilities would consistently match the empirical probabilities of events. The notion of being well calibrated is not only an aspect of personality; it is also affected by a person's profession. We now explore the phenomenon of optimism among engineers as well as within other professions.

Optimism in Engineers

To develop insight about optimism bias, a survey was administered to 80 systems engineers attending the 2008 International Council on Systems Engineering (INCOSE) Symposium in Utrecht, The Netherlands. A mixed group of both practitioners and academics made up the population, ranging in experience levels from relatively new in the community to well-informed experts from various countries. The goal of the survey was to gather a quantitative understanding about systems engineering estimation bias at the 90% confidence interval and at varied confidence levels—with the general hypothesis that other types of engineers are similarly optimistic.

The survey consisted of two sections, each comprising ten questions. Participants were informed that the survey was voluntary, and they were also made aware that understanding estimation habits—not testing intelligence—was the intent of the exercise. Participants were not allowed to consult other people or the Internet for assistance, and they were advised that the survey should take approximately 3 minutes. The questions were not scientific in nature, but rather were common knowledge questions that all systems engineers at the conference should have had relatively the same exposure and ability to answer. For instance, participants were asked to estimate the population of China in the first section and asked whether Italy beat Brazil in the last World Cup Final in the second section. We now expand more on the goals and results of each respective section.

The first section of the survey asked participants to provide a 90% confidence interval of their certainty to the answers of 10 different common knowledge questions. In short, they were to provide a "lower bound" and an "upper bound" in which they were to be 90% certain that their answer to the question would lie within that range. For example, one of the questions asked was "How many days does it actually take the Moon to orbit the Earth?" If one were to think the answer was 27 days, a typical confidence interval may have been 25–31 days or some other range depending on the individual and their degree of certainty.

To depict the results from this set of questions, a histogram was created to show the scores of the 80 participants across the range of possible accuracy levels (0% to 100%). In the cases where participants failed to answer certain questions, those that went unanswered were not counted and their overall score was rounded up to the nearest 10%. By rounding up, we ensured that the results were not slanted to show optimism. In theory, all 80 participants would have been in the 90% category or at least distributed around the 90% category. However, as shown in Figure 10.3, most systems engineers were around 30% correct when they should have demonstrated 90% accuracy in their estimates. This illustrates a significant degree of optimism to the extent that only one participant actually met the 90% accuracy target.

Understanding the optimism bias of individual systems engineers with respect to a set accuracy target, we now visit the second section of the survey to examine the extent of estimation bias across a range of confidence levels.

The second section asked participants to provide a binary response, true or false, to 10 common knowledge statements and provide a confidence level between 50% and 100%. The lower bound to the confidence level is 50% because if one were less than 50% confident the answer was true, that would be equivalent to indicating they were more than 50% confident the answer was false. Thus, a truly unknown statement, such as "The coin will land on heads," should yield either 50% certainty of true or false from any rational decision maker.

The results of the second section can best be summarized in the form of the accuracy with respect to confidence diagram shown in Figure 10.4. To construct a similar diagram, the entire pool of answers from the 80 participants was segmented according to the confidence levels declared and then grouped on the chart seen in Figure 10.4 with respect to their cumulative accuracy (i.e., point "(50, 49.4) $n = 176$" reads when 176 people asserted to be 50% confident in an answer, they were correct 49.4% of the time).

In general, this figure depicts that as confidence increases, accuracy diverges significantly from the perfectly calibrated diagonal where confidence equals actual. Note that the two clear outliers, (65, 66.7) and (85, 37.5), had too few samples, 3 and 8, respectively, to be statistically significant.

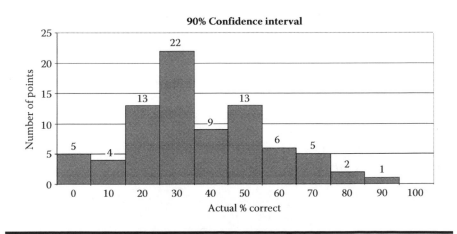

Figure 10.3   Results from 90% confidence interval survey.

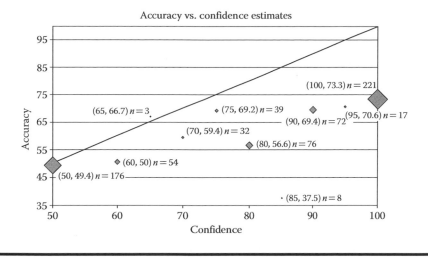

Figure 10.4   Results from accuracy versus confidence survey.

Results from these two sets of questions support our general hypothesis that engineers are inherently optimistic in estimation practice. With this understanding now accepted, we focus our attention on addressing the question *how can engineers better manage optimism?* Since optimistic estimates about a program's cost, schedule, effort, or other attributes could lead to unattainable situations for decision makers, it is imperative that engineers are aware of this optimism phenomenon. As we can see from Figures 10.3 and 10.4, there are no general rules of thumb that can (or should) accurately be employed in attempts to discount the effect of optimism in an estimation. Rather, it is important that engineers take the time to engage in estimation exercises that move them closer to the calibration line previously discussed. In fact, calibration seminars exist that use similar questions to those employed in our survey to help individuals learn a better understanding for connecting subjective probabilities and objective outcomes [22]. Now that we have quantitatively demonstrated optimism in engineers, we will discuss trends in other professions.

Differences across Professions

When one considers the calibration studies of doctors, accountants, IT professionals, strategists, analysts, and psychologists, it is common to see optimistic bias. One of the corrections for this is to provide training on calibration, similar to that mentioned previously, so that individuals can reduce their level of optimism. However, each of these professions has their own incentives for being calibrated judges of certain types of events. Accountants, IT professionals, strategists, and analysts may greatly benefit from being less optimistic, while doctors and psychologists may simply need to decide when to turn "on" or "off" their optimism depending on a particular patient's situation. Optimism of doctors has been shown to improve the psychological and physical health outcomes of their patients [26]. However, doctors are careful not to communicate a false sense of optimism in cases where expectations of eventual success are sufficiently unfavorable [27,28]. Optimism in health care presents a different environment for considering calibration because it has less to do with comparing confidence to accuracy and more to do with treating each case as unique given the scientific facts and knowing when it is reasonable to be optimistic based on experience with particular diseases.

There are other professions that can never afford to be optimistic because of the asymmetrical costs of the outcomes. We consider these to be well-calibrated professions: bookies and weather reporters. These professions are unique for three reasons. First, they receive immediate feedback on whether their predictions are correct or not based on the comparison between their confidence levels and the occurrence of actual events. Second, providing accurate predictions have career rewards. Bookies have financial incentives to be calibrated because they can earn more money when they are more realistic in the probabilities of sporting events. Weather reporters who are more accurate tend to earn respect in their field and may get promoted faster. Third, they do not overreact to extreme events since they understand that outcomes will eventually regress towards the mean. For example, bookies exploit the fact that chance events make outcomes an imperfect measure of abilities [29]. Weather reporters similarly understand that certain weather conditions are anomalies and damage can sometimes be concentrated on a small geographical area. This has created the need for specifically targeted weather alerts that do not affect large geographical regions.

Bookies do not want their profits to depend on the outcome of games. In American football, their objective is to set a point spread to equalize the number of dollars wagered on each team and to set the total line to equalize the number of dollars wagered "over and under," which relates not to which team wins and by how much, but to the total number of points scored by both teams. Bookies attempt to account for all the factors that gamblers take into account: player strengths and weaknesses, injuries, home-field advantage, and historic rivalries. If bookies are aware of systematic bettor irrationalities, they will factor them into their forecasts [30,31]. The ability to adjust their level of optimism based on what others think the outcome will be is certainly a learned skill that is perfected over time.

Conversely to bookies and weather reporters, some historically not well-calibrated professions include those who are forced to bid on proposals. For example, in software project bidding, engineers and managers tend to have over-optimistic cost estimates. Jørgensen [20] explains how the bidding process makes this profession especially susceptible to various factors that breed optimism, two of which are referred to in economics as the "winners' curse" and "adverse selection." Winners' curse occurs in bidding auctions when there are many bidders, wherein economic theory dictates that one is likely "to win only when being over-optimistic about the value of the bidding object" [20]. Thus, there is a great chance that the lowest bidder cannot actually deliver the promised low cost. With respect to adverse selection, the theory can be read that those with lower bids are more likely to be less competent. The more competent bidders who understand the problem better will have a higher bid—acknowledging the higher development cost that will ultimately yield lower life-cycle costs [20]. The prime takeaway from this understanding is that the bidding process needs a selection mechanism in place that accounts for these potential optimism-induced phenomena and mitigates its effects.

The question becomes *how can engineers be more like bookies or weather reporters and less like software project bidders in their judgments of probabilities?* By examining the performance of a field that relies more on scientific measurement, weather forecasting, we can gain an appreciation for the promise of calibration. The data for the weather reporters demonstrate that their predictions exactly match what actually happened for very large samples of predictions, as shown in Figure 10.5.

It should be noted that the 100% prediction estimates resulted in 90% precipitation. This is reasonable considering most weather reporters are significantly accurate for all other confidence levels. However, weather reporters are trained to do this deliberately because the penalties of predicting that it is going to rain 90% of the time are asymmetrical. If people interpret this as a 10% probability of no rain, then there is a chance that at least some of them will decide not to carry an umbrella when they go outside. To avoid this, weather reporters adjust their prediction to 100% chance of rain to encourage people to carry their umbrellas and prepare for at least some rain. In the event that the 10% chance of no rain actually takes place, it becomes only a slight inconvenience for those carrying umbrellas.

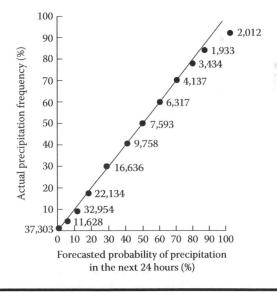

Figure 10.5 US National Weather Service forecasting accuracy. (From Koehler, D. J., and N. Harvey. 1997. *J Behav Decis Mak* 10:221–42. With permission.)

Optimizing Optimism

Can we calibrate engineers to become less optimistic? Fortunately, the answer is "yes"; there are several strategies that can help people be less optimistic about the weather, the performance of their favorite sports team, etc. Some of these strategies are presented here, but it is up to individuals to decide which are most appropriate for their circumstances. A method for combining some of these strategies is likely to work the best.

The simplest technique is betting money or pretending to bet money. One study showed that people do not necessarily have to bet money; as long as you pretend to bet money their accuracy automatically improves [32]. Pretending that there is money involved tends to help individuals be more realistic judges of events because they associate their accuracy with a financial reward.

Another technique is to separate the observation from the task itself so that judgments can be made independent of outcome. One study found that separating "doing" from "observing" a task has an impact on optimism. Actually doing a task makes individuals more optimistic compared to those who simply observe it [33]. Decision makers can reduce their optimism simply by removing themselves from tasks and positioning themselves as neutral observers.

There are many things to learn from people who are well calibrated and from the underlying reasons for their accuracy. It is clear that personality plays a significant role, but professions, and associated rewards structures, also determine a person's sensitivity to the calibration. In some circumstances, optimism may lead to positive results in areas such as mental and physical health, while in others it can lead to financial disaster. The medical profession has learned to manage optimism so that it is present when it is needed and absent when it may give a sense of false hope. With respect to the engineering community, one might implement best practices similar to those of more calibrated professions discussed previously, such as the following: (1) constantly providing mechanisms of feedback about prior estimates, (2) creating an incentive structure that values accuracy in estimation, and (3) ensuring there is no overreaction to atypical events. In the Optimism Calibration section, we further explore the notion of optimism calibration by performing a simple calibration exercise.

Optimism Calibration

To understand better the phenomenon of optimism calibration, we performed a trial calibration exercise on a group of engineering students in an MIT graduate class—Cost Estimation and Measurement Systems. The sample size consisted of five students, which although small, can still provide valuable insight. Moreover, this exercise was performed at the end of the course, such that students were well educated with respect to estimation methods and principles. Next, we discuss the process we took to calibrate the students and the results from the exercise. The questions and answer forms used for this exercise can be made available upon request.

First, at the end of one class, students were informed how to fill out the calibration answer form (similar to those given to the INCOSE population) for both 90% confidence interval and binary questions. Ten confidence interval and ten binary questions were asked to each students for the first round. Next, everyone was shown the results of the first round of the INCOSE exercise, wherein we facilitated a review of the optimism phenomenon that was seen, as discussed earlier in this chapter. Students were then shown the results from their original trial—in the same format as the results from the INCOSE population. After discussing optimism similarities to the INCOSE group, despite a smaller sample size, we reviewed some of the principles identified in this chapter—pertaining to underlying reasons for optimism as well as some of the strategies for improvement.

Once this discussion concluded, the students were asked to complete 20 more confidence interval and 20 more binary questions. While they were shown their results relative to round 1, it was consensus opinion that there had been some improvement. In the ensuing discussion, improvement strategies were again considered, such as pretending to bet money. Moreover, it was noted that the constant reinforcement of seeing scores immediately after testing improved the group's confidence in understanding their estimation capabilities and limitations.

Finally, a third round of questioning was performed, which similarly to round 2 consisted of 20 final confidence interval questions and 20 final binary questions. Following the expected trend, the group again came to the conclusion that noticeable improvements in calibration had been made. In the final discussion, we considered the variability across participants—who seemed to improve the most and why. In general, it was believed that the more cognizant one was of their estimation habits and improvement methods, the more they were able to improve. Those who saw minimal improvements believed they did so because they had an exceptional first round, either by good estimation or due to the smaller amount of questions. The group results are discussed below and can be seen in Figures 10.6 and 10.7.

With respect to the calibration exercise, one can see a slight improvement from round 1 to 2 and a more noticeable improvement from round 2 to 3. In fact, we note that four of the five students achieved 80% or higher accuracy in the third round, whereas only two students were at 80% accuracy in round 1. However, since only one student was at 90% accuracy by round 3, there are obviously improvements that can be made. At the end of the session, we discussed the concept of anchoring, which often throws off many confidence interval estimators. This phenomenon occurs when estimators think of the answer and then add and subtract error accordingly. Although this strategy seems intuitively acceptable, it often yields tighter ranges than appropriate for 90% confidence. A more beneficial strategy for this exercise pertains to thinking about upper and lower bounds individually—by declaring you are 95% certain the answer lies below your upper bound and 95% certain the answer lies above your lower bound—as opposed to focusing on a central arbitrary number.

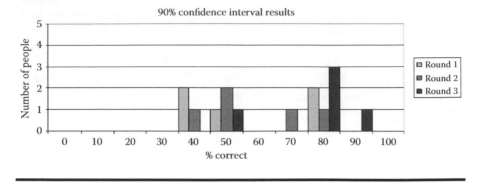

Figure 10.6   Class calibration exercise—90% confidence intervals over three rounds.

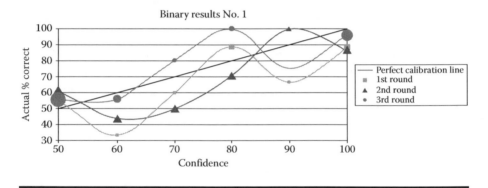

Figure 10.7   Class calibration exercise—accuracy versus confidence over three rounds.

Regarding the group binary results, there was also fair improvements. Most notably, the confidence levels that accumulated the most data points, 50% and 100%, saw improvements from round 1 to round 3. Additionally, the 60% confidence interval saw significant improvements from round 1 to round 3, despite less data points than the 50% and 100% levels. In general, the 70%, 80%, and 90% points were less clear—or failed to show improvements. Conversely, if one were to combine results from round 2 to round 3 for a more statistically relevant depiction of estimation accuracy relative to round 1, it appears the results would fall much closer to the perfectly calibrated line. Moreover, an interesting result of this exercise was the fluctuation between optimism and pessimism throughout the exercise, a result we hypothesize can be attributed to optimism bias overcompensation. However, with the exception of the 50% confidence interval, most of the other pessimistic points (those lying above the calibration line) had less data points than their optimistic counterparts.

From the positive results of this exercise, we believe similar practices and techniques can be used to calibrate engineers. Although there could be some logistical concerns regarding data input and consolidation of larger groups, we believe this experiment can effectively be executed with a larger group. In short, even though the sample size was too small to yield definitive conclusions, insight from this exercise indicates that engineers can be calibrated for both better estimation accuracy and precision.

Conclusion

This chapter provided a connection between the literature on happiness, judgment, decision-making, meteorology, and gambling to explore the concept of optimism and consider a method to measure and calibrate it. A logical next step is the development of a formal methodology to train engineers in becoming better-calibrated judges of future events.

One implication of this work is the ability to demonstrate that experience does not matter in terms of becoming a better judge. Common sense would suggest that more experienced professionals are better estimators, but it can be shown that calibration exercises are an adequate substitute for experience [34]. This understanding is important because it can save time, resources, and potential errors that may otherwise take decades to learn. Furthermore, this result would demonstrate that better calibrated people do not necessarily have better information or possess superior guessing skills, but that they are more in tune with their cognitive abilities and more realistic about their judgments—a skill that requires the connection between subjective probabilities and objective outcomes.

References

1. Miller, G. A. 1956. The magical number seven, plus or minus two: Some limits on our capacity for processing information. *Psychol Rev* 63:81–97.
2. Webster Dictionary. 2011. http://www.webster-dictionary.org (accessed on July 12, 2011).
3. Brier, G. W. 1950. Verification of forecasts expressed in terms of probability. *Mon Weather Rev* 78:1–3.
4. Seligman, M. E. P., T. A. Steen, N. Park, and C. Peterson. 2005. Positive psychology progress: Empirical validation of interventions. *Am Psychol* 60:410–21.
5. Aristotle. 1974. The Nichomachean Ethics. J. A. K. Thomson, Trans. New York: Penguin.
6. Gaskins, R. W. 1999. Adding legs to a snake: A reanalysis of motivaton and the pursuit of happiness from a Zen Buddhist perspective. *J Educ Psychol* 91:204–15.
7. Bower, J. E., C. A. Low, J. T. Moskowitz, S. Sepah, and E. Epel. 2008. Benefit finding and physical health: Positive psychological changes and enhanced allostasis. *Soc Personal Psychol Compass* 2:223–44.

8. Lyubomirsky, S., L. King, and E. Diener. 2005. The benefits of frequent positive affect: Does happiness lead to success? *Psychol Bull* 131:803–55.

9. Peterson, C., M. E. P. Seligman, K. H. Yurko, L. R. Martin, and H. S. Friedman. 1998. Catastrophizing and untimely death. *Psychol Sci* 9:127–30.

10. Danner, D. D., D. A. Snowdon, and W. V. Friesen. 2001. Positive emotions in early life and longevity: Findings from the nun study. *J Pers Soc Psychol* 80:804–13.

11. Estrada, C., A. M. Isen, and M. J. Young. 1994. Positive affect influences creative problem solving and reported source of practice satisfaction in physicians. *Motiv Emot* 18:285–99.

12. Isen, A. 1987. Positive affect, cognitive processes, and social behavior. *Adv Exp Soc Psychol* 20:203–53.

13. Harker, L., and D. Keltner. 2001. Expressions of positive emotions in women's college yearbook pictures and their relationship to personality and life outcomes across adulthood. *J Pers Soc Psychol* 80:112–24.

14. Russo, J. E., and P. J. H. Schoemaker. 1992. Managing overconfidence. *Sloan Manage Rev* 33:7–17.

15. Myers, D. G., and E. Diener. 1995. Who is happy? *Psychol Sci* 6:10–19.

16. Ben-Shahar, T. 2007. *Happier: Learn the Secrets to Daily Joy and Lasting Fulfillment*. Columbus, OH: McGraw-Hill.

17. Matlin, M. W., and D. J. Stang. 1978. *The Pollyanna Principle*. Cambridge, MA: Schenkman Publishing Co.

18. Charles, S. T., C. A. Reynolds, and M. Gatz. 2001. Age-related differences and change in positive and negative affect over 23 years. *J Pers Soc Psychol* 80:136–51.

19. Brickman, P., D. Coates, and R. Janoff-Bulman. 1978. Lottery winners and accident victims: Is happiness relative? *J Pers Soc Psychol* 36:917–27.

20. Jørgensen, M. 2009. How to avoid selecting bids based on overoptimistic cost estimates. *IEEE Software* 26:79–84.

21. Roy, M. M., N. J. S. Christenfeld, and C. R. M. McKenzie. 2005. Underestimating the duration of future events: Memory incorrectly used or memory bias? *Psychol Bull* 131:738–56.

22. Hubbard, D.W. 2010. *How to Measure Anything: Finding the Value of Intangibles in Business*. Hoboken, NJ: John Wiley & Sons.

23. Buehler, R., D. Griffin, and M. Ross. 1994. Exploring the "planning fallacy": Why people underestimate their task completion times. *J Pers Soc Psychol* 67:366–81.

24. Babad, E. 1987. Wishful thinking and objectivity among sport fans. *Soc Behav: Int J Appl Soc Psychol* 4:231–40.

25. Seligman, M. E. P. 2006. *Learned Optimism: How to Change your Mind and Your Life*. New York: Vintage Books.

26. Kubzansky, L. D., P. E. Kubzansky, and J. Maselko. 2004. Optimism and pessimism in the context of health: Bipolar opposites or separate constructs? *Pers Soc Psychol Bull* 30:943–56.

27. Peterson, C., and L. M. Bossio. 1991. *Health and Optimism*. New York: The Free Press.

28. Scheier, M. F., and C. S. Carver. 1987. Dispositional optimism and physical well-being: The influence of generalized outcome expectancies on health. *J Pers* 55:169–210.

29. Lee, M., and G. Smith. 2002. Regression to the mean and football wagers. *J Behav Decis Mak* 15:329–42.

30. Bird, R., and M. McCrae. 1987. Tests of the efficiency of racetrack betting using bookmaker odds. *Manag Sci* 33:1552–62.

31. Bruce, A. C., and J. E. V. Johnson. 2000. Investigating the roots of the favourite-longshot bias: An analysis of decision making by supply- and demand-side agents in parallel betting markets. *J Behav Decis Mak* 13:413–30.
32. Bukszar, E. 2003. Does overconfidence lead to poor decisions? A comparison of decision making and judgment under uncertainty. *J Bus Manag* 9:33–43.
33. Koehler, D. J., and N. Harvey. 1997. Confidence judgments by actors and observers. *J Behav Decis Mak* 10:221–42.
34. Murphy, A. H., and R. L. Winkler. 1984. Probability forecasting in meterology, *J Am Stat Assoc* 79:489–500.

About the Author

Ricardo Valerdi is an associate professor at the University of Arizona in the Department of Systems & Industrial Engineering. Previously he was a research associate in the Engineering Systems Division at the Massachusetts Institute of Technology. His research focuses on systems engineering metrics, cost estimation, test & evaluation, human systems integration, enterprise transformation, and performance measurement. Ricardo is the co-editor-in-chief of the *Journal of Enterprise Transformation* and served on the board of directors of the International Council on Systems Engineering (INCOSE). He received a PhD in Industrial & Systems Engineering from the University of Southern California and a Master's in Psychology from Harvard University.

FUNCTION POINTS INTRODUCTION

Sivasubramanyam Balasubramanyam

Introduced by Allan Albrecht at IBM in the year 1979, Function Points have come a long way. Function Points are a unit of measure to express the amount of business functionality provided to a user by the software. They are used both for estimation during early stages of the project and later to measure the actual size of the application delivered. It goes without saying that what you cannot estimate you cannot plan; the fundamental aspect of project planning hinges with estimating the size of the project and getting it right. In this section, on Function Points, there are two chapters written by authors who address different dimensions of the Function Point counting exercise.

Claudia Hazan is a specialist in software metrics and estimation, working for SERPRO—the Brazilian government data processing service company. She has also taught at prestigious Brazilian universities. Claudia's chapter "The 13 Mistakes of Function Point Counting" begins with a discussion on the utility of Function Points during estimation; the reader is then guided on a step-by-step path of identifying the mistakes that take place during any Function Point counting process. Claudia gives the reader examples of the mistakes and suggestions on aspects that have to be taken care of during a Function Point counting session.

Lori Holmes is a Director of Q/P Management Group, specializing in software measurement and process improvement. Lori's chapter "Facilitating Function Point Counts: How to Ask the 'Right' Questions and Get the 'Right' Answers for an Accurate Count in an Efficient Manner" discusses how to facilitate a Function

Point review session. Lori then shows the reader how to plan the role of a facilitator and the prerequisites for a person identified as a facilitator. The discussion ends by highlighting the right questions to be asked for different types of transactions and data functions along with hints that can be utilized during a review session.

Chapter 11

The 13 Mistakes of Function Point Counting

Claudia Hazan

Contents

The Main Uses of Function Point Metrics

The use of the Function Point (FP) metric provides a number of benefits, such as the availability of the Counting Practices Manual (CPM) [1] that has well-defined rules for FP counting. The use of FPs also provides independence in requirements modeling, programming language, and software development process. There are several additional uses of the FP metric, among which are productivity indicators (hour/FP), quality indicators (defects/FP), and support for "make or buy" analysis of software products. The main uses of the FP metric are FPs as a monetary unit ($/FP) in contracts for software development and maintenance and FP as a basis for software estimation.

The use of the FP metric as a basis for pricing decisions in software contracts has increased dramatically in the industry and for the Brazilian government. There is a recommendation to Brazilian Government organizations to use the FP metric on software factory contracts, instead of a man-hour effort metric. In this context, the supplier is remunerated based on the functional size of the software project delivered. The software project size is measured by the FP metric, which represents an asset to the client. This contract type allows a better risk balance between the customer and the contractors. It is very important to ensure the correctness of the FP count and estimations by both parties: customer and contractor.

The FP metric has been used in support of software estimation processes, too. According to software quality models, the first estimate to be generated is the estimate of project size. The estimates of effort, schedule, and costs have to be derived using the estimated project size. Figure 11.1 shows a software estimate process based on use of the FP metric.

The first step is acquiring the available project documentation to collect and analyze the requirements. The estimates are generated in the early stages of the software project's lifecycle, when requirements have not yet been completely defined. The source for the estimate lies within the documentation of initial requirements, such as descriptions of business needs and records of meetings. The professional producing the estimate needs to identify the functional requirements for the next step—estimating project size. The functional size could be estimated using the FP estimate method, for instance Estimated FP Count [3]. Project effort, cost, and schedule are estimated, considering the following: functional size, non-functional requirements, and historical data of projects completed in the organization. The next step is getting the approval for the software estimate from the client. It is common to see the scope of the negotiation change when a client requests a reduction in the schedule. It is important to track the estimates (planned vs. actual)

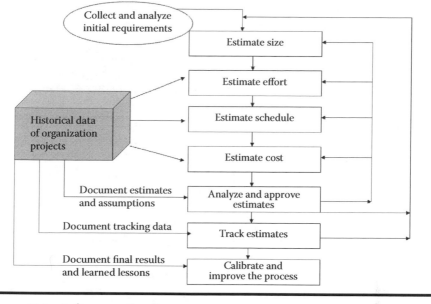

Figure 11.1   Software estimating process.

during project construction until its completion. At the end of the project, it is a best practice to collect data and analyze the results and learned lessons to improve the software estimating process. Therefore, an incorrect size estimate impacts other project estimates: cost, schedule, and effort. The end result is an unsuccessful software project with cost overrun or schedule delays.

The Main Causes for Mistakes in Function Point Counting

The International FP Users Group CPM defines objective and comprehensive rules for FP counting. Although professionals have used the CPM, I have found several mistakes when reviewing their FP estimates and counts. The two main causes for these mistakes are as follows:

- Lack of knowledge of the CPM counting rules by the professionals responsible for performing the FP count. Some IT professionals suddenly receive a new task to perform: completion of FP counts and estimates. In most cases, they undergo quick training in FP analysis. In some cases, they receive brief guidelines on FP counting, with an overview of the FP analysis technique. Therefore, they perform FP counting without a full understanding of the CPM counting rules. The result is incorrect FP counting. A false paradigm is "a system analyst can define requirements, construct software, test software, and count FPs." I agree that any person without proper training can count FP without adequate quality.

■ Poor quality in the requirements documents. FP counting is based on the user view; thus, a requirements document should be clear enough to allow the software metrics professional to identify the functional user requirements. The correctness of FP counting depends on the correct understanding of the requirements document. In most cases, the software metrics professional does not know the system they are measuring. Frequently, there are several missing, incomplete, and incorrect requirements in the requirements document, especially for enhancement projects. In some cases, the requirements document for the enhancement project is an updated system requirements document, hindering the identification of the logical functions affected (inserted, updated, or deleted). In some cases, the requirements document resembles a technical programming document by describing the SQL statements, for instance, "Change this SQL statement in stored procedure X." It is a good document for programmers but a bad one for the software metrics professional who is identifying the user view. The software metrics professional has to possess solid knowledge in requirements engineering to perform the activities of requirements analysis and elicitation during FP counting or estimating. In fact, FP counting and estimating supports the improvement of requirements documents [2].

It is best practice to define the guidelines for software metrics in contracts for software development and maintenance services. This is a recommended practice in Brazilian government organizations. These guidelines, prepared by the contractor, define rules for counting FPs in maintenance projects based on the changes to non-functional requirements. These projects have zero FPs, following the CPM counting rules, as there are no changes in functional requirements. Functional requirements are the basis for sizing the software project. Often, local software metric guidelines clarify the application of some CPM rules. When creating local guidelines, consider specific activities performed in the organization, such as how to count FPs in data warehousing projects. Sometimes, software metric guidelines modify the CPM formulas, for instance, creating an Impact Factor for the FPs of changed and deleted functions in the Enhancement Project. It is common to see an Impact Factor of 40% for Deleted FPs and an Impact Factor of 75% for Changed FPs. Software metric guidelines can define FP counting rules differently from the CPM rules such as counting Code Tables with one FP. In contrast, if you follow the CPM rules, Code Tables are not counted—zero FPs. Therefore, these software metric guidelines constitute another object that must be studied by software metrics analysts. They need to have the correct understanding of the specific rules and the concepts for maintenance projects. On the other hand, the use of the software metric guidelines can easily be another source of mistakes in counting FPs.

Main Mistakes in Function Point Counting

When FP analysis is performed by staff without the proper skills and experience, the mistakes can be quite significant (e.g., greater than 100%). Even if the results of this FP count are not being used as the basis to generate effort, schedule, and cost estimates for the project and the project is not contracted by the FP metric, it is still important to produce an accurate FP count. Indeed, this is still an issue when used in the analysis of productivity indicators (hours/FP), which the organization uses to set targets.

In one situation, I observed errors resulting in the FP count being 200% less than it should have been. When reviewing FP analysis of contracted software projects, in some case 1000 FPs could be 100 FPs. As you can see from these illustrations, incorrect FP analysis can cause extremely inconsistent results. In some cases, the FP count may be too small, but in others too large. In addition, an incorrect FP count can be 100% smaller than a correct count, failing to count functional requirements while including aspects that should not be counted such as non-functional requirements (e.g., usability aspects). This chapter will discuss the 13 main mistakes in FP counting that have been most frequently observed during FP auditing or review. I performed the audits and reviews to promote the correct application of the FP counting rules described in the CPM. Other reasons for the audits and reviews were to improve software projects estimates, provide correct data for productivity and quality analysis, and promote the use of FPs as standard metrics. Another reason was to avoid conflicts between the customer and the contractor in software factory contracts based on FP metrics. The following sections describe the mistakes in FP counting.

Error in the Definition of Functional Size versus Development Effort

Let us start with the most frequently observed error in the industry.

This is a common dialogue between a software metrics consultant and a project manager: The consultant says, "I am researching functional size estimating methods based on FP." The manager replies "Why FP? Why don't you research the Constructive Cost Model (COCOMO)?"

The consultant answers "COCOMO does not estimate software project size."

Many people think FP counting is a method for estimating schedule, cost, and effort. This is incorrect. The use of FPs allows you to estimate the functional size of the software project. Of course, the size estimate is an important input in deriving cost, effort, and schedule estimates. Thus, the FP size is an input to cost and effort estimate models, such as COCOMO II.

The consequences of this mistake are "How do I count the FP size of this online help? Its construction was very laborious. I spent a lot of time working on this help functionality." The help facility is a usability requirement, which is a non-functional requirement. FPs are a measure of functional size; therefore, non-functional requirements are not counted with FPs, even though their development may be laborious.

In some cases, a non-functional requirement can generate functional requirements, which equate to user identifiable functions. For example, the user requires functionality to maintain the help information by creating, updating, inquiring, and deleting the help content. In this example, the data entity maintained by the user counts as an Internal Logical File (ILF) and the functions, that is, elementary processes, count as External Inputs (EI) and External Inquiries (EQ).

Additionally, there are a lot of technical requirements that are very laborious from the standpoint of a programmer. These technical requirements have zero FP, as FP is not an effort metric.

Error in the Use of Function Point Counting Formulas Described in the Counting Practices Manual

This error may occur as a consequence of the previous error described earlier. To maximize returns in fixed price contracts by FP, some contracted organizations wish to artificially "increase" the FP counts. A reason for this practice is the high development effort for software projects with high complexity non-functional requirements. These organizations create components for the CPM formulas such as additional adjustment factors, which enable them to reach their goals. For example, if the database of a project is complex, an organization may use an adjustment factor of 1.2 multiplied by FPs counted. This practice is incorrect.

FP counting must be based on CPM counting rules and formulas. This type of error can also frequently occur due to the lack of knowledge of the CPM as in an example presented at a workshop on requirements engineering. The example shows the FP count of a web system where the initial calculation of Unadjusted FPs (UFP) was 130. After calculating the Adjusted FPs of the development project, it was found that a function of data model conversion was developed, with an effort estimated at around 10% of the total. Therefore, the Conversion FP (CFP) was calculated as CFP = 10%UFP, thus CFP = $0.1 \times 130 = 13$. The Value Adjustment Factor (VAF) calculated for this project was 1.14. The Adjusted FP size of the Development Project (DFP) was calculated by the formula DFP = (UFP + CFP) * VAF; therefore, DFP = $(130 + 13) * 1.14 = 163.02$.

There is a mistake in the calculation of the CFP component of the DFP formula as presented above. Although the study refers to the use of an older CPM release, there is not a rule in the CPM that considers effort within the FP calculation formula. FP is a functional size metric independent of the effort to develop the application. The functions of data conversion should be identified and counted according to the CPM counting rules. The functions of data conversion, associated with the initial data loading, are run only once during the application installation task. Generally, they are classified as External Inputs (EI). Sometimes, these functions are also identified as External Outputs (EO) as they are associated with the load control reports containing summarized and totalized data. These reports are required by the users and must be counted as an independent elementary process.

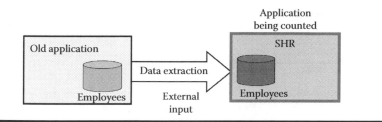

Figure 11.2   Human resources system—data conversion function.

Errors in the data conversion function are often seen in FP counting and FP exam results when training in FP analysis. Figure 11.2 provides an example of a data conversion function in the Human Resources System (SHR). The user requires the migration of employee data from the old SHR application to the new SHR. We have to count the data load function as an EI. The counting of an External Interface File (EIF) to read and load the data is very common. And it is a mistake. In this example, the logical data in the physical employee data file from the old application is counted only as a Data Element Type (DET) of the EI: Initial Data Load of Employee.

There are several counting rules in the CPM that are not intuitive to the FP Counter. A full understanding of the CPM counting rules requires training and practical experience in FP counting. Mentoring by an experienced individual is an excellent way to train new FP Counters.

Error: External Inquiries versus External Outputs

This mistake is produced by a lack of knowledge of the identification rules of EO and EQ. It is also very common. Some people count FP based on the following "rule": "all reports should be classified as EO and all inquiries are EQ." Unfortunately, this simple "rule," as easy as it seems to apply, is incorrect. Notice that the "rule" is not compliant with CPM counting rules.

For example, the functionality of "Student Inquiry" presents a student list containing the name of the student and the age of the student in the Training System (Figure 11.3). This function retrieves the student birth date from the ILF on students to compute the student age. The inquiry function "Student Inquiry" should be classified as EO due to the student age calculation. The functionality of "Report on Students" retrieves the student name and identification code from the ILF on students. The "Report on Students" presents the information in alphabetical order. This report should be classified as an EQ. It is not an EO as it does not contain calculation, derived data, update of an ILF, or system behavior change. The "a set of data is sorted" processing logic may be performed by an EQ, following the CPM counting rules.

Another common mistake is associated with the functions to "send an e-mail." Often, this function is erroneously counted as an EO. The functionality that

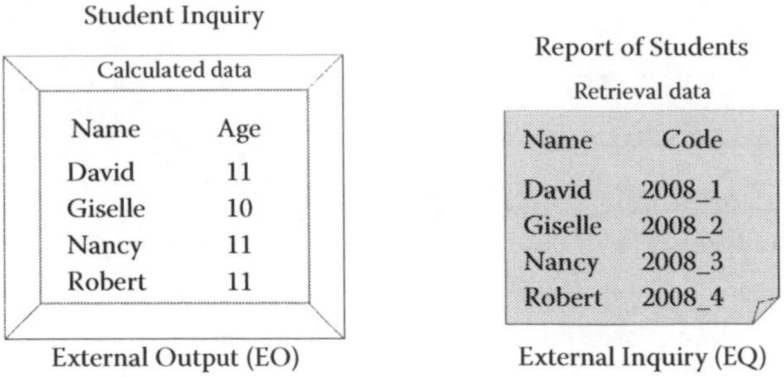

Student Inquiry

Report of Students

Calculated data	
Name	Age
David	11
Giselle	10
Nancy	11
Robert	11

Retrieval data

Name	Code
David	2008_1
Giselle	2008_2
Nancy	2008_3
Robert	2008_4

External Output (EO)

External Inquiry (EQ)

Figure 11.3   Training System—External Outputs × External Inquiries.

allows a user to send a message to "Contact Us" is very common in websites. With this kind of functionality, the user chooses a theme, completes the name, e-mail address, and message fields, and finally clicks on the OK button. The functionality retrieves the e-mail of the person responsible for the selected theme from the ILF Contact Us and sends the data to the email address field. This functionality has the primary intent of sending data outside the application boundary and it retrieves the e-mail of the person responsible from the ILF. However, it does not meet any mandatory logic processing for an EO. So, this functionality is counted as an EQ. Sometimes, the "Contact Us" functionality updates a Control File, which is an ILF that stores when a message was sent, so it counts as an EO. The "maintain one or more ILFs" processing logic may be performed by an EO and is not performed by an EQ. In some cases, the function "send an e-mail" must be performed together with a function that updates data. For example, within a web application, the user fills out a registration form and the application automatically sends an e-mail with the registration identifier. There is only one independent elementary process, that is, only one complete transaction in this example. The function "send an e-mail" must be counted as a part of the elementary process "update registration form." The primary intent of "update registration form" is to maintain an ILF called the registration form ILF. Therefore, this elementary process is counted as an EI.

Error in the Identification of Logical Files

I found this mistake in the majority of FP counts during the auditing and reviewing of these counts. Commonly many physical entities are counted incorrectly as an ILF or EIF. This is another incorrect "rule" where "every physical table or file should be counted as an ILF or EIF." This incorrect "rule" is not compliant with the CPM counting rules. It is important to emphasize that files in FP analysis are a group of logically related data or control information and not physical tables or files. Some physical tables or files may be counted as a part of an ILF or EIF;

however, some are not counted. This error frequently results in a FP count larger than the correct size of the projects.

In reality, many novice FP Counters forget the Record Element Type (RET) concept. Note that the ILF is an independent data entity; the dependent data entities are counted as a RET of the ILF. For example, in a Project Management System, the physical data files Project and Project Team should be counted together as one single ILF.

In addition, Code Data, that is, code-description tables, temporary files, and others files created to meet technical requirements, are not counted in FPs.

Another common mistake related to the data functions is the counting of the same logical data group as an ILF and as an EIF. If a logical data group is read and maintained, then count this data group only once as an ILF. For example, suppose that the Training System read the supplier table, which is identified as an ILF to the Contract System, and updates some attributes in the supplier table. Therefore, the supplier data is counted as an ILF for the Training System. The supplier data is an ILF of the Contract System and is read and updated by the Training System. The Training System does not count it as an EIF, as it is counted as an ILF, and the same data group, considering the user view, cannot be counted twice.

Error in Elementary Processes Identification

A difficulty in the identification of elementary processes has frequently been seen in the industry. The most common error is the identification of sequential activities as independent elementary processes. The incorrect "rule" is: "each application screen is an elementary process." According to the CPM counting rules, "an elementary process constitutes a complete transaction, is self-contained, and leaves the business of the application being counted in a consistent state." This means that an elementary process should be an independent activity.

In the example shown in Figure 11.4, consider an Employee Inquiry function that has one input parameter screen and an output screen, which presents the retrieved results. Some people count this functionality as two elementary processes: one EI for the parameter screen and an EQ for the results screen. This practice is incorrect. The two screens are part of one single inquiry activity, that is, a single elementary process of inquiry. One of these screens does not leave the application business in a consistent state and does not constitute a complete transaction. Therefore, the Employee Inquiry function should be counted as only one EQ.

An automatic e-mail transmittal is part of the functions that are frequently counted incorrectly as an independent elementary process. The right way to count an automatic e-mail transmittal is as part of the elementary process associated with the functionality. For instance, consider the functionality Insert Participants in the Meeting. When the manager inserts a new participant in the meeting, the application updates the Meeting ILF, retrieves the participant e-mail from EIF Employee,

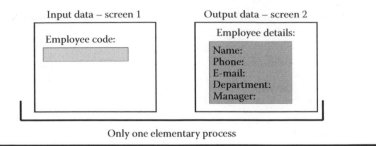

Figure 11.4   Elementary process identification.

and sends an e-mail to the participant. Note that there is only one elementary process: insert a new meeting participant, where the primary intent is to update the meeting ILF, which is counted as one EI. The sending of an e-mail to the participant is not counted separately as an EQ. It is not a complete transaction, that is, it is not an elementary process. It is a part of the EI.

Let me provide a hint here, which will help to identify the elementary processes: sequential functions are part of the same elementary process and independent functions are part of different elementary processes. Another incorrect "rule" related to this error is "all requirements identified in the software requirements document constitute an elementary process." This incorrect "rule" has been seen in some FP counts. For example, consider the use case "Update Student Information." There are functions such as "Cancel" and "Clear," which are not elementary processes, as they are related to non-functional requirements such as usability. The "Cancel" function provides support to application browsing and the "Clear" function provides user efficiency improvement as the function erases the data entered by the user on the screen. In this example, the functional requirement "Update Student Information" is one single elementary process, counted as an EI.

Error in the Identification of User Requirements

A solid knowledge of requirements engineering is an essential skill for the FP Counter, especially requirements analysis techniques. The input to FP counting is the requirements document, so the FP Counter needs to review the document to understand it to identify the functional requirements. Often, the quality of the requirements document is poor, especially when considering the initial requirements document as the basis for the FP estimate. It is common to see a standard requirements document using the term "Maintain" for CRUD (Create, Read, Update, and Delete) functions. Therefore, the FP Counter needs to clarify the required functions. For example, consider the requirement "Maintain Project Tasks" where we can identify these lower level functions: Insert New Project Task, Update Project Task Data, and Delete Project Task. In some cases, there are no delete functions. In addition, there is an implicit inquiry that precedes the update task. In some cases, there are two inquiries, one for a list of tasks and one for the inquiry of detailed tasks. The FP Counter should ask detailed questions of the requirements analyst while reviewing the requirements document to identify the elementary processes.

The common mistake is the treatment of all the "Maintain" requirements as CRUD. In the majority of cases of requirements to "Maintain," the user requirement is only an update function. We would then count an EI for the update function. We can count an implicit inquiry too. In the example shown in Figure 11.5, the user from a travel agency needs functionality that will update the currency conversion rate. Even though the requirements document shows "Maintain Currency Conversion Rate," there are only two elementary processes: the EI for Update Currency Conversion Rate and the EQ that precedes the update called Inquire Currency Conversion Rate.

The hint is to observe the user view. FP counting considers the functionality required and received by the user. Note that the functions not required by the user are not counted. Some examples of uncountable functions are those provided by browsers and business intelligence (BI) tools.

Error in the Identification of Implicit Inquiries

This error is also related to the identification of elementary processes. Some FP Counters do not identify implicit inquiry functions associated with updating data. This mistake occurs when the FP Counter performs the count based on application screens, instead of functional requirements. Consequently, the implicit inquiry (viewing of the data prior to update) is not counted. Note that the data inquiry that precedes the update is an elementary process, independent from the data update process. The user may only query the data without updating anything. Therefore,

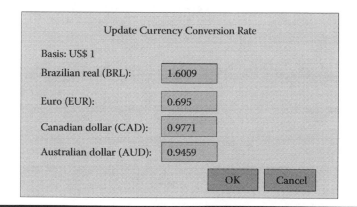

Figure 11.5 User requirement identification.

according to the rules of what constitutes a unique elementary process as described in CPM, the implicit inquiries should be counted as they have not been counted already. In the example shown in Figure 11.6, there are two functions on the screen: the Professor Data Update External Input and the Professor Data Query External Inquiry, which retrieves professor data from the Professors ILF and presents it to the user.

Another common mistake associated with queries considers the kind of inquiry, either lists or details. There are two separate functions. For example, List of Projects retrieves and presents minor information on the projects such as project name, project manager, and project status. Inquiry of Project Details retrieves and presents all the information on the project selected by the user. There are two EQs. Sometimes, the user requires information about the total number of records retrieved in the list; therefore, the list is counted as an EO due to the calculation of the sum of retrieved records. In some cases, list and details present the same data and have the same logical processing; therefore, they should be counted only once, in accordance with the CPM rules of uniqueness of elementary processes.

Error in Determining the Uniqueness of Elementary Processes

According to the CPM counting rules, "When compared to an elementary process already identified, count another similar elementary process as the same elementary process if they require the same set of DETs, require the same set of FTRs, and require the same set of processing logic to complete the elementary process." Note:

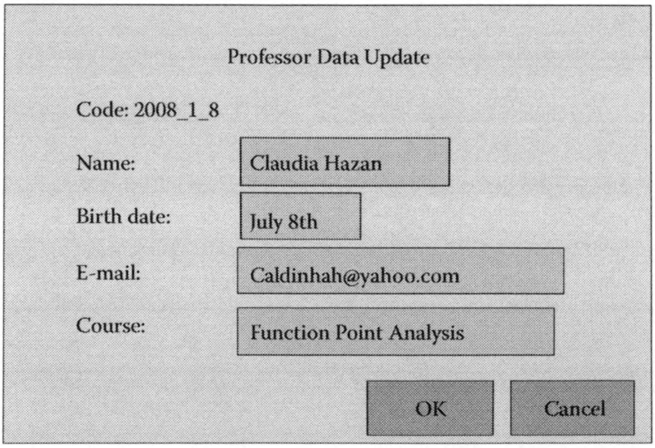

Figure 11.6   Implicit inquiry identification.

The implementation of the functionality does not influence the determination of the uniqueness of an elementary process.

In the example shown in Figure 11.7, the Training System has two course inquiries implemented as List Box of Courses and Box of Courses. These inquiries were implemented by different programmers in different system modules. In addition, the requirements are not the same. List Box of Courses is arranged alphabetically and Box of Courses is arranged by registration date. In analyzing the description of the functions, some FP Counters identify two EQs, although this is incorrect. There is only one EQ as there is only one elementary process to be considered when performing the FP count, which is the Inquiry of Courses. There are two inquiries, two programmers, two modules, and only one elementary process. This is a possible and common scenario in several software applications. Let us check the CPM counting rules. The two inquiries have the same set of DETs such as the name of course. The two inquiries have the same set of FTRs such as the Courses ILF. They also have the same set of processing logic as recognized by the CPM. At this point, the FP Counter notices that the processing logic type of "sorting or arranging a set of data" is different within the two inquiries. However, within the CPM counting rules, this form of processing logic does not impact the singleness of an elementary process, that is, the orientation (sorting) of the data does not constitute a unique elementary process.

Error in Determining the Value of the Adjustment Factor

The majority of Brazilian organizations do not use the adjustment factor in FP counting. The CPM 4.3 standard metric is UFP. The control organization in the Brazilian government has recommended the use of UFP in software factory contracts since 2008. Counting of UFP is contemplated in most of the software contracts in the industry while some others use a fixed adjustment factor. It is a mistake to use a fixed adjustment factor for all software projects as the value of the adjustment factor should be calculated for each development or enhancement project according to the CPM counting rules. In addition, many mistakes have been observed in the determination of the degree of influence of the 14 General Systems Characteristics (GSCs) when calculating the value of the adjustment

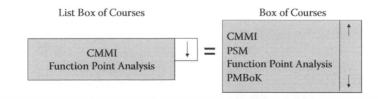

Figure 11.7 Determination of uniqueness in an elementary process.

factor. In spite of improving the definition of the GSCs as documented in the CPM 4.2 release, there is still a lot of difficulty in identifying the Degrees of Influence (DI) of the GSCs. For instance, the characteristic of reusability is one that has presented evaluation mistakes. It is very common that the FP Counters believes that it should have a DI of four or five due to the reuse of components from other applications and for having internal reuse only. In this example, the correct DI is one.

According to CPM 4.3, ISO/IEC 14143-1:2007 and to the Brazilian Government, I do not recommend the use of an adjustment factor in FP counting, as FP is a functional size metric and the GSCs of the adjustment factor consider non-functional requirements. It is odd to evaluate non-functional requirements that influence the calculation of a functional size metric. In addition, the incorrect assessment of GSCs constitutes another source of error.

Error in the Calculation Formula Implemented in the Function Points Counting Spreadsheet

Many organizations create spreadsheets to automate FP calculations. It is important to note that function types do not have the same contributions to the FP count. The functional contributions of data function ILFs and EIFs are different. The functional contributions of transactional function EIs and EQs are the same, but the functional contribution of an EO is different. In an actual case, the FP counting spreadsheet of an organization has only three functional contributions for all function types: Low is set at 3 FP, Average is set at 4 FP, and High is set at 6 FP. In another real case, the functional contribution of ILFs and EIFs are the same: Low is set at 7 FP, Average is set at 10 FP, and High is set at 15 FP. This is incorrect. Table 11.1 shows the correct functional contribution of the function types according to the CPM counting rules.

Error in Counting Data Functions in Enhancement Projects

Most software projects necessitate the enhancement and maintenance of non-functional requirements. FP counting rules for enhancement projects are not intuitive. Therefore, some people without training in FP counting make several mistakes. The most common mistake is the counting of data functions that are not affected by the enhancement project. In a development project, we count the logical data entities as ILFs or EIFs, analyzing them using the CPM counting rules. However, in enhancement projects, the CPM counting rules process states that "in order for a data function to be counted as a changed function, the general guideline is that it should be structurally altered (e.g., adding or removing an attribute or changing the characteristics of the attribute)." If a data function is only referenced by transactional functions in the enhancement project, then the data function is not counted in the enhancement project.

In the example shown in Figure 11.8, the user of the Training System requires the addition of instructor information in the "Generate Training Certificate" function. The instructor name is stored within the Table of Courses. Within the baseline count of this functionality is counted as an EQ called Generate Training Certificate. There are two FTRs referenced (Employee, Course) with a total of six DETs (Course Name, Participant Name, Training Hours, Training Period, Print action button) that leave the application boundary. The function is of Average complexity and is equal to 4 FP.

The FP counting result for this enhancement project is as follows:

One changed EQ for the Generate Training Certificate transaction. This transaction references two FTRs (Employee, Course) and seven DETs (Course Name, Participant Name, Training Hours, Training Period, Name of Instructor, Print action button) across the boundary of the application. The function is of Average complexity and is equal to 4 FP.

The functional size of this enhancement project is 4 FP.

The referenced files Employee and Course are not counted in the enhancement project, as these files are not impacted by the enhancement project.

Table 11.1 Determination of the Contribution of Function Types

Function Type	Low Complexity	Average Complexity	High Complexity
Internal Logical File (ILF)	7 FPs	10 FPs	15 FPs
External Interface File (EIF)	5 FPs	7 FPs	10 FPs
External Input (EI)	3 FPs	4 FPs	6 FPs
External Output (EO)	4 FPs	5 FPs	7 FPs
External Inquiry (EQ)	3 FPs	4 FPs	6 FPs

Course Name
Participant Name
Training Hours
Period of Training
Training Location

Course Name
Participant Name
Training Hours
Period of Training
Training Location
+ Name of Instructor

Figure 11.8 Enhancement project—certificate information.

This mistake has dramatically increased the FP counting for the enhancement project in the example shown, as the project could have been sized at 16 FP (7 FPs for the Course ILF; 5 FPs for the Employee EIF; 4 FPs for the Generate Training Certificate EQ). The incorrect count would be four times more than the correct project size. Recently, I reduced a FP count for an enhancement project similar to the example above, which had been sized at 35 FPs, to 7 FPs. The functionality changed was one EO with four FTRs. The contractor had counted this as a High complexity EO, which was worth 7 FP. They also incorrectly counted an extra 4 ILFs of Low complexity worth 28 FPs.

Error in Determining the Complexity of Changed Functions in Enhancement Projects

Another very common error in the FP counting of enhancement projects is difficulty in identifying the complexity of changed functions. For example, think about the change in a High complexity EI. The change is to add one more DET to the function. This function continues to be identified as High complexity. In practice, this function is counted incorrectly as a simple function since the change was the addition of only one DET in an implemented function. The CPM mentions that the CHGA (FP of functions modified by the enhancement project) considers the new functionality available to the user by the application. In spite of that, the modification in a high complexity function is small; it should be rated as high complexity as it remains with a complexity that is considered high.

Error in Counting Practices Manual Use: Function Point Counting of Maintenance Projects

The majority of the software factory contracts based on FPs mention that the size of development and maintenance software projects is measured using the FP counting method described in the CPM. However, the CPM considers FP counting for development and enhancement projects only. The other types of maintenance projects such as corrective maintenance, cosmetic maintenance, and adaptive maintenance with changes to non-functional requirements are measured incorrectly when following the CPM enhancement formula. According to the CPM, these modification requests cannot be measured in FP. In fact, the FP metric is a functional size metric. When considering business requirements for these maintenance projects, they do not have a functional size, as there are no changes to the functions (add, change, or delete) based on the user viewpoint.

Maintenance projects with changes to non-functional requirements have zero FP following CPM counting rules. However, in a software factory contract based on the FP metric, the contractor should be remunerated, and so it is important to define formulas to deal with maintenance projects. The metrics guidelines of the organization should provide definition and formulas to cover maintenance projects.

For example, the maintenance of an interface, called cosmetic maintenance in the literature, is related to the demands of interface changes. Additional examples are font type, color, logos, buttons, and changes in the position of fields or text on a screen or report. Additional items that fall into this type of maintenance include changes to text messages from a specific functionality, such as error, validation, warning, alerts, or completion of processing messages. The suggested formula proposed in the metric guidelines of some Brazilian government organizations is

$$FP\_Cosmetic = 0.6 \times Number\ of\ elementary\ processes\ impacted$$

The formula above considers each elementary process changed due to the maintenance project with the lowest functional contribution of 3 FP. In addition, a 20% Impact Factor is applied so that 3 FP × 20% = 0.6. Each organization has to define its own kind of maintenance projects and formulas based on their historical data on projects.

The metrics guidelines of the organizations constitute another source of error, as the FP Counter needs to understand the definition and formulas for maintenance projects. The main difficulty found is in establishing whether the demand is classified as an enhancement project following the CPM counting rules or as the non-functional requirement of adaptive maintenance. One difficulty is in defining the functional and non-functional requirements. For instance, inserting a new filter in an existing report is an enhancement project; inserting page numbering in an existing report is an adaptive maintenance project.

The definitions and formulas of the metrics guidelines developed within organizations should be simple, clear, and consistent. It is important to present practical examples providing fact-based information obtained from analyzing the functions in existing applications of the organization. The Brazilian Ministry of Planning published a Software Metrics Guideline in December, 2010, to support other government organizations that contract out software factory services. These other government organizations then customize the standard to enable them to create their own Software Metrics Guideline. The Metrics Workgroup of the Ministry of Planning is working on the second release of the Software Metrics Guideline based on feedback from the group members of several Brazilian government organizations. The guideline is available only in Portuguese at the website http://www.governoeletronico.gov.br.

This chapter presented some direction to FP Counters and to the individuals who are auditing or reviewing FP counting. It is very important to ensure the correctness of FP counts and to ensure that the counter is following the CPM rules. Incorrect FP counting generates useless information and high costs. The consequences of incorrect FP counting include inadequate payment to contractors in contracts based on the FP metric. Additionally, poor effort, schedule, and cost estimates will be created. When taking inaccurate sizing processes based on the FP metric into consideration, problems may arise when considering the results obtained from quality and productivity indicators that use FP as the standard metric, such as hour/FP and defect/FP.

References

1. The International Function Point Users Group. 2010. *Function Point Counting Practices Manual, Release 4.3.1.* Princeton Junction, NJ: IFPUG Standards.
2. Hazan, C., D. M. Berry, and J. S. P Leite. 2005. E possivel substituir processos de Engenharia de Requisitos por Contagem de Pontos de Funcao? In *8th International Workshop on Requirements Engineering (WER2005)*, 197–208. Porto, Portugal. http://wer.inf.puc-rio.br/WERpapers/artigos/artigos_WER05/claudia_hazan.pdf.
3. NESMA. Netherlands Software Metric Association. 2005. The application of Function Point Analysis in the early phases of the application life cycle. In *A Practical Manual: Theory and case study.* http://www.nesma.nl/download/boeken_NESMA/N20_FPA_in_Early_Phases_(v2.0).pdf.

About the Author

Claudia Hazan is a high-technology specialist in the software metrics and estimation area, having been a Certified Function Point Specialist (CFPS) since 2001. For the last 10 years, Claudia has worked for SERPRO, the Brazilian government data processing service company. She has taught classes and seminars at prestigious Brazilian universities such as SERPRO Corporate University. A frequent keynote speaker on topics such as Function Points, CMMI, software measurement, information technology governance, and strategic planning of information technology, Claudia holds a degree in Information Technology from the Universidade Estadual do Rio de Janeiro (UERJ) and a Master's degree in Quality Engineering/Software Quality from the Instituto Militar de Engenharia (IME). In addition to her academic activities, Claudia supports SERPRO clients in the following areas: software measurement and estimation process implementation, Function Point-based contract assessment, CMMI management approaches, and definition of IT strategic plans. She has had several articles published on Brazilian seminars and workshops.

Chapter 12

Facilitating Function Point Counts: How to Ask the "Right" Questions and Get the "Right" Answers for an Accurate Count in an Efficient Manner

Lori Holmes

Contents

Organizations strive to be as efficient as possible while conducting Function Point (FP) counts while still maintaining the highest level of accuracy. Counting sessions that include both the FP expert and the project/application Subject Matter Expert (SME) are proven to be the best way to achieve both the efficiency and accuracy objectives. This avoids the need for continual follow up and/or assumptions being made due to counting sessions occurring in a vacuum separate from the SMEs. However, facilitated sessions can be difficult and time consuming without the necessary skills or a structured process for preparing and conducting the counting session. This chapter addresses the following:

- The role of the FP facilitator
- The preparation necessary to conduct a successful counting session
- The skills and process necessary to conduct a successful counting session
- Appropriate follow-up procedures

FP Facilitator Roles

The first step to being a successful FP facilitator is to understand the various roles that the FP facilitator must fulfill. Although the FP facilitator should be an expert in FPs, it takes much more than that expertise to run an efficient and accurate counting session. The FP facilitator needs to be viewed as both the leader of the session and the FP expert in order for the session to flow smoothly and accomplish its objectives. First, it is important that the FP facilitator be a neutral and unbiased resource. The objective of the counting session is to end up with an accurate FP count. The FP facilitator cannot be influenced by the SMEs, potential political fallout, or the eventual results when conducting the counting session. For FPs to be accepted in an organization and the subsequent measures to be useful, it is imperative that all parties see the counting sessions as objective and following the same process each and every time. To provide accurate counts, the FP facilitator must involve all of the participants and ensure that everyone is comfortable that the appropriate information is being presented so that consensus can be met. If the correct preparation is completed, the participants will be the right individuals to discuss the project, and so the session should be very participative and include relevant discussions. Determining who should be participants is discussed later in this chapter.

To be efficient, the FP facilitator must monitor the time spent on discussions and keep the participants focused on the objective of completing the FP count. The session should not be used to design the system or correct problems. It is to discuss the functionality delivered or planned for delivery so that it can be described in FP terms. Since the facilitator is the FP expert, they will know when discussions need to continue and when they can be stopped. For instance, if the complexity of a report is determined to be high given the number of logical files referenced and a large number of Data Element Types (DET), in most cases it is not necessary to argue whether the DETs are 35 or 36 because it will not impact the final count. However, it is important for the FP facilitator to know the organizational standards to determine if actual DETs must be determined.

It is also important that the results of the counting session be documented and understood by all participants. It is the FP facilitators' role to make sure the FP information is being recorded and explained to the SMEs as the session is being conducted. If everyone understands what was included in the count as the session is progressing, it will avoid questions, objections, and potential errors after the fact.

As previously stated, there are numerous roles that the FP facilitator must fulfill to successfully conduct a counting session. There are specific skills that are necessary in order to execute these roles effectively. The FP facilitator must be organized, communicate effectively, be adept at handling difficult situations, and effectively use meeting mechanics. These skills will be shown as they relate to the following sections that describe planning, facilitating, concluding, and following up on the counting sessions.

Planning

Everything is better with preparation. Specific to FP counting, the FP facilitator will be much more comfortable leading the session if they are prepared. In addition, participants will appreciate the planning efforts and feel comfortable that the meeting will be effective and efficient. To effectively plan a FP counting session, it is important to do the following:

■ Understand the purpose of the count
■ Identify the appropriate people to involve
■ Identify the required documentation
■ Schedule the session
■ Understand how the resulting FP count should be documented

Without fully understanding the purpose of the FP count, it is nearly impossible to reach the appropriate and accurate outcomes. Understanding the purpose of the count allows the FP facilitator to involve the correct people, obtain the appropriate documentation, schedule the appropriate amount of time, identify the scope of the session, and be prepared for any situations that may arise. For instance, a FP counting session may be requested to provide FP counts as input into the effort and cost estimation process. It seems simple enough, but perhaps a portion of the functionality is going to be developed in-house, a portion developed by a contracting firm, and a portion implemented via a package. It is important to know what the estimation group is looking for to know the scope of the FP count. If the estimate is only to plan for the in-house development, then that is the only portion that should be FP counted. It is important to determine this in the planning phase prior to walking into the counting session to ensure the appropriate participants are present, they know the objectives of the session, and they are prepared to participate with the appropriate documentation. Often we are asked who should be in the meeting and what documentation should be provided. Clients specifically ask if certain positions should be invited (e.g., project managers, test team, etc.) or if specific documents are required (e.g., data model, context diagram, etc.). The answer to this is "it depends." When determining who should attend and the required documentation, the question should be who and what would allow for the most accurate FP count. The question should be who knows the most about the functionality that is included in the project/application under consideration and what documentation best explains the functionality from a logical perspective. The individual(s) who best meet these criteria should be invited and they should be told to have access to the supporting documentation needed to discuss the impacted functionality. The participants should not be selected based on their position, but by their knowledge. In addition, the development life cycle should not be changed for the sole purpose of producing documentation for FP counting. Whatever documentation is used by the development staff to deliver the functionality will aid in the FP counting session. Having supporting documentation will lessen the chance of functionality being missed and will support the results of the session if questions arise.

Often organizations ask, "Why can't a count be completed from documentation alone?" or "Why do we need documentation when we have an SME?" Certainly, FP counts can be conducted using either approach, but neither is the best way to ensure the most accurate count. When only documentation is used, then the FP facilitator may make incorrect assumptions based on how things appear or are worded in the document. Even if an SME is "on call," they will only be utilized if the FP facilitator feels they do not understand something, which is subjective. Or they will be bothering the SME with a multitude of questions, interrupting them multiple times and dragging the count out based on the SME's responsiveness. In addition, counting from documentation only is not very productive and will typically take longer than conducting a facilitated meeting with an SME. Meeting with an SME without documentation requires the SME to remember everything about a project/application, which can be difficult and likely impossible for a very large project. The most effective and efficient FP counting sessions that obtain the most accurate and repeatable FP counts is to schedule a facilitated session between the FP facilitator and SME to discuss the functionality and have documentation to support the discussion and the results.

For a first time FP facilitator, determining how much time to schedule may be difficult. It will become easier over time as the FP facilitator gains experience. The following are some things to consider when planning the session time.

- Approximate size of the project/applications involved—By knowing the over-all requirements or the effort involved in the project, the FP facilitator may be able to determine if the project impacts a handful of functions or a large amount. Based on that, the FP facilitator can determine if the duration of the meeting should be 1 hour, 1 day, or somewhere in between.
- Availability of staff, documentation, and facilities—The schedule and session times may be dictated by the availability of the participants. It is important that the FP facilitator be flexible. The SMEs may be working on a high priority project and only be available for various 1-hour meetings instead of one long session. Or perhaps the project involves multiple applications or SMEs. The FP facilitator may want to start with a specific application, but if the SME of a different application is leaving on holiday, then they will need to be scheduled first.
- Number and personalities of the SMEs involved—The size of the group may also play a part in the scheduling. With a large amount of people there will be more discussion and stronger facilitation will be required. The FP facilitator should also consider the personalities of the participants. If there are FP skeptics in the session, the FP facilitator may need to allow time for some "sales" discussion, but these can be kept to a minimum by making sure everyone understands the purpose and objective of the session. There may also be "talkers" in the session, people who like to give the entire history of the company. It is important to be respectful, but keep things on track. Pay attention to these variables when scheduling the length of the session.

If an FP count involves a large group of SMEs that have knowledge about various portions of projects/applications, then the FP facilitator may want to schedule the sessions a little bit differently. Initially one session can be held to complete the overviews and establish the type, scope, and boundaries. The subsessions can be scheduled with the appropriate individuals on the sections where they are knowledgeable. This frees up the other SMEs from sitting in sessions where they cannot participate. When possible, start with the Data functions since they are necessary to determine the complexity of the functions.

- Time constraints related to the counting results—Even with all of the above, the session may be dictated by time constraints driven by the objective (e.g., an estimate is required by the corporate headquarters in 1 week, the

Table 12.1 Planning the Session Time

FP Size	Development Effort	FP Counting Effort
5–20	4 hours to 1 month	15–30 minutes
20–100	1–10 months	30 minutes to 1 hour
100–500	10–72 months	1–5 hours

monthly reports are due in 1 week, and the CIO wants this project included). Again, the FP facilitator needs to be flexible, efficient, and organized to meet the deadlines dictated by the time constraints.

■ Experience of the FP facilitator—When first practicing these facilitation techniques, the initial counts may not go as quickly as desired due to the facilitators' experience level. However, with practice, efficiencies will be realized and productivity will increase. When scheduling the session, take into consideration the experience level of all participants (FP facilitator and SMEs) and allow the appropriate time for discussion, explanations, and documentation.

■ Corporate meeting expectations and culture—Think about how things work at your company (e.g., do people always show up late, do people take phone calls during meetings, is there a rule restricting meetings on Fridays). Be sure to schedule sessions based on the acceptable meeting culture in your organization.

The chart shown in Table 12.1 is useful in planning the session time for beginning FP facilitators. It is based on the ability to count 100 FPs per hour and is only to be used to aid in planning the initial FP counting sessions, not for estimating projects.

For example, if the FP facilitator knows the project is impacting five reports, it would be 5–20 FPs and would take 15–30 minutes to count. Or if the project was 4 hours to 1 month of development effort, it can probably be counted in 15–30 minutes. This is on average and may be over or under from project to project but it is a way to get started if you have never scheduled a counting session before. Once an organization has developed historical measurement data, the FP facilitator can use the effort and productivity rates to customize this chart for ongoing use. Once proper planning occurs, it is time to facilitate the session.

Facilitating

Effective planning will aid in a successful counting session; however, there are specific items related to the meeting itself that should also be considered. The FP facilitator needs to establish a comfortable meeting environment, utilize good meeting mechanics, conduct the meeting in an efficient manner, and provide closure at the end of the meeting to confirm objectives have been met and/or address outstanding items.

Communication is essential to obtaining an accurate FP count. Communication is more effective when the participants are at ease with the process, expectations, and objectives. The planning previously discussed will aid in this comfort level for the participants because it will ensure that everyone is prepared and knows what to expect. An open and trusting environment also enables a more comfortable setting. Participants need to be able to express themselves and know there are no "hidden agendas." If the FP facilitator wants the participants to be open in their discussions, then the FP facilitator needs to be open as well. The FP facilitator should be open about the objectives, the process, and the results. If it appears that something is not being shared or that a hidden agenda exists, the participants may become suspicious, and therefore argumentative and less communicative. They may feel the need to "protect" themselves. Much of this can be avoided if the FP facilitator is a good active listener and pays attention to the participants' tone and demeanor. It is important to listen quietly to what is being stated by the SMEs, question to clarify, and restate to confirm understanding. Do not assume where the discussion is going, listen and confirm. The FP facilitator should not be working on a response or thinking "How am I going to count this?" instead of listening to what is being said by the SME. Often when mentoring a new FP facilitator, it is not uncommon to see this behavior taking place. The FP facilitator will ask an SME to tell them about a function that changed. The SME might say "we added fields to a report that uses customer data, calculates when they are due for billing, and produces a report." A new FP facilitator is so focused on the FP rules that they do not listen fully, so they may figure out that a report changed and then ask if it has calculations or what groups of data are used. If they were actively listening, they would realize that this information was already provided and they just need to confirm their understanding. SMEs are much more open to communicate if they know the FP facilitator is interested and listening. Curiosity is a favorable trait for a FP facilitator to have. Curiosity leads one to be interested in what is being discussed and will generate questions that can lead to uncovering key details that will contribute to the counting session. To obtain an accurate FP count, it takes asking questions and figuring out how the business works. Someone who is genuinely interested in learning about new systems and how businesses function will find it much easier to ask questions and gain the necessary knowledge to count accurately. This curiosity leads to a full understanding of the application capabilities rather than just focusing on the first thing that sounds like an Elementary Process (EP) and then moving on.

In addition to achieving a comfortable environment, the FP facilitator should use good meeting mechanics. In part, this means that the meeting starts on time and that everyone understands the purpose and objective of the session. The FP facilitator should review the agenda/process and make revisions as appropriate. During the meeting, the FP facilitator should take thorough notes and use visual aids to keep participants focused and aid in explaining the outcomes of the session. In addition, the FP facilitator should monitor progress and time to allow for any final discussion at the end of the session and planning for any follow-up assignments.

To obtain the most accurate FP count in the most efficient manner, the FP facilitator should consider the following:

■ Follow a defined process
■ Know the International FP Users Group (IFPUG) rules
■ Be aware of any local counting standards and/or templates
■ Know what questions to ask
■ Understand the relationship between functions
■ Know how to diagram and document the outcome of the session
■ Utilize helpful hints

Each of these is discussed below.

Follow a Defined Process

The IFPUG Counting Practices Manual (CPM) provides a step-by-step process for conducting counts and is widely used and proven to be effective. This is the process that should be followed. The FP facilitator may need to be flexible based on the expertise of the SME and the available documentation. For example, the documentation may flow better by going through each requirement one by one rather than doing all of the data and then all of the transactions. However, for each requirement you can still follow the data-transaction order, it just repeats itself. In this case, be careful to make sure that functions are not counted multiple times. Figure 12.1 presents the IFPUG process diagram.

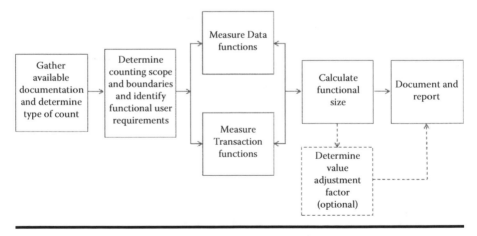

Figure 12.1   International Function Point User Group* process diagram.

* International Function Point Users Group Counting Practices Committee, *Counting Practices Manual 4.3, 2009.* This document contains material that has been extracted from the IFPUG Counting Practices Manual. It is reproduced in this document with permission of IFPUG.

Know the International Function Point Users Group Counting Practices Rules

In addition to following the IFPUG process, it is important to understand fully the IFPUG counting practices rules. Often the SMEs are not familiar with the IFPUG terminology, so the discussions are not focused on Internal Logical Files (ILFs) or External Inputs (EI) but more on the business functionality such as "a customer uses this screen to maintain their detail information." It is much easier for the FP facilitator to focus on the conversation if they do not have to spend time in their head trying to figure out "what is an ILF, and what are the rules that allow me to count one." Obviously, a new FP facilitator will take time to fully memorize the rules, so initially they will have to work harder at focusing first on listening to the description of the functionality and then secondly trying to figure out how to apply the FP rules and count it. For a FP facilitator just starting out, they should let the SMEs know that they are new and ask them to be patient if things take a little bit longer the first time. As long as the FP facilitator is open and honest about the situation, the SMEs will typically be patient and understanding.

One way to get up to speed quickly on the rules is to memorize the steps in the process, the basic definitions of the functions and their complexities, and the rules around what can be counted when. During training sessions, using rote methods of learning such as flash cards or oral quizzes helps participants get familiar with the terminology and the rules much quicker.

Be Aware of Any Local Counting Standards and/or Templates

Often organizations establish local counting standards or templates to document the application of the IFPUG counting rules to specific situations. The FP facilitator should review these prior to the counting session to ensure consistent counting across projects/applications. This will also save time since the FP facilitator will not have to determine how to apply the rules in situations where discussions have occurred and decisions have already been made.

Know the Questions to Ask

Knowing the rules enables FP facilitators to ask the right questions to draw information from the SME participants. This is one of the keys to becoming a successful FP facilitator. The questions asked and the questioning technique used is extremely important to conducting successful and consistent FP counting sessions. If a FP facilitator follows the same process every time, it increases the support from the SMEs because they feel that there is a method to the madness and that everything will be covered. Asking the common questions each time ensures consistency and accuracy from count to count and keeps the FP facilitator from overlooking things. It is important to mention that the following questions are a guide to the session flow. They are not intended to be used alone for the interview, but rather to solicit information and lead to a two-way interactive discussion about the functionality. The answers to each question should dictate what to ask next. Be a detective, and look for clues that will lead to more questions and answers in order to fully understanding what is being described. The FP facilitator should use the answers to draw out the information needed to complete the FP count.

One key to knowing what to ask is following the structured process described above. Following the steps outlined lays out a format of what areas to focus on. This is a good standard order to go through, but remember that the FP facilitator may need to be flexible depending on the documentation and the personality and expertise of the SME.

Always start by asking the SME to provide a short overview of the project/application under discussion. Having an overview from the SME enables the FP facilitator to get an overall understanding of the project/application that they can keep in mind as the FP count moves to the detail level to make sure the functionality counted relates to the overview. It also enables the FP facilitator to use their past experience with other similar projects/applications to ask questions regarding functions the SME may not have mentioned.

Next the FP facilitator should provide an overview of what is to be covered and how the process will flow to make sure that everyone is on the same page. They should discuss the Purpose, the Process, and the Payoff.

Share the Purpose with the participants. Present what you plan to accomplish in the meeting. Stating the Purpose will answer questions that the participants may have such as: Why are we here? What can I offer? How will what I offer be used? The FP facilitator should specifically state the goal (e.g., to conduct a FP count for a feasibility study or develop an estimate). The FP facilitator should also state that the SMEs do not need to know how to count FPs, but that they are there to share their expertise on the project/application being considered. It is also good to share how the FP count will be used and who will be receiving it (e.g., it will be provided to the estimation group to feed into their tool and produce an effort estimate).

Next the FP facilitator should explain the Process that will be used for the FP counting session. Since the Process follows the flow of the FP functions (e.g., data and transactions, complexity, etc.), this may also be a good time to do a quick overview of FPs if the SMEs are not familiar with them. This should not be a training session, but just a quick description of what will be discussed when, pointing out the key pieces of information that the participants are expected to supply. This is also a good time to review the documentation the SMEs have brought to determine if the flow of the session will need to change or not. It also ensures that the SMEs have brought useful documentation and are prepared for the meeting. Conversely, it allows the FP facilitator to adjust the meeting agenda or cancel the meeting if the SMEs are not prepared. Finally, before diving into the counting, the FP facilitator should share the Payoff. Share how the participants will benefit from the meeting. The Payoff discussion answers questions such as "What is in it for me?" and "How can I really benefit?"

Reviewing the Purpose, Process, and Payoff should be done quickly. This is not to be a full blown discussion on FPs and how and why the organization is using them. Hopefully, the organization has provided education to all of the staff involved on the details. This is just a 5–10 minute introduction to make sure all participants are ready to go.

Finally, the FP facilitator can get into FP specifics for the count being conducted. The FP facilitator needs to confirm the Type of Count being conducted (Application, New Development, or Enhancement) and the Scope and Boundaries involved. Again, this is to confirm that all participants are focused on the same functionality being discussed.

Now that the count has started off on the right foot and all participants understand the type and scope of what is being counted, the FP facilitator can proceed with conducting the count itself. The FP facilitator should control the flow of the count. They should not just ask the SME "What did you change?" and hope they tell you everything. You also do not want the SME to jump around too much or things may get missed. Take a structured approach to decomposing the functionality being discussed to minimize random discussions. Do not be afraid to slow the session down so that your understanding is fully developed. The FP facilitator needs to maintain the structure of the meeting and keep everyone focused. Use the documentation available, but do not rely on it alone. Make sure to ask about all types of functions that are relevant even if they are not specifically mentioned.

Typically, it is easier to start with the Data functions first and then move on to the Transaction functions; however, this may change based on the available documentation. For example, if the SME does not have anything available to show the data (e.g., data models, entity-relationship diagrams, file layouts, etc.), the FP facilitator may need to use the transactions to determine the Data functions.

The questions to ask are divided into Inclusion questions, Defining questions, and Complexity questions, and those are separated for Data and Transaction functions. The first sets of questions that will be discussed are the Data function questions.

Data Functions—Inclusion Questions

Even if the documentation does not mention data or the SME does not offer anything, ask about the data. Make sure to ask all of the questions. It is important to ask open-ended questions that solicit more than just a yes/no answer. For instance, the FP facilitator should not say "You did not have any data changes did you?" Instead, the FP facilitator should ask and/or ascertain the following:

- Were any logical files of data added?
- Were any logical files of data changed (structure)?

- Were any logical files of data deleted.
- For application counts ask to see all of the data referenced and/or maintained.

If possible, focus on one data type at a time. ILFs are a good place to start, so you can add the word "maintained" to the questions (e.g., were any logical data files added that the application maintains, etc.). Keep in mind that when you move on to the External Interface Files (EIF), they may be a little more difficult for the SMEs to identify. Mention that you are looking for data referenced only by the application and try to identify the EIFs. However, pay close attention when Transaction functions are discussed because often this is when the SMEs think of the EIFs. They will start to list File Types Referenced (FTR) and suddenly remember a reference group of data that is new or changed. If this happens, document it and come back to the Data function questions to get the specifics.

Data Functions—Defining Questions

Once the SMEs mention a group of data, the FP facilitator can proceed to the Defining Questions:

- What is the logical view of the data? Are there multiple physical tables that make up the logical group?
- Does a user recognize the data as being used by the application?
    - If no, do not count it. If yes, proceed.
- Is the data maintained by a user through an EP of this application or is it used for reference?
    - If maintained, ILF. If referenced, EIF.

Data Functions—Complexity Questions

After the FP facilitator knows what Data function to count, they can determine the complexity with the following questions:

- What data subgroupings do the users recognize as being used in the application being counted for the Data function under consideration (Record Element Types [RET])?
- What data fields do the users recognize as being used in the application being counted for the Data function under consideration (DET)?

The FP facilitator may need to provide RET examples to the SMEs to help them understand the question. The FP facilitator can also use this opportunity, if there is time, to educate the SMEs on FP terms. Depending on the purpose and use of the count and local counting standards, the FP facilitator should determine if they need exact numbers for RETs/DETs or if they can use ranges. Knowing the complexity grids is helpful in this area. If the FP facilitator knows there is only one RET on an ILF, then time spent discussing whether the DETs are 35 or 36 is moot because the ILF will be low complexity either way. This is where the FP facilitator can save time in the counting session. At this time, the FP facilitator should be documenting the outcome of the discussion using the organization's standard templates and documentation guidelines.

Once the discussion of a Data function is complete, the FP facilitator should loop back to the Data Inclusion questions and start over again through the question flow until all appropriate Data functions have been identified and documented.

After all of the Data functions have been completed, the FP facilitator can begin to discuss the Transaction functions. It is important to include all transactions such as online screens, data feeds (in and out), online and printed reports, signals, conversion, etc. Often it helps to go through one category of transactions as a time. As with Data functions, there are Inclusion, Defining, and Complexity questions for Transaction functions as well.

Transaction Functions—Inclusion Questions

- What transaction functions were added?
- What transaction functions were changed (DETs or processing logic)?
- What functions were deleted?
- For application counts ask to see all transactions.

When discussing changed transactions, the FP facilitator should not just stop at what functions were changed, but ask the SME to explain the change. The FP facilitator needs to make sure the function can be included in the count per IFPUG rules. If the SME just says "the logic changed," the FP facilitator should ask them to provide an explanation of a specific logic change. At the end of the day, the FP facilitator needs to be able to defend their FP count, so they need to fully understand the changes and ensure that the count is accurate according to the IFPUG rules.

After the FP facilitator determines that a Transaction function can be included in the count, they can move on to the Defining questions.

Transaction Functions—Defining Questions

- What is the Elementary Process (EP) of the transaction?

First the FP facilitator needs to understand the entire EP being included from the logical perspective. To obtain this information, they should ask the SME how the function works from the user perspective (e.g., how does it start and when does it finish?). Once the EP is known, it is easier to determine how it should be classified.

- Is the primary intent of the EP to receive data into the system or to send data out of the system?
  - Receive data in, EI. Send data out, External Output (EO) or External Inquiry (EQ) and proceed to the next question.
- If the intent is to send data out, does the process
  - Derive any data?
  - Update an ILF?
  - Perform any calculations?

If yes to any of the above, then count it as an EO. If no to all three, then count it as an EQ.

While everyone is focused on this specific transaction, it is the best time to determine its complexity.

Transaction Functions—Complexity Questions

The following are questions that will help in identifying FTRs and DETs on EIs, EOs, and EQs:

- What data groupings are utilized during the EP (FTRs)?
  - Count them each once.
- What data fields enter the boundary (DETs)?
  - Count them each once.
- What data fields exit the boundary (DETs)?
  - Count them each once (count data fields that both enter and exit the boundary only once).
- Is there capability for error or confirmation messages?
  - If yes, add 1 DET.
- Is there a capability to specify an action (OK button, Enter key—causes the transaction to be executed)?
  - If yes, add 1 DET.

The FP facilitator may need to reiterate that only ILFs and EIFs can be FTRs and can use this opportunity to educate the SMEs on additional FP terms. As with Data functions, the SME should determine from the purpose of the count and the organization's standards whether to use exact numbers or ranges and what level of detail is necessary for documenting the transaction functions. Once the FP facilitator is completed with a transaction function, they should go back to the Inclusion questions and start again. Transaction functions may be done in groupings (e.g., the function identified has add, change, delete, and inquiry capability). It is okay to examine all of these at one time, but when determining Inclusion and Complexity make sure to focus on one at a time for complete accuracy.

The FP facilitator does not need to use the exact wording of the questions listed above and should not just go through the questions as a script. The questions should be used as a reminder of what type of information should be obtained from the SME to conduct an accurate count and are used as a flow to ensure consistency and repeatability in the counting process itself.

Understanding the Relationship between Functions

Something else that can assist the FP facilitator in knowing how to expand on the questions above is understating the relationship between functions. This can also help avoid functions being missed. Hopefully the SME is very knowledgeable and has good supporting documentation, but sometimes not everything is presented. Based on how functions interact with each other, there are tips to know if certain functions should be expected to show up in a project/ application count. For instance, if ILFs change or are added, then there should be a way to maintain it. If the FP facilitator does not see any EIs or EOs maintaining ILFs that have been documented, then they should ask about it. On the other hand, if data is being added to a transaction it has to come from or be stored somewhere, which can indicate a change to a logical file. Also, if data is being stored, chances are a user will want to see it or report on it, so the FP facilitator should expect to be discussing functions in this area. Applications typically communicate with other applications, so it is good to ask about these interactions to determine if additional functionality should be included. In addition, data that is added can often be changed or deleted, and so if that is not specifically mentioned, the FP facilitator should ask about it. This list is not all inclusive and the FP facilitator should use their prior knowledge of counts to determine if other related functions should be discussed. It is a good practice to develop a mental list of the interactions and dependencies and use it as a guide as you are completing the count.

Overall, the FP facilitator needs to maintain control of the session and relate the functions to one another. The SME should not just rattle off the functions quickly. The FP facilitator should also remember the overview and make sure the functions are relating to what they were told about the project/application under consideration.

Finally, the FP facilitator needs to pay attention to how functions relate to one another to recognize changes that may need to be made to the count. For example, based on discussions, the FP facilitator may realize the application boundary is incorrect or that a security FTR should have been counted for specific transactions. If this is discovered late in the count, the FP facilitator needs to understand what functionality it relates to in order to go back and make adjustments to functions previously counted.

Diagram/Document

It is imperative that the results of the session be documented in detail so that everyone understands what was counted and why. Recording the results of the counting session as it progresses enables the participants to know what is being done and therefore stay focused and participate effectively. Good recording during the count also helps data entry and provides an audit trail of the count.

They say a "picture is worth a thousand words"; well this is true with FPs as well. Most people appreciate when they can see the project/application functionality presented in a visual fashion, so diagramming as the count is being conducted can be a useful tool. This does not mean that the FP facilitator always needs to be standing at a flip chart or a white board. If only two people are in the session, the diagram can be done on a piece of paper. At the end of the count, it is always good to show what has been discussed and ask the SMEs if there is anything else that needs to be covered. It is usually easier for them to answer this question when they have a diagram to look at rather than a list of functions in a tool/spreadsheet or notes in a design document. Figure 12.2 shows an example of a diagramming technique that can be used.

Whether or not a diagram is used, the FP facilitator should document the count in a clear and detailed manner. Make sure to use specific function names that are recognizable to the SME. To save time and space, the FP facilitator can consolidate common functions (e.g., Add Customer, Change Customer, Delete Customer, etc.) on one line; however, make sure they are counted separately. The number of RETs, DETs, and FTRs should be included on the diagram or the spreadsheet. For RETs and DETs, it is a good idea to document the specific names for later reference. It is also a good idea to document why the function is included in the count

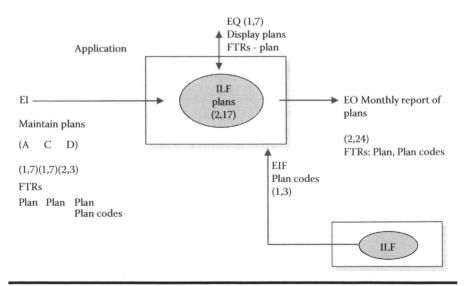

Figure 12.2 Example of a diagramming technique.

(e.g., added function, changed function). If a changed function, document what changed (e.g., added DETs, logic change to calculate taxes based on a fixed rate rather than percentage of sales).

Utilize "Helpful Hints"

All of the above information can be summarized into the following "helpful hints."

- Stay focused—avoid distractions and unnecessary conversations. Make sure discussions occur, but focus on topics that are relevant and keep the session moving in an effective and efficient manner.
- Follow the process—using the structured flow of the counting process helps with the learning curve and with consistency from session to session.
- Diagram—this is most effective with large and/or complex counts or with large groups of SMEs. It allows the participants to see visually the FP count progress.
- Use the IFPUG CPM —this is where the rules are, so it can be very helpful when difficult situations arise and the FP facilitator needs to go back to the basic rule. It is available to help, so use it.
- Document completely—this provides support for this count and future counts and can aid in clarification if questions arise.
- Do not rush—although the session should be run efficiently, take time to ask all the questions. This aids in the accuracy of the count and ensures that things do not get missed.
- Get detailed answers—if you need clarification get it while you have access to the SME. It is often harder to get a hold of people once they leave the session and it delays the completion of the count. Do not let the SME "skim" over things. Make sure, as the FP facilitator, that you fully understand the functionality yourself and get all of the information to determine the count. This is your job as the FP facilitator. It is not the SMEs job to tell you how and what to count. Also make sure the responses you get are specific. Do not accept "there was a logic change." Make sure to ask specifically what the logic change was.

Concluding the Count

You have finally completed all of the discussions related to the project/application functionality, so now it is important to end the session appropriately. The count may or may not be completed in one session, and so it is important that all participants understand the status of the count. The FP facilitator should recap what has been accomplished and inform participants of the "next steps." Participants need to know if there is anything else that they need to do. Even if the count is finished, the SMEs should be informed about where the data is going and how it will be used. If there are activities outstanding, make sure to assign responsibilities and get completion dates for those activities. Often when people leave a counting session they forget all about it. You want to finish things up while the discussions are fresh in everyone's mind, so providing deadlines is imperative. Finally, take the time to thank participants for their participation. SMEs take time out of their day to provide information, and even though we hope they get something out of it also, the FP facilitator should recognize the contribution of the SMEs and thank them.

Following Up

After the completion of the counting session itself, there may be some follow-up activities required of the FP facilitator. Reporting and follow up on FP counting sessions will aid in gaining support from staff on the FP process and keep the overall process updated and consistent. The following are potential follow-up activities that may occur:

- Data entry—although the FP facilitator is documenting the count during the session, there may be data entry required in a specific FP repository tool or some cleanup required to the documentation.
- Outstanding questions—during the counting session, the SMEs may not have all of the answers and there may be some difficult situations where the FP facilitator is unsure of how to proceed. This may require some offline research or discussions. If this occurs, it is important to address them as quickly as possible so that the FP count can be completed.
- Reviews and audits—although not required, it is recommended that FP counts be reviewed by another FP expert to ensure consistency across facilitators and the organization. Also, people are not perfect, so errors in data entry may occur. A review process can avoid errors getting through to the final count.
- Provide results to the appropriate area and the count participants—of course, it is necessary to provide the counting results to the sponsor/area that required the FP count to occur, but it is also helpful to have a process for providing the information back to the SME participants as well. They have taken time out of their schedule to provide expertise and should see the results of their work. This demonstrates an "open" environment and will aid in gaining good support from the SMEs in the future.
- Update company-specific guidelines—there may be situations that arise during a counting session that will occur again at the organization (e.g., a package was used to deliver some functionality). The approach to handling these situations may be based on the company objectives, not necessarily IFPUG rules. To ensure consistency, it is a good idea to document these types of things in company-specific guidelines. The document can be updated as new situations are encountered during additional counting sessions.

The follow-up activities close the loop on the counting sessions and ensure that all parties are comfortable with the results. The count is now complete.

Summary

It is important to remember that although there are IFPUG rules to follow for FP counting, completing accurate and consistent counts is not automatic. It takes thinking and analysis by the FP facilitator to be successful. However, with proper planning and a strong, focused, interested facilitator, the sessions do not have to be difficult. The information discussed in this chapter will lay the foundation to becoming a better FP facilitator and counter. In summary, remember the following:

- FP facilitation gets more comfortable with experience.
- Planning and preparation make a big difference.
- Follow the process, but be adaptable.
- Good follow-up paves the way for future counts.
- Do not feel you are out there alone—use your support system (e.g., other FP facilitators).
- Enjoy the learning experience.

About the Author

Lori Holmes is a director with Q/P Management Group, specializing in software measurement, process improvement, and quality assurance. Her areas of expertise include establishing measurement programs, project estimating, software quality assurance, Function Point Analysis, and managing customer satisfaction. Lori is recognized as an international consultant, speaker, and instructor. She focuses on organizations implementing quality and productivity improvement programs using measurement techniques. She is an experienced instructor in measurement, process improvement, quality inspections, problem solving techniques, and Function Point Analysis.

Previously, Lori was a quality associate for First Data Corporation, an organization providing support for bankcard processing, cable television processing, and WATS marketing. Prior to this, she was the quality assurance manager within a systems and programming organization. She was responsible for developing and monitoring processes and procedures to assure quality in all application development efforts. The processes included measurement and development methodologies. She also implemented a software measurement process that relied on Function Point counting of all software designs as a primary metric. Lori was also an applications programming manager, leading four technical teams. She was responsible for applications development and day-to-day production issues.

Ms. Holmes received her Bachelor of Science in Business Administration, with a Business Information Systems focus, from Illinois State University in 1984. She became a certified quality analyst through the Quality Assurance Institute in Orlando, Florida, in 1990. She is also certified to facilitate workshops in the areas of software metrics, benchmarking, customer service, teamwork, empowerment, and organizational change. Lori has been certified by the International Function Point Users Group as a Certified Function Point Specialist.

Q/P Management Group, Inc.

10 Bow Street, Stoneham, MA 02180
    Tel: 781-438-2692
    Fax: 781-438-5549
    Web site: www.qpmg.com

Q/P Management Group, Inc. (Q/P) specializes in software measurement, estimating, quality, and process improvement. Company expertise includes Measurement Program Design and Implementation, IFPUG Certified Function Point Analysis and Training, Outsourcing Evaluation and Vendor Management, Software Engineering Institute (SEI) Capability Maturity Model Integration (CMMI) Assessments and Training, and Software Quality Assurance techniques.

Q/P's Software Benchmark Database is one of the world's largest sources of metrics data. The database is used by numerous companies and government agencies to benchmark software development and support, establish estimates for software development projects, and establish fair market prices for software products.

Q/P also develops and distributes software tools that estimate software projects, support software measurement programs, and aid in Function Point Analysis activities. More information is available at www.qpmg.com or by contacting our offices at (781) 438-2692.

MEASUREMENT PROGRAMS INTRODUCTION

Dawn Coley

Establishing a software measurement program still remains a relevant topic in the Information Technology industry. Topics addressing the basics continue to be as current as they were 20 years ago. Organizations still struggle with selling, defining, implementing, supporting, improving, and adjusting their measurement activities. In addition, as the software measurement discipline has grown and matured, many new topics have emerged. This section has chapters that address basics in addition to more advanced discussions of specific aspects of measurement programs. The section spans chapters from one that is a discussion of case studies giving a clear message about the value of performing software measurement all the way to a discussion of motivation and measurement.

Jan-Paul Fillié is an experienced business intelligence (BI) consultant at IBM Global Business Services in The Netherlands. He is the editor of the NESMA Counting guideline for Function Point Analysis in data warehousing. He has participated in the successful delivery of several data warehouses, both as an architect and as a project manager. He shares this depth of experience in his chapter "Measurement of Business Intelligence." In it, he discusses several aspects of how measurement can enable and enhance business intelligence or data warehouse projects.

Scott Goldfarb is the President of Q/P Management Group. He has served as an international consultant, instructor, and speaker with over 30 years of software experience. Scott specializes in helping organizations improve software quality and productivity through measurement. His chapter "Case Studies in Measurement-Based Decision Making" highlights compelling real-life case study information that provides examples of dramatic improvements realized by organizations implementing measurement programs. He includes case studies demonstrating the benefits of measurement programs that focus on baselines, benchmarking, outsourcing, vendor management, ongoing measurement, and scope control.

Dr. Tara Kelly is a Function Point Analyst currently working in the Irish office of MDS. Her chapter "Measurement and Motivation" provides a comprehensive look at the relationship between the two. She discusses the history of Function Point Analysis along with an overview of the theoretical body of knowledge surrounding motivation. Tara then discusses how measurement was implemented in an Information Technology organization with an understanding of this body of knowledge and how problems and issues were addressed.

Jim Mayes is a Senior Consultant with over 35 years of IT experience in software development and life cycle management. His last 16 years have involved providing software metrics support across many disciplines including project estimation, project tracking, predictive analysis, data analysis trending, benchmarking, and process improvement. His chapter, "Achieving Business Objectives: Building a Software Metrics Support Structure," addresses the crucial topic of aligning the organization to provide the needed support that enables a software metrics program to succeed. Jim uses the analogy of building a structure, including the floor, walls, and roof to drive home his point.

Chapter 13

Measurement of Business Intelligence

Jan-Paul Fillié

Contents

Introduction

The high rate of failure of business intelligence (BI) or data warehouse projects combined with a growing demand for BI solutions is creating a major gap between supply and demand. Predicting the cost of a BI project that realizes a specific functionality has proven to be very difficult in practice. This is the reason why so many of these projects get into trouble. The best-known estimating method is Function Point Analysis, a method of objective- and technology-independent prediction of the size of an information system. A counting guideline for sizing data warehouses has been available since 2009. Function Point Analysis for BI can also be used to support project control, forecasting, productivity improvement, and benchmarking.

Return on Information

Many articles have been written about determining the Return on Investment (ROI) of BI, but a clear, consistent vision still does not exist. It sometimes seems that BI is a new phenomenon for which the business value is not easily understood. However, it has been more than 50 years since Luhn [1] wrote his article coining the term "business intelligence." The field has developed into an essential component of current business operations and management [2]. BI provides not only the information to coordinate day-to-day operations but also the knowledge to cope with change in the organization.

There is a growing awareness of the possibilities of BI and an increased use of BI applications in recent years. When it comes to planning innovation, Chief Information Officers (CIOs) apparently place "insight and intelligence" at the top of their focus list (Figure 13.1). IBM® (IBM Corporation, Armonk, NY) draws this conclusion in a published CIO study [3], on the basis of evidence provided by 3000 CIOs globally. This study also shows that our businesses depend more and more on data for decision making.

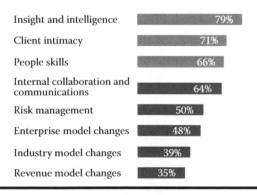

Insight and intelligence	79%
Client intimacy	71%
People skills	66%
Internal collaboration and communications	64%
Risk management	50%
Enterprise model changes	48%
Industry model changes	39%
Revenue model changes	35%

Figure 13.1   Focus of CIOs over the next 5 years.

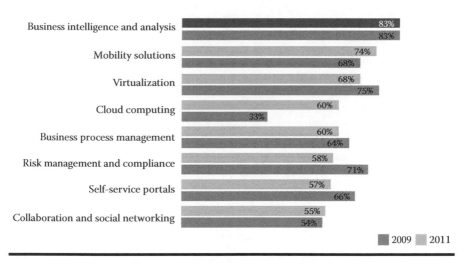

Figure 13.2   **Most important visionary plan elements of CIOs to help create the future organization.**

Furthermore, "business intelligence and analysis" remain a constant in the plans of CIOs as shown in Figure 13.2. For the past 3 years, this element has stayed fixed in first place with 83% of the CIOs questioned mentioning it as important.

Investment Decision

The value of "normal" systems like Enterprise Resource Planning or Customer Relationship Management can be determined by looking at savings on administrative cost or improved efficiency. The question that needs to be asked when dealing with BI is: What is the value of a good decision for the company? The answer is not clear and is difficult to translate into monetary terms.

When buying a standard BI package, the investment itself is relatively easy to determine. However, when a custom solution is needed, the bulk of the cost is spent on specialized labor. It appears to be very difficult to predict the cost of a BI project when specific functionality is needed. This is the reason why many of these projects get into trouble.

Counting and Estimating

General application development theory includes a range of methods to determine total functionality of an application or a project. The best known is Function Point Analysis (FPA), a method of objective- and technology-independent forecasting of the size of an information system. However, as Van Heeringen [4] argues, FPA practitioners find it hard to carry out Function Point Analysis on data warehouse systems. In combination with the reluctance of BI specialists to apply methods derived from application development to their field of expertise, the application of this method to BI is not common practice.

A counting guideline for sizing data warehouses has been available since 2009 [5]. This guideline developed by Nederlandse Software Metrieken Gebruikers Associatie (NESMA) finally makes it possible for FPA practitioners to perform a FPA count on a data warehouse system. The guideline can also be used for other BI solutions such as master data management or report systems because of their similarity to a data warehouse solution. Such a count measures the available or changed functionality of a BI solution or project.

To determine the value, it is necessary to forecast not only the yield but also the investment. The bulk of the cost is determined by the needed specialist labor. Various BI suppliers use their own method. It is difficult to compare these methods objectively. It is better to determine the functional size of a BI solution or project, translate this to the estimated effort, and then to the needed investment. Roughly, this can be accomplished by multiplying the number of Function Points with the estimated number of hours per Function Point. A more refined investment calculation is possible using the data of comparable projects. This way the influence of environment, project size, and duration can be taken into account. The remainder of this chapter is based on this preferred approach.

Function Point Analysis

Function Point Analysis is a method to determine the functional size of an information system based on the functionality from the viewpoint of the end user. The functional size is measured in Function Points as defined by Albrecht [6] in 1979. This method is ISO-approved and maintained by Function Point user groups such as NESMA and IFPUG (International Function Point Users Group).

Data Warehouse Application

Why is it so difficult to use Function Point Analysis on data warehousing? If you look at a data warehouse application (see Figure 13.3) from the perspective of a regular application, the boundaries appear straightforward. Data flows into the application from multiple sources and is presented to the user through reports and other visual presentations. If you count only this direct interaction and the functions involved, then the bulk of the complexity is disregarded.

As shown in Table 13.1, the main function of a data warehouse is information retrieval and analysis. This is accomplished by the transformation and integration of information resulting in a central data model, which contains the combined information of the enterprise. Not all of this information will be made available to

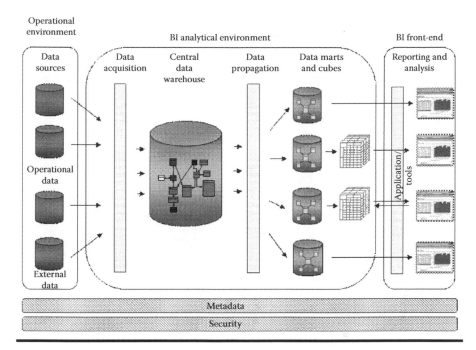

Figure 13.3   The elements of a data warehouse environment.

end users through the provided reporting. The total of enterprise information and company history represents valuable functionality in itself for future use and a flexible platform for new information applications and requests. In addition, the data warehouse will relieve the various source systems of data and information requests that may hinder their performance and business availability.

Guideline for Data Warehousing

The guideline for data warehousing helps FPA practitioners to count the elements of a data warehouse or BI solution as shown in Figure 13.4.

An explanation of the terms is given as follows:

- *Facts and dimensions*: These are the two types of entities in a dimensional model. The facts represent the process events, and the dimensions describe the facts from common viewpoints such as time/date, customer, product.
- *Hubs, links, and satellites*: Within a data vault model, the hubs are the common entities and the links describe the relationship between the different hubs. Satellites add flexibility to both hubs and links by splitting off the attributes that change over time.

Table 13.1   Comparison of a Transactional System with a Data Warehouse

Operational Application	Enterprise Data Warehouse (EDW)
Support day-to-day operations	Information retrieval and analysis
Operational use	Analytical use
Record level access	Result set access
Predictable OLTP transactional queries through predefined custom interfaces	Unpredictable analytical queries for ad hoc reporting and other BI usages
Direct user input through applications	Fully controlled update path from operational applications
Optimized for fast updates and fast query responses (often 3NF)	Optimized for large bulk uploads and large volume result set queries
Small data packages	Large periodic batch volumes
Data integration for specific purpose (single subject area)	Data integration for multiple purposes (multiple subject areas)
Operational construct	Informational construct
Used at operational tactical level	Used at analytical strategic level
Day-to-day operational needs	Long-term decision support needs
(Near) current data	Both current and historical data
(Near) real-time data upload	Batch data uploads
Event driven data uploads	Time-driven data uploads
Highly detailed data	Detailed and summarized data
Data are updated (volatile)	Data are appended (nonvolatile)
Fast updates of small datasets	Bulk uploads of large snapshots
High velocity and high frequency	Low velocity and low frequency

- *OLAP cubes*: Online analytical processing describes a technique for analysis based on a multidimensional model or cube. This provides a flexible solution for users to analyze a limited set of data from different angles (dimensions) and levels of detail.
- *Master data*: These are common data elements such as customer, product, account, or other referential data, centralized in the organization. Master data management provides a solution for central or federated maintenance and distribution to applications.

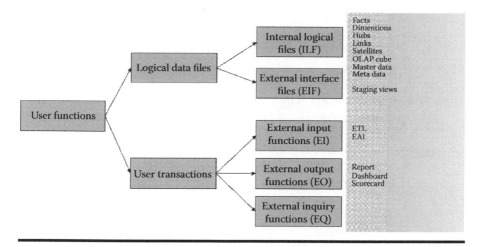

Figure 13.4 FPA user functions and their BI counterparts.

- *Metadata*: These are descriptive data or data on data. Metadata contain information on purpose, accuracy, computation, and availability of data.
- *Staging views*: In the acquisition layer of the data warehouse, source data can be either loaded directly or accessed by views.
- *ETL*: Extraction, Transformation, and Loading is the data transfer and transformation technique used in the data warehouse. ETL processes are usually batch oriented.
- *EAI*: Enterprise Application Integration is the real-time data exchange between applications through messaging in an enterprise service bus.
- *Dashboard*: This is a management overview based on multiple reports.
- *Scorecard*: This is a report of key performance indicators with their current value and trend behavior. The scorecard is based on a strategy map of the organization.

As can be assumed from the concentration of elements listed behind the internal logical files, the bulk of data warehouse functionality is found in the central data model. Specific data modeling techniques have been developed for data warehouse applications. There are three main data modeling techniques:

1. *Relational modeling* for the data warehouse as described by the data warehouse pioneer Inmon [7]. In this normalized approach, the data in the data warehouse is stored following database normalization rules in a third normal form (3NF) relational database using entity-relationship (E-R) modeling techniques. Tables are grouped by subject areas that reflect general data categories (e.g., data on customers, products, finance). The normalized structure divides data into entities, which creates several tables in a relational database. In the

Corporate Information Factory approach of Inmon, Imhoff, and Ryan [8], the atomic data in the data warehouse is stored in a relational model, but the data marts contain dimensionally modeled summary data.

2. *Dimensional modeling* is a design technique for databases intended to support end-user queries in a data warehouse. It is oriented around ease of use and query performance. Dimensional modeling always uses the concepts of facts (measures) and dimensions (context). Facts are typically (but not always) numeric values that can be aggregated. Dimensions are groups of hierarchies and descriptors that define the facts. Dimensional modeling was first described by Kimball [9] in his book *The Data Warehouse Toolkit*.

3. *Data vault* is a hybrid approach, first described by Linstedt, Graziano, and Hultgren [10], between 3NF and star schema. The design is created to be flexible, scalable, consistent, and adaptable to the needs of the enterprise.

Finally, in modern data warehouses, the use of pre-described data models is expanding. Instead of using a custom model, an industry model based on relational or data vault modeling techniques can be an accelerator for data warehouse design and development and an integration point for complex organizations. Vendors like Teradata® (Teradata Corporation, Dayton, OH) and IBM have data warehouse models for specific business processes like banking or telecom. These models have clearly defined levels of abstraction, supporting the translation from a conceptual to a logical model and from a logical to a physical model. This prevents losing business or technical context when changes are applied, thus improving the model's flexibility. All data warehouse modeling techniques including specific industry models can be counted using the counting guideline for data warehousing.

Sizing BI and Data Warehouse Systems

The Counting Guideline for Data Warehouses allows Function Point Analysts to size BI systems and projects. An example of such a count is shown in Figure 13.5. Collected project data from IBM show that this Counting Guideline can also be used for several other BI solutions and data migration projects. More insights provided by this gathered evidence are described in the section Business Intelligence Insights.

Estimation Scenarios

Project estimation starts with sizing the to-be-developed new functionality (step 1a) or changes on an existing application (step 1b) as shown in Figure 13.6. The accuracy of the size estimate depends on the level of available documentation.

The levels of estimation with limited to high certainty are as follows:

Indicative count: This is usually performed when only requirements are defined and a rough indication of size is needed. The rule of thumb is to multiply the number of expected data warehouse entities by 35.

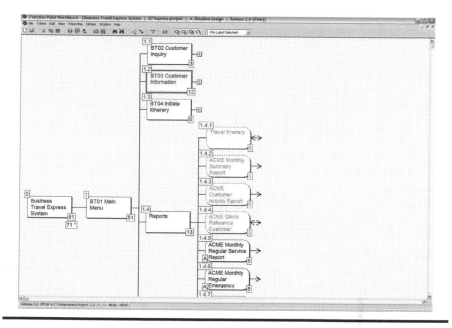

Figure 13.5 A Function Point count with Function Point Workbench™ (CHARISMATEK Software Metrics Pty Ltd, South Melbourne, Australia).

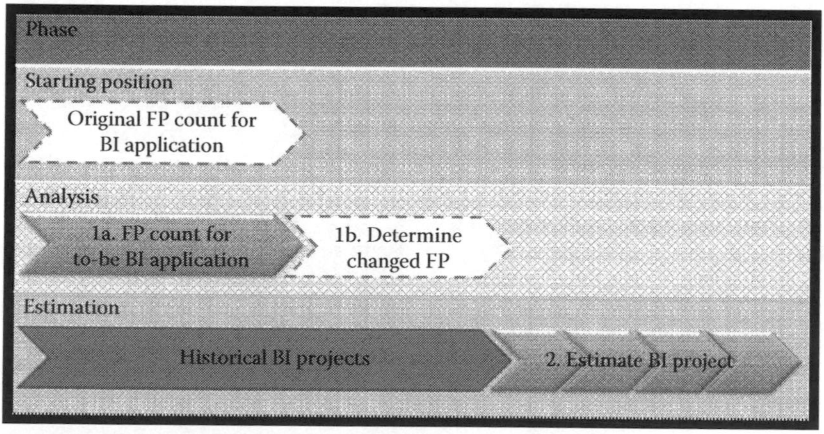

Figure 13.6 Overview of estimation activities.

Global count: This type of count can be performed when the basic architecture and data model for a new BI solution are defined. At the very least, the number of entities and reports in the various layers of the data warehouse needs to be known. For a global count, the functions are counted for all defined user data files and interactions. For this count, the assumption is made that transactions

(external input or output) are valued as average complexity and the logical data files (internal logical file or external interface file) as low complexity.
Detailed count: With a full design and consequent documentation, a detailed count with high certainty can be performed. Such a count takes into account the number of attributes and file types for each user function. In most cases, this level of detail is not available for new development.

Many organizations work with a fixed effort per Function Point. However, this is not a reliable method when the project size varies or different constraints apply to projects. Shortening the project time, for example, exponentially increases the team size, the number of defects, and, therefore, the total effort.

With the help of tools like SLIM Estimate from QSM® (QSM Inc., McLean, VA), it is possible to make estimates based on size, project time, and several other restrictions (Figure 13.6, step 2). The underlying calculation models are based on more than 8000 software development projects. This is the basis for the estimated effort, project time, team size, and defects. Another method is using specifically chosen comparable projects as the basis for the estimate. This estimation scenario is based on history. An example is shown in Figure 13.7.

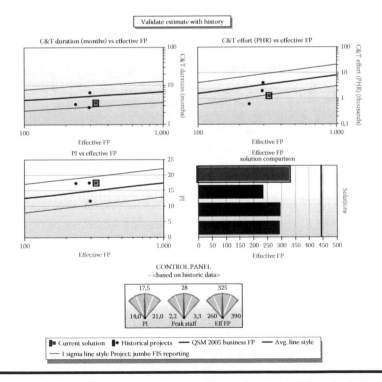

Figure 13.7   Comparison of an estimate with a selection of historical BI projects in QSM SLIM Estimate.

By varying constraints such as limiting the team size or project duration or incorporating contingency into overall effort, an optimal estimate can be determined. Common practice is to provide multiple scenarios to the project manager with the associated risks and likelihood of meeting the constraints. The project manager can choose the most applicable estimate for starting his or her project plan.

Other Uses within the Business Intelligence Domain

Estimation is only the first step when applying measurement to the software development projects as visualized in Figure 13.8. The following step in measurement is control of ongoing projects, and finally, metrics of completed projects need to be gathered to support analysis and improvement of accuracy for all measurement stages.

From these basic steps in BI measurement, further use of BI project insight can be through improving productivity, benchmarking, and exchange of experience with other organizations.

Control of Projects

Besides creating the estimates, it is also highly recommended to monitor an ongoing project by using solid metrics. By using QSM SLIM Control, it is possible to check whether a project is proceeding according to plan, as shown in Figure 13.9.

This process starts with collecting the actuals of the project (step 1). These actuals can be compared with the plan (or chosen estimation scenario, step 0) in the tool. In addition, a forecast (step 2) can be made based on current data as shown in Figures 13.10 and 13.11. These steps can be repeated periodically throughout the life cycle of the project (steps 3 and 4). This makes it much easier to preserve the metrics of the project at project closure.

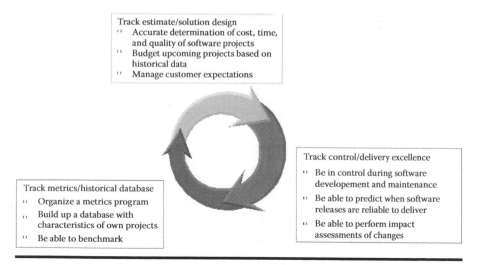

Figure 13.8   The three continuous stages of the BI measurement process.

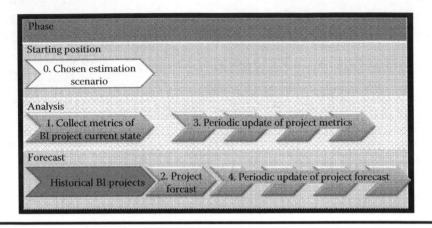

Figure 13.9   Overview of control activities.

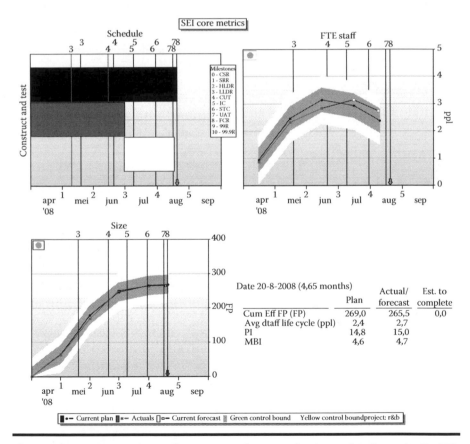

Figure 13.10   Comparison of current project metrics (completed results [in FP], effort, and PI) with the plan.

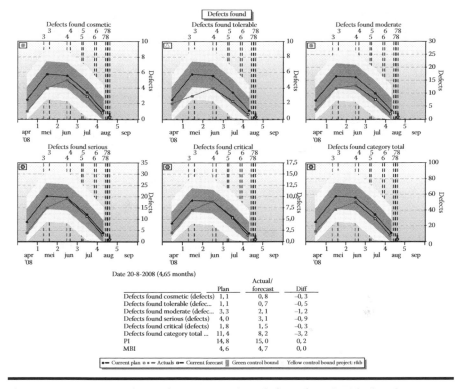

Figure 13.11   Comparison of current project defects found with the plan.

Moreover, the combination of Function Point Analysis and QSM SLIM can be used to make measurable agreements with suppliers of BI services.

Building a Knowledge Base

Besides estimating the project, it is also important—at the end of the project—to determine what has been achieved, what effort has been expended, and how long it took to complete, as shown in Figure 13.12.

Capturing project results starts with the collection of metrics (step 1), possibly facilitated by the use of control or a similar tool. The results are added to the project database (step 2) and analyzed for validity and lessons learned (step 3). Optionally, the trend line can be updated for new estimates or forecasts (step 4). The possible metrics/characteristics to be captured on a BI project for building a knowledge base are:

- Size (FP)
- Effort (person hours)
- Duration (days)

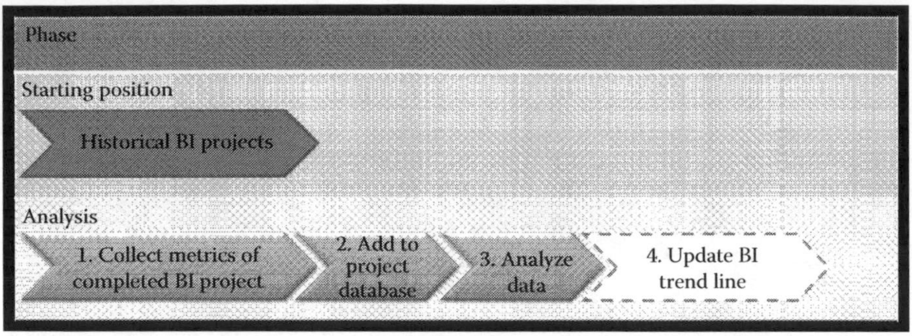

Figure 13.12 Overview of metrics activities.

- Team size
- Number of defects
- Number of source systems
- Data intake method (flat file/xml/db connection)
- BI tooling (ETL/OLAP/Reporting)
- Development method (waterfall/agile)

It is clear that the standard curves in QSM SLIM for IT projects also apply to BI. In the section "Business Intelligence Insights," the conclusions of the analysis performed by IBM are revealed, showing interesting differences between BI and regular projects.

Improving Productivity

From the knowledge gathered in the project database, the significance of project factors and constraints can be derived. These factors, for example, project size, duration, and team size, have either a positive or negative impact on productivity. On the basis of these observations, it can be recommended to, for example, take more time (duration) or combine several smaller projects into one to increase the productivity of the BI team. In addition, the simple fact of measurement can have a positive effect on the team's performance.

Benchmarking

When organizations want to make sure that their BI projects are performing well or when they want to compare their BI projects with the best in class, it may be beneficial to benchmark these projects against a reference database. This process is shown in Figure 13.13. This can be either an internal or an external evaluation, depending on the availability of a BI project database within the organization.

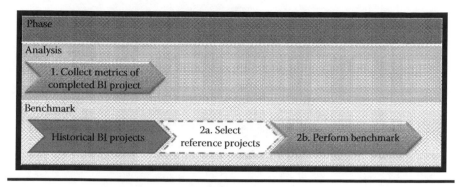

Figure 13.13   Overview of benchmark activities.

The process starts with collecting the data of the project to be benchmarked (step 1). These data can be compared with either a selection of reference projects (step 2a) or the complete database with BI projects (step 2b). Such a benchmark can highlight the differences, best practices, and risks involved in the execution of BI projects.

Exchanging Experience

What has been found so far is that the NESMA Counting Guideline can be used for more than just data warehouses and that the ratios of BI projects are quite similar to that of "normal" software development projects. For the near future, it is important to gather experience on both the figures and the application of the Counting Guideline. The workgroup of NESMA holds representatives from the following major organizations: ABN AMRO, Atos Origin, Capgemini, and IBM. The Counting Guideline for Function Point Analysis in data warehouse projects is also used by several Dutch companies.

Business Intelligence Insights

The 260+ BI projects captured at this point in time in IBM's BI database have been analyzed for statistical verification. In Figure 13.14, the overview of projects is shown. The distribution of the projects follows an expected Gauss distribution with some outliers.

Looking at these first experiences, it seems that the projects are not evenly distributed in size. The majority of the BI projects are relatively small as shown in Figure 13.15. Perhaps this is due to the type of BI projects that IBM performs or this is a specific feature of BI projects. One explanation is the ever-growing nature of data warehouse systems, which implies that one major first implementation is followed periodically by smaller releases. This phenomenon certainly deserves further investigation in the future.

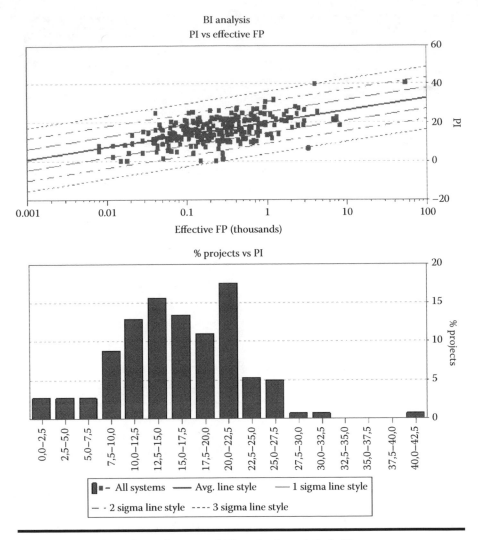

Figure 13.14 Overview of captured BI projects and their PI.

The software process Productivity Index (PI) is a QSM metric as described by Putnam [11]. It represents the level of an organization's software development efficiency. The PI is a macro measure for the total development environment. For analysis of BI projects, PI can be used as a metric to compare project performance: the higher the PI value, the better the project performance.

In comparison with the standard software development trend line, the additional duration (Figure 13.16) and effort (Figure 13.17) increase much more slowly with increasing project size in BI. In conclusion, the striking difference between

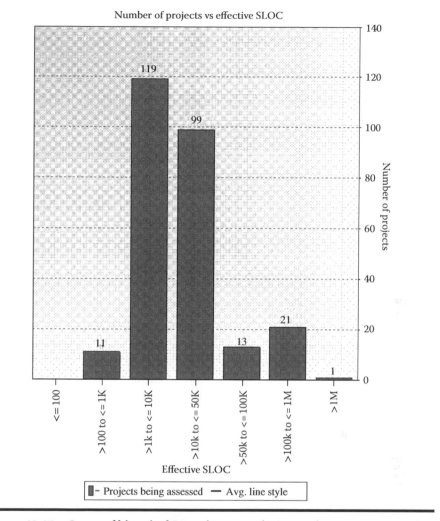

Figure 13.15 Count of historical BI projects per size group in QSM SLIM metrics.

BI projects and other software projects is that the PI is high, especially for large projects as shown in Figure 13.18.

Other project factors are similar to regular software development factors. In other words, the productivity increases with larger projects for BI. Of course, this analysis needs refinement with more "large project" metrics collected. The expectation is that, with growth and maintenance of the BI knowledge base, the accuracy of estimations and forecasts will increase as well as the confidence of the people using these results.

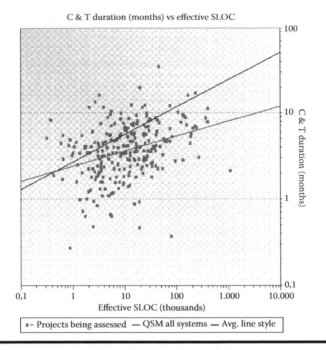

Figure 13.16 Comparison of duration of historical BI projects against the QSM trend line in QSM SLIM metrics.

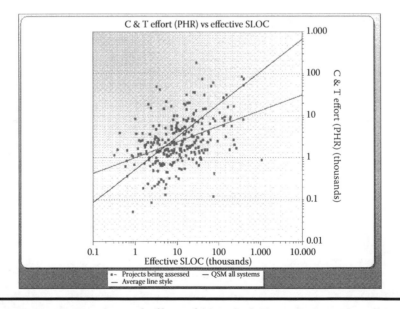

Figure 13.17 Comparison of effort of historical BI projects against the QSM trend line in QSM SLIM metrics.

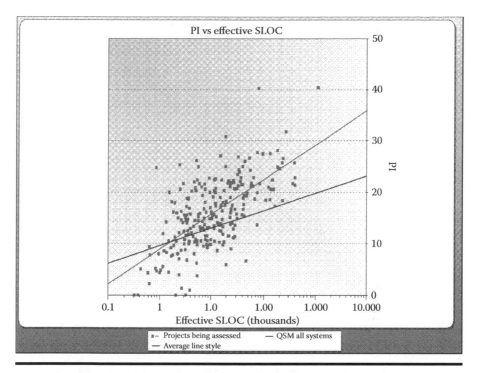

Figure 13.18 Comparison of PI of historical BI projects against the QSM trend line in QSM SLIM metrics.

Added Value for Business Intelligence

In conclusion, every BI project would benefit from preliminary cost calculations to underpin the business case. This is obviously important for the customer as well as the supplier. To calculate the cost, the expected functionality has to be determined, and an estimate for the implementation of the project has to be made. In addition, every organization that frequently executes BI projects (e.g., by working in releases) can benefit from using this experience to estimate new projects and possibly even to control the delivery. Combining Function Point Analysis and tools such as QSM SLIM makes it possible to build up a knowledge base and experience on the implementation of BI projects.

References

1. Luhn, H. P. 1958. A business intelligence system. *IBM Journal of Research and Development,* 2(4): 314–319.
2. Fillié, J. P. 2010. Half a century of BI: From BI inception to BI 2.0. *Cutter IT Journal.*
3. IBM. 2011. The essential CIO, insights from the Global Chief Information Officer Study, http://www-935.ibm.com/services/us/cio/ciostudy/.

4. Van Heeringen, H. Measuring the size of a data warehouse application using COSMIC-FFP, http://www.gelog.etsmtl.ca/publications/pdf/120.pdf.
5. NESMA. FPA Applied to Data Warehousing (version 1.1; English), http://www.nesma.nl/download/boeken_NESMA/N25_FPA_for_Data_Warehousing_(v1.1.0).pdf.
6. Albrecht, A. J. 1979. Measuring application development productivity. In *Proceedings of the Joint SHARE, GUIDE, and IBM Application Development Symposium*, Monterey, CA, October 14–17, 83–92, Armonk, NY: IBM Corporation.
7. Inmon, W. H. 2005. *Building the Data Warehouse*. New York, NY: John Wiley & Sons.
8. Inmon, W. H., C. Imhoff, and S. Ryan. 2000. *Corporate Information Factory*. New York, NY: John Wiley & Sons.
9. Kimball, R. 1996. *The Data Warehouse Toolkit: Practical Techniques for Building Dimensional Data Warehouses*. New York: John Wiley & Sons.
10. Linstedt, D., K. Graziano, and H. Hultgren. 2008. The new business supermodel. In *The Business of Data Vault Data Modeling*, Cambridge, MA: The MIT Press.
11. Putnam, L. H. 2000. Linking the QSM Productivity Index with the SEI Maturity Level, McLean, VA: Quantitative Software Management, Inc., http://www.qsm.com/sites/www.qsm.com/themes/diamond/docs/LINKING6.pdf.

About the Author

Jan-Paul Fillié is an experienced business intelligence (BI) consultant at IBM Global Business Services in the Netherlands with an interest in innovation of information management. His main focus is improving BI project delivery through agile and iterative processes.

He is an expert in estimation and measurement of BI and data warehouse projects. As a member of the Data Warehouse workgroup of NESMA, he is the editor of the NESMA Counting Guideline for Function Point Analysis in Data Warehousing. At IBM, he supports the sizing and estimation for BI client proposals and has been harvesting the results of BI projects in a global historical database. So far, more than 260 projects have been collected as a basis for analysis, trend line development, and benchmarking.

Some of the highlights in Jan-Paul's experience are the development of information analysis and benchmarking products for hospitals delivered through a BI portal in 2000/2001. He participated in the successful delivery of several data warehouses, both as an architect and as a project manager. In 2005, he helped set up a development factory for BI projects based on Rational Unified Process (RUP) and supported several BI and data warehouse implementations for clients in this environment. One of his more recent accomplishments is the design and delivery of a Data Quality as a Service solution for a global organization in electronics.

Besides his involvement in consulting and project delivery, he regularly publishes BI-related articles for several Dutch magazines and internationally in *Cutter IT Journal*. He also frequently uses his experience for training clients and colleagues in various BI subjects.

Chapter 14

Case Studies in Measurement-Based Decision Making

Scott Goldfarb

Contents

Introduction—Achieving Management Goals through Software Measurement

In today's challenging economic times, organizations need to make the most of their resources. Unfortunately, many improvement initiatives have been slashed. Even measurement staff and initiatives are being cut or underfunded. This is very disturbing because experience has proven that measurement enables performance improvement, resulting in lower costs. This has been demonstrated numerous times by organizations willing to measure productivity and implement improvements. This chapter documents eight case studies from different organizations that I have worked with over the years to demonstrate how software measurement can help companies achieve quantifiable goals, especially those of cutting costs. These examples can help organizations promote measurement and identify similar opportunities for improvement and cost cutting.

Questions and Benefits

The following are common questions that many senior managers want answered:

- How do we make sure resources are being utilized effectively?
- What is the appropriate funding level for application maintenance and support?
- Is offshore development cost effective?
- How do we control vendor costs and manage vendor performance?
- How do we make sure we are doing the best job in selecting package software?
- How do we manage changes in scope?
- Are we productive and how do we improve productivity and quality?

The answers to these questions highlight the benefits that can be gained through software measurement. The following eight case studies will illustrate these benefits, which involve using measurement for quantifying change of scope, managing outsourcing agreements, analyzing the cost effectiveness of offshore development, and performing a baseline in combination with benchmarking to identify opportunities for improvement.

Baselines and Benchmarking

The first two case studies involve establishing a baseline. A baseline is the result of a process that collects quality and productivity data as well as process information in order to identify productivity and quality levels. The baseline analysis also provides an understanding of what practices are in place and which practices are producing favorable results. The baseline process, as depicted in Figure 14.1, begins with the selection of projects and applications that are a representative sample of

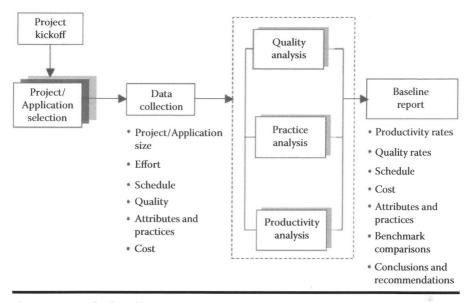

Figure 14.1   The baseline process.

the organization's performance in terms of new development, enhancement work, and maintenance of existing applications. Data is collected including the size of projects and applications, cost and effort by activity, schedule duration for projects, quality based on defects, information that describes the environment, and practices that are utilized in maintaining and developing software. Based on the data collected, productivity, quality, cost, and practice analyses are performed. The results are documented in a baseline report that includes productivity rates, quality rates, and schedule information. In addition, processes and practices are analyzed to identify process improvement opportunities. A benchmark comparison can also be performed and provide valuable insight into the baseline analysis. The benchmark compares the organization's performance to industry averages and/or best in class performance. This comparison will highlight the strengths and weaknesses of the organization, help identify opportunities to implement best practices, and set expectations for future improvement including potential productivity gains.

Case 1: High-Tech Company

The first case study involves a large high-tech company whose specific focus was on trying to improve productivity and reduce costs. The company had tripled the size of their development staff over a fairly short period of time, and senior management was convinced that significant change was necessary to improve the environment and make it more productive. The high-tech company's goal was to "implement process improvement opportunities that would increase productivity and quality." They did this by establishing a baseline, identifying opportunities, and developing a comprehensive process improvement program. The program included 18 initiatives to improve productivity and quality as well as reduce costs. A subset of those initiatives included the following:

- Redefining the software development life cycle to make it more streamlined
- Developing a test bed facility and database
- Creating a project management function
- Establishing a measurement program to improve the estimating process
- Redesigning the physical office space to improve productivity
- Improving requirements gathering and management
- Implementing reviews and inspections to improve quality

This was an extremely aggressive process improvement program. It took 18 months to implement the initiatives and the results were measured following a learning curve period. The company's new measurement program quantified a 62% increase in productivity over a 2-year period, compared to a 5% per year improvement experienced by most companies. They also measured their defect rates and were able to quantify a 20% improvement in quality based on a reduction of defects per development hour. Overall, there was a tremendous improvement in productivity and a very good improvement in quality as well.

Case 2: Financial Services Company

The second case study that utilized a baseline approach is a financial services organization. This organization employed several outside suppliers to help develop and maintain software. They were highly pressured by senior business management to cut costs year after year. Their goal was to "significantly cut development costs through process improvement and staff reduction." They performed annual baselines and benchmark comparisons over a 5-year period. They used the baseline to identify process improvement opportunities as well as to measure progress each year. To do this, they established an ongoing measurement process intended to report performance information required for the annual baseline. The benchmark comparisons helped the company to identify improvement initiatives each year and to measure the impact of the improvements made in each previous year.

The improvement initiatives that the company put in place over the 5-year period included the following:

- Adjusting project schedules to optimize productivity
- Bundling small unproductive projects into larger projects
- Redesigning poorly performing critical applications

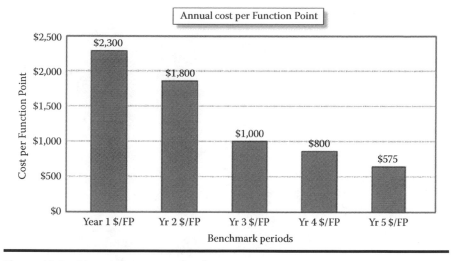

Figure 14.2   Measuring cost reduction.

- Implementing software engineering tools
- Transitioning resources offshore
- Increasing user involvement in requirements definition
- Improving life cycle methods

These initiatives for the most part were either implemented or actively supported by the outside service providers. These service providers were also very cooperative in establishing the baseline and planning improvements.

The results from the improvement initiatives (see Figure 14.2) showed consistent annual cost reduction. In year 1, their cost per Function Point was $2,300. By year 5, their cost per Function Point was down to less than $600. This represented a 75% development cost reduction over a 5-year period. As a bonus, they also greatly improved customer satisfaction.

Benefits of Metrics in Outsourcing and Vendor Management

The next three cases are related to outsourcing. Figure 14.3 depicts a model used in consulting engagements to help organizations maximize the benefits of outsourcing and improve vendor performance management. Two out of the three cases used this model and began by establishing a baseline to measure quality, productivity, and cost prior to outsourcing. That information was used to assess alternatives for outsourcing. Based on that analysis, they established the scope of the contract and defined terms and conditions. Performance levels were then negotiated including

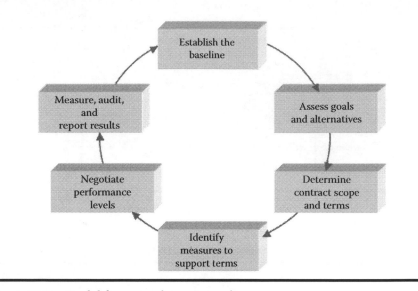

Figure 14.3   Model for managing outsourcing.

percent improvements in quality, productivity, and cost. Results were measured, audited, and reported quarterly, and an annual baseline was conducted to determine if performance goals were achieved.

The use of productivity-related metrics in outsourcing has evolved significantly over the years. Initially, productivity measurement was primarily used as a tool to manage performance and to help provide incentives for achieving goals or assessing penalties. Contract terms were established and often a productivity improvement goal of between 5% and 15% per year was set. If not achieved, a significant penalty would be assessed, sometimes as much as 10% of the overall revenues of the outsourcing agreement. Measurement has also been used in the past to evaluate vendor bids against industry benchmarks. Often, these productivity measures are based on Function Points per hour, or in the maintenance area, Function Points being maintained per year per full-time person.

Over the past 5 years, "pay by the metric" terms have become much more common as a mechanism for managing productivity and costs in outsourcing agreements. This is when a company establishes a payment schedule based on the output delivered. It is often the number of Function Points developed, enhanced, or maintained. This is demonstrated in the next case.

Case 3: Major Insurance Company

The third case study, involving a major insurance company, utilized a pay by the metric approach. The company's goal was to "outsource software development functions and guarantee major cost reductions for their business partners." The action they took was to establish an initial baseline in order to quantify current productivity, cost, and quality levels. They then structured an agreement with an outsourcer that would guarantee annual reductions in IT expenses.

The results of the baseline can be seen in the matrix shown in Table 14.1. Over a hundred projects that were a representative sample of the development work that went on within the organization were selected and analyzed. Function Points were counted on each of the projects and the costs associated with those projects were gathered. The matrix is broken down by platform (client server, web, and mainframe) and size of the project. Small-sized projects in this particular case are classified as less than 50 Function Points, medium is 50–300 Function Points, and large is greater than 300 Function Points. Project categories are broken down this way because it has been found that productivity varies significantly by the size as well as the platform of the project. For instance, client–server productivity for this organization is typically lower, meaning that it has a higher cost per Function Point than web development where there are better methods and tools to develop web-based applications and therefore a more productive development platform. Size can have an even bigger impact on productivity. For example, for most organizations, very small projects, like adding a new file or report to an application, are by far the least productive. In this company's case, medium-sized projects turned out to be the most productive and least costly. Therefore, when a baseline is established, it should be broken down by project size category and platform because the cost will vary by these different criteria.

Table 14.2 focuses only on the Small Project category. This table is similar to a contract schedule that can be found in an outsourcing agreement. Medium and Large Projects will have their own unique tables as part of the contract schedule. The schedule dictates the first year's cost (cost per Function Point) and the annual cost reductions over the duration of the contract. This particular organization negotiated and signed an agreement with a major outsourcer to reduce the cost per Function Point by 10% per year or 35% over the lifetime of the contract. The guaranteed cost reductions year after year are based on the outsourcer's belief that productivity can be improved. The outsourcer was also factoring in the transition to a less expensive offshore resource as part of this process. From the customer's perspective, they are guaranteed an annual budget reduction and total projected savings of over $100 million, which they are well on their way to achieving.

Table 14.1 Pay by the Metric Approach

Cost per FP by Project Size and Platform			
Platform	Project Size		
	Small	Medium	Large
C/S	$2,200	$1,750	$1,900
Web	$1,750	$1,400	$1,600
MF	$1,950	$1,600	$1,850

Table 14.2 Pay by the Metric Table

	Contract Future Pricing–Cost per FP Small Projects–Annual Schedule				
Platform	Baseline Year	Year 1	Year 2	Year 3	Year 4
C/S	$2,200	$1,980	$1,782	$1,604	$1,443
Web	$1,750	$1,575	$1,418	$1,276	$1,148
MF	$1,950	$1,755	$1,580	$1,422	$1,279

Case 4: Major Worldwide Bank

This next case is a major worldwide bank that had been in an outsourcing agreement for several years when they decided to act on one of the contract terms related to benchmarking. Many outsourcing contracts include terms and conditions that give the customer the right to benchmark performances. Based on the results of the baseline and benchmark, the outsourcer might need to cut costs, improve productivity, or improve quality. In the case of this worldwide bank, the goal was to "re-establish the maintenance head count (the number of full-time people or FTPs) as dictated by the contract terms." The action was to perform a benchmark study and then negotiate resource levels. This organization had been counting Function Points as part of their measurement initiative and knew the size of their application portfolio. They also knew they had 850 full-time people maintaining that portfolio. Also important to the benchmark comparison was knowing the mix of application Function Points by platform and by application age.

Maintenance productivity is impacted tremendously by the age of the application. For instance, very new applications (less than 3 years old) have high maintenance and poor productivity. This is due to the fact that newly built applications have latent problems (defects) from the original development effort and often major enhancements will continue for years. Very old applications (over 20 years old) also have poor productivity due to a different set of factors. In general, applications that are in the 10–12 year time frame typically have the highest productivity and the lowest cost. These are applications that are well established requiring only minor functional changes but are not so old that they require geriatric care. For these reasons, a benchmark comparison based on age as well as platform is important.

The company's baseline was compared to an industry average benchmark. The benchmark was based on the same application mix in terms of application age and platform. The benchmark industry average comparison indicated that a staff of 550 developers should be able to maintain a portfolio of that size, type, and age. The top quartile benchmark was 350 developers, meaning that if the environment was very productive, 350 developers could maintain the portfolio. The customer was wary about trying to reduce staff from 850 to 550 over a short period of time, so they negotiated with the outsourcer and agreed to a cut of 150. This staff reduction was implemented over a 6-month period and resulted in a $15 million annual savings that continued for many years without any noticeable impact on service levels.

This case also included an analysis and benchmark comparison of labor rates for both onshore and offshore resources, which were found to be high. This led to a renegotiation of labor rates that further reduced the contract cost by $6 million per year.

Overall, the measurement baseline analysis, benchmark comparison, and renegotiation resulted in an ongoing annual savings of over $20 million per year.

Case 5: Government Agency

The fifth case study is from a government agency that wanted to redesign and enhance a travel system for tracking their staff's reservations and travel expenses. Their goal was to "analyze a vendor bid from a preferred vendor to determine if it was a fair price." To accomplish this, they decided to compare the vendor bid to an in-house development option. In order to do this, they analyzed the existing travel system and any additional requirements in order to approximate the size of the new application in terms of Function Points. They then utilized industry average productivity rate data combined with their own historical data in order to estimate the cost to develop the new application in-house. When that analysis was performed, the estimated cost for in-house development was $2 million compared to the vendor bid of $12 million.

Based on the results of the measurement analysis, the vendor bid was rejected and the vendor was removed from the preferred vendor list. The organization developed the system in-house at a cost of $3 million resulting in an overall cost avoidance of $9 million.

Benefits of Ongoing Measurement Programs

Ideally, organizations should have an ongoing measurement program that is continually available to provide information by which to manage. Usually, these types of programs measure and report at the project and application level and also provide periodic reporting often on a monthly or quarterly basis. In addition, annual baseline reports are often produced and include comparisons to the previous year. This allows the organization to track and identify trends in productivity and identify process improvement opportunities. When enough historical measurement data has been collected, organizations will often begin to utilize this information in order to produce better project estimates and forecasts for application support.

Case 6: Large Manufacturing Company

This is a case study from a large manufacturing company that had a well-established ongoing measurement program. Their goal was to utilize software measurement to improve project management, resource utilization, and productivity. Their ongoing program revealed possible issues related to staffing practices. To better understand the issues, they performed a deep dive analysis of staffing practices and identified a major problem in the use of offshore resources. Offshore projects were being staffed with 3 to 10 times the head count of similar sized onshore projects and typically cost more. As depicted in Figure 14.4, their projects that were 100% staffed by onshore resources cost approximately $1,000 per Function Point. Those projects that were 100% offshore were about double that price at slightly over $2,000 per Function Point. Finally, the cost of projects that were mixed with onshore and offshore resources were well over $3,000 per Function Point. Unfortunately, mixed projects represented the majority of the work performed.

The onshore versus offshore cost analysis provided a compelling reason for the manufacturing company to make major changes related to the staffing of projects. The biggest change was the development of guidelines on how to better utilize offshore development staff. The guidelines included target head count ranges based on the size of the project. For example, for a project that is 500 Function Points in size, the head count should be between 20 and 30 people and the project schedule duration should be between 7 and 10 months. They also changed the practice of assigning offshore resources to projects early in the development life cycle in order to avoid the charging of unproductive time against the project budget. To resolve this issue, they went to an on-demand approach for resource utilization where developers only worked when they were needed and only on productive tasks. They also modified their time accounting practices allowing both offshore and onshore developers to charge time against unproductive and overhead activities not related to project work. This greatly improved the accuracy of time being reported.

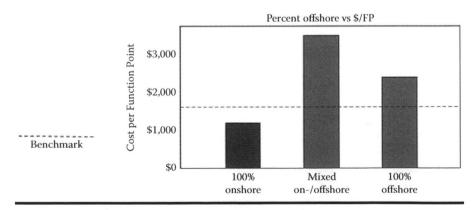

Figure 14.4 Measuring offshore resources.

The new staffing guidelines and practices had an immediate and significant payback. The overall cost per Function Point went from $2,800 to $2,000 per Function Point. This represented a 35% cost reduction with minimal investment and a great example of productivity improvement resulting from working smarter not harder.

Case 7: Government Agency Human Resource Management Applications

The seventh case study to be examined utilized Function Fit Analysis (see Figure 14.5). This is a way to identify the requirements of a project and put them into Function Point terms, then compare commercial off-the-shelf software (COTS) offerings against the actual business requirements. Based on that, a functional gap analysis is performed to identify what the COTS is and is not delivering in terms of satisfying requirements. After that analysis is completed, project estimates are established, and an appropriate make/buy decision can be made based on information provided.

The government agency was considering replacing all of their human resource management (HRM) systems that were supporting several departments with very unique requirements. Their goal was to evaluate various package solutions to determine the best solution and the funding requirements to purchase the package and make any necessary modifications. As part of their research, we performed a Function Fit Analysis. Three major projects were analyzed to determine functional fit and gaps. Many large packaged personnel systems do not meet very specific

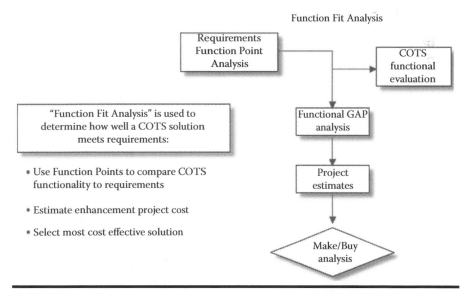

Figure 14.5 Measuring functional fit.

Table 14.3 Measuring Functional Fit

	Function Points			
	Added	*Changed*	*Unchanged*	*Total AFP*
Total FPs	20,375	636	434	21,445
Percent, of Total Project	95%	3%	2%	100%

government requirements, and in this case, all of the COTS that were evaluated had limited satisfaction of requirements. As depicted in Table 14.3, the COTS that the organization initially preferred only had a 2% out-of-the-box fit. That is based on a total requirement for this HRM system of over 21,000 Function Points of software development, a very large application for any organization. The initial front runner package that they were hoping to purchase only gave them 434 Function Points of those requirements out of the box, which equates to the 2% function fit. There was an additional 636 Function Points in the package, or 3% of what was needed, that partially satisfied the requirements but still had to undergo some modification. Finally, they were left with over 20,000 Function Points, or 95% of the application, that would still have to be developed. It was a shocking analysis to the managers and architects who thought the package would be a good fit for their requirements.

This analysis resulted in solutions that were selected and funded based on real data, not politics or gut feel. One of the COTS solutions was rejected and another with a better fit to requirements was selected. The Function Fit Analysis also provided a solid funding estimate for the customization work needed and provided critical information to one of the organizations that eventually decided to change their business processes in order to better fit the COTS software and reduce the funding for customization.

Managing Change of Scope—Case 8: Major IT Service Provider

The final case study is based on a major IT vendor with a project that had gotten out of hand. The vendor knew that requirements had been constantly changing on a daily basis and that they had to get things under control quickly. Unfortunately, the project was a fixed-price contract. Supposedly, the requirements were fixed as well, but in reality they were not. Changes in scope are a common occurrence. Even small projects on average increase approximately 35%. For instance, a project starts out at 100 Function Points in the requirements phase, but during the functional design phase increases by 20%. During detail design, the size increases by 10% and suddenly the project is up to 135 Function Points for a total scope creep of 35%.

Large projects that are thousands of Function Points commonly experience scope creep of over 100%. It happens all the time but companies are usually not very good about measuring it and managing it. This major IT service provider decided to put the proper controls and measures in place and began with the counting of Function Points as defined by the original requirements.

At the start of the project, the fixed price was determined based on an application that had requirements related to about 920 Function Points. This is about the size of an average-sized application. A year later, when we measured the size during the functional design phase, the Function Point count had increased to 1650 Function Points. This represented an 80% increase in functionality. It doubled in size the following year and kept on growing.

The change of scope analysis (see Figure 14.6) opened the eyes of the customer. They finally had a mechanism to quantify the changes in requirements that they had requested and could now justify the vendors request for increases in funding. The contract was renegotiated because the vendor had implemented a process to track, document, and quantify changes in scope. The customer, who was very unhappy in the early years of the project, was transformed into a satisfied customer. The major IT service provider saved their reputation as a top notch vendor and was able to secure additional funding. The increase in the contract price helped the vendor avoid a $4 million loss.

Getting Started with Measurement

As documented by the case studies, measurement can be a valuable tool for decision making that can often result in improving productivity and reducing costs. So, how do organizations get started using measurement? The answer depends on a number of factors including the following:

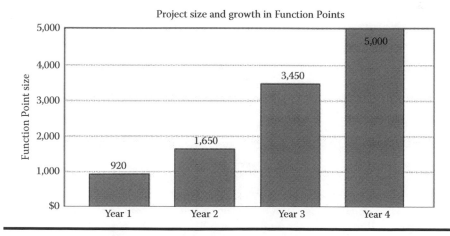

Figure 14.6   Measuring change of scope.

- Size of organization
- Past history with measurement
- Need to improve and reduce cost
- Need to address a specific problem
- Availability of funding a measurement initiative

In the best of circumstances, establishing an ongoing organization-wide measurement program is desirable because it provides decision-making information as issues are identified. Establishing an ongoing program typically starts by defining the goals of the organization and then determining what measures should be in place to track progress against those goals. Defining the high-level measures is followed by a more detailed analysis of what data needs to be collected and what type of reporting is required. A strategy and plan for implementation should also be developed. The strategy and plan should address the following:

- Marketing and communicating measurement to the organization
- Training and education requirements
- Resource and funding levels
- Pace of implementation and evolution of the program
- Measurement tools and systems

Not all organizations can afford a full-blown measurement program. Others are not totally convinced of the benefits. In these situations, piloting measurement on a small number of projects and/or applications is often a good choice for getting started. This allows the organization to collect and report measurement information without the initial expense of establishing an ongoing process and support organization. In most cases, the pilot will provide management with the right perspective so they can see the potential benefits and make a decision to move forward.

Many organizations prefer to start a measurement program by conducting a quality and productivity baseline or benchmark study. This is a particularly good option for organizations that want to quickly identify and implement productivity and quality improvements. A baseline also collects a lot of information in a relatively short period of time in order to establish a repository for the measurement program early. In addition, the organization gains a great deal of experience when performing a baseline or benchmark because they are often led by an experienced external expert.

Many measurement programs are established because organizations are considering or have decided to enter into an outsourcing agreement. In this case, measurement is needed as a way of managing supplier performance. Many of these agreements, as demonstrated in some of the case studies, will base cost or improvement terms and conditions on measurement. This typically requires a baseline and benchmark comparison to establish the initial targets.

Lastly, you can get started by finding the right opportunity that targets a specific issue. There are many opportunities to provide measurement analysis for good decision making, for better managing a project, or to find specific ways to improve quality and productivity and reduce costs. As demonstrated by the case studies, these opportunities include assessing vendor bids, estimating software projects, evaluating packaged software, determining proper staffing levels for maintenance support, determining the effectiveness of offshore resources, and managing change of scope.

Measurement as quantified by the case studies almost always results in significant improvement. Those organizations that measure typically increase productivity by 2 to 3 times more than those organizations that do not measure. So, start measuring and start saving.

About the Author

Scott Goldfarb, president of Q/P Management Group, is an international consultant, instructor, and speaker with over 30 years of software experience. Scott specializes in helping organizations improve software quality and productivity through measurement. He has assisted dozens of organizations involved in outsourcing arrangements and is considered an industry expert in outsourcing, measurement, and estimating. His other areas of expertise include Function Point Analysis, benchmarking, software development methodologies, quality assurance, and project management.

Prior to the founding of Q/P Management Group, Scott was vice president of Professional Services for Software Productivity Research, Inc. (SPR), specializing in software measurement and estimating. Scott was also a managing consultant with Nolan, Norton and Company, where he was responsible for the management of various client assignments, including 2 years of international engagements working with European companies. Scott worked as a manager and systems analyst for Varian/Extrion, a high-tech manufacturer, where he assisted in the establishment and management of an MIS department and distributed data processing installation. Prior to this, he served as an account executive and customer service/production manager for Automatic Data Processing (ADP), a data processing service bureau specializing in financial applications.

Scott received his B.S. degree in Business Administration from Boston University in 1975 and attended the M.B.A. program at Suffolk University in 1979–1980. Scott has been certified by the International Function Point Users Group (IFPUG) as a Certified Function Point Specialist (CFPS) and served as IFPUG president in 2001–2003.

Scott has spoken at numerous conferences, including the International Function Point Users Group (IFPUG), the Better Software Conference, the Software Technology Conference (STC), and the Quality Assurance Institute (QAI). Scott has also written a number of articles published in industry magazines and association journals.

Company Information

Q/P Management Group, Inc. (QPMG) specializes in software measurement, estimating, quality assurance, and process improvement to increase productivity and reduce costs. Company expertise includes Measurement Program Design and Implementation, IFPUG Certified Function Point Analysis and Training, Outsourcing Evaluation and Vendor Management, Software Engineering Institute (SEI) Capability Maturity Model Integration (CMMI) Assessments and Training, and Software Quality Assurance techniques.

QPMG's Software Benchmark Database is one of the world's largest sources of metrics data. The database is used by numerous companies and government agencies to benchmark software development and support, establish estimates for software development projects, and establish fair market prices for software products.

QPMG also develops and distributes software tools that estimate software projects, support software measurement programs, and aid in Function Point Analysis activities. More information is available at www.QPMG.com or by contacting their offices at (781) 438–2692.

Chapter 15

Measurement and Motivation

Tara Kelly

Contents

Introduction

This chapter will investigate the topic of measurement as a motivational tool. Measurement can be used to motivate software professionals and managers, and a by-product of this is an improvement of the overall software development process.

The chapter will first look at software measurement and Function Point counting in particular as a measurement method. Following this, the subject of motivation will be reviewed. These two topics will then be examined using a case study. This will describe the implementation of a software measurement program in a medium-sized software organization.

Software Measurement

Why measure software? There is a myriad of reasons why a company would measure their software. They may use the data to plan, to make decisions, or to improve process [1–4]. However, the practice of establishing a software measurement program can produce many questions. What do we measure? How do we measure? At what point in development should we measure? How should we produce the results? Who will be reading the results? Over the years, organizations have found answers to these questions and have gone on to set up effective measurement programs. Due to this, software measurement has become widely recognized as an effective means to understand, monitor, plan, control, and aid in the development of software [5]. As software techniques and languages have evolved, so too have the measurement methods that can be used. The earliest method to take hold was the lines of code (LOC) measure [6]. This was used to measure a programmer's productivity (how many LOC they produce per day/month) and program quality (defects per LOC or kilo lines of code [KLOC]). However, this measure is open to the criticism that different programmers will produce different numbers of LOC depending on their programming style. In addition, this method is limited by not allowing projects or tasks to be compared if they are developed on different platforms or using different languages. For example, how to compare LOC in Java versus LOC in RPG? This led to a focus on technology-independent software measurement techniques [7, 8], which prompted Albrecht in 1979 to pioneer Function Point (FP) counting [9].

Due to the independent nature of FP counting, it could be used to compare projects that use different technologies. In its essence, FP counting is a technology-independent method of observing/measuring a software system from the functional viewpoint. While a large amount of the work effort of Function Points is contained in the actual counting activity, the value of the method can only really be seen in the analysis of the resulting data. A measurement program using FP as its basis can carry out analysis on productivity, quality, reliability, and many other areas within the software development process. In essence, the FP figures can be used to analyze most elements involved in a software project once the counting practices are reliable. As with most statistical methods, the benefit also increases with the amount of data gathered for analysis. If a small amount of FP counts are available, this will reduce the reliability and relevance of the resulting data. Therefore, the key to success is to build up a large store of FP counts and project data for any software that is to be measured [10].

History of FP as a Measurement Tool

After Function Point Analysis (FPA) was introduced in the late 1970s, the International Function Point Users Group (IFPUG) was established and succeeded in bringing FP to a much wider audience. The development and publication of the Function Point Counting Practices Manual introduced consistency to the method and became the recognized industry standard for FP [11].

In the late 1980s and early 1990s, FP was used by a large number of companies (AT&T, Xerox, General Electric) [12]. However, during the 1990s, there was a drop-off in use; this is a well-known pattern of the Gartner "hype curve" [13]. In this curve, methodologies enjoy a large acceptance after initial implementation and reach a maximum "hype"; this happened to FP in the late 1980s and early 1990s. Then a methodology tends to fall into a "trough of disillusionment," usually prompted by misuse and unaddressed problems. In the late 1990s, FP suffered from this trough because of a number of issues. Symons [14] carried out an investigation into this and found the reasons were the following:

- Often the gathering of the software metrics for projects was delegated too far down in the organization. Junior metrics staff found it too difficult to obtain reliable data and because of this the resulting analysis data was unreliable— an example of "garbage in, garbage out."
- If the programs did not fail because of poor data, then the reason tended to be poor analysis and presentation of the data. Senior managers did not give feedback on the type of information they wanted to see, and because of this, they regarded the reports as useless, which led to FP being cut out of budgets.
- A large number of companies were using FP because they produced bespoke software for themselves, and when packaged software became more accessible for their needs, they reverted to using this instead. The result of which was that they no longer needed to measure their software productivity and discontinued their FP projects.
- In a similar vein to the previous issue, some companies started outsourcing their software production and again, no longer needed to measure internal productivity. Unless it was part of the outsourcing contract, FP was not necessarily being used in the outsourcing organization.

These issues related more to company culture and process rather than a problem with the FP methodology. Other concerns that arose related to the stability and consistency of FP counting within organizations, a number of studies investigated these and proposed solutions:

- Low and Jeffery's study [15] indicated that there was a variance of FP results between analysts due to experience. They concluded that experience in the application of Function Points is important to achieving consistent results.
- Emrick [16] and Symons [17] both recommend that the key to consistency with FP counts is keeping the number of people carrying out the counts and analysis to a minimum and ensuring that there is a process in place. Decisions reached between the analysts should become internal standards and should be documented for auditing purposes. Additionally, the counters should receive frequent practice rather than carrying out sporadic counts.
- The use of FP software also leads to consistency between counters and allows for a constant application of FP practices and calculations.

However, these problems were not addressed in time and caused the downward trend in FP use. Since then, nothing else has filled the requirement for a technology–independent measurement technique. In the meantime, the evolution of software meant that most companies were beginning to work across multiple platforms, technologies, and languages. The FP measurement technique was perfectly suited to this form of environment, and since 2000, FPA has been climbing out of this trough with renewed interest and the benefit of hindsight to address any issues that may have occurred with the method [17]. The renewed interest in FP has brought about an increase in publications in the area and an increase in the number of companies using it, including the MDS software company on which the case study in this chapter is based.

Overview of Measurement in MDS

MDS (www.martindawessystems.com) is a medium-sized IT company that produces telecom billing solutions. Up until 2009, there was no software measurement program within the organization. The company had grown its product base over the years and had branched into new technologies and languages. Due to this, there was an inability and reluctance to compare projects to each other due to the differences in platforms. The decision was made to establish a software measurement process in order to aid with management decisions, measure productivity, and for use as a motivational tool. The results of measurements would be used as the basis for a KPI system for reviewing the development process. The next decision was which measurement tool to use in this new process. The products being developed are mainly end user focused, and the functionality supplied is an important part of the development process. For all these reasons, FP counting was chosen as the appropriate method for measurement in MDS.

For MDS, the advantages of FP analysis mainly arise from its technology independence. This independence means all projects and products can be measured in the same way and all developers can be measured as well, regardless of area of expertise. The result is consistency of measurement in an organization [14]. Another advantage is the capability of Function Points to be used at very early stages of development, such as specification stages, making it possible to use the method for estimation [15, 18]. These estimates can then feed into a motivational methodology to motivate engineers to reach their deadlines and feed into a KPI process at review time. The use of Function Points also supplies a measurement "language" that can be understood by technical and non-technical personnel in the organization because of its focus on a system user's external view [19]. This is important in an organization where the product stakeholders include salespeople, project managers, customer managers, and other groups who may not be familiar with technical specifications.

As discussed above, any difficulties with FP relate to the implementation of the method within the organization, and these can be solved with the use of a dedicated counting team that is well trained and uses consistent counting practices. The advantages that can be gained from using the FP measurement method outweigh any difficulties that may arise. A number of studies carried out have found that there is a clear relationship between FP components and work effort, and they have concluded that Function Points are a more consistent measure of system size or production functional size than other metrics [15, 20, and 21].

Summary

Function Point counting is not without its issues as a measurement technique, but these would seem to relate more to the implementation of the method than the method itself. By identifying and addressing these issues at the start of the software measurement initiative in MDS, the reliability and use of the produced analysis figures are significantly increased. This is very important if one of the outputs of the process is data that will be used as employee review and motivation tools.

Therefore, in order to use measurement for motivation, it is first necessary to understand motivation as a management activity. What does it take to motivate people? What is needed for people to engage with a motivational process? Can employees ever see measurement as a positive thing? For answers to these questions, we must turn to motivational theory.

Motivation

The definition of motivation is "internal and external factors that stimulate desire and energy in people to be continually interested in and committed to a job, role, or subject and exert persistent effort in attaining a goal" [22]. It is the role of management to ensure that employees remain motivated in their job and thus ensure high productivity and quality of work. Management can only control the factors internal to the organization, such as work environment and remuneration. However, they must also be aware of any external factors that may be influencing an employee. These can range from personal family matters to the point that an individual is at in their career. What motivates a newly graduated developer can be quite different to what motivates an experienced manager. Therefore, an organization can have many different motivational methods being used at any one time to motivate people at different levels and in different roles. Over the years, there have been many different theories of motivation, all attempting to identify the correct mix of elements that can be used to keep people motivated. The following sections will review some of the more commonly used motivation theories.

Hawthorne Experiments

Between the years 1924 and 1932, a series of experiments were carried out in a factory called the Hawthorne Works that produced telephone relays. These studies were devised and carried out by George Elton Mayo [23]. The main objective was to study the impact on productivity by changing factors in a workers' environment and varying elements in their routine.

The first of these studies was called the Illumination Experiments. The objective of the investigation was to determine if varying the level of lighting being used in the factory would increase output. The results of the experiments were measured by counting how many finished relays each worker produced. Mayo wanted to discover if there was a direct correlation between lighting and productivity. Two groups of workers were used. They were placed in separate rooms and while the light was changed in one room, it remained constant in the other. The findings showed that output actually increased in both groups. This was attributed to the fact that the test subjects were aware they were being monitored. Therefore, the increase in productivity was due to an awareness of being monitored rather than a changing of lighting [24].

This led to another experiment named the Relay Assembly experiment. This was designed to study the effects of rest breaks, length of working day, and refreshments. Two participants were selected from the factory floor and they were allowed to select another four colleagues to join them. The group was moved to a separate room to work. Over a period of 5 years, a supervisor worked with and monitored the group. During the study, a number of variables were changed; when this happened the supervisor would discuss the changes with the group and sometimes they would act on the suggestions of the group. The variables included the following:

- Breaks—first giving them two 5-minute breaks and then changing to two 10-minute breaks
- Providing food during breaks
- Shortening the day by 30 minutes

Each time the variable changed, productivity increased. Researchers concluded that the increase in productivity was again due to monitoring rather than any particular factor [25]. Mayo believed that the reason for productivity increase was due to the test subjects becoming a team and working well together rather than any specific variable [23].

The last of these experiments investigated the impact of payment incentives on productivity. This study had the opposite effect on productivity than expected. The workers involved in the study were afraid that the management would use the results to lower the base rate of pay. In order to combat this and sabotage the experiment, they worked at an artificially slow rate. Observation of the group showed that informal "cliques" had formed, and these groups enforced this unproductive rate of work. The researchers interpreted this as evidence of how informal work relations can have an enormous influence on motivation and performance [26].

Since these experiments were carried out, there has been some criticism leveled at them. Academics contend that any number of elements could have impacted the productivity levels [27–29]; it may not have been the variables that Mayo was influencing. However, most are in agreement that these were among the first studies that recognized that the very act of monitoring people could impact their behavior for better or worse. This "Hawthorne Effect" is now taken into consideration when reporting on in vivo experiments [30]. This can be implemented in a practical way by applying monitoring within an organization; it is the responsibility of management to identify the level of monitoring necessary to increase productivity. The level and type of monitoring will differ from organization to organization and will also differ depending on the level and role of the employee. Measurement of people's work can be used as one method of monitoring, and thus can be used to motivate and in turn increase productivity and quality.

Maslow's Hierarchy of Needs

In 1943, Abraham Maslow put forward his theory on motivation [31]. This theory proposes that human motivation can take the form of a pyramid with the largest and most fundamental needs at the bottom and the needs becoming more focused as the pyramid climbs. The theory states that rather than being motivated by one need, humans are motivated by multiple needs and these needs exist in a hierarchical order. The hierarchy of needs with examples of how these needs are fulfilled in employment can be seen in Figure 15.1.

The lowest and first motivational level of the hierarchy contains physiological needs. These cover the most basic of human needs. In a person's private life, these are satisfied by the availability of food, water, and shelter. However, there are equivalent needs in an employment environment, for example, a warm place to work with basic pay for a job done. Once this level is satisfied, then the next level of needs is activated and can be used as a motivator. A person desiring physical safety will devote their efforts to securing a safer environment, and they will not be

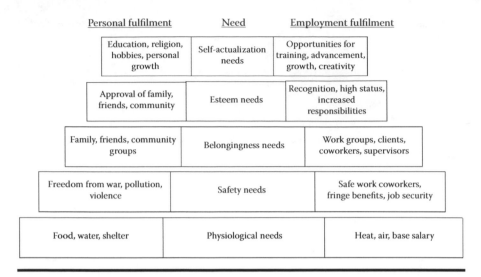

Figure 15.1   Maslow's hierarchy of needs.

concerned with higher level needs. If an employee has access to a basic salary and a warm place to work, they are no longer motivated by these things. The next level becomes a motivator, so once physiological needs are met, a person starts to aim for safety needs.

The safety level of the hierarchy refers to the need for a safe and secure physical and emotional environment and freedom from intimidation. In order to satisfy this in a working environment, employees must be supplied with a safe workplace and job security. In times of uncertainty in an organization, employees can be motivated to work harder to achieve the need of job security.

In software development organizations, the lower level needs are generally satisfied, as workers have a safe environment to work in and are financially remunerated for their work. Therefore, for the purpose of this chapter, the higher levels of Maslow's theory are of more interest.

The third layer is concerned with social needs and involves feelings of belonging. These needs reflect the desire to be accepted by one's peers, have friendships, and be part of a group. Within a workplace, people want to feel that they are an important part of the organization. This is often achieved by placing workers in teams or lines and also organizing team meetings and social events. This encourages people to get to know their colleagues and fulfill these belonging needs. This relates back to Mayo's findings that productivity increased when people worked in groups in the Relay Assembly experiment [23].

The esteem level can be further broken down into low-level and high-level esteem needs. The lower level is focused on recognition from others, as well as gaining status and responsibility. This can be satisfied by being promoted within an organization, or being awarded or singled out for praise. This higher level of esteem is a need for self-respect. This can be achieved by knowing that a job has been done well. One way of helping a person achieve this is to allow them to self-monitor and determine their own best work and areas for improvement. This is often done by using a self-appraisal process in organizations.

This highest level in the hierarchy is self-actualization needs. These represent the need for self-fulfillment. At this level, the focus is on developing one's full potential, increasing one's competence, and becoming a better person. An organization can help a person achieve this by giving them opportunities for training, advancement, and growth in the company. This type of need becomes more evident as someone progresses in their careers, as they have satisfied the lower levels of needs. They have a good job, are well remunerated, and have good relationships with people they work with. At this point, they may become demotivated if there is no chance for growth in the company. Sometimes this can mean a new role or new training. This causes a person to become motivated again because of new challenges.

Using measurement as a motivator would be connected to the esteem needs level. If measurement is used correctly, it can allow an employee to feel good about their work by being compared to their group as a whole. They will be able to identify areas where they need improvement, which will motivate them to work on these areas. In addition, they should receive recognition when they are achieving high results. At the highest level of the needs hierarchy, self-actualization, measurement can also be a useful tool. An employee's measurement results can help to identify training possibilities, or could identify a new role an employee would be suited to, or when they could be used as a mentor for other groups in the organization.

In 1969, Clayton Alderfer expanded on Maslow's theory in an effort to simplify it and respond to criticisms of its lack of empirical evaluation [32]. Alderfer's theory became known as the ERG theory and was similar to the Maslow hierarchy by also being hierarchical in nature and presuming that individuals move up the hierarchy one step at a time. However, Alderfer reduced the number of need categories to three. He grouped the lower two levels into one category called existence needs. The belongingness needs were categorized as relatedness needs. Finally the two upper levels, esteem needs and self-actualization needs, were placed in a category called growth. He also suggested that the movement through the hierarchy was more complex than Maslow suggested. The notion of a frustration–regression principle was introduced. This proposed that the failure to meet a high-order need might trigger a regression to an already fulfilled lower-order need [33]. Thus, a worker who cannot fulfill the need for personal growth may revert to a lower order social need and redirect his or her efforts toward financial remuneration. This would imply that in order for an employee to be motivated enough to move through a needs hierarchy, the goals must be realistic and attainable. If they are not and the person fails, they will then regress back down the hierarchy. When we examine this in terms of the impact of measurement on motivation, it can be concluded that measurement will help in identifying realistic goals for an employee. Each member of a team can be measured against their own performance and the performance of the team as a whole, leading to goals and objectives that are tailored to the individual.

Herzberg's Two-Factor Theory

In 1959, Fredrick Herzberg developed another popular theory of motivation called the two-factor theory [34]. Herzberg interviewed hundreds of workers about times when they were highly motivated in their jobs and other times when they were dissatisfied and unmotivated in work. His findings suggested that the work characteristics associated with dissatisfaction were quite different from those pertaining to satisfaction, which prompted the notion that two factors influence work motivation. This can be seen in Figure 15.2.

On either side of the neutral space, two entirely separate dimensions contribute to an employee's behavior at work. The first of these are called hygiene factors and involve the presence or absence of job dissatisfiers such as working conditions, pay, company policies, and interpersonal relationships. When hygiene factors are poor, work is dissatisfying. However, good hygiene factors simply remove the dissatisfaction; they do not in themselves cause people to become highly satisfied and motivated in their work.

For motivation to occur, there is a need for the second set of factors that influence job satisfaction. These motivators are high-level needs and include achievement, recognition, responsibility, and opportunity for growth. Herzberg believed that when motivators are absent, workers are neutral toward work, but when

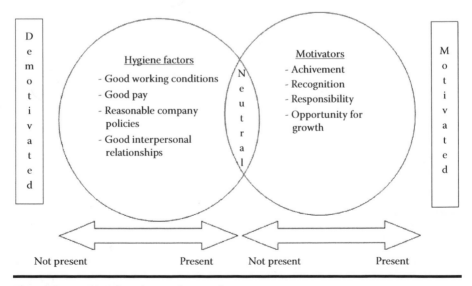

Figure 15.2   Herzberg's two-factor theory.

motivators are present, workers are highly motivated and satisfied. Thus, hygiene factors and motivators represent two distinct factors that influence workers [35].

Hygiene factors work only in the area of dissatisfaction. Unsafe working conditions or a noisy work environment will cause people to be dissatisfied. However, the correction of these will not lead to a high level of motivation and satisfaction. Motivators such as challenges, responsibility, and recognition must be in place before employees will be highly motivated to excel at their work. The implication of the two-factor theory for managers is clear. Providing hygiene factors will eliminate employee dissatisfaction but will not motivate workers to high achievement levels. On the other hand, recognition, challenges, and opportunities for personal growth are powerful motivators and will promote high satisfaction and performance. The manager's role is to remove dissatisfiers—that is, provide hygiene factors sufficient enough to meet basic needs—and then use motivators to meet higher level needs and propel employees toward greater achievement and satisfaction.

In terms of using measurement as a tool to aid motivation, its place in relation to this theory would seem to be in the dimension of the motivators. As with the needs hierarchy theories, in order to identify and measure an employee's achievements and goals, they must be measured against other colleagues and also against past metrics. This way, if a person has excelled, then he or she can receive recognition and a feeling of self-worth. If they are not achieving a certain standard, then areas for training and improvement can be identified and rather than damaging an employee's self-esteem, they can instead be used as an opportunity for growth and improvement. However, according to Herzberg, before any of this is possible good hygiene factors must be in place otherwise people will not be in a position to be motivated.

Job Characteristics Theory

Within software engineering, a commonly cited model of motivation is the Job Characteristics Theory [36]. This is mainly focused on the area of job satisfaction, but there would seem to be a connection between that and an employee feeling motivated. Hackman and Oldham [36] defined five characteristics that impact job satisfaction. They are the following:

1. Task identity—a piece of work can be identified as having a beginning and an end
2. Autonomy—level of choice an employee has over their schedule and work procedures
3. Skills variety—number of different activities performed by the employee
4. Task significance—impact of employee's work on the final product, other colleagues, or the work environment
5. Job feedback—information provided to the employee regarding his performance

These characteristics can be combined to reflect the overall motivating potential of a job; this potential is given a score called the Motivating Potential Score (MPS). First, an employee completes a questionnaire that consists of 23 statements. They have to indicate whether each statement is an accurate or inaccurate description of their present job. The scoring system ranges from 1 to 5, where 1 is very inaccurate and 5 is very accurate. Once the questionnaire is complete, a scoring key is used to allocate a score to each of the five characteristics above. Five of the statements relate to skill variety, four to task identity, four to task significance, four to autonomy and six to feedback. An average is then calculated for each of the characteristics. The resulting figures are then used to calculate the MPS using the formula:

$$MPS = (\text{skill variety} + \text{task identity} + \text{task significance}/3) \times \text{autonomy} \times \text{feedback} \tag{15.1}$$

This displays the relationships between the characteristics and three psychological states:

- Experienced meaningfulness
- Experienced responsibility for outcomes
- Knowledge of actual results

The skill variety, task identity, and task significance affect the experienced meaningfulness of an employee's experience. If an employee experiences meaningfulness, then they feel that the work they are doing is valuable and worthwhile, which in turn gives them a feeling of self-worth. Autonomy then affects the employee's experienced responsibility for the outcome of their task. If the individual experiences personal responsibility, they feel accountable for the work they are doing and the results. Then finally, the feedback characteristic supplies knowledge of the actual results of the work activities [37]. Therefore, a person who has knowledge of the actual results knows and understands how effectively they are performing the job. In order for an employee to be motivated, all three of these psychological states must be present. The outcomes of this situation are the following:

- High internal work motivation
- High "growth" satisfaction
- High general job satisfaction
- High work effectiveness

Internal work motivation is considered the most important of these outcomes. This will lead to an employee being self-rewarded for a good performance. They do not need any external motivators, for example, financial or promotion. The knowledge of achieving their own goals and doing well inspires them to work hard. The "growth" satisfaction comes when a person feels that the challenges and tasks that they are carrying out are leading to personal and professional growth. They recognize this as a positive thing, and it encourages them to take on more challenges. The general job satisfaction outcome reflects a general happiness with their job and tasks while work effectiveness is more directly related to the tasks themselves and is measured by quality and quantity of work. If any one of the three psychological states is not present, some of these outcomes will be weakened, which will lead to the motivation of the employee being weakened.

In order for this theory to work, three "moderators" are needed; these refer to the characteristics of the people who are carrying out the task.

1. Knowledge and skill—the necessary knowledge and skills to carry out the task; the employee must know they are capable of achieving the results necessary to complete the task.
2. Growth need strength—the strength of a person's need to grow professionally.
3. Work context—this refers to the general conditions of work such as pay, job security, coworkers, and managers.

These personal characteristics need to be strong in order for the psychological states to be achieved, and in turn, to result in strong motivational outcomes [38].

Similar to the other theories reviewed above, it is easy to see how measurement can fit into this motivational theory. One of the characteristics of the model is job feedback, and this can be achieved using measurement techniques. If an employee has a well-defined set of objectives and goals, then their performance can be measured and compared to these, which will allow them to reach the psychological state of gaining knowledge of the actual results of their tasks. If they have reached their goals, then the results will be a strong set of the listed outcomes. Their internal work motivation will be high due to good self-esteem and personal recognition of a job done well. If they have improved their performance since last measured, then they will be aware of their "growth" within their role. Both of these lead to a general job satisfaction, and if an employee is performing well, then this will impact positively on their team, which will then improve the work environment. Finally, an employee's work effectiveness can be measured as it relates to quality and productivity. Therefore, a measurement technique as a motivator plays a large part in the Job Characteristics Model.

Motivating Software Engineers

As demonstrated in the earlier sections, much work has been done on developing motivation techniques and theories over the years. It has now become an accepted standard in organizations to use some form of motivation for staff, whether it be bonus incentives or promotions. However, within the software engineering field, motivation is increasingly noted as a damaging problem. It has even been cited as being one of the main reasons for software development project failure [39]. When software engineers are viewed as an independent group rather than being part of the larger generic group of "employees," studies have shown that there is a distinctive personality profile for them [40]. They tend to be less motivated by the traditional methods of rewards and recognition and are more motivated by the nature of the job, their successes, and challenges [41, 42]. This profile would suggest that the Job Characteristics Model would suit software engineers much more than an attempt to apply a hierarchy of needs to them.

Therefore, in order to motivate software engineers, we must first have a profile for them. A number of papers have identified characteristics that can be used to build this profile. Beecham et al [43] have placed these characteristics into three linked categories. The first of these contains the "raw" characteristics. The following are the straightforward attributes of a software engineer.

- Need for organizational stability [44–48]
- Technically competent [44, 46, 49–51]
- Seek out promotion [45, 52–54]
- Growth oriented [47, 50, 52, 55–60]
- Need for competent supervision [45, 46, 51, 61]
- Low need for social interaction [41, 55–57, 40, 62, 63]
- Need to be involved in setting their own goals [57]
- Need to receive feedback [57, 58]
- Need to have a geographically stable workplace [46]
- Need to believe their job is worthwhile and meaningful [46, 47, 51]
- Need to be independent in their role [41, 46–48, 54, 56, 60]
- Need to have variety in their tasks [46, 48, 60, 64]
- Are marketable (this is probably due to a number of the preceding characteristics) [48, 60]
- Need to be challenged within their role [48, 54, 60, 62]
- Creative [60, 65]
- Need to be identifiable by a group/role title [47, 51, 52, 60, 66]

These characteristics help to build a general image of a software engineer as a creative, driven individual who needs feedback on their performance in order to believe their job is worthwhile and ensure they are valuable to the organization. This type of profile would seem to correspond to the job characteristics that impact job satisfaction [36].

- Task identity and autonomy = need their role to be identifiable, need to be independent, and need to set their own goals
- Skills variety = need to have variety
- Task significance = need to believe their job is worthwhile and meaningful
- Job feedback = need to receive feedback

However, these characteristics do not appear in every software engineer in equal measure. Beecham et al [43] have identified control factors that relate to an individual's personality. These control factors then determine the strength of these "raw" characteristics within each individual. The control factors are as follows:

- Personality traits [49, 53, 61, 65, 67–69]
- Desired career paths [46, 47, 70]
- Competency in their role [49, 54, 71, 72, 73]

There are another set of factors that impact on the characteristics, and Beecham et al [43] call these moderators. These also influence the level of software engineering characteristics but are external to the individual rather than personal factors.

- The stage they are at in their career [49, 68, 73–79]
- Culture (country they work in) [45, 48, 52, 56, 58, 62, 66, 79]
- Job type/role [59, 62, 80, 81]
- State of the IT profession [41, 78, 80, 82, 83]
- Opportunities/policies within the organization they work in [47]

These moderators dictate the strength of the characteristics of a software engineer. Although a general profile of a software engineer can be built using the main characteristics, not every individual will have all 16 characteristics and the presence or absence of them is dictated by control factors. In addition, the characteristics that are present will be at varying levels and this is dictated by the moderators that are influencing an individual.

In terms of motivation, a general motivational technique can be developed for software engineers based on the characteristics you would expect to find and the moderators that are dependent on cultural and organizational environment, but there must be allowance for each individual's control factors and personality.

Motivating Factors

Once we have built up a profile of the software engineer and understand what characteristics are most likely to be present in employees, the next step is to apply this knowledge to identifying motivators. The following motivators have been identified by studies over time, and these are in no particular order:

- Rewards and incentives [50, 64, 77, 84–93]
- Training and specialization [46, 50, 41, 66, 84, 89, 90, 94–97]
- Variety of work [52–54, 66, 70, 78, 84, 85, 89, 91–93, 96, 98]
- Clear career path and opportunity to climb within an organization [46, 52, 54, 66, 70, 78, 84, 85, 88, 89, 90–93, 96, 98]
- Assigning responsibility to a person [50, 54, 85, 95, 98, 99]

- Good management and good communication [50, 53, 61, 41, 66, 78, 85, 87, 89, 90, 92, 94, 95, 97, 100, 101]
- Put supportive relationships in place [41, 51, 53, 63, 66, 84–86, 90, 97, 102–105]
- Allow for a good work/life balance [47, 66, 84–86, 105, 106]
- Working for a successful company [47, 85]
- Allow employees to work in groups and participate in the company as a whole [53, 64, 66, 74, 84, 85, 90, 93, 95, 99, 101, 104, 107–109]
- Giving feedback on performance [52, 53, 62, 64, 74, 78, 86, 97, 108, 110]
- Recognition for a job well done, not in terms of rewards but just personal recognition [41, 50, 51, 53, 64, 66, 87, 89, 90, 92, 95, 109]
- Equity [93, 108, 111]
- Trust/respect for employees [51, 74, 99, 111]
- Ensure employees have technically challenging work [41, 54, 83, 87, 89, 95, 100, 105, 106, 108, 109]
- Ensure a secure and stable working environment [64, 66, 84, 87–89, 91, 97, 100, 112]
- Ensure an engineer can identify with their tasks [41, 50–52, 54, 61, 62, 64, 74, 88–92, 94, 95, 97, 108, 109, 113]
- Allow an employee to have autonomy [50, 52–54, 74, 97, 108–110]
- Appropriate working conditions, tools, environment, etc. [47, 52, 88, 105, 108, 114, 115]
- Ensure that the engineer knows their task is significant and making a contribution [51, 52, 54, 74, 89, 102]
- Ensure there are sufficient resources available [66, 89]

A number of these motivators would be considered as things that would be standard in most organizations, that is, clean, appropriate working environments with all the tools a person needs. If we look back at Herzberg's two-factor theory [34], these could be regarded as hygiene factors and as such are not motivators alone, rather they place the employees in a neutral space at which point other elements can be used to motivate them. There are factors that need to be considered when putting in place any of the above motivators.

- Job fit—if the job does not fit a person and their abilities, then no amount of motivators will impact a person [41, 55, 56, 58, 78, 79, 104, 115–121]
- Tailoring practices—how tasks are assigned to people within the organization [54, 84, 100, 103, 112, 116]
- Long-term/short-term strategies—the organization's plans for the future and how it runs its business [84]
- Temporal effects—issues that may be occurring within the organization at any one time [44, 83, 97, 113, 119, 122–126]
- Individual differences—these are the moderators discussed in the Job Characteristics Model [48, 70, 96, 97, 108, 127–133]

These factors will have influence over how successful motivators will be in an organization. For example, if the job fit is poor for a large number of employees, then no amount of rewards will force them to be motivated. Therefore, the above factors should be taken into consideration when implementing motivation.

Another factor that needs to be considered is whether or not new strategies need to be put in place in order to motivate staff. A number of the motivators listed above can only be achieved if there is some form of measurement taking place in the company.

- Rewards and incentives cannot be decided upon unless performance is being measured and a baseline is being used. Then employees who perform above this baseline are rewarded.
- Identifying training needs is much easier if employees can be compared across a role and gaps in their expertise can be identified, but this can only be done if there is an objective method to measure expertise.
- Similar to the above, an employee's career path can have very definite steps and growth if there are measurement methods in place to decide when someone should move up levels in their role.
- Feedback should be given in a measured way as well as anecdotal evidence. This way, employees can see how they are performing across the organization and within their own role.
- As above, a person's contribution to the organization/team should be measurable, this way any feedback people receive is objective and factual, rather than being possibly emotionally driven or subjective.

Motivating software engineers is not as straightforward as just financially rewarding them at various points depending on performance. The various characteristics that have been identified for software engineers make up a complex picture, which must be addressed when setting up a motivating program. Studies have identified a number of motivators that can be used for this type of employee and a number of these require a measurement technique to be in place before they can be used effectively [128, 129, 130, 131, 132, 133].

Summary

Over the years, a large number of motivational theories have been put forward, and for all their differences, a number of elements are common to them all. People have a series of needs that exist in a hierarchy, and as each need is met, the person climbs up the hierarchy and the next need is activated. Some needs are quite basic and when these needs are satisfied, a person is not necessarily motivated but rather is in a neutral state. Once in this state they are in a position to be motivated. Motivators can differ depending on the person, culture, environment, etc. When we investigate software engineers' characteristics, we can build a profile of an individual who is motivated by more than just a basic needs hierarchy. They require a number of elements to be present in order for them to be motivated. These are discussed in detail above, but in general, they reflect a group of people for whom financial reward is not enough in and of itself. Rather, engineers need to know they are valued, doing important work, and are appreciated within the organization. They relish the chance to develop and learn, and because of this, enjoy being challenged in work. In order to ensure that an employee of this type is kept motivated, it is important that any motivating procedures in place are objective and allow for tracking of performance, growth, and training for individuals/groups in the organization. This information should be made available to the employees as their profile indicates that they appreciate and expect feedback.

All of this would indicate that measurement could be used as a motivator for software engineers. It allows for all the feedback and motivators discussed above and allows for objective feedback that comes from a scientific place rather than an anecdotal feedback mechanism that has a lack of transparency and is open to criticism. Measurement and motivation would seem to sit comfortably together. The following sections will detail a case study where a measurement process was put in place in order to motivate and measure employees in a software development company. This in-vivo study will highlight the difficulties of implementing such a process and how to overcome these problems.

Measurement and Motivation in an Organization

In order to understand how introducing measurement as a method of motivation impacts an organization, it is best to examine it in a real-life setting. For this purpose, the following case study will review a software measurement program in a medium-sized software company called MDS (www.martindawesystems.com).

Background of the Company

MDS is a software company that is headquartered in the United Kingdom and has a satellite office in the southwest of Ireland. The software development process operates across both of these offices to produce software solutions for corporate billing in the telecom arena. Over the years, the organization has built up a product catalog containing a number of applications, each of which fulfills a specific function. The product development department is concerned with constantly evolving these products and producing releases for existing telecom customers as well as the conception and development of new products.

Within this department, the software process used follows a traditional waterfall-style life cycle of design, development, test, documentation, and deployment into a live customer environment. Once this point has been reached, the product or specific release is supported using a helpdesk function within MDS. Approximately

50 developers within the organization work across a number of different platforms using many different languages including Java, SQL, Oracle, XML, RPG, and Lavastorm.

Due to this proliferation of languages and platforms, in the past it was considered very difficult to compare projects/products to each other. There was resistance to software measurement processes being put in place, because it was believed that they would not fairly represent the work that went into the development activity. There were concerns from various groups within the organization that measurement would lead to inaccurate comparisons between projects and more importantly people. Until a technique could be found that addressed these problems, there was no formal software measurement carried out in MDS.

After investigation into this issue, the method of Function Point counting was considered a suitable technique for measurement in this type of organization. Its user functionality focused ethos matched the type of software being produced. In addition, the technology-independent nature of the approach meant that the same technique could be used across the entire product range, allowing for consistent comparison of projects, products, and teams. Once the method had been selected, the measurement process then had to be developed fully and introduced to the organization.

Introducing Measurement to MDS

A measurement process in an organization is not just a case of measuring software and putting out results. There are a large number of questions that must be asked first:

- What is being measured?
- When is it being measured (at what point in the life cycle)?
- Why is it being measured?

In the case of MDS, the answer to what is being measured is that all software produced by the organization was to be measured. Next, in order to answer when it should be measured, we must first look at the reasons for measurement. Within MDS, these reasons were twofold, firstly the productivity of the projects and people was to be analyzed, and then based on this analysis the measurement process was to be used for estimation of future work. To measure how productive a project/piece of work is, the best point for measurement is when the work is complete. For software products in MDS, the work is considered complete when it has been deployed to a live customer environment. Before this occurs, a change could be made to the software due to testing, customer requests, or changes to the environment. For these reasons, the end of the development phase is too dynamic to be a measurement point. A different point was needed to measure software for the purpose of estimation. This measurement needs to take place at the earliest point as possible in the life cycle, early enough that the result is useful but late enough that you are measuring the correct information. It was decided that the ideal point for estimation measurement was after the production of a specification document, as this way the resulting data could be used for pricing and planning purposes. The three questions above had been answered, and the next stage was to set up a measurement team and ensure all information necessary was available.

Measurement Team and Process within MDS

As discussed earlier in this chapter in the section "History of FP as a Measurement Tool," there are a number of recognized pitfalls that can occur when setting up a measurement process. Each of these issues was addressed in MDS in order to ensure the process was stable and produced the desired results.

- Specific FP analysts were selected and formed a team.
- This team was small and focused to allow for experience to build and consistency to develop across the FP counts.
- FP software was purchased to record counts and allow for detailed analysis.
- All software metrics data necessary was gathered.
- Stakeholders from all levels of the organization were included in order to ensure the analysis and representation of data was correct.

The first activity of the team was to carry out a large amount of Function Point counting on existing products that were already in a live state with various customers. Once this was complete, the next step was to determine how long it had taken to develop this work. Using these two pieces of data, the FP count and the time taken to develop the work, it would be possible to calculate the productivity of the software in terms of the number of Function Points developed per day.

The most effective way to collect data on development times is to take it directly from a time logging system. In MDS, every employee logs their time using a web-based time sheet system. This allows project managers to create specific tasks for developers. The developers then log time against these tasks and the time logged can be input into a project plan to track the progression of a project. Tasks are categorized into functional phases, for example, design, development, and non-functional project management. Once a project is complete, the time spent on it can be extracted and input into the measurement system for productivity calculation. This way there is a pureness to the data that allows for true analysis, and it has not already been filtered by someone else's view of the work.

Using this information, a productivity database was built up, containing data relating to functional phases. The type of development activity was split into different categories in order to increase accuracy for the estimation process in the future. Once the database was considered large enough, the second stage of the measurement process was put in place. Each new piece of work undertaken by the organization was measured using FP counting once the specification document had been produced. Using the productivity metrics produced, an estimate was developed for the piece of work. The figures produced represented "effort in man-days." It was decided to express the time in man-days for quotation reasons. The database could just as easily have expressed the time in man-hours as the time is logged this way. Now every piece of work has a target of the amount of days it should take to complete, based on work done in the past.

It is at this point that the measurements can be utilized as a motivational tool. When the estimate is produced, it is placed in a process engine used by MDS, which allows for transparency of procedure. The developer who is assigned the work can then view the estimate and is expected to complete the work within this time frame. Once the work is complete and has been deployed to the customer, the actual time taken can then be extracted using the productivity process detailed above. For every piece of work a developer is involved in, the productivity can be calculated and analyzed. It was decided to incorporate this information into the biyearly reviews for the development team in MDS. Every developer would have a productivity number that they would be expected to reach. This number would not be the same for everyone but would take into consideration their experience, type of work they had been involved in, etc. This process of motivation fulfills a number of the motivational factors as discussed above:

- Assigns responsibility to the engineer—they know what is expected from them and they have the ability to plan and manage their time because of this.
- Challenging—there are times when the estimate may be aggressive and this represents a challenge to the engineer and allows them to stretch themselves.
- Allow for growth—because each developer has their own productivity number, it allows them to track their own process and growth, and experience becomes evident over time.
- Identifies areas for improvement or training—due to the ability to split the data into different categories, it can be easily identified when there is a gap in a person's knowledge or experience.
- Recognition—by including the productivity analysis as part of an employee review, it allows for the employee themselves to recognize when they are performing well and also allows for the organization to reward improved performance.
- Feedback—as well as giving feedback in a review setting, the developers also receive feedback week by week. The time sheet system that operates in MDS logs time week by week. Once a week, the data is extracted from this time sheet database. The productivity for each piece of work is calculated for each developer. All of this information is then placed in a website, called the "KPI website." Every developer has their own log on for the website where they can view the productivity figures for their own work. This feedback allows the developers to take control of their work and track it.

The estimation and productivity system within MDS can be seen in Figure 15.3.

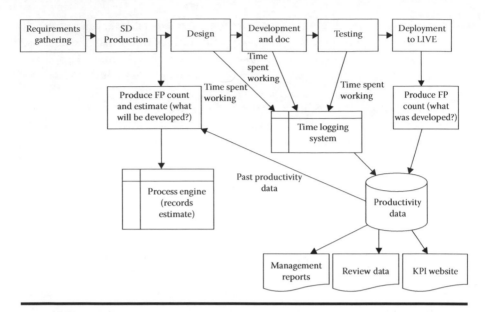

Figure 15.3   MDS software measurement process for estimation and productivity.

Issues Arising from the Measurement Process

As the new measurement process was introduced to MDS, a number of issues arose that had to be dealt with to ensure its success. The main issues were the following:

- Lack of understanding
- Reluctance to be measured
- Uncertainty of the data

Each of these had been expected, and action was quickly taken to counteract the issues before they became embedded in the organization. A series of presentations were given on Function Point counting and the new process for estimations and productivity. Complete transparency of the entire process was the only way to gain the understanding and trust of the stakeholders involved. During the presentation sessions, feedback was welcomed and acted upon where possible. This allowed the employees to feel part of the process rather than victims of it.

The reluctance to being measured was again an expected outcome of introducing a measurement technique. Another set of feedback sessions were organized to explain how the productivity figures worked in terms of each employee's reviews. It was also decided that the productivity figures would not be the only element considered in a review, and there would still be a place for peer and management feedback as a counterbalance. The KPI website allowed developers to track their progress and make management aware if there were going to be delays in work for various reasons. It also allowed developers to prepare for reviews by being aware of their own productivity before it was discussed in a review.

An unexpected issue was the uncertainty that people felt about the data being input to the productivity process. Although they were comfortable with the FP counting due to the presentations given, they were not confident in the time being recorded in the time management system. This was taken onboard by the measurement team and was actioned by carrying out a large cleanup activity on the data in the time logging system. The importance of logging time correctly was impressed upon every team leader and employee in the organization. Because people were able to see the consequences of poor time recording, it brought about a complete change of culture within the organization. Developers now insist on having the correct tasks within the time logging system and are very active in ensuring the information is correct on reports and the KPI website that is produced. They often contact the measurement team if they believe that information is inaccurate. The same applies to the estimation stage; developers now understand the impact that an estimate will have on them so they have become stakeholders in the process. They often give feedback on an estimate and help to identify the development category it belongs to in order to ensure the correct productivity numbers are used to produce the estimation data.

By ensuring complete transparency, allowing developers to become stakeholders in the process, and encouraging their input and feedback, any issues that arose in the early implementation stages of the measurement process are beginning to resolve as time passes. The future for measurement in MDS is bright; it has become embedded in the existing software development process and is being engaged with at all levels of the organization. Since countering the issues above, the estimates are now, on average, within 13% of the actual time taken to develop projects. The use of FP as an estimation tool has proved to be much more successful than the traditional knowledge-based method of estimation that was used in the past.

The use of it as a motivational tool is also growing although it has only been in place for three review cycles. The weekly updating of the KPI website is allowing an ongoing personal review for developers, and based on the feedback received by the measurement team, they are utilizing this on a regular basis. The introduction of measurement to MDS would seem to be a success, and the intent is to constantly evolve the process to ensure it remains relevant and important to the organization as it expands.

Summary: Measurement and Motivation

Motivation has become an integral part of managing people within an organization. The ideal situation is to have inspired, enthusiastic employees who want to do their best work for their employer. However, as the theories described above show, this is not a simple matter of just giving people a job to do and paying them for it.

The process of motivating people is much more complex and has to consider many different internal and external factors. In addition, the motivational tool that works so well for one department of an organization may not have any impact at all in another department. What motivated a person a year ago may not motivate them now due to a change in circumstances. The motivational process is not a static "one size fits all" program that can be plugged into any organization. Rather it should be a dynamic, evolving process, using many different methods and rewards to encourage people to do their best for the organization as well as themselves.

Software measurement can be utilized at many different points of a motivational process. As well as evaluating how motivated someone is based on his or her productivity, it can also identify when a person is not motivated. This can be just as important because once management are aware of this they can take steps to correct it. Measurement can be used to track a person's improvement and encourage them to do better when compared to their past results or the results of their colleagues. Software measurement allows people to challenge themselves and be recognized and rewarded when they exceed expectations. Software measurement provides a scientific, transparent, and subjective method of feedback that can be used to motivate software engineers to work to the best of their ability.

References

1. DeMarco, T. 1983. *Controlling Software Projects: Management, Measurement, and Estimates*. New York: Yourden Press.
2. Gilb, T. 1994. *Principles of Software Management*. Addison Wesley, Reading, Mass.
3. Fenton, N. E., and S. L. Pfleeger. 1996. *Software Metrics: A Rigorous and Practical Approach*. 2nd ed. London and Boston: International Thomson Computer Press.
4. Jones, C. 1991. *Applied Software Measurement*. Boston: McGraw Hill.
5. Briand, L. C., C. M. Differing, and H. D. Romback. 1997. Practical guidelines for measurement-based process improvement. *Softw Process Improv Pract J* 2(4):253–80.
6. Akiyama, F. 1971. An example of software system debugging. *Inf Proc* 71:353–79.
7. Halstead, M. 1977. *Elements of Software Science*. New York: Elsevier.
8. McCabe, T. 1976. Software complexity measure. *IEEE Trans Softw Eng* SE-2(4): 308–20.
9. Albrecht, A. J. 1979. Measuring application development. In *Proceedings of IBM Applications Development joint SHARE/GUIDE symposium*, 83–92. Monterey, CA: IBM Corporation.
10. Jensen, G. 2000. Estimating life-cycle effort and duration. In *Australian Conference of Software Measurement*. Sydney, Australia, Software Engineering Australia Metrics New South Wales.
11. International Function Point Users Group (IFPUG). www.ifpug.org (accessed May, 2011).
12. Jones, C. 1986. *Programming Productivity*. New York, Boston: McGraw-Hill.
13. Linden, A., and J. Fenn. 2003. *Understanding Gartner's Hype Cycle*. Strategic Analysis Report. Gartner Research.
14. Symons, C. 1988. Function Point Analysis: difficulties and improvements. *IEEE Trans Softw Eng* SE-14(1):2–11.

15. Low, G. C., and D. R. Jeffery. 1990. Function Points in the estimation and evaluation of software process. *IEEE Trans Softw Eng* 16(1):64–71.
16. Emrick, R. D. 1987. In search of a better metric for measuring productivity of application development. In *The International Function Point Group Conference Proceeding*, 23–25 September, San Antonio, TX: International Function Point Users Group.
17. Symons, C. 2001. Come back Function Point Analysis (modernised) – all is forgiven. In *Proceedings of FESMA-DASMA 2001*. Heidelberg: FESMA Publ.
18. Ince, D. 1989. Software metrics. In *Measurement for Software Control and Assurance*, ed. B. A. Kitchenham and B. Littlewood. New York: Elsevier Science Publishing.
19. Kemerer, C. F. 1987. An empirical evaluation of software cost estimation models. *Commun ACM* 30(5):416–29.
20. Abran, A., and P. N. Robillard. 1996. Function Point Analysis: an empirical study of its measurement process. *IEEE Trans Softw Eng* 22(12):171–84.
21. Laranjeira, L. A. 1990. Software size estimation of object-oriented systems. *IEEE Trans Softw Eng* 16(5):510–22.
22. www.businessdictionary.com (accessed May 24, 2011).
23. Mayo, E. G. 1949. Hawthorne and the Western Electric Company. In *The Social Problems of an Industrial Civilisation*, ed. E.G. Mayo, 60–76. London: Routledge.
24. Adair, G. 1984. The Hawthorne effect: A reconsideration of the methodological artefact. *J Appl Psychol* 69(2):334–45.
25. Rosenthal, R. 1966. *Experimenter Effects in Behavioural Research*. New York: Appleton-Century-Crofts.
26. Henslin, J. M. 2008. *Sociology: A Down to Earth Approach*. 9th ed. Boston: Pearson Education.
27. Kolata, G. 1998. *Scientific Myths That Are Too Good to Die*. New York: New York Times.
28. Clark, R. E., and Sugre, B. M. 1991. Research on instructional media. In *Instructional Technology: Past, Present and Future*, ed. G. J. Anglin, 327–43. Englewood, CO: Libraries Unlimited.
29. Parsons, H. M. 1974. What happened at Hawthorne? New evidence suggest the Hawthorne effect resulted from operant reinforcement contingences. *Science* 183(4128):922–32.
30. Kelly, T., and J. Buckley.2006. A context-aware analysis scheme for Bloom's taxonomy. In *Proceedings of the 14th International Conference on Project Comprehension*, 67–76. Washington DC: IEEE Computer Society.
31. Maslow, A. H. 1943. A theory of human motivation. *Psychol Rev* 50(4):370–96.
32. Alderfer, C. P. 1969. An empirical test of a new theory of human needs. *Organ Behav Hum Perform* 4(2):142–75.
33. Alderfer, C. P. 1972. *Existence, Relatedness and Growth: Human Needs in Organizational Setting*. New York: Free Press.
34. Herzberg, F., B. Mausner, and B. B. Snyderman. 1959. *The Motivation to Work*. New York: John Wiley.
35. Herzberg, F. 1969. One more time: how do you motivate employees? *Harv Bus Rev* 46(1):53–62.
36. Hackman, J. R., and G. R. Oldham. 1976. Motivation through the design of work: Test of a theory. *Organ Behav Hum Perform* 16:257–79.
37. Hackman, J. R., and G. R. Oldham. 1980. *Work Redesign*. Reading, Mass: Addison-Wesley.
38. Faturochman. 1997. The job characteristics theory: a review. Bul Psikol 5(2):1–13.

39. DeMarco, T., and T. Lister. 1999. *Peopleware – Productive Projects and Teams*. New York: Dorset House.

40. Capretz, L. F. 2003. Personality types in software engineering. *Int J Hum Comput Stud* 58 (2):207–14. Academic Press.

41. Tanner, F. R. 2003. On motivating engineers. In *Engineering Management Conference 2003. IEMC '03 Managing Technologically Driven Organization: The Human Side of Innovation and Change*, 214–18. Albany, NY: IEEE.

42. Ramachandran, S., and S. V. Rao. 2006. An effort towards identifying occupational culture among information systems professionals. In *Proceedings of the 2006 ACM SIGMIS CPR Conference on Computer Personnel Research: Forty Four Years of Computer Personnel Research: Achievements, Challenges and the Future*, 198–204. Claremont, CA: ACM Press.

43. Beecham, S., et al. 2008. Motivation in software engineering: a systematic literature review. *Inf Softw Technol* 50(9–10):860–78.

44. Agarwal, R., P. De, and T. W. Ferratt. 2002. Explaining an IT professional's preferred employment duration: empirical test of a causal model of antecedents. In *Proceedings of the ACM SIGCPR Conference*, 14–24. Kristiansand, Norway: ACM.

45. Burn, J. M., L. C. Ma, and E. M. Ng Tye. 1995. Managing IT professionals in a global environment. *SIGCPR Comput Pers* 19(3):11–9.

46. Crepeau, R. G., et al. 1992. Career anchors of information systems personnel. *J Manag Inform Syst* 9(2):145–60.

47. Garza, A. I., S. E. Lunce, and B. Maniam. 2003. Career anchors of Hispanic information systems professionals. In *Proceedings of Annual meeting of the Decision Sciences Institute*, 1067–72. San Diego, CA: DCI.

48. Ituma, A. 2006. The internal career: an explorative study of the career anchors of information technology workers in Nigeria. In *Proceedings of the 2006 ACM SIGMIS CPR Conference on Computer Personnel Research: Forty Four Years of Computer Personnel Research: Achievement, Challenges and the Future*, 205–12. Claremont, CA: ACM.

49. Darcy, D. P., and M. Ma. 2005. Exploring individual characteristics and programming performance: implications for programmer selection. In *Proceedings of the 38th IEEE International Conference on System Sciences, HICSS '05*, 314a. Hawaii: IEEE.

50. Frangos, S. A. 1997. Motivated humans for reliable software products. *Microprocess Micro Syst* 21(10):605–10.

51. Ferratt, T. W., and L. E. Short. 1986. Are information systems people different: an investigation of motivational differences. *Manag Inform Syst Q* 10(4):377–87.

52. Burn, J. M., J. D. Cougar, and L. Ma. 1992. Motivating IT professionals. *Hong Kong Challenge Inf Manag* 22(5):269–80.

53. Linberg, K. R. 1999. Software developer perceptions about software project failure: a case study. *J Syst Softw* 49(2–3):177–92.

54. Smits, S. J., E. R. McLean, and J. R. Tanner. 1992. Managing high achieving information systems professionals. In *Proceedings of the 1992 ACM SIGCPR Conference on Computer Personnel Research*, ed. A. L. Lederer, SIGCPR '92, 314–27. Cincinnati, OH: ACM.

55. Couger, J. D. 1989. Comparison of motivating environments for programmer/analysts and programmers in the US, Israel and Singapore. In *System Sciences, Vol IV: Emerging Technologies and Applications Track, Proceedings of the Twenty-Second Annual Hawaii International Conference*, Vol. 4:316–23.

56. Couger, J. D., and H. Adelsberger. 1988. Environments: Austria compared to the United States. *SIGCPR Comput Pers* 11(4):13–7.

57. Couger, J. D., et al. 1990. Commonalities in motivating environments for programmer/analysts in Austria, Israel, Singapore and the U.S.A. *Inform Manag* 18(1):41–6.
58. Couger, J. D., and A. Ishikawa. 1995. Comparing motivation of Japanese computer personnel versus those of the United States. In *System Sciences, Vol IV, Proceedings of the Twenty-Eighth Hawaii International Conference*, Vol. 4:1012–19.
59. Couger, J. D., and S. C. McIntyre. 1987. Motivating norms for artificial intelligence personnel. In *Proceedings of the Twentieth Hawaii International Conference on System Sciences*, Vol. 4:370–4.
60. Sumner, M., S. Yager, and D. Franke. 2005. Career orientation and organizational commitment of IT personnel. In *Proceedings of the 2005 ACM SIGMIS CPR Conference on Computer Personnel Research*. SIGMIS CPR '05, 75–80. Atlanta, GA: ACM.
61. Mata-Toledo, R. A., and E. A. Unger. 1985. Another look at motivating data processing professionals. *SIGCPR Comput Per* 10(1):1–7.
62. Khahil, O. E. M., et al. 1997. What motivates Egyptian IS managers and personnel: some preliminary results. In *Proceedings of the ACM SIGCPR Conference*, 187–92. San Francisco, CA: ACM.
63. Kym, H., and W. W. Park. 1992. Effect of cultural fit/misfit on the productivity and turnover of IS personnel. In *Proceedings of the ACM SIGCPR Conference on Computer Personnel Research*, 184–90. San Francisco, CA: ACM.
64. Peters, L. 2003. Managing software professionals. In *IEMC '03 Proceedings. Managing Technologically Driven Organisations: The Human Side of Innovation and Change(IEEE Cat No. 03CH37502)*, 61–6. Albany, NY: IEEE.
65. Wynekoop, J. L., and Walz, D. B. 1998. Revisiting the perennial question: Are IS people different? *Databases Adv Inf Syst* 29(2):62–72.
66. Jordan, E., and A. M. Whiteley. 1994. HRM practices in information technology management. In *Proceedings of Computer Personnel Research Conference (SIGCPR) on Reinventing IS: Managing Information Technology in Changing Organization*, 57–64. Alexandria, Virginia: IEEE.
67. Enns, H. G., T. W. Ferrat, and J. Prasad. 2006. Beyond stereotypes of IT professionals: implications for IT HR practices. *Commun ACM* 49(4):106–9.
68. Moore, J. E. 1991. Personality characteristics of information systems professionals. In *Proceedings of the 1991 Conference on SIGCPR*, 140. Athens, GA: IEEE.
69. Miller, W. C., J. D. Cougar, and L. F. Higgins. 1993. Comparing innovation styles profile of IS personnel to other occupations. In *IEEE International Conference on System Sciences, HICSS '93, Proceedings of the 26th Annual Conference*, 378–86. Hawaii: IEEE.
70. Igbaria, M., G. Meredith, and D. C. Smith. 1995. Career orientations of information systems employees in South Africa. *J Strateg Inform Syst* 4(4):319–40.
71. Kandeel, H., and K. Wahba. 2001. Competency models for human resource development: case of Egyptian software industry. In *Managing Information Technology in a Global Environment. 2001 Information Resources Management Association International Conference*, 117–21. Hershey, PA: Idea Group Publishing.
72. Turley, R. T., and J. M. Bieman. 1995. Competencies of exceptional and nonexceptional software engineers. *J Syst Softw* 28(1):19–38.
73. Argarwal, R., and T. W. Ferratt. 2000. Retention and the career motives of IT professionals. In *Proceedings of the ACM SIGCPR Conference*, 158–66. New York: ACM.
74. Cheney, P. H. 1984. Effects of individual characteristics, organizational factors and task characteristics on computer programmer productivity and job satisfaction. *Inform Manag* 7(4):209–14. Amsterdam: Elsevier Science Publishers.

75. Crook, C. W., R. G. Crepeau, and M. E. McMurtrey. 1991. Utilisation of the career anchor/career orientation constructs for management of IS professionals. *SIGCPR Comput Pers* 13(2):12–23. Amsterdam: Elsevier Publishing.
76. Goldstein, D. K. 1988. An updated measure of supervisor-rated job performance for programmer/analysis. In *Proceedings of the ACM SIGCPR Conference on Management of Information Systems Personnel*, 148–52. College Park, Maryland: ACM.
77. Hsu, M. K., et al. 2003. Career satisfaction for managerial and technical authored IS personnel in later career stages. *SIGMIS Database* 34(4):64–72.
78. Zawacki, R. A. 1992. Motivating the IS people of the future. *Inform Syst Manag* 9(2):73–5.
79. Smith, D. C., and H. L. Speight. 2006. Antecedents of turnover intention and actual turnover among information systems personnel in South Africa. In *Proceedings of the 2006 ACM SIGMIS CPR Conference on Computer Personnel Research: Forty Four Years of Computer Personnel Research: Achievements, Challenges and the Future*, 123–9. Claremont, CA: ACM.
80. Cougar, D. J., and S. C. McIntyre. 1987. Motivation norms of knowledge engineers compared to those of software engineers. *J Manag Inform Syst* 4(3):82–93.
81. Im, J. H., and Hartman, S. 1990. Rethinking the issue of whether IS people are different from non-IS people. *MIS Q* 14(1):1–2.
82. Myers, M. E. 1991. Motivation and performance in the information systems field: a survey of related studies. *SIGCPR Comput Pers* 13(3):44–9.
83. Ramachandran, S., and S. V. Rao. 2006. An effort towards identifying occupational culture among information systems professionals. In *Proceedings of the 2006 ACM SIGMIS CPR Conference on Computer Personnel Research: Forty Four Years of Computer Personnel Research: Achievements, Challenges and the Future*, 198–204. Claremont, CA: ACM.
84. Agarwal, R., and T. W. Ferratt. 2001. Crafting a HR strategy to meet the need for IT workers. *Commun ACM* 44(7):58–64.
85. Agarwal, R., and T. W. Ferratt. 1998. Recruiting, retaining and developing IT professionals: an empirically derived taxonomy of human resource practices. In *Proceedings of the ACM SIGCPR Conference*, 292–302. Boston: ACM.
86. Agarwal, R., and T. W. Ferratt. 2002. Enduring practices for managing IT professionals. *Commun ACM* 45(9):73–9.
87. Baddoo, N., T. Hall, and D. Jagielska. 2006. Software developer motivation in a high maturity company: a case study. *Softw Process Improv Pract* 11(3):219–28.
88. Burn, J. M., et al. 1994. Job expectations of IS professionals in Hong Kong. In *Proceedings of the 1994 ACM SIGCPR Computer Personnel Research Conference on Reinventing IS: Managing Information Technology in Changing Organization*, 231–41. Alexandria, Virginia: ACM.
89. Garden, A. 1988. Maintaining the spirit of excitement in growing companies. *SIGCPR Comput Pers* 11(4):10–2.
90. Klenke, K., and Kievit, K. A. 1992. Predictors of leadership style, organizational commitment and turnover of information systems professionals. In *Proceedings of the 1992 ACM SIGCPR Conference on Computer Personnel Research*, ed. A. L Lederer. 171–83. Cincinnati, OH: ACM.
91. Mak, B. L., and H. Sockel. 2001. A confirmatory factor analysis of IS employee motivation and retention. *Inform Manag* 38(5):265–76.

92. Niederman, F., and M. R. Sumner. 2001. Job turnover among MIS professionals: an exploratory study of employee turnover. In *Proceedings of the 2001 ACM SIGCPR Conference on Computer Personnel Research*, 11–20. San Diego, CA: ACM.

93. Ridings, C. M., and L. B. Eder. 1999. An analysis of IS technical career paths and job satisfaction. *SIGCPR Comput Pers* 20(2):7–26.

94. Thatcher, J. B., Y. Liu, and L. P. Stepina. 2002. The role of the work itself: an empirical examination of intrinsic motivation's influence on IT workers attitudes and intentions. In *Proceedings of the ACM SIGCPR Conference*, 25–33. Kristiansand, Norway: ACM.

95. LeDuc, A. L. J. 1980. Motivation of programmers. *SIGMIS Database* 11(4): 4–12.

96. Niederman, F., and M. Sumner. 2003. Decision paths affecting turnover among information technology professionals. In *Proceedings of the 2003 SIGMIS Conference on Freedom in Philadelphia: Leveraging Differences and Diversity in the IT Workforce*, 133–42. Philadelphia, PA: ACM.

97. Santana, M., and D. Robey. 1995. Perceptions of control during systems development: effects on job satisfaction of systems professionals. *SIGCPR Comput Per* 16(1):20–34.

98. Garden, A. 1988. Behavioural and organizational factors involved in the turnover of high tech professionals. *SIGCPR Comput Pers* 11(4):6–9.

99. Checchio, R. A. 1990. Creating a motivating environment in software development. Experience with the management of software projects. In *Proceedings of the Third IFAC/IFIP Workshop*, 81–6. Pergamon, New York.

100. Li, Y., et al. 2006. Motivating open source software developers: influence of transformational and transactional leaderships. In *Proceedings of the 2006 ACM SIGMIS CPR Conference on Computer Personnel Research: Forty Four Years of Computer Personnel Research: Achievements, Challenges & the Future*, 34–43. Claremont, CA: ACM.

101. Smits, S. J., E. R. McLean, and J. R. Tanner. 1997. A longitudinal study of I/S careers: synthesis, conclusion and recommendations. In *Proceedings of the 1997 ACM SIGCPR Conference on Computer Personnel Research*, 36–48. San Francisco, CA: ACM.

102. Andersen, E. S. 2002. "Never the twain shall meet": exploring the differences between Japanese and Norwegian IS professionals. In *Proceedings of the 2002 ACM SIGCPR Conference on Computer Personnel Research*, 64–71. Kristiansand, Norway: ACM.

103. Lee, P. C. 2002. The social context of turnover among information technology professional. In *Proceedings on the 2002 ACM SIGCPR Conference on Computer Personnel Research*, 145–53. Kristiansand, Norway: ACM.

104. Reid, M. F., et al. 2006. Affective commitment in the public sector: the case of IT employees. In *Proceedings of the 2006 ACM SIGMIS CPR Conference on Computer Personnel Research: Forty Four Years of Computer Personnel Research: Achievements, Challenges & the Future*, 321–32. Claremont, CA: ACM.

105. Richens, E. 1998. HR strategies for IS professionals in the 21st century. In *Proceedings of the ACM SIGCPR Conference*, 289–91. Boston: ACM.

106. Morales, A. W. 2005. Salary survey 2005. *Softw Dev* 13(11):32–42.

107. Dittrich, J. E., J. D. Cougar, and R. A. Zawacki. 1985. Perceptions of equity, job satisfaction and intention to quit among data processing personnel. *Infor Manag* 9(2):67–75.

108. Gambill, S. E., W. J. Clark, and R. B. Wilkes. 2000. Toward a holistic model of task design for IS professionals. *Inform Manag* 37(5):217–28.

109. Procaccino, J. D., et al. 2005. What do software practitioners really think about project success: an exploratory study. *J Syst Softw* 78(2):194–203.

110. Carayon, P., et al. 2003. Job characteristics and quality of working life in the IT workforce: the role of gender. In *Proceedings of the 2003 SIGMIS Conference on Computer Personnel Research: Freedom in Philadelphia – Leveraging Differences and Diversity in the IT Workforce*, 58–63. Philadelphia, PA: ACM.
111. Agarwal, R., and T. W. Ferratt. 2002. Toward understanding the relationship between IT human resource management systems and retention: an empirical analysis based on multiple theoretical and measurement approaches. In *Proceedings of the ACM SIGCPR Conference*, 126–38. Kristiansand, Norway: ACM.
112. Hsu, M. K., et al. 2003. Perceived career incentives and intent to leave. *Inform Manag* 40(5):361–69.
113. Rubin, H. I., and E. F. Hernandez. 1988. Motivations and behaviours of software professionals. In *Proceedings of the ACM SIGCPR Conference on Management of Information Systems Personnel*, 62–71. College Park, Maryland: ACM.
114. Honda, K., et al. 1985. Research on work environment for software productivity improvement. In *Proceedings of COMPSAC 85. The IEEE Computer Society's 9th International Computer Software and Applications Conference*, 241–48. Washington: IEEE Comput. Soc. Press.
115. Fujigaki, Y. 1990. Stress analysis of software engineers for effective management. Human factors in organizational design and management – III. In *Proceedings of the 3rd International Symposium*, 255–58. North-Holland, Netherlands.
116. Nelson, A. C. and C. LeRouge. 2001. Self esteem: moderator between role stress fit and satisfaction and commitment? In *Proceedings of the 2001 ACM SIGCPR Conference on Computer Personnel Research*, 74–7. San Diego, CA: ACM.
117. Lee, P. C. 2002. Career plateau and professional plateau: impact on work outcomes of information technology professionals. *SIGCPR Comput Pers* 20(4):25–38.
118. Tanniru, M. R. and S. M. Taylor. 1981. Causes of turnover among data processing professionals – some preliminary findings. In *Proceedings of the 18th Annual ACM SIGCPR Computer Personnel Research Conference*, 224–47. Washington, DC: ACM.
119. McLean, E. R., S. J. Smits, and J. R. Tanner. 1996. The importance of salary on job and career attitudes of information systems professionals. *Inform Manag* 30(6):291–99.
120. Thomas, S. A., S. F. Hurley, and D. J. Barnes. 1996. Looking for the human factors in software quality management. Proceedings of *Int Conf Softw Eng Educ Pract*, 474. California: IEEE.
121. Cougar, J. D. 1992. Comparison of motivation norms for programmer/analysts in the Pacific Rim and the U.S. *Int J Inform Syst* 1(3):16–30.
122. Cougar, J. D. 1988. Motivators vs. demotivators in the IS environment. *J Syst Manag* 39(6):36–41.
123. Bartol, K. M., and D. C. Martin. 1982. Managing information systems personnel: a review of the literature and managerial implications. *MIS Q* 6:49–70.
124. Almstrum, V. L. 2003. What is the attraction to computing? *Commun ACM* 46(9):51–5.
125. Baroudi, J. J., and M. J. Ginzberg. 1986. Impact of the technological environment on programmer/analyst job outcomes. *Commun ACM* 29(6):546–55.
126. Lending, D., and N. L. Chervany. 1997. The changing systems development job: a job characteristics approach. In *Proceedings of the 1997 ACM SIGCPR Conference on Computer Personnel Research*, 127–37. San Francisco, CA: ACM.
127. Mannaro, K., M. Melis, and M. Marchesi. 2004. Empirical analysis on the satisfaction of IT employees comparing XP practices with other software development methodologies. *Proceedings of 5th International conference on Extreme Programming and Agile Processes in Software Engineering*, 166–74. Germany: Springer.

128. Hertel, S., S. Niedner, and G. Hermann. 2003. Motivation of software developers in open source projects: an Internet-based survey of contributors to the Linux kernel. *Res Policy* 32:1159–77.

129. Roberts, J., I. Hann, and S. Slaughter. 2004. *Understanding the Motivations, Participation and Performance of Open Source Software Developers: A Longitudinal Study of the Apache Projects.* New York: Carnegie Mellon University Working Paper.

130. Ferratt, T. W., H. G. Enns, and J. Prasad. 2003. Instrument validation for investigating a model of employment arrangement fit for IT professionals. In *Proceedings of the ACM SIGMIS CPR Conference*, 168–78. Philadelphia: ACM.

131. Ferratt, T. W., H. G. Enns, and J. Prasad. 2004. Employment arrangement fit for IT professionals: an examination of the importance of fit components. In *Proceedings of the ACM SIGMIS CPR Conference*, 25–9. Arizona: ACM.

132. Goldstein, D. K. and J. F. Rockart. 1984. An examination of work-related correlates of job satisfaction in programmer/analysts. *MIS Q* 8(2):03–115.

133. Rash, R. H. and H. L. Tosi. 1992. Factors affecting software developers' performance: an integrated approach. *Manag Inform Syst Q* 16(3):395–413.

About the Author

Dr. Tara Kelly is a Function Point Analyst, currently working in the Irish office of MDS. Previously she has worked as a lecturer at the University of Limerick and Limerick Institute of Technology. Her research interests include software metrics, software estimation, and program comprehension.

Chapter 16

Achieving Business Objectives: Building a Software Metrics Support Structure

Jim Mayes

Contents

> "The business objectives of software projects should include balancing time, cost, and quality with the expected business value of the software produced. Software metrics are critical to this endeavor."

The benefits of a metrics program must be continuously justified in terms of business value and "raison d'être." This is true whether we are trying to initiate a software metrics program or trying to sustain one due to organizational changes, budget constraints, or other factors. Unfortunately, a metrics program is often perceived as an intrusive and unnecessary interference with getting "real work" done. The bottom line is that the metrics program must be directly aligned with business objectives at the project level to be successful and provide value. This chapter focuses on building a structural model to illustrate how this can be accomplished. Like building a house, this structure has four layers—foundation, floor, walls, and roof—with each layer supporting the layers above it.

The primary component of this model is the establishment of a Software Estimation Metrics Group (SEMG) within the foundation layer. Just as the CMU/SEI Capability Maturity Model (CMM) establishes a Software Engineering Process Group (SEPG) for managing software processes, an SEMG should be established for managing software metrics. The SEPG and SEMG functions complement each other and have common goals in relation to achieving business objectives.

Background

In 1994, after 20 years as a software programmer and development manager, I read Ed Yourdon's book, *The Decline and Fall of the American Programmer* [1]. It was an epiphany for me, as if someone opened the curtains and turned on the lights for the first time. It was like Information Technology (IT) had been stuck in the dark ages, but now there was hope that the IT environment could be significantly improved. The evolution of process, metrics, and quality initiatives over the years has certainly enhanced these prospects, but there remains a long way to go. Since reading Yourdon's book, I immediately became engaged in process improvement initiatives as an SEPG Manager, SEMG Manager, and Metrics Consultant, primarily focusing on estimation.

Why did initially I focus on estimation? As a software development manager, one of my most difficult, yet critical tasks, was providing justifiable software project estimates. At that time, our basis for estimation, as one of my coworkers once put it, was more *religious in nature, based on faith in our ability to deliver*, rather than based on historical data; we provided *hysterical* estimates instead of *historical* estimates. Therefore, as I focused my energy on process improvement related to software estimation, I realized that software metrics are an integral part of estimation, continuous improvement, risk management, and project management. As to the importance of process improvement related to estimation, Putnam and Meyers put it this way: "An organization can accomplish its estimates only if it has a software development process it can repeat" [2].

The importance of project-level metrics (actual project results) cannot be overstated, because "if we don't know where we are, a map won't help." If our current capabilities are not quantified, it would be difficult to determine what needs to be improved and what baseline to use for measuring improvement.

"So You Can Measure, So What!"

At every International Function Point Users Group (IFPUG) conference, Bill Hufschmidt handed out buttons with catchy phrases on them. At one conference, he gave out buttons with the phrase: "So You Can Measure, So What!" I loved that button, and this is what it meant to me:

> Merely measuring things or counting Function Points isn't what soft-ware metrics is all about. It is what you can do with the information, and the metrics derived from the data, that matters. When metrics are only used for management reporting, the primary benefits are lost. In order to maximize the potential benefits, software metrics should be traceable to the project level, so they can be put to work, providing value to the overall software development process.

In this context, it is important to understand the definition of what is meant by *measure, metric,* and *indicator (MMI)*. Basically, a measure is a standard unit of measurement, such as Function Points for size or hours for effort. A metric combines two or more measures into a meaningful derivation, such as using hours per Function Point as a productivity metric. An indicator is something that draws attention to a particular situation, such as a flag or deviation outside predetermined tolerances or control limits. These MMI terms distinguish the difference between software metrics and project management status reporting [3].

It is also important to understand these MMI terms in relation to how software metrics are perceived by the software organizations being measured. In his book *Why Does Software Cost So Much?* Tom DeMarco wrote, "I observe there are at least three different reasons we collect metrics, as follows:

- To discover facts about our world
- To steer our actions
- To modify human behavior" [4]

DeMarco goes on to suggest a metrics spectrum, as shown in Figure 16.1, with behavior modification on the left, steering in the middle, and discovery to the right. The objective of the SEMG is to provide discovery metrics for continuous improvement and steering metrics for risk management. DeMarco suggests that the further to the right you are on the metrics spectrum, the more successful your use of metrics will be. As you move toward the left side of the spectrum (behavior modification), you must beware of the Hawthorne effect, where people respond differently just because they are being measured. An example of behavior modification that

Behavior —————— Steering —————— Discovery
modification

Figure 16.1 DeMarco's metrics spectrum. (Reprinted from: Tom DeMarco. Why Does Software Cost So Much? And Other Puzzles of the Information Age, 16–17. Dorset House. Copyright © 1995. All rights reserved. With permission.)

you do not want was illustrated in a *Dilbert* comic strip several years ago. In the first frame, the pointy-haired boss said that he was going to pay a "bonus of ten dollars for every bug found and fixed." A subsequent frame showed Wally shouting: "I'm going to write me a new minivan this afternoon" (Adams 1996). As this illustrates, a software metrics program should focus on the connection between steering and discovery and stay away from behavior modification metrics of this type. It should be clear that the MMIs are related to continuous improvement, managing risk, and balancing time, cost, and quality (TCQ). A balanced set of software metrics is important. To quote Karl Wiegers [5]:

> A risk with any metrics activity is dysfunctional measurement, in which participants alter their behavior to optimize something that is being measured, rather than focusing on the real organizational goal. For example, if we are measuring output productivity but not quality, expect some developers to change their coding style to expand the volume of material they produce, or to code quickly without regard for bugs. I can write code very fast if it doesn't actually have to run correctly. The balanced set of measurements helps prevent dysfunctional behavior by monitoring the group's performance in several complementary aspects of their work that lead to project success.

Blueprint for a Software Metrics Support Structure

A multilayered metrics support structure is shown in Figure 16.2, with each of the four layers building onto the layers below it. Each layer is also dependent on the other layers for achieving business objectives, just as a building is dependent on its foundation, floor, walls, and roof in order for it to be structurally sound and to achieve its functional goal. There are many similarities in managing the construction of buildings and software. (Okay, so I have a degree in building construction from an engineering school, and *This Old House* is one of my favorite television programs.) How easy would it be to construct a building without any measures? It would be impossible, right? Because the construction mantra is: "Measure twice, cut once." Of course, software products can be constructed without measures, metrics, or processes; however, there are plenty of industry figures showing the high percentage of project failures each year. There are also an equally high percentage of projects that are completed, but fail to provide the appropriate business value due to cost or schedule overruns. It is

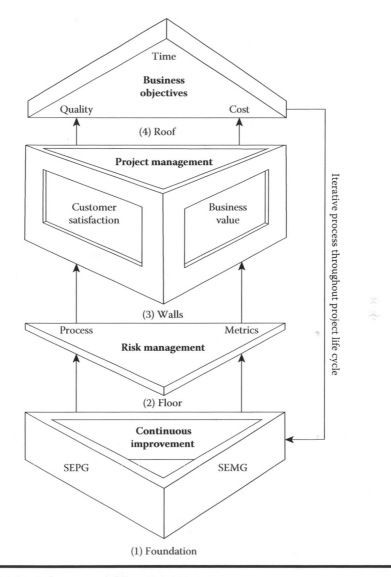

Figure 16.2   Software metrics support structure.

important, therefore, to quantify project results and use empirical analysis to manage these risks, improve estimates, improve processes, and assess business value.

The environment needed to support this initiative consists of the following structural components (layers):

■ Foundation—continuous improvement
■ Floor—risk management

- Walls—project management
- Roof—business objectives

The SEMG provides support related to each of these components, as described in the paragraphs that follow.

Foundation: Continuous Improvement

An SEMG that is established in relation to a continuous improvement program and a process management group (SEPG) lays the foundation for achieving business objectives. The concept of establishing a group for managing CMM measurement practices is supported by CMU/SEI-92-TR-25 Technical Report, "Software Measures and the Capability Maturity Model" [6], which states:

> ...many of the potential benefits that an organization can derive from a sound measurement program are often not achieved due to a half-hearted commitment to a measurement program. The commitment cannot be just a policy statement; it must be total commitment. The policy must be followed with the allocation of resources to a measurement program. This includes allocating staff as well as tools. It is important that an individual or group be assigned responsibility for the measurement program. This group identifies the measures to be collected, establishes training in measurement, monitors the consistency of the measures across the projects throughout the organization, and can help initiate measures. This group can also provide composites of historical data that managers can use in planning and monitoring projects. The human element in a measurement program should not be taken lightly. Success and failure are tied to people. All staff members need to see the benefits of the measurement program and understand the results will not be used against them.

Another Technical Report, CMU/SEI-97-HB-003, "Practical Measurement for Process Management and Improvement," by William A. Florac, Robert E. Park, and Anita D. Carleton, "shows how well-established principles and methods for evaluating and controlling process performance can be applied to a software setting to achieve an organization's business and technical goals." This report focuses on "Process Management" related to operational software processes. Its primary focus is on the "enduring issues that enable organizations to improve not just today's performance, but long-term success and profitability of their business and technical endeavors" [7].

These CMU/SEI reports describe different aspects of software measurement and metrics that should be managed by the SEMG for achieving business objectives.

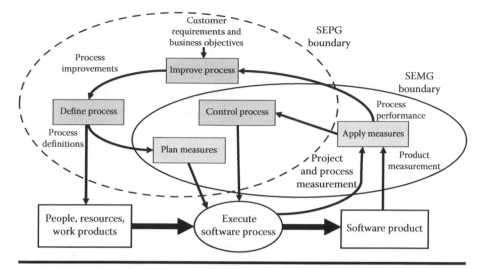

Figure 16.3   Continuous improvement, SEPG, SEMG relationship model.

As stated in CMU/SEI-97-HB-003, "Every organization asks the question, 'Are we achieving the results we desire?' This gets couched in many ways, such as, Are our customers satisfied with our product and services? Are we earning a fair return on our investment? Can we reduce the cost of producing the product or service? How can we improve the response to our customers' needs or increase the functionality of our products? How can we improve our competitive position? Are we achieving the growth required for survival?" The vital SEMG role in this layer is shown in Figure 16.3, which illustrates the process management relationship between continuous improvement, the SEPG, and the SEMG, in order to answer these questions. It is a chart provided in CMU/SEI-97-HB-003 that I have adapted to show the SEPG functional boundary, the SEMG functional boundary, and where the boundaries overlap.

The SEMG provides the measurement capability and expertise necessary to analyze process improvement opportunities using statistical analysis techniques for process control, root cause analysis, and solution analysis, which include the following:

■ Control charts
■ Scatter plots (trending)
■ Run charts
■ Cause-and-effect diagrams
■ Histograms
■ Bar charts
■ Pareto charts

Floor: Risk Management

"Risk Management is project management for adults" [8]. This was the title of a keynote presentation that Tom DeMarco gave at the Quantitative Software Management (QSM), Inc. Users Conference. In the presentation, he stated that the software industry today is developing process sophistication and orderliness, via the CMM; however, the use of the term *maturity* in the CMM is deviant to the term that he would use to recognize project management: *adulthood*. A great manager is one who deals with uncertainties, not certainties, and this is the fundamental reason that we are not mature. To effectively manage a software project, managers must be aware of the real world and must have the capacity to deal with the real world. The SEMG can help quantify and identify these uncertainties via discovery and steering metrics, so they can be managed.

If you go back to Figure 16.2, you see the risk management layer, which includes process and metrics, adds a floor on to the foundation layer supported by the functions of the SEPG, SEMG, and continuous improvement. Of course, one of the primary reasons for implementing CMM processes is to reduce risks associated with software projects. Therefore, the SEPG's primary role in this layer is to reduce risk by insuring adherence to process, which includes a risk management process as well. The SEMG role is to provide statistically quantifiable data for managing risks related to project estimates and indicators for triggering alarms during a software project's life cycle. DeMarco describes the *Circular Definition of Risk* as follows:

> A *Risk* is a problem that has not occurred. A *Problem* is a risk that has occurred. A *Transition* is a problem going from risk to problem, such as in the *Trucker's Maxim*: behind every ball comes a running child (transition), apply brakes when you see the ball, and do not wait until you see the child.

The triggers and alarms (indicators) provided by the SEMG can identify a *transition*, and help prevent a *risk* from becoming a *problem*. Project managers will then be able to "apply brakes when they see the ball" (indicator). The SEMG functions that facilitate this ability include the following:

- Validation of top-down versus bottom-up estimates to compare them to historical results and identify the risks related to estimates
- Project monitoring of estimated versus actual data (size, schedule, effort, defect rates, etc.)
- Predictive analysis as to probable project outcomes based on in-flight results
- Providing indicators for managing risks associated with in-flight data variation outside of acceptable tolerances

Walls: Project Management

The triangular relationship in this layer includes project management for providing customer satisfaction and business value associated with the business objectives of the software project. The processes and metrics supported in the continuous improvement layer (the foundation) and risk management layer (the floor) carry forward to the project management layer of the structure. With the foundation and floor to build upon, the project management layer builds the walls, or software product, that will support the roof (business objectives) of the structural model. This layer operationalizes software development processes and project level metrics. It includes the following steps in the TCQ process for balancing time, cost, and quality that are supported by the SEMG and software metrics:

- Prioritizing business objectives and project constraints
- Time-sensitive estimation for balancing TCQ
- Providing alternative estimate solutions for partnering negotiation

Time-sensitive estimation is a critical component of the TCQ process. One of the primary reasons for projects failing to achieve business objectives is trying to deliver too much too fast. As schedules are compressed, project effort, cost, and defects exponentially increase. It does not take much compression to cause this effect. On the other hand, if the schedule is lengthened, effort, cost, and defects are exponentially decreased—balance is the key. One way or another the scale stays balanced as shown in Figure 16.4.

The nonlinear TCQ relationships associated with time-sensitive estimation are illustrated in Figures 16.5 and 16.6. This is not a theory, but is based on the empirical evidence as to how software projects actually behave, as proven by the work of Tom Demarco, Larry Putnam, Ware Myers, and others [9,10]. By applying the TCQ principles, the project schedule, cost/effort, and quality components can be

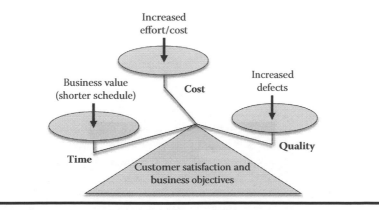

Figure 16.4 Balancing time-cost-quality versus business objectives.

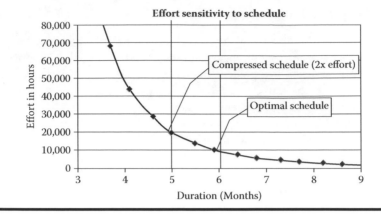

Figure 16.5 Effort sensitivity to schedule compression.

prioritized and balanced in relation to business value and objectives. If the TCQ components are set in stone, then other alternatives may include de-scoping the project or assigning more highly skilled resources.

Software project estimates are not one-size-fits-all commodities. Alternative solutions should be provided for each project estimate, and the one that provides the most business value and has the most reasonable probability of success should be chosen. Signing up for an unachievable estimate serves the interest of no one. It may provide short-term gain in customer satisfaction with an estimate that satisfies the customer demand for an unrealistic completion date, but usually results in long-term pain for IT and the customer. Therefore, balancing TCQ with business value is achievable only when alternatives are provided and there is a long-term partnership between the client and IT organizations. Sharing information and trust are key elements to achieving customer satisfaction.

Roof: Business Objectives

Just as a roof completes the structure of a building, this layer is the culmination of the structural components below it in the metrics model. In this layer, the achievement of business objectives is realized via the TCQ project results that drive business value. With partnering negotiation, the client organization determines the TCQ drivers related to the business, and the IT organization determines the TCQ drivers related to the software. Joint ownership of the business objectives as a mutual goal is the way to work through the issues objectively. A partnership between the client and the IT organization is required to achieve balance between software project estimates and business objectives. The layers below this level, continuous improvement, risk management, and project management are essential for successfully accomplishing this goal.

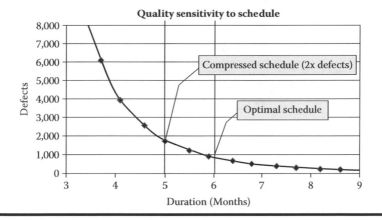

Figure 16.6   Quality sensitivity to schedule compression.

Also in this layer, the SEMG quantifies and analyzes the overall project results as they relate to achieving business objectives. This analysis leads to the identification of continuous improvement opportunities related to software processes, predictive analysis for risk management, and balancing TCQ. This is an iterative process with the experiences of previous projects being used to help new projects achieve greater success.

Conclusion

The benefits of a software metrics program must be justifiable in relation to business value and business objectives. The software metrics support structure and SEPG, SEMG, and TCQ initiatives illustrate how project-level software metrics provide value and are essential to achieving business objectives. Establishing an SEMG in this context provides the focus, continuity, experience, backup, and reinforcement of professional skills needed for sustaining and improving an organization's management capabilities for achieving business objectives. To provide these benefits, it must be a centralized function staffed by dedicated metrics and estimation specialists.

Without a metrics program supported by an SEMG, it would be difficult, if not impossible, to effectively achieve business objectives or to continuously improve project results. To quote Michael Mah: "Your history will help you better manage the future." The SEMG provides the corporate memory needed to learn from the past and build a better future [11].

References

1. Yourdon, E. 1992. *Decline and Fall of the American Programmer.* New Jersey: Prentice Hall.
2. Putnam, L. H. and W. Myers. 1996. *Controlling Software Development.* Los Alamitos, CA: IEEE Computer Society Press.

3. Ragland, B. 1995. Measure, Metric, or Indicator: What's the Difference? *CrossTalk*, Vol. 8, No. 3 (March 1995), www.stsc.hill.af.mill.

4. Demarco, T. 1995. *Why Does Software Cost So Much?* New York: Dorset House Publishing.

5. Wiegers, K. 1999. A software metrics primer. *Softw Dev*, July 1999.

6. Baumert, J. H., and M. S. McWhinney. 1992. *Software Measures and the Capability Maturity Model*. CMU/SEI-92-TR-25, ESD-TR-92-24. Pittsburgh, PA: Carnegie Mellon University.

7. Florac, W. A., E. P. Robert, and D. C. Anita. 1997. *Practical Software Measurement: Measuring for Process Management and Improvement*. CMU/SEI-97-HB-003. Pittsburgh, PA: Carnegie Mellon University.

8. DeMarco, T. 1997. *Risk Management: Project Management for Adults*. McLean, VA: Presentation, QSM Users Conference.

9. Demarco, T. 1982. *Controlling Software Projects*. New York: Yourdon Press.

10. Putnam, L. H., and W. Myers. 1992. *Measures for Excellence: Reliable Software, On Time, Within Budget*. Englewood Cliffs: PTR Prentice-Hall.

11. Mah, M. 2000. Sizing up your promises and expectations. In M. Mah, ed., *IT Metrics Strategies*, Vol. VI, (12). Arlington, MA: Cutter Information Corp.

About the Author

Jim Mayes is a senior consultant with CGI Technologies and Solutions, Inc. in Atlanta, GA. He has over 35 years of IT experience in software development and life cycle management in the corporate environment at BellSouth (AT&T) and as an industry consultant with CGI, QSM Associates, and Mayes Consulting LLC. Over the past 16 years, he has been directly involved in providing software metrics support for project estimation, project tracking, predictive analysis, data analysis/ trending, benchmarking, process improvement, outsourcing, productivity measurement, SLIM estimation/metrics tools, and Function Point Analysis.

During his 28 years at BellSouth, he gained telecom IT experience as a systems analyst, applications development and maintenance manager, Software Engineering Process Group (SEPG) manager, and Software Estimation Metrics Group (SEMG) manager. This experience included both in-house software development and out-sourced development environments for various disciplines such as billing, network engineering, provisioning, and customer support.

Jim has a Bachelor of Science degree from the Georgia Institute of Technology and has been a Certified Function Point Specialist (CFPS) for over 15 years. He has had numerous articles published, is a frequent speaker at conferences, and has been a member of the following organizations: Atlanta SPIN, AQAA, IEEE Computer Society, and the International Function Point Users Group (IFPUG).

METRICS FOR THE CIO—BUSINESS VALUE

INTRODUCTION

Pierre Almén

IT doesn't deliver value. IT enables it!

The business challenges for Chief Information Officers (CIOs) have changed over time. Historically, productivity, cost, and quality have often been the main ones needing attention. However, we now see creating business value among the top challenges, with it possibly becoming the major and most focused challenge for today's CIO. Is the option for IT then to either decrease the cost or increase value or revenue? My opinion is that IT can do both and must do both. IT must be focusing both on efficiency—doing things right—and on effectiveness—doing the right things. By succeeding with both perspectives, IT will be recognized as a strategic partner and recognized as delivering value to the business. Therefore, it is up to the IT managers and the CIO to define, measure, improve, and communicate the value that IT adds to the business.

Paul Below is working as a consultant at Quantitative Software Management (QSM); he has over 25 years of experience in the area of measurement technology and is a Certified Software Quality Analyst and Six Sigma Black Belt. Paul describes a limited set of statistical terms and techniques that can be used for analysis of software metrics in his chapter. He also provides important points to remember when doing this analysis and includes practical examples.

Dr. Christof Ebert from Germany is the managing director of Vector Consulting Services, an instructor at Stuttgart University, and an internationally renowned keynote speaker and author of several books within IT. In his chapter, you will learn how to set improvement objectives and implement objective-driven process improvement through the E4 (Establish, Extract, Evaluate, Execute) process. A case study is included to show productivity improvement results.

Miranda Mason is a Partner within Accenture, and she has more than 15 years experience with implementing software development and maintenance metrics programs. In her chapter "A Framework for Implementing an Effective Software Development and Maintenance Metrics Program for the CIO," Miranda gives you the steps needed to define and implement a successful metrics program within software development and maintenance.

Stavros Pechlivanidis is a Senior Management Consultant at IBM Global Business Services in Germany and holds a position as a Subject Matter Expert on metrics and as a Lead Estimator. He has developed an approach to help derive measures for business value, the Competitive Advantage Flower (CAF), which uses seven dimensions to describe the original strategy behind any business initiative. The result of the CAF process describes measures and communicates the business value of IT initiatives.

Chapter 17

Maximizing Value: Understanding Metrics Paradoxes through Use of Transformation

Paul Below

Contents

Introduction

This chapter describes a set of statistical terms and techniques, suitable for dealing with problems commonly encountered in analysis of software metrics. The purpose is to give the reader an appreciation for the techniques, but further aid may be needed to actually apply the concepts.

Software metrics are useful to help manage and improve software processes. However, measured software systems and processes exist over a large range of complexity, size, and quality, often with a skewed distribution. Care must be taken to prevent serious blunders in the analysis of skewed metrics. (Skewness is a measure of the tendency for the distribution of values to be more spread out on one side than on the other. Skewness is discussed in more detail later in this chapter.)

Data Analysis

The first part of the measurement process is the collection of the data. Next, the data is analyzed in various ways. Finally, the results are presented. The purpose of analysis is to take action based on the information contained in the data.[1]

Analysts often examine the relationship between two metrics (either primitive or computed) to help determine if a causal or predictive relationship exists between the metrics. If it does exist, the nature and strength of the relationship is usually pursued.

This study considers only two metrics at a time and not the more complex (multivariate) case where a response to a simultaneous combination of several related metrics is examined.

The graphs in Figures 17.1 and 17.2 each show a relationship between two variables.

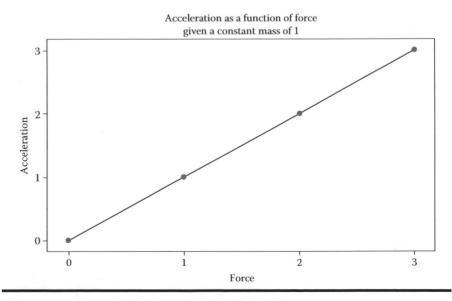

Figure 17.1   Example of a deterministic relationship.

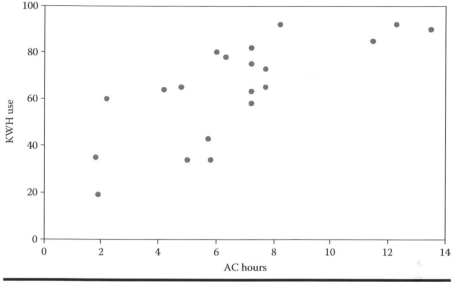

Figure 17.2   Scatter plot example.

In Figure 17.1 (a graph of the acceleration of an object as a function of the force applied to that object, with the object's mass equal to one), the relationship is deterministic. That is, if you know the value of the independent variable (force), you know the value of the dependent variable (acceleration), given that the mass of the object does not change.

In Figure 17.2, however, there could be several values of the dependent variable for each given value of the independent variable. The graph in Figure 17.2 is the amount of electricity used in a house (kWh use) plotted against the number of hours the home air conditioner ran that day (AC hours).

Drawing a straight line to connect the points in Figure 17.1 is easy, because there is no scatter and because the relationship is linear. ($F = MA$: force equals mass times acceleration. Force is commonly expressed in Newtons, mass in kilograms, and acceleration in meters per second squared.) You can use the line to predict what acceleration will result from putting a given force on an object of mass equal to one.

Drawing a line in Figure 17.2 is a bit more complicated (there are other appliances in the house, besides the air conditioner, that use electricity). Since there is some scatter, no one line passes through all the points, but there must be a line that in some sense is a best fit to those points. The process of drawing a best-fit line through scattered data points is called *regression*.

The mathematical techniques for regression are not described in this chapter. Any statistical tool will be able to apply them. The important point is that the mathematical techniques will produce a best fit *if they are properly applied.* Of course, in some cases, there really is no underlying relationship and no model will fit.

Unfortunately, if the data contains a few outliers, the regression derived from the data can be influenced greatly by those few observations and may not be representative of the whole data set. Even worse, the dependence of conclusions on those few observations can be hidden in the final presentation. As Box, Hunter, and Hunter wrote in their classic Design of Experiments text:

Most of the methods of analysis we discuss are totally appropriate and efficient when the models (a) are *structurally adequate* and the (supposedly independent) errors (b) have *constant variance* and (c) are *normally distributed.* The possibility of transforming the response *y* makes these three desiderata less burdensome and greatly broadens the class of problems to which the methods may be applied, for we then need ask only that the requirements be approximately satisfied for *some transformation of y* and not necessarily for the measurement *y* itself.[2]

As will be demonstrated, transformation is a technique for dealing with these issues.

It should be pointed out that if the intent is solely to create a control chart, then the normalization transformation is usually not required. This is because control charts work well even if the data are not normally distributed.[3] However, for other graphical and statistical methods, normality is either desired or required.

Skewness

Before fitting any model, it is appropriate to look at the data. A simple way to display data is with a scatter plot. Figure 17.3 is taken from a set of validated closed project data collected during the first half of 2008 by one organization. It shows a plot of the software-related effort needed to complete the project versus the Function Points added and modified.

The most striking feature of Figure 17.3 is how the data is distributed. Most of the values (on either axis) are very small and a few are relatively large. This is an indication that some sort of transformation may be required.

One potential regression pitfall is that the few large values will determine the fit of the regression equation.

A scatter plot is effective in showing two variables simultaneously. To look at the distribution of one variable, we can use a histogram or a box plot. A histogram uses groupings to display the frequency of observations for several intervals. A box plot displays quartiles.

A histogram for the project Function Points is given in Figure 17.4. Note the long tail of distribution to the right (the small bars that occur to the right of the highest bar), which indicates *skewness*. When a distribution is symmetrical about the mean, the skewness is equal to zero. If the histogram has a longer tail to the right than to the left, we say the distribution is skewed positively or to the right. If the probability histogram has a longer tail to the left, the measure of skewness is negative or to the left.

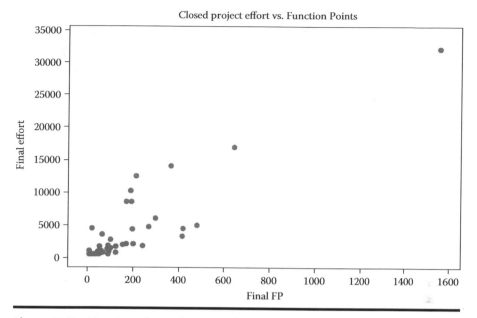

Figure 17.3 Non-transformed scatter plot.

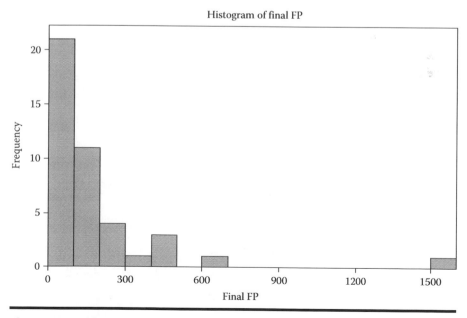

Figure 17.4 Histogram of project size.

Another way to examine the distribution is by the use of probability or normality plots. A probability plot does not use groupings and so is more effective than a histogram for small samples. Refer to a statistics text or tool for more information.

Many types of metrics commonly have a skewed distribution, including project metrics, application portfolio metrics, code complexity metrics, and others.

Transformation

If the distribution of the data is skewed, a family of transformations may be applied to the data.[4]

The nine transformations in Table 17.1 form a ladder. If the data is skewed to the right, it is appropriate to take a step down the ladder and try the next transformation. If the data is skewed to the left, take a step back up the ladder.

Histograms for each step in the ladder for the project Function Point size presented in Figure 17.4 are depicted in Figure 17.5.

Starting with the top of the ladder in the top left, the distributions change from skewed right through approximately normal to skewed left. It is apparent that the log transformation (center histogram in middle row) does the best job of removing skewness in this dataset. The log transformation is the closest to having a normal (commonly called a "bell-shaped") distribution. The first four histograms are skewed to the right, and the last four are skewed to the left.

Experience has shown that, for many pairs of software metrics, a log transformation successfully removes skewness and linearizes the relationship. In addition, they are useful for examining metrics over a large range of values. "Log–log diagrams are convenient because many orders of magnitude can be contained on one small piece of paper."[5]

Table 17.1   Normalization Transformation Ladder

y^3
y^2
Y
$\sqrt{(y)}$
$\log(y)$
$-1/\sqrt{(y)}$
$-1/y$
$-1/(y^2)$
$-1/(y^3)$

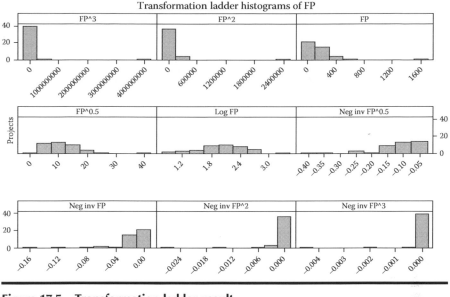

Figure 17.5   Transformation ladder result.

Box–Cox

Another method for dealing with data that do not have a normal distribution is to use a Box–Cox transformation.

Minitab (one of the commercially available statistical tools) provides a facility for implementing Box–Cox transformations in which the original variable Y is transformed to $W = Y$ raised to lambda when lambda is not equal to zero and to the natural log of Y when lambda is zero. The software contains a procedure to select the optimum value for the lambda.

As with the transformation ladder and histograms, the Box–Cox graph can be used to assess the appropriateness of the transformation.

For example, you can use the 95% confidence interval for lambda to determine whether the optimal lambda value is "close" to 1, since a lambda of 1 indicates that a transformation should not be done. In the case that the optimal lambda is close to 1, you would gain very little by performing the transformation.[6]

In the example project Function Point data, the Box–Cox transformation returns an estimate of the optimum lambda of 0.18. This result can be seen in the Box–Cox plot in Figure 17.6, at the point where the plotted curve has a minimum value.

The Box–Cox transformation produced a distribution that was almost as good as the one achieved through use of the transformation ladder, and it was somewhat quicker to complete.

Skewness measures the departure from symmetry by expressing the difference between the mean and median relative to the standard deviation. A skewness of zero

Table 17.2 Comparison of Transformation Methods

Variable	N	Mean	Standard Deviation	Median	Skewness
Log FP	42	1.9804	0.5135	1.9864	−0.19
FP^0.18	42	2.3224	0.4897	2.2781	0.46

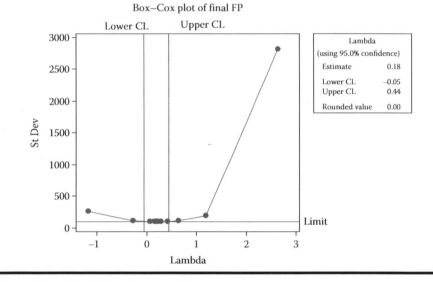

Figure 17.6 Lambda estimate plot.

indicates a symmetrical distribution. Table 17.2 compares the summary numerical results of the log transformation to the Box–Cox transformation.

The box plot in Figure 17.7 compares the summaries of the two distributions. Both boxes appear symmetrical, and so for practical purposes, either should suffice.

Linearity

Not all relationships between a dependent and an independent variable are linear. In fact, linear relationships are probably the exception rather than the rule for software metrics datasets. However, linear regression is more useful than might be suspected.

For example, while a relationship may be nonlinear over the entire range of independent values, it may behave as if it were approximately linear over a restricted range. If we fit a linear model that is appropriate for a specific range of independent

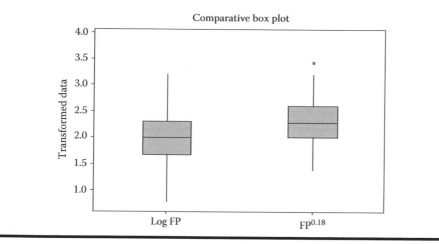

Figure 17.7   Box plot comparison of transformation.

Table 17.3 Linearizing Transformation Ladder

$\log(y)$	$\log(x)$
$\log(y)$	x
y	$\log(x)$
$1/y$	$1/x$
$1/y$	x
y	$1/x$

variables, extrapolation to other values not fit by the model may produce unreliable and inaccurate results. However, useful information can be obtained inside the region that was successfully modeled.

Fortunately, for situations where the relationship is nonlinear over the entire range, transformations of data can frequently be found that will reduce a nonlinear model to a linear form. Linearizing may require transforming both the independent and the dependent variable.

Table 17.3 is a list of some common linearizing transformations.[7]

Residual plots can be used to help decide where to start. (*Residuals* are the differences between the actual and the predicted values. Residual plots are an important diagnostic to determine the success or failure of a model.) Alternatively, work down the list of linearizing transformations as needed.

Not all functions are linearizable, and in some cases, it is not desirable to transform for linearity. These functions are best handled by nonlinear methods.

The relationship between effort and size for industry software development projects has been successfully linearized by use of the log–log transformation.[5] In addition, since it is at the top of the linearizing ladder, it might be a good place to start for software project data, especially since the log transformation successfully adjusted for the size skewness as seen in Figure 17.5. Therefore, regression will be undertaken on the log transformed project effort and size.

Paradox

Transformation is a valuable tool for understanding relationships between metrics. These relationships are not always intuitive. Yet, understanding of these relationships and reasons for the behaviors is necessary to derive optimum staffing strategies and to determine project schedules.

Industry data definitely shows an upward trend in productivity as application size increases. This is true whether we use measures like Quantitative Software Management (QSM)'s productivity index (PI) or ratio-based productivity measures (FP or some other size measure per person month of effort). The QSM industry benchmark trends behave similarly: as projects get larger, average productivity increases as well.

No matter how we look at productivity, the data and the regression trends tell us the same thing: on average, team productivity increases with project size.

Figure 17.8 is a trend graph of productivity versus size for business applications completed between the years 2000 and 2010. The trend slope is typical for other application types or historical eras. The vertical productivity measure is Function Points per man month of effort for the "main build" (all tasks from detailed design through implementation). The cloud of points is overlain with an average line (regression) and ±1 standard deviation lines. Note that Figure 17.8 uses a log–log transformation to normalize the distribution and aid in analysis.

Similar relationships are seen with individual metrics such as duration, effort, and staff. They are also positively correlated with software size. Therefore, on average, larger projects take longer, use more effort, and have more people working. This is not surprising, larger jobs should take longer and require more people than small ones.

But how do we reconcile the increase in productivity on larger projects? The way to do that is to use transformation.

Other studies have shown that productivity tends to decrease as teams become large. We have just seen that productivity increases with project size. And staff size increases with project size. How can this be?

Though they do confirm that conventional productivity declines as project size increases, two variable charts do not tell us why this is true. To answer that question, we need a way to visually examine *three* variables at once: size, productivity, and team size. This can be done with a three-dimensional (3D) plot, but since we cannot visually rotate the 3D cube in space, it is still hard to tell what is going on.

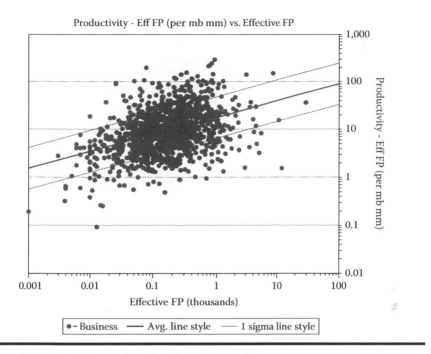

Figure 17.8   Trend lines of productivity versus size.

Clustered box plots provide more insight into the relationship between our three variables. Each box in the Figure 17.9 box plot represents the interquartile range of the data:

■ The bottom of the box represents the first quartile (25th percentile).
■ The horizontal line inside the box is the median (50th percentile).
■ The top of the box represents the third quartile (75th percentile).
■ "Whiskers" extending from either end of the box show the range of the values (minimum to maximum).
■ Individual outliers show up as circles and extreme values as asterisks.

We divided the projects into size quartiles. Quartile 1 in Figure 17.9 contains the smallest 25% of projects and quartile 4 contains the largest 25%. Productivity (FP/PM) is on the vertical axis.

The projects were also divided into four staffing (peak staff) quartiles, with the first quartile containing the smallest teams (the bottom 25%) and the fourth quartile containing team sizes at the 75th percentile or above.

Within each size bin (quartile), the behavior is the same: productivity as shown by the four shaded size quartile boxes declines as team size increases. This is the behavior that was shown by researchers who examined team size versus productivity. However, now with the box plot we can see a bigger picture.

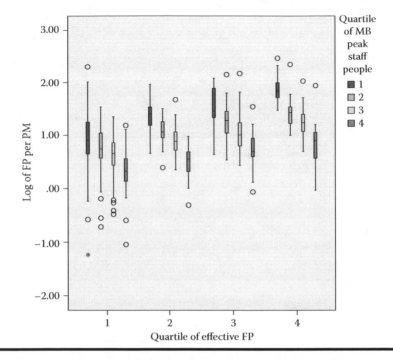

Figure 17.9 Box plot of productivity versus size stratified by staff.

Compare boxes of the same shade, which represent a quartile of staff size. For a given staff quartile, productivity increases as software size increases. This is the behavior we observed on the trend line of productivity versus size. For a given team size, productivity is higher for larger projects.

In general, smaller teams are more productive. And in general, larger projects are more productive. This interaction would not have been clear without the use of transformation combined with a multivariate box plot.

The relationships between metrics such as productivity, size, duration, and staff are not simple, but they can be understood. When examining two variable graphs, it is important to remember that it is the relative rates at which the factors change that are important. This is how we can understand that productivity increases with project size even though effort increases with project size. Relationships such as these are not linear, which introduces a possible pitfall to avoid.

Regression Pitfall

Now that we have determined that a log transformation is necessary to adjust for the skewness of the data, we are ready to fit a regression line to the project data. Figure 17.10 is a plot of the project data following a log–log transformation. A linear regression line was applied to the transformed data.

In Figure 17.10, the log–log transformation achieves two important goals: reduce skewness and increase linearity.

The transformation made the relationship linear, and the transformation was done before we plotted the data to account for the skewness.

A caution for those using graphical tools that allow for the scale to be transformed without modification to the regression. If the linear regression is on the raw (untransformed) data, the regression line will not make a good fit because the data is skewed. This is an example of the type of mistake that can be made by ignoring skewness—the regression is influenced by a few large values. Figure 17.11 is a regression of the non-transformed data. Note that the regression line passes directly through the largest project. Compare that to the regression in Figure 17.8 where the line passes under the largest project.

This situation can arise in Excel, if the raw data is plotted with regression and the scale of the graph is later changed to log–log. Compare the regression line in Figure 17.12 to the one in Figure 17.10. Figure 17.10 provides a better fit to the data.

The regression line in Figure 17.12 appears curved, because it was linear on the non-transformed data and then became curved when the scale was changed to logarithmic.

The effects of not transforming skewed data are more severe for smaller data sets and those that are highly skewed. Many of our software metrics data sets are of this type.

A final point: remember that the equation for the regression line will assume transformed data, as shown on the scale of the scatter plot. If the equation is used for prediction, the data must be transformed before and after the equation is used.

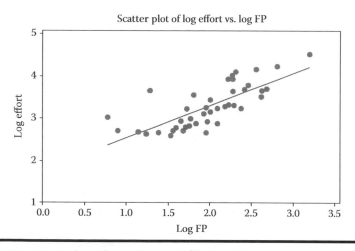

Figure 17.10   Regression of transformed effort and size.

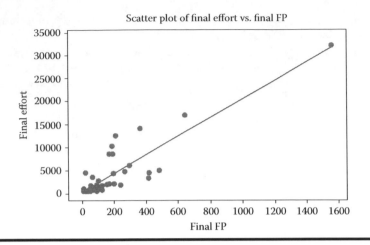

Figure 17.11   Example of poor regression using non-transformed data.

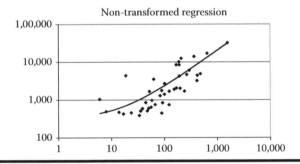

Figure 17.12   Example of poor regression.

Summary

The purpose of analysis is to take action on the information contained in the data. Analysts often examine the relationship between multiple measures to determine if there is a predictive or possible causal relationship between the metrics.

The methods presented in this chapter represent only initial steps of data analysis, but they are perhaps among the most important steps.

This may be an oversimplification, but there are two important points to remember when analyzing software metrics:

1. Metrics tend to have skewed distributions, and relationships tend to be nonlinear.
2. Analyzing skewed data directly, without the use of transformations, can result in misleading conclusions.

Good statistical practice is required not only to determine if relationships exist, but also to understand the nature and strength of the relationships.

Graphical methods are important not only to the presentation of results, but also during the data analysis. The analyst can use graphical methods to explore the data. Prior to regression analysis, graphical methods can be used to examine the data for skewness or linearity.

Endnotes

1. This sentence is a paraphrase of a concept frequently taught by W. E. Deming.
2. Box, G. E. P., W. G. Hunter, and J. S. Hunter. 1978. *Statistics for Experimenters: An Introduction to Design, Data Analysis, and Model Building.* New York: John Wiley and Sons, 239.
3. Wheeler, D. J. and D. Chambers. 1992. *Understanding Statistical Process Control,* 2nd ed. Knoxville: SPC Press, 65–76.
4. Tukey, J. W. 1977. *Exploratory Data Analysis.* Boston: Addison Wesley, 172–3.
5. Putnam, L. H. and W. Myers. 1992. *Measures for Excellence: Reliable Software on Time, Within Budget.* Upper Saddle River, New Jersey: Prentice Hall.
6. Minitab help text, version 14 (2005).
7. Weisberg, S. 1980. *Applied Linear Regression.* New York: John Wiley and Sons, 125.

About the Author

Paul Below has over 25 years experience in the subjects of measurement technology, statistical analysis, estimating and forecasting, Lean Six Sigma, and data mining. He has provided innovative engineering solutions as well as instruction and mentoring internationally in support of multiple industries.

He serves as services consultant for Quantitative Software Management (QSM), where he provides clients with statistical analysis of operational performance, helping strengthen competitive position through process improvement and predictability.

Paul is a Certified Software Quality Analyst and a past Certified Function Point Specialist. He is a Six Sigma Black Belt. He has been a course developer, instructor, and conference speaker on estimating, Lean Six Sigma, metrics analysis, Function Point Analysis, along with teaching statistics in the Masters of Software Engineering program at Seattle University.

He is a member of the IEEE, the American Statistical Association, and has served on the Management Reporting Committee of the International Function Points User Group as well as on CMMI high maturity assessment teams. He has one US patent and two patents pending.

Chapter 18

Objective-Driven Process Improvement: Connecting Improvement with Business Objectives

Christof Ebert

Contents

Introduction

Reducing product cost, improving product quality, and optimizing the overall product strategy from positioning to reuse, are goals in practically all companies to stay competitive, to continuously improve business, and to survive in a fast changing environment. It is thus crucial for most companies to simultaneously improve project management, product development, and engineering processes. However, the integration of these activities often falls back due to methodology wilderness, lack of vision, or organizational misalignment. To effectively improve IT and software development, first of all, the current situation and status must be understood. Based on this situation analysis, gaps are identified and compared to economic goals, benchmarks and process frameworks. Then an improvement program is started to close these gaps. Despite an increasing body of knowledge with improvement frameworks such as Capability Maturity Model Integration (CMMI) or Six Sigma, many organizations still struggle in practice. This chapter goes beyond such method frameworks and looks to setting improvement objectives. Objective-driven process improvement (ODPI) underlines the need to start with clear business objectives. From those, a specific and tailored approach towards achieving engineering excellence is derived. The E4-measurement (Establish, Extract, Evaluate, Execute) process is applied to instrument and drive ODPI and show how to measure throughout an improvement project. Improving productivity and efficiency is selected as a hands-on example of how to practically implement ODPI.

Objective-Driven Process Improvement

Today, software is a major asset for many companies. In industrial and consumer sectors, it is increasingly software that defines the value of products. For instance, value generation in the automotive industry already depends over 50% on innovative software-driven technologies. Not surprisingly, engineering investments are heavily spent on software development of applications and products. In our fast-changing world, a company will only succeed if it continually challenges and optimizes its own engineering performance. At the same time, engineering of technical products is currently undergoing a dramatic change. Ever more complex systems with high quality must be developed at decreasing cost and shortened time to market. Competition is growing and the entry barriers to established markets are diminishing. The result is more competitors claiming that they can achieve better performance than established companies can. An increasing number of companies are aware of these challenges and are proactively looking at ways to improve efficiency and productivity of their development processes.

Development processes along the product life cycle determine how things are done—end to end. They provide guidance to those working on the product and focus on what to do. Guidance means understanding and ensures repeatability. Focus means achieving targets both effectively and efficiently, without overhead, friction, and rework. Good processes are as lean and agile as possible, while still ensuring visibility, accountability, and commitment to results. Insufficient processes reduce business opportunities and performance due to not keeping commitments and delivering below expectations. Processes must be usable by and useful to both practitioners and managers. They must integrate seamlessly, and they must not disturb or create overhead.

Process improvement will fail if we do not consider these basic requirements. By focusing on the essence of the processes, integrating processes elements with each other, and providing complete tool solutions, organizations can tailor processes to meet specific needs and allow localized and problem- or skill-specific software practices, while still ensuring that the basic objectives of the organization are achieved.

To continuously improve and thus stay ahead of competition, organizations need to change in a deterministic and results-oriented way. If you do not know where you are and where you want to go, change will never lead to improvement. Looking toward improved process maturity will help in setting up an improvement trail.

The concept of process maturity is not new. Many of the established quality models in manufacturing use the same concept. This was summarized by Philip Crosby in his bestselling book *Quality Is Free* in 1979 [1]. He found from his broad experiences as a senior manager in different industries that business success depends on quality. With practical insight and many concrete case studies, he could empirically link process performance to quality. His credo was stated as "Quality is measured by the cost of quality which is the expense of non-conformance—the cost of doing things wrong."

However, over half of all process improvement programs fail. Why is that? It is for two reasons, namely the following:

■ Lack of systematic change management
■ Insufficient management support

Both observations have one common denominator. Many improvement activities have insufficient objectives and for that reason no motivation to change and no possibility to follow through with the implementation of changes. Projects without clear goals will miss their goals clearly, as Tom Gilb once stated.

We have introduced the concept of ODPI in order to focus processes—and their improvement—on the objectives they must achieve [2]. Processes are a means to an end and need to be lean, pragmatic, efficient, and effective—or they will ultimately fail, despite all the effort one can imagine.

Objective-driven improvement is a goal-oriented improvement approach towards measurable and sustainable performance improvement. It has several components that distinguish ODPI from the more traditional approach with a focus on certification and therefore insufficient buy-in from stakeholders:

■ Focus on concrete business needs
■ Incremental deliveries of tangible progress
■ Broadening scope of the improvement project from engineering to a product and customer perspective
■ Usage of improvement frameworks as support for methodology and best practices, but not as an end in itself

Process improvement frameworks such as the CMMI offer the benefit to improve on a determined path, to benchmark with other companies, and to apply worldwide supplier audits or comparisons on a standardized scale. Combined with ODPI, they provide the "tools" to implement changes, while ODPI ensures staying on track and delivering the right results in due time. Figure 18.1 shows the basic steps in ODPI, starting from business objectives and ending with sustainable results being delivered. There are seven steps to emphasize this:

1. Create urgency
   Derive concrete change needs from the organization's business goals. The status quo must appear more dangerous than the journey to the new state. Employees and management must feel the pressure resulting from business needs.
2. Ensure sponsorship
   Sustainable changes start at the top and then grow top-down. Change needs to be pushed by senior management. "You need to be the change that you want to see in the world."
3. Establish vision for action
   Establish a compelling vision. The change vision must energize employees towards being part of the change. Ensure a sound methodology and the right actions. You have just one shot.
4. Create room to change
   Change needs resources and competences. Organize change as a project with a small energetic team. Provide a budget and ensure expert support. Agree on project targets, responsibilities, milestones, and deliverables—tuned to business goals. Rigorously manage the change project. Monitor performance, looking to usage and use, pre- and post-change. Manage risks.

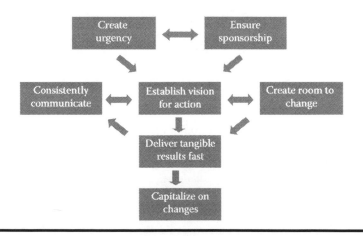

Figure 18.1 Objective-driven process improvement: Seven steps to success.

5. Consistently communicate

   Mobilize stakeholder support. Vision, content, progress, and results must be consistently communicated. Use different communication channels. Do not confuse leadership and democracy. Engrain change into management behaviors. "Walk the talk."

6. Deliver tangible results fast

   Change where there is a pressing need. Fast and sustainable results create trust. Set up the transformation in incremental steps to periodically deliver tangible value. Monitor the implementation and institutionalization of the change with a few measurements, such as use and usage.

7. Capitalize on changes

   Success motivates more changes. Show how new ways of working actually deliver better results. Anchor new behaviors within your organizational culture. Consolidate achieved results by updating organizational templates, such as budgeting. Ensure that changes are engrained to culture and periodically reassessed. Results are sustainable only when they are delivered without management pressure.

We show in this chapter how ODPI is used for productivity improvement. Specifically, we show how adequate measurement is used as a precondition to define the right objectives and later on systematically follow through.

Improvement Needs Measurement

Process improvement needs software measurement. Objectives need to be framed quantitatively. The progress in achieving these objectives must be tracked with adequate measurements. Figure 18.2 shows the dependencies between the execution of a process, its definition, and the improvements. It introduces to the goal-oriented E4-measurement process (Establish, Extract, Evaluate, Execute) starting with objectives (Establish), through executing the process and measuring results (Extract), evaluating results (Evaluate), and deriving and implementing concrete improvements (Execute) [2]. This E4-measurement process is well suited to implement ODPI as it starts with a breakdown of business-oriented objectives.

Obviously, if there is no process, some initial definition has to happen to determine a measurement baseline. Improvements are feasible only if they are quantitatively tracked against such a baseline that then serves as a yardstick on progress and a pointer on directions to take. Processes must be quantitatively judged whether they are good or bad, or whether they are better or worse than before. To make change sustainable, it is based on realistic improvement objectives. The interaction of objectives and feedback is obvious in day-to-day decision making. Different groups typically work towards individually controlled targets that build up to business division-level goals and corporate goals.

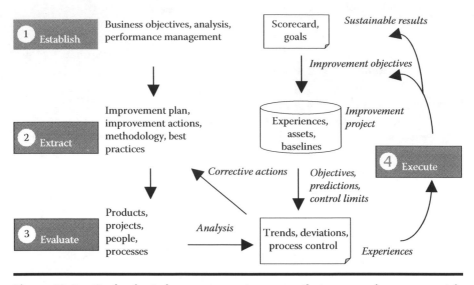

Figure 18.2   Goal-oriented measurement ensures that process improvement is embedded in a closed feedback loop.

Let us look at a specific example to better understand these dependencies. A department or business division-level goal could be to improve maintainability within legacy systems, as it is strategically important for most software and IT companies. Design managers might break that down further to redesigning exactly those components that are at the edge of being maintainable. Product and project managers, on the other hand, face a trade-off with time to market and might emphasize on incrementally adding functionality instead. Clearly, both need appropriate indicators to support their selection processes that define the way towards the needed quantitative targets related to these goals. Obviously, one of the key success criteria for process improvement is to understand the context and potentially hidden agendas within the organization to find the right compromises or weigh alternatives.

Objectives related to individual processes must be unambiguous and agreed upon by their respective stakeholders. Stakeholders are those who use the process or who benefit from it. These are not just management, but could comprise engineers and suppliers, amongst others. This is obvious for test and design groups. While the first are reinforced for finding defects and thus focus on writing and executing effective test suites, design groups are targeted to delivering code that can be executed without defects. Defects must be corrected efficiently, which allows for setting up a quantitative objective for a design group, that is, the backlog of faults it has to resolve. This may uncover one of the many inherent conflict situations embedded in an improvement program. Setting an overall target of reducing defects found by the customer, for instance, triggers immediate activities in design, such as improved coding rules, establishing code inspections, and so on. Finding such defects up front means better input quality to integration test that as a result might not be able to accomplish efficiency targets, such as a distinct rate of faults per test case. For testers, this change, however, has dramatic consequences, as it will be more expensive to detect remaining defects. Besides maybe enhancing test coverage, a successfully running test case has little worth from a cost reduction perspective. They also have to change their own performance measurements to achieve better customer quality combined with more efficiency.

Productivity Improvement

We focus in this chapter on process improvement for better productivity. Productivity improvement is a major goal for many companies due to increasing global competition and the need to focus scarce resources on what really matters for value creation. Let us therefore work in four steps that will guarantee that you will get a grip on productivity. Figure 18.3 shows this stepwise approach to productivity improvement based on the E4-measurement process.

1. Agree on objectives. The first step is to set a business-driven objective. This implies that you understand what you mean by productivity (Establish).
2. Determine where you are. The next step is to determine where you are and what should be improved (Extract).

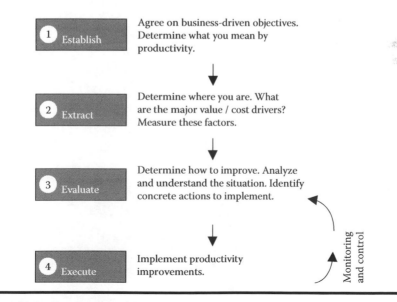

Figure 18.3 Productivity improvement.

3. Determine how to improve. Then you analyze in detail how you are doing, compare with others, evaluate how specific industry best practices might help, and agree on concrete actions for productivity improvement (Evaluate).
4. Implement improvements. With this basis you will systematically improve and subsequently repeat the previous steps (Execute).

How can software engineering productivity be effectively improved? Based on an understanding of what productivity is (step 1) and where we are (step 2), it is a simple step to move forward and determine what must be changed. Figure 18.4 shows the different levers to improve productivity.

The first thing we realize is that in order to improve productivity, it is wrong to simply talk about cost reductions. Often the one and only mechanism that is triggered when it comes to R&D or IT productivity is to reduce cost, which is done mostly by cutting out what does not matter at present or by outsourcing. Both have detrimental effects on overall enterprise performance and long-term stability. Reducing investments to new products will create short-term yields but will equally reduce market attractiveness. Productivity improvement means looking at both numerator and denominator.

In improving productivity, start always on the output side and reflect whether you are truly delivering value to your customers—inside or outside the company.

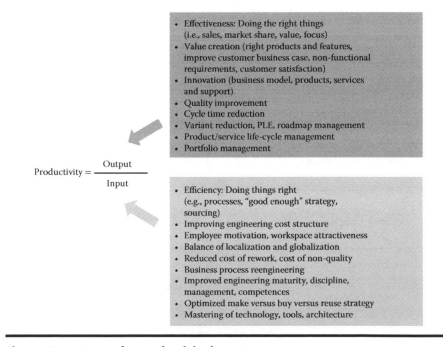

Figure 18.4 Levers for productivity improvement.

Do you sufficiently manage product content and roadmaps? Are the business case and needs of your customers understood and considered in the product portfolio? Do you have too many variants for different markets and waste efforts on customization that is not paid for? Which of your products have the highest market share and market growth? Analyze and manage your portfolio to ensure that scarce resources are spent on critical portfolio elements (i.e., focus on cash cow products to safeguard today's cash flow, and focus on future stars for new technologies). Reduce the number of versions and spend more time on strategic management together with your product managers, marketers, and sales personnel. Reduce the number of versions and rather spend more time on strategic management together with your product managers, marketers, and sales. Are you doing the right thing? Note that cost reduction while doing the wrong things will reduce expenses, but will not improve performance.

Then look to the input side. It is about efficiency, but certainly not only about cost of labor, although this matters most in software engineering. Evaluate where you are spending your effort. Embark on a rigorous activity-based accounting to determine which processes consume effort and how much they contribute to value creation. Look to your rework along the entire product life cycle. Rework is not only created with changing requirements, insufficient variant management, or defect corrections. Rework also comes from insufficient processes and lack of automation. Investigate which of your processes need more guidance or management control. Focus on the cost of non-quality, because it typically is a huge share in software development and maintenance. If the test consumes 40% of resources, this is the process to look into, because the test is not value creation. Are there techniques that could improve quality during design and development and thus reduce test overhead? How much of your test is redundant? How do you determine what to test and how much to test? Rarely do companies have rules to find out what is good enough and build this notion around a business case.

Starting from the 1980s, several studies were performed to understand what impacts on productivity in a software or IT project. The general finding by researchers like C. Jones or F. Brooks shows that there are productivity factors that can be controlled (process-related: accidental) and factors that cannot be controlled (product-related: essential) [3,4]. Jones found that product-related and process-related factors account for approximately the same amount—roughly one-third—of productivity variance.

Often hardware productivity improvement is used as a benchmark to raise demands on the software side. Admittedly hardware productivity exploded over several decades, but this was above any other industry experience ever. The anomaly is not that software progress is so slow, but that computer hardware progress is so fast. No other technology since civilization began has seen seven orders of magnitude price-performance gain in just 50 years. In hardly any technology can one choose to blend the gains from improved performance and reduced cost. We cannot expect to see twofold productivity gains every 2 years in other engineering fields. However, we should strive to continuously improve software productivity.

By applying this basic insight, we identified two basic approaches towards improving productivity in software projects, namely the following [2]:

■ Reduce accidental barriers (e.g., improve engineering and management discipline, processes, and tools; apply standards—from cradle to grave [languages, templates, IDEs, and so on]; design to quality, change, cost, and so on; introduce lean and agile concepts such as smaller teams, components, iterations, and so on).

■ Control essential barriers (e.g., understand what the real needs are and implement those in the product; do not implement each single change request; carefully evaluate the customer's business case behind a feature and do not implement when there is no clear business case; improve domain understanding; use suitable modeling languages to achieve a "unified" understanding; develop self-generating and self-updating software; reuse components).

CASE STUDY   Productivity Improvement

We conclude with a short case study on productivity improvement [2]. Figure 18.5 shows how a productivity improvement project was launched and implemented in a company with

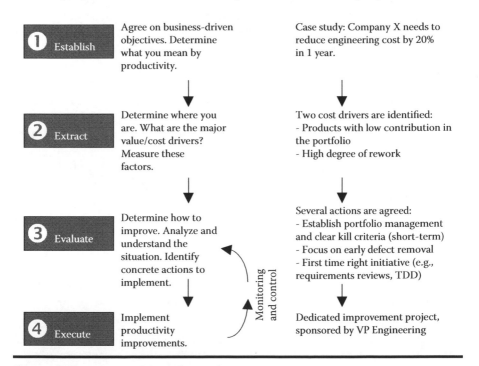

Figure 18.5   Case study: Implementing productivity improvement.

which we worked. Our starting point is the business objective to reduce cost of engineering by 20%. We will not discuss the story behind it, as it might reveal the situation of the client. Suffice it to say that senior management immediately suggested outsourcing parts of development to India. Our proposal was to first look into what drives productivity, before embarking on a mechanism that in fact might not create the benefits which are hoped for. Outsourcing is such an example. It is often demanded, because it looks attractive. However, what is missed in this thinking is the long learning curve of 2 years until tangible results are achieved, and the relatively low—compared to expectations—savings potential of 15–20% if executed well [2].

In that company, we found two major cost drivers, first, an overly high amount of small customization projects, which did not create much value. Some had been started simply because sales claimed that they would otherwise lose that market. What was missing, however, was a sound business case and valuation that could prove this statement. A second observation was that a high cost of non-quality (i.e., cost for defect correction etc.) was created by finding defects too late. We proposed and evaluated a set of potential improvements, where we agreed on three concrete actions after careful analysis of cost, impacts, duration, and feasibility in the specific contact of our client. The first was to install portfolio management with a clear decision-making and execution process. This meant that all projects and products were screened based on their contribution and strategic adherence. Within 6 months, we could remove projects with an effort contribution of over 20% compared to the overall engineering cost. However, this was just a one-time effect. We had to move further in a second step.

We therefore also embarked on early defect removal and a dedicated "first time right" initiative in engineering. Unexpectedly, this latter initiative got very good buy-in from engineering because they realized that many changes and thus rework was introduced from the outside. A strengthened portfolio management helped in controlling such changes and having clear criteria to decide and prioritize change proposals. Therefore, portfolio management introduced a decision-making approach to focus on value-creation in engineering rather than defect corrections.

Some concrete actions will show how we achieved early defect removal and implementing the "right the first time"

principle. A key change was to establish a strong requirements management process with reviews of requirements and
their changes by a defined expert group of product management, systems engineering, testers, and the project manager.
Requirements without the customer's business case and clear
internal business forecast were not accepted and had to pass
a monthly steering board under the lead of the business unit
vice president. Test-driven development (TDD) was installed
to ensure that requirements were consistently broken down
to the design specifications and finally code. We used TDD
specifically to create unit test cases that could be reused with
each iteration where code was changed and redelivered. This
caused a strong reduction of defects found by integration and
system test and therefore helped after some 10–12 months to
gradually reduce these late testing activities. Another action
was to use automatic code analysis tools that would be used by
the engineer before delivering her code complete milestone in
the current increment. While it took a while to tailor and adjust
the screening rules to the most relevant defects, it helped to
give ownership of defect removal to designers, rather than testers. These combined changes helped to deliver work products
right the first time along the development process, and thus to
improve efficiency.

Conclusions

The chapter showed how to set up and drive a process improvement program
with business goals and concrete development challenges and how to deliver tangible value. We showed that often the reason for failures in implementing process
improvement is that objectives are unclear or overly abstract (e.g., reduce cycle time
by 20%), and as a consequence, the entire project is handled ad hoc with no concrete benefits.

The notion of ODPI has been introduced to underline the need to start with
clear business objectives and from those derive a specific and tailored approach
towards achieving engineering excellence.

Our message is clear: Productivity improvement needs several related steps that
are carefully implemented. There is no silver bullet, despite all the promises by
tool vendors and others. Broad experience in engineering and product life-cycle
management helps in selecting the right actions with the most value in a certain
environment. Clear objectives, an objective-driven improvement program, and
excellent change management are keys in introducing such changes.

Acknowledgments

Some parts of the chapter appeared first in Software Measurement by C. Ebert and R. Dumke [2]. Copyright: Springer, Heidelberg, New York, 2007. Used with permission. We recommend reading respective portions of that book as an extension of the quantitative concepts mentioned in this chapter.

References

1. Crosby, P. B. 1979. *Quality is Free*. New York: New American Library.
2. Ebert, C., and R. Dumke. 2007. *Software Measurement*. Heidelberg, New York: Springer. ISBN 978-3-540-71648-8.
3. Brooks, F. P. 1987. No silver bullet, essence and accidents of software engineering. *IEEE Comput* 20(4):10–9.
4. Jones, C. 1986. *Programming Productivity*. New York: McGraw-Hill.

About the Author

Dr. Christof Ebert is managing director at Vector Consulting Services. He supports clients around the world to improve product strategy and product development and to manage organizational changes. He sits on a number of advisory and industry bodies and teaches at the University of Stuttgart. Before that, he held engineering and management positions for 15 years in IT, transportation, and aerospace. An internationally renowned keynote speaker, SEI certified CMMI Instructor, area editor of the Software Engineering Body of Knowledge, and steering chair of the IEEE conference series on Global Software Engineering, he has authored several books including his most recent books *Global Software Engineering* published by Wiley/IEEE in 2011 and *Software Measurement* published by Springer in 2007. Contact him at christof.ebert@vector.com.

Chapter 19

A Framework for Implementing an Effective Software Development and Maintenance Metrics Program

Miranda L. Mason

Contents

Many Information Technology (IT) organizations struggle with defining and implementing an effective metrics program for application development and maintenance. Common issues include too many metrics, data overload, no clear alignment to strategy, no end-to-end perspective or ability to drill down, and unclear accountability. Any of these issues can lead to an ineffective program and frustrated IT leadership. This chapter will detail a proven framework to establish quickly an actionable Software Development and Maintenance (SDM) metrics program and scorecard based on data that is generally available in most SDM organizations.

Common Metrics Program Challenges/Pitfalls

While the majority of SDM organizations have an IT Scorecard and are reporting metrics, the Chief Information Officer (CIO) and IT leadership often feel that the metrics are not effective or are not giving them the information they need to manage their organization. Common challenges and pitfalls observed across many organizations include the following:

- *Inefficient*—Too many metrics collected or no clear alignment to strategy.
- *Distributed*—Data collection and reporting. No enterprise visibility across IT and SDM, or each functional area and region have scorecards that do not "roll up" into a cross IT view.
- *Unclear accountability*—Lack of end-to-end perspective or accountability for key metrics (e.g., availability, restoration time) making it difficult for leadership to analyze which tower, group (e.g., infrastructure or application team), or individual is accountable for restoring from an outage.
- *Unaligned*—Metrics are not linked to strategic objectives and cascaded into individual objectives, and therefore, do not drive accountability and improvements.
- *Unfocused*—High volume of metrics diffuses management attention, operational/detailed metrics included on executive reports.
- *Unclear business expectations*—No standard Service Level Agreement (SLA) approach across IT or consistent, updated SLA metrics and targets agreed with the business.
- *Inwardly focused*—End-to-end perspective is missing. Internal Operational Level Agreements (OLA) between IT towers is lacking.
- *Metrics are inconsistent* across towers or calculations are different for metrics that are consistent (e.g., availability, resource management).

- *No visible root cause analysis and results are not actionable.*
- *Lack of standard processes and tools* results in data quality issues and lack of data in some areas (i.e., project delivery metrics).

Steps for Defining and Implementing an SDM Metrics Program

Define the Metrics Architecture
Confirm the Organization Objectives
Identify and Select Metrics for Each Objective
Define the Metrics
Determine Metrics Phasing Based on Data Availability and Data Quality
Design the Strategic Scorecard and Supporting Reports
Start Reporting on the Initial Set of Metrics
Define the Longer Term Metrics Program

Step 1: Define the Metrics Architecture

A Metrics Architecture is an essential starting point for defining or improving a metrics program. Not all metrics are equal and a common pitfall of IT organizations is information overload or too many metrics for the CIO and IT leadership. The Metrics Architecture provides a framework for defining the right audience and governance levels, and the metrics and level of detail needed to support each level. The Metrics Architecture contains several levels of metrics. In designing the Metrics Architecture, begin with the highest level objectives and metrics, in this case the objectives for the Software Development and Maintenance organization, and cascade those objectives and metrics down to the organization level, then to the regional and team level, and finally down to a process or individual level. Using a top-down approach helps to ensure alignment of objectives and measures at all levels of the organization. This approach also allows a drill down on metrics to understand performance at each level.

The sample Metrics Architecture in Figure 19.1 leverages a top-to-bottom metrics approach both to demonstrate performance and to provide data for analysis. This enables management to make informed decisions at each level of governance. The levels in this metrics framework are further defined as:

- *Strategic performance*—measures overall health of the IT organization against targets. These metrics are the "vital few" CIO or executive level metrics used by the leadership team to assess the state of IT "at a glance." The metrics are commonly organized in a dashboard format with stoplight or green/yellow/red indicators to report performance against standards. The number

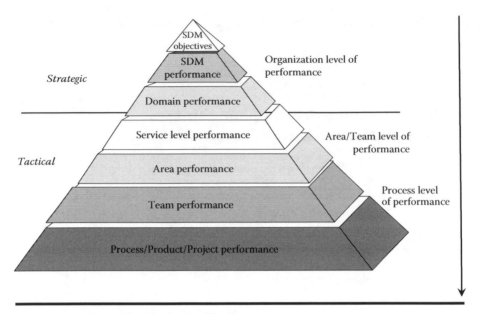

Figure 19.1 Example Metrics Architecture.

of metrics at this level should be no more than 10–20 key indicators with the ability to drill down to further levels of detail as required to understand negative trends or yellow/red results. Metrics at this level are typically reported monthly and should be a combination of "leading" and "lagging" indicators. The leading indicators are more predictive in nature and can enable the leadership team to take corrective actions to prevent yellow or red status versus always looking in a "rearview mirror" of past results.

■ *Tactical performance*—the next level down in terms of measuring performance. The top-down objectives and metrics should cascade to each level of the organization down to team and individual levels. The amount of data and metrics required increases as the structure breaks down into management units and teams. There will be higher volumes of reports and transactional data required to manage day-to-day operations, so it is important to ensure that the teams have the right data at the right times to support the strategic and tactical metrics and targets and that the calculations and interpretation are consistent.

The tactical level includes the measurement of delivery against service level commitments to the business. The service levels are the metrics that the business (i.e., buyers and users of IT services) care about such as availability, stability, response and resolution time, and on-time and on-budget delivery. An organization performing application development and maintenance work should have SLAs—support models, metrics, and target levels of performance—defined and agreed upon with the business units regardless of whether there are sourcing arrangements in place. This ensures that IT understands key business objectives and drivers and how applications, projects, and IT investment support the business operations, and promotes improved alignment of IT results in support of business goals. If a sourcing arrangement is in place or is pursued, IT suppliers can align to an existing SLA structure and targets.

Metrics at the tactical level are typically reported daily, weekly, or monthly depending on the frequency required for tactical deliver management. Service level metrics are typically reported monthly to the business.

Step 2: Confirm the Organization Objectives

It is important that the metrics align with and support the overall SDM organization objectives. Determining Strategic metrics begins with identifying the organization's goals and objectives and determining the measures that will be used to measure those goals and objectives. The SDM or IT objectives may align with or support the corporate objectives by cascading to objectives that IT can control. An example of this is a corporate objective of Faster Time to Market for specific products. The SDM organization objectives to support this corporate goal could be increasing the predictability of delivery and improving productivity levels for new development. Another example related to Maintenance is an SDM objective of reducing Cost to Serve for manufacturing application support to align with a corporate objective of reducing the cost to produce a widget.

Strategic metrics identified top down for each SDM objective and are then reported on the SDM organization's executive scorecard. If your SDM organization already has objectives defined, then those should be used as the starting point. If there are no objectives defined or if there is a desire to compare the metrics against "standard" SDM goals, the following list is a good starting set of common SDM goals.

- Reduce *Cost to Serve* and overall IT spend per unit of output
- Increase *customer satisfaction*
- *Response/turnaround time* that meet business targets
- Increase *throughput*
- Improve *quality and reliability*
- Increase *predictability* of delivery
- Improve or maintain *productivity* levels
- Effective *resource management*
- Increase *employee morale and satisfaction*

There may be other goals that are more difficult to measure such as demonstrating the business value of IT to the business. A metrics program can quickly be derailed by the challenges of defining and implementing business value metrics such as return on investment (ROI). It is suggested that a metrics program begin with the goals that are easiest to measure and tackle the more complex and less quantitative goals at a later time as the program matures.

Step 3: Identify and Select the Metrics for Each Objective

A "Top-Down" Metrics Identification Matrix can serve as a useful tool for identifying metrics that align to each organization objective and select the most appropriate metric(s) for each objective. The strategic objectives are a required input for this step.

Complete the Top-Down Metrics Identification Matrix to identify metrics that could be used to measure and manage strategic initiatives and goals. This matrix will help select the metrics that will be implemented.

List strategic objectives.

Identify critical success factors—things that you can do or put in place to accomplish the goal. This translates high-level objectives into actionable and measurable components.

Identify metrics that can measure critical success factors and measure progress toward goals and objectives.

For each metric, determine the metric type—leading or lagging.

An effective leadership scorecard is based on a set of hypotheses about cause and effect, which can be expressed in if-then statements. An example of a hypothesis statement is as follows: *If we provide employees with the training and skills they need to do their jobs, then they will be able to perform their jobs more efficiently and effectively. If employees can perform their jobs more efficiently and effectively, then productivity will increase.*

Top-down metrics should identify cause and effect relationships of strategic objectives and should include a mix of leading and lagging indicators. This column of the matrix helps to identify the balance of metric types that you have decided to implement.

Leading indicator—A leading indicator drives or causes the desired outcome. Leading indicators tell us what type of outcome may be expected down the road and are an early indicator of progress toward achieving the outcome or objective.

Lagging indicator—A lagging indicator measures outcomes and results. Lagging indicators report past performance after it is too late to change or influence the results.

Using the example above, productivity would be a lagging indicator. Productivity results are based on several drivers or leading indicators that could be used to predict productivity results in the future. Leading indicators such as low training hours per full-time equivalent (FTE), low employee satisfaction, attrition, poor process compliance, and large amounts of time spent on rework and fixing defects will be red flags indicating that productivity results will also be low.

Analyze the metrics—An analysis of each metric is completed to assess strengths and weaknesses of implementing the metric as input into selecting the most appropriate metrics in support of the objectives. Guidelines for assessing a metric's strengths and weaknesses include the following:

Prior to selecting a metric, the behaviors that each metric will encourage should be assessed in order to select metrics that reinforce positive behaviors. If the behavior that the metric will drive is not desired, it should not be implemented or the behavior should be carefully managed.

Evaluate ease and cost of collecting the data for the metric. If a metric is difficult or expensive to collect, weigh the value of the metric with the cost to collect to determine if it is worthwhile to implement. If the metric is valuable, seek ways to reduce the cost or difficulty of data collection (e.g., automate data collection).

Determine the frequency of data collection. Most metrics should be available monthly if not more frequently; however, some metrics such as Employee Satisfaction may only be available quarterly or annually.

Assess the balance of leading and lagging indicators. Balancing leading and lagging indicators will ensure that you have some opportunity to predict and even change outcomes rather than always looking at past performance.

Determine which metrics to implement—Based on metric type and the metrics analysis, use the far right column to note which metrics on the matrix you will implement. Metrics that are not planned for implementation at this time should remain on the matrix. You may decide that the metric should be implemented at a later time when circumstances change.

A sample Top-Down Metrics Identification Matrix completed for one strategic objective can be found in Table 19.1.

It is recommended that you start with a smaller set of metrics (no more than 20) and keep it simple, so you may choose a subset of the metrics below to get started and add additional metrics in later phases.

These are strategic level metrics for the executive scorecard and are typically reported monthly. There will be many more detailed metrics and reports required to support the strategic metrics. A strategic scorecard level metric should have supporting metrics and data in order to "drill down" on the results to analyze trends, understand why a status is yellow or red, or view results by domain (such as Department), area (such as Geography or Business Unit), or team.

As an example, Percent Projects on Schedule and Percent Projects on Budget are reported monthly for all projects completed during the reporting period. This metric summarizes the ability to deliver a project predictably and within the original estimates. However, the metric is a "rearview mirror" view or "lagging indicator" as the projects are already completed. The Program Management office and project managers should be tracking and managing to the project plan and in-flight metrics

Table 19.1 Sample Top-Down Metrics Identification Matrix

Strategic Objective	Critical Success Factors	Metric	Type	Strengths	Weaknesses	Data Available?	Implement?
Increase Predictability of Delivery	Successfully implement releases on budget and on schedule	Percent Projects on Budget	Lagging	Data is available in project management tool Can be measured on completed and in-flight projects (ETC, EAC)	Lagging indicator unless reported on in-flight projects Could cause staff to pad estimates to increase chances of completing within the estimate	Yes	Yes
		Percent Projects on Schedule	Lagging	Data is available in project management tool Can be measured on completed and in flight projects (End Date Variance, Schedule Variance)	Lagging indicator unless reported on in-flight projects Could cause staff to pad estimates to increase chances of completing within the estimate	Yes	Yes

Better manage release churn and scope changes which impact our ability to deliver to estimate	Requirements Volatility	Leading	Great leading indicator as we believe most projects are late due to business frequently changing requirements especially after test has already started	Data is not available today but will be in place after the testing tool is fully implemented in Q3	No	Yes – Q4
	Change Request Impact (in Hours)	Leading	Can be an effective shorter term measure of degree of change to projects	Need to work with project managers to ensure change requests are completed for every change and the project is re-baselined	Yes	Yes
Improve prioritization of projects upfront to reduce effort spent on low priority or cancelled projects	Positive Return on Investment for Each Project	Leading	This measure would ensure that we do not start on any project unless the business benefits are quantified and the project cost is justified	Difficult to measure Would require significant involvement from the business to define the estimated dollar value	No	No

(Continued)

Table 19.1 Sample Top-Down Metrics Identification Matrix (*Continued*)

Strategic Objective	Critical Success Factors	Metric	Type	Strengths	Weaknesses	Data Available?	Implement?
		Percent Projects with Approved Business Case	Leading	Could be quick to get in place using the business case template defined last quarter Could significantly reduce low value or cancelled projects by requiring governance approval based on business case prior to starting		No but quick to put in place	Yes
		# Cancelled Projects	Lagging	Easy measure to track and be able to quantify to the business the volumes and hours spent on cancelled projects		Yes	Yes

throughout the software development life cycle. Typical project metrics that are leading indicators, more predictive, or tracked "in-flight" while the project is in progress include Estimate to Complete (ETC), Estimate at Completion (EAC), Variance at Completion (VAC), End Date Variance, Cost Variance, Schedule Variance, Cost Performance Index (CPI), Schedule Performance Index (SPI), Deliverable Timeliness, Requirements Churn, Change Request Impact, Defect Rates, and Defect Removal Efficiency.

If leadership sees a yellow status or downward trend in the predictable delivery of completed projects on the scorecard, they may desire to drill down into Completed Projects by area or team, by project size, or other characteristics to better understand the trend. Leadership may also view the in-flight project reports to understand if those projects still in progress are on track and what the monthly results will be.

There may also a need to identify metrics bottom up by area or team or in support of process improvement initiatives. In this case, there should be a checkpoint to map the process level metrics that ensures that the process metrics are in alignment with the strategic objectives and are measured consistently with the strategic metrics. Bottom-up metrics will often roll up into organizational level metrics that are reported on the executive scorecard; however, many process level metrics will be too detailed or specific to that process to roll up at a higher level. It is important that the bottom-up metrics support the overall objectives or team leads and individuals may be managing to and focusing on the wrong things or reporting metrics that conflict with the strategic metrics on the scorecard.

Step 4: Define the Metrics

Once the metrics are identified, they need to be defined in sufficient detail to understand how the metric should be used, how the metric is calculated, where to obtain the data, frequency of data collection and reporting, and how to analyze the results. A metrics definition manual can be created as the reference for all the metrics definitions. A suggested format for defining an individual metric is as follows, using Percent Projects on Budget as an example.

Metric Name: Percent Projects on Budget

Description of Use: Percent Projects on Budget is the percentage of projects that are completed on or under budget where the actual hours spent is within +/5% of budgeted or estimated number of hours.
Category:
    Internal Process—Leading and Lagging Indicators

Goal: Ensure that projects are being delivered within budget, thus meeting Business Partners' expectations and financial targets. The goal is to increase the percentage of projects delivered on budget over time.

Formula: (Number of Projects or Enhancements Completed on or under Budget/ Total Number of Project or Enhancement Requests Completed) × 100   (19.1)

Measurement Unit: Percent
Data Elements and Data Sources:

- Planned Effort (hours)—Planned hours to complete the project from the detailed estimate from the Detailed Estimate field in the project management tool.
- Actual Effort (hours)—Actual effort for all completed project and enhancements from the project management tool; includes all phases of the project including Plan and Analyze through Unit Test and Deployment.
- Total Number of Projects or Enhancements Completed—Total number of projects and enhancements completed during the reporting period.

Data Slices Available: *Business Unit, Domain*
Target: 90%
Target Range:

- Green: >85%
- Yellow: 80%–85%
- Red: <80%

Data Quality:
   Requires Improvement—A standard project management tool (and methods) is implemented across the organization as a whole; however, estimates and actuals are not consistently entered and updated in project plans.
Frequency and Reporting—Monthly for all projects and enhancements completed during the reporting month. However, project leads should be monitoring project performance more frequently and using standard project management metrics.
Analysis:
   Potential causes of decrease in Percent Projects on Budget:

- Unqualified or inadequately trained team members causing more work than estimated
- Work process inefficiencies
- Inability to monitor budget and actuals of project
- ETCs not being updated by team members
- Changing scope or schedule requirements
- Inaccurate estimating

Potential corrective actions:

■ Provide needed training
■ Implement consistent project management processes/tools across regions/ functional areas
■ Control scope and schedule churn
■ Improve estimation model

Associated metrics:

■ Percent Projects on Schedule
■ Budget (Effort) Variance
■ Schedule Variance
■ Change Impact in Hours
■ Requirements Volatility
■ Defect Density

Step 5: Determine Metrics Phasing Based on Data Availability and Data Quality

After selecting the desired set of metrics for implementation, you may find the number of metrics that need to be reported to be overwhelming. Initially, the focus can be on a set of readily available metrics where data is readily available with decent data quality. Incorporate metrics that will require some effort to set up collection or improve current processes/tools into the long-term plan. The phasing phase may have three or more target timeframes—Initial Metrics, Medium Term Metrics (i.e., 2–3 months later; these are metrics that could be available or have improved data quality after a short term or quick hit project is completed), and Longer Term Metrics (3–6 months or greater; these are metrics dependent upon longer term/large continuous improvement initiatives and/or require standard process adoption/maturity).

When planning future metrics requirements, consider when metrics may need to be retired or replaced with a more relevant metric or one with more alignment to the overall objectives. The metrics should continually be kept "evergreen" and relevant to leadership that may require removal or refreshing of metrics from time to time.

Step 6: Design the Strategic Scorecard and Supporting Reports

Once the metrics are identified, the efforts to start collecting the data can begin in parallel with defining how the database and reports will look and what tools to use. Many people start with this step and are too caught up in designing how the data will be reported than they are about finalizing and getting the data. Whether you purchase a robust business intelligence tool and data warehouse, build your own, or just create a simple Excel-based report you first need to start with what the metrics are, what data will be collected, where it will come from, and how frequently. These requirements should be defined before advancing on how the data will be summarized and reported.

If the intent is to implement an automated reporting system, it is recommended that you start designing and reporting with a manual design in Excel. Starting simple with a manual report has a number of benefits including (1) getting a useful report for leadership to start using up faster and that (2) designing and implementing a manual report serves as a prototype and helps in defining better requirements for a more effective automated solution.

Some tips in designing a strategic scorecard solution are below:

- The executive scorecard typically follows a *Balanced Scorecard* format with the leading and lagging metrics grouped by four quadrants. The four common Balanced Scorecard perspectives are Financial, Customer, Business Process, and Learning and Growth [1].
- The metrics should represent the entire SDM scope where possible with the ability to "drill down" to more detailed levels of the organization by domain, tower, and team.
- It is helpful to define the catalog of reports upfront—audience, level of organization, governance, purpose of report, and expected actions—and then map the metrics and level of detail to the required reports.
- The executive level scorecard should be simple and contain the vital few metrics that enable leadership to view the organization's performance against objectives "at a glance." Additional levels of detail should be a "drill down" or other supporting report.
- The executive scorecard should show performance against targets, a trend over time (at least 6 months of history) and ideally a "stoplight" status for each metric of results against target green, yellow, and red performance ranges.
- If data quality for certain metrics is poor and requires improvement, they can be reported now to kick start the focus and desired behaviors, and a Data Quality Indicator can be added to the scorecard to indicate that the data quality is Poor—Requires Improvement versus Good. This helps to keep the pressure on to improve data quality so that the metric will be representative of actual performance.

In addition, it is a good idea to inventory current reports that are being produced and rationalize them against the new direction. If reports do not support the organization's objectives or could potentially be in conflict with the strategic metrics and scorecards, they should be eliminated or revised. If there are good supporting reports that will support the strategic metrics, those may be leveraged in rolling out the strategic SDM metrics.

Step 7: Start Reporting on the Initial Set of Metrics

This step is straightforward, once the initial metrics and scorecard formats are defined just get started! The first reports will not be perfect, but leadership will quickly get some initial data they can use to assess and manage and much will be learned from actually reporting the metrics in the desired format. Once the initial reports are being published, the focus can be turned to longer term planning.

Step 8: Planning the Long-Term SDM Metrics Program

Once initial metrics are established and being reported, the more difficult work begins to plan an effective longer term program. This is more difficult because an effective metrics program that is truly being used to drive the organization's performance is typically a major change initiative for an organization. It requires a solid structure and team to support it, effective leadership buy-in and sponsorship, active use each day, week, and month to manage outcomes, and a link to each individual's performance. In order to achieve an SDM program that meets these goals, there are many program components to consider beyond just data collection and reporting. Figure 19.2 contains a sample Metrics Program Roadmap that suggests the components and high-level tasks within each component that should be considered in a long-term metrics program plan. The Metrics Program Roadmap example contains tasks related to the metrics themselves as well as Change Management components, as in Figure 19.3, that are very important to address to truly drive performance and ensure the right behaviors are supported.

Summary of the Critical Success Factors for an Effective SDM Metrics Program

The steps outlined in this chapter can increase the chances of implementing an effective Software Development and Maintenance metrics program that avoids common pitfalls, that the CIO and the SDM leadership team will find invaluable for steering the organization toward meeting its objectives, and that is truly ingrained in the organization down to the team and individual level. In closing, below is a summary of the critical success factors that should be in place to support an effective metrics program. Although you may not have all of these at the start it is important to incorporate any gaps into your long-term planning to keep your metrics program on track and successful. The most important success factor is having SDM leadership on board and sponsoring the program from the start. If you do not have this in place, it is not likely the program can ever be successful.

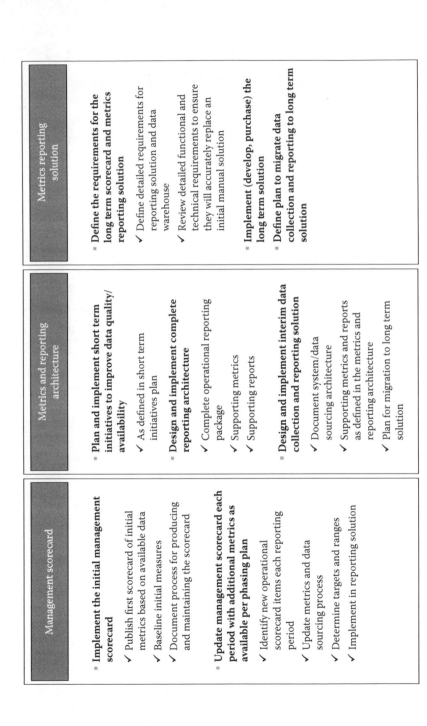

Management scorecard

※ **Implement the initial management scorecard**
- ✓ Publish first scorecard of initial metrics based on available data
- ✓ Baseline initial measures
- ✓ Document process for producing and maintaining the scorecard

※ **Update management scorecard each period with additional metrics as available per phasing plan**
- ✓ Identify new operational scorecard items each reporting period
- ✓ Update metrics and data sourcing process
- ✓ Determine targets and ranges
- ✓ Implement in reporting solution

Metrics and reporting architecture

※ **Plan and implement short term initiatives to improve data quality/availability**
- ✓ As defined in short term initiatives plan

※ **Design and implement complete reporting architecture**
- ✓ Complete operational reporting package
- ✓ Supporting metrics
- ✓ Supporting reports

※ **Design and implement interim data collection and reporting solution**
- ✓ Document system/data sourcing architecture
- ✓ Supporting metrics and reports as defined in the metrics and reporting architecture
- ✓ Plan for migration to long term solution

Metrics reporting solution

※ **Define the requirements for the long term scorecard and metrics reporting solution**
- ✓ Define detailed requirements for reporting solution and data warehouse
- ✓ Review detailed functional and technical requirements to ensure they will accurately replace an initial manual solution

※ **Implement (develop, purchase) the long term solution**

※ **Define plan to migrate data collection and reporting to long term solution**

Figure 19.2 Sample Metrics Program Roadmap—Metrics program components.

Operationalize

* **Design and implement central process standardization and metrics function**
* **Refine operational review and management process**
  ✓ Senior SDM Leadership
  ✓ Functional Areas
  ✓ Department
* **Clarify accountability for each metric**
* **Integrate into individual performance plans**
  ✓ Available metrics and targets
  ✓ Data quality improvement initiatives
  ✓ Individual and team actions that will contribute to strategic metrics
  ✓ Process and tool compliance
* **Update organization structure and roles descriptions**
* **Refine/Implement support processes**

Change adoption

* **Define value proposition and metrics tree/ strategy map**
* **Linkage of metrics to strategic goals**
* **Develop change adoption plan**
* **Establish change adoption network**
  ✓ Change agents
* **Enable desired culture**
  ✓ Link individual performance with SDM objectives
  ✓ Map desired and undesired behaviors for strategic metrics
  ✓ Update communications plan to reinforce expectations

Communications

* **Initial Kickoff communication and Intent from CIO or SDM leadership**
* **Implement metrics program communication plan**
* **Execute communication events:**
  ✓ Leadership summits
  ✓ Town hall meetings
  ✓ Newsletter / Postcards / FAQ's

Training

* **Develop metrics program training plan**
* **Develop / acquire training materials**
* **Conduct role based training**
  ✓ Senior leadership
  ✓ Management/ Team Leads
  ✓ Staff
* **Institute continuous learning**
  ✓ Establish ongoing training opportunities
  ✓ Job-Aids and support tools

Figure 19.3   Sample Metrics Program Roadmap—Change Management components.

- Leadership *is accountable for metrics, and an employee performance* reward structure is linked to the metrics.
- Defined metrics are aligned to the intended *business outcomes* and driving the *desired behaviors.*
- Every metric has *a target* so that you know how you are doing.
- Top-to-bottom IT *performance goals alignment*—shared objectives/goals that cascade down to each individual in the SDM organization.
- Supporting *governance structure*—clarity around who receives what data and what actions are expected.
- An *operating model* is defined including roles, responsibilities, hand-offs, and dependencies for the IT internal organization and across service providers. This is a key to establishing clear accountability for each metric. There may be several metrics that may be impacted by several towers within the IT organization such as Application Availability. Availability can be impacted by the Application Maintenance or Development towers as well as the Infrastructure organization. Availability can be measured by tower responsibility using the root cause of the outage (i.e., downtime caused by the code vs. downtime caused by infrastructure), which establishes clear accountability but does not measure from a business perspective. Alternatively, there can be one owner for end-to-end Availability, with OLAs defined with dependant towers.
- Comprehensive time reporting—understands *where people are spending time* at the appropriate level of granularity.
- *Standardized methods, processes, and tools* are in place and being used consistently across the organization.
- *Defined metrics/reporting architecture*—the hierarchy for data, metrics, and reports starting top down—how data is sliced, drill downs, supporting metrics, and reports for each level of governance.
- *Quality data capture* at the source. If there are data quality issues currently, you can start collecting the metric and incorporate "Data Quality Indicators" to indicate if a metric has "Good" data quality or if it "Requires Improvement." This enables the metric to get the right focus and start driving the right behaviors while data quality improvement efforts are underway.
- A *centralized function* to collect and produce metrics/reports and facilitate continuous improvement. Centralizing the metrics function ensures a "single source of truth" and prevents conflicting reports coming from different towers or departments.
- Planning for and addressing the *Communication/Change Management* aspects of a metrics program. Implementing metrics will drive behaviors and can be a major change initiative within an organization if done properly. Focusing on the people side facilitates a broad understanding of the metrics and how they link to overall IT and corporate objectives. This can be cascaded down to each individual who can impact the metrics in their daily responsibilities.

References

1. Kaplan, R. S. and D. P. Norton. 1996. *The Balanced Scorecard: Translating Strategy into Action.* Boston, MA: Harvard Business School Press.

About the Author

Miranda Mason is a partner with Accenture and has more than 15 years of experience in design and implementation of SDM metrics programs, productivity measurement, and outsourcing SLAs. Miranda is the global lead of Accenture's technology performance commitments capability and led the design and rollout of Accenture's patented performance management system and standard metrics across the global outsourcing business.

Chapter 20

Deriving Business Value Measures for Business Initiatives

Stavros Pechlivanidis

Contents

Introduction

Motivation

Most discussions about IT and software measurements are not or only slightly integrated into other business measurement topics, like measuring corporate, strategy, or investment success. This may be the case because measuring IT as a cost center usually fits the perspective of most organizations. Business value is created elsewhere in their value chain, and therefore, more resources are spent for measurements within those value chain links. From an IT point of view, this situation is not satisfactory, as it makes it even more difficult to communicate the business value contributed by IT or software, beyond the financial perspective.

In this context, the author observed that the underlying strategy of IT initiatives tends to be abstract and sometimes not even explicitly stated. This in turn makes identification and measurement of generated business value complicated. In such cases, the observed behavior was to either focus on project success metrics or on a couple of financial figures to measure the IT initiative's business value. In the end, these measures do not really support the message of IT (or the initiative as such) contributing any business value.

To resolve this communication problem, the author developed the Competitive Advantage Flower (CAF), an approach to help derive measures for business value of business initiatives by utilizing seven dimensions to describe the original strategy behind any initiative. The resulting description supports the clear description, measurement, and communication of business value of IT initiatives.

Chapter Objective

The objective of this chapter is to introduce the reader to the CAF approach developed by the author and his lessons learned from applying it. To accomplish this, the two competitive advantage types (cost and differentiation advantage) are introduced first, together with the terms business initiative, business value, and a brief summary of the common Goal Question Metric (GQM) approach to derive measures. Then CAF will be defined. The definition includes the seven dimensions (Expense, Technology, Productivity, Innovation, Business Process, Customer Satisfaction, and Product and Service Quality), their relationship to the competitive advantage types, the dimension maturity levels, and the process of application. The chapter concludes with lessons learned from applying CAF onto a business initiative within IT.

Fundamental Concepts

Before the CAF approach is introduced, the concepts it is based on are briefly introduced, as well as its methodological positioning within the process of deriving measures.

Value and Competitive Advantage

In the mid-1980s, Michael E. Porter introduced the concepts of *value* and *competitive advantage* into corporate strategy analysis [1] to answer two questions:

1. How attractive is an industry? (Potential market profitability.)
2. How good is an organization positioned within it? (Advantage against competitors.)

Value defines the extent of competitive advantage an organization has, as Porter writes: "Competitive advantage grows fundamentally from the value a firm is able to create. ... Value is what buyers are willing to pay, and superior value stems from offering lower prices than competitors for equivalent benefits or providing unique benefits that more than offset higher prices" [1, p. 3].

Porter distinguishes between two primary types of competitive advantage, which result in three generic strategies [1, 2]:

1. *Cost advantage* is about having lower cost than the competitors while producing an identical product. A strategy built on cost advantage is generically called a *cost leadership strategy*. The primary intent within this strategy is to constantly reduce expenses in order to sustain Cost Leadership.
2. *Differentiation advantage* is about producing a differentiated product, where the buyer is willing to pay a price premium for the difference, which exceeds the expenses to provide this difference. A strategy built on differentiation advantage is generically called a *differentiation strategy*. The primary intent within this strategy is to invest in differentiation (i.e., quality, branding, etc.) while taking into account cost constraints.

Both generic strategies have an industry-wide competitive scope. The third generic strategy called *focus strategy* has a single segment competitive scope and incorporates both types of advantages [1, 2].

Although the conceptual difference between cost and differentiation advantage is obvious, in reality cost advantage may lead to differentiation and differentiation advantage may lead to significant expense reduction [2]. The key point to remember for this chapter is the primary intent when pursuing cost or differentiation advantage.

Life Cycle of Business Initiatives

The term *business initiative* is very broad. It can be an action within established processes done by a single employee [3], a project or program of several months [4], a multiyear transformation program with several parallel and consecutive projects, or the creation of a start-up to enter a market. Due to size restrictions, the following definition will be used in the rest of this chapter:

> A *business initiative* is a project or program of up to two years duration, where a significant part (>30%) of its activities are IT-related (i.e., organizational, services, software, hardware, etc.).

On the strategic level, an organization may pursue both competitive advantage types, either for different kinds of products and services they offer or in different time frames as a response to changed external factors or internal capability and resource levels. Within such a strategic chain of activities, a single action or response can be seen as a business initiative to implement or sustain the competitive advantages of an organization.

Well-defined business initiatives do implement either cost advantage or differentiation advantage, in order to avoid being stuck in mediocrity. Based on this hypothesis and the life cycle of a business initiative as illustrated in Figure 20.1, the primary strategic intent of an initiative should be clearly stated.

In practice, poorly defined business initiatives are not uncommon. Even if they are well defined, their primary strategic intent becomes diluted during implementation. Before approval and funding, the strategic intent is very important. A business case is developed, showing the value of the candidate initiative. After approval, implementation activities like project setup and operational implementation become more important. Then at project closing, the focus is not switched back again, so that the question *"Was the project successful?"* is asked although the real question should be *"Was the business initiative successful?"*

The difference between those two questions is that *business initiative success* and *project success* are two different things. Project metrics are used to describe project success by measuring project characteristics as on-time, on-budget percentage of

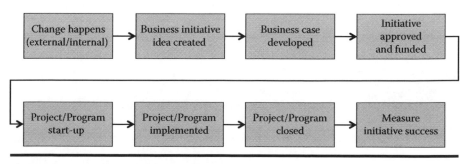

Figure 20.1   Business initiative life cycle.

planned activities being performed (i.e., education classes, etc.). Business initiative metrics on the other side describe the business value gained through the initiative. A project may be executed perfectly but still result in zero improvement of the business. Reformulating the second question into *"Will the promised business value be realized?"* makes the difference more obvious.

Methodologies to Derive Measures

One commonly used methodology to derive software metrics is the Goal Question Metric (GQM) approach described in [5]. In this approach, based on defined goals, questions are formulated in order to grasp the goal achievement. In the final step, metrics are derived from the questions, in order to quantitatively measure the goal achievement [5].

The CAF approach is used to rediscover and sharpen the strategic business initiative *goals*. This result is then used as input to derive metrics using the GQM methodology.

The Competitive Advantage Flower Approach

In this chapter, the seven dimensions of the CAF approach and the dimension maturity levels will be defined. This will be concluded with a description of the seven process steps to derive business value of business initiatives using CAF and GQM.

CAF Definition—The Seven Dimensions

CAF consists of seven dimensions, describing cost and differentiation advantage aspects, as illustrated in Figure 20.2.

Strategies pursuing cost advantage are described by the following three dimensions, depicted as leafs:

1. *Expense*: Expense describes the cost associated with providing the business object. A business object can be a product, a service, or some subprocess. Examples for business objects are a consumer product and its production line or a Customer Relationship Management system or the communication subprocess within human resources (HR). Although a low expense level can also be achieved through a differentiation strategy, it is the key aspect of a cost leadership strategy.
2. *Technology*: This dimension describes the effectiveness of technology (hardware, software, machines, etc.) and its deployment extent within the business object. An example would be the automation level of the business process to handle insurance applications in order to create insurance policies. Increasing the existing technological support of a production or service process is a way to reduce the resources needed to perform this process. Adding technology support to differentiate a service is included in the Innovation dimension.

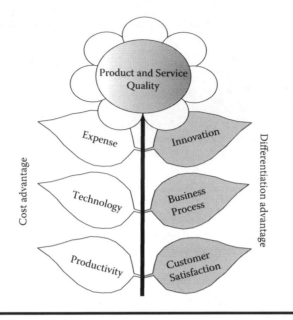

Figure 20.2   Competitive Advantage Flower.

3. *Productivity*: Productivity describes the output volume per unit of time. Examples are developed Function Points per 100 hours, produced television sets per day, or settled insurance claims per person day. Increasing productivity is another main aspect of a cost leadership strategy. There are some instances where the productivity is improved by major changes in the process area or by introducing new innovative solutions. Those are differentiation advantage instances and are handled through the Business Process and Innovation dimensions.

Strategies pursuing differentiation advantage are described by the following three dimensions (leaves):

4. *Innovation*: This dimension describes the innovation level of a product or service. As the term *innovation* is very broad, the two-dimensional typology of [6] will be used in this chapter. The first describes the type of innovation (product, process, position, or paradigm innovations), whereas the second describes "the degree of novelty involved" [6, p. 11] (incremental to radical). As incremental innovations happen in all CAF dimensions, it is difficult to classify them based on their type only. Incremental innovations of a business object should be classified case by case through expert interviews.

5. *Business Process*: This dimension focuses on the effectiveness of the business process, in contrast to the Technology dimension, which looks at efficiency. It includes two main aspects of a business process: cycle time of the product or

service produced and cost effectiveness. Cost effectiveness is not about decreasing the cost of the process (cost advantage) but increasing the value per invested dollar, in order to support the price premium of a differentiated offering.

6. *Customer Satisfaction*: This dimension describes the customer satisfaction level associated with the product or service provided and includes all direct activities to increase customer satisfaction. Examples are marketing, customer community activities, or after-sales services. Customer satisfaction is not unimportant in cost leadership strategies, but as a direct dimension it is a main aspect of differentiation strategies. Customer satisfaction in the context of cost leadership is a facet of the following dimension.

The blossom or seventh dimension is the quality of the product or service offered in the business object. This dimension fits equally to cost and differentiation advantage. It is based on the other six dimensions but also adds a more complete point of view:

7. *Product and Service Quality*: This dimension describes the quality of products and services provided. *Product* or *service* in this context should be understood as the output of an examined process and not only for example end products. Examples for quality characteristics are defect proneness, longevity, or response time. Quality is important in both strategy types. A cost advantage cannot be realized, for example, if the offered product is not as reliable as the competitor's product. This holds true also for a differentiated product, where low quality offsets the extent of price premium the buyer is willing to spend for a superior, but unreliable product.

In a nutshell, the CAF dimensions describe characteristics of the business object (product/service/subprocess) changed, not the business initiative itself. The question is not how innovative or productive the project was implemented, but rather to what innovation or productivity level the business object was increased through the business initiative.

CAF Assessment—Dimension Maturity Levels

In the CAF approach, the business object is assessed in two process steps on a scale from 1 to 5. In the first step, the current object status per dimension is assessed. In the second step, the expected object status after the initiative is successfully implemented is assessed. The difference of the two assessments indicates the expected type of business value. Table 20.1 shows the maturity level description for the dimension assessment.

The maturity level definition is based to a large extent on dimension measurability, because it is a strong indicator for the needed level of "heroism" and implicit knowledge within the particular dimension. If, for example, the dimension *Business*

Process is assessed with level 1, this means that the process is neither documented nor measurable. Success depends on head monopolies of key personnel involved. From an organizational point of view, this is a major business risk because if, for

Table 20.1   Maturity Level Description for Dimension Assessment

Level	General Description
1	The dimension is not measurable. Even without measures the ineffectiveness is obvious.
	Efficiency is not considered at all.
	If in place, the wrong measures are used for measuring.
	Success depends solely on implicit knowledge and chance.
2	The dimension is measured on a basic level. Results are below average.
	Efficiency and effectiveness can be improved very easily.
	The measures lead to misinterpretations. They are not aligned to the business perspective.
	Success depends heavily on implicit knowledge.
3	The dimension is measured. Results are average if benchmarked with peers.
	Efficiency and effectiveness can be improved easily.
	The measures are technical in nature. They are loosely aligned to the business perspective.
	Success depends to a reasonable degree on implicit knowledge.
4	The dimension is measured. Results are above average if benchmarked with peers.
	Efficiency and effectiveness are competitive, as they were often improved in the past.
	There are technical and business measures in place, reflecting the business perspective.
	Success depends punctual on implicit knowledge.
5	The dimension is measured. Results are best in class if benchmarked with peers.
	Efficiency and effectiveness are state of the art, by using the best technological solutions.
	Technical and business measures are in place. They are used to steer the business.
	Success does not depend on implicit knowledge.

example, those people are suddenly not available anymore due to a traffic accident, the business process will simply not function anymore. Depending on the importance of the business process, this could have a catastrophic impact on the overall business.

Based on those two assessments, the following insights can be gained in another step:

- The *strategic intent* of the business initiative (cost or differentiation advantage)
- The *expected type of business value* of the business initiative
- The *likelihood of realizing the expected value*

The *strategic intent* of the business initiative can be derived by looking at the differences between the two assessments. It should be checked if the initiative has a clear strategic intent, or if it wants to realize "everything" in equal intensity. From a strategic perspective, the latter case should be avoided. It may be better to split up the business initiative into a cost advantage and a differentiation advantage initiative. This approach will make realization, communication, and measurement of business value at the end of the initiative easier. Be aware that a clear strategic intent does not prohibit any improvements or secondary objectives on the "opposite" side; it is a question of intensity.

The *expected type of value of the business initiative* is derived by looking at the dimensions with the highest differences between the assessments. Differences in the Expense dimension should bring some financial value by lowering cost, while business value from the Business Process dimension could result in a shorter cycle time or less process errors. The expected value size itself cannot be derived using only the CAF approach because it depends on the specific business object and its importance within the organization, that is, improving the main product versus improving some minor subprocess.

The *likelihood of realizing the expected value* is derived by analyzing the current level with the business initiative itself. The *general means for improvement* listed in Table 20.2 are examples of possible business initiatives on a particular level. On paper, it is easy to go from level 1 directly to level 5, for example, by applying new technologies or processes. In reality, the likelihood for such an initiative to face severe change management problems at implementation time is very high. This likelihood stems from affected personnel not willing or being able to change so quickly, as well as not knowing exactly what the object specifications (i.e., process description, inputs, outputs, etc.) really are. As level 1 indicates a strong bargaining position of the personnel, change management activities are "damned to perfection" in order to deliver business initiative success. The conclusion here is that even though some organizations manage to successfully implement such initiatives, the chances for success are lower than using adequate means for improvement.

Table 20.2 General Means for Improvement per Maturity Level

Level	General Means for Improvement
1	• Introduce controlling • Strategy and business alignment • Business Process Reengineering (BPR) on a green field
2	• Introduce/improve controlling • Strategy and business alignment • Rationalization and automation, BPR • Knowledge management
3	• Rationalization and automation • Operational innovations • Product or process innovations
4	• Apply new technologies • Operational innovations • Product or process innovations • Position innovations
5	• Apply new technologies • All innovation forms (product/process/position/paradigm)

CAF Process—Deriving Business Value Measures

After describing dimensions and maturity levels, the process to implement the CAF approach can be introduced. As can be seen in the process overview illustrated in Figure 20.3, the process consists of seven process steps, which are described in detail in this chapter.

The default starting point assumed in the following process description is the step *Business case developed* within the business initiative life cycle (Figure 20.1). Deviations rooted in another starting point are described as optional parts.

1. *Analyze business object to be changed*: In the first step, the business object has to be defined. This could be a certain offering (product/service) needing improvement, but it could also be a specific business subprocess. In the case of a subprocess, the output or outcome has to be defined, becoming the offering to be improved. If the object is too general for analysis, it can be broken down by identifying its business drivers. The output of this step is a well-defined business object, additionally described by business drivers.

2. *Assess current dimension maturity levels*: The current dimension maturity levels are assessed through expert interviews. If the outcome of the first step

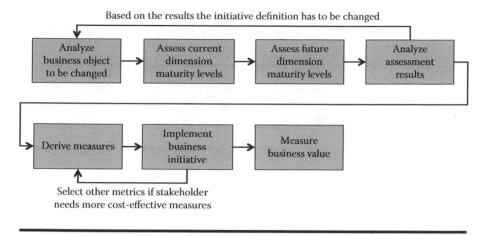

Figure 20.3   CAF approach process overview.

includes business drivers, then all business drivers are assessed separately. The assessment level does not need to be a natural number (i.e., 1.75 is possible). The overall assessment is the average of the business driver assessments. It may be reasonable to weight the business drivers if their impact is not similar. The output of this step is the current dimension maturity levels of the business object.

3. *Assess future dimension maturity levels*: This process step is an analogue to step 2, with the output being the future dimension maturity levels of the business object.

4. *Analyze assessment results*: In this step, the insights gained from the assessments are analyzed. If the strategic intent of the business initiative is not definite, the business initiative should be split, as described previously. The insight on the expected type of business value is used in step 5 to support deriving the right metrics. If the likelihood of realizing the expected value is questionable, then the implications should be discussed with stakeholders. An alternative to lowering the expectations is to increase investment into change management and/or project management.

Optional: When the CAF approach is used after the business initiative is already implemented, ambiguous insights on strategic intent and expected type of business value are discussed with the stakeholder in order to understand the original strategic intention of the business initiative. The insight on the likelihood to realize the expected value is documented, as it may be useful to justify the results of step 7. Remember that a project may be implemented successfully without any business value being realized, that is, no lasting change being achieved.

The output of this step is the primary strategic intent of the business initiative and the expected type of business value as well as the likelihood of initiative success.

5. *Derive measures*: Based on the goals and support information analyzed in step 4, measures for business value can be derived using the GQM methodology, as described in [5]. After defining the metrics, the expected values have to be defined. The height of those values is sanity checked against the assessment results from steps 3 and 4. Based on this information and the investment planned for the business initiative, a business case can be derived to support initiative approval.

    Optional: When the CAF approach is used after the business initiative is already implemented, the resulting business case can be compared against the original business case. Based on this comparison, stakeholder expectations can be adjusted.

    The output of this step is the definition of a measurement system, capable of measuring the business value of the business initiative.

6. *Implement business initiative*: After approval in the business initiative life cycle, the initiative is implemented. From the CAF process point of view, it is important to look at the effort to implement the defined measures. If possible actions should be included in the project plan to lower the implementation effort for the defined measures (i.e., by configuring certain systems, etc.)

    Optional: When the CAF approach is used after the business initiative is already implemented, the defined measures have to be prioritized in case the cost to implement them is higher than the cost stakeholders are willing to bear to measure business value. This could result in revisiting step 5 in case stakeholders need more cost-effective measures.

    The output of this step is the implementation of the defined measurement system.

7. *Measure business value*: The measurement of the business value should be time constrained, in order to be able to allocate any measured business value to the initiative. The time span is derived from the business case and adapted to the measures defined in step 5. A final report is compiled after this time has elapsed, illustrating the achieved business value.

Lessons Learned

The author applied the CAF approach outlined previously onto a real business initiative after it was implemented. Although the project team had some financial measures in place, they still needed additional metrics to measure the business value because the main objective of the initiative was to improve customer communication, not only saving cost. Based on this application, the author derived some strengths and weaknesses concerning the implementation of the CAF approach.

Strengths of the CAF Approach

The strength of the CAF approach lies in its *speed of implementation*, its *support for strategy communication*, and its *flexibility*.

Speed of Implementation

CAF is a *lightweight approach*, based on the well-known competitive advantage concept and utilizing the widespread GQM method for deriving metrics. The seven dimensions (3 + 3 + 1) and the dimension maturity levels are easy to understand. The assessment can be conducted based on expert interviews only (i.e., executive level, project management, subject matter expert, etc.). This characteristic increases the *speed of assessment*, as it does not need prerequisite information or any analysis results in order to assess dimension maturity.

Support for Strategy Communication

Depending on when in the business initiative life cycle CAF is applied, it supports strategy communication. The seven dimensions enable the interviewed expert to achieve a *structured view* on the business object. If CAF is applied after implementation, it helps to *rediscover the strategic intent of the initiative*. This can be utilized in the communication of the derived measurement system to measure business value. If CAF is applied before implementation, its results can be utilized in the *communication of the business case*.

Flexibility

The CAF approach is *flexible enough to be applied at any time* within the business initiative life cycle. This is important, as most business initiatives with IT-related activities do not necessarily originate in IT. Therefore, in real life it is very likely that the chance to apply CAF will arise only after the business initiative is approved and has started.

But even for organizations being able to apply CAF at business case development, it gives them additional incentives to do so, for example, by outlining the primary intent of the initiative in terms of competitive advantage or assessing the likelihood of realizing the expected business value based on the initiative's topic and operational setup.

It is also *flexible enough to be applied on all types of business initiatives*, even those without IT-related portions. This is rooted in the initial selection of the seven dimensions, as none of them is purely IT related. Even the Technology dimension can be found in any business object (product/service/subprocess), as technology support is omnipresent.

Finally during business object assessment, the *option to define (weighted) business drivers*, if the assessment of the object itself is not trivial, also increases flexibility.

Weaknesses of the CAF Approach

Although the CAF approach is flexible, it has some weaknesses. By being developed specifically for business initiatives, that is, activities with a defined end, it is not suitable for deriving business value of line organizations. The main reason is the *missing support for n-tier breakdown strategy structures*, for example breaking down the corporate strategy to business unit strategy to operational strategy, etc.

In the context of business initiative application, it does not support *historization* or the *determination of expected value increase*.

Historization

As competitive environments constantly change, sustaining competitive advantage requires continuous improvement. This also holds true for business object dimensions assessed with maturity level 5. The most cost-efficient way to offer a service today (expense dimension with a maturity level of 5) may not be the most cost-efficient way in one year. In the Technology dimension, such changes happen even faster than, for example, in the Business Process dimension.

To mitigate this weakness, the author currently develops an aging function for the dimension maturity levels, in order to map such developments. The aging function currently depends on the dimension itself, the industry environment, and the internal resources and capabilities of the organization.

Determination of Expected Value Increase

The dimension assessment and analysis (process steps 2 to 4) result in a likelihood of realizing the expected value as well as the type of business value to expect, but it gives no hint as to the expected increase. If, for example, an initiative is increasing the Expense dimension maturity level of a service by 2.5, what percent expense reduction can be expected for this service?

Conclusion

By determining the primary strategic intent of a business initiative in terms of competitive advantage (cost or differentiation advantage) through seven dimensions, the CAF approach supports the identification of business value measures in order to measure initiative impact. Its lightweight character as well as its flexibility makes a low-risk pilot implementation within an organization feasible. Even if the CAF approach is not adapted on a regular basis, all of its strengths can be utilized in each single implementation. From an IT measurement perspective, the CAF approach is important because with competitive advantage, it introduces a key business concept into IT measurement and its communication. This supports the demonstration of IT contributions to business value beyond the financial perspective.

References

1. Porter, M. E. 1985. *Competitive Advantage—Creating and Sustaining Superior Performance.* 1st ed. New York: The Free Press.
2. Grant, R. M. 2005. *Contemporary Strategy Analysis.* 5th ed., chap. 7, 8, and 9. Oxford: Blackwell Publishing.
3. BusinessDictionary.com. What is initiative? Definition and meaning. http://www .businessdictionary.com/definition/initiative.html, WebFinance, Inc., June 8th 2011, (accessed on June 8, 2011).
4. BusinessDictionary.com, What is initiatives? Definition and meaning, http://www. businessdictionary.com/definition/initiatives.html, WebFinance, Inc., June 8th 2011, Last Access: June 8th 2011.
5. Basili, V. R., G. Caldiera, and H. D. Rombach. 1994. The goal question metric approach. In *Encyclopedia of Software Engineering,* ed. John J. Marciniak. New York: Wiley.
6. Tidd, J., J. Bessant, and K. Pavitt. 2005. *Managing Innovation: Integrating Technological, Market and Organizational Change.* 3rd ed., chap. 1.2 and 1.3. Chichester: John Wiley & Sons.

About the Author

Stavros Pechlivanidis holds the position of senior managing consultant within IBM Global Business Services. He has over 9 years of project experience within the insurance industry. Additionally he has had project assignments in logistics, paper, automotive, research, and defense.

His roles on projects range from metrics consultant to project manager. As a project manager and consultant, he is responsible for international projects, including global delivery resources. In his role as a metrics consultant, he has been involved for over 9 years with effort estimation, measurement, benchmarking, quality assurance of benchmarks, and KPI systems.

In his position as a subject matter expert on metrics and lead estimator within IBM, he supports GBS service projects in effort estimation, receiving the IBM Quality Leadership Award in January 2007. He uses this experience to develop and introduce metrics solutions or KPI systems for customers in the context of project engagements on a strategic as well as operational level. He is a subject matter expert in IFPUG Function Points, giving internal and external classes and coaching. He has been an elected board member of the German metrics organization DASMA e.V. (http://www.dasma.org) since 2004. He has been a member of the technical advisory board of ISBSG (http://www.isbsg.org) since 2005 and an executive assistant since 2009.

NEW TECHNOLOGIES AND ENVIRONMENTS INTRODUCTION

VII

Sivasubramanyam Balasubramanyam

A proliferation of new devices and their uses are causing the technology landscape to keep changing. Smart phones and other mobile devices have created a whole new paradigm of mobile applications and are hastening the shift toward cloud computing in the corporate and consumer spaces. Cloud computing is also being embraced by the corporate community both large and small due to the ability to scale up and reduce the total cost of ownership. Originally coined by Gartner group, Enterprise Resource Planning (ERP) integrates management information encompassing the entire organization. In this section, there are three chapters written by authors who address measurement as applicable to mobile applications, cloud computing, and ERP.

Loredana Frallicciardi is an expert in performance management and software engineering, working for Computer Sciences Corp. She has been a past chair of the International Function Point Users Group (IFPUG) Certification Committee, director of applied programs, and has represented Italy at the International Organization for Standardization (ISO). Loredana's chapter, "ERP Function Point Analysis: A Possible Approach and a Practical Experience," begins with a description of the initial phases of an ERP implementation, moving on to discuss how to apply Function Point Analysis to an ERP project. Along the way she highlights the assumptions to be made and the counting process, ending with an example of FP counting in an ERP project.

Tammy Preuss is a Senior Business Manager at AT&T specializing in customer experience for IT systems—retail and online applications. She is also Vice Chairman of the IFPUG New Environments Committee. Tammy's chapter, "Mobile Applications, Functional Analysis, and the Customer Experience," focuses on the evolving mobile app space. She starts off by defining what constitutes a mobile app and how customers use such apps. The discussion then moves on to classifying mobile apps, the means of their distribution, and the revenue models associated with these apps. Tammy helps the reader understand the development cycles and languages of these apps and the role of measurement and functional point analysis in her context. She ends the discussion by highlighting the benefits measurement brings to the developer and customer experience.

Steven Woodward is CEO of Cloud Perspectives, specializing in cloud computing, and is a member of the National Institute of Standards and Technology (NIST) Cloud Computing Working Group. He is also a director of conferences and education at IFPUG. Steve's chapter, "Cloud Computing Solution Measurement," explores the cloud computing environment as it is today. He describes the characteristics of what cloud computing is and then goes on to elaborate on the various service models in prevalence. Steve then discusses the critical measurement fundamentals; the goals, measurement as applicable for business success, and how customers can be invoiced for the services provided. Along the way, he gives examples of various scenarios to illustrate the usage of the metrics.

Chapter 21

Enterprise Resource Planning (ERP) Function Point Analysis: A Possible Approach and a Practical Experience

Loredana Frallicciardi

Contents

Preface

The actual market trend shows an increase in purchasing of Enterprise Resource Planning (ERP)/Commercial Off-the-Shelf (COTS) products rather than the development of custom systems. This choice is made by the companies usually after a Make or Buy Analysis activity [1].

Make or Buy Analysis is a cost analysis methodology used for evaluating the benefits of buying a software package rather than developing a custom solution or vice versa. The main activity of this methodology is to analyze the features offered by the software against the user needs to identify the following:

- Functionality offered by the product that does not need to be modified
- Functionality offered by the product that must be changed
- Functionality offered by the product, but not required by the user
- Functionality not offered by the product to be developed ad hoc

Usually, the decision to Make or Buy software is taken by comparing the effort and costs required to make the software package compliant with the user's requirements, with the effort and costs required to make a custom solution.

When an ERP product is selected and adopted in a company, it is very usual that a preliminary project having in scope to make the product perfectly compliant with the user's requirements is created. The typical application of this type of project provides a preliminary analysis that determines the gap between the user's business processes and the standard features offered by this product.

This activity is usually documented in a business requirements document (typically the Business Blueprint for the ERP SAP product), containing the following:

- The list of standard functional transactions offered by the product that have to be activated, usually with parameterization activities
- The list of standard functional transactions offered by the product that have to be modified or deleted (inhibited for the usage), usually with parameterization activities and/or software developed ad hoc
- The list of transactions and tables required for the solution but not offered by the product, usually created with software developed ad hoc
- The list of tables of the product requiring a preloading of data, usually made with data entry or batch input

A project aiming at the enhancement of an ERP already adopted usually provides the same type of analysis described earlier.

For these characteristics, both the project for the first implementation and the project for the enhancement of ERP products are classifiable as Enhancement Projects in terms of Function Point Analysis (FPA), and are both measured by using the procedure for "Enhancement Project Function Point Counts," as described in the International Function Point Users Group (IFPUG) Counting Practices Manual (CPM) 4.3.1 [2].

Approach to Apply Function Point Analysis to ERP Projects

The approach used successfully in a practical experience at a large Italian company ICT to study how to apply FPA to ERP projects is described below [3,4].

This approach consisted of the following main steps:

1. A sample of ERP projects to be submitted to the trial was identified.
2. For these projects, the Measurement Procedure for Function Point (FP) counting as defined in the IFPUG CPM 4.3.1 was applied, determining the Counting Scope and Boundary; identifying the Functional User Requirements; measuring the Data Functions; measuring the Transactional Functions; calculating the functional size (Unadjusted Function Points [UFPs]); and documenting and reporting the FP counts.
3. Each need to make assumptions regarding the rules of IFPUG CPM 4.3.1 was identified.
4. The results of FP counts were validated for repeatability and effectiveness aspects.
5. The productivity rate (FP/day) for project management purposes and for the determination of the economic value ($$) of a FP was identified.

All the above steps are described below in more detail.

Identify a Sample of ERP Projects

In this first step, a sample of projects was selected (at least 20 to represent a statistically significant sample) to be submitted to the experiment.

All the selected projects had the following characteristics:

- They included the first implementation of the ERP SAP product or the enhancement of it.
- They were implemented in a limited time (i.e., 1 year).
- They had a well-defined analysis and design documentation submitted to the quality control procedures, which conforms to the UNI EN ISO 9001:2000 standards (to guarantee consistency between projects' documentation).
- They were easily measurable, as their project managers had been actively involved in the trial.

The above features were crucial for the effectiveness of the trial and the feasibility of the next steps. It was also crucial to collect all the project documentation produced during the phases of requirements definition, analysis, and design.

Apply the Measurement Process for Function Point Analysis

After collecting the necessary documentation, the next step was probably the most difficult: it was to create the FP counts for all projects under consideration, identifying the key elements of the FPA from the following:

- The formalisms used by the methodology of analysis and design (for example, the accelerated SAP (ASAP)* methodology for the SAP ERP package)
- The textual description of the functional user requirements detected by appropriate documentation
- The interviews with the project manager and/or end-user application

---

* The ASAP methodology was developed by SAP AG with the aim of making faster and smoother the phase of implementation and development of all SAP systems. For this purpose, the methodology provides the following:
  - A sequence of activities geared to the implementation of the package
  - Extensive documentation and collection of templates and links to additional resources, the so-called accelerators, aimed at simplifying and speeding up the configuration
  - A series of highly integrated tools with the applications
  The ASAP methodology provides the following phases for a SAP project implementation:
  - Project Preparation
  - Business Blueprint
  - Realization
  - Final Preparation
  - Go Live and Support

The task force to analyze the documents, to count the FPs, and to identify any assumptions to be made was composed of a few people, all having the same level of knowledge of the IFPUG FPA and all IFPUG Certified Function Point Specialists (CFPSs).

Identify Any Need to Make Assumptions

During the trial, there was the need for assumptions. This need may occur when a specific rule of the IFPUG CPM 4.3.1 does not apply well to the element you are counting.

Once agreed by all the involved CFPSs (possibly with the support of the Delphi* technique), the assumptions are documented and they are reapplied each time the conditions recur.

Validate the Results of Function Point Counts

The results of FP counts were validated [5,6] for their repeatability and the effectiveness of the information they were showing.

The repeatability was assured because the projects under examination were counted by the all the CFPSs involved in the experimentation and the difference between the results of the various FP counts was always less than 10% (6.2% on average).

Being effective for the FP size of the ERP projects under examination was a "must" of the measurement program. In fact, the company sponsoring the experimentation was looking for a sizing method of ERP that was supported by international standards (such as the IFPUG CPM 4.3.1), repeatable and reliable, but at the same time effective for the immediate understanding of the results.

In other terms, the information given by the FP size of ERP projects would have to give an immediate idea to the project managers about the effort, the time, and the schedule needed for the implementation of the project.

For this reason, the assumptions made during the experimentation, in particular those relating to the "intermediate user," were intended to properly define the boundaries of the application, limiting or excluding those cases in which an

---

* The Delphi technique in this case is based on the involvement of at least three experts (on FP counting, project domain, ERP/COTS product) and on the following steps:
  1. The Team Leader presents the same specification to each expert.
  2. The experts independently analyze the specification. A meeting may be called where the experts can discuss issues.
  3. The experts independently develop a solution and give it to the Team Leader.
  4. The Team Leader analyzes and consolidates the solutions gathered and distributes a summary to the experts, excluding any rationale for the solutions.
  5. The Team Leader calls a group meeting to discuss solutions, focusing on where the solutions vary widely.
  6. Experts review the solutions and steps 4–6 are repeated until a consensus is reached.

"oversized FP" or "undersized FP" of ERP projects could occur due to the nature of these projects.

In addition, the main information required by the sponsor as a result of the experimentation was a reference value of FP productivity rate and the economic value (which is the cost) for 1 FP.

So, the correlation between the size of ERP projects and the effort needed for their implementation was analyzed. To enable this, the results of the activities in the previous phases were stored in a database containing the following:

- Project ID
- Type of project (new implementation or enhancement)
- Domain user (who is targeted by the project)
- Phase of the life cycle in which the FP count was made (definition of user requirements, technical analysis, after the realization)
- UFPs, with the detail of logical files, elementary processes
- Effort spent for the project's implementation, broken down by the various phases
- Main factors that may influence the FP productivity rate of the project (such as percentage of customized transactions versus the standard activated ones; user domain; percentage of standard transactions deleted (inhibited for the usage) versus the standard activated ones; percentage of added transactions ad hoc versus the standard activated ones; number of table files requiring a data loading; etc.).

This database was the basis for the estimation model used by the company to provide estimates of time, cost, schedule, and resources.

As mentioned previously, the most important factor that was analyzed was the correlation between the effort spent to implement ERP projects and their size in FP, which is crucial for the success of the trial. In fact, the higher the correlation between the two variables, the more the applicability of FPA rules in the context of ERP. That means the assumptions made, the quality and effectiveness of the documentation used, the models used for the interviews, etc., would be all considered adequate in the context of the experimentation.

After this analysis, the way to proceed with the experimentation was decided on the basis of the following considerations:

- If the coefficient of determination (R^2) between effort and FP size was not less than 0.65, the experimentation would be validated, and the operating procedures and assumptions made during the experimentation would become standards internal to the company to be used as a unique reference by all the personnel involved in the project estimation process.
- If the coefficient of determination (R^2) between effort and FP size was less than 0.65, the following should be verified:

- Whether the selected projects had characteristics consistent with each other (if not, the projects with inhomogeneous characteristics should be eliminated from the experimentation, being careful not to reduce the number of projects (observations) to a number less than 12, that is, the minimum significant number from the statistical point of view)
- Whether the measured size (or estimated, depending on the phase where the FP counting was made) of the selected projects was made in an accurate way, where if required, a new FP counting has to be made by a different CFPS
- Whether the assumptions made were repeated in the same way for all the projects
- Whether the documentation collected and analyzed for the FP counting was accurate and had the same degree of granularity for all the projects

If all the above checks were successful, the next point of attention was on the process used and the assumptions made during the experimentation. Indeed, in this case, all the steps of the experimentation (or most of them) would be remade. The practical experimentation carried out with the described approach for the company who sponsored it has provided more than satisfactory results. In fact, it immediately detected a high correlation between Effort (mm/dd) and FP size, with a coefficient of determination (R^2) greater than 0.75, thus as an ease of use of the FP counting rules and of the assumptions identified, which have had the consensus of all the CFPS involved.

Assumptions for ERP Projects

The most relevant assumption for the application of FPA to ERP projects was for the first implementation of the ERP product, when all or most of the functionality offered by the product cannot be used by the user without their preliminary activation, usually made with parameterization and/or data entry activities and sometimes with a minimal effort.

In cases like this, all the functionality of the baseline of the product, when activated, are identifiable as "added functionality."

This gives a very poor effectiveness to the FP size of ERP projects. In fact, in this case, the FP counting of the ERP project would give the same result of the FP counting made for the software completely developed ad hoc!

Therefore, an assumption becomes necessary for the concept of USER (see definition in IFPUG CPM 4.3.1: "User—Any person or thing that communicates or interacts with the software at any time"). For the cases described above, the user may represent both the end user (one who gives the Functional User Requirements, one who uses the final system) and the intermediate user (the

ERP/COTS product specialist, one who uses the system for parameterization, data entry, preloading table files activities, etc., to deliver the appropriate functionality to the end user).

During the FP counting of ERP projects, there will be situations where the user is identifiable as the end user and situations where the user is identifiable as the "intermediate-user."

In the following section, it has been described in detail when to use one type or the other type of definition. When not specified, the usage of the end user definition is implied.

Function Point Counting Procedure

Following are the steps for the FP counting procedure, as described in IFPUG CPM 4.3.1. For each step are indicated, where applicable, the assumptions to be made.

Determine the Type of Counting

As anticipated earlier, both the projects for the first implementation of ERP products and for the evolutionary maintenance of ERP products consist of adding, changing, and deleting some functionality starting from the baseline functionality offered by the product. Therefore, for both types of projects, the type of counting is the Enhancement Project Function Point Counts as described in IFPUG CPM 4.3.1.

Determine the Counting Scope

For the Enhancement Project Function Point Counts, the functionality to include in the FP counting is as follows:

- The functionality added *ex-novo* to the baseline of standard transactions offered by the product (usually added through software developed ad hoc)
- The standard transactions offered by the product and activated to meet the end-user Functional User Requirements (usually activated through parameterizations of the product)
- The standard transactions offered by the product and changed or deleted (inhibited for the usage) to meet the end-user Functional User Requirements (usually made through parameterizations of the product and/or software developed ad hoc)
- The functionality for preloading the information necessary for the proper operation of the product (usually made through data entry, even manual, and/or batch input).

Determine the Boundary of the Application

As referred to in CPM 4.3.1, the application boundary defines the border between the software being measured and the user, allowing the identification of the following:

- Elements "internal" and "external" to the system under FP counting
- Interactions between the system under FP counting and the external world (the end user, the intermediate user, and/or other systems)

One can assume that for the first implementation of ERP adopted in a company, it is identification of one or more applications depending on the modularity of the ERP product.

If, for example, the ERP product is composed of a set of independent modules, it is possible to identify as many applications (and boundaries) as the independent modules implemented.

As an example, for ERP SAP R/3, there are various modules grouped by the macro processes they represent, such as Maintenance and Logistic (SD, MM, PP, QM, and PM modules), Accountability and Finance Control (FI, CO, TR, and PS modules), Human Resource (HR module), and Vertical Solutions (IS, WF). Each of these macro processes may represent an application.

However, the boundary of an application depends on the end user's point of view and needs to be analyzed from time to time.

Measure Data Functions

As referred to in CPM 4.3.1, a Data Function represents functionality provided to the user to meet internal and external data storage requirements. A Data Function is either an Internal Logical File (ILF) or an External Interface File (EIF), where the term file does not mean physical file or table, but refers to a logically related group of data.

In many ERP products, the database is designed to be highly reusable for several different purposes and contexts, and for this reason it is highly fragmented in numerous tables.

So, within this step, it is necessary to analyze the database used by the product from the logical point of view of the end user and aggregate the various tables at a level of abstraction such that each group of data identified may have the meaning of an entity in an entity-relationship diagram, designed at a conceptual level (i.e., CUSTOMER, SUPPLIER, ORDER, etc.).

Because of the type of count, the Enhancement Project Function Point Count, the Data Functions identified in this step should be added, changed, or deleted from the database of the ERP product. However, for these products, it is very unusual to create new tables or alter the structure of the existing ones. Thus, only a few Data Functions may be identified during this step.

When determining which Data Functions are included in the FP count, they will be classified as ILFs or EIFs applying the standard "Data Function Identification Rules" of CPM 4.3.1.

No assumption is made for the determination of ILF or EIF complexity (Low, Medium, or High), for which "Data Function—Complexity and Contribution Definitions and Rules" of CPM 4.3.1 are applied.

Measure Transactional Functions

As referred to in CPM 4.3.1, a Transactional Function represents an elementary process that provides functionality to the user to process data. A Transactional Function is an External Input (EI), External Output (EO), or External Inquiry (EQ).

So, within this step, it is necessary to analyze, for each Functional User Requirement, the standard transactions offered by the ERP product and identify the following:

- If one or a group of them meets (as they are) the Functional User Requirement
- If one or a group of them meets (with modification) the Functional User Requirement
- The new transactions to develop ad hoc to meet the Functional User Requirement
- All the elementary processes related to the above transactions

Of course, all these details (also known as "Gap Analysis") are available in the business requirements document (typically the Business Blueprint, for the ERP SAP product) and thus, the work to do during this step is simply to compare all the transactions (standard to the product and the new ones to be developed ad hoc) with the Functional User Requirements and identify for each of them the related elementary processes.

An elementary process is the smallest unit of activity that is meaningful to the user, constitutes a complete transaction, is self-contained, and leaves the business of the application being counted in a consistent state.

For example, for the Functional User Requirement "Invoice Data Capture," more than one transaction of the ERP product may be involved (such as Capture Header, Capture Elements of Detail, etc.), and all of them will contribute to identify one single elementary process.

It will be the next step, the one for determining the complexity (Low, Medium, High) of the elementary process, which will take into account of how many transactions are required for its completion. In fact, it will be identified as much Data Element Types (DETs) as is the data used from all of the above transactions.

Once the elementary processes are identified, to classify them as EI, EO, or EQ, their primary intent must be determined.

Below is the list of the different scenarios that can occur when we are going to identify and classify the Transactional Functions.

Project for the First Adoption of an ERP Product

The activities to be carried out are the following:

- The functionality included in the scope of the FP counting (see "Determine the Counting Scope" step of the Function Point Counting Procedure) are analyzed and the related elementary processes are identified, as described below:
    1. For the activation of standard functional transactions of the product, the concept of intermediate user is used and the elementary processes of the technical transactions that have to be used by the intermediate user to activate the functional transactions required by the end user are identified.
    2. a. For the changing/deleting of functional transactions of the product that entails the automatic changing/deleting of other functional transactions logically correlated but not included in the scope of the FP counting, the concept of intermediate user is used and the elementary processes for the technical transactions that have to be used by the intermediate-user to change/delete the functional transactions required by the end user are identified.
       b. For the changing/deleting of functional transactions of the product that does not entail the automatic changing/deleting of other functional transactions logically correlated but not included in the scope of the FP counting, the concept of end user is used and the elementary processes related to the functional transactions required by the end user are identified.
    3. For the preloading of data necessary for the proper working of functional transactions in the tables of the product, the concept of intermediate user is used and the elementary processes for the technical transactions that have to be used for this preloading are identified.
    4. For adding new functionality to the baseline provided by the product, the concept of end user is used and the elementary processes related to these new functionalities are identified (no assumptions here).
- The type of each elementary process identified is determined. It will be the following:
    - Always an EI, for the cases referred to above in points 1 and 2a. In fact, parameters, flags, set values, etc., are identifiable as control information that enters the boundary of the application, and the processing logic required to complete the elementary process has the primary intent to alter the behavior of the application (see "Transactional Function Counting Rules" of CPM 4.3.1).
    - Consistent with the type of elementary process identified for the changed/deleted functional transaction (so, it can be an EI, an EO, or an EQ) for the cases referred to above in point 2b.
    - Always an EI (one unique, regardless of the number of records to be entered in the table!), for the cases referred to above in point 3. In fact, the

values entered in the tables needed for the proper working of the functional transactions of the product are identifiable as data that enter the boundary of the application, and the processing logic required to complete the elementary process has the primary intent to maintain one or more ILFs (see "Transactional Function Counting Rules" of CPM 4.3.1).

- Consistent with the type of process elements identified for the new functionality released to the end user (so, it can be an EI, an EO, or an EQ) for the cases referred to above in point 4.

■ The complexity of each elementary process is identified by following the additional rule explained below, in addition to those already described in CPM 4.3.1:

  - EI—Count a DET for each unique, intermediate-user recognizable, non-repeated attribute that crosses (enters and/or exits) the boundary during the process of altering the behavior of the system (parameterizations) and/or preloading data in the standard tables of the product
  - EO—No additional rule
  - EQ—No additional rule

The introduction of the concept of intermediate user can be used only when the implementation made for a functional transaction implies the same implementation for other functional transactions correlated but not required by the end user, and as such, not included in the scope of the FP counting.

This assumption is necessary to limit the scope of the count and not produce FP counts with poor significance and effectiveness when compared with the effort of the related project's implementation.

Therefore, this assumption is applied in the following cases:

■ Activation of standard functional transactions of the product, which drags with it the activation of many other functional transactions not required by the end user and, therefore, is not used.

■ Change of standard functional transactions of the product, which drags with it the change of many other functional transactions not required by the end user and, therefore, is not used.

■ Preloading in the standard tables of the product of data necessary for the proper functioning of functional transactions (e.g., to enter a new Organizational Unit, code, and description, in the appropriate table of the ERP product).

Project for the Evolutionary Maintenance of an ERP Product

As stated before, the only difference between a project for the first implementation of an ERP product and a project for the evolutionary maintenance of an ERP product is the evident availability, for the second one, of the baseline of functionality immediately operational.

Therefore, all assumptions/rules described at previous paragraph are valid also for this kind of project.

Calculate the Value Adjustment Factor

In accordance with the requirements of ISO 14143 standard Part 1 [7], the adjustment factor to the UFP was not used at all. This value was therefore assumed equal to 1.

The Function Point Analysis Measurement Program

The validation of the experiment ensures that the process used for applying FPA to ERP projects is successful and that it may be included as a standard in the Software Measurement Program of the company.

If the company has not yet implemented any Software Measurement Program, following are briefly the main steps create it at least for the aspects (and metrics) related to FPA, by following a "project-based" approach [8–10].

Plan the Function Point Analysis Measurement Program

This is the most important activity, where the processes, the goals, the objective, and the benefits of the program are determined, the sponsorship is established, and the roles and responsibilities are identified.

Generally, a stable team of FP Counting Specialists is created and a Lead for the team is identified. The main responsibility of the team is to monitor and validate constantly the correct application of FPA for uniformity and accuracy aspects. This team acts as a reference for all the FP counters of the company and should be composed by CFPS people, being also responsible for the FP training internal to the company.

The team has the following duties/responsibilities:

- Review FP size for accuracy and consistency
- Provide FP measurement support to the people involved
- Provide and distribute software measurement reporting
- Maintain measurement data
- Establish and maintain internal counting standards
- Provide training and mentoring on all the aspects of FPA

Implement the Function Point Analysis Measurement Program

The activity consists of putting in place the processes determined for the FPA Measurement Program, pursuing the goals and the objectives determined for the program during the previous step.

The requirements requested for the projects under experimentation are now extended to all projects, even if this may mean changing some internal standard, such as the way to deliver the project's documentation, the quality control activities on the project's documentation, etc.

The FPA is applied to all the projects which, based on their characteristics, fall in the scope of the FPA Measurement Program. The team of FP Counting Specialists provides FP counts, monitors and supports the FP counts made by others FP counters, provides periodic training to all the people involved in the program, gathers measurement data that is stored in the historical database, and provides periodic reporting to the sponsors and the management of the company about the "health" of the program.

Monitor the Function Point Analysis Measurement Program

The data gathered for the projects, first of all, the FP size, are systematically reviewed and analyzed by the team of FP Counting Specialists responsible for the FPA Measurement Program. During this step, all the anomalies found are recorded and analyzed, with the aim to verify the causes of those anomalies most frequently detected. Then, the corrective actions for the FPA Measurement Program are identified and promoted (i.e., additional FP training, a better support to FP counters, a better detailed project documentation, etc.).

The Continuous Improvement of the Function Point Analysis Measurement Program

The improvement of FP Measurement Program may involve the following aspects:

- Additional training for FP counting rules not well applied or not applied with uniformity
- More attention to the quality control activities on the projects' documentation
- More attention on gathering all the measurement data as defined at the start of the program, for each project and for each phase of the software life cycle (i.e., effort, defects, schedule, elapsed time, costs, and so on)

Additional actions for the improvement of FPA Measurement Program may be suggested, thanks to a continuous analysis of the data stored in the database of the company.

The improvement of FPA Measurement Program may also be induced by the improvement of the FPA method itself. In fact, it is known that the FPA method is subject to periodic improvements studied and implemented by the IFPUG Counting Practice Committee. Therefore, the FPA Measurement Program will be periodically updated to receive the evolutions of the FPA method.

Also in this case, the updates will involve training, and updating the Counting Practices Manual and the historical data collected, thus causing, depending on the extent of the changes, the provision of new versions of training, and an update to projects' sizes, recalculated with the new FP counting procedure or a conversion factor, if available.

An Example of Function Point Counting

The following is a very simple case study that describes the functionality to be implemented by an ERP SAP Enhancement Project and its FP counting.

Description

The user requires that the reference date of a contract is not modifiable by all users anymore. The inhibition of this modification has to be valid after the first insertion. However, he requires also the creation of a user enabled to change this field.

The SAP standard transaction involved for this Functional User Requirement is "Edit Master WBE." It manages in total the insertion/updating of five fields.

After the change, the users not authorized will update four fields, while the enabled user will continue to update five fields.

The user enabled to change the reference date of a contract has to be inserted with his particular level of authorization in the SAP table Authorization Levels. The SAP table Transactions Groups also has to be updated associating the new type of authorization to the transaction Edit Master WBE.

The SAP tables involved in the transaction after the change are REGISTER WBE, AUTHORIZATION LEVELS, and TRANSACTIONS GROUPS.

Function Point Counting

Determine the Type of Counting

The type of counting is the Enhancement Project Function Point Counts.

Determine the Counting Scope

The functionalities to include in the FP counting are as follows:

- The standard transaction SAP Edit Master WBE that needs to be changed to meet the end-user Functional User Requirements
- The functionality of preloading the information necessary for the proper working of the above transaction

Measure Data Functions

The ILFs identifiable are the following:

- REGISTER WBE (recognized by the end user)
- AUTHORIZATION LEVELS (recognized by both the end user and the intermediate user)
- TRANSACTIONS GROUPS (recognized at least by the intermediate user)

All the identified ILFs have a Low complexity, but they do not contribute to the UFP because they are neither added nor modified.

Measure Transactional Functions

The SAP transaction Edit Master WBE itself represents an elementary process from the point of view of the end user, classifiable as a changed EI.

Additional Transactional Functions are as follows:

- The loading, in the SAP table AUTHORIZATION LEVELS, of the identification data (code and description) of the user enabled to change the reference date of the contract
- The loading, in the SAP table TRANSACTIONS GROUPS, of the transaction code Edit Master WBE and the related new authorization.

The above Transactional Functions represent two elementary processes from the point of view of the intermediate user, classifiable as two EIs added.

The Edit Master WBE has an Average complexity, due to seven DETs (five fields, plus one more for the ability to initiate the action and another one for the ability to send an application response message) and two FTRs (only those recognized by the end user). Its contribution to the UFP count is four UPFs.

The elementary process of loading, in the SAP table AUTHORIZATION LEVELS, of the identification data (code and description) of the user enabled to change the reference date of the contract has a Low complexity due to three DETs (code and description of the enabled user; code of the authorized level) and one FTR. Its contribution to the UFP count is three UPFs.

There are no additional DETs for the ability to initiate the action and for the ability to send an application response message (this is, very probably, a manual task).

The elementary process of loading, in the SAP table TRANSACTIONS GROUPS, of the transaction code Edit Master WBE and the related new authorization has a Low complexity due to two DETs (transaction code and code of the new authorization) and one FTR. Its contribution to the UFP count is three UPFs.

There are no additional DETs for the ability to initiate the action and for the ability to send an application response message (this is, very probably, a manual task).

It is important to include those last two transactions in the FP counting scope because they are transactions (technical) not seen by the end user, but without them the Functional User Requirements cannot be met.

The technical transactions useful to meet a Functional User Requirement are visible and usable only when you enter in SAP as an intermediate user (designer). The intermediate user of SAP is still a user, though with different purposes than the end user. Thus, they both have to be considered in accordance with all the limitations made in the previous paragraphs.

The UFPs counted from the point of view of the end user may be kept separated from the UFPs counted from the point of view of the intermediate user in the historical database. This, in order to have a part of project size "standard" (perfectly compliant with the CPM 4.3.1 rules) and the other part (that counted from the point of view of intermediate user) ready to be studied, if applicable, as Non-Functional User Requirements and counted as such by using the new IFPUG SNAP methodology, when completed.

Finally, it should be highlighted that the analysis of data collected during the experiment was performed individually on the UFPs counted for projects with a prevalence of customization activities, for which the need to include the intermediate-user perspective occurs more heavily, and on the UFPs counted for projects with a prevalence of custom software developed ad hoc, for which the FPA is applied about exclusively compliant with the IFPUG CPM 4.3.1 rules (a minimal usage of the intermediate-user perspective is needed).

Below are two graphs containing the results of the analysis of data carried out, respectively, on the projects with a majority of "customizing" activities (Figure 21.1) and on projects with a majority of software development ad hoc activities (Figure 21.2).

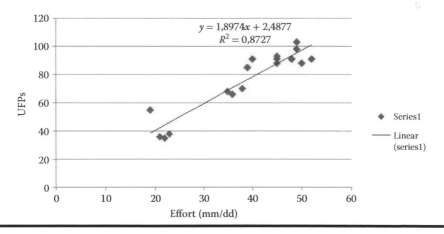

Figure 21.1 Unadjusted Function Points (end-user point of view) versus effort (mm/dd).

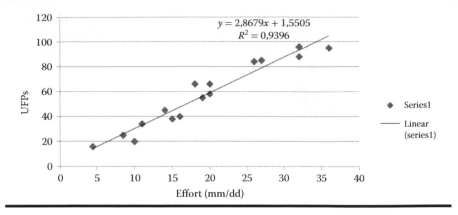

Figure 21.2 Unadjusted Function Points (intermediate-user point of view) versus effort (mm/dd).

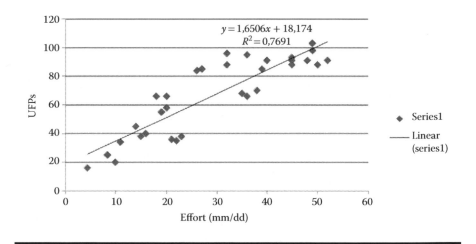

Figure 21.3 Unadjusted Function Points versus effort (mm/dd).

The third graph above shows the results of the same analysis carried out on all projects submitted to the experiment (Figure 21.3).

It is probably immediately intuitive that the FP productivity rate is significantly higher for projects with a majority of "customizing" activities (2, 96 FP/dd) than the one for projects with a majority of software development ad hoc activities (1, 91 FP/dd).

So, as a result of the experimentation we were provided two different values of the FP productivity rate as a reference, one for each of the two above cases and a third for those projects not immediately classifiable under one or the other type (2, 37 FP/dd).

References

1. Holmes, L. 2008. *Evaluating COTS Using Function Fit Analysis.* Q/P Management Group. http://www.qpmg.com/pdf/presentations/evaluating_cots_using_function_fit_analysis.pdf. Accessed October, 2010.
2. The International Function Point Users Group. 2010. *Function Point Counting Practices Manual, Release 4.3.* Princeton Junction, NJ: IFPUG Standards.
3. GUFPI-ISMA. 2006. *Metriche del software. Esperienze e ricerche.* Rome: Franco Angeli Editore.
4. Beckett, D. 2009. Sizing and estimating ERP implementations. *Paper presented at the 4th Annual International Software Measurement & Analysis Conference,* September 13–16, 2009. Chicago.
5. Jones, C. 1999. *Software Portfolio Analysis with Function Points Metrics.* Software Productivity Research. http://www.spr.com/templates/computer/pdf/SoftwarePortfolioArticle.pdf. Accessed January 2008.
6. Goldfarb, S.G. 2008. *Establishing a Measurement Program.* Q/P Management Group, http://www.qpmg.com/pdf/articles/establishing_a_measurement_program.pdf. Accessed May, 2009.
7. ISO: International Organization for Standardization. 2007. *ISO 14143-1: Information Technology—Software Measurement—Functional Size Measurement. Part 1: Definition of Concepts.* Geneva, Switzerland: ISO.
8. Morris, P. 2007. *Case Study of a Successful Measurement Program Version 1.2. Total Metrics.* http://www.totalmetrics.com/total-metrics-articles/Software-Measurement-Case-Study.pdf. Accessed July 2009.
9. The International Function Point Users Group. 2002. *IT Measurement Practical Advice from Experts.* Boston: Addison-Wesley Professional.
10. The International Function Point Users Group. 2004. *Guidelines to Software Measurement Release 2.* Princeton Junction, NJ: IFPUG Standards.

About the Author

Loredana Frallicciardi is an expert in the Performance management and software engineering disciplines, working for CSC Italy—Computer Sciences Corporation, a worldwide company leader for system integration and outsourcing services.

She has more than 20 years of experience in the software engineering field, spent through the study of methodologies, techniques, and tools assisting the development of structured and engineered systems.

She holds a degree in Mathematical Science from the University of Naples. She is a CFPS (Certified Function Point Specialist) and has been one of the first CSMS (Certified Software Measurement Specialist) level 3.

She is author of several articles, published and/or presented at national and international conferences; in the *IT Measurement—Practical Advice from the Experts* IFPUG book, and in the *Metriche del software. Esperienze e ricerche* GUFPI book.

For several years she has been an Italian representative for ISO-UNINFO working in Working Group WG12, dedicated to the development of an International Standard for Functional Size Measurement Methods.

She has been an IFPUG volunteer since 1993, becoming at first the Chair of the IFPUG Certification Committee and then the IFPUG Director of Applied Programs, until November 2010.

As the past IFPUG Director of Applied Programs, she has contributed to assist IFPUG members to understand, plan, manage, and improve software engineering processes and practices, thanks to the definition and publication of the Guidelines of Software Measurement, to the IFPUG Software Measurement Specialist Certification (CSMS), and the first IFPUG book *IT Measurement—Practical Advice from the Experts.*

Chapter 22

Mobile Applications, Functional Analysis, and the Customer Experience

Tammy Preuss

Contents

Mobile applications, their use and popularity, have increased exponentially in the past 5 years with the introduction of Apple's iPhone, Google's Android operating system, and mobile gaming platforms such as the Nintendo DS. This increase in applications and the data used has challenged communication service providers to provide the needed bandwidth. New business models, revenue models, and even companies have been created on the success of one mobile application or a new piece of functionality.

Customers experience mobile applications differently than applications on computers. In addition to their portability, customers interact with mobile applications through different interfaces. Using multi-touch screens, voice, rotation/alignment, camera interfaces, and blowing air on the screen, these applications are changing our communication methods and allowing customers to personalize their interactions.

Functional Analysis, as defined by ISO/IEC 14143-1:2007 and documented in the International Function Point Users Group (IFPUG) Counting Practices Manual (CPM) 4.3.1 [1], can quickly identify the functionality provided to the customer by documenting data and transactional functions. This method assists the developer in improving both quality and the customer experience.

What Is Meant by Mobile in Mobile Application?

A mobile application is one that will work on a wireless network: cellular, Wi-Fi, or Bluetooth. From a regulatory perspective, this includes both the licensed spectrum (cellular) and the unlicensed spectrum (Wi-Fi and Bluetooth). Frequencies and average distances serviced by different wireless networks are listed in Figure 22.1 [2,3,4,5,9].

Developers of mobile applications need to be aware of the frequencies, network protocols, and distances needed by the mobile device to communicate with these networks. Developers also need to understand how to initiate and terminate the application's connection to the network in an efficient manner. Holding a session

Regulation	Network Protocols	Radio Frequencies in the United States	Distance	Primary Use
Licensed	Cell towers (GSM and CDMA standards)	Various frequencies between 700–2100 Megahertz	Up to 10 square miles	Cellular coverage
Licensed	Femtocell (GSM and CDMA standards)	Various frequencies between 700–2100 Megahertz	5000 square feet	Provide cellular coverage in little to no-coverage areas and residences
Licensed and Unlicensed	Wi-MAX (GSM and CDMA standards)	2.5 Gigahertz	30 miles	Cellular coverage
Unlicensed	Wi-Fi	2.4 or 5 Gigahertz	300 feet	Connect 2 or more devices
Unlicensed	Bluetooth	2.4–2.485 Gigahertz	33 feet	Connect 2 or more devices; very close range

Figure 22.1   Spectrum allocation in the United States.

open too long consumes network resources. Closing it too soon may disrupt what the customer was doing with the application. This all impacts the application's performance and customer's experience with the application. U.S. smart phone handsets have the ability to use all three major wireless networks (cellular, Wi-Fi, and Bluetooth).

How Does a Customer View a Mobile Application?

Customers view mobile applications on their smart phones, tablets, and gaming devices as tools that increase their connectivity and interactivity with the world around them. Technology is bridging the vast age and distance gap that has long divided the generations [6]. Browsing through a mobile store can be just as enjoyable as browsing in a book store. Customers closely identify with the devices and in many cases give their devices personalities or create avatars (virtual selves) within the mobile application environment.

Wireless applications include those that provide connectivity for other devices (e.g., USB modem connecting a laptop with a cellular network) to very sophisticated software such as the instant queue in an online movie library, instantaneous updates on social networking sites, Voice over Internet Protocol (VoIP), or the connection between two seemingly unrelated devices (such as the smart phone and a car using Bluetooth).

Mobile data through cellular networks has been available since the first Cellular Digital Packet Data (CDPD) networks were introduced in the late 1990s in the United States. The applications that ran on these networks were simple by today's standards, using text menus for interactivity. As data networks have evolved allowing increasing throughput, mobile applications are presenting customers with richer visual and tactile experiences. Given this relatively new environment for software and the consumer, what measurements will have value to those who design mobile software? What technical and functional measurements will assist in software development and the customer's experience? Before we can answer these questions, we need to classify the types of mobile applications and provide examples of the functionality these applications are providing.

Classification of Mobile Applications

Mobile applications come with many functions provided to the user. The most basic applications are those that establish connectivity with a network. Although most laptops/netbooks are provisioned with Wi-Fi capabilities, some require a separate device (e.g., USB modem) to connect with the cellular network. The software on the modem provides connectivity to the cellular network. Mi-Fi devices, which create a personal mobile hot spot, offer similar functionality.

- Functionality provided: Application connects the customer's device(s) to a wireless network.
- Data connectivity: Continuously open data connection with a cellular network.

Next are applications that use the wireless network for short, bursty data from the originating device or service to another device. These include applications supporting e-readers, pill bottles, and pet collars. The applications are designed to do specific tasks on behalf of the user.

- Functionality provided: Applications that locate the customer's lost pet.
- Data connectivity: Short, bursty traffic either at regular intervals, when needed, or when a special event occurs.

A variation on this model is an application where the initial download and application updates are the only data used on the wireless network. These applications are using the capabilities of the device exclusively. Wireless coverage while the application is in use is not needed.

- Functionality provided: Applications to do Sudoku puzzles.
- Data connectivity: Short, bursty traffic on downloads and updates. Application can function on the device without wireless connectivity. It is self-contained on the device.

Next are more complex applications that include device functionality and web or server functionality. This is where the design of thin client as compared with thick client on the device and thin server as compared with thick server need to be carefully considered by the application developer. Does most of the data and functionality reside on the device, the server, or is there a 50/50 balance? These decisions will help architect a solution that supports the performance needed, the amount of data exchanged between the client and server, and the speed and bandwidth of the wireless network. Massive multiplayer games, social networking applications, and cloud services fall into this category.

- Functionality provided: Applications that access social networks.
- Data connectivity: Continuous while application is up. Architecture of application determines amount of data needed to interact among device, network, and server/cloud.

Last are the real-time streaming services of music and video. Although these take up the most wireless bandwidth, they are simpler in design than the massive multiplayer game software. Their performance is determined by the carrying capacity of the wireless network they are on. Faster networks that do not drop packets improve the customer experience with these applications. For slower networks, significant buffering on the mobile device may be required. In some cases, even buffering does not help the user experience.

- Functionality provided: Application to watch a live sports event.
- Data connectivity: Continuous, real-time streaming with buffering required by application if network throughput is too slow.

Application Stores—Distributors of the Mobile Applications

Most of today's mobile applications are sold in online application stores and marketplaces. The distribution of the applications is controlled by the companies that own the operating systems of the devices. While there are unaffiliated stores, the most popular application stores are those owned and managed by these companies. To entice developers to write applications for their stores, each operating system company has software development kits (SDKs) that include programming language assistance, sneak peeks of future releases, tutorials, testing support, device simulators, and tools to upload the software and publish it to the store. For a small up-front fee, developers are given access to this wealth of resources and support. The application stores make their money by receiving a percentage of any sales (usually 30%).

Mobile Commerce

Different revenue models are being pursued for mobile applications. Common revenue models include: free, free trial then pay, pay per application, free with advertising, location-based services, recommendations/social networking/product placement, subscription based, daily discounts at local businesses, and buying accessories within the application/ecosystem (e.g., farm equipment and seed). All software applications need to consider the revenue model that they will use with their application store, wireless carrier, and advertisers. The revenue model selected and the methods of payment are key functionality for a mobile application.

Development Life Cycles

Each mobile operating system has a ramp-up time for developers new to the ecosystem. In 2010, according to a study by Online Marketing Trends, Google's Android had the shortest ramp-up time at 5 months, followed by Apple's iOS at 7 months. With experienced developers, the development cycle is short for mobile applications, typically 2 months or less [7]. Most follow an agile life cycle and releases are quickly coded, tested, and beta tested through the arrangement between the mobile developers and the application stores/marketplace. Enterprise applications may have longer development cycles due to the complexity of functionality required by the company as well as security and data protection/encryption concerns. Successful companies that develop applications for consumers can be very small (100 employees for Rovio—maker of Angry Birds) [8] given the revenue they produce. Companies in many industries are developing their own in-house mobile applications for use by their employees. Internal instant messaging and social networking are among these areas being rapidly developed for use on mobile devices.

Native Operating System or HTML5 (Hypertext Markup Language Fifth Revision)

The five major mobile device operating systems in the United States (iOS, Android, Windows Phone 7, Blackberry OS, and WebOS) are causing quite a challenge for mobile developers. Do companies have development teams working on five different operating systems or do they code in a common language such as HTML5 which may or may not take advantage of the native operating system and hardware functionality? Do application developers code for the most common operating systems based on number of devices sold (e.g., iOS and Android) or do they go after specific deals/arrangements with less popular operating systems? The decision to code for the native operating system or to use a common language such as HTML5 will depend on the mobile application, the device, the functionality being provided to the customer, and the volume of customers.

Software Measurement

In this fast-paced development life cycle, what software measurements make sense? For most developers and entrepreneurs, the key measures are revenue and/or popularity. This is expressed in the company's balance sheet and the application's ranking in the Top Paid Applications and/or the Top Free Applications lists. Companies look for new and creative ways to market their applications to make the most money and get to the top of the favorite charts. Besides revenue and popularity, are there measures that as part of good software practices help facilitate the quality of the product and insure a good customer experience? Two methods, functional analysis and source lines of code, will be briefly discussed.

Functional Analysis

Functional analysis provides a good opportunity to quickly prototype an application from a user's point of view, without regard to the programming language used, to produce the functionality. It is a good tool to document the customer experience and can be used early in the requirements phase of the software development life cycle.

The analysis can be done at any phase in the development life cycle. In cases where a prototype to final code happens in weeks, the functional analysis will aid in quality and validate the functionality that is being provided to the customers. Functional analysis supports productivity and quality measures. Productivity is expressed in Function Points/time period. Quality is expressed in defects/Function Point.

Source Lines of Code

Source lines of code (SLOC) is a metric that many developers are comfortable with. It is easy to understand and quantify. It has some key differences from functional analysis. This method does not capture the functionality provided to the user. It is not applicable during the requirements phase of the project as coding has yet to start. Each developer may code differently depending on experience level producing a wide variation in SLOC. Like functional analysis, it can be used to define productivity measures. Productivity is usually expressed in KSLOC (1000 lines of code)/time period. Quality is expressed in defects/KSLOC.

What Is the Key Takeaway on Measurement?

While the author's preference is using functional analysis on mobile applications, the key takeaway is to be consistent in the measurement system used from release to release.

When Do Mobile Application Companies Consider Measurement?

Because of the small numbers of employees at many mobile application companies, software measurement and the benefits it provides may not be on the priority list. The focus of the company is generating that first hit application. Good software practices are dependent on the engineers and their training rather than company best practices. Functional analysis can help improve the quality and customer experience leading to success in that first hit application.

What Is Functional Analysis?

As defined in IFPUG's CPM release 4.3.1, Function Point Analysis measures software by quantifying the tasks and services (i.e., functionality) that the software provides to the user based primarily on logical design. The objectives of Function Point Analysis are to measure the following:

- Functionality implemented in software that the user requests and receives
- Functionality impacted by software development, enhancement, and maintenance independently of technology used for implementation

The process of Function Point Analysis is as follows:

- Simple enough to minimize the overhead of the measurement process
- A consistent measure among various projects and organizations

A Function Point Analysis count consists of six steps; see Figure 22.2. The steps will be discussed at a high level [1].

Step 1: Gathering Documentation

To do the analysis, gather all the information that is available about the application. Requirements, prototypes, data models, Unified Modeling Language (UML) models, and Subject Matter Expert (SME) interviews are all good sources to start with.

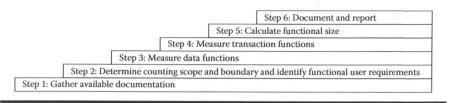

Figure 22.2   Steps of Function Point Analysis.

Step 2: Determine Counting Scope and Boundary and Identify Functional User Requirements

Define the customer or user role. A user can be a person, server, a network, a cloud-based service, and even another mobile phone. Set the boundary of the application you are analyzing. The user is always outside this boundary. List the functions from the user's perspective. What benefits are the users receiving? What roles are users performing? What benefits are your users getting from the application?

What Are the Different Application Boundaries?

Mobile applications have some of the most diverse logical application boundaries in the industry as shown in Figure 22.3. A mobile application can be self-contained on the device, client-server, cloud based, contained entirely within another application or ecosystem, part of an application, a mobile optimized website, or a non-optimized website.

A boundary indicates the scope of the analysis and also defines what you are interested in from a logical perspective. The user is always outside the boundary.

Another question to consider for boundary definitions is the following: Are you only interested in the application that you developed or are you also interested in third-party boundaries (such as the cloud) too?

Step 3: Measure Data

Functional analysis has its own vocabulary. Data and the transactions that support them are closely related.

Logical data that is maintained (adds, updates, etc.) within the boundary of the application is called an Internal Logical File (ILF). The primary intent is to store data being used by the application's transactions.

Data that is referenced outside the boundary of the application is called an External Interface File (EIF). The EIF also has stored data but the data is being referenced by our application, not maintained. The EIF of one application is the ILF for another application.

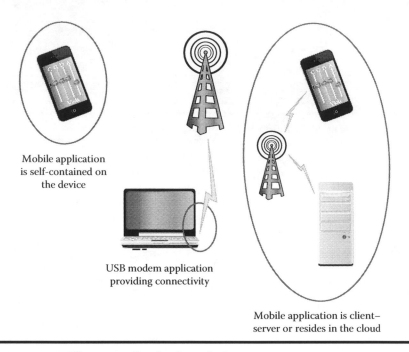

Mobile application
is self-contained on
the device

USB modem application
providing connectivity

Mobile application is client–
server or resides in the cloud

Figure 22.3   Different application boundaries.

Step 4: Measure Transactions

There are three transaction types: External Inputs (EI), External Outputs (EO), and External Inquiries (EQ). External inputs are transactions that originate outside the boundary of an application and have the primary intent of maintaining an ILF or altering the behavior of the application. Typical examples are Add, Change, and Delete functions.

EOs are transactions that send data outside the boundary of the application. The primary intent is to present data to the user that uses processing logic above/beyond simple data retrieval. Examples include reports with calculated summary totals.

EQs are transactions that send data outside the boundary of the application. The primary intent is to present data to the user through retrieval of data. A typical example is selecting a choice from a pick list and being presented with more information on the item you selected.

Steps 5 and 6: Calculate Functional Size and Document and Report

Once all data and transaction functions have been measured, points are assigned to the level of complexity of the function based on a scoring system of high, medium, or low. All transactions are assigned points and the final value of the count is documented.

Value to Application Developers and Customer Experience

Using these steps, one can easily map out the data and transaction functions, assign points, and determine a function's complexity. The real value of the method is the logical analysis of the application that shows the application from the customer's point of view. It is used to forecast potential technical problem areas.

More information on counting using Function Points can be found in the Counting Practices Manual, case studies, training classes, and the annual International Software Measurement and Analysis Conferences—all available at www.ifpug.org.

Let us look at an example of a mobile application developer who uses functional analysis, sales, and operational measures to help her with her mobile application.

Introduction—The Terrific Tuner, A Mobile Application

A senior university music student, for a required assignment, has developed a chromatic string tuner mobile application (see Figure 22.4). The application helps the string musician tune by ear (aurally) by providing a pitch to match. It helps the string musician tune visually by using pictures of the musician's favorite hot drinks. The drinks move up and down the strings to show the sharpness or flatness of the note. When the note is in tune, the drink matches an arrow to the side and the drink steams.

Figure 22.4   The Terrific Tuner, a mobile application.

The application is preloaded with common string instruments and their tunings as well as a few hot drinks. The application will be free and runs on one mobile handset. It is coded to work with the handset's native operating system. The application can determine where the customers are when using the application through Global Positioning System (GPS), Wi-Fi hotspot, or cellular tower information available to the application from the operating system. The student receives customer usage reports from the application. The student also receives sales reports from the application store.

- Application Classification: Self-contained on the mobile device
- Users: String Instrumentalists (customers), Application Administrator (preloads data into application)
- Revenue Model: Free
- Application Boundary: Except for initial download from the application store and periodic software updates, the software is contained entirely on the handset and uses the handset's microphone, speaker, and touch screen. The application sales reports, while a part of the mobile ecosystem, are not created by the developer and are outside the boundary of the application. The student's computer, which stores the customer usage reports, is outside the boundary; see Figures 22.5 through 22.8.

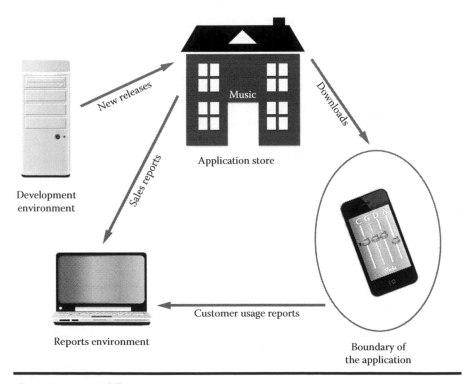

Figure 22.5   Mobile ecosystem.

Data Supporting the Application

Logical Data	Data Elements	Data Type
String instruments	Name of instrument	ILF
	Picture of instrument	
	Number of strings	
	Common note names	
	Common tunings (in hertz)	
Favorite Drinks	Name of drink	ILF
	Picture of drink	
Customer Data	Number of times customer opens application	ILF
	Customer's favorite drink	
	Customer location when using application	
	Length of time application is open	
Location	GPS longitude and latitude	EIF
	Wi-Fi registered name	
	Wi-Fi longitude and latitude	
	Cellular tower identification	
	Cellular tower longitude and latitude	

Figure 22.6   Data analysis.

Mobile Ecosystem

Transactions above the double line are used by the customer. Transactions below the double line are used by the application administrator and/or support reporting.

Transactions Using the Data	Logical Data Used	Transaction Type
Select string instrument to tune	Strings	EQ
For tuning by ear (aural tuning), present screen to select pitch. Sound pitch.	Strings	EQ
Select Favorite Drink	Favorite Drinks	EQ
For visual tuning, present screen to match pitch. Use pictures of favorite drinks on a string to indicate closeness to pitch. Drinks steam when exact pitch is attained.	Strings, Favorite Drinks	EO
Add new string instrument	Strings	EI
Delete string instrument	Strings	EI
Add new favorite drink	Favorite Drinks	EI
Get Customer Location GPS	Customer, Location	EI
Get Customer Location Wi-Fi	Customer, Location	EI
Get Customer Location Cellular	Customer, Location	EI
Report: Most popular drink	Favorite Drinks	EO
Report: Most popular location	Customer, Location	EO
Report: Average length of use by customer	Customer	EO
Report: Number of times customer opens application in a day	Customer	EO

Figure 22.7   Transactions using the data.

Summary of Functional Analysis

Number	Quantity	Data or Transactions
Internal Logical Files	3	Strings, Favorite Drinks, Customer
External Interface Files	1	Location
External Inputs	6	Add & delete strings, Add drinks, Get Customer Location GPS, Get Customer Location Wi-FI, Get Customer Location Cellular
External Inquiries	3	Select string instrument, Aural tuning, Select Favorite Drink
External Outputs	5	Visual tuning with drinks, All reports (4)

Figure 22.8   Summary of functional analysis.

How Does This Analysis Help the Developer?

The developer has a clear list of the functionality provided to the customer and application administrator. These lists show the data and the transactions that are using the data. This then allows the developer to concentrate on technical issues associated with her application (such as the lowest practical speed that the application can be downloaded, and analyzing customer information).

Customer Experience

The customers are happy with the application's fun interface, ease of downloading through the application store, and price. If the musician plays by ear, then he is given the option to match pitch. If the musician prefers a visual representation, then a picture of a favorite hot drink with steam rising occurs when correct pitch is attained. He likes using this simple application and takes it on his next gig where he shows the application to his fellow musicians. He was pleased that a new guitar tuning used by his favorite band was available.

Two Months Later

As the application's popularity expands among the music students, the local businesses (coffee shops, bars) ask to have the drink pictures branded with their names. They also want the application to link to their shops' websites. They pay product placement dollars to the developer for the branded drinks. The developer contracts with the local businesses to get click-through revenue and a very small percentage of any food and drink that are sold via the web from the application. The application will send a code to the websites, so that if drinks or food are ordered, the developer receives credit. The application remains a free download.

- Application Classification: Self-contained on the mobile device
- Users: String Instrumentalists, Application Administrator
- Revenue Model: Free to customers. Product placement dollars, click-through revenue, and a percentage of food and beverage sales from local businesses for orders placed via the web.
- Application Boundary: Handset; see Figure 22.9.

A renamed ILF, Branded Drinks, contains information from the original Favorite Drinks ILF (with new brand pictures) and a new data element, web link of local business. Two new ILFs, Commission Codes and Click-through, are created. Commission Codes will store the unique code for each business' website—so our developer will get credit for food and beverage sales. Click-through records the user's clicks/taps to the local businesses' websites; see Figure 22.10.

A new transaction is added linking the mobile application to local businesses' websites for information, food, and drink orders. A new report, Click-through to Businesses, is created. One updated function (Add Branded Drinks) and five new administrative functions, Change and Delete Branded Drinks and Add, Change, and Delete Commission Codes, are included.

How Is Analysis Helping the Developer?

Although the developer is pleased that her application is proving popular at her university, she finds that the administrative functions are taking up a lot of her time. With the revenue she is making, she is able to pay part-time students to analyze her reports and help with administration. Using functional analysis, she is able to explain the functionality and expected customer experience quickly to her new hires.

Customer Experience

Her customers are pleased with the opportunity to link to their favorite beverage's website. This allows her customers to place drink and food orders in the morning when they get up or after a gig at night. The businesses are happy for the increase in sales.

Data Supporting the Application

Logical Data	Data Elements	Data Type
String instruments	Name of instrument	ILF
	Picture of instrument	
	Number of strings	
	Common note names	
	Common tunings (in hertz)	
Branded Drinks (formerly Favorite Drinks)	Name of drink	ILF
	Picture of drink (with brand)	
	Web link of local business	
Customer Data	Number of times customer opens application	ILF
	Customer's favorite drink	
	Customer location when using application	
	Length of time application is open	
Location	GPS longitude and latitude	*EIF*
	Wi-Fi registered name	
	Wi-Fi longitude and latitude	
	Cellular tower identification	
	Cellular tower longitude and latitude	
Click-through	*Click-through URLs*	*ILF*
Commission Codes	*Local business code*	*ILF*

Figure 22.9   Updated functionality (in italics).

Four Months Later

Through social networking sites, other university students in other cities download the application. Local businesses in those cities wish to be featured too. More and more local businesses are contacting the developer to have their branded drinks added to the application with links to their menus. She now links the current location of the customer with a branded drinks list that is applicable within 5 miles of his/her location. She also needs to add business GPS location coordinates and street

Transactions Using the Data	Logical Data Used	Transaction Type
Select string instrument to tune	Strings	EQ
For tuning by ear (aural tuning), present screen to select pitch. Sound pitch.	Strings	EQ
Select Branded Drink	*Branded Drinks*	*EQ*
For visual tuning, present screen to match pitch. Use pictures of favorite drinks on a string to indicate closeness to pitch. Drinks steam when exact pitch is attained.	*Strings, Branded Drinks*	*EO*
Link to local business website	*Branded Drinks, Commission Codes, Click-through*	*EO*
Add new string instrument	Strings	EI
Delete string instrument	Strings	EI
Add Branded Drinks	*Branded Drinks*	*EI*
Get Customer Location GPS	Customer, Location	EI
Get Customer Location Wi-Fi	Customer, Location	EI
Get Customer Location Cellular	Customer, Location	EI
Report: Most popular drink	*Branded Drinks*	*EO*
Report: Most popular location	Customer, Location	EO
Report: Average length of use by customer	Customer	EO
Report: Number of times customer opens application in a day	Customer	EO

Figure 22.10 (*Continued*)

Transactions Using the Data	Logical Data Used	Transaction Type
Change Branded Drinks	*Branded Drinks*	*EI*
Delete Branded Drinks	*Branded Drinks*	*EI*
Add Commission Codes	*Commission Codes*	*EI*
Change Commissions Codes	*Commission Codes*	*EI*
Delete Commission Code	*Commission Codes*	*EI*
Report: Click-through to businesses	*Branded Drinks, Click-through, Commission Codes*	*EO*

Figure 22.10   Updated transactions (in italics).

address of the businesses. She uses a geocode/reverse geocode third party function to populate this information as part of the Add, Change, or Delete Branded Drinks administrative functions.

Although her revenue model is working well, our developer is worried about application performance and the amount of data the application has on the handset. She and her team are currently supporting 45 cities and more are being loaded every day. Her staff size in now 10 part-time students. She takes a leave of absence from the university to run her business.

- Application Classification: Self-contained on the mobile device
- Users: String Instrumentalists, Application Administrator
- Revenue Model: Free to customers. Product placement dollars, click-through revenue, and a percentage of food and beverage sales from businesses in 45 cities.
- Application Boundary: Handset; see Figure 22.11.

The Branded Drinks logical file is updated with the GPS location and street address of the local businesses. If a business provides a street address, the geocode function can provide the GPS coordinates. If a business provides the GPS coordinates, the reverse geocode function can provide the street address, as shown in Figure 22.12.

The visual tuning transaction becomes more complex with the addition of the Location file and the logic to show only branded drinks within 5 miles of the user's current location in addition to unbranded drinks.

Data Supporting the Application

Logical Data	Data Elements	Data Type
Branded Drinks	Name of drink	ILF
	Picture of drink (with brand)	
	Web link of local business	
	Business GPS location coordinates	
	Street address of business	
	City of business	
	State/Province of business	
	Country of business	
	Zip code of business	
Geocode (3rd party functionality)	*Business GPS location coordinates*	EIF
	Street address of business	
	City of business	
	State/Province of business	
	Country of business	
	Zip code of business	

Figure 22.11 Functionality updated (in italics).

How Is Analysis Helping the Developer?

Because the developer is concerned with performance, she takes her functional analysis and starts working different scenarios with her application simulator. How large can the drink file get before it too big? Is the more complex branded drink location algorithm slowing down the application's performance? She is alarmed at the reports that show the average usage time is increasing. She is concerned that this is due to the time it takes the application to start up with all the data. She and her team are just starting to run the scenarios when…

Customer Experience

The application breaks. With so many businesses in different locations now being added, the self-contained model is not working any longer. Downloading updates of the application from the application store takes time. Users are not happy that a new update is pushed to them every week. The application takes a long time to

New & Updated Transactions Using the Data	Logical Data Used	Transaction Type
Visual Tuning with Drinks	Strings, Branded Drinks, Location	EO
Get Geocode/ Reverse Geocode	Geocode	EQ
Add Branded Drinks	Branded Drinks, Geocode	EI
Change Branded Drinks	Branded Drinks, Geocode	EI
Delete Branded Drinks	Branded Drinks, Geocode	EI

Figure 22.12   New and updated transactions.

start on the handset. Her customers are complaining on social networking sites, on blogs, and on e-mails to her.

Five Months Later-Post Crisis

She and her team redesigned the application to work using a thin client approach on the handset with a server handling and storing most of the data. Fortunately, an angel investor allowed her to buy servers that would handle most of the data transactions. The customer is now limited to three locations worth of information with one location being the customer's current location. In this new model, our developer has to worry about cellular network performance. She has to optimize her data transactions across the network, so the customer's bucket of data is not used excessively. She has to make sure the application will continue to work if it is unable to reach the network. When the customer starts the application, if the network is not available, it uses the settings from the earlier session. Other challenges she is working on include the need for geographically redundant servers.

Her angel investors urge her to develop the application for the second most popular operating system, expand into that application store, and expand into Europe and Asia.

■ Application Classification: Thin client on handsets with servers handling bulk of data processing. Cellular and Wi-Fi networks need to support real-time connectivity for most functionality. If networks are not reachable, application will run with settings from earlier session.

■ Users: String Instrumentalists, Application Administrators
■ Revenue Model: Free to customers. Product placement dollars and a percentage of food and beverage sales from local businesses for orders placed via the web. The business is expanding into Europe and Asia.
■ Application Boundary: Handsets + servers; see Figures 22.13 through 22.15.

Data Supporting the Application

Logical Data	Data Elements	Data Type
String instruments	Name of instrument Picture of instrument Number of strings Common note names Common tunings (in hertz)	ILF
Branded Drinks	Name of drink Picture of drink (with brand) Web link of local business Business GPS location coordinates Street address of business City of business State/Province of business Zip code of business Country of business	ILF
Customer Data	Number of times customer opens application Customer's favorite drink Customer location when using application Length of time application is open	ILF
Location	GPS longitude and latitude Wi-Fi registered name Wi-Fi longitude and latitude Cellular tower identification Cellular tower longitude and latitude	EIF

Figure 22.13   (Continued)

Logical Data	Data Elements	Data Type
Location	GPS longitude and latitude	EIF
	Wi-Fi registered name	
	Wi-Fi longitude and latitude	
	Cellular tower identification	
	Cellular tower longitude and latitude	
Click-through	Click-through URLs	ILF
Commission Codes	Local business code	ILF
Geocode (3rd party functionality)	Business GPS location coordinates	EIF
	Street address of business	
	City of business	
	State/Province of business	
	Country of business	
	Zip code of business	

Figure 22.13   Data functions.

Transactions Using the Data	Logical Data Used	Transaction Type
Select string instrument to tune	Strings	EQ
For tuning by ear (aural tuning), present screen to select pitch. Sound pitch.	Strings	EQ
Select Branded Drink	Branded Drinks	EQ
Select up to three locations	Branded Drinks, Location	EQ
For visual tuning, present screen to match pitch. Use pictures of favorite drinks on a string to indicate closeness to pitch. Drinks steam when exact pitch is attained.	Strings, Branded Drinks, Location	EO

Figure 22.14   (*Continued*)

Transactions Using the Data	Logical Data Used	Transaction Type
Link to local business website	Branded Drinks, Commission Codes	EO
Add new string instrument	Strings	EI
Delete string instrument	Strings	EI
Add Branded Drinks	Branded Drinks, Geocode	EI
Get Geocode/Reverse Geocode	Geocode	EQ
Get Customer Location GPS	Customer, Location	EI
Get Customer Location Wi-Fi	Customer, Location	EI
Get Customer Location Cellular	Customer, Location	EI
Report: Most popular drink	Branded Drinks	EO
Report: Most popular location	Customer, Location	EO
Report: Average length of use by customer	Customer	EO
Report: Number of times customer opens application in a day	Customer	EO
Change Branded Drinks	Branded Drinks, Geocode	EI
Delete Branded Drinks	Branded Drinks, Geocode	EI
Add Commission Codes	Commission Codes	EI
Change Commission Codes	Commission Codes	EI
Delete Commission Codes	Commission Codes	EI
Report: Click-through to businesses	Branded Drinks, Click-through, Commission Codes	EO
Save previous settings	Strings, Branded Drinks	EI

Figure 22.14   Transaction functions.

Summary of Functional Analysis

Number	Quantity	Data or Transactions
Internal Logical Files	5	Strings, Branded Drinks, Customer, Commission Codes, Click-through
External Interface Files	2	Location, Geocode
External Inputs	12	Add & Delete Strings; Add, Change, Delete Branded Drinks; Add, Change, Delete Commission Codes; Get Customer Location GPS, Wi-Fi and Cellular; Save previous settings
External Inquiries	5	Select string instrument, Aural tuning, Select Branded Drink, Select up to three locations, Get Geocode/Reverse Geocode
External Outputs	7	Visual tuning, All reports (5), Link to local business website

Figure 22.15   Summary of functional analysis.

How Is Analysis Helping the Developer?

The developer has to hire different developers to write the application for the second operating system. Because she has the functionality documented, it is easy to train the new developers in the functionality that needs to be provided. Does coding the application in two native operating systems increase the application's functionality? Ideally, the application's functionality is the same whichever operating system and coding language are used. Even if the functionality is similar, there may be key technical differences in the handsets, operating systems, and application stores that make the second version of the application a different application than the first and worthy of its own analysis.

Customer Experience

Customers are pleased with the application performance improvements. They mention in areas of no wireless coverage, the application works. The application is mentioned in popular music blogs. It hits #2 in the free application popularity chart. While #1 would have been nice, there is no way of getting ahead of a very popular game.

Coda

The developer sells her company to a larger application company 3 years later. She resumes her last semester of school and graduates. She returns to playing gigs at the local coffee house and spends time managing her charitable foundation.

Summary

As the mobile application industry evolves, software measurement will continue to play an important part in the customer experience and quality of the mobile application. This chapter has discussed the wireless networks that support mobile applications, how customers are interacting with their mobile devices, the classifications of mobile applications, mobile commerce, software development life cycles, and the debate on coding in a native operating system or HTML5. Software measurements compared functional analysis to SLOC in three areas: functionality, quality, and productivity. High level definitions of functional analysis, as provided by the IFPUG Functional Sizing Method, are presented. An example of a mobile application and its evolution from initial release to final sale to a larger firm demonstrated how functional analysis assists the developer and delivers a great customer experience.

References

1. International Function Point Users Group (IFPUG). 2009. *Function Point Counting Practices Manual*, Release 4.3.1, Part 1.
2. http://support.apple.com/kb/ht3887 (accessed April 15, 2011).
3. http://en.wikipedia.org/wiki/Spectrum (accessed April 14, 2011).
4. http://electronics.howstuffworks.com/cell-phone1.htm (accessed April 14, 2011).
5. http://www.wimax.com/wimax-faq/ (accessed April 15, 2011).
6. OMG! My Grandparents are my BFF! 2011. *Wall St J*, The Journal Report. May 9, 2011.
7. http://www.onlinemarketing-trends.com/2011/01/life-cycle-of-mobile-application.html (accessed April 15, 2011).
8. http://www.bgr.com/2011/05/18/angry-birds-creator-rovio-sets-2-3-year-goal-for-ipo/ (accessed May 18, 2011).
9. http://www.att.com/shop/wireless/devices/3gmicrocell.jsp#/features (accessed April 15, 2011).

About the Author

Tammy Preuss, AT&T Senior Business Manager IT, analyzes and designs the customer experience from an IT systems and architecture perspective with special focus on AT&T's retail and online sales applications for both consumer and business. She is a Certified Function Point Specialist, a Lean Six Sigma Black Belt, and a Project Management Professional. She has extensive experience in information technology, process improvement, training, project management, methodology alignment, and software measurement. Tammy is chairman of the IFPUG New Environments Committee and has 20 years of experience in the telecommunications industry. She regularly presents at industry conferences including Mobile World Congress and 4G World.

Tammy holds a Masters in Telecommunications Management from Stevens Institute of Technology, a Masters in Music from Yale University, and an undergraduate degree from California State University, Fresno.

Chapter 23

Cloud Computing Solution Measurement

Steven Woodward

Contents

The world of information technology continues to change at an accelerated pace. Cloud computing solutions are very much leading the pack, driving various models, solutions, and standards. The returns-on-investment can be tremendous, but likewise, so are the risks. Without solution-based measurement, the full benefits cannot be realized from the cloud, nor can the risks be adequately managed. This chapter will use several real-life scenarios and outline how measurement can be leveraged in cloud computing environments, while driving solutions. However, before we get there, first we need to understand what is "cloud computing"?

What Is Cloud Computing?

This chapter will not be an all encompassing set of information for cloud computing, but rather, it will focus on some of the most important basics to consider for those interested in solution measurement.

There are several communities and companies who have published cloud computing models and frameworks. For this particular chapter, I use the National Institute of Standards for Technology (NIST) guidelines from the United States Department of Commerce. This is the community that has been driving many of the accepted definitions in the cloud computing marketspace and is also one of the cloud communities where I personally focus my efforts and contributions. Information is available from the NIST website at www.nist.gov.

The objectives at NIST are to provide thought leadership and guidance around cloud computing and catalyze its use within industry and government. NIST provides guidelines and support to help governments and companies fulfill the cloud computing objectives of interoperability, portability, security, and privacy [1].

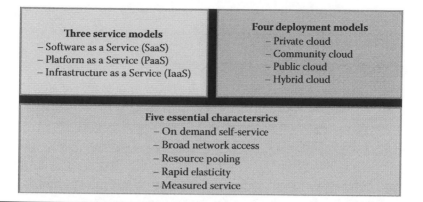

Figure 23.1   National Institute of Standards for Technology cloud model [3]. (From: National Institute of Standards for Technology—Cloud Computing Reference Architecture and Taxonomy Working Group Status Presentation. 2011. *Washington Cloud Computing Workshop*.)

The accepted NIST definition for cloud computing is as follows:

Cloud computing is a model for enabling ubiquitous, convenient, on-demand network access to a shared pool of configurable computing resources (e.g., networks, servers, storage, applications, and services) that can be rapidly provisioned and released with minimal management effort or service provider interaction. This cloud model promotes availability and is composed of five essential characteristics, three service models, and four deployment models [2] (see Figure 23.1).

NIST has recently identified the five primary roles in cloud computing that I will also outline, as this concept is very important to provide context for measurement activities [1].

I will condense and simplify the detailed definitions for the purpose of this study.

The Five Essential Characteristics

On-Demand Self-Service

A consumer (customer) can self-provision computing capabilities, such as server time and network storage, as needed.

Broad Network Access

Capabilities are available over the network and accessed through standard mechanisms and channels (e.g., mobile phones, laptops, and PDAs).

Resource Pooling

The provider's computing resources are pooled to serve multiple consumers using a multi-tenant model. This means that physical and virtual resources are dynamically assigned and reassigned according to consumer demand. Examples of resources include storage, processing, memory, network bandwidth, and virtual machines.

Rapid Elasticity

Capabilities can be rapidly and elastically provisioned; the capabilities often appear to be unlimited and can be purchased in any quantity at any time.

Measured Service

Cloud systems automatically control and optimize resource use by leveraging a metering capability to some degree, appropriate for the type of service (e.g., storage, processing, bandwidth, and active user accounts). Resource usage monitoring and reporting also provides transparency for both the provider and the consumer of the utilized service.

The Three Service Models

Cloud Software as a Service

The capability provided to the consumer is to use applications running on a cloud infrastructure. The application's functionalities are accessible from various client devices through a thin client interface such as a web browser (e.g., web-based e-mail).

Cloud Infrastructure as a Service

The capability provided is to provision processing, storage, networks, and other fundamental computing resources (provision the infrastructure virtually).

Cloud Platform as a Service

The capability provided to the user role is to deploy onto the cloud infrastructure created, enhanced, or acquired applications created using programming languages and tools supported by the provider. Platform as a Service (PaaS) also includes middleware and other services that are not specifically Software as a Service (SaaS) or Infrastructure as a Service (IaaS) (e.g., reusable services, development, testing, deployment).

The Three Deployment Models

Private Cloud

The cloud infrastructure is operated solely for an organization. It may be managed by the organization or by a third party and may exist on premise (internal) or off premise (external). The internal and external consideration is often called "hosting" and is a separate discussion from the deployment model, although it is a significant consideration.

Community Cloud

The cloud infrastructure is shared by several organizations and supports a specific community that has shared concerns (e.g., mission, security requirements, policy, and compliance considerations). It may be managed by the organizations or by a third party and may be "hosted" on premise (internal) or off premise (external).

Public Cloud

The cloud infrastructure is made available to the general public or a large industry group and is owned by an organization selling cloud services. Usually it will be hosted externally, although in some cases it could be hosted internally, for example, your company itself is the cloud provider.

Hybrid Cloud

The cloud infrastructure is a composition of two or more clouds (private, community, or public) that remain unique entities but are bound together by standardized or proprietary technology that enables data and application portability (e.g., cloud bursting for load balancing between clouds). Similarly, these could be internally or externally hosted.

The Five Roles

Cloud Carrier

The cloud carrier is the intermediary that provides connectivity and transport of cloud services from cloud providers to cloud consumers (e.g., your Internet service provider or carrier).

Cloud Provider

The provider is the person, organization, or entity responsible for making a service available to cloud consumers (e.g., organization hosting your cloud).

Cloud Consumer

The cloud consumer is the person or organization that maintains a business relationship with, and uses service from, cloud providers (e.g., user of cloud services; note: can also be using services provided by cloud brokers).

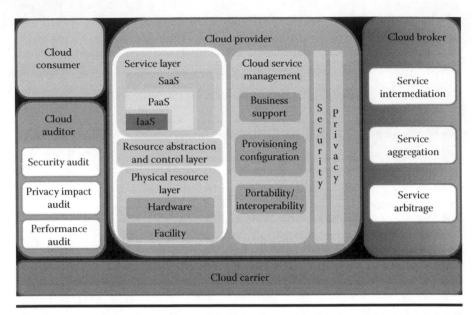

Figure 23.2 National Institute of Standards for Technology cloud computing reference architecture.

Cloud Broker

The cloud broker is an organization that manages the use, performance, and delivery of cloud services and negotiates relationships between cloud providers and cloud consumers (e.g., party who provides services that amalgamate cloud providers services into more meaningful services as required by the cloud consumer).

Cloud Auditor

The cloud auditor is a party who can conduct independent assessments of cloud services, information system operations, performance, and security of the cloud implementation (e.g., a neutral third-party assessor to evaluate appropriate cloud solutions).

Figure 23.2 is the NIST Reference Architecture; this model is of tremendous help, fostering communication to clarify your specific roles, activities, and accountabilities. For the purpose of this chapter, I am not walking through the entire model. I do suggest that you read the various NIST documents that are available to the general public, if you get involved with cloud computing solutions.

Measurement Fundamentals

Cloud measurement is critical for successful cloud computing initiatives, from the perspective of trust, accountability, transparency, optimization, and service level agreements. Most organizations lack robust measurement capabilities and, therefore, are essentially ill prepared to collect, analyze, and use cloud computing measurement information.

"Measured service" is one of the five characteristics of cloud computing (using the NIST definition [2]), but it does not mean that it is well done, or for the purposes that support your organization's goals at this time.

Measuring for the sake of measuring is a waste of resources and money. Too often companies forget why they are measuring, what they wish to accomplish, and what decisions need to be made by leveraging measurement information. Measurement is not an "end unto itself" and you need to pay close attention to the value that measurement analytics provides to stakeholders, so that they can accomplish and demonstrate their goals [4, 5].

Measures should not be selected based on those easiest to obtain (e.g., automatically collected from a tool) or what you always have collected in the past. The reality is that the technical world of today does not reflect that of just 5 years ago. Measures need to provide the most valuable timely perspectives in a cost-effective manner to communicate key information that can improve decision making [6].

The measures need to be consistent, but the approaches need to be agile, enabling timely, meaningful, pertinent information to be exchanged. The rate of change in technology is moving too fast to consider a "one size fits all" mentality.

Cloud Goals

In cloud computing environments, you must understand who you are (roles), goals, and expectations. Each cloud role has different perspectives, questions, and goals; additionally, different individual stakeholders will have potentially different prioritized goals. Figure 23.3 identifies the concept regarding different goals and questions based on the cloud roles.

We will use two scenarios in this chapter to help provide real-life examples that will drive specific measurement and analytics. The categorizations that I use are from a combination of resources with the intent to generate early discussions, identifying measures and analytics that provide the best value at a reasonable price point.

The intent of the scenarios examples are to help explain the process of selecting appropriate specific measures based on communicated goals or objectives expressed by stakeholders. The goals, therefore, are not formalized or contain a standardized structure for the purposes of this chapter.

Scenario 1: Consumer—Functionality

Role: Cloud consumer

Deployment Model and Hosting: Public—external

Goal: Strategic—The expectation is that by using cloud services you can be more responsive to your customers' business needs (functionality requests) at a

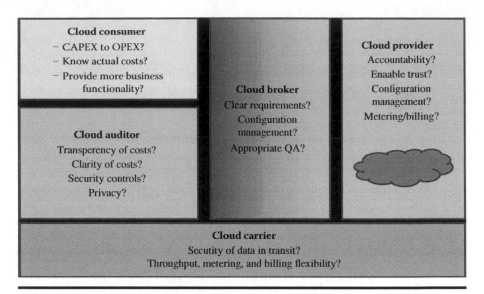

Figure 23.3 National Institute of Standards for Technology roles with some goals and questions identified.

lower price point and faster time-to-market. This will result in higher satisfaction and therefore better retention of customers.

Considerations and assumptions:

1. The goal is improved delivery of business functionality.
2. This will start small and expand, based on successful migration and realized benefits from specific business applications leveraging cloud services.
3. Software measurement and business perspectives will be valuable.
4. The software application functionality existed previously and was simply migrated to the cloud and leveraged various cloud services (business functionality did not change).
5. Some cloud services need to be developed internally or by cloud brokers (middleware, for example).
6. The focus is from business functionality, and therefore, is aligned with SaaS "Service Model," although PaaS and IaaS may be used, but the realized benefits from the cloud are related to business functionality.
7. Measurement maturity at this company is limited; therefore, measurement analytics will be basic in nature.

Cultural Considerations

Since measurement experience is limited, this infers that we need to establish a "before" and "after" cloud baselines. The stakeholders also need to understand that it might take several months before improvements are realized and quantified. The organization's culture and experience is always a major consideration; do not give someone a Ferrari when they do not know how to drive. The answer is also not to hire someone who knows how to drive a car. Skills and capabilities that align with your tools, goals, and objectives must be considered.

Business Measures Consideration and Identification

We first identify the key business measure that pertains to "customer retention." What questions do the stakeholders want answered about customers? Is it the number of customers? Is it the revenue retained overall for customers? You will need to have specific discussions relating to what are and will be your core questions pertaining to this goal. You may find that during interviews and discussions, different processes and directions for the measurement need to be considered.

For example, it is agreed that the key question is "How much customer revenue did we retain pre-cloud and post-cloud?" Your discussions then lead to a realization that customer revenue needs to be for the entire customer experience with your organization, not just for an application. Therefore, this is a very strategic measure that has several influencing factors, not just the cloud initiative. You make the decision to collect the pre-cloud measurement data and determine that 1 year after the cloud deployment, the post-cloud measurement collection will take place. In these discussions you also realize that the "invoiced" amounts will provide the most valuable perspective.

Business Measure 1

Measurement Name: Customer Revenue Invoiced

Measurement Type: Business

Audience: CEO, CIO, Executive Team, and Customer Relationship Management Managers

Summarization: Total customer revenue invoiced over a 1-year period, with subtotals by month

Description: Total revenue invoiced in U.S. dollars from customers; this is exclusive of any rebates and other promotions offered during reporting period, but it is inclusive of taxes.

Reporting Period: A yearly report will be generated for the C Level executives and marketing directors. The report will contain the customer revenue invoiced broken down by month; no other reporting breakdowns will be available.

Data Collection Method: The revenue information is obtained directly from the monthly invoice information within the billing system.

Format: Currency maximum: $99,999,999,999

Decision Making and Benefits: This information is valuable outside the cloud computing initiative. This measure and information is valuable in several contexts to highlighting customer revenue, offering an early indication of the impact from various initiatives (positive or negative). Future decisions can consider this information and make better decisions.

Data Collection Costs: Estimated $2000 initially and $1500 yearly (includes reporting)

During this discussion, you quickly realize that other more operational measures are needed to support the business goal and monitor progress towards this goal, rationalizing why and how this goal is expected to be enabled [7]. These measures are more technical or software in nature.

Here is some supporting text from discussions around technical measurement.

The functionality is provided to the users in meaningful releases. Releases vary in scope, some significantly larger than others. It was, therefore, determined that releases were not the best measure to communicate the volume of functionality. Likewise, the organization uses an agile methodology, and while the teams have used "story points" with good success, they realized that story points are not comparable or consistent release to release. We really need a standard way to evaluate and size user recognizable functionality to help provide context around features or functionality being delivered.

The expectation is to deliver more functionality to the user; therefore, we need to measure the scope of business functionality. The International Function Point Users Group (IFPUG) method provides a very good standard to generate the necessary discussions, measures, and metrics. The decision was made to leverage the IFPUG method and extend with local guidelines for our particular type of software. Following the IFPUG guideline we realize that our company focus is generally limited to enhancements.

Schedule or time-to-market is also important and was stated in our goals. This needs to be measured in context with quantified functionality.

Effort is important, but it was decided to use monetary measures where possible; therefore, all effort hours are converted to U.S. dollars. This is also traceable to our stated goals.

Quality and defects were discussed, but it was decided that the organization does not have the maturity or the interest to collect defect data at this time.

Reporting was discussed and it was decided that some pre-cloud reporting is needed for comparative post-cloud analysis. This led to discussions and communication that categorizations should be used, as all software/functionality is not created equally. It was decided to categorize based on plans for the next 2 years for the cloud computing initiative. Therefore, the decision was made to have three business categorizations: Customer Relationship Management, Billing, and Human Resources; and four size categorizations: less than 100 Function Points, 100–299 Function Points, 300–999 Function Points, and greater than 999 Function Points [6].

Reporting will be completed for every release and summarized for the quarter. It was also suggested to collect relevant observations that could have impacted the project, as well as other general comments regarding the project, staff, processes, and any assumptions. Therefore, stakeholders understand that the measures will require some analysis in conjunction with the other subjective comments. This consideration also influenced the conscious decision to collect the functional size information manually. We can then collect the additional project attributes and other key observations, in conjunction with the Function Point Analysis. For the purposes of this chapter, I will not go into the details of such analysis.

Measure 1

Measurement Name: Function Points Enhanced

Measurement Type: Software

Audience: CEO, CIO, Executive Team, Customer Relationship Management Managers, Project Managers—Note: A manager is only provided reports for assigned projects.

Summarization: Need to categorize according to business (three categories) and size (four categories), quarterly reporting summarization.

Description: Use the IFPUG (CPM X.XX) method in conjunction with our local company extensions.

Reporting Period: Pre-cloud projects need to be sampled, agreed that 10–15 in each business category that are determined to be a good representative cross section of projects. Pre-cloud projects will have individual detail reports generated and will be contained on the summarized quarterly reports. Post-cloud projects will have detail reports generated at project end. Information will also be included on the quarterly reports. (The detail report requirements will be defined under a separate initiative and is outside our scope.)

Data Collection Method: Manual Function Point Analysis using spreadsheets or Function Point Analysis repository tools.

Format: numeric 99999

Decision Making and Benefits: This information is valuable outside the cloud computing initiative. This measure and information is valuable in several contexts to highlight and clarify requirements and demonstrate functionality delivered. Future decisions can be better made by using this information. Helps governance, accountability, and management of service level agreements.

Data Collection Costs: $90,000 initially, plus $20,000 ongoing yearly (includes all software reporting, not just Function Point collection related). This includes Function Point collection costs, but excludes detailed project reporting.

Measure 2

Measurement Name: Schedule Duration Days

Measurement Type: Software

Audience: CEO, CIO, Executive Team, Customer Relationship Management Managers, Project Managers—Note: Managers are only provided reports for projects where they are the assigned manager.

Summarization: This information will be used in context with other measures such as "Function Points." We will determine the average delivery cycle in days for 50, 200, 600, and 1200 Function Point enhancement projects. This will be repeated for each of the three business categories. In the project detail report this information will be also reflected.

Description: Schedule days start when the formal request is received at Information Communication Technology (ICT) and ends when it is deployed to production (the cloud, unless we are dealing with a thick client).

Reporting Period: Schedule day information is reflected on the project detail reports, plus the quarterly reports.

Data Collection Method: Can be obtained from the project/release management tool in use. Further refinement may be needed to calibrate for consistency or account for anomalies such as project suspended and restarted.

Format: numeric 9999

Decision Making and Benefits: Schedule compression can require budgets to double or even quadruple; therefore, it can significantly impact the effort and costs. By optimizing your schedule to your capabilities, significant cost savings can be realized. Schedule data is needed to gain perspectives to improve decisions. Time-to-market considerations are also critical from the perspective of the business.

Data Collection Costs: $1000 ongoing yearly—already collected easily calibrated and usable to support cloud computing analysis.

Measure 3

Measurement Name: Enhancement Cost

Measurement Type: Software

Audience: CEO, CIO, Executive Team, Customer Relationship Management Managers, Project Managers—Note: Managers are only provided reports for projects where they are the assigned manager.

Summarization: This information will be used in context with other measures such as "Function Points." We will determine the average costs per Function Point for projects (detail reports) and will also categorize based on average costs/Function Point for projects in the size ranges identified earlier. This will be repeated for each of the three business categories. The project detail report will reflect the cost per Function Point for the individual project.

Description: Costs are calculated based on effort and in U.S. dollars. Foreign exchange rates used are based on rates at time of project completion. See our company standard chart of accounts for specific details regarding costs that are included or excluded. This will only include software-related activity and does not include hardware investments, but does include management effort for the project. All SaaS costs related to the enhancements also must be included and categorized consistently.

Reporting Period: Cost information is reflected on the project detail reports, plus the quarterly reports.

Data Collection Method: Can be obtained from the project release management tool in use. Further adjustments will be needed to calibrate effort into U.S. dollars or to account for anomalies such as known reporting inconsistencies (reporting to incorrect accounts or missing known effort). SaaS costs need to be included and reported appropriately.

Format: currency $99,999,999

Decision Making and Benefits: Effort and associated costs for software development, enhancements, and maintenance are the largest investment in any ICT budget. Many cloud objectives are driven with the expectations of improving delivery efficiency; therefore, cost information must be collected to demonstrate that goals are being realized or moving in positive directions. Effective use of cost information with other measures, to form metrics, such as dollars per Function Point will lead to better perspectives and decision making.

Data Collection Costs: $50,000 initially, plus $4,000 ongoing yearly—already collected easily calibrated and usable to support cloud computing analysis.

Special Note: Project detail reporting and measures are excluded and are yet to be defined under scenario 1.

Scenario 2: Security

Role: Cloud consumer

Deployment Model and Hosting: Private—external

Goal: Strategic—Company "FP Security Inc" experienced several security breaches involving the internal server. It has been communicated by the cloud provider that the cloud offers robust security appropriate for your privacy sensitive applications.

Considerations and assumptions:

1. The goal is to improve security to an appropriate level and demonstrate that security expectations are realized and fines reduced.
2. There are four key health business applications where security and privacy improvements are needed.
3. The applications are already operational on virtual machines (VM), which are hosted internally.
4. Privacy acts need appropriate considerations (Health Insurance Portability and Accountability Act [HIPAA] and Health Information Technology for Economic and Clinical Health Act [HITECH]).
5. Last year you were fined $1.5 million dollars due to software system security breaches (HIPAA and HITECH related).

Business Question:

In your existing internal VM environment, you have good detection for security breaches and have recognized when this has occurred, reported to authorities, and taken steps to mitigate the impact from the breach. Since the applications are health-related, they need to comply with HIPAA and HITECH [8]. These acts hold organizations to a higher level of accountability. Penalties are assessed based on the breaches reported to the required authorities. The key business perspective and objective is to reduce the assessed fines. This is the key improvement indicator.

Technical Question:

It was determined that technical perspectives are less critical at this time. Based on the prioritized measure, no additional technical measures were prioritized at this time. This may sound surprising, due to the technical description and recognizing the technical complexities of identifying a "security breach."

Business Measure 1

Measurement Name: HIPPA and HITECH Associated Fines

Measurement Type: Business

Audience: CIO, CEO, Legal, Marketing, Application Manager

Summarization: Total HIPPA and HITECH penalties assessed summarized monthly.

Description: Total assessed penalties from HIPPA and/or HITECH.

Reporting Period: Each month will report the previous 12 months of assessed penalties. An existing report already exists and we just need to use a different selection value, "7788," for this expenses type.

Data Collection Method: The information pulled directly from Accounts Payable using the accounting code "7788" specifically distinguishes these expenses.

Format: Currency maximum: 999,999,999

Decision Making and Benefits: The overall objective is to demonstrate that the SaaS is more secure and the financial penalties from breaches have been reduced.

Data Collection Costs: You are already collecting this information; minimal additional cost is incurred. Minor costs associated with running an expenses report with a different expense type. Ongoing reporting is estimated at $500 per month.

The key for this scenario is that the simple measures are the best and easiest to obtain at the best value-cost ratio. This scenario also highlights the importance of non-technical considerations that might be critical perspectives for measurement initiatives.

Summary

Cloud computing offers tremendous value and benefits; however, solid measurements are needed to help plan, manage, govern, and benefit from the cloud.

Cloud computing has many objectives, cloud types, characteristics, and behaviors. Organizations pursuing cloud computing need to understand their specific role(s), responsibilities, and boundaries. Clear communication channels are critical to gain trust between the roles, optimize the cloud resources, and manage risks.

The Goal—Question—Metric approach remains viable in cloud environments, helping focus your measurement definitions on what you need, rather than what you have. Too often, measures are identified and collected based on the ease of collection, rather than the value they provide in context to business and technical needs.

The cloud computing model requires new considerations as this is a very flexible model and therefore requires flexible thinking regarding the measurement approaches. The responsibilities for a given contractor may stop at calling a PaaS, rather than providing a comprehensive business solution [4, 5]. These component deployment options in conjunction with other physical considerations for the infrastructure itself (IaaS) make the entire solution very dynamic and challenging.

Measurement and the processes followed help generate meaningful discussions that clarify expectations, roles, responsibilities, accountabilities, and governance between multiple actors in the cloud.

The measures and the analytics provide key ongoing information, helping organizations optimize solutions, improve transparency, and improve trust between the roles and stakeholders.

This chapter provided a short introduction to cloud computing, with specific real-life scenarios, to help communicate an approach, identify some of the key measures, and report considerations selected to provide meaningful information in context with the scenario objectives.

Cloud computing changes the way that technology solutions are provisioned, developed, managed, deployed, and supported. Several concepts require different considerations including which measures will provide the best and most valuable perspectives at a reasonable cost point. The measures and analytics of early 2000 often does not reflect valuable perspectives for cloud computing. Cloud computing requires different and flexible ways of thinking, but one can still leverage some of the foundations from proven methods and approaches.

The measurement initiatives and quests may involve estimation, sizing, and governance or may include some new and innovative perspectives. The NIST cloud computing models provide a strong foundation to improve communication and consistency of terminology. Measurement initiatives need to understand the terminology and models that are being applied to ensure responsible value for money from the measurement activities.

Every cloud computing initiative is unique and needs to be treated as such. There are dozens of cloud computing standards and methods, plus other industry best practices (such as IFPUG, ISO, and TM Forum), which compliment cloud guidelines in specific situations.

References

1. National Institute of Standards for Technology Cloud Computing Standards Roadmap. 2011. *NIST CCSRWG—070*, Eleventh Working Draft. Washington, DC: National Institute of Standards for Technology, U.S. Department of Commerce.
2. National Institute of Standards for Technology. 2011. *DRAFT Cloud Computing Synopsis and Recommendations*, special publication 800–146. Washington, DC: National Institute of Standards for Technology, U.S. Department of Commerce.

3. National Institute of Standards for Technology—Cloud Computing Reference Architecture and Taxonomy Working Group Status Presentation. 2011. *Washington Cloud Computing Workshop.* Washington, DC: National Institute of Standards for Technology, U.S. Department of Commerce.
4. Woodward, S. M. 2010. *Cloud Planning and Governance.* Webinar Series.
5. Woodward, S. M. 2011. *Introduction to Cloud Computing using NIST Frameworks.* OCRI session for technical law cluster.
6. Woodward, S. M. 2002. Using project metrics to more efficiently manage projects. In *IT Measurement Practical Advice from the Experts,* ed. International Function Point Users Group, 271–92. Boston, MA: Addison Wesley.
7. Brooks, P. 2006. *itSMF Metrics for IT Service Management.* Zaltbommel, Netherlands: Van Haren Publishing.
8. US Department of Health and Human Services. 2002. Health Insurance Probability and Accountability Act, Health Insurance Information Technology for Economic and Clinical Health. http://www.hhs.gov (accessed August, 2011).

About the Author

Steven Woodward is a member of the NIST Cloud Computing Working Groups and Cloud Standards Customer Council, a TM Forum Cloud Computing activist, and is a founding company of the Ottawa Center for Research and Innovation Cloud Computing Cluster. Steven is director of conferences and education at IFPUG ISMA events. He is a frequent international presenter and instructor at various cloud and measurement venues, including Mobile World Congress (Barcelona), Interop (New York), Quality Assurance Days (Vienna), and the International Software Measurement Analysis (Richmond) conference. Cloud Perspectives has worldwide partners and associates to help further evaluate performance, security, and privacy for cloud computing initiatives. Cloud Perspectives are leaders in helping companies investigate vendor agnostic cloud computing opportunities, establishing plans and roadmaps that maximize value from ICT investments while managing risks.

NON-FUNCTIONAL AND AGILE INTRODUCTION

Luigi Buglione

Measure what is measurable, and make reasonable what is not so

Galileo Galilei

One of the hardest challenges is to try to quantify and make measurable something that is not easy to define because it is made up of multiple facets; and each facet is an attribute. If we subscribe to the well-known motto from Tom Demarco, "you cannot control what you cannot measure," this challenge is so difficult because you cannot measure what you cannot define and you cannot define what you do not know. It is quite easy to agree on the definitions provided by ISO/EEE standards about what "functionality" is, and it is also easy to accept Albrecht's 1979 proposal about Function Points, where functionality needed to be perceived from the user viewpoint. This year (2011), 32 years since the publication of Albrecht's idea, a new International Function Point Users Group (IFPUG) guide for sizing non-functional attributes for an IT project has been released. It is not an issue of missing or poor knowledge in the software/systems engineering domain, but more a question of determining the right product or project scope and attaining agreement on the definition of which attributes to measure, as in Galilei's quote. The more we know, the easier it is to define and find a measurable way to quantify a certain object of interest. Under the "non-functional" umbrella, there is, in fact, plenty of possible product attributes. The chapter from the IFPUG Software Non-functional Assessment Process (SNAP) team is about an overview of the IFPUG proposal for the new Assessment Practices Manual (APM), which proposes a way to size non-functional requirements (NFR) using a series of categories. The calculation of the SNAP points will allow IT organizations who are using Function Points to have two product sizing units for better approximating the final project effort. An organization can also use SNAP points when a maintenance project contains only NFR that cannot be sized using a method such as the IFPUG CPM.

The second issue dealt with in this section is agile, which has quickly become one of the typical buzzwords in IT projects during last 15 years. It has been 10 years since the writing of the "Agile Manifesto," which addresses the need for satisfying more customers, reducing the internal bureaucracy, and remaining sufficiently flexible on both sides (customer-provider) in order to achieve the customers' business goals. Looking at agile, there has been a huge amount of attention paid to the so-called Agile Software Development (ASD) techniques such as XP, Agile Unified Process (AUP), and TDD. Less attention has been paid to Agile Project Management methods such as Scrum or DSDM. In particular, the way agile projects deal with measurement is not often consistent and well defined; they use subjective measures more than objective ones. The chapter by Ray Boehm has the aim to propose a review of those ways typically adopted from the agile domain. On the other side, the chapter by Thomas Cagley intends to propose a way to manage an agile project using functional measures, by discussing the adoption of the Quick and Early Function Points (QEFP) methodology by two case studies.

Chapter 24

Software Measurement and Agile Development

Raymond Boehm

Contents

Agile development teams are springing up in large organizations and working side-by-side with teams that use traditionally planned software development approaches. Traditional managers are often uneasy about the perceived misalignment between agile development practices and the metrics and measures with which they are familiar. This chapter introduces some agile measurement concepts. It also explains why and how some traditional estimating techniques should be used to gain control of agile software development.

This chapter begins with the fundamentals of agile development. People familiar with agile development can safely skip this section. The chapter goes on to describe the techniques of measurement used in agile development and how they are used to predict the time required to achieve the next software release. Many agile developers are only superficially familiar with these topics. Then, the use of traditional techniques to measure and estimate agile development is discussed. Both agile developers and traditionally trained measurement personnel will benefit from this. Finally, the chapter will be summarized.

The Fundamentals of Agile Development

Figure 24.1 summarizes the current state of agile development. In February of 2001, 17 methodologists met in Snowbird, Utah, to discuss approaches to software development. The result of that meeting was the Agile Manifesto. The manifesto expresses the values that they held and a set of principles that should be adhered to in order to produce quality software. Based on this manifesto, they and other methodologists developed several agile development methodologies. Examples of some of these are shown in the figure. Two of the best known, eXtreme Programming (XP) and Scrum, are described below. The bottom of the figure shows some of the techniques that have emerged as important agile techniques. They are each used in several of the methodologies. One of them, the development of user stories, must be understood by measurement professionals. It is described below.

The Agile Manifesto

"We are uncovering better ways of developing software by doing it and helping others do it. Through this work, we have come to value the following:

> *Individuals and interactions* over processes and tools
> *Working software* over comprehensive documentation
> *Customer collaboration* over contract negotiation
> *Responding to change* over following a plan

That is, while there is value in the items on the right, we value the items on the left more" [1].

The agile values were agreed to by the Agile Alliance. This is the 17 members who authored it and countless other signers of the manifesto over the years. The values make intuitive sense to most software developers. However, the fourth value has been a stumbling block for measurement professionals. Many agile developers

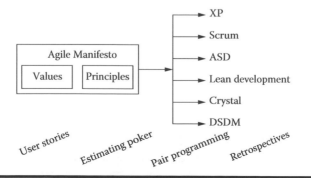

Figure 24.1   Current state of agile development.

use it as an excuse to skip any up-front estimating or planning. This is a mistake. As stated in the quote, the items on the right do have value. The section below, titled "Why Use Traditional Estimating for Agile Development," explains why up-front estimating is an important part of the agile development process.

The Agile Alliance also presented 12 principles of agile software development. They can be found at http://agilemanifesto.org/principles.html. They should be understood by measurement professionals working with agile teams. Furthermore, they can be mined to identify quantities that need to be measured. For example, one principle encourages frequent release of software and another dictates that the working software be the primary measure of progress. This justifies the use of a measure such as Function Points to size frequently the software being developed. Yet another principle discourages the use of overtime for extended periods in order to develop software. Measuring the actual time worked, even for workers who are exempt from paid overtime, is necessary to insure the adherence to this principle.

The principles do capture the essence of agile development and should be understood to work effectively with agile teams. Fast delivery of software is the hallmark of agile development. Frequent, "from a couple of weeks to a couple of months," release of working software is a must. There are only two principles that have explicit quantities associated with them. This is one of them.

The other principle with an explicit quantifiable criterion is the one that states that business people work with the developers *daily*. For agile development to work, the domain experts must be available to answer questions on a continual basis.

Incorporating these principles into methodologies is a design process. For example, welcoming changes to requirements is both an agile value and principle. However, the chaos of agile development must be controlled. When Scrum is described, it will be shown that stories and priorities are basically locked down for the 30-day long sprints that make up development. Of course, everything can change at the end of the sprint. In extreme cases, the results of the entire sprint can be thrown away.

Agile requires constant communication among the team members. The domain experts are considered part of the team. Because of this, less documentation is produced than in traditionally planned projects. This means that agile measurements should be independent of the type of material that is in a requirements or high-level design document. Any attempts to generate traditional measurements like Function Points must be based on communication with the team, the source code, or the application itself.

eXtreme Programming

Kent Beck actually introduced XP just before the release of the Agile Manifesto. It would be fair to say that Beck influenced the Agile Alliance as much as he was influenced by them. In fact, Beck claims that he has not designed XP; he has discovered and organized it. According to Beck, "most of the practices in XP are as old as programming" [2].

The best way to explain XP might be to describe what Kent Beck calls an "ideal XP project." The project is broken into the following phases: Exploration, Planning, Iterations, Maintenance, and Death.

Exploration

During this first phase, business people are developing the user stories that will drive development. User stories are described in a later subsection titled User Stories. Technical people are experimenting with the tools and software architecture that will be used to develop the application. This phase should take a few weeks. If the problem domain or technology is completely new to the team, that is, business and technical people, then this phase can take a few months.

Planning

During this phase, the customers and programmers agree on a date for the first release of the software. This software should implement the smallest set of user stories that the customers would find useful. It should also be the most valuable set. This first release should be implementable in 6 months or less. If the proper groundwork has been laid during exploration, then this planning phase should take a day or two.

Iterations

The release is built in a series of iterations that each take between 1 and 4 weeks. The iteration begins with a planning game that identifies the stories that will be implemented during that release. The quantitative details of the planning game will be described in the section "Agile Measurement and Planning." The first iteration puts the architecture in place.

The subsequent iterations begin with an identification of the most important stories to implement at that time. There are some programming practices that occur during iterations that are new to people who are unfamiliar with agile development. These include the following:

Test-driven development: Where test cases are developed before the code is written so that the code can be continuously checked for proper execution.

Pair programming: All production code is written with two programmers at one machine.

40-hour weeks: Programmers are encouraged to limit their workweeks to 40 hours and forbidden to work overtime 2 weeks in a row.

On-site customer: A customer is available to answer questions full time.

The last few iterations of the release are referred to as "productionizing." This is where the emphasis shifts from developing new functionality to making sure the program is fit for production. These iterations usually take 1 week each.

Maintenance

The first release consisted of the smallest number of user stories that would deliver value to the user. This means that there is usually a backlog of stories to implement after the first release. This means that the maintenance phase is simply additional iterations where more functionality is added to the application. The good news is that application is delivering value to the users while this work is being done. The bad news is that the needs of the installed base of users must be considered. This is the case whenever maintenance is performed on system that is in production. In XP, developers are encouraged to put enhancements into production as often as possible, even before the iteration is complete.

Death

According to Beck, there are two reasons for a system to die. First, everyone is happy with the system. The customers cannot think of any new user stories to implement. The system just continues to perform the function it was designed to. This almost never happens.

The other reason a system dies is that it becomes impossible to maintain. When enhancements are attempted, the defect rate becomes intolerable. This happens with applications that have been developed with traditionally planned methods as well as those that were developed using agile methods. These applications usually get replaced.

Scrum

The Scrum methodology was developed by Ken Schwaber and Jeff Sutherland. In some ways, Scrum is a methodology that competes with XP. In other ways, it is a complementary technique. Jim Highsmith sums it up nicely: "whereas XP has a definite programming flavor (pair programming, coding standards, refactoring), Scrum has a project management emphasis" [3].

In Scrum, the actual work is accomplished through a series of Sprints. Each Sprint has a fixed length of 30 days. The Scrum process consists of pre-sprint planning, the sprint, and a post-sprint meeting.

Pre-Sprint Planning

The purpose of pre-sprint planning is to develop and maintain three backlog lists:

- The Product Backlog contains a list of all product and technology features that are planned for the product as a whole.
- The Release Backlog is the subset of the Product Backlog that needs to be implemented for the next release.
- The Sprint Backlog is the subset of the Release Backlog that needs to be implemented for the sprint.

The product owner meets with the technical team to insure that the right amount of features goes into the Sprint Backlog. The team decides this by decomposing the features that the product owner suggests into tasks and then estimating the tasks. Then the sprint is planned based on the resources available.

The pre-sprint planning also produces a Sprint Goal. This is the business purpose of the sprint. Even if all of the features of the Sprint Backlog are not implemented, the Sprint Goal should be achieved by the end of the sprint.

Sprint

The 30-day sprint is where the coding gets done. Scrum strongly discourages any product changes during the sprint. This adds some control to the process and allows the development team to actually see the completion of something. Of course, it is possible that the organization's requirements or priorities may have shifted during the sprint, and the product owner decides to throw away the results of the entire sprint.

The defining activity of the sprint is a daily meeting called a scrum. By the way, the word scrum is taken from the sport of rugby. It is the point where the forwards of each team meet to essentially restart the game. The daily scrum meeting serves a similar purpose for the development team.

Scrum meetings are short—around 15 minutes. They are conducted with everyone standing in order to keep them short. Participants report three things: what they did since the last scrum, what they will do before the next scrum, and any impediments that exist. Managers listen, but do not talk. The purpose of the scrum is to present status and raise problems, not solve them. Practitioners of other agile methodologies, like XP, have incorporated these types of daily stand-up meetings into their processes.

Post-Sprint Meeting

After the sprint, a meeting is held to review progress and demonstrate any software that was developed during the sprint. The project is reviewed from a technical perspective. At this point, the next sprint can begin. This meeting may accomplish the pre-spring planning for this next sprint.

User Stories

The development of user stories is common to most agile methodologies. User stories are written by the customer. They are often handwritten on cards. Thus, the terms story cards and user stories are synonymous. The writing of user stories is one of the many agile techniques that have become common among many different agile development methodologies. Refactoring and pair programming are others. User stories are being presented here because it is an important part of agile measurement and planning.

Figure 24.2 shows a story card from a hypothetical accounting or personal finance application. Is it a good requirements statement? Probably not. It leaves too many unanswered questions in the mind of the developer. Will everyone agree on what the data items on a check are? Will the check number be entered by the user or generated by the computer? Does the payee have to be drawn from a list of approved payees? However, this does not matter. User stories are not meant as a substitute for user requirements.

At best, story cards are specifying the scope of the application to be built. This is why they are a critical part of the measurement, planning, and estimating activities of an agile software development project. Agile project requirements are not completely discovered until a developer discusses a story with a user. At that point, it becomes locked in the code of the system, not in a separate document.

Is Figure 24.2 a good story card? Mike Cohn wrote a book about user stories and included Bill Wake's INVEST criteria for evaluating user stories [4]. According to Wake, stories should be independent, negotiable, valuable, estimable, and testable. The following subsections show that Figure 24.2 is a good story.

Independence of User Stories

With agile development, the customer should be able to choose the implementation order of the stories. In order for this to be possible, the stories should be relatively independent. For example, breaking Figure 24.2 into separate stories to choose the next check number and then input data would make the second story dependent on the first. This should be avoided.

User Stories Are Negotiable

Figure 24.2 shows negotiable functionality. How much like a check does the screen have to look like? If the payee must be chosen from a list, what happens if the payee is not on the list? Giving the user a chance to update the list at that point might be helpful. Simply issuing an error message might be simpler.

The user will enter information for checks that are written.

Figure 24.2 A story card.

User Stories Are Valuable

In general, user stories must be valuable to the purchaser of the application. Note that there is a distinction between user and purchaser. The person funding the development of an application might never actually use it. Regarding Figure 24.2, there is no question that entering a check would make a valuable contribution to an accounting application.

User Stories Are Capable of Being Estimated

Implementers should be able to estimate the card in Figure 24.2. Obviously, if the card is negotiable, then the estimate will have some uncertainty associated with it. However, it is still unambiguous enough to be estimated relative to other stories that the team may be considering.

User Stories Are Small

User stories can be too small or too big. A story like "Get the next check number" might be too small. When a story is too small, it frequently violates one of the other criteria. The story about getting the next check number is also not independent. The other extreme is the story that is too large. These are called epic stories. For example, "The user can keep track of his cash position" would be an epic story. It would be difficult to estimate. It would be difficult to implement without getting much more information from the user. For all practical purposes, large stories must be split into smaller ones. Relatively speaking, Figure 24.2 depicts a small story.

User Stories Are Testable

It is basic project management that there needs to be a way to declare that something, such as a task, is complete. When considering a user story, someone must be able to say when it is done. In the world of agile test driven development, it is best if the story can be automatically tested for proper functioning. Figure 24.2 certainly depicts a testable story. The customer can verify that it is part of the program. It can be tested to verify that it is functioning properly.

Comparison of Agile and Traditional Development

In 2004, Barry Boehm (no relation to the author) and Richard Turner wrote a book to explore the phenomenon of agile development [5]. They explored the differences between agile development and traditionally planned development. They considered four dimensions of differences: the applications being developed, project management, technical characteristics of the development process, and characteristics of the personnel who do the work. Table 24.1 summarizes their findings.

Table 24.1   Agile versus Traditionally Planned Development

	Agile	*Traditionally Planned*
Application	Usually highly changeable, both during and after development.	Usually larger applications, often having fixed requirements.
Management	The customer is part of the development team. Communication is more personal.	Plans are thoroughly documented. Communication is more formal.
Technical	Development done in short increments, with frequent releases of software to the user community. User acceptance is usually captured in executable test cases.	Requirements are captured in formal requirements documents. Development may be outsourced. User acceptance requires voluminous test cases and plans.
Personnel	Customers are usually co-located with the developers. The developers are highly skilled generalists. They thrive on chaos.	Work is usually done by specialists, such as analysts, designers, programmers, and testers. These people thrive on order.

Agile Measurement and Planning

Agile purists have two areas where measurement and planning are critical. The first is the selection of user stories to be implemented during the next iteration. This is partially driven by the value of the stories to the customer. The amount of effort required for each story also plays a part in making this determination. An illustration should make this clear.

Table 24.2 shows five user stories that must be implemented to have an automated checkbook program. They are entered in the order that the customer values each story. The customer considers the first one the most valuable and the last one the least valuable. Each story also has the number of days that are required for implementation. Assume for now that there is a way to get this estimate. Furthermore, assume these values are in calendar time. It will be shown shortly that neither of these assumptions reflects the reality of how agile estimating and planning are done. In any case, these values have been chosen for the illustration.

Suppose that the iteration is 1 week long and there are four developers involved. This means there are 20 workdays. Obviously, the first story should be implemented. However, there is no time also to implement the second story.

Table 24.2 User Stories for Checkbook

Reference	User Story	Days to Implement	Story Points
1	The user will enter information for checks that are written.	12	8
2	The user can get the checking account balance from the bank.	10	8
3	The user can print checks.	8	5
4	The user can reconcile the bank statement with the checkbook program.	12	8
5	The user can print a check register.	5	5

Therefore, the third must be implemented in the first iteration. Some people may feel that work could be done on the second, but this is just not done.

There were two simplifications in this example that need to be addressed. First, where did the number of days come from? They could have been estimated, but in practice they are not. Instead, story points are established. The definition of story points is explained in the next subsection. A later subsection, "Estimating Poker," shows how they are often assigned.

The other simplification has to do with the time available for development. Is there time for meetings, sick days, and the like being considered? This is addressed by the concept of velocity that will be addressed below.

The other place where agile purists find measurement and planning necessary is when performing tasks during the iteration. Developers do not usually implement an entire story at one time. Stories get decomposed into tasks. Different developers may be working on the tasks that make up a single story. The tasks have to be estimated. Tasks are usually estimated in ideal time. Ideal time will be defined below, but suffice to say that it is related to regular time as we all know it.

The developer's performance against the task estimates is tracked and used to make future estimates. It is necessary to ascertain how closely the developer has estimated the task that was just completed. It is also necessary to see how much task-related work the developer was able to perform relative to calendar time. All this must be taken into account to decide the next steps to be performed during the iteration. This tracking, estimating, and planning cycle occurs every few days during the iteration. The date for the end of the iteration is cast in concrete. The continual tracking and planning is an attempt to get all of the tasks done by the end of the iteration.

During this tracking and planning, it may become obvious that a developer may not be able to finish all of their tasks. If tasks go into jeopardy, then one of two actions must be taken to rectify the situation: renegotiate the scope of the task or rebalance the workload by assigning the task to another developer. Renegotiating scope is consistent with the idea that good user stories are negotiable. Their functionality can be simplified to get them done in a given iteration.

In addition to story points and ideal time, one additional measure will be discussed below. This measure is test points. It is still considered experimental. At some point in the future, it might take the place of story points.

Story Points

Using story points is one way to assign estimates to user stories. Every story is assigned one of the following values: 0 (for extremely small), 1, 2, 3, 5, 8, 13, 20, 40, and 100. Some practitioners allow a value of 4 instead of both 3 and 5 [6].

Story points are abstract. They do not represent days, hours, or any other time unit. Fred Grossman et al. found this to be a key advantage of story points and discouraged any attempt to equate them to real time [7]. Tying story points to a time period introduces too much complexity too soon. If you attempt to predict effort, you introduce technical considerations prematurely. There becomes a natural tendency to start to think about staffing levels and delivery time. At this point, it is overwhelming and seldom successful. It is better to have an abstract measure at this point.

Story points are relative. In other words, it should take the team twice as long to implement a 40-story-point story as it does to implement a 20-story-point story. Developers tend to be able to specify this without becoming overwhelmed by attempting to assign anything like actual hours to the story.

The reason there are only 10 different values of story points between 0 and 100 is to emphasize the imprecision of the measure. It does not make sense for anyone to agonize about the difference between a 20- and a 21-story-point story when an individual estimate might be off by 50% anyway. The values are also not uniform between 0 and 100. There are six or seven values between 0 and 20 and only three from 20 to 100. This is because developers can usually estimate the relationship between smaller stories much better than they can for larger stories. The larger values tend to be assigned to epic stories. These stories usually get broken down into smaller stories in later planning sessions. When this happens, they get estimated with smaller numbers of story points.

Conceptually, assigning the number of story points is easy. The team agrees on a medium-size story. In Table 24.2, that would be story 2; assign that a medium-size story point value, which might be 4, 5, or 8. Table 24.2 shows the result of choosing 8. The two stories that took 12 days are 20% larger than story 2, which would make the estimate 9.6 story points. However, there is no valid story point value of 9.6. This value is closer to 8 than to 13. Therefore, these stories have 8 story points. Using similar logic, story 3's predicted value of 6.4 story points is closer to 5 than to 8. Story 5 could have been either 3 or 5 story points. Under those circumstances, an old project manager cannot help but pick 5 story points.

Choosing a different medium-size story or choosing to center that value at either 4 or 5 story points would not have made any difference. Story points do not have any tangible significance. They cannot be expressed in terms of time, lines of code, or anything else that exists in the real world. A different team working on the same application might estimate stories differently and actually implement at a different rate. If any of the same stories showed up in different projects, then the story points would be expected to be different. When arrived at properly, story points are accurate relative to one another in the same project. In addition, as Table 24.2 shows, because of the imprecision of estimating at this point, two stories that are only close in terms of the amount of effort will end up with the exact same number of story points.

At this point, someone might question how something like this can be used to estimate effort and plan iterations. Estimating effort is not really necessary. Iterations can be planned by calculating the velocity, in story points per iteration, at which work can be done. This will be explained in the "Velocity" subsection below.

Ideal Time

According to Kent Beck, ideal time is the measure where you ask yourself, "How long would this take without distractions and disasters?" Even this definition is troublesome. Is it a distraction when a customer calls to clarify something that was said about the story that is currently being implemented? Is a corporate reorganization a disaster or just business as usual in your environment?

In the early days of agile development, stories were estimated in terms of ideal time. Story points have largely replaced ideal time for that. Ideal time continues to be used to estimate tasks during the iterations. During the iteration, the responsible programmer estimates how much ideal time will be necessary to perform each task. The time might be conditioned on something. For example, it might be based on the assumption that some other programmer who is familiar with some part of the system will help understand something.

The ideal time estimate does not contain an allowance for any non-task items. For example, time spent helping other programmers, clarifying requirements with customers, processing e-mails, and attending meetings is not considered in the ideal time. In agile development, this non-task time can be considerable. In XP, for example, all changes to production code must be made by two programmers working together. This time is only counted in the ideal time for one of the programmers. This is not an example of inefficiency. In agile development, it is the way things are done.

XP uses a term called load factor. It is the ratio between ideal time and calendar time. In a 15-day long iteration, a team member new to the team, technologies, and domain might only deliver 3 days of ideal time. This would correspond to a load factor of 5. An experienced team member might deliver 7 or 8 days of ideal time. This corresponds to a load factor of 2. This is about as low as the load factor should get.

All team members have to be involved in helping other members in order for agile development to work. As can be seen from these examples, load factors may be different for different team members during the same iteration.

Test Points

In the Israeli Air Force's agile metrics suite, the number of test points is considered a product size metric [8]. The following is a method of calculating the test points metric:

1. A test point is one step in an acceptance testing script or a line in a unit test. These are identified for each software module.
2. When the software is run, a test point might be executed or it might not. If it is executed, then it might pass or it might fail. To be included in the test points metric, the test point must have been executed and it must have passed.
3. For the iteration, sum the test points for all of the software modules.

This measure is calculated at the iteration level. Even for modules that do not change, it is possible that the test points will vary between iterations. A later iteration may stop executing a test point or the test may fail after other changes are made to the system.

The test points metric measures size because the more functionality and the more complex that functionality is, the greater the number of test cases that are necessary. This correlation has not been found in lines of code or in the size of specification documents. Of course, in agile development there are few, if any, specification documents.

In agile development, these test cases should be generated as part of implementation, not by a test or QA group after the fact. Having developers generate the test cases also leads to higher values for testing points. This is desirable. While the measure of testing points is not considered a quality measure, using it encourages practices that lead to higher quality systems. Its use becomes a win–win for everyone concerned.

Comparison of Agile Measures

Table 24.3 summarizes the pros and cons of each of the agile measures. However, the state of the practice might best be summarized by the way these measures are currently used. Story points are the preferred method of sizing and planning user stories. Ideal time is still the most common way to estimate tasks that must be performed during iterations. Even though they were first suggested over 5 years ago, the testing points metric is still too new and untested (no pun intended) to evaluate fully.

Table 24.3   Comparison of Agile Measurements

	Pros	*Cons*
Story Points	Story points are easy to learn and easy to calculate. You can estimate the relative amount of time without worrying about the actual amount of time.	Story points are completely non-standard. They cannot be compared between applications.
Ideal Time	Ideal time makes intuitive sense. You are using time to estimate time. Making calendar time closer to ideal time should be an organizational objective.	To some, the difference between ideal time and calendar time sounds like something that should be made up with unpaid overtime.
Test Points	In test-driven development, making test cases and scripts are part of the process, so test points are a normal side effect that encourages good programming practice.	The measure is not widely used at this time. In addition, the test cases are usually developed later than they would be needed for estimating purposes.

Planning Poker

A method to specify the number of story points was discussed when story points were defined. This method was conceptual, not practical. It required an estimate for each story to be in place. If you had estimates of time, you would not need story points.

When a collection of stories needs to be estimated in practice, estimating poker is a good approach. It is a workshop technique designed to achieve consensus on the relative sizes of the stories. Estimating poker is sometimes called planning poker.

Estimating poker is played by all of the developers on the team. If there are more than 10, it may be necessary to break the developers into groups. Each player gets a set of cards with the numbers 0, 1, 2, 3, 5, 8, 13, 20, 40, and 100 on them. The numbers on the cards should be large enough for everyone at the table to see them.

The following process is followed for each story that is to be estimated:

1. Someone reads the story card. That person might be any of the developers or it might be the customer. People can ask questions about the story.
2. Each person decides how many story points should be awarded to the story. They choose the appropriate card and place it face down in front of them. When everyone's cards are in front of them, then everyone turns their card

over. It is important that people do not see each other's choices before they make their own. They should not be influenced by anyone else's choices.

3. If everyone has chosen the same value, then this round is done and the value for the story has been established. This is uncommon. If there are different values, then the people with the smallest and the largest values explain why they chose those values. There can be questions and discussions. This will give everyone more information to consider, and they can go to the previous step to estimate again and see if they reach consensus. If they do not reach consensus after two or three rounds, the dealer may have to do something to force agreement. It might be to average the values people have chosen or to go with the majority value.

It is important to keep this game moving. If questions or discussions start to drag out, then they should be halted with a 2-minute warning. Cohn suggests having a 2-minute timer available that anyone can set when they feel questions or discussions are taking too long.

The ambiance of the estimating poker game should mimic that of a friendly poker game. The discussions should be informal. Some type of refreshments could be served. Mike Cohn's company, Mountain Goat Software, makes a planning poker web application available. It takes the place of physical cards in estimating poker. Some people collect players in the same room with their laptops to play it. It prevents people from seeing each other's cards in the event that anyone turns over their card prematurely. It also allows people to play if they are not co-located. Co-location has been an agile principle that many teams have found impossible to impose. The web application is at http://www.planningpoker.com.

Velocity

When using story points, calculating the velocity of the iteration is easy. If two 13-story-point stories are implemented during the iteration, then the velocity is 26 story points per iteration. It would be prudent to plan for 26 story points of stories in the next iteration.

Calculating velocity for tasks that were estimated using ideal time is a little more complicated. Suppose a programmer has three tasks to perform that each have ideal time estimates of 16 hours. If the iteration takes 3 weeks and the first task is done by the end of the first week, can we assume that the next two will be completed? No, we cannot!

When working on a task, the programmer has to track the actual time spent. This is basically actual ideal time. Suppose that the task only required 12 hours of work during that week and the other 28 were spent in other activities such as working with other developers. Then, the velocity is 12 ideal hours per week. If the remaining tasks are estimated correctly and the velocity remains constant, then completion of the next two tasks is in jeopardy.

At any time during the iteration, you should be ready to re-estimate the remaining tasks. In the example just given, the first estimate was off. Some of the experience gained in doing that task might help to estimate the next two better. You can also wish for an increase in velocity. This is a wish that seldom comes true! In XP, this type of analysis should occur every 3 days during the iteration.

Predicting the Next Release

An important use of velocity is to predict the completion of a release. Suppose that after two iterations there are 180 story points left to implement. Also suppose that the velocity of the last iteration was 30 story points per iteration. Dividing 180 by 30 would show that there were six iterations left. This is illustrated by the burndown chart in Figure 24.3.

The example chart is consistent with many agile development projects. It shows eight iterations leading to a release. If they are 1-week long iterations, then the release is ready in a little under 2 months. This is consistent with the agile principle of releasing software every 2 weeks to 2 months.

An agile practitioner looking at the chart might expect the team to beat the eight release estimate. That is because the first release only delivered 20 story points and the second delivered 30. Lower productivity on the first release is to be expected. The team is often learning to work together. They face learning curves associated with the problem domain and the technologies being used. They may have infrastructure tasks

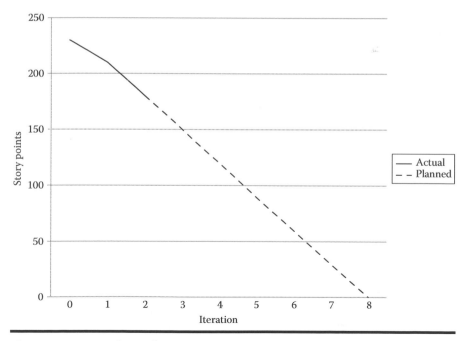

Figure 24.3   Burndown chart.

associated with putting some of this technology in place. Those tasks are frequently overlooked when story points are being estimated. These productivity constraints often plague the second iteration as well. If the velocity of the second iteration is 30 story points, then there is a good chance it will improve on the third iteration. The practitioner may believe this, but it should not be reflected in the chart until it actually happens.

The burndown chart must take project changes into account. For example, if new stories are written or if the story points estimated for existing stories changes, then this must be reflected in the chart. For example, if 10 more story points worth of stories had been written during the second iteration, then the remaining story points would have been 190 instead of 180. The velocity would still have been 30 story points per iteration. That would be the value used to reduce the backlog of story points. Then, the release would take an additional seven iterations instead of six.

The burndown chart is a common chart used by agile practitioners. The *x*-axis could be in ideal time or test points. In any case, it is always used to indicate the number of iterations that are expected until the next release.

Using Traditional Measures for Agile Development

When managers schooled in traditionally planned development talk about measures, they are usually thinking about up-front project estimating. Some have heard of use case points, and most are familiar with Function Points. While most agile practitioners realize that up-front project estimating is necessary, some still do not. The next subsection explains the importance of up-front estimating and subsequent subsections describe some of the traditional techniques that might be applied to agile development.

Why Use Traditional Estimating for Agile Development?

There are two primary reasons why up-front estimating is necessary for agile development. The first can be summed by saying there is more to life than software development. The second reason is to insure that the required team size is not too large for agile development. Both reasons are elaborated on below.

There Is More to Life Than Software Development

An illustration of this reason for up-front estimating was taken from the author's blog:

> *In the late eighties, I had over 15 years of experience in all phases of software development. I had a MS degree in computer science. I had taught computer science in two colleges. I had worked as a programmer, analyst, and project manager. I had taught structured analysis and design in college and was helping a life insurance company. The point is that I loved software*

development as an activity in itself. That is probably true of many of the people reading this.

As part of the methodology development engagement that I just mentioned, I was asked to develop an estimating process. As a project manager, I was often called upon to provide estimates. However, this was the first time I began to look at formal estimating approaches like Function Point Analysis and the Constructive Cost Model (COCOMO). I applied some of this thinking to a project that was just kicking off. I became concerned that the project would take twice the resources that were currently being estimated. I wrote this in my status report. I doubted that there would be any follow-up.

I was wrong! Someone had read my status report and I was called to the product manager's office. The product manager was outside of the IT department. I have no idea what his position in the company was, but he had the largest office of anyone I had worked with on that engagement. As soon as I entered, he told me that he had heard that I had doubts about the current estimate for the system development. I told him I thought it would be twice as expensive as currently estimated. His response was, "oh, that's O.K."

He must have realized that I was surprised, maybe even shocked, by his nonchalance. He explained why he was unconcerned. He took out a spreadsheet that explained the product launch. The product was a new insurance offering. The first number on the spreadsheet showed the expected revenue from the project. The remaining numbers were expenses in order from largest to smallest. The first expense, roughly the same order of magnitude as the revenue, showed the mortality expense; people would buy the insurance, die, and a claim would have to be paid. The next was the cost of training the agents to sell the new product. The third was the cost of producing sales literature. The next was the cost of the system.

The product manager showed that even if the cost of system development doubled, the insurance product itself would still be profitable. In fact, the cost of the system would still be lower than the cost of sales material! For him, the cost of system development was not a big concern! For me, it illustrated a point that I knew intellectually but did not fully understand: computer systems are usually only a part of the solution to a business problem, not an engineering feat in and of itself.

After discussing costs, the product manager took out another spreadsheet that showed timelines for the various activities. He was concerned about the time for development. The system should be ready once the agents were trained. Otherwise, they would not be able to sell the new product immediately and would lose their momentum. This illustrated another point. The estimate and plan often have business significance beyond managing the system development activities, they are often driven by the organization's business needs, and often the estimate and plan must be done before there is a commitment to bring in developers [9].

Controlling Team Size

Planning for the size of the team is necessary for any software development project. With agile development projects, it is necessary to make sure the team size does not get too large. Linda Rising has written the "No More than 10" pattern to limit the size of an agile team to 10 members [10]. Up-front estimating will allow management to decide whether they are willing to attempt certain projects using agile development.

Use Case Points

Gustav Karner introduced use case points in the early nineties. It is a process that assigns a size measure to an application based on its use case model. In very broad terms, the points are calculated using the following steps:

1. Generate a weight for each actor based on its complexity. Low complexity actors are usually other applications. High complexity ones interact through a graphical user interface. The weights associated with each level of complexity are 5, 10, and 15, respectively. Then sum these weights to arrive at the unadjusted actor weights.
2. Generate a weight for each use case also based on its complexity. Karner based the complexity on the number of transactions in the use case. Simple complexity use cases have 3 transactions or less and a weight of 1. Average complexity use cases have between 4 and 7 transactions and a weight of 2. Complex use cases have more than 7 transactions and a weight of 3. These weights are summed. Recognizing transactions in a use case is not always trivial, and so there have been suggestions that complexity be established in other ways [11].
3. Technical complexity for the entire application is calculated based on 13 system attributes. These are shown in Bente Anda's thesis [12] along with their weights. Each attribute is assigned a value between 0 (no impact) and 5 (very high impact). That value is multiplied by the weight of the factor. These products are summed, divided by 100, and added to 0.6 to yield a technical complexity factor.
4. Environmental complexity considers the tools, techniques, and personnel used to implement the system. These are shown in Bente Anda's thesis along with their weights. Each attribute is assigned a value between 0 (not the case) and 5 (very much the case). That value is multiplied by the weight of the factor. These products are summed, multiplied by −0.03, and added to 1.4 to yield an environmental complexity factor.
5. The actor and use case weights are summed and multiplied successively by the technical and environmental complexity factors to calculate the use case points.

Use case points were designed to be a stand-alone estimating technique. It was thought that a use case point took 30 person hours to implement. Benta Anda had conducted several studies comparing the accuracy of use case points–based estimates with both actual results and with estimates generated by experts. The use case points–based estimates were closer to the actual values than the expert estimates were.

The use case point method does not address how to calculate the duration of the project. A quick first estimate of this can be calculated using what Steve McConnell calls the Basic Schedule Equation [13]. It is reproduced in Equation 24.1, below.

$$\text{Schedule in Months} = 3 \cdot \text{Staff Months}^{1/3} \qquad (24.1)$$

Use case points are a natural estimating technique to use when use cases are being used to capture user requirements. When used in an agile development, use case points could take the place of story points. If so, the burndown chart in Figure 24.3 would have use case points on its *x*-axis instead of story points.

Function Points

Function Points were developed at IBM by Allen Albrecht in the late 1970s. It was designed as an estimating methodology. Since that time, it has come to be used both for estimating and for the governance of outsourcing contracts. The calculation of Function Points is explained in the International Function Point Users Group's (IFPUG) Counting Practices Manual [14]. It is not repeated here.

Estimating with the International Software Benchmark Standards Group Database

The International Software Benchmark Standards Group (ISBSG) makes a database of over 5000 software projects available to the public. The database contains size information on the projects, usually in the form of IFPUG Function Points. It also shows the effort and duration of the project. It shows the development technologies and methodologies that were used. Technologies include the programming languages and CASE tools. Methodologies include some agile-related development techniques like Rapid Application Development (RAD).

Estimators can acquire the ISBSG database. It can be used for comparison purposes. If the ISBSG database contains a project similar to the one being estimated, then the effort and duration values can be considered in the estimate. There are dangers in just accepting these values as the estimate. There is often confusion regarding what was actually in the scope of the project. For example, was the conversion of any existing data considered part of the effort and duration of the project reported in ISBSG? Was the team familiar with the development approaches? Even people familiar with the project may be unable to answer these types of questions after some time has elapsed. Also, consider that project effort and duration must be planned, not predicted. The estimator might be instructed to estimate for minimum duration, even at the cost of extra effort. This would give a different, but still valid, estimate for the project.

Estimating with the Constructive Cost Model Suite

Barry Boehm's Constructive Cost Model (COCOMO) is one of the best known software estimating models. The current release of COCOMO is COCOMO II. Unfortunately, "the COCOMO II schedule, as presently implemented in COCOMO II.2000 does not reflect any of the currently accepted alternatives such as iterative, spiral, or evolutionary development. Obviously, COCOMO II does not address any of the RAD strategies that are being employed to reduce schedule and sometimes effort as well" [15].

Fortunately, there is more to COCOMO than COCOMO II. There is an entire COCOMO suite of models. One of these is the Constructive RAD Model (CORADMO). Figure 24.4 shows the CORADMO output that was run for the Bomb Shelter Studios case study that appeared in Mike Cohn's *Agile Estimating and Planning* book.

Figure 24.4 estimates that the project will be done in 3.7 months with an average team size of 5.3 people. The estimate of 3.7 months is equivalent to about 16 weeks. There is a point with almost seven people involved. The case study depicted the project as taking 18 weeks. There was a team of five full time people and two more with part time involvement. The CORADMO run approximates the case study.

Figure 24.4 does mention COPSEMO, the Construction Phase Schedule and Effort Model. CORADMO simply calls this model. It is simply part of the implementation of CORADMO. Likewise, CORADMO requires that COCOMO II.2000 be run for the same system and then have its output post-processed by CORADMO. Appropriate cost drivers must be input for both COCOMO II and CORADMO.

COCOMO II required a size for the case study. That size was calculated by counting Function Points. Because the case study depicts user stories from early in the file cycle, the Early Lifecycle Functional Estimating (ELFE) process was used to estimate the number of Function Points. ELFE has been taught as part of IFPUG's FP-221, "Estimating Project Size Early in the Lifecycle," course since 2006. The details of the counts and the selection of cost driver values are explained in the author's thesis [16].

Summary and Comparison of Measures

This section summarizes and compares the measures discussed in this chapter.

Story Points

Story points estimate the implementation effort to implement stories in abstract terms, that is, not tied to time, lines of code, or functionality. Their values are relatively accurate, that is, a 40-story-point story should take twice as long to estimate as a 20-story-point story. They must be estimated by the development team.

CORADMO	Currently implemented only for projects (not modules)						© Copyright 1998-2000 USC Center for Software Entingineering.		
Step	**BOLD: required values carried forward from COPSEMO;**				*Italic: optional values carried forward from COPSEMO*				

1 Get COCOMO II.2000 data and adjustments from COPSEMO

	Project:	*Havannah*		Totalsize=	10282		PM_C=	17.944	M_C=	6.13				P_C=	2.928
Including schedule parameters				SCED_R=	VL	SCEDinc:	0%	SCEDV=	1.43						
Including scale factor ratings				PREC_R:	H	FLEX_R:	N	RESL_R:	N	TEAM_R:	H	PMAT_R:	L		

2 Get COPSEMO distribution information: values specified or calculated in COPSEMO. Baseline/Input vales: BOLD

Eff% & Sched % per stage (per CoPSEMo)

	Inception			Elaboration			Construction			Total E&C			Total		
Effort %	6.0			24.0			76.0			100.00			118.00		
Schedule %	12.5			37.5			62.5			100.00			125.00		
P/Ave(P)	0.5			0.64			1.22			1.00			Does not apply		
	PM	M	P	PM	M	P	PM	M	P	PM	M	P	PM	M	P-ave
PSE Distributed	1.08	0.44	2.43	4.31	1.33	3.24	13.64	2.21	6.16	17.94	3.54	5.07	21.17	4.43	4.78

3 Get the schedule multipliers values.

RVHL L | N | CLAB N | RESL N | PPOS H

		Inception			Elaboration			Construction		
		PM	M	P	PM	M	P	PM	M	P
L	RVHL	1.000	1.000	1.000	1.000	1.000	1.000	1.000	1.000	1.000
N	DPRS	1.000	1.000	1.000	1.000	1.000	1.000	1.000	1.000	1.000
N	CLAB	1.000	1.000	1.000	1.000	1.000	1.000	1.000	1.000	1.000
N	RESL	1.000	1.000	1.000	1.000	1.000	1.000	1.000	1.000	1.000
H	PPOS	1.030	0.930	1.108	1.030	0.930	1.108	1.030	0.930	1.108
	II	1.030	0.930	1.108	1.030	0.930	1.108	1.030	0.930	1.108

4 Apply the product of user selected schedule and effort multipliers to each PM, M and P in each stage.

input vales: BOLD

	Inception			Elaboration			Construction			Total E&C			Total		
	PM	M	P	PM	M	P	PM	M	P	PM	M	P	PM	M	P-ave
PSE Distributed	1.08	0.44	2.43	4.31	1.33	3.24	13.64	2.21	6.16	17.9	3.5	5.1	19.0	4.0	4.8
II	1.03	0.93	1.11	1.03	0.93	1.11	1.03	0.93	1.11						
RAD Eff&Schd	1.11	0.41	2.69	4.44	1.24	3.59	14.05	2.06	6.82	18.5	3.3	5.6	19.6	3.7	5.3

Ave(P) refers to the average number of persons on the project; in the absence of Schedule Multiplier effects,
it is the same as PM_BS/M_BS for the entire project, and each stage's P/Ave(P) is the same as stage's Effort%/Schedule%.

5 Plot of P vs M. Input values in BOLD

RVHL= L | DPRS= N | CLAB= N | RESL= N | PPOS= H

	Inception			Elaboration			Construction			Total E&C			Total		
Effort %	6.0			24.0			76.0			100.0			106.0		
Schedule	12.5			37.5			62.5			100.0			112.5		
P/Ave(P)	0.48			0.64			1.22			1.00					
	PM	M	P	PM	M	P	PM	M	P	PM	M	P	PM	M	P-ave
PSE Distributed	1.08	0.44	2.43	4.31	1.33	3.24	13.64	2.21	6.16	17.9	3.5	5.1	19.0	4.0	4.8
II	1.03	0.93	1.11	1.03	0.93	1.11	1.03	0.93	1.11						
RAD Eff&Schd	1.11	0.41	2.69	4.44	1.24	3.59	14.05	2.06	6.82	18.5	3.3	5.6	19.6	3.7	5.3

Persons (P) vs Months (M)

NOTE: Transition values taken directly from COPSEMO

—✕— Inception   —●— Elaboration   —■— Construction   - -△- - Ave   —○— E+C_P   —◇— P_C   —●— Transition

Figure 24.4 Constructive RAD Model estimate of Bomb Shelter Studios project. (From Boehm, R., An Approach to Early Lifecycle Estimating of Agile Projects, unpublished. With permission.)

Ideal Time

Ideal time estimates the amount of time a task will take to complete without distractions. It must be estimated by the developer. It is usually one-half to one-quarter of actual, or wall clock, time.

Test Points

Test points are an experimental measure of software component size. Its use encourages developers to enter the correct amount of test scripts and cases. It is not usually counted until implementation is under way.

Use Case Points

Use case points measure the functionality of the application. When use cases are part of the development methodology, they are fairly quick and easy to count. At this point, few sophisticated estimating models use them to generate estimates.

Function Points

Function Points measure functionality. They can be estimated early in the lifecycle, before developers are brought into the project, by using processes like ELFE. If they are also being used to govern an outsourcing agreement, then there calculation is part of the development process. Otherwise, it tends to be the most difficult and time consuming of the measures discussed here. It is also the most widely accepted. This allows the Function Point size estimate to be compared to completed projects in the ISBSG database. Function Points can also drive sophisticated estimating models like COCOMO.

References

1. Beck, K., M. Beedle, A. van Bennekum, A. Cockburn, W. Cunningham, M. Fowler, and J. Grenning, et al. 2001. http://agilemanifesto.org (accessed April 15, 2005).
2. Beck, K. 2000. *Extreme Programming Explained: Embrace Change*, xx, chap 3, 178. Boston, MA: Addison-Wesley.
3. Highsmith, J. 2002. *Agile Software Development Ecosystems*, 242. Boston, MA: Addison-Wesley.
4. Cohn, M. 2004. *User Stories Applied For Agile Software Development*, 17. Boston, MA: Addison-Wesley.
5. Boehm, B., and R. Turner. 2004. *Balancing Agility and Discipline: A Guide for the Perplexed*. Boston, MA: Addison-Wesley.
6. Cohn, M. 2006. *Agile Estimating and Planning*, 56–60, chap 23. Boston, MA: Addison-Wesley.
7. Grossman, F., J. Bergin, D. Leip, S. Merritt, and O. Gotel. 2004. One XP experience: introducing agile (XP) software development into a culture that is willing but not

ready. In *Proceedings of the Conference of the Centre for Advanced Studies on Collaborative Research*, 242–54. Markham, ON.

8. Dubinsky, Y., D. Talby, O. Hazzan, and A. Keren. 2005. Agile metrics at the Israeli Air Force. In *Proceedings of the Agile 2005 Conference*. Denver, CO.

9. Boehm, R. 2009. Why estimate & plan? (Cont.), http://agileestimator.com/2009/10/26/why-estimate-plan-cont/ (accessed April 30, 2011).

10. Rising, L. 2010. The benefits of patterns. *IEEE Softw* 27(5):15.

11. Nunes, N., L. Constantine, and R. Kazman. 2010. iUCP—Estimating interactive software project size with enhanced use-case points *IEEE Comput* 27(3): 64–73.

12. Anda, B. 2003. Empirical Studies of Construction and Application of Use Case Models. Dr. Scient., University of Oslo, http://simula.no/research/se/publications/SE.3.Anda.2003 (accessed February 14, 2005).

13. McConnell, S. 2006. *Software Estimation: Demystifying the Black Art*, 221. Redmond: Microsoft Press.

14. Brown, B., R. Edwards, E. J. Fischer, D. Garmus, J. Russac, A. Timp, and P. Thomas. 2010. *Function Point Counting Practices Manual*, Version 4.2.1. Princeton Junction: International Function Point Users Group (IFPUG).

15. Boehm, B., C. Abts, A. W. Brown, S. Chulani, S. K. Clark, E. Horowitz, R. Madachy, D. Reifer, and B. Steece. 2000. *Software Cost Estimation with COCOMO II*, 17, 215. Upper Saddle River, NJ: Prentice Hall PTR.

16. Boehm, R. 2011. *An Approach to Early Lifecycle Estimating of Agile Projects*. unpublished DPS thesis.

About the Author

Raymond Boehm is the principal consultant for Software Composition Technologies. He has over three decades of experience in software development, teaching, and consulting. Before founding Software Composition Technologies, he was the metrics manager for one of the divisions of CSC and was a professor at the New York Institute of Technology (NYIT). He received an MBA from NYIT and is completing a Doctor of Professional Studies (DPS) Degree in Computing at Pace University. His thesis, "An Approach to Early Lifecycle Estimating for Agile Projects," served as the basis for much of this chapter. He is an IFPUG Certified Function Point Specialist (CFPS) and a Quality Assurance Institute (QAI) Certified Software Quality Analyst (CSQA). He is a member of the IEEE Computer Society, the ACM, and the Agile Alliance.

Software Composition Technologies was founded in 1996 to help people gain control of software development. Primarily, it applies Function Point Analysis and software estimation techniques to provide clients with answers to their business challenges. It also trains and mentors organizations in these same techniques. In addition, it provides assistance in the areas of software development methodology and quality assurance.

Chapter 25

Agile Estimation Using Functional Metrics

Thomas M. Cagley Jr.

Contents

The term agile has come to mean many things to many people. The definitions and connotations range from how work is organized within a project to a description of the speed at which work is completed or alternately a radical rethinking of organizational culture. Regardless of how you define agile, I would suggest that we all would agree that agile methods are now maturing. Part of the process of maturing is the incorporation of best practices from other methods and frameworks creating

479

a hybrid. The fringe is influencing the center and the center is influencing the fringe. The hybrid is at once better than any of the absolutes and threatening to those who believe in absolutes.

Estimation has been a lightning rod for the discussion of all methods (agile, waterfall, iterative, or water fountain) with the issues of predictability and standardization radiating outward. Because of the controversy, this is an area where a wide range of hybridization has always occurred. Organizations adjust techniques to fit governance structures, culture, and risk profiles. There is no one-size-fits-all solution. This chapter provides a path for incorporating the use of Function Points into agile estimation techniques. The process will yield an estimation process that combines one part functional metrics and one part parametric estimation techniques with two parts agile estimation (heavily influenced by Mike Cohn's book, *Agile Estimating and Planning*). I would suggest that functional metrics provides a path for incorporating the best practices of robust software sizing with the collaborative techniques championed by the agile community in a manner that increases standardization without ignoring the principles of the Agile Manifesto (http://www.agilemanifesto.org/).

Budgeting, Estimation, and Planning

I would like to begin this discussion by challenging your preconceived notion of estimation as compared to the activities of budgeting and planning. These three concepts shown in Figure 25.1 are sometimes thought of as being synonymous; however, I believe it is important to understand just how different these concepts are. Each has different inputs and outputs, uses different tools and techniques, and

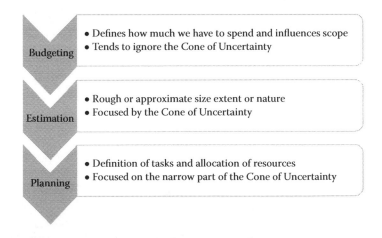

Budgeting
- Defines how much we have to spend and influences scope
- Tends to ignore the Cone of Uncertainty

Estimation
- Rough or approximate size extent or nature
- Focused by the Cone of Uncertainty

Planning
- Definition of tasks and allocation of resources
- Focused on the narrow part of the Cone of Uncertainty

Figure 25.1 Estimation versus planning versus budgeting.

is generally used by different groups within the organization. A quick overview of the macro differences are as follows:

- Budgeting
  - Defines how much we have to spend based on the influence of scope
  - Tends to ignore the Cone of Uncertainty
- Estimation
  - Presents an approximation of effort and duration based on size and project nature
  - Focused by the Cone of Uncertainty (a range based on knowledge)
- Planning
  - Defines tasks and allocates resources
  - Focused on the narrow part of the Cone of Uncertainty (a much smaller range)

Estimation, planning, and budgeting might be related but they are certainly not the same. The use of functional metrics in agile estimation is targeted at the estimation layer of this three-layer cake but provides support for planning. Developing a basic understanding of the components of estimation (we are going to ignore budgeting as a bastion of guesses) and its relationship to sizing is critical to using these techniques.

Estimation

Estimation is several parts science and at least one part magic. This strange confluence of science and magic defines the transformation of requirements size, skills, people, and equipment into how much the project will cost and how much effort it will take. The whole process of transformation is bound by a Cone of Uncertainty. The "Cone of Uncertainty," originally shown by Barry Beohm [1] and later described in *Software Estimation: Demystifying the Black Art* [2], written by Steve McConnell, builds boundaries around the false precision of the estimate, providing a range around the estimate based on what is known and unknown. Collaborative estimation techniques are good at increasing team knowledge while reducing the amount of self-deceit that can occur when knowledge is discussed.

The amount of art needed to create an estimate increases as estimation discipline is replaced by planning discipline. The art of planning matches specific tasks with people through a process of assignment. In a perfect world, estimates and planning could be done together in seamless workflow but estimates happen generally earlier in the project life cycle before you can decompose work into tasks that is required for planning.

The simplest form of any estimation model, human- or tool-based, is a mathematical mash-up of size (implied or counted), team, and organizational behavioral attributes and degree of difficulty (technical complexity) applied to a productivity signature as shown in Figure 25.2. As the level of sophistication in the mathematics increases,

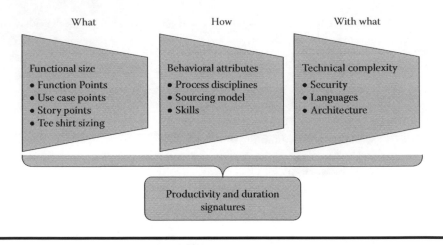

Figure 25.2 Basic estimation model.

tools such as SEER-SEM (http://www.galorath.com), SLIM (http://www.qsm.com), or KnowledgePLAN (http://www.spr.com) make sense. Other methods raise the level of collaboration and do any of the required maths in the heads of the participants. These techniques include Delphi (http://en.wikipedia.org/wiki/Wideband_delphi), analogy, or planning poker (http://planningpoker.com). The process in this chapter splits the difference, leveraging collaboration to increase participation and self-knowledge, while suggesting the use of a simple spreadsheet-based parametric model to increase consistency and standardization.

Sounds simple, right? Estimation has been a nagging pain in every IT manager's backside since a user asked how much a project would cost and when it would be done. We have gotten pretty good at budgeting using techniques like "x number of people times 20 hours in a day and you'll get something next year" methods. It is when we try to figure out how much functionality will be delivered in real life that things start to break down or at least get very, very complicated.

There are three main categories of problems that cause estimation to be problematic in the real world:

1. Uncertainty: How much do you know about what you are building?
2. Self-knowledge: What do you do really know about yourself and your team?
3. Consistency of method: Do you have a process for estimating?

Uncertainty

A lot has been written about uncertainty, mostly from the point of view of requirements; however, the impact of uncertainty extends further than requirements into factors that can be purely technical (whether specific coding languages can do the job) to the complexities of the real world (cue the changing economy as an example). If we change our perspective to completion of the project, I propose that we will all admit that the level of project uncertainty is substantially reduced the closer you are to completion of the project. Moving back toward the beginning of the project where most estimation exercises occur, one simple truth becomes apparent: Knowledge dispels uncertainty.

Basic human psychology drives a need for certainty, and many times we think in binary terms: black and white. The certainty we seek is unfortunately unattainable, which causes conflict within ourselves and within the communities that we join or are forced to join. Managing the conflict that the need for certainty generates is a cost that does not need to be borne if we accept a rational dose of uncertainty. The cost of conflict is generated by two flavors of mechanisms.

1. Compensation
2. Conflict avoidance

There are similarities and differences between the mechanisms.

Deepak Chopra has pointed out that in quantum physics, matter fluctuates between a wave and a particle, only "collapsing into manifestation" in response to an observer [3]. Not only do differing levels of awareness lead people to perceive the world differently, but through our awareness and conscious and unconscious layers of intention, we all participate in creating what manifests. This is an uncomfortable level of uncertainty for anyone seeking to estimate a project.

To compensate for the lack of certainty, we create theories about how things occur. As we seek to understand uncertainty, the natural extension is to formulate explanations. Explanations are mechanisms to shift variability back to a deterministic mode. Models are a mechanism to explain variability. The thought is that what we can explain, we can control. Whether our model is true or untrue is not as material as the exercise of creating theories and models to compensate for a lack of order in the outside world. Mike Copeland suggests that humans choose to create theories that have been elevated to "knowns" or beliefs to lessen the uncertainty of ambiguity. It is as if the creation of models can create order and relationships where causality does not exist [4].

Models, theories, and abstractions are mechanisms to compensate for the disconnection between a need for certainty that an estimate seems to require and the real world that is far more uncertain. I would suggest that estimates and abstractions continue at high and higher levels until a mass audience can relate quickly. The problem with this compensation technique is that as simplifications are simplified, so they are easier to understand they lose predictive power and decisions made from simplifications of simplifications are significantly riskier.

Conflict within organizations can represent an interesting dichotomy: constructive conflict and destructive conflict. Constructive conflict can help forge ideas, removing the scale revealing the core of the idea by forcing people to confront possible defects in a solution so that the best idea survives and adds value. However, for all of the possible good constructive conflict can deliver, destructive conflict is always injurious to the organization. The distinction between constructive and destructive is often hard to discern, increasing the risk of any perceived conflict. The difficulty discerning the difference and the downside risk of getting the distinction wrong makes being conflict avoidant a viable strategy. Talking in abstractions and abstractions of abstractions such as single numbers or high-level estimates are tools to avoid conflict. This is true for a number of reasons. The first is that the more abstract an idea is, the more easily the similarities of worldviews can be emphasized smoothing over potential divisions within a group. In competitive environments, abstractions are a means of withholding information or as a tool to emphasize conformity. In all of these cases, rather than risking conflict even though it might be constructive, abstractions such as high-level estimates or single number estimates are used to defuse conflict.

Dispelling uncertainty without resorting to abstractions is critical to agile estimation. We need to gather better knowledge by leveraging history, mathematical algorithms, and/or project-specific information to make better estimates. Integrating agile techniques for knowledge capture in projects are tools for reducing uncertainty. Techniques to use include incorporating a user or user proxy on the team, focusing on short predefined time horizons, implementing processes that foster communication, and periodic replanning.

Self-Knowledge

Two psychologists, Joseph Luft and Harry Ingham, developed a construct to understand personal awareness. The tool named Johari's Window [5] divides personal awareness into four different categories, as represented by its four quadrants: open, hidden, blind, and unknown. The lines dividing the four panes are like window shades, which can move as an interaction progresses. The concept is adaptable to teams. Team-level blind spots complicate estimation, planning, and ultimately performance. Techniques to improve a team's self-knowledge include forming stable teams, fostering intimate communications, and ensuring retrospectives actually happen often. These tools minimize what is not known by the team and bring misunderstandings to the surface quickly.

Consistency of Method

There are several types of estimation that can be leveraged during any project.

Estimation Types

Let us quickly review the most popular estimation techniques in very broad terms, which are the following:

- Analogy
- Bottom-up
- Parametric
- Delphi

Note that there are many classification schemas for estimates. Lionel C. Briand and Isabella Wieczorek provide a summary of schemas in their article, *Resource Estimation in Software Engineering* [6].

Estimation by analogy starts with the selection of a similar project (building a new bathroom based on the results of building a bathroom last week), which acts as a central metaphor for the new project. The estimator will then decide how closely the two projects resemble each other and whether there are any mitigating circumstances that will affect the effort required to finish the project, how much the project might cost, and how long it will take. Based on these differences, the estimator will apply a correct factor and, *voila*, an estimate is created. The second general category of estimation techniques is the bottom-up estimate. An estimate of this type typically starts by identifying a set of technical deliverables (a shower stall, sink and pipes for a bathroom with a shower if building a house) or work breakdown structure (the tasks needed to build a bathroom for our house). The identified low-level deliverables are estimated based on some form of history, then rolled up to higher and higher levels until the cost or effort for the entire project is known. The third category of estimation is called parametric estimation. This form of estimation builds and leverages statistical relationships between historical data and one or more variables that define scope such as functional size (the number of square feet in the bathroom times the productivity of the builders). The fourth type of estimation techniques can be grouped broadly into the category of Delphi. The central theme of Delphi techniques is the use of collaborative techniques to leverage groupthink to decide on an estimate (the plumbers, electricians, and carpenters get together and use a process to come to consensus on how much time is required to build the bathroom). These techniques work best when the requirements being estimated can be stated at a level of granularity that can be understood by those participating in the estimation session.

Mike Cohn has described the planning continuum using an onion analogy [7], where strategy is the outer layer followed by layers for portfolio, product, release, and iteration segments as you approach the onion core. I suggest that there is no one tool or technique perfectly suited for each level in the onion.

Integrating Cohn's planning onion into our earlier conversation of budgeting, estimation, and planning, I would suggest that strategy and portfolio levels are budgeting tasks. The product and release layers are estimation tasks where tools like parametric estimation make sense. Iteration and day-to-day organization are planning tasks where planning tools like schedules, kanban boards, and standup meeting make sense to direct activity. The method we are introducing in this chapter combines the use of functional metrics and tools in the estimation step in a manner that fosters usage in the planning layers of the onion. This set of techniques provides a consistent strategy and answers the changing information needs as the project evolves—all this, while providing a collaborative environment for both the team and the client.

Agile estimation using functional metrics is designed to cover the product and release rings of Cohn's planning onion using a synthesis of parametric and Delphi estimation techniques with the emphasis shifting from parametric to Delphi as events dictate. The technique leverages the ability to size requirements in terms of Function Points to develop parametric estimates and then dovetails collaborative techniques to refine those estimates based on memories and self knowledge. Figure 25.3 provides a process view of the agile estimation using functional metrics.

The process flow is as follows:

Stage One—Backlog estimation

1. Identification of functional requirements (or stories)
2. Sizing using Quick and Early Function Points
3. Simple parametric estimation for each story

Stage Two—Sprint or iteration planning

1. Break requirements into more granular pieces (if needed) and refine size
2. Team level re-estimation of requirements using delphi techniques
3. Team level commitment

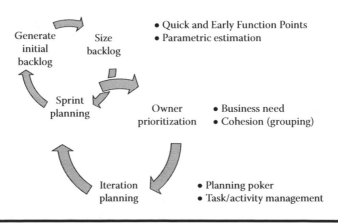

Figure 25.3 Proposed solution.

Developing a quantitative size for requirements is a critical component in developing an estimate and for planning; however, size and estimates are not synonymous. Sizing the requirements is merely a step along the path from point A to point B. As we move along the path, the sized requirements we develop will be revisited twice.

The sizing process begins by segregating the functional requirements from the nonfunctional requirements. The functional requirements are then sized using the Quick and Early Function Points (QEFP) methodology developed by David Consulting Group [8]. Function Points for all their warts are the easiest way to consistently size software requirements. This is accomplished by focusing on the basic building blocks of functionality found in all software projects. The QEFP method leverages the relationship between action verbs and transactions to identify the transaction functions found in Function Points and the subject of the requirement to identify the data functions found in Function Points. The application of this technique is similar to sentence diagramming that you learned during grade school or high school. This relationship between words and size has been observed and investigated over the past few years by a number of different people within the functional sizing community including myself (see "Turning Perfect Good Words Into Numbers" originally presented at the IFPUG Functional Sizing Summit at http://www.davidconsultingroup .com). Function Points or any functional metric has at its heart the goal of converting requirements or stories into a number in a consistent manner. The number then must be interpreted based on the abilities of the team or organization. At the level of the overall project, the technique described in this chapter leverages parametric estimation. A simple parametric estimation equation could be

$$Y = -(7^{-6} \cdot (X^2)) - Z \cdot X + 26.587 \qquad (25.1)$$

where
  X = Size in Function Points
  Y = Productivity rate for the type of project
  Z = Behavior or Process Index

This equation is an application of software-estimation principles noted by Capers Jones in book, *Estimating Software Costs* [9, p.6]. The result is a productivity rate for the project. Collection of historical data on a selection of projects will be required to build an equation. I would further suggest that you would need to augment internal data with external data to increase the validity of the estimation equation. Note that the factor can be applied to a disaggregated requirement, epic, or story. This estimate is created for organizational planning purposes.

The "Behavior or Process Index" is a weighted aggregation of estimating adjustment factors that typically specify methodologies, work patterns, team skills, team dispersion, tools, and languages to be used.* The weighted aggregate can then be

---

* See [9], Section 4.

correlated to project performance and used to predict future projects. This technique is similar to those used in commercial parametric estimation tools. A list of possible attributes can be found in the appendix of *Software Assessments, Benchmarks, and Best Practices* [10].

Stage 2 begins when sprints or iterations are kicked off. The sprint teams (we will use Scrum terminology [11, pp.141–142]) breakdown the stories into pieces that can be accomplished during the sprint, then resize the pieces using the QEFP method. The goal of using QEFP at this point is to take one source of variance out of the estimation discussion that will be had when the Delphi or planning poker method is applied. This focuses the group on expanding the team-level self-knowledge needed to coalesce on an appropriate level of effort needed to complete the story. For example, the QEFP technique has been combined with planning poker into a process that was quickly learned by the sprint teams. The results were a marked reduction in stories that were not completed during the sprint that they were committed to complete. By removing size as a variable, the team that initially piloted this method indicated that they were better able to focus on discussing team capabilities and technical considerations when doing their initial sprint planning.

Role of Measurement and the Project Management Office in Agile Estimation

Measurement plays a crucial role both at a project and organizational level. An interesting concept that has emerged from sorting out the Project Management Office's (PMO) role in an agile world is measurement. Measurement needs to be part and parcel of the team's feedback loop. Whether it is a function of the calculation for velocity or knowing how far away it is done, measurement as feedback belongs to the team. This can be another point of conflict between the team and the PMO.

Self-managing teams are self-measuring because without data no one can consistently manage. This might sound like a truism but it is true. Measurement belongs within the development team so that the team can actively manage the work. Typical measures may include task time expended and planned, cycle time, sprint duration, story throughput, Function Points delivered in the sprint, and rework. Many of these measures are tracked through burndown charts, burnup charts, and backlogs. The team measures what it needs to get its job done effectively and efficiently and nothing more.

Here again the PMO and team roles and data needs differ. The PMO's job is to analyze and interpret information for the organization's consumption, rather than pre-chewing it for the project team's consumption. Focusing on the overall measurement data for the purpose of forecasting the overall project's outcome is a PMO role. Self-managing teams require data; the PMO should be positioned to ensure that the agile teams have the right external data so that they can be self-managed.

The PMO's role in measurement is to provide information and data. If the project team does not have the data, they cannot be self-managed.

One of the normal roles of a PMO is to facilitate getting things back on track when the overall project outcome is not expected to meet management and customer expectations. This is typically done through active intervention at granular level (task and person). Instead, using our three voices, the Scrum master/coach will actively influence the team to deal with the internal blockers while the PMO will focus on the macro external blockers. The PMO's role would be to help fix those things that are outside of the team's boundary, get the things out of the way of the team, and then get out of the way—letting the team do what they need to do internally to get the job done. Issues and blockers inside the team will be dealt with on a day-to-day basis using self-managing and collaborative techniques facilitated by the Scrum master.

Finally, the PMO keeps the team informed about the outside world through information and data versus simply trying to coordinate and manage them based on what is happening in the outside. An example of the information the PMO can provide for sprint teams are the true goals of the project from the organization's perspective. In how many projects does the team understand the true goals? This piece of data is critical to make the day-to-day decisions on individual tasks and activities that all self-managed teams must make. Knowing the goals allow the team to make the correct trade-offs without having to go and seek external qualification of those decisions.

Another interesting potential conflict point between the project team and the PMO is that he or she who prioritizes directs. Directing is a role that most project managers feel that they should at least have a hand in, whereas in an agile project, the Voice of the Customer does the prioritizing supported by information from the other voices. The customer defines what gets done and in which order; the team defines how the work is done leaving the PMO to play a different role than they are used to. I liken the difference in approach to the seeming difference between a line dance and a mosh pit. Both are dancing, both are fun, but both are very different.

Real life examples will help drive home how organizations synthesized what could be considered conflicting methodologies into something greater than the sum of the two parts.

Case One

- ▪ Firm: Small custom technology organization
- ▪ Project Types: Internal and external projects
- ▪ Culture: Highly collaborative
- ▪ Current Methodology: Mixed waterfall and Scrum

Other notes: All external projects are bid with many using a fixed fee structure. Internal projects were continually re-scoped to fit the internal development budget that changes as the economy waxes and wanes. Before rewriting the estimation process and leveraging functional metrics, approximately 30% of bids were successful and budgets tended to be a suggestion. The lack of estimation success meant that there was a significant risk of losing money if the business was won and going out of business if the business was not won.

The firm adopted QEFP for sizing the backlogs for all projects, both internal and external. Where backlogs were not being used to manage requirements, they were developed. A quick baseline was developed to determine a productivity factor. During the initial implementation of backlogs sized using the QEFP method, it became apparent the level of non-functional requirements was relatively small (less than 10% of the requirements) and the amount of non-functional requirements was stable. This allowed the firm to simplify the estimation process by only focusing on functional requirements (unless there was a special case) as the productivity factor based on their historical data incorporated the typical level non-functional requirements. The productivity factor was then used to translate individual stories into effort. Each team spent a day reviewing how they worked together to generate a baseline of self-knowledge and trust. Collaborative story-level estimation was redone using planning poker. It became apparent quickly that a lot of disaggregation was needed to actually estimate the backlogs. After applying QEFP and the productivity factor to the in-flight projects, the firm progressed to applying QEFP to all bids.

The results were that won bids increased 20% and negative misses were nearly eradicated. A negative miss was defined as underbidding on a fixed bid contract. Retrospectives from projects and sprints after steady state was attained (2 months) anecdotally, suggesting that using this method has reduced the effort required for estimation and planning by over 70% from the pre-agile scenario.

Case Two

- ■ Firm: Large software development firm
- ■ Project Types: Internal projects (software for resale)
- ■ Culture: Hierarchy, classic command and control
- ■ Current Methodology: Mixed waterfall (but Scrum recently introduced)

Other notes: The methodology in the environment was predominantly classic waterfall with central PMO. Just before we readdressed the estimation process, a team had implemented Scrum and some components of extreme programming (XP); this was done in sort of a guerilla fashion. One very large project was consuming the majority of the organization's resources. Significant requirements were still being discovered after construction had begun. Estimates had been developed based on a bottom-up process very early in the project and they were of questionable validity. The top managers just returned from begging for more money from the board of directors. The project was being capitalized.

The solution in this case was for the company to more firmly embrace the Scrum framework for project management at the team level. Teams were tweaked to make them as cross-functional as possible. The iteration cadence was set at 4 weeks. The iterations were bounded by a single large planning session that included all sprint teams and an overall end of sprint demo. Each team used the standard Scrum tools of daily standup meetings, retrospectives, and burndown charts (generated from TFS) to self-organize, self-measure, and self-manage. Three senior product managers from the business were assigned to the project on a full-time basis with authority to make decisions about the project.

The PMO was redirected to focus on external governance. They managed the overall backlog, removing completed requirements (after the demo) and adding requirements or returning those that were partially completed. Functional and non-functional requirements were incorporated into one common backlog. The PMO also performed initial sizing of all new or returned requirements using the QEFP method for functional requirements and story points for non-functional requirements. A senior project manager also chaired the scrum of scrums that kept all of the teams synchronized. The PMO led a management roundtable to facilitate communication and release planning at an executive level.

Rearranging the roles redirected energies to get more work done faster, better, and cheaper. The change separated roles to focus on tasks either inside or outside the team but not on both. The change allowed the teams to function with far less overt management and to continuously hone their methods to get the work done faster, better, and cheaper.

A product backlog was developed and QEFP were adopted to size the backlog. The sizing process exposed a number of functional blind spots (Function Points can be leveraged as a form of analysis). Team members were trained in using QEFP that allowed them to size new stories or resize changed stories at an individual sprint planning level. The impact of these changes was to allow the PMO to size and preplan the backlog with development leaders and the primary product owner. The PMO used a set of standard productivity rates to estimate both the functional requirements. The set of productivity rates included five basic rates that were developed for development and infrastructure teams so that non-functional requirements sized in story points had their own special rate for estimation. The full product owner team selected stories to formulate sprints during the sprint planning meetings. Teams re-evaluated (sized and estimated) the selected stories and then committed to the stories they could do.

The initial result was improved product owner satisfaction—involvement allowed them to be part of the solution. After the first few sprints, there was an increased perception of estimate consistency both at the product backlog level and sprint team level. It was also noted that the teams that had been using Scrum before adopting the new estimation methods had a reduced number of stories that had not been completed at the end of the sprint. In teams that had been using SCRUM before the change, the stories that failed the sprint (did not complete) averaged approximately 40%. It had once been said that almost no sprints were successful.

After the implementation had reached steady state, the percentage of escaped stories fell to under 5%. The teams attributed this improvement during retrospectives to a better capacity to size and commitment to work that they are actually able to accomplish during the sprint. Retrospectives indicated that using the QEFP methodology did not add any significant time to the planning game. Early in the deployment there were occasional comments about difficulties estimating some non-functional requirements. In at least one instance the team requested adding personnel with broader skill sets to the team to deal with non-functional requirements.

Summary

The process proposed in this chapter begins at the backlog level where requirements or stories are managed at the project level. Leveraging a sizing technique such as QEFP for functional requirements and story points for non-functional requirements can be used to estimate individual requirements so that data can be used to prioritize work before sprint planning. There is a secondary benefit to this process that enforces granularity and understanding of the requirements. It can be said that what cannot be sized cannot be built. As stories transition into sprint planning, the knowledge gained in the estimation process transfers into the sprint teams so they can focus on complexity and other technical factors that improve the quality of planning as evidenced by fewer stories not completing during the sprint.

Estimating the backlog using parametric estimating techniques integrates management's need to estimate how much a project will cost, when deliveries will happen, and whether work is being done efficiently. The use of sizing techniques as an input to the sprint planning process adds a level of discipline to the process that increases the performance as defined by completed sprints without perceived overhead.

Agile methods have matured and are now being integrated into many different approaches to the development of software. Estimation has been problematic for all methods, from agile to plan based, and therefore it tends to be a lightning rod for experimentation and synthesis such as is being described in this chapter. This chapter has presented a path for integrating the discipline found in functional metrics with the collaborative approaches found in agile estimation.

References

1. Boehm, B. 1981. *Software Engineering Economics*, 311. Upper Saddle River, NJ: Prentice Hall.
2. McConnell, S. 2006. *Software Estimation: Demystifying the Black Art*. Microsoft Press.
3. Deepak Chopra and Intent. 2010. http://bit.ly/o4yWNu (accessed June 11, 2009).
4. Copeland, M. 2008. Why People Think the Way They Think. http://bit.ly/pZszCS (accessed June 11, 2009).
5. http://en.wikipedia.org/wiki/Johari_window (accessed June 14, 2009).

6. Briand, L. C., and I. Wieczorek. *Resource Estimation in Software Engineering*. International Software Engineering Research Network, Technical Report. ISERN 00–05, 5.
7 http://www.mountaingoatsoftware.com/presentations/51 (accessed June 14, 2009).
8. David Consulting Group. Webinar, "Agile Estimation Using Functional Metrics", Febraury 2011.
9. Jones, T. C. 1998. *Estimating Software Costs*, 6. New York: McGraw-Hill.
10. Jones, C. *Software Assessments, Benchmarks and Best Practices*, 567. Boston: Addison-Wesley.
11. Schwaber, K. 2004. *Agile Project Management With SCRUM*, 141–42. Redmond, WA: Microsoft Press.

About the Author

Thomas Cagley Jr. is a Certified Function Point Specialist (CFPS), author, blogger, podcaster, and former president of IFPUG. He is currently the vice president of the David Consulting Group (DCG), where he manages consulting practices. He is the coauthor of *Mastering Software Project Management: Best Practices, Tools and Techniques*. Cagley has over 20 years experience in the software industry in which he has been a consultant since 1997. He was previously metrics practice manager at Software Productivity Research. Earlier, he held technical and managerial positions in different industries as a leader in software methods and metrics, quality assurance, and systems analysis. As an agile evangelist, he has infused agile and lean techniques into software development process consulting at DCG. He is a frequent speaker at international conferences on software measurement and process improvement.

About the David Consulting Group

DCG was formed in 1994 by David Garmus and David Herron, two of the industry's acknowledged authorities in the field of sizing, measurement, and estimation of software application development and maintenance. In 2006, Michael Harris bought the company.

DCG's consultants are drawn from industry and have decades of practical hands-on experience across multiple industries and government in the United States and internationally. DCG has provided services on every continent from North America to South America, Europe, Africa, the Middle East, and Asia. All of our consultants are at the top of their profession, highly qualified, and well used to translating the results of sizing and measurement exercises into practical business-driven recommendations.

At the David Consulting Group, we believe in the value of software measurement, estimation, and process improvement. Our mantra is, "Measure. Improve. Deliver."

Our approach is agile. We deliver value to our clients regularly and frequently, irrespective of the best practices we utilize.

Chapter 26

Software Non-Functional Assessment Process

Christine Green*, Dan Bradley†, Talmon Ben-Cnaan‡,
Wendy Bloomfield‡, David Garmus§, Jalaja
Venkat§, Steve Chizar§, and Luca Santillo§

Contents

---

* SNAP project manager, ITPC vice-chair.
† ITPC Chair.
‡ ITPC member.
§ SNAP team member.

Introduction

In building software, as with any construction project, many factors influence the cost and effort required to complete the product. Customers indicate the project's purpose, operation and expected outcomes, and functional requirements. Engineers and builders apply technology, performance, and quality criteria to produce the desired functions and non-functional requirements.

International Function Point Users Group (IFPUG) Function Points (FP) effectively measures the functional aspects of a product from the customer's perspective and provides a good measure of the value delivered. However, extensive analysis shows that there exists no close correlation (*R*-Square < 0.5) between Unadjusted Function Points (UFP) and the effort required to deliver the product. In an attempt to resolve this discrepancy, the IFPUG method may use the General Systems Characteristics (GSC) to modify the UFP count by a Value Adjustment Factor (VAF) derived by answers to a set of questions focused on the project's non-functional requirements.

Recognizing the need for a closer correlation between FP and effort, in 2005, the IFPUG IT Performance Committee (ITPC) distributed a survey to collect and prioritize project attributes. The survey results were to be used to derive a new set of GSCs updated to current technologies to provide a better correlation between FPs and effort. After initial analysis, the ITPC determined that a different approach was required to achieve a project "count" that would more closely correlate to total development effort. What was needed was a project sizing framework that included both the functional and the non-functional factors contributing to effort.

In 2007, the ITPC initiated a project approved by the IFPUG Board to define a framework for a new form of measurement to be used with the existing IFPUG CPM 4.2.1 [1]. The project charter described a project to be called "Technical Size CPM" until an agreement on final naming. The original charter described a project that would require a team of international experts who would develop a final framework for non-functional sizing on the basis of the initial concepts put forward by the ITPC. This project charter only covered project elements for the first year of the project, although it was recognized that the entire concept would take several years to develop.

In late 2007, the ITPC invited IFPUG members to participate in the "Technical Size" project and indicated the commitment (5–10 hours monthly including one to two conference calls) it would take to be on the team. By February 2008, more than 80 people had volunteered. This was the first external indicator of the tremendous interest in a more comprehensive sizing method. From this pool of volunteers, 15 individuals from diverse industries, countries, and background experience were selected to join the Technical Size Core Team. In conjunction with the ITPC, this team developed the initial framework for non-functional sizing. Early decisions made by the core team narrowed the focus of the initial framework to concentrate on technical and quality aspects and determined that environmental characteristics were too organizationally specific to become part of the method.

At the September 2008 ISMA Conference, the core team presented the Technical Size Framework and launched the next phase of the project to develop a method to size the non-functional requirements. To name this new method, a contest was held at ISMA. After consideration of more than 30 entries, "Software Non-functional Assessment Process" was selected, and SNAP was born.

After release of the initial framework, the core team met over the period of January to August 2008. Sub-teams were identified midway through the project. The sub-teams worked on defining an assessment process and a counting process and identifying the ISO and IEEE definitions [3,4]. More than 20 presentations were given by members of the core team with different views on how to size the non-functional requirements. Final determination to use an assessment method was made at a "face-to-face" meeting of the core team in September 2009, and laid the groundwork for the initial draft of the Assessment Practices Manual (APM) that was completed in March 2010 [2].

The current stage of the IFPUG APM when the chapter was written was that the APM was in beta testing. Changes might have occurred to the final version of the APM between the creation of this chapter and the first released version of the APM.

Objective of SNAP

SNAP defines a framework and method for determining non-functional sizing and establishes a link between non-functional sizing and effort without reinventing the General System Characteristics (GSCs). The framework uses definitions and terminology from organizations such as IEEE, ISO, and IFPUG and reuses the definitions, terminology, and structure of the functional size framework.

SNAP sizing is performed separately from functional size measurement; therefore, traditional Function Point data is not impacted. Non-functional sizing includes all technical and quality aspects and can be performed with varying levels of resources depending on the required accuracy of the result. It is anticipated that the sizing process will be adjusted for new technologies and changing business needs through modifications to categories and subcategories.

The SNAP process has the following characteristics:

- Non-functional requirements within an application are assessed using various subcategories that are grouped under logical categories.
- The distinction between the non-functional requirements and the categories that are used to size them should be comprehensible to SNAP users.
- Categories do not describe the non-functional requirements; hence, they do not replace or explain the standards that describe and classify the non-functional requirements (such as ISO 9126) [6].
- The categories and subcategories describe how the assessed project or product will meet these non-functional requirements.

The SNAP results (called SNAP Points) have the following characteristics:

- They can be used in conjunction with the functional size and will help explain the additional development effort required to meet the non-functional requirements.
- Along with functional size, they can be used as input to estimating models.
- They are determined from a non-functional user's view, but understood and agreed to by the functional user.

The process of SNAP is defined in the APM.

The Assessment Practices Manual

The primary objective of the APM is to provide a clear and detailed description of the SNAP assessment process. Adherence to the guidance provided by the APM will result in consistent assessments that can be used for both internal and external benchmarking. Although able to be used independently, the manual was developed to resemble the IFPUG Counting Practices Manual to facilitate the addition of another dimension to project measurement programs.

Metrics professionals and technical experts are the intended audience for the APM. APM provides a structured approach that may be used by persons experienced and those new to the assessment process. Used in conjunction with FP measures, the APM provides standards for non-functional assessment that will enable software professionals to better manage, estimate, and improve the development process.

IFPUG Assessment Practices Manual Link to IFPUG Counting Practices Manual

The objective of the Software Non-functional Assessment Process (SNAP) was to define a sizing method using a defined framework for sizing non-functional requirements that could be used to establish a link between non-functional size and effort. Functional requirements in software development and maintenance were already covered by the functional size measure known as IFPUG Function Points as defined in the IFPUG Counting Practices Manual (CPM).

Functional information is quantifiable today using IFPUG Function Points and represents a good measure of project and/or application size. Providing a quantifiable measure for the non-functional information enables organizations to build historical data repositories that can be referenced to assist in decision making for the technical and/or quality aspects of projects and/or applications. Used in conjunction with IFPUG Function Point measures, the non-functional assessment will provide information that can identify items impacting quality and productivity positively as well as negatively.

Having both functional and non-functional measures enables software professionals to do the following:

- Better plan and estimate development project cost
- Better plan and estimate application maintenance cost/resource requirements
- Better plan and estimate the return on investment (ROI) for application replacement
- Identify potential categories for process improvement
- Assist in determining technical and quality strategies

- Quantify the impact of current technical and quality strategies
- Provide specific measurement data when communicating technical and quality issues to various audiences

SNAP Method

Non-Functional Assessment Process

The non-functional assessment process uses a series of questions, grouped by categories, to measure the size of non-functional requirements for the development and delivery of the software product.

Figure 26.1 describes the assessment process.

Determine Assessment Purpose and Scope

The Purpose

The first step in the SNAP process is to determine the purpose of the assessment. Organizations may choose to perform the assessment based on project specifications and technical standards in order to provide the non-functional size of a development project as an additional input to the estimation process for the first release of an application.

The SNAP method can also be used to determine the non-functional size of an enhancement to an existing application. This will allow for a better estimate of the effort involved in the change, even if the enhancement does not impact the functional size of the application. Completed projects may also be assessed to provide an additional component of portfolio size. The total of Function Points and non-functional size may be combined for use in support cost reporting and ongoing support estimates.

The purpose influences the desired accuracy and scope of the assessment and, therefore, the assessment effort. Once determined, the next step in the process is defining the scope of the assessment.

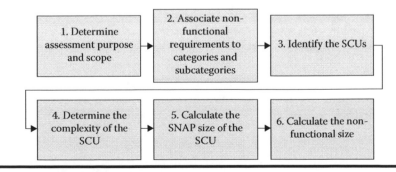

Figure 26.1   Assessment process.

The Scope

The assessment scope defines the set of non-functional user requirements to be included in the assessment. The scope is used to determine the boundary and to define the set of partitions to be included in the assessment. Depending on the assessment, it is possible the scope could include more than one application. At this point, the assessor also identifies which categories and subcategories will be included in the non-functional size measurement.

Characteristics of Scope

- A development project non-functional assessment includes all non-functional requirements for the development and delivery of the software product.
- An assessment of an installed base of applications includes all non-functional requirements for the support of the installed applications.
- An enhancement non-functional assessment includes all non-functional requirements for the development and delivery of the enhancement project; the boundary of the application(s) impacted remains the same.
- A maintenance assessment includes all non-functional requirements for a selected set of partitions.

Boundary

The boundary (also referred to as application boundary) is a conceptual interface between the software under study and its users. The boundary defines what is external to the application and indicates the border between the software being measured and the user. It can be perceived as a "membrane" through which data processed by transactions pass into and out of the application. Determination of the boundary is dependent on the user's external business view of the application and independent of non-functional and/or implementation considerations.

Note: The purpose, scope, and logical application boundaries need to be consistent between the FPA and SNAP process.

Partition

A partition is a set of software functions within an application boundary that share homogeneous assessment criteria and values. Within a boundary, partitions cover all software functions that constitute the application being assessed. They may cooperate between themselves to provide complete software functions to the application user and shall not overlap.

The characteristics of a partition are as follows:

■ May be used to meet non-functional requirements
■ Requires development effort that may not be reflected when sizing the functional aspect of the project/product, using FPA
■ Can be sized using SNAP categories and subcategories
■ Might coincide in simple cases with the overall application

Associate Non-Functional Requirements to Categories and Subcategories

After identification of scope and boundary, non-functional requirements are assessed using standardized categories and subcategories. The association of the non-functional requirements with categories and subcategories is performed as follows:

Identify the non-functional requirement under scope (e.g., requirements for data security; requirements to improve performance).

Category

■ A category is a group of components, processes, or activities that are used to meet the non-functional requirement.
■ Categories are divided into subcategories. Each subcategory has common features (within the subcategory) to simplify the assessment.

Subcategory

■ Subcategory is defined as a component, a process, or an activity executed within the project to meet the non-functional requirement.

Identify the SNAP Counting Unit

The SNAP Counting Unit (SCU) is unique to each subcategory; it is determined by the nature of the subcategory. For each subcategory, a unit of size is used to assess the measure of the category depicted by an SCU result. The SCU is part of the subcategory definition.

Sizing is done separately per each SCU. The definition of an SCU is important to understand. The SCU is the component or activity in which complexity and size are assessed.

The SCU can be a component, a process, or an activity identified according to the nature of the subcategory/subcategories. In some cases, the SCU is identical to the functional elementary process. In such cases, sizing of the elementary process will be performed both for its functional sizing, using Function Point Analysis, and for its non-functional sizing, using SNAP. The SCU is different for each of the subcategories so that the assessment is done against measures that are appropriate for the subcategory being assessed.

Determine the Complexity of Each SCU

The complexity of an SCU is determined by parameters or assessment questions. The assessment questions are related to specific attribute(s) that allow for the non-functional assessment of a given subcategory. The resulting answers can be:

- Ranges such as high and low
- Qualitative values such as the number of incidents of the attribute that is being rated
- Ordinal values such as 1st, 2nd, 3rd

The assessment questions and resulting values are dependent on the SCU.

The complexity parameters may include more than one type. For example, count the number of systems, then measure the percentage of those systems that are of a certain type, and finally count the number of interfaces. Then, the complexity level of the SCU within each subcategory is mapped to a non-functional size.

Calculate the Non-Functional Size of Each SCU

Based on the complexity of the SCU, a table of values will be provided to translate the complexity into SNAP Points (SP). The SNAP Points will be an arithmetic sum of the size of all the SCUs whose complexity has been determined.

Calculate Non-Functional Size (SNAP Points)

The non-functional size is the sum of SNAP Points obtained by combining all category values.

The requirement of the organization may be to provide the non-functional size for a set of non-functional requirements. Alternatively, the organization may require a non-functional size for a category such as Internal Data Movement. SNAP Points are allocated to requirements and to categories as related to the SCU. Therefore, a breakdown by category or a set of non-functional requirements can be reported.

An example may be that security is more important to the organization than usability. In such a case, the non-functional size can be determined using the categories and subcategories related to Security and then determining the SNAP Points. The same process can be repeated for the categories and subcategories related to Usability to determine the SNAP Points. The non-functional size can then be used to verify that categories related to Security have a greater complexity than those related to Usability.

Categories and Subcategories

The SNAP Assessment Model is structured to four broad level categories. Every category has subcategories facilitating measurement of a detailed assessment on the application requirements. Tables 26.1 through 26.22 provide detail on the Categories and their corresponding Subcategories. They are taken directly from the The SNAP Assessment Practices Manual [2].

Category 1: Data Operations

Table 26.1 Category 1: Data Operations

Data Operations	This Data Operations category relates to how data is processed within the SCU to meet the non-functional requirements in the application. This process does not cross the assessed application boundary.

Subcategory 1.1: Data Entry Validation

Table 26.2 Subcategory 1.1: Data Entry Validation

Definition	Operations that are taken either to allow only certified (predefined) data or to prevent the acceptance of uncertified data.
SCU	The functional elementary process.
Example	Application ABC requires preparation of specific set of restricted data depending on the Client Access level. The restricted data performs multiple validations before displayed to user. Number of complex field validations performed are assessed SNAP Points.

Subcategory 1.2: Logical and Mathematical Operations

Table 26.3 Subcategory 1.2: Logical and Mathematical Operations

Definition	Logical decisions, Boolean operations, and mathematical operations applied on the process (for functional or non-functional purposes).
SCU	The functional elementary process.
Example	Application requires generating multilevel complex reports from very high volume of data. To meet this requirement, it is required to create joins to combine folders that are not joined when tables are loaded from the database. Number of data elements and number of independent paths are assessed in SNAP Points.

Subcategory 1.3: Data Formatting

Table 26.4   Subcategory 1.3: Data Formatting

Definition	Any change in a transaction that deals with structure, format, or administrative information not directly relevant to functionality that is seen by the user.
SCU	The functional elementary process.
Example	Application requirement needs to store the data in specific structure and format. The change in data format should not be visible to an end user. Number of data elements formatted or transformed are assessed in SNAP Points.

Subcategory 1.4: Internal Data Movements

Table 26.5   Subcategory 1.4: Internal Data Movements

Definition	Data movement within application boundary.
SCU	The functional elementary process.
Example	Application functionality requires taking internal data from one partition to another within the application boundary. Number of data element moves between the partitions are assessed in SNAP Points.

Subcategory 1.5: Delivering Functionality by Data Configuration

Table 26.6   Subcategory 1.5: Delivering Functionality by Data Configuration

Definition	Functionality that is provided by adding, changing, or deleting reference data information from the database with no change of the code or the database structure.
SCU	The functional elementary process.
Example	Requirement to add/change the data to enable access to a specific user on multiple functionalities. This data level change or data configuration is assessed.

Category 2: Interface Design

Table 26.7 Category 2: Interface Design

Interface Design	This category relates to the end user experience. This category assesses the design of UI processes and methods that allow the user to interface with the application.

Subcategory 2.1: UI Changes

Table 26.8 Subcategory 2.1: UI Changes

Definition	Changes or information added to user interface (UI) that does not change the functionality of the system but affect non-functional characteristics (such as usability, learnability, attractiveness, accessibility).
SCU	Each SCU is a set of screens as defined by the functional elementary process.
Example	ABC application has a requirement to adopt UI standards as client mandate. This high-importance user interface has complex processes to display graphics, UI control validations, and complies with ADA standard 508.
	SNAP assesses the number of UI data elements and the complexity of UI change.
	Note: The functional process counts the sets of screens within one elementary process.

Subcategory 2.2: Help Methods

Table 26.9 Subcategory 2.2: Help Methods

Definition	Information provided to the users that explains how the software provides its functionality.
SCU	Set of screens as defined by the functional elementary process.
Example	ABC application has help feature that has to be dynamically supported with pop-up context help aid.
	SNAP assesses the type of help and number of help items impacted—added/changed.

Subcategory 2.3: Multiple Input Methods

Table 26.10   Subcategory 2.3: Multiple Input Methods

Definition	The ability of the application to provide its functionality while accepting multiple input methods.
SCU	The functional elementary process.
Example	ABC application added operations that support multiple language; function keys; auto fill; dynamic menus; shortcut key; common keys; navigation— screen/page level. SNAP assesses the number of media (fax, PDF, Office document, screen, voice message, SMS) and number of UI controls within the elementary process.

Subcategory 2.4: Multiple Output Methods

Table 26.11   Subcategory 2.4: Multiple Output Methods

Definition	The ability of the application to provide its functionality while using multiple output methods.
SCU	The functional elementary process.
Example	ABC application added operations that support multiple language; control for page wise data display, data sort of various order, content/literal add or change, third party UI controls for navigation— screen/page level. SNAP assesses the number of media (fax, PDF, Office document, screen, voice message, SMS) and Number of UI controls within the elementary process.

Category 3: Technical Environment

Table 26.12   Category 3: Technical Environment

Technical Environment	This category relates to aspects of the environment where the application resides. It assesses technology as well as changes to internal data and configuration that do not provide added or changed functionality from a FP perspective.

Subcategory 3.1: Multiple Platforms

Table 26.13   Subcategory 3.1: Multiple Platforms

Definition	Operations that are provided to support the ability of the software to work on more than one platform.
SCU	The application within the boundary.
Example	ABC application is a large distributed system that needs to be built on multiple platforms. This system is composed of multiple software and hardware platforms.
	Note: Application that has more than one S/W, H/W and O/S platform—each is qualified to SNAP assessment under this subcategory.

Subcategory 3.2: Database Technology

Table 26.14   Subcategory 3.2: Database Technology

Definition	Features and operations that are added to the database without affecting the functionality that is provided.
SCU	The physical tables/number of FTRs (File Type References).
	Count complexity of each physical unit as SCU.
Example	An application has non-functional requirements to improve performance, need to study its DB, tables, and data volume. The requirement is that the application will have to perform lookup and respond with higher volume of data.
	Number of tables impacted in this SCU are assessed in SNAP Points.

Subcategory 3.3: System Configuration

Table 26.15   Subcategory 3.3: System Configuration

Definition	System configuration provided by adding, changing, or deleting information from the database with no change in the code and the database structure.
SCU	The application within the boundary.
Example	Application requires data connection via single/multiple connectivity. The requirement refers to the configuration file for any addition/changes in the connectivity details.
	Application requires to connect with Hardware has Device Configuration wireless device or any wired devices setup. The requirement refers to the device configuration file for any addition/changes in the connectivity.

Subcategory 3.4: Batch Processing System

Table 26.16   Subcategory 3.4: Batch Processing System

Definition	Multiple batch job executed thru a single elementary process.
SCU	The elementary process.
Example	ABC application must perform EOD jobs including interest calculation, payment processing, data backup within the application, etc. Number of batches or transactions executed with this elementary process gets assessed in SNAP Points.

Subcategory 3.5: Multiple Technology

Table 26.17   Subcategory 3.5: Multiple Technology

Definition	Transaction that executes on more than one technology.
SCU	The functional elementary process.
Example	ABC application has multiple components that interface with other components to be compatible with more than one technology. Number of technologies on which the application executes is assessed here **Rule:** Application that has more than one technology is qualified to SNAP Point under this subcategory.

Category 4: Architecture

Table 26.18   Category 4: Architecture

Architecture	This category relates to the design and coding techniques utilized to build and enhance the application. It assesses the complexities of modular- and/or component-based development.

Subcategory 4.1: Mission Critical (Real-Time System)

Table 26.19   Subcategory 4.1: Mission Critical (Real-Time System)

Definition	Critical transaction to business that instantaneously transacts the data within stipulated time.
SCU	The elementary process that contains critical transactions.
Example	Applications must run critical functionalities to process information within agreed/mandated time frame (6–8 seconds) for highly critical data or user must sense that it is immediate.
	Number of critical transactions within the elementary process.

Subcategory 4.2: Component-Based Software

Table 26.20   Subcategory 4.2: Component-Based Software

Definition	Pieces of software used to integrate with previously existing software or to build components in the system.
SCU	The functional elementary process.
Example	An application made of multiple components. The components may be business objects, UI control objects, service objects, remote procedure calls.
	Number of unique components interfaced within the SCU process is assessed here.

Subcategory 4.3: Design Complexity

Table 26.21   Subcategory 4.3: Design Complexity

Definition	Support for growing number of users and data over time. Also refers to modular design that helps to localize changes and identify reusable components.
SCU	The assessed application within the boundary.
Example	An application must be designed to be modular that helps localize changes, and identify more reusable components. The application should also support a growing number of users and data over time.
	SNAP assessment count.
	Number of applications interfacing across application boundary and components within application boundary.
	Number of reusable components.

Table 26.22   SNAP Calculation Table

# of Items	Logical and Mathematical Operations	Data Formatting
2	2 × Simple	2 × Simple
2	2 × Simple	2 × Medium
4	4 × Medium	4 × Complex
2	2 × Complex	2 × Complex

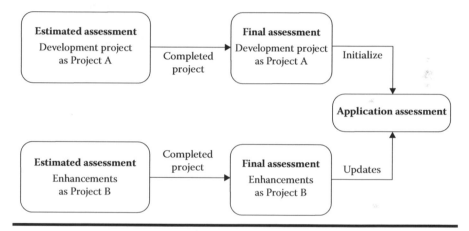

Figure 26.2   Types of SNAP assessments and their relationships.

Determine the Type of Assessment

This section explains the types of SNAP assessments.

Non-functional requirements assessed at the early stage of development or enhancement gets more clarity and identifies additional non-functional characteristics during its life cycle than the original requirements. It becomes important to realize the actual non-functional requirements delivered to the user. Therefore, it is essential to update the application size upon completion of the project.

If the size changes during development, the non-functional size at the end of the life cycle should accurately reflect the full non-functional characteristics delivered to the user.

Figure 26.2 illustrates the types of SNAP assessments and their relationships. (Project A is completed first, followed by Project B.)

The functional size and the non-functional size can be measured for either projects or applications. From the above schematic representation, the types of assessment are determined based on the purpose, as one of the following:

- Development project assessment
- Enhancement project assessment
- Application assessment

Development projects develop and deliver the first release of a software application. The project's non-functional size is an assessment of the non-functional requirements provided to the users with the first release of the software.

Enhancement projects develop and deliver adaptive maintenance. The project's non-functional size is a measure of the non-functional characteristics added, changed, or deleted at the completion of an enhancement project.

An application is a cohesive collection of automated procedures and data supporting a business objective; it consists of one or more components, modules, or subsystems. An application's non-functional size is a measure of the non-functional characteristics that an application provides to the user, determined by the application SNAP assessment. It is also referred to as the baseline or installed non-functional size. This size provides a measure of the current non-functional characteristics the application provides to the user. This number is initialized when the development project SNAP assessment is completed. It is updated every time the completion of an enhancement project alters the application's size.

SNAP Examples

The examples below provide an explanation on applying the SNAP model in project scenarios. This section intends to facilitate the user's gaining of an initial understanding, appreciation, and application of the model in projects.

The title of the section provides a brief one line summary of the example, with the requirement type and the transaction type. The "Overview of the Requirement" section details the project requirements as documented in the project's requirement specification. The "SNAP Explanation" section helps in understanding and deciphering these project requirements.

Example 1: Security Requirement: Encoding/Decoding Transaction

Overview of the Requirement: The proposed system has new hardware that defines a set of requirements and tests for a new category of devices. This device allows the encoding of screen data for virtual machines (VMs). This is required to be offloaded from the CPU to another dedicated remote hardware. This enables higher levels of scalability on a remote server. These tests ensure fidelity and compatibility, which verifies core functionality of the remote library interaction with the remote hardware. This design ensures that all supported resolutions can be handled by the device and that the quality of compression is within the functional requirements.

SNAP Explanation: This design process involves two SNAP subcategories:

1. Data Formatting—this transaction deals with the change in the structure and/or format of the data.
2. Logical and Mathematical Operations—this transaction deals with some logical decisions and mathematical operations, when testing for compatibility.

For both of them, the SCU is the elementary process.

Identify the elementary processes from the requirements. Assume the counting has identified 10 different elementary processes. At the elementary process, identify the applicable category and map to its subcategories. As per the definition, group the process as illustrated below.

- Two processes have Simple calculations and a small amount of data.
- Two processes have Simple calculations and a medium amount of data.
- Four processes have Medium calculations and a "complex" amount of data.
- Two processes have "Complex" calculations and a "complex" amount of data.

Figure 26.2 describes the types of SNAP assessments and their relationships.

Note: For details on subcategory parameters and complexity, refer to the SNAP APM.

Map the process to the SNAP subcategories. The count will be as follows:

Total count of Logical and Mathematical Operations: four Simple, four Medium, two Complex

Total count of Data Formatting: two Simple, two Medium, six Complex

Example 2: Availability Requirement: Information Available within Acceptable Time Interval

Overview of the Requirement: ABC Corp. manages an embedded real-time system. These distributed real-time systems must enforce constraints of both real-time and embedded paradigms. One of the key requirements is that the system must present the user with a display of the number of records in a database. This count of records needs to be updated in real time, and hence, the system needs to be capable of updating the displayed record count within an acceptably short interval based on the number of records changing/updating.

SNAP Explanation: The system is required to present the user with a display of the number of records in a database. This is a functional requirement. How up-to-date this number needs to be is a non-functional requirement. If the number needs to be updated in real time, the system architects must ensure that the system is capable of updating the displayed record count within an acceptably short interval of time. Further sufficient network bandwidth may also be a non-functional requirement of a system.

This process involves two subcategories:

1. Database Technology—Features and operations that are added into the database without affecting the functionality provided. The SCU is each physical unit.
2. Mission Critical (Real-Time System)—Critical transaction to business that instantaneously transacts the data within stipulated time. The SCU is the elementary process.

This requirement has three physical units and two different elementary processes:

■ Two physical units are Simple temporary files
■ One physical unit is Complex with changes in queries and views
■ One process has a "Simple" timely management report
■ One process has a "Complex" transaction that manages application performance on a large enterprise server

Note: For details on subcategory parameters and complexity weightage, refer to the SNAP APM.

The SNAP count will be as follows:

■ **Total count of Database Technology:** two Simple, one Complex
■ **Total count of Mission Critical (Real-Time System):** one Simple, one Complex

The FPA and SNAP Link

SNAP Points can be used in conjunction with Function Points to provide an overall view of the project or application including both functional and non-functional sizing. Organizations should collect and analyze their own data to determine technical productivity impacts.

Figure 26.3 illustrates the link between the FPA process and the SNAP process. The purpose, scope, and logical application boundaries need to be consistent between the FPA and SNAP processes.

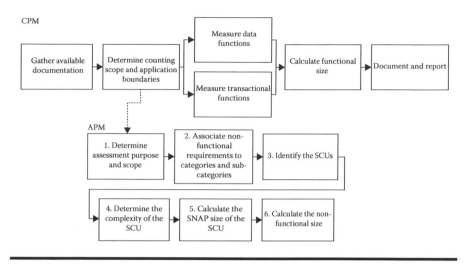

Figure 26.3   Link between the FPA process and the SNAP process.

Use of SNAP Points to Plan and Estimate Development Project Cost

Count Function Points for a project, and utilize established productivity rates based on Function Point size and project type to estimate the functional project effort.

Complete a SNAP assessment, and utilize historical data to determine the impact of SNAP Points on the project effort. Adjust the project effort up or down depending on the SNAP score to provide a functional or technical effort estimate. The relationship between non-functional size and effort is typically specific to a particular organization. Once significant SNAP assessment data is collected, a "rule of thumb" relationship should be established by industry, platform, and so on from data contained in repositories such as the International Software Benchmark Standards Group (ISBSG) benchmark repository.

Complete a risk/attribute assessment for the organizational factors that impact productivity. Utilize historical data for the risk/attribute impacts on project effort, and adjust project effort up or down appropriately to provide a functional/techni-cal/risk effort estimate.

Use of SNAP Points for Application Maintenance Cost/Resource Estimation

This would be similar to the process identified above to use SNAP Points to plan and estimate development project cost. SNAP Points should be used to estimate the overall cost and resource requirement for application maintenance.

Function Points would be used to size an application. SNAP Points would be used to size the non-functional characteristics of the application. Historical data would then be used to estimate the maintenance cost and resource requirements for the functional and non-functional size for each application in order to better plan future resource utilization and to aid in determining maintenance strategies and annual budgeting.

Use of SNAP Points to Estimate Return on Investment for Application Replacement

Count Function Points for an application to determine its functional size. Complete a SNAP assessment to determine the non-functional size of the application. Compare the estimated cost of the replacement project with the maintenance cost of the existing application to determine the potential ROI.

Use of SNAP Points to Identify Candidates for Possible Process Improvement

Complete a SNAP assessment, and utilize historical data to determine the impact of SNAP Points on the project effort. Analyze poor SNAP scores that have an adverse impact on effort, and determine if improvements in any of the subcategories could be achieved for the project or application.

Use of SNAP Points to Quantify the Impact of Current Non-Functional Strategies for Projects or Applications

The detailed responses to the SNAP assessment can be compared to the ISO 9126 characteristics to ensure the appropriate focus for either a project or application; for example, a project with more SNAP Points allocated to accuracy versus attractiveness indicates that there is more emphasis on accuracy in the project on accuracy [8].

Use of Non-Functional Alternatives to Compare Options for Delivery

Non-functional alternatives can be compared by estimating total functional and non-functional costs, for example, cost of development versus purchasing a COTS item, or by comparing technologies to deliver functionality in order to select the most appropriate technology.

SNAP, FP, and Benchmarking

A benchmark is an assessment of the current productivity of a project or an organization and is an important input to be used for improving estimation of things such as effort, staff, duration, and quality.

Benchmarking should have the following characteristics:

- It should be objective.
- It should be comparable.
- It should use historical information.
- It should be a simplification of reality.

In many organizations, benchmarking for productivity is based on two major measures: (1) size and (2) effort. The correlation between these factors has usually been impacted by things such as complexity of the project, and the methods to be used within the project.

From ISBSG data, the benchmarking between IFPUG Function Points and effort is a commonly used productivity factor.

Introducing SNAP will make it possible to compare productivity for both functional and non-functional requirements:

- FP versus effort
- SNAP versus effort

It is the hope that, in the future, it will be possible to find a further correlation between FP and SP versus effort. This can be done only by an analysis of how the combination of FPs and SPs relate to each other, which requires benchmark data.

By using the different types of productivity measures, it is possible to compare the functional productivity, the non-functional productivity, and the productivity on the basis of requirements of the project (functional and non-functional). Be aware that the productivity will still be impacted by influencers such as method, staff skills, and maturity of process.

Figure 26.4 describes a scatter plot of normalized effort against functional size.

Figure 26.5 describes a scatter plot of normalized effort against non-functional size.

This means that the usual benchmarking indicators that are used where size is a part of the equation could, in the future, be used to monitor not only quality and productivity for functional requirements, but also for non-functional requirements and the combination of both functional and non-functional requirements.

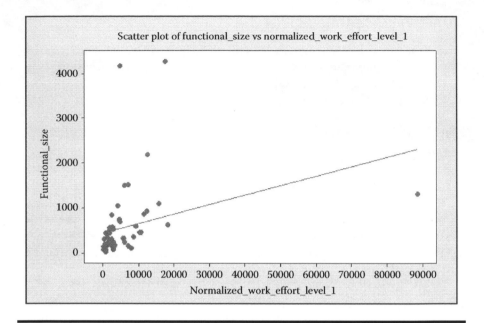

Figure 26.4   Scatter plot of normalized effort against functional size.

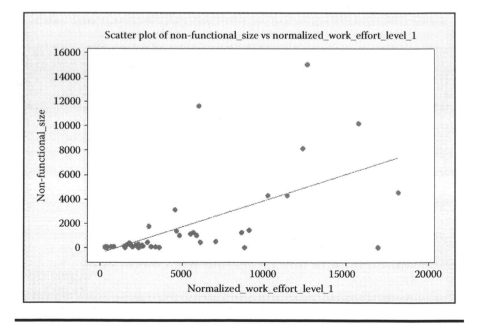

Figure 26.5   Scatter plot of normalized effort against non-functional size.

SNAP Institutionalization

This section briefly discusses how the SNAP assessment process should be implemented in an organization. Since the assessment of non-functional software aspects will most likely be carried out in parallel with other software product metrics (such as functional sizing), while being a novelty to most practitioners, a correct implementation of SNAP within the ongoing measurement program in the organization is crucial for its success.

Similar to the introduction of a general measurement program, or a benchmarking program [5], implementing SNAP might require some setup steps, and possibly an iterative approach, such as the PDCA cycle (Plan-Do-Check-Act).

Plan

In the planning phase, the scope of the SNAP program should be determined, together with its stakeholders and roles involved in the organization. The scope should derive from the general goal of the program, which generally speaking might be one of the following: estimation, assessment, or audit (or a combination). The SNAP program scope should be defined in terms of the criteria applied to identify the software systems being assessed and for each practical instantiation of SNAP, it should explicitly list the system(s) being assessed. In addition, in the planning phase, the relationships between the non-functional measure and other product (or process) metrics should be clearly identified, if any, with respect to the general goal of the assessment.

Do

Once the above has been identified in the planning phase, the first SNAP iteration should be carried out by expert practitioners, so as to carefully collect SNAP values and to report issues, feedbacks, weaknesses, and strengths of the program being applied.

Check and Act

The first iteration might therefore suggest, through the "check" phase, several improvements or refinements to "act" upon, including the definition of the scope, stakeholders, and measures being defined and collected. In order to standardize the SNAP process in the organization, lessons learned should be clearly identified and documented, and the IFPUG ITPC (SNAP team) should be informed and questioned in order to exchange clarifications and recommendations. Until a global (open, public) benchmarking process is in place, internal data collection regarding the SNAP iterations over time should be documented and analyzed in order to guarantee that the process is applied uniformly. Non-functional requirements are a natural counterpart to functional requirements, typically measured through Function Points. Particular emphasis should be put on the analysis of the relationship between functional and non-functional sizes being measured for the same software system(s), or their components. This does not mean that strong correlation should always be expected. A combination of functional and non-functional sizes might be found to provide a better means for the general measurement goals (such as estimation, for instance). Typically, one might find that one size (e.g., FP) can be used to normalize the other size (e.g., non-functional), or that one size (e.g., non-functional) can be used to characterize separate portions of the software system (measured in FPs).

After the first iteration, training material and guidelines for SNAP implementation should also be set up to expose and teach the SNAP program to beginners and new practitioners.

Training Requirements

Usability evaluations of this publication have verified that reading the APM alone is not sufficient training to apply the non-functional assessment process at the optimum level.

Training is recommended, particularly for those who are new to SNAP. To speak a language as a native, learning the grammar and the words alone are not sufficient. They just provide a framework. You need language experience to understand how the language is spoken in practice, how the grammar rules should be applied, what idiomatic expressions are common, and so on. The same is true for SNAP. The knowledge of process and rules is a necessity, but the knowledge alone is not a sufficient condition to apply SNAP correctly.

This APM is one module in the IFPUG documentation. All documents complement one another, particularly the Function Point Counting Practices Manual (CPM) and the APM.

IFPUG has not yet developed an official training certification or training path for SNAP, but it will occur in the future.

Benefit for Organizations Using SNAP

A non-functional assessment will assist IT organizations in multiple ways. It will provide insight into projects and applications to assist in the estimation and analysis of quality and productivity. Used in conjunction with FP measures, the non-functional assessment provides information on items that impact quality and productivity in a positive or negative way. Having this information enables software professionals to do the following:

■ Better plan, schedule, and estimate projects
■ Identify areas of process improvement

- Assist in determining future technical strategies
- Quantify the impacts of the current technical strategies
- Provide specific data when communicating non-functional issues to various audiences

Having both Function Point (FP) data and non-functional requirements provides a more complete picture of software development. The FP information is quantifiable and represents a good measure of the functional project and/or application size. Providing a quantifiable measure for the non-functional information allows organizations to build historical data repositories that can be referenced to assist in decision making for the technical and/or quality aspects of projects and/or applications.

References

1. IFPUG. 2004. *Counting Practice Manual, version 4.2.1.* International Function Point Users Group. www.ifpug.org/publications (accessed December, 2011).
2. IFPUG. 2011. *Software Non-functional Assessment Process (SNAP) Assessment Practice Manual (APM).* www.ifpug.org/publications.
3. International Organization for Standardization (ISO) website: www.iso.org (accessed December, 2011).
4. Institute of Electrical and Electronics Engineers (IEEE) website: www.ieee.org (accessed December, 2011).
5. IFPUG. 2004. *Guidelines to Software Measurement (GSM), Version 2.0.* International Function Point Users Group, website: www.ifpug.org/publications/guidelines.htm (accessed December, 2011).
6. ISO. 2001. *ISO 9126-1:2001, Software Engineering – Product Quality – Part 1: Quality Model.* International Organization for Standardization, website: www.iso.org.

About the Authors

The authors are made up of the ITPC solicited volunteers from the IFPUG membership that became part of the core team for the Software Non-functional Assessment Process (SNAP). The team was selected based on the experience of the members and their demographics. The ITPC wanted to ensure that an international group of members would be included on the team. The team was made of members from Canada, Denmark, India, Israel, Italy, and the United States. The team was made up of a diverse group of IT professionals. Therefore, there were a number of different views and ideas on how to solve the problem. The solution was not easy or straightforward. The members were, however, eager to create a solution and reach a consensus. The members of the core team worked very hard and devoted many hours. The team participating in the chapter was a sub-team of the core team.

Christine Green has been involved in measurement and estimating for the last 10 years and is currently leading a team of estimating and measurement specialists at HP in Europe. She is the vice-chair of the IFPUG IT Performance Committee and has acted as the project manager for the SNAP project.

Dan Bradley has 40 years experience as a developer, manager, and champion of information technology. In this capacity, he has led the migration of IT development from unit record based 2 GLs to the current object-oriented, GUI, client/server, web-targeted environment. As IFPUG's ISBSG representative, IT Performance Committee Chair and IFPUG member for over 20 years, he has broad experience with industry benchmarking of the software development process.

Talmon Ben-Cnaan is a quality manager at Amdocs (Amdocs is a market leader in telecommunication business support and operational support systems with more than 19,000 employees). He led the quality measurements in his company, responsible for collecting and analyzing software measurements from software development projects and providing quality reports to senior management, based on measurements. The author was also responsible for implementing Function Points in his organization. He is an IFPUG member and a PMP.

Wendy Bloomfield is a Certified Function Point Specialist (CFPS) since 1998, currently working as a metrics analyst at a large Canadian insurance company. She has over 25 years of experience in the IT industry, specifically in the areas of software development, analysis, design, quality assurance, and Function Point Analysis. Her focus of the last 10 years has been on Function Points, metrics, compliance, and balanced scorecards. Wendy is currently a member of IFPUG IT Performance Committee.

David Garmus is an acknowledged authority in the sizing, measurement, and estimation of software application development and maintenance. Cofounder of the David Consulting Group, he serves as a Past President of the International Function Point Users Group (IFPUG), a past member of the IFPUG Counting Practices Committee and a current member of the Software Non-functional Assessment Process Working Group. Garmus is a Certified Function Point Specialist, has a BS from UCLA and an MBA from Harvard University. He has been a frequent speaker at ITMPI, IFPUG, QAI, PMI, SEI and IEEE Conferences, and he has authored numerous articles and four books.

Jalaja Venkat is a Certified Function Point Specialist (CFPS), currently leading the software estimation program for a large Indian IT organization. Her areas of experience in the IT industry are software development, quality assurance, and software estimation processes. For the last 14 years, she has been focusing on process compliance, software training, estimation process definition, implementation, and Function Point consulting for IT clients.

Steve Chizar is a retired IT specialist from the Navy Supply Information System Activity (NAVSISA), now known as the Naval Supply System Business Solutions Activity. He has 25 years of experience in the IT industry, specifically in the areas of software development, analysis, design, quality assurance, and Function Point

Analysis. His focus of the last 10 years of his career was on Function Points, metrics, and processes. Steve is currently a member of IFPUG Education Committee and a member of the Software Non-functional Assessment Practices team.

Luca Santillo is a Certified Function Point Specialist (CFPS) since 1996, CEO at Agile Metrics, and a metrics consultant and trainer in Italy and worldwide. He developed several techniques and guidelines for Function Point counting in data warehousing, ERP packages, middleware applications, and early & quick sizing. His focus of the last 10 years has been on Function Points, software process productivity, and benchmarking. Luca is currently the president of the Italian Function Point Users Group—Italian Software Metrics Association (GUFPI-ISMA) and Honorary Treasurer and director at the International Software Benchmarking Standards Group (ISBSG).

OUTSOURCING
INTRODUCTION

Sivasubramanyam Balasubramanyam

Almost all large corporations outsource today, procuring some goods or services under contract from an outside supplier, for a variety of their requirements. This has become a reality in the globalized world we live in. Organizations evaluate vendors using various measures or hire the services of a consultant to help them evaluate prospective vendors and their services. This section presents four chapters that touch on this topic.

Barbara Beech is a Senior Business Manager with over 27 years of IT experience working for AT&T. She also serves the International Function Point Users Group (IFPUG) on the Education Committee. Barbara's chapter "Software Measurement and Service Levels" starts with a discussion on the challenges people face when defining service level agreements. She outlines an approach that starts with the understanding of the current performance level, which will help in arriving at a meaningful and achievable service level agreement. Barbara explains the process of constructing a service level, making it operational, and reporting on it and ends with how a service level agreement can be assessed.

Harold van Heeringen is a Senior Metrics Consultant at Sogeti Nederland, specializing in software estimation models and benchmarking practices. He is also a member of various metrics related organizations like NESMA, COSMIC, and ISBSG. Harold's chapter, "Request for Proposal Management—Answering Metrics-Based Bids," presents the appropriate way of requesting and responding to metrics-based requests for proposals (RFPs). He talks about the problems facing the IT industry in the context of outsourcing. Harold highlights the issues on the outsourcer and supplier sides and what must be done to correct them; he finally ends with guidelines on how to ask the right questions and how to respond to a RFP more objectively.

Pierre Almen is an IT management consultant at ImproveIT, specializing in software metrics. Pierre's chapter, "SOS—Application Quality Issues!" examines issues and measures that have to be considered by the Chief Information Officer (CIO) before embarking on outsourcing software development or maintenance. He starts off with the required metrics and their possible sources. Almen presents two case studies that explore the subject from the vendor and the outsourcer perspectives. Along the way he gives examples of the metrics used in the case studies and guides the reader on how and what to measure to gauge the performance of the outsourcing process.

Roberto Meli is the CEO of DPO Srl and was a past chairman of the COSMIC measurement practices committee. Roberto's chapter, "Software Measurement in Procurement Contracts," starts by introducing concepts used in software contracts. He then describes the customer–supplier relationship, the tender process, execution of the contract, and the termination of the contract. Roberto goes on to talk about how the measurement model is applicable to contract execution, and the why, what, how, and when to measure for development and enhancement projects, and ends with who will measure.

Chapter 27

SOS—Application Quality Issues!

Pierre Almén

Contents

Background

Outsourcing of application development and maintenance continues to grow worldwide.

An unspoken reason for outsourcing is often dissatisfaction with in-house ability, competence in new areas, service, cost, and quality. A survey done by IDC Nordic shows the top five business challenges for Chief Information Officers (CIOs) in 600 Nordic companies [1]; see Figure 27.1.

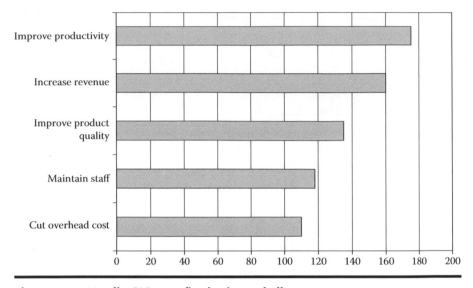

Figure 27.1   Nordic CIOs top five business challenges.

When outsourcing companies onshore, nearshore, or offshore are tempting with low hourly rates, it is easy to decide to let someone else take care of software development and/or maintenance. However, how many CIOs have knowledge of the whole process, the complete delivery chain that will be affected when outsourcing? Often not before the outsourcing decision, but for sure they will acknowledge that when the outsourcing supplier has started to deliver what was agreed in the outsourcing contract. That is a bit too late. Unfortunately, a majority of all CIOs do not take advantage of existing internal and external data for development of projects or maintenance of applications when a contract is negotiated and written. It is not enough to have the data; you must understand how to match the data with the services you want to outsource. It does not stop there; you should avoid having services that mix fixed-price components with time and material components. With a mix, no one really knows if the supplier performs as was wished and expected, from the client side or from the supplier side. It often seems that the thoughts in the CIOs minds are "I'm making a decision! Stop confusing me with facts!" The only way to assure that outsourcing of application development and maintenance is effective and reaches the goal of the outsourcing is to measure the services produced by the outsourcing supplier and have metrics that are relevant and allow you to monitor and control the outsourcing arrangement, though that is not enough. The metrics produced will only show the current performance, cost, quality, etc., they do not say if they are competitive. To know that, you need to benchmark your services and their related metrics. That can be done against either internal or external data. There are pros and cons with both types of data.

Some advantages with internal data are the following:

- You know a little more about the projects and applications that are included in the reference data.
- You can follow the internal progress.

Some advantages with external data are the following:

- You will get the market perspective and comparison.
- It is normally of better quality and consistency especially if the data is from a benchmarking company that can map and collect data of services regardless of how each company is organized.

No matter if you use internal or external data to measure the services from an outsourcer, you need a baseline as a starting point. That will give you an excellent possibility to both follow up on the outsourced services and to communicate any progress against the current challenges for your IT organization. So do not wait, make sure you implement a measurement program before you start your outsourcing.

Following are two outsourcing cases in which quality issues have been discovered.

The first is from an outsourcing supplier view when they realize shortly before delivery of an application package to a client that they probably have assured a quality level that it too high for the developed application package. Was their suspicion right and, if so, what is the market quality level?

The second is from a company view, where the company offshored maintenance of an application package. They suddenly discovered that the contract quality key performance indicators (KPIs) and metrics created by the offshoring supplier did not match the signals the manager got from his own department.

SOS Case 1

A Nordic outsourcing company was developing a package of applications for a Nordic company. At the end of the developing process, the outsourcing company suddenly realized that the quality level (very few defects and with no critical defects at all in the installed software) for the delivered package did not seem to be realistic. The contract had been written without using any kind of benchmarking data, neither internal nor external quality data. The project manager (PM) sent an SOS: "We have a quality issue!" Can we help him to show the market application quality level and how the quality level in the contract related to the market? The following were the assumptions for this assignment:

- Very limited budget to do this.
- Need the result within a couple of days.

- A ballpark figure was enough.
- The project was in the coding and testing phase (waterfall development method used).
- Use Function Points (FPs) based quality level KPIs.
- Use fast counted FPs.
- Count FPs for one application within the application package.

Although the application quality level was the trigger for this assignment, we agreed to extend the scope a little. The reason was that with a small extension to the budget we could calculate a couple of more KPIs/metrics as this list shows:

- Create estimated KPIs/metrics for the application and a baseline from a reference database
  - Application quality as number of monthly discovered defects in production
  - Distribution of defects based on severity (only from reference database)
  - Application productivity as number of Full Time Equivalents (FTEs) needed to maintain (support, defect fixing, technical enhancement) the whole application package
- Create estimated KPIs/metrics for the project and a baseline from a reference database
  - Project productivity as number of FPs per person month (120 working hours)
  - Project delivery capacity (time-to-market) as number of FPs per project calendar day (from project start until end of code and test phase)
  - System test defects to be found (based on system test defects per 1000 FPs from reference database)
  - Acceptance test defects to be found (based on system test defects per 1000 FPs from reference database)

We decided to use the following fast FP counting method:

- Count only Transaction functions without defining their complexity, for example, just record all Transaction functions
- Assume the same complexity of all Transaction functions
- Assume the Data function share of the total FP count

The project manager selected the application within the application package that we should use when counting the FPs. This application was still in the development phase. One of the developers showed us the functionality specifications and based on that, the user functionality that could be FP Transaction functions was derived. More information about the FP Analysis (FPA) method and how you count FPs can be found on the International Function Points Users

Group (IFPUG) website [2] and in other abstracts within this book. Chapter 41 in this book shows an overview of the FPA process and accuracy of the counted FP size.

To get an additional and even rougher estimate for this application, information was collected about the number of lines of code for each programming language used. The lines of code can be used for backfiring of FPs, but with a pretty low accuracy [2].

Results Based on Counting One Application within the Application Package

Based on our walkthrough of the functionality specifications, we estimated the functional size for the whole application package to be just over 4900 FPs based on following assumptions:

■ All transactions have medium complexity (+5% based on our own international experience).
■ +10% for missing functions or functions that will be added to the functionality specifications.
■ The share for the Data functions is estimated to be 30% (often-used rule of thumb).
■ The share for this application out of the total application package was estimated by the project manager to be around 13%.

With the same counting data, we used ratios from a study done at Cologne University (presentation at the 2006 IFPUG ISMA conference) to calculate the total FPs for the application package [3]:

■ Ratio is based on the Transaction functions External Input (EI) and External Output (EO).
■ +10% for missing functions or functions that will be added to the functionality specifications.
■ The total application package based on assumptions above is estimated to be between around 4160 FPs to around 4530 FPs (depending on if it was a pure host or PC system).

These results based on the "Cologne study" indicate that the accuracy of the size of this selected application itself seems to be reasonably good, especially when considering the minor effort spent for the counting session.

Using the backfiring method for the lines of code for the whole application package, we calculated the functional size to be between 12,700 and 24,000 FPs.

The backfiring method indicated a much higher FP value and although it is a method with low accuracy, the backfiring result could be an indication that the counted part of the application package could have a lower functional share of the total application package, that is, the estimated functional size of the total package should be higher.

The next step was to select comparable data from the benchmarking database. This database consists of data collected from thousands of projects and applications when benchmarking companies all around the world. Using a documented and consistent method when collecting this raw material will return high-quality reference data. Keep that in mind when you consider using external reference data and are comparing different sources. The data presented as the "Ref Grp" is the average for a selected number of good performing companies. It is not a general market average. It is more a target for very good performance, but it can be used as a target and the performance by the reference group companies is achievable.

Based on the result of counting just one of the applications, the project productivity and delivery capacity was calculated and presented in Figure 27.2 as "Proj Appl 1." "Ref Proj" is the average for similar projects (size, type, environment, etc.).

With the available data, we calculated the number of hours per project day, as shown in Figure 27.3. Together with the fact that this project, for example, had a quite high scope creep, the high number of worked hours per calendar day can explain a reasonable part of the low productivity.

Using the benchmarking database, we could estimate the number of defects to be found in the system test and the acceptance test derived from defect levels found for similar projects in the benchmarking database. The result is shown in Figure 27.4.

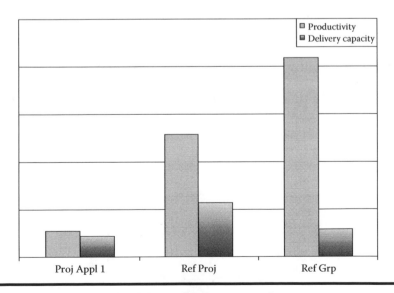

Figure 27.2　Project productivity and delivery capacity.

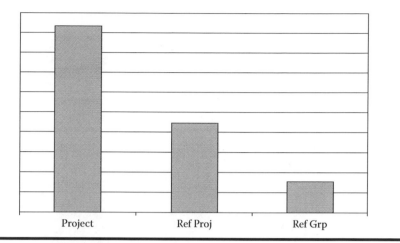

Figure 27.3 Hours/project day.

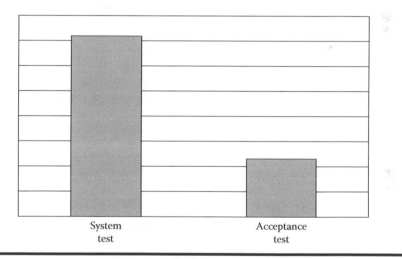

Figure 27.4 Number of defects predicted in test.

The trigger for this assignment, the SOS from the project manager asking for benchmarking data showing quality levels, was of course calculated and presented. In Figure 27.5, you can see the estimated reported number of defects per month for the whole application package based on the benchmarking data for similar big applications. The quality levels shown for big applications in the benchmarking database (Ref Appl) and for the reference group data (Ref Grp) are number of reported defects in a year per maintained 1000 FPs, that is, they have different values in the *y*-axis. In this figure, you can also see the predicted number of FTEs that will be needed to maintain this application during one year. The reference data (Ref Appl and Ref Grp) shows the number of FTEs needed for maintaining

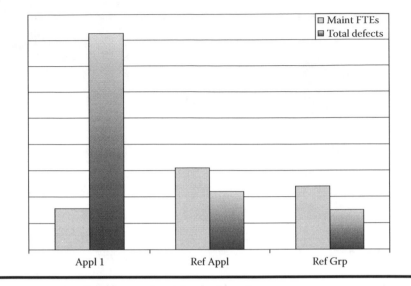

Figure 27.5   Application productivity and quality.

10,000 FPs. For the reference data, you can observe that the quality level and the productivity are lower (needs more personnel to maintain the same FP size) for a similar big application compared to the average for the reference group. Remember that the reference group value is the average of selected good performing companies and not an average in the benchmarking database.

The last metric we created was how the reported defects for an application are distributed based on severity levels. The project manager could now see how many defects of different severity levels that his application probably would have in the first year after implementation. The most important aspect here was to show that the customer could normally expect to find critical errors in a new developed application of this kind.

The outsourcing company was very pleased to get these kinds of facts without spending a lot of money and resources. Based on that and the indication that we presented that the functional size of the application package could be a bit bigger, they decided to raise the accuracy of the presented result by letting us include one more of the applications in this application package. The application package consisted of different kind of applications and with two applications of different types included in the results, we increased the chance to get more accurate and representative KPIs/metrics.

Results Based on Counting Two Applications within the Application Package

The counting process including a second application was the same as for the first application. The only difference is in the calculation and presentation of the results, where we now could show the total result based on each of the included applications and a total result based on both these two applications.

After our walkthrough of the functionality specifications for this second application within the application package to be developed, we estimated the functional size for the whole application package to be just under 8200 FPs based on the following assumptions:

■ All transactions have medium complexity (+5% based on our own international experience).
■ +10% for missing functions or functions that will be added to the functionality specifications.
■ The share for the Data functions is estimated to be 30% (often-used rule of thumb).
■ The share for this application out of the total application package was estimated by the project manager to be around 20%.

With the same counting data, we used ratios from a study done at Cologne University (presented at the 2006 IFPUG ISMA conference) to calculate the total FPs for the application package for this second application [3]:

■ Ratio is based on the Transaction functions EI and EO.
■ +10% for missing function or functions that will be added to the functionality specifications.
■ The total application package based on the assumptions above is estimated to be between around 6860 FPs to around 7450 FPs (depending on if it was a pure host or PC system).

This fast counting method gives a small difference compared to the fast counting method that was used and the difference is about the same order of magnitude as when counting the first application.

When combining the two fast FP counted applications from the application package using our fast counting method, an estimated functional size for the total application package was calculated to be just under 6900 FPs.

With the functional size estimated for the two selected applications, the project productivity and delivery capacity KPIs were calculated and presented (Figure 27.6).

The next step was to estimate the total number of defects to be found in the system test and the acceptance test, now with a functional size estimated from a second application and based on deriving the total functional size from the two counted applications. The number of defects per 1000 FPs is shown for the "Ref Proj" as one of the results in Figure 27.7.

We could now finally answer the SOS question from the project manager as to whether the quality level in the contract was achievable and the market comparable quality level they had to deliver. In Figure 27.8, we presented the estimated number

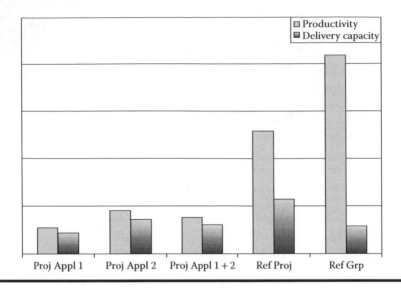

Figure 27.6   Project productivity and delivery capacity.

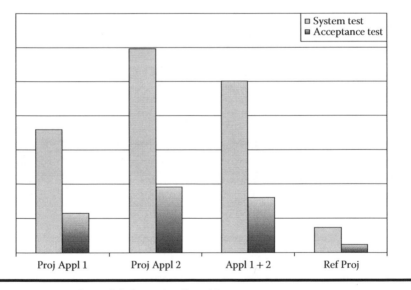

Figure 27.7   Number of defects predicted in test.

of defaults that the client can expect to find the first year in production based on quality levels for similar applications (size, age, type, environment, etc.). Because we had already presented the distribution based on defect levels for similar applications, we could in addition break down the estimated number of defects to find the first year in defect levels. This break down is not included in the figure. We could

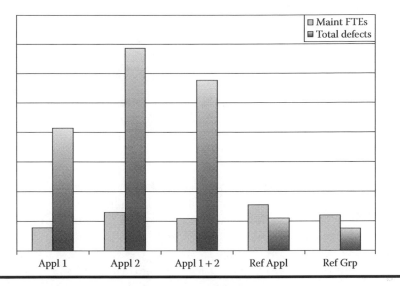

Figure 27.8 Maintenance productivity and quality.

further present the estimated number of FTEs that will be needed to maintain this application package, also shown in Figure 27.8. Please note that the data shown for "Ref Appl" and "Ref Grp" are based on a fix number of FPs.

Case 1 Summary

Using a software measurement expert and a functional sizing metric, the IFPUG FPs, together with external benchmarking data, the project manager could get the facts he wanted when he sent his SOS very quickly and without spending a lot of the project budget! Based on market data, the Nordic outsourcing company was able to show the client that, they had to expect a certain amount of defects for this application package after being implemented in production. Furthermore, the project got an indication of how many defects they will find within their system and acceptance testing, and the outsourcing company now knows how they can use facts to predict quality levels and resources needed for a new application to be maintained. With the help of the facts, they are now aware that shorter and smaller projects are more productive and easier to predict. Going over to a more agile project approach can help them improve their business.

SOS Case 2

A Nordic company offshored the application maintenance of a part of their application portfolio. In the contract, several KPIs and metrics were included. There was a penalty included if the offshoring supplier failed to meet the KPIs. There were a couple of KPIs and metrics related to the quality. One KPI was measuring the resolution time for defects and another KPI was measuring the defect reduction for the offshored application package. The application management (AM) manager at the Nordic company could not understand why the KPI report from the offshoring supplier showed green for the defect resolution time KPI. At the management meetings, he was told that it often took a long time to fix the defects found in those applications. He was also told that there were many open defects in those applications. The KPI for defect reduction that the offshoring supplier presented showed a much lower number of defects.

SOS—Can you have a look at this and explain what is going on!

We started to study the KPI reports, followed up by interviewing both people from the Nordic company and from the offshoring supplier.

The KPI for defect resolution time had four levels of resolution time depending on defect severity. In the definitions within the contract, the defect resolution time should be calculated as the time from which the supplier was notified about the defect until the offshoring supplier had presented either a temporary solution including a workaround or a permanent fix, and the solution was accepted by the Nordic company. For three of the severity levels, the KPI was measured in hours and for the fourth severity level, the KPI was measured in days. When we investigated how the KPI was calculated by the offshoring company, we found two things of which the AM manager was not aware:

1. The offshoring supplier only counted hours within "business hours," not 24 hours a day. Using that way of counting the hours, the maximum defect resolution time for defects with the high severity levels was in fact about the same as the maximum defect resolution time for defects with the lowest severity level (the level where the KPI was presented with days).
2. The offshoring supplier only counted the time that the defect was assigned to them. The offshoring supplier, for example, did not have access to production data, so they sent a database query in a mail to the application responsible at the Nordic company and stopped the clock at the same time. Sometimes, I found conversations like a ping-pong match where the offshoring supplier always was really fast to send a query to the responsible contact at the Nordic company. The total defect resolution time was far more than the KPI stipulated.

The KPI for defect reduction was calculated as a percentage reduction period over period for the open backlog of defects. When we studied this KPI, we found the same situation as for the previous KPI. The offshoring supplier excluded all the open defects where they had sent a query, etc., about the defect.

For both of the KPIs, the AM manager expected and of course wanted to get a report that showed the quality from a business perspective, that is, the perspective of the AM manager's clients! New reports were created that now included total resolution time and total backlog of open defects regardless of to whom it was assigned.

Case 2 Summary

As this shows, it is not enough to include KPIs and metrics in a contract, no matter how good and useful they seem to be, if the purpose of the KPIs is not defined and the definitions are not mutually communicated and understood.

And remember—"You can't control what you can't measure," but try to make sure that you measure the right thing and with the right data! [4]

References

1. IDC. 2009. Nordic CIO Survey.
2. http://www.qsma.com/pdfs/ITMSVol_VI11.pdf (accessed August 15, 2011).
3. Bundschuh, M. 2006. Presentation, "Early Project Estimation with Early FP Prognosis" at IFPUG ISMA Conference September 2006.
4. DeMarco, T. 1986. *Controlling Software Projects: Management, Measurement, and Estimates.* Upper Saddle River, NJ: Prentice Hall.

About the Author

Pierre Almén is a Certified Software Measurement Specialist (CSMS) and was the first in northern Europe to be a Certified Function Point Specialist in 1994. He has more than 37 years of experience within software development and maintenance. He worked 25 years for IBM Sweden, both at the IBM internal software development and maintenance department and as a management consultant at IBM clients with roles like systems analyst, test leader, project leader, project manager, and manager for a software development group and for 10 years in benchmarking and performance improvement for Compass Consulting, Sweden. Pierre is since 2008 an independent IT management consultant (ImproveIT) with a focus on software measurement and improvement. He started a Function Point network in Sweden 15 years ago and started a software measurement network at the Swedish Computer Association in 2006. Pierre has been a member of the Management Reporting Committee since 2006.

Chapter 28

Software Measurement and Service Levels

Barbara Beech

Contents

Making the Transition from Software Measurement to Service Levels

Software measurement is a topic widely written about in various areas of cost, quality, and schedule adherence. Service levels, sometimes referred to as service level agreements (SLAs), are not as widely written about and therefore, when faced with the task of implementing service levels, most people struggle with how to develop the specific service levels needed and then also how to "operationalize" them. This chapter covers more about operationalizing in the "Operationalizing the Service Level" section. This chapter discusses how to develop service levels from existing software measurements as well as how to construct new service levels that might be needed where there are no existing software measures.

Software measurements are those measurements that an organization or individual application or team develop from existing data to determine how they are performing. The data may be used to improve internal processes or procedures. The data many times captures in-process measurements and may be reported to upper management or kept in the local application group. Service levels are measurements that are developed with either an external supplier or internal supplier within the same company. They are developed because of the need to maintain a certain level of performance for an application or business process where impacts to the level of performance can have financial or operational impact on a company. Most times service levels do not measure in-process measures but instead measure the final product or a major milestone during the development process. Understanding what should be a service level versus what might just be a software measurement is critical and takes much analysis of the type of work that is being performed by the application as well as the type of business functions that might be impacted by any poor performance. Service levels should only measure performance that can have an impact on business operations where the failure would cause either missed revenue or higher operational expense. It is not necessary that every software measurement be a service level. There are many in-process measurements that have value to monitor, but if their performance was missed, it would not have a significant business impact.

So how do you identify what service levels are needed? The first area that needs to be identified is the type of work that is being performed.

Is it application development, data center operations, select application development functions such as testing or production support or some combination? Once this is understood, then you can begin to look at what service levels would be appropriate to establish for the type of work being performed.

The right service levels for application development should cover the following areas:

- Operations
    - For example, impacts to system availability, batch file processing, or system response time
- Development
    - For example, defect measures, cost measures, or on-time delivery measures
- Business process impact
    - For example, billing accuracy or order fulfillment

The best place to begin identifying service levels is to determine what currently is being measured today. It does not matter how well it is being measured at this point. You just want to know what types of measures are collected today for the various systems. Later you will deal with how well the data is being collected and what current data exists. This also includes any business measures that are being collected. If you have spent time researching and there is no current measurement data being collected, then you need to do either one of the following:

- Partner with the business or your client to determine critical applications to the business and critical processes to the business. From this information and identified measures for the type of work being performed, you will be able to begin the process of defining the service levels.
- If the client has a hard time identifying these, then the Goal, Question, Metric (GQM) [1] approach should be used where the following are asked:
    - What goal are you trying to achieve?
    - *Reduce development cost*
    - What questions do you need to answer to achieve the goal?
    - *How much is being spent on projects?*
    - What metrics support answering the question?
    - *Cost per project*

After identifying what type of measurement data exists, you can begin the task of turning these measures into service levels. More measurement detail will be needed when you begin to establish service levels. Existing measurement data is usually not very well defined, and many times how the results are calculated is left open to interpretation. Therefore, this leads to misinterpretations of data. Various groups can measure the same thing but calculate things differently. Developing a service level requires that great care put into being as specific as possible about what is included and how results are calculated. If you do not take the time to define all the details needed, then the end result can be interpreted in various ways and data can be very difficult to compare across organizations. The section "Constructing a Service Level" will review the various components of constructing a service level.

Constructing a Service Level

There are two components to developing service levels and they are looked at as part of a pyramid. They are service level definitions and service level targets.

Figure 28.1 shows the service level pyramid.

In order to develop an appropriate target for a service level, the definition needs to be completed first. Without a clear definition, it will be impossible to determine what target should be set for a particular service level.

Here is a service level checklist that can be used, which is discussed in more detail in the following:

- Types of service levels needed—what type of work is being performed (development, operations, finance). Identify what applications and functions are included.
- Identify critical applications or functions.
- Identify critical and key service levels to support applications and functions.
- Develop definition and calculation for each service level.
- Identify when the service level will be assessed against the target for performance.
- Identify how often the service levels are reported.
- Gather historical data for the service level and analyze to set a target.
- Ability to operationalize the service level—ensure data can actually be reported and is accurate.

Following is a list of components of service levels that you will need to consider when developing service levels:

- Service level name
  - Include the exact service level name here. This should be the name that is used for reporting the service level.
- Service level category
  - In other words, which category does this measure fall within (e.g., cost, quality)?

Figure 28.1 Service level pyramid.

- Service level type
  - Is this a critical or key service level being measured? When setting up service levels, some may have financial penalties, whereas you will want others to be merely reported and not tied to any financial penalties. Critical service levels are measures associated with financial penalties. Identify those service levels most critical to the business and put them in this category. Key service levels are those that should be reported but are not tied to financial penalties because they are less important to the business. Different service levels can be in the critical or key categories, or they can be the same service level but reported for only a portion of the systems (e.g., defect density for critical systems, defect density for non-critical systems).
- Definition
  - Describe the measure and how it will be calculated. This area should include exactly what the service level is meant to measure and how it will be calculated. This is a critical component as it is important that there is a clear understanding of what the service level is and how to calculate it. Any misunderstanding here will lead to the reporting of inaccurate data. Be as specific as possible here; include formulas if they are appropriate. In addition, other items to consider are the following:
    - Include start and end times for any time span during which the service delivery will be measured. Include days of the week and time of day here.
    - If a service level involves days be sure to specify if they are business days or calendar days. For example, providing a cost estimate back in 10 business days is different from 10 calendar days. That can mean the difference of 2 additional days.
    - For defect service, levels include if they are open or closed defects, and what severity levels are included. These specifics can make a big difference in the results.

The calculation should be very specific and indicate the numerator and denominator involved in the measure. It should also be specified if rounding applies. For example, should results be reported as 95% or 95.4% or 99.98%? This is very important, as it will affect service level results. There could be a big difference in a measure if the result is 99.98% or 99.9%.

Be careful in the calculation of aggregating too much data or you will end up with a lot of data washout. That is the good and bad data will get washed out based on the amount of data that is being combined. For example, if there is one large project that has good results but many small projects that do not have good results, the large project will carry more weight and hide the fact that the small projects are not doing well. In this case, splitting the results into several categories and reporting the measures separately is preferred. For example, projects greater than 1000 hours and projects less than or equal to 1000 hours, or data reflected in various Function

Point ranges (Function Points greater than 1000 and Function Points less than or equal to 1000). If data must be aggregated into one measure, try to ensure that it is weighted appropriately so that good and bad results do not cause the data to be skewed. In many cases, it is best to look at individual service level data by itself rather than trying to combine results in an aggregate view, for instance, listing any system file deliverables separately for assessments and targets. These file deliverables can relate to different systems and have different time and day requirements, so it makes more sense to evaluate them separately rather than in aggregate. Also consider breaking out specific service levels by application or groups of applications and evaluating them separately. For example, critical applications might be grouped together and non-critical applications might be grouped together.

■ Base measures
  – Should include the specific data elements that are part of the measures.
  – For example, number of severity 1 defects for each application, and base-line Function Point size for each application.
■ Reporting frequency
  – Should specify how frequently the data should be reported. All data should be reported at least monthly so trends can be monitored. Reports at the lowest level of detail should be provided even if you are not assessing or establishing a target at these levels. It is important to see as much detail as possible to understand the components of any measure. Determine if the data is reported in the month it occurred or in the month resolved.
  – For example, if a defect is opened in June and closed in July, decide if the data is reported in June or July.
■ Data source
  – If the service level is comprised of several base measures, indicate the source for each of them. This is a critical component of the service level. If it is not clear where the data comes from, then the data will either not be reported or could be reported incorrectly. If there is no automated data source, then the data source might be an Excel spreadsheet. However, it should still be specifically identified who will maintain and provide the data. Having an unclear data source is one of the biggest problems in obtaining accurate service level data.
■ Service level assessment period
  – This is the time period for collecting the service level data and when the service level results will be assessed against the service level target (in some cases for a financial penalty). The assessment period can be annual, quarterly, monthly semi-annual, or tri-annual.
  – This area takes a lot of thought and is coupled with the setting of a target. It is important to note that this can have a different value than report-ing frequency. The data may be reported monthly, but assessed against a target at a different time interval. Consider the behavior you are trying

to drive and what you want it to focus on. There are several options that can be used here:

- Annually: Use this when you care about the overall yearly results and you expect a service level to fluctuate monthly but do not necessarily want to penalize the service provider monthly. This option, in many cases, will get to a better annual target than you would be able to achieve if the service level was assessed monthly. For example, it might make sense to assess system availability on an annual basis. This allows for monthly variations in data but still meets the overall organizational performance goal.

- Quarterly: Use this when the number of opportunities for a service level may not be high enough each month to warrant a monthly target. With each service level, look at the number of possible opportunities and what the impact would be if the service provider missed one. This will allow you to have a better quarterly target than you would be able to achieve if you assessed a service level monthly. For example, on-time delivery of enhancements might be best assessed quarterly based on the number of enhancements. Let us look at a specific example. If there are only five enhancements in a month and one was missed during a month over the course of a 3-month period, the monthly result for the miss would be 80% (4/5). However, if this was assessed quarterly and there were fifteen enhancements and one was missed, the result for the quarter would be 93% (14/15). If you had a 90% service level target, the service level would be missed for the month but not for the quarter.

- Monthly: Use this option when a monthly miss of a service level can have a major impact on the business. For example, it probably makes sense to assess defect data and business impact data on a monthly basis.

■ Target

- This is a critical component of the service level that requires care and thought. In order to set a target, look at any historical data that has been collected to see what would be an appropriate target to set. This is called the baseline period. If you are working with a service provider, most will require a baseline period of collecting data prior to a target being set, unless there is historical data that can be used to develop an appropriate target. This baseline period is typically 6 months. After that, an analysis will be done on the data and a recommendation made as to what would make an appropriate, initial target. However, there are still times that targets are established by the business or at the corporate level that need to be adhered to. If, however, the current performance does not support the corporate target, then an improvement plan over time will need to be put into place to achieve the corporate target.

- Sliding targets are another method of setting a target based on the number of opportunities of a particular service level. For example, when measuring on-time delivery of enhancements, set various targets based on the actual number of enhancements that you have in an assessment period. For example, if there are greater than X requests, the target can be Y%; if there are less than X requests, the target can be lower than Y% (such as Y–5%) since there are fewer opportunities and, therefore, a greater opportunity to miss the target.

 - It is recommended that this information be kept in a separate contract document from the service level definitions included in the contract since this will be the area that will change most frequently, and you will want to minimize how much of the contract language needs to be updated as these targets change. They will change annually, but they will also change in the process of gathering and baselining data and setting targets.

■ Exclusions
 - As each service level is defined you will encounter data that for one reason or another is agreed upon to be excluded from some measures. Document any known exclusions that will not be incorporated into the service level results. For example, certain types of applications from a service level or certain severity levels from a defect measure might be excluded.

Baselining the Data and Setting Targets

Forrester [2] says the challenges in establishing service levels are the following:

■ Missing historical data
■ Lack of mechanism for data collection and resolution
■ Ill-defined requirements from business customers

Once the service levels have been identified and defined, the next challenge will be to determine an appropriate target based either on historical data, on industry data, or on an organizational goal. Unless the service level has been measured as a software measurement and data has been rigorously collected in the past, it will be very difficult to establish a target with historical data or at least to establish a target that reflects the performance that is acceptable. Rigorous in the above sentence means attention has been paid to ensure that all the base measures or data elements of the service level are accurate and complete. For example, for a defect measure if the data shows defects are closed on time only 60% of the time, you will not want to use that data to set a target. It could be the results are poor because the data has not been maintained rigorously. Therefore, in these types of instances, you will want to baseline your service level. This means collecting data over a period of months (e.g., 6 months), ensuring the data collected is accurate and the processes in place to collect the data are established, and then establishing your target. Baseline periods can be different based on the type of measure. They can be 6 months, 9 months, 12 months or if the measure is quarterly, they can be two quarters or three quarters of data. If an external supplier is involved, decide up front what the appropriate baseline period should be prior to beginning measurement. Of course, even though the service level is being baselined, data should still be reported monthly so results can be tracked.

When setting a target a number of methods can be used, and it is also important to define the method that will be used prior to the baseline period. Some options for a 6-month baseline period are the following:

- Take the monthly data and average over 6 months. For example, the average of 99%, 98%, 75%, 96%, 99%, and 95% is 93.67%, or about 94%.
- Drop the high value and the low value and then average to remove any anomalies. For example, in the same example as above, drop the high value of 99% and the low value of 75%, and then average 98%, 96%, 99%, and 95% to get 97%.
- Use the 6-month aggregate results. For example, 60 projects delivered over 6 months with 5 not being delivered on time equals 55/60 or 91.67%, or about 92%.

Operationalizing the Service Level

Reporting the Service Levels

Now that the service levels have been defined and the data sources have been identified, reporting needs to begin on the service levels. This is where the rubber meets the road to see if results can actually be produced and reported. This is what is called operationalizing. Many times, definitions and data sources are listed, and when it comes time to actually report data either the definition was not correct or there are problems with the data source so nothing really get reported and the service level really becomes abandoned. Everything can be documented but a report with valid data will be unable to be produced for various reasons. So, always question staffs who have worked on this to ensure they *really* can report the service level that has just been defined. If it cannot be reported, then you are back to the drawing board to determine if the definition is correct or there are problems with the data source, but assuming the service level can be operationalized then expect to see reports on the results. Usually there are several levels of reports produced. One is a high-level overall summary or scorecard and the other a more detailed view of the data that makes up the overall summary. Reports are typically produced monthly. Depending on the type of service level being measured, the reports can list the monthly results as well as a year to date result if the service level is being assessed annually. For certain service levels, it also makes sense to have a report that depicts a rolling average so that the monthly reports become more normalized. If there will be large fluctuations in your monthly data, consider a rolling average that smoothes out the monthly differences.

Figure 28.2 shows an example of an overall scorecard.

Figure 28.3 shows an example of a summary scorecard.

Figure 28.4 shows an example of a detailed report.

IT Example Health Report
June

February Status	EOY Outlook	Metric	Actual	Target	12 Month Trend	Good
●	●	IT	100.00	99.99		↑
●	●	Availability Critical	100.00	99.98		↑
●	●	Deliverables Key	99	98		↑
▲	●	Deliverables Response	95	97		↑
●	●	Time Delivered Defect	0.005	0.030		↓
⬡	●	Density Residual Defect	0.000	0.000		↓
●	●	Density PADs Resolved Within Commitment	90.00	90		↑

Legend: ● Green ▲ Yellow ⬡ Red

Figure 28.2 Overall scorecard example.

Assessing the Service Levels

Service levels can be assessed against their target differently from the time frame they are reported. For example, a service level might be reported monthly but assessed against its target on an annual basis. Some typical time frames for assessment are the following:

- Monthly
- Quarterly
- Tri-annually
- Semi-annually
- Annually

There are many reasons to assess a service level other than on a monthly basis. Many times based on the type of work occurring in the system and based on the number of opportunities, it is best to assess the service level quarterly. As each service level is developed, look at the historical data or current data that needs to be analyzed to determine the best method for assessment. For example, for a measure

SLA Example Performance Report

Critical Service Level - Monthly Summary

Reporting Month : **August**

CSL #	Critical Service Level Metrics	Monthly Targets Expected	Jan-10	Feb-10	Mar-10	Apr-10	May-10	Jun-10	Jul-10	Aug-10	Sep-10	Oct-10	Nov-10	Dec-10	Annual YTD Actual (Jan10-Dec10)
	Application Development & Maintenance (ADM)														
1)	On - Time Delivery of Projects														
1.1)	On - Time Delivery of Projects	99.00%	100.00%	100.00%	100.00%	100.00%	95.45%	98.85%	100.00%	100.00%					99.43%
1.2)	On - Time Deliver of Development	99.00%	100.00%	100.00%	100.00%	100.00%	100.00%	100.00%	100.00%	100.00%					100.00%
3)	**IT Availability**														
3.1)	IT Availability - Billing	100.000%	100.00%	100.00%	99.99%	100.00%	100.00%	99.98%	100.00%	100.00%					100.00%
3.2)	IT Availability - Call Center	100.000%	100.00%	100.00%	100.00%	100.00%	100.00%	99.63%	100.00%	100.00%					99.88%
3.4)	IT Availability - Sales	100.000%	99.99%	99.99%	100.00%	100.00%	100.00%	100.00%	100.00%	100.00%					100.00%
4.1)	Mean Time to Restore (MTTR) within 60 min - MC applications	65.0%	100.00%	80.00%	100.00%	N/A	60.00%	83.33%	100.00%	100.00%					86.36%
	Key Business Deliverable														
5)	**Critical Batch Job Executions**														
5.1)	Bill Files to Billing Operations On-time	99.980%	100.00%	100.00%	100.00%	100.00%	100.00%	100.00%	100.00%	100.00%					8
6)	**Business Measures**														
6.2)	Billing Accuracy - Accounts Impacted	99.66%	100.00%	99.95%	99.98%	99.98%	100.00%	100.00%	99.96%	Not Received Yet					99.99%
	Problem Management														
2)	Production Defects Closed within Commitment Timeframe for Severity 1 Defects	99.00%	100.00%	NA	100.00%	NA	NA	NA	NA	NA					0
	Governance														
7)	Customer Satisfaction(Annual)														

Figure 28.3   Summary scorecard example.

SLA Example Performance Report

Critical Service Level - ADM Monthly Summary

Reporting Month : August

CSL #	Critical Service Level Metrics	Actual Performance											YTD Actual
		Jan-10	Feb-10	Mar-10	Apr-10	May-10	Jun-10	Jul-10	Aug-10	Sep-10	Oct-10	Nov-10	Dec-10	
	Application Development And Maintenance (ADM)													
	On - Time Delivery of Projects													
	1.1) On - Time Delivery of Projects	100%	100%	100%	100%	95%	98.9%	100%	100%					99.43%
1)	Number of Projects Deployed on time	22	96	34	31	21	86	29	27					346
	Number of Projects scheduled to be deployed	22	96	34	31	22	87	29	27					348
	1.2) On - Time Delivery of Development	100%	100%	100%	100%	100%	100%	100%	100%					100.00%
	Number of Projects delivered on time	17	15	47	40	21	45	37	37					259
	Number of Projects scheduled to deliver code	17	15	47	40	21	45	37	37					259
	IT Availability													
	3.1) IT Availability - Billing	100.00%	100.00%	99.99%	100.00%	100.00%	99.98%	100.00%	100.00%					100.00%
	# Occurrences	0	0	1	0	0	1	0	0					2
	Degraded Mins	0	0	39	0	0	108	0	0					147
	Scheduled Mins	673,530	614,280	685,020	661,440	673,530	661,440	681,750	676,800					5,327,790
	3.2) IT Availability - Call Center	100.00%	100.00%	100.00%	100.00%	100.00%	99.83%	100.00%	100.00%					99.96%
3)	# Occurrences	0	1	1	0	0	9	2	0					13
	Degraded Mins	0	2	3	0	0	987	3	0					996
	Scheduled Mins	590,100	543,120	609,720	587,520	590,100	587,520	608,820	591,000					4,707,900
	3.4) IT Availability - Sales	99.99%	99.99%	100.00%	100.00%	100.00%	100.00%	100.00%	100.00%					100.00%
	# Occurrences	6	4	0	0	2	2	0	2					16
	Degraded Mins	183.35	164	0	0	59	1.84	0	59					467
	Scheduled Mins	1,926,990	1,761,600	1,967,865	1,898,850	1,927,260	1,899,090	1,957,665	1,937,190					15,276,510
4)	4.1) Mean Time to Restore (MTTR) within 60 min - MC applications	100.00%	80.000%	100.00%	N/A	50.000%	83.333%	100.00%	100.00%					86.364%
	Total Number of outages	3	5	1	0	2	6	2	3					22
	Outages resolved within 60 min	3	4	1	0	1	5	2	3					19

Figure 28.4 Detailed report example.

that looks at number of outages, it might be best to assess that annually especially if there are a small number of outages and there will not be data each month. Do not report results for one month that are really not indicative of performance. In the example of outages if there is a month in which there are 10 outages and 5 are resolved on time for a result of 50% and there is another month in which there are 2 outages and 1 is resolved on time for a result of 50%, these two situations are not equal even though the result is the same. It is better to have a lower number of outages. Therefore, it would be best in this situation if the number of outages will fluctuate monthly to have this as an annual measure. Consider having a service level assessed annually if the monthly results can fluctuate and you are mainly concerned with the overall annual view of the measure. However, remember to set the target appropriately for an annual measure versus a monthly measure. A better target should be established for an annual measure than a monthly measure since you are allowing some monthly fluctuations in the measure.

Table 28.1 shows service level examples.

Table 28.1   Service Level Examples

Cost	Responsiveness
• Cost per Function Point for projects • Cost per Function Point for maintenance • Estimate accuracy (on budget)	• Project estimates within commitment time frames • Projects delivered within commitment timeframes (on-time delivery) • Production application defects closed within commitment time frames • Project time to market • Responding to incidents within commitment time frames
Quality	*Customer Satisfaction*
• IT availability • Mean time to restore (MTTR) • Critical batch deliverables • Release quality (project defect density) • Application quality (application defect density) • Total defect containment • Defect backlog • Business process metrics	• Customer satisfaction survey

Service Level Examples

Critical and Key Batch Deliverables

- Measures the ability to meet the negotiated service level for system outputs that are determined to be critical or key to business operations, assessed by opportunities/achieved for each deliverable.
- For example, *X file delivered by 8 a.m. Monday through Saturday to X system 97% of the time.*
- Note that it is critical to specify the days and time. A poor example of a service level would be X file delivered by 8 a.m. Monday through Saturday to X system. Without mentioning the percent of time the file is to be delivered on time, the service levels would be meaningless.

System Availability

- Measures the sum of the minutes a system is available for use as scheduled divided by the number of minutes the system was scheduled for use times 100% to convert into a percentage.
- *(Total scheduled minutes for all applicable systems—minutes not available for use for all applicable systems)/Total scheduled minutes for all applicable systems * 100.*
  - For example, 99.99%.
- Note this service level could be developed in aggregate to cover 10 applications or look at each application separately.

Mean Time to Restore (MTTR)

- Measures the number of outages restored on time.
- For example, 65% of all outages restored in <60 minutes.
- The number of outages restored in <60 minutes/number of outages * 100

$$12 / 15 = 0.8$$
$$0.8 * 100 = 80\%$$

Cost per Function Point for Projects

- Measures the cost of a project based on the Function Point size of the work effort, looked at by categories of size and type of work (client/server, mainframe, and web).
- For example, $1000 per Function Point.
- For example, $300 per Function Point.

Estimate Accuracy (on Budget)

- Measures the accuracy of a time and cost estimate (given at the end of business requirements to the commitment Time and Cost).
- For example, 90% of projects meeting specified dollar range (±25%).

Business Process Metrics (BPM)

- This metric is used to measure the "quality" of a business process. It is focused on measuring the accuracy, completeness, and timeliness of a specific deliverable, business process, or business process component.
- For example, 99% of bills delivered on time.

Release Quality

- Measures the total number of defects with severity levels 1, 2, and 3 per delivered Function Point for each application release.
- Uses project Function Point count.
- For example, 0.15 = 15 defects per 100 Function Points.

Application Quality

- Measures the total number of defects with severity levels 1, 2, and 3 for an application over an annual time frame, uses application baseline count.
- For example, 0.0005 = 5 defects per 10,000 Function Points.

Total Containment

- Measures the containment of defects from production environment.
- For example, 98% of defects found prior to production.

Production Application Defects Closed within Commitment Time Frames

- Measures the number of severity 1 and severity 2 production defects attributed to application defects closed during the reporting month that met service level commitments.
- For example, 90% of severity 1 production application defects resolved within 24 hours.

Defect Backlog

- Measures the improvement in the backlog of production defects and provides a beginning balance of open defects at the start of the calendar year. Provides

a count of opened and closed (including cancelled) production defects monthly, and at the end of each calendar year, for all applications.
■ For example, 11.1% reduction in defects.

Project Estimates within Commitment Time Frames

■ Measures the percentage of project estimates that are completed within the turnaround time specified and should include all estimates (initial and final).
■ For example, 90% of all estimates returned within X days.

Projects Completed on Time

■ Measures the percentage of projects that are completed by the vendor commitment date.
■ For example, 95% of projects completed by the agreed upon commitment date.

Project Time to Market (Schedule Duration)

■ Measures the calendar duration of a project minus any work stoppages and compares duration to a targeted cycle time range based on Function Point size. Used to ensure projects are completing within reasonable cycle times based on the size of work.
■ For example, 90% of all projects meet their target cycle time range.

Customer Satisfaction Metrics

Measures satisfaction with the organization based on a survey of key stakeholders. Two different satisfaction scales are typically used with this measure. The scale from 1 to 10 can be used or the scale from 1 to 5 can be used depending on the survey needs.

Table 28.2 shows details of categories for a 10-point scale.

Benchmarking

It is natural once you have data to want to know how you compare internally as well as externally. Be very careful that you ensure you are comparing "apples to apples" when you do this. Things to consider are the following:

■ Standard definitions
  – Is the definition of the service level for the other internal or external organization the same?
  – For example, for defect measures, do both definitions include the same severity levels?

Table 28.2 Details of Categories for a 10-Point Scale

Falls far below expectations Unacceptable performance Very dissatisfied		Falls below expectations Less than satisfactory performance Dissatisfied		Sometimes meets, sometimes misses expectations Adequate (satisfactory) performance Somewhat satisfied but somewhat dissatisfied, too		Consistently meets and occasionally exceeds expectations More than satisfactory performance Satisfied		Always meets and frequently exceeds expectations Excellent to outstanding performance Very satisfied	
At **low** level	At **high** level	At **low** level	At **high** level	At **low** level	At **high** level	At **low** level	At **high** level	At **low** level	At **high** level
1	2	3	4	5	6	7	8	9	10

- Type of work being done
  - Is the application work similar?
  - For example, business applications versus defense applications.
- Application platforms
  - What types of platforms are being compared: mainframe, web, client server? There are differences in all platforms as well as the age of applications.
- A size measure
  - There needs to be a way to normalize data such as Function Points.
- Phases of development included
  - This is especially important to cost measures.
- Type of work included
  - Are the specific tasks the same?
- Type of contract and terms with supplier
- Labor rates
- Onshore/offshore mix

Once you have established similar data, then you can feel free to compare internally and externally. Just make sure that the data you are comparing is valid and accurate. One way to compare is to compare each organization to their own

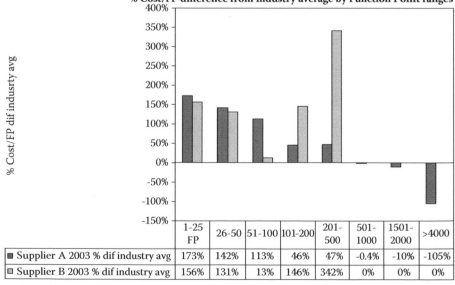

	1-25 FP	26-50	51-100	101-200	201-500	501-1000	1501-2000	>4000
Supplier A 2003 % dif industry avg	173%	142%	113%	46%	47%	-0.4%	-10%	-105%
Supplier B 2003 % dif industry avg	156%	131%	13%	146%	342%	0%	0%	0%

Figure 28.5 Example of a comparison of two suppliers using their own table of industry averages.

industry average value and then to measure the percentage difference from the industry average.

Figure 28.5 shows an example of a comparison of two suppliers using their own industry averages.

References

1. Park, R. E., W. B. Goethert, and W. A. Florac. 1996. *Goal-Driven Software Measurement - A Guidebook*. HANDBOOK CMU/SEI-96-HB-002. Pittsburgh, PA: Carnegie Mellon University.
2. Martorelli, B., A. Parker, and S. Galvin. 2008. *Building a "Starter Set" of SLAs for Managed Application Outsourcing Relationships*. Cambridge, MA: Forrester Research Inc.

About the Author

Barbara Beech is currently a senior business manager at AT&T Services, Inc. in the IT Sourcing Vendor Management Organization. Her current responsibilities include defining, reporting, and evaluating service levels for new and existing external supplier contracts. She is also responsible for the benchmarking of external supplier contracts. She has worked at AT&T for over 27 years in the area of software development. For the past 15 years, her focus has been on process and metrics. She is located in Piscataway, New Jersey. Barbara has been a member of IFPUG for 8 years, has served on the Management Reporting Committee, and currently serves on the Education Committee. Barbara received her IFPUG CSMS certification in 2006.

Barbara has a B.A. in Business Administration and Economics and completed course work for an M.S. in Educational Research. Barbara has presented at numerous conferences on the topics of software measurement and service levels. Barbara can be reached at barbara.beech@att.com or at 908-996-2128.

Chapter 29

Software Measurement in Procurement Contracts

Roberto Meli

Contents

Introduction

Software has become a competitive factor in the market for companies in the software business and for any other organization because of the pervasiveness of the Information and Communication Technologies (ICT) embedded into almost any commercial product or process. Most of the organizations have now become "software intensive." When any organizational asset enters in the "critical success factors club" of a competitive market, it is doomed to be observed at an X-ray level. In addition, the difficult global economical situation of recent years has led private and public organizations to look for a major cost and time efficiency in the ICT field maintaining or even increasing the expectations in terms of quantity and quality of software products required. These pressures have raised a project's risks and consequently increased the already high rate of unsuccessful projects to an unacceptable level. Nevertheless, the new customer expectations are not avoidable anymore and the supplying organizations must face the goal of improving the management capabilities of software development and maintenance processes in a transparent and measurable way.

At the same time, a clear trend has been found in the market: the outsourcing of increasing parts of the production process of any "customer" organization. There are many reasons for that: to keep fixed costs at a low level, to gain rapidly access to new revolutionary technologies and competencies, etc. Therefore, as a massive phenomenon, software has exited the company's closed environment to become an economical market asset and ICT outsourcing has become an important business in the world. Most of the large, medium, and small organizations buy increasing amounts of software products and services on the market instead of developing them "in house." This means that they need to quantify software just to allow the adequate draft of a contract and to reduce the potential for endless litigation.

Any efficient and effective economical transaction is based on the capability to measure the promised and then released performances as well as the relative economical reward, in a highly competitive and well balanced (between offer and demand) environment.

Unfortunately, what is considered a rule in most fields of business trades, is perceived as difficult to apply to the software market. The so-called immateriality of the software product has induced practitioners and accounting staff to consider input measures (i.e., person-hours) of a production process as if they were output measures. In this way, a software product supply has often been sold on a "person-time" basis without any guarantee that the final product met the product expectations and was worthwhile.

Excluding some qualified exceptions, software managers usually consider software measurement as a "dessert" in the project meal. If they have some extra money and time, they would get and even appreciate it, but the main course of "real productive" activities is usually the only one consumed in the "fast food" environment that the software development arena has become today. Using measurement practices, instead, might raise the rate of project success to a higher level, statistically. However, this is a valid topic at the organization level, not at the individual project level. Projects usually have very short-term strategies (they have very tight deadlines) and show an opportunistic behavior; it is not liked, in this context, to accept certain direct costs in exchange for eventual organizational-wide indirect benefits.

For these reasons, measurement has become a true issue only when it has been needed to establish and regulate contractual relationships based on a transparency concept.

In the global marketplace, a big effort has been made, in the last few years, to apply economical reward processes based on measurable parameters that are objective as much as possible. In the ICT domain, this effort led to the spreading of broad (multi-project) agreements based on an economical appreciation of software development activities derived by the amount of delivered functionality, measured by the use of the Function Point (FP) method.

However, the amount of delivered software functionality is only one of the many factors to be considered for deriving software project costs: software systems, which may differ both by "nature" (web applications, MIS, workflow systems, and so on) and by implementation aspects (architecture, hardware, programming language, tools, quality requirements, and so on), require development efforts that differ very much even when the functionality amount to deliver is the same—the effort deviation being eventually as large as 800%. Using FPs in contracts is not only a matter of writing appropriate requests for proposal or supplier's offers, it is also a matter of designing and operating an estimation and measurement process that is compliant with formal contractual provisions and with customer–supplier informal expectations. The process should be characterized by a good compromise among several attributes like precision of estimation and measurement, repeatability of results, easiness of execution, low impact on production processes, and the like. A relevant component of this system is the measurement's dashboard, an information management tool that is indispensable for contract governance.

One of the key success factors for the utilization of measurement practices in a contractual agreement is the "control" task. If no verification and validation over the quality and quantity supplied is made at the end of the supply, then the measurement process becomes useless, formalistic, and unreliable. In these cases, the FPs unitary price becomes only a variable used to win a tender with no relation with the effective cost of delivery. This will lead to market confusion and unreliability of publicly known unitary prices in transactions and finally to the opacity of any procurement process.

When managing software procurement in a market environment, the customer–supplier contractual relationship is one of the most important issues to be considered. In the case of a delivery including software development or maintenance, the economical evaluation approach adopted either in the tender process or in the day-by-day management of the contract can make that relationship very difficult to manage. As already pointed out, FPs are only a small part of the problem's solution, and in addition, they have to be used in an advanced way to give good results.

A Contractual Framework

One of the main reasons why organizations are interested in software measurements, then, is the need of estimating and controlling the effort, duration, staff, and cost of a software new development or maintenance project. Measurements are also indispensable for any successful process improvement program, but the typical actual organization (public or private) is still less sensible to methodological or internal issues than to contractual and external ones.

In Figure 29.1, we see a simplified model of a market transaction regarding a software supply.

In this customer–supplier relationship model, some requirements and constraints are "transferred" from the customer to the supplier who transforms them in a preliminary logical/technical design. The supplier then estimates the production costs and produces a requested selling price (cost to the customer), a deadline (time) together with a quantification and qualification of the offered solution. A formal/informal negotiation then takes place on the main contractual aspects, usually time,

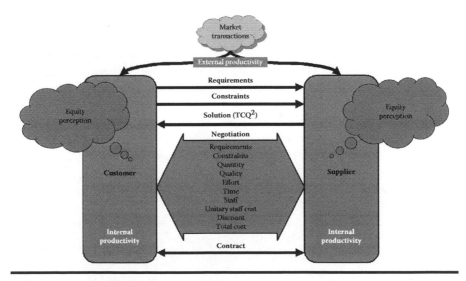

Figure 29.1 Software as a market good.

cost, quantity and quality (TCQ²), till the final agreement is (eventually) reached and a contract is drawn. After that, the supply will enter its operational life and a control process will continuously verify that the initial assumptions are fulfilled. Meanwhile, a change request process is put in place to deal with the unavoidable requirement turbulence found in modern environments. A new formal or informal transaction cycle will then be eventually started to lead to a new negotiated agreement. Eventually, the supply might be terminated by the parts involving a shared compensation for the activities already done. This scheme, apparently tailored on a "waterfall" process model, can be applied, with some variances, to an incremental, evolutionary, or agile approach as well.

In the negotiation phase, the customer is not particularly interested in the development process characterization on which she/he has no complete access (even if in an ISO 9001:2008 certificated quality framework, this is not completely true). Therefore she/he will tend to compare the economic indicators of the supplier proposal(s) to the market and internal averages ratios regarding productivity and unitary prices for a given TQ². We should keep in mind that the customer is not interested in a specific quantity of software (whatever it is defined), but in the resolution of his/her business problems and, eventually, in the acquisition of the logical software features that are promised to be decisive with respect to those problems. For these reasons, she/he will be interested in the measurement of the logical features more than of the technical aspects of the system. Logical features are much more related to user needs than technical features. The customer will tend to compare suppliers in terms of capability in releasing logical functionalities of an expected quality irrespective of technical issues (unless they represent constraints). In the same negotiation phase, two indicators will influence the supplier: the external average productivity ratio and unitary prices—for competitive reasons—and the internal specific production unitary cost in realizing the system required for cost-benefit analysis. The knowledge of both of them is important to be a successful supplier on the market. The first measure of productivity is (must be) the same used by its customer, and the second one is totally internal and is related to the supplier-specific production environment. Both the customer and the supplier are then interested in external benchmarking data to conduct a successful negotiation. These are usually supplied by independent consultants, associations like ISBSG (International Software Benchmarking Standards Group) or public authorities.

As we have seen, for some time now, software has taken on the appearance of a market good and has been the subject of important economic transactions on par with other, more traditional products (i.e., hardware). The age of software developed entirely in house has certainly passed and organizations are making more extensive use of the software suppliers market. This means that the mechanism for forming the price of software is influenced by the empirical laws of supply and demand. It is quite often said that a tender process is capable of giving the "automatic situational equity" needed to manage a market transaction. Unfortunately, this is often an illusion for some reasons:

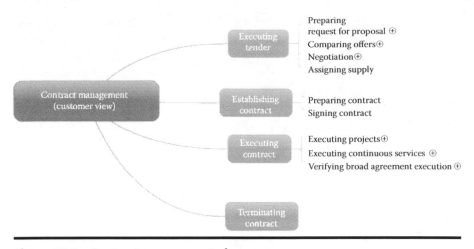

Figure 29.2   Contract management phases.

■ When the number of different suppliers capable (or allowed) to answer a tender is low (i.e., less than 10), it is difficult to consider the transaction as a real "competitive" one; "hidden agreements," "compensation agreements," and the like are common issues; in this case, the price will surely be overestimated (supplier's predominance).

■ When the market is dominated, on the other side, by an offer exceeding the demand, then the price will be underestimated and it will be difficult for a supplier (engaged in a surviving battle) to respect the agreements (demand's predominance).

■ When the requirement specifications are too ambiguous or synthetic, then different suppliers might understand different meanings and their proposals will be barely comparable in the substance although formally equivalent. The risk here is to assign the contract to the supplier that has the minimum understanding of the requirements and hence the minimum proposed cost.

The main contract management phases are illustrated in Figure 29.2.

Executing Tender

Figure 29.3 shows the main activities needed to select the supplier in a specific procurement situation. There are three different situations to deal with. A broad agreement is a contract in which a general production capability is acquired at specified conditions (maximum size, technical constraints, quality expectations, unitary prices, etc.). Specific services are then acquired within the agreement framework in a simplified way. The other two approaches are for procurement of a specific project or a specific continuous service. The main difference between them is the granularity of a single request to be satisfied. Offers may be compared using various types of indicators like

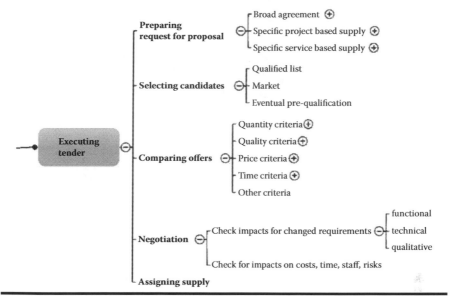

Figure 29.3 Executing tender.

quantity, quality, price, time, and derived ones like productivity. A clear set of rules for assigning value to the offers must be produced and communicated.

Establishing Contract

After the assignment, it is necessary to prepare and sign a contract that must be compliant with all the provisions of the request for proposal using the elements that will be clarified later.

Executing Contract

Figure 29.4 describes several activities that are needed to execute a contract. Many of them are related to measurement issues. Projects are managed differently than services while the broad agreement has one more level of management: the process level. At this level the regularity of the estimations and measurements is taken into account while deriving statistics and trends. The goal is to identify and correct eventual systematic errors or behaviors based on multiple instances.

Terminating Contract

A final verification and validation of the supply is needed to close formally the contract. Payments might follow the closure of activities by several months since a clause of guarantee might be specified in the contract.

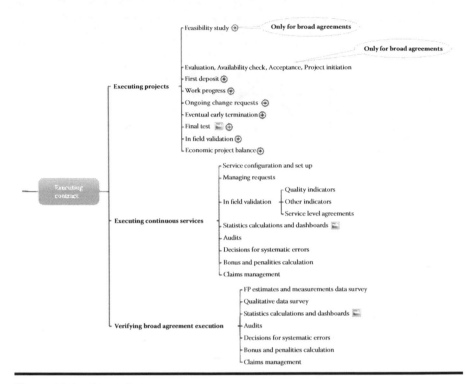

Figure 29.4   Executing contract.

A Contractual Measurement Model

Sizing Methods Supporting Market Transactions

When we consider software from the economical point of view—as an asset capable of satisfying buyers' needs—then a functional measurement method like FPs seems to be more appropriate to the context of use than a technical measure (lines of code [LOC], number of physical files, etc.), since it is related to a quantification of the different "user based services" that are supplied by the software application under consideration. Any Functional Size Measurement Method (FSMM), indeed, is strongly correlated to the "use value" of the software application itself, so it seems appropriate—from a customer viewpoint—to pay more for systems that show a higher functional measure.

Focusing contracts on functional measurements then has, among the others, a very positive advantage: it motivates the producer to optimize the ratio between functional services and the technical software items that are needed to implement those functionalities. Since the producer will be paid in proportion to the "services" that the software would release to the users, than she/he will have an interest in realizing the minimum number of software technical items (i.e., LOC, classes, objects, etc.) that will meet the functional requirements needed at the expected quality level. On the contrary, if the contract assigns value directly to the technical software items, we should expect—and we often have—an unjustified increase of those measures, the functionalities required being equal. This will generate non-maintainable, incomprehensible, inefficient systems, and customers would pay more to suppliers who are less efficient than others as they deliver the same functionality using more code.

It is nevertheless true that the effort needed to release a given software product is more dependent on the number and intrinsic nature of the technical items that should be designed, built, and tested than on the logical functionalities that those items aim to implement. This is why functional measures alone, although they may be definitely considered a primary cost driver, are not particularly well correlated to effort in ISBSG benchmarking databases, as it may be seen in the Figure 29.5.

Clear evidence of the previous statement is reached when we consider the practice of reusing software items as module libraries, component catalogs, and the like. There are many situations in which, despite the fact that a single reused item does not correspond to any logical functionality taken in itself, all these items aggregated and assembled together may rapidly and economically allow the implementation of many different logical functionalities with a small amount of working effort. In this case, the effort needed to realize the overall system will not be proportional at

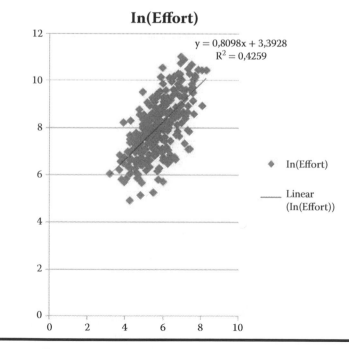

Figure 29.5 Effort correlation with FP.

all to the logical "services" required (FPs), but it will be proportional to the number and nature of the new items to be build and to the number and difficulty of the integrations of already available items that should be carried on in the general system architecture. At this point, it is necessary to explicitly discourage attempts to transform technical measures into functional measures and vice versa (like the too widespread practices of FP backfiring from LOC to measure existent applications or the transformation of FP into LOC to permit the use of a LOC-based effort estimation method). For the reasons explained before, the two measures are derived from different, incompatible models and are focused on different dimensions of a software product. Therefore, these attempts will only generate confusion and a higher level of entropy in the ICT universe.

Summarizing, we may state that the (market) price of a software application is more meaningfully associated to a functional measure because of the "external" and higher level of interest of the customer represented in a contract, whereas the "internal" cost of production is often determined by the technical activities to be carried on. Consideration of the reuse and replication level and of the productivity factors analyzed later may let the two approaches become closer.

Why to Measure

There is a straightforward answer to this question: because supplier's remuneration for a software ad hoc development or enhancement should be proportional to quantity, quality, and other product and process attributes. The business goal is to pay for the results (FP + quality) and not for the used resources (person-hours). If we pay for the resources, we might be in the situation of paying more for a less efficient supplier with a lower productivity that needs more person-hours to produce the same number of FP (results) of a certain quality in a predefined environment.

What to Measure

Nature of an ad hoc Software Supply

An ICT contract that regulates an ad hoc software supply (among the other products) might include different types of interventions:

- New Application Development
- Functional Enhancement Maintenance of an already existing application (it adds, changes, and/or deletes functionalities)
- Non-Functional Enhancement Maintenance of an already existing application (it changes the quality characteristics of the application: i.e., performances, usability, maintainability, etc., the functionalities being the same)
- Adaptive Maintenance of an already existing application (it makes the same functionalities available in a changed technological environment)

- Corrective Maintenance of an already existing application (it detects and removes the causes and effects of software errors)
- Mixed requests

Crossing the previous classification, there is another one based on the level of resources needed to complete the single software intervention required and on the supply process followed.

- Extraordinary Maintenance
- Ordinary Maintenance

It is useful to state, at this point, that even if any kind of ad hoc software might be conceptually modeled in terms of FSMM, it is not always cost effective or useful to do it to support adequately a software contractual process. For example, a customized Enterprise Resource Planning (ERP) system is definitely a software set of applications and it is possible to measure it by the use of a FSMM. The point is that the final measure is not reasonably correlated to the effort of customization, since this effort (and the consequent cost to the customer) is more related to the activities of organizational analysis, process analysis, "gap" analysis, calibration of parameters, etc. An ERP development project might even end up without any traditional programming effort. This is why, for this kind of supply, it is more convenient to establish and use different productivity models. The same is true for web-systems where the "functional" size of the software needed is only a part of the stuff to be produced (graphics, clip arts, video, animations, etc.). In all these cases, the contract needs to be partitioned into several components, each of them with its own measurement method.

Although the FSMMs have been developed to deal directly with the "functional" types of change in the software applications, they might be usefully applied to the other kinds of changes with some variations and supplementary rules. We will not consider here the acquisition of commercial off-the-shelf (COTS) software since it follows other procurement standards.

New Application Development

This is a very simple case. Any FSMM states how to measure a new software application. The only additional suggestion here is to consider the "reuse" and "replication" aspects adequately, since, today, even new applications could be built up using previous "chunks" of applications already in existence or by the use of technical "components," or may have to be used in a multichannel environment.

Functional Enhancement Maintenance

This case is very similar to the previous one but the reuse aspect is more relevant here.

Non-Functional Enhancement Maintenance

This is a hard case to deal with. Improving the performance (non-functional attributes of a software product) could be a very simple or complex task. Sometimes, the effort of "perfecting" a software application may be proportional to the functional size of the application, sometimes not. It should be decided on a situational basis whether to consider the cost as influenced by the amount of FPs or by other parameters.

Adaptive Maintenance

This is a difficult case too, but simpler than the previous one. Usually, a "translating" project consists in the redeveloping of an existent application into a different technical architecture. For such a situation, there is a great level of "functional reuse" associated with a minimum level of "technical reuse" (see later). It is possible to save the analysis costs, but it is necessary to spend for the realization and testing phases. The functional measure of the application could be used as an input to a productivity model that cuts off 90% of the analysis effort. The remaining 10% should be used by the supplier to "understand" the existing application to rebuild it in a different technical architecture. The Construction phase is usually performed entirely in order to implement the already known requirements in a different technical environment, but sometimes it is possible to use some kind of "automatic" translator (i.e., COBOL to C++) so that the construction cost could be reduced by a significative amount. The testing phase is, obviously, performed completely. The final cost per FP is significantly lower than the development-from-scratch unit cost.

Corrective Maintenance

This is, typically, a "service" supply more than a "product/project" supply: it is not possible to measure the FP of a correction activity since it usually impacts the "technical aspect" of the software. The cost of discovering and correcting a fault in the programs and the consequent damages in the actual data is not usually proportional to the FP of the functionalities impacted by the error (eventually the whole application!). For this reason, a single correction is not measurable using a FSMM. A very well known exception to this rule was the Y2K correction effort that assumed the form of very large projects and where the total amounts of functional measures of the applications to be corrected were useful to estimate project costs. After that, the "project" situation is very rare in the corrective maintenance area.

Mixed Requests

In the actual market, it is very common for a customer to commit to a set of different types of interventions at the same time and on the same software objects (applications). For example, a project might involve the development of a new application, the enhancement maintenance of two existing applications to interface with the new one, and some non-functional and adaptive maintenance on qualified portions of the existing applications plus a correction of "cosmetic" minor errors. In these cases, it is suggested to articulate the contract in separate portions, each of them with its own quantification method and explicitly considering the overlap of the different interventions, reducing, consequently, the cost of all the shared components. For example, the analysis phase of the two maintained applications, in the previous case, will take in account, at one time, the needs for functional enhancements, non-functional enhancements, and adaptive transformation. It is not appropriate here to charge the customer for three different analysis tasks as if they were conducted separately by scratch.

Extraordinary Maintenance

When a single required software change is estimated to be completed over a certain (conventional) threshold of effort/cost/time, the supply process model is project-oriented. It is necessary to have a plan and to allocate the resources over the goals, activities, and products to be released. The response time is usually set up in terms of weeks or months. The decision process is relatively slow and articulated. The impact of the single intervention is high. This is a "step"-like type of change management. This model might be related to any one of the previous classifications (enhancement, adaptive, corrective, i.e., Y2K). Functional measurement standards might be appropriately used here.

Ordinary Maintenance

When a single required software change is estimated to be completed under a certain (conventional) threshold of effort/cost/time, the supply process model is "service"-oriented. The resources are pre-allocated permanently on the process and are "used" on a rapid demand-answer basis. The response time is usually set up in terms of hours or days. The decision process is very quick and simple. The impact of the single intervention is low. This is a "continuous" type of change management. Any one of the previous maintenance types might be included in this category (enhancement, adaptive, and corrective).

Functional measurements of single interventions are not very useful here but the total functional measure of the applications to be "monitored" and "maintained," might be useful to determine the overall "annual fixed" cost to be spent by the customer to receive an adequate "maintenance" service on a work-on-demand basis. At the end of the "covered period," this cost will not necessarily be strictly correlated to the actual effort supplied, since it is formulated as an "insurance" type of cost. In addition, there are many other factors impacting the total cost of a service supply such as the service level agreement shared between the parties (i.e., response times).

The more frequently used cost model, for ordinary maintenance, is a fixed cost amount over a certain period of time based on the estimated frequency and entity of interventions needed.

Another ordinary maintenance cost model is of a variable type and might be based on some simple estimating formulae, specific to the local applications and environment, by which customer and supplier could rapidly agree upon the cost of any standard task.

Types of standard maintenance tasks might be defined at various levels of complexity; for example, the number and size of files or screen fields that have to be changed. The effort estimated to complete each standard task is established in units of "standard-hours." So when any user needs a maintenance change, a cost could be given according to the agreed formulae. Performance improvement targets could be set for the supplier, in terms of target reductions in the standard-hours for specified tasks, and hence also reductions in costs.

In the following sections, we will consider only the sizing of a "project"-type approach.

Scope of Supply

A contract for a new development or extraordinary maintenance must indicate which specific products and activities are included/excluded from the provision. Is the complete project life cycle commissioned or only a part of it? How many and which deliverables are included in the software supply? Sometimes it is possible to make the user requirements, the system requirements, and the architectural design "in house" and to acquire the rest of the project phases; in other cases, it is preferable to outsource the project from the user requirements definition; in even other cases, it is possible to make two different contracts for the specification phase and the realization phase. The functional measurement of the supplied products is not influenced by this choice, whereas the price for the customer must be. The scope must be clipped on a high-level work breakdown structure consistent with the model of the production process adopted or required. The scope will contain activities proportional to the FP and non-proportional to them but to other quantitative measures (e.g., number of installations, number of training courses).

Ongoing Change Request

In a software project, requirements are often subject to rapid change that may impact on the cost, development time, and the amount of work needed to implement the project itself. To quantify the economic impact due to changes during construction is necessary to refer to a procedure for managing these changes to calculate and negotiate the impact. The impact must be managed according to the contractual framework of reference.

A change in requirements during the work requested by the customer may have a functional impact and/or non-functional impact. The functional impact may result in the creation of new functions or logical data structures and/or may have an impact on how other logic functions or data structures must be changed or deleted. If there are changes during implementation of functional requirements, the calculation might be as follows:

- Conversion functionalities (CFP), if present in the change requests, must be identified and added to the original CFP count.
- Added functionalities (ADD), if present in the change requests, must be identified and added to the original ADD count.
- Changed functionalities (CHG), if present in the change requests, must be identified and added to the original CHG count.
- Deleted functionalities (DEL), if present in the change requests, must be identified and added to the original DEL count.
- A function (ADD or CHG) that is changed two or more times during construction will be multiplied by a factor of 1.4 (a conventional value that may be customized).
- A feature added with a change request (ADD), which is then removed later with a new change request, will be excluded from the counter ADD and inserted into the counter DEL with a coefficient of reduction given by the following formula:

$$\text{UFP} = \text{UFP recognized for the deleted requirement} \cdot \% \text{ of cumulative progress} \qquad (29.1)$$

where percentage of cumulative progress to use is that of the last phase completed at the time of the cancellation like in Table 29.1 below.

When there is a non-functional impact on the change request, a direct estimation of its cost should be done separately and added to the cost of the functional impact.

Table 29.1 Cumulative Percentage of Effort and Progress for Every Life Cycle Phase

Phase	Effort (%)	Cumulative Progress (%)
Analysis and design	35	35
Detailed design	10	45
Construction	30	75
Test	20	95
Roll out	5	100

Cancelled Activities

When there is a cancellation of a current initiative at the end of one phase of work subsequent to the analysis and design, for reasons not attributable to the supplier, compensation will be recognized at the same value calculated using the following formula:

$$\text{Reduced Price} = \text{UFP} \cdot \text{unitary UFP price} \cdot \% \text{ of Cumulative Progress} \qquad (29.2)$$

Percentage of cumulative progress is calculated as before. UFP stands for unadjusted FP.

Reuse and Replication

Among the factors that are becoming increasingly important to determine the cost of production in the software market is the capability of reusing previous software assets. "Reuse" is a word that could be attributed to two different software viewpoints: the logical organization and the technical organization of the software items. Both of them are important and show a different aspect of reuse.

Functional reuse may be defined as the reutilization of user recognizable and existing logical data structures and functionalities to build up new logical features. Depending on the particular architectural environment, we might have an extreme situation in which the functional reuse is very high but the technical capability of reusing existing "physical" software items is very low: we must rebuild the desired logical item almost by scratch. This is the case, for example, when, in a multi-level client-server architecture, we want to deliver a functionality logically similar to an existing one, but in a technical environment completely different from the original one.

Technical reuse may be defined as the reutilization of existing physical data structures and software items (modules, objects, programs, etc.) to build up new technical items to be used in the construction of new logical features. Depending on the particular functional requirements, we might have an extreme situation in which the functional reuse is very low but the technical capability of reusing existing "physical" software items is very high: we can build the desired new logical feature using almost effortlessly some existing technical "items." This is the case, for example, when we want to deliver a set of functionalities to manage (CRUD) a number of logical files which are similar in structure (i.e., unique ID, description, numerical values) but different in contents (i.e., money conversion table, time conversion table, length conversion table, etc.). Functional and technical reuse may combine them in any possible way, as shown in Figure 29.6. The most significant savings due to a reuse strategy derive from the combination of both the reuse types.

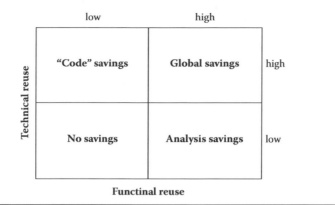

Figure 29.6   Types of reuse.

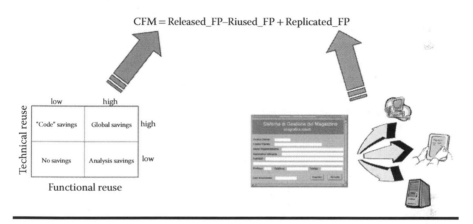

Figure 29.7   Contractual functional measurement.

At this point, a relevant question is, is it "appropriate" to consider the reuse level in a market transaction regulated by a formal contract? In other words, is this factor a visible or a transparent one? Is it a negotiation element or a supplier's competitive factor?

The answer is, again, situational. If the customer makes its own software assets or components available to the supplier to produce a new item or it is inclined to ask (and pay) for a generalization of the software commissioned to create savings in the future, then the reuse is an explicit and evident parameter and must be included in the contract; otherwise, it is an internal competitive factor of the supplier.

Reuse may be considered by the use of a "decreasing" coefficient to lower the UFP measure to be used for cost calculations as shown in Figure 29.7.

Replication is the opposite concept of reuse. Any FSMM has a step in which the identical functions are eliminated from the count. This is also known as the multiple media issue. There are situations in which replication of the same functionalities on different technology platforms involve programming different code, to integrate it with other platforms, and then testing the functionalities again again (multichannel availability). Other times the replication is simply a matter of a different editing format (pdf, spreadsheet, print report). In the first case, replication may be considered by the use of an "increasing" coefficient to raise the UFP measure to be used for cost calculations as shown in Figure 29.7.

How to Measure

Contractual Schemes

Three main "pure" contractual schemes of an ad hoc software supply are frequently used: Fixed Cost for Specified Product (also called Turnkey Supply), Variable Cost for Time and Material, and Variable Cost for Released Product.

The Fixed Cost for Specified Product model is based on the preliminary estimation of the resources needed to release a software product requested in such a way that the global price, once it has been agreed on, is not reviewed at the end of the supply unless the final testing of the system demonstrates that the initial requirements have not been properly satisfied. The responsibility to deliver a complete and adequate product is in the hands of the supplier.

According to the second model (Variable Cost for Time and Material), a global price for the final system is not established and "locked" but unitary costs for the available resources are agreed. Sometimes a maximum and (eventually) a minimum amount of money is established to help the customer and the supplier to budget the initiative. The actual cost of the supply is determined at the end of the initiative in proportion to the resources needed to satisfy the initial (and ongoing) requirements. Sometimes, to facilitate contract control, a minimum productivity in terms of FP per workday is agreed and monitored during the project life. This implies the need to measure the products during the intermediate or final phases, even if these measures are not strictly necessary to the economic transaction. Similarly to the previous contractual scheme, a preliminary estimation of the resources needed to release a requested software product is made, but only to fix the maximum and eventually the minimum cost of the supply. Both functional derived effort and non-functional derived effort should be estimated. At the delivery of the final product, a measurement of quantity, quality, and technical aspects is made to verify the minimum granted productivity constraint, if present. These measures are not essential to the economic transaction that is based on the resource usage.

According to the Variable Cost for Released Product model, a preliminary estimation of the quantity, quality, and technical aspects is made to "price" the final product, but only to fix the maximum and eventually the minimum cost of the supply. This is made to help the customer and the supplier to budget the initiative. Both functional derived cost and non-functional derived cost should be estimated.

The final price of the supply is determined on the basis of the actual measurements of product attributes instead of the forecasted values, within the established range of values. The product measures are essential to the economical transaction. Figure 29.7 shows the flow of information needed to "construct" the price of supply in the first and last case.

To calculate the Productivity Adjustment Factor (PAF), it is possible to adopt the following steps:

- Evaluation of the impact level (e.g., very low, low, normal, high, very high, extremely high) for each factor
- Quantitative definition of each factor based on the shared table describing the various adjustment factors (like COCOMO)
- Calculate the PAF through the multiplication of all values

Broad Agreement

Broad general contracts are characterized by wide "scope" and long durations between the time the contract is drafted and the time the service is provided. In these cases, usually, spending limitations, unitary prices, general contract objectives, and technical architectural constraints are the only items defined with some accuracy. The pricing approach that applies to this type of contract can be a problem, since the cost of the whole contract should be estimated together with the cost of the various transactions that are envisaged under the contract without adequate knowledge of what to do. In this contract, it is really important to define the rules that the parts will follow during the execution of it. All of the three "pure" schemes may be articulated and used. All nominal unitary costs and tables of numerical parameters must be defined and agreed. All non-functional costs should be regulated.

Contract Fulfillment

The contract should be monitored by the verification of quantity, quality, and adequacy of the deliverables explicitly included in the supply. The functional measurement verification is directly related to the monitoring activity, and it is also needed to normalize other "quality" attributes. If, during an intermediate measurement, it turns out that the "amount agreed upon" is going to be exceeded, the regulating mechanism including both the client's management and the supplier's management must be initiated. There are two alternatives shown in Figure 29.8:

- The specifications are reduced at least to the "amount agreed upon."
- A new amount of FPs must be agreed upon. A new budget must be determined according to the shared rules, based on the unitary prices already included in the original contract. This helps to prevent disagreements later on between both parties.

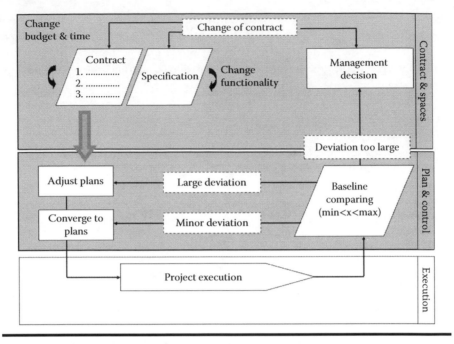

Figure 29.8   Contract size monitoring.

Any new project started from a broad agreement decreases the global quantity of money or size of the entire contract till it becomes empty. Using the approach described here, it is possible to allow a different mix of delivered systems with respect to the estimated one without any conflict and unfairness since it is possible, for example, to exchange more "simple requirements" with less "complex but reusable requirements" by the use of the formulae established. The equity perception is granted in a situational way.

When to Measure

Figure 29.9 shows the positioning of the estimation and measurement task in the software life cycle, depending on the contractual scheme, the relative importance of size estimation, and measurement changes. An effective way of predicting the FP values early in the life cycle is the Early and Quick FP Analysis available in the public domain.

Who Will Measure

In a contractual environment, the responsibility of making estimates and measurements may be given to the customer or the supplier indifferently, but the customer has the need (right) to review all the deliverables supplied by the supplier. Where there is disagreement on the measurement results, arbitration by a third party may be the solution.

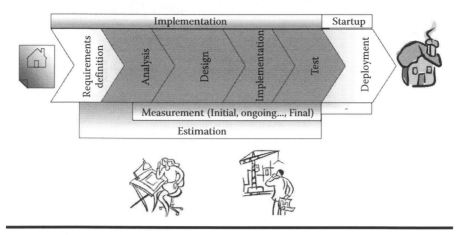

Figure 29.9   Estimates and measurements in the life cycle.

Conclusions

Software is a market good like many other products today, but the relative procurement processes are far less rigorous and mature than in other business areas. Too frequently, an otherwise skilled acquirer or seller behaves as a novice when dealing with a software supply. The desire to oversimplify the content of the agreement is strong, but the problems overlooked at the negotiation and contractual phase will always explode in the implementation phase, leading to illegal practices or damaging conflicts. An independent third party, in these situations, might help both the supplier and the customer set up and control a good agreement based on high professional skill. In this chapter, some classification parameters to be used in preparing good software contracts and some new methods to support the measurement and cost of a software supply have been outlined. In this area, a crucial role might be played by government authorities and metrics associations, which are important "opinion makers" and rulers for the market.

Bibliography

1. ISO/IEC. 2007. *14143-1:1998 Information Technology—Software Measurement— Functional Size Measurement—Part 1: Definition of Concepts.* 2nd ed., JTC 1/SC 7, ISO/IEC, Geneva: ISO/IEC.
2. Meli, R. 1998. Software Reuse as a Potential Factor of Database Contamination for Benchmarking in Function Points. *ISBSG Workshop*, Rome, Italy, February 12, 1998.
3. Meli, R. 2000. Functional and technical software measurement: Conflict or integration? *FESMA 2000*, Madrid, Spain, October 2000.
4. Grant Rule, P. 2001. The Importance of the Size of Software Requirements. *The NASSCOM Conference*, Mumbai, India, 7th–10th February, 2001. http://www .software-measurement.com/.

5. Symons, C. 1997. Controlling Software Contracts. *European SEPG Conference*, Amsterdam, June, 1997. http://www.software-measurement.com/.

6. Raysz, P., and D. Lisak. 1999. Method for Well-Defined Terms of Agreement in Software Contracts Using Function Points. *ESCOM-SCOPE 99*, Herstmonceux Castle, East Sussex, England, 27–29 April.

7. IFPUG, and R. Meli, et al. 2002. Early & Quick Function Point Analysis: from summary user requirements to Project Management. In book *IT Measurement—Practical Advice from the Experts*. Boston: Addison-Wesley.

8. Meli, R. 2004. The Software Measurement Role in a Complex Contractual Context. *SMEF2004*, Italy.

9. Boehm, B. W., et al. 2000. *Software Cost Estimation with COCOMO II*. Upper Saddle River, NJ: Prentice-Hall.

10. Iorio, T., and R. Meli. 2005. Software measurement and Function Point metrics in a broad software contractual agreement. *SMEF ROMA*.

11. Meli, R., and F. Perna. 2008. Practical experiences of Function Points estimation and measurement in a complex outsourcing context of an Italian public administration. *SMEF2008*. Milano, Italy.

12. Meli, R. 2008. Risk Measurement & Perception: A Critical Issue. Keynote at *SMEF2008*, Milano, Italy.

13. Meli, R. 2009. IFPUG Functional Size Measurement & Modern Software Architectures. *Workshop at SMEF2009*, Roma, Italy.

14. DPO. *Early & Quick Function Points Reference Manual—IFPUG version*. http://www .dpo.it/sito %20 inglese/eqfp/index.htm (accessed 2011).

About the Author

Roberto Meli graduated with a degree in Computer Science in 1984. In 1996, he became CEO of DPO Srl. During the past 20 years, he has developed focused competences in the project management and software measurement areas and has written papers for technical magazines and international conferences. He was a Certified Function Points Specialist (CFPS) from 1996 to 2004. He is a consultant and lecturer in training courses on project management and software measurement for many major Italian companies and public organizations. He developed the Early and Quick Function Point Analysis method, managing the implementation of the Sfera product. In the last 15 years, he has had the following roles: chairperson of the Board of Directors of GUFPI–ISMA (Gruppo Utenti Function Points Italia—Italian Software Measurement Association), coordinator of the GUFPI–ISMA Counting Practices Committee, Italian delegate to the MAIN (Metrics Association's International Network), chairperson of the COSMIC Measurement Practices Committee, and Conference Chairperson of the SMEF event (Software Measurement European Forum), one of the leading European events in this area. He has managed the GUFPI–ISMA working group that released the Italian Guidelines for the Contractual Usage of Function Points. This document has been then used to feed the Italian Government ICT Authority Guidelines to be used by all Italian public administrations. Currently, he is the president of the Simple Function Point Association (SiFPA; http://www.SiFPA.org).

the ICT knowledge broker

DPO (Data Processing Organization Srl) is a qualified supplier of services in the ICT market. DPO's excellence areas are Software Measurement and Estimation, Requirements Management, and Project and Risk Management. DPO provides specialized services and products to promote the continuous evolution of production and management processes for both public and private organizations. DPO's high quality standards come from its active role in research at the international level and the certified expertise of its personnel (e.g., IFPUG CFPS). DPO's professionals collaborate with acknowledged technical national and international bodies in the software measurement area. DPO is the first Italian company that is ISO 9001:2008 certified for Function Point consultancy.

Chapter 30

Request for Proposal Management: Answering Metrics-Based Bids

Harold van Heeringen

Contents

Introduction

Worldwide, many requests for proposals (RFPs) are sent out every day to a large number of potential suppliers. In RFPs, client organizations (RFP senders) are trying to gather objective criteria, with which they can analyze and evaluate bids from different suppliers (RFP responders). Although the questions asked in these RFPs are often hard to answer for not so mature organizations, they are sometimes even harder to answer by more mature organizations. In this chapter, the focus is on so-called metrics-based questions in RFPs regarding the selection of a supplier for a software realization project.

Metrics-based questions in RFPs are often stated as follows:

- What is your productivity rate in hours per Function Point for .Net projects?
- What is your standard duration for a project of 1000 Function Points?
- What is your price per Function Point for a Java project?

Of course, at first sight these questions seem like perfectly reasonable questions, making it possible to decide objectively which supplier is the best. When we consider certain "laws of metrics," however, it turns out that in fact these questions are "unanswerable." For instance, there is no such thing as a standard productivity rate, but there is a number of factors, like duration, size, and complexity, which together lead to a realistic productivity rate.

This also means that in the software industry, quotations of suppliers are often not realistic. In this chapter, the danger of this will be addressed. Client organizations should become aware of the questions they should ask in RFPs and they should learn how to evaluate the quotations from the suppliers and the risks that are involved with the often used "just select the cheapest one" option. In this chapter, both topics are discussed. Readers who operate on the demand side see which questions should be asked in RFPs and how to identify the quotations of suppliers that are not realistic. Readers on the supply side learn about the present and the future in RFP management and the questions that they should be able to respond to in the near future.

The Information Technology Industry Has a Huge Problem!

In general, client organizations are not satisfied with the performance of information technology (IT) suppliers, resulting in low levels of customer satisfaction. In practice, the IT organizations are often blamed for many things that go wrong, not least in the case of software realization projects, where many projects fail. The often quoted

Standish Chaos Report (2009) [1] reports that only 32% of all projects were successful in 2009, being defined as on time, in budget, and delivering all the functionality that was agreed upon, while 44% of the projects investigated were unsuccessful. In this chapter, the question is raised to which extent the way RFP management is carried out by client organizations contributes to this low success rate. The focus is on software realization projects in which suppliers (internal and/or external) are asked to offer a fixed price or a price per Function Point to deliver the software described in a document containing the user requirements of the users in the organization.

Usually, the RFP is sent out to various external suppliers who are experts in providing technical solutions and delivering software, usually the so-called preferred parties selected at an earlier stage. Many organizations believe that outsourcing is the perfect solution for managing a part of the (usually "non-primary") functions in the organization in an efficient and effective way. This may be true for certain tasks that are relatively easy to understand, like for instance catering or security of an organization. In these cases, knowledge transfer from the outsourcing company to the service supplier is relatively easy and the characteristics of the service to be delivered and its price are easy to agree on.

IT development projects, however, are usually very complex. There is a lot of tacit knowledge in the heads of the people in the IT department, which is not written on paper. This tacit knowledge is absolutely crucial for delivering software that is going to match the expectations of the users. Knowledge transfer from the outsourcer to the supplier is, therefore, often a very difficult task. Only when the outsourcing company succeeds in specifying the functional and non-functional requirements in a complete and detailed way, it may be possible for the supplier company to understand exactly what the client requests.

Outsourcing companies try to select the right outsourcing partners by trying to compare the different suppliers based on quantitative data. Although this idea is very good, the way it is done in practice is unfortunately quite the opposite. A number of models from software metrics literature show us that there are certain "software metrics laws" indicating that selecting the cheapest supplier blindly often results in failing projects, in which both the supplier and the outsourcer are not happy. This means that client organizations could be blamed for at least a percentage of the unsuccessful projects, just because of the fact they did not ask the right questions and therefore did not select the right supplier.

Requests for Proposals

The Wikipedia definition of an RPF is as follows:

An RFP is an early stage in a procurement process, issuing an invitation for suppliers, often through a bidding process, to submit a proposal on a specific commodity or service. The RFP process brings structure to the procurement decision and allows the risks and benefits to be identified clearly upfront. The RFP may dictate to varying degrees the exact structure and format of the supplier's response. Effective RFPs typically reflect the strategy and short/long-term business objectives, providing detailed insight on which suppliers will be able to offer a matching perspective [2].

Usually, an RFP is a document in which specific questions are asked about the submitting company itself, the people who are going to work on the project, the technical solution proposed, and the costs involved. Submitting organizations are usually very limited in the way they can answer the questions asked. They are not allowed to describe any context of the answers, because this would make it harder for the client organization to compare the answers. In many cases, only one word or a number is allowed as an answer on a question, without a chance to explain the specific word or number.

In many cases, RFPs are also submitted to select outsourcing partners (or "preferred suppliers") for a period of time. During this period of time, the supplier may or may not do any work agreed upon in the contract. This is not the focus of this chapter, however, it is relevant for RFP management. In this chapter, RFP management is considered for a single software development project, not for a contract for a period of time.

In general, the company that sends out an RFP has to provide all the necessary information to the potential suppliers for them to be able to draw up a sound proposal. In general, the following information has to be submitted for an RFP on a specific project:

- Client corporate information
- The bidding process—like a deadline for the definitive proposal, but also possible scheduled sessions for asking and answering questions
- The functional requirements that have to be delivered in the system
- The non-functional requirements that have to be satisfied, like for instance security requirements and the development language to be used
- The set of questions that are asked to select the right proposal
- Decision criteria that the client organization is going to apply to select the most appropriate proposal

Client Issues

For the party that submits an RFP, it is crucial to select the right outsourcing party and to do so in a legal acceptable way. Of course, the client organization should provide general information like the following:

- Schedule of the bid process. Are there going to be any information sessions for suppliers to ask questions? What date is the submission deadline for the quotation? When will the decision be communicated? What date should the project start?
- Organizational information. Who are the responsible persons in the client organization and how is the organization structured? What is the mission of the organization?

- General requirements that a supplier has to meet to be allowed to be in the bid process. An example could be a requirement that the organization must hold a CMMI Level 3 certification.
- Solution details. Are there any limitations to the solutions that the suppliers have to take into account, like architecture or programming language?
- Decision criteria. What are the criteria that will select the winning bid in an objective way? How many points can the supplier earn for each question and what are the criteria to decide which answer is best?

When preparing an RFP, the client organization also has to think of the criteria on which it will judge and select the most appropriate proposal. This usually means that they will have to think of the most important characteristics of the project itself and of the party that will realize it. Characteristics that are usually considered are (not limitative) the following:

- Price
- Quality
- Productivity
- Duration
- Supplier creditability
- Supplier references
- Solution details

To be able to compare the different supplier quotations in an objective way, the questions are usually as quantitative as possible. To be able to compare the answers in an objective way, Function Points are usually used to define the metrics in the questions. The main advantage of the Function Point size unit (either IFPUG [3], NESMA [4], or COSMIC [5]) is that it is an objective size unit that is independent of the technology being used. An application of 500 Function Points in Java is just as big as an application of 500 Function Points in Cobol. Project estimations, therefore, have to take into account realistic productivity rates (for instance, in number of hours per Function Point or price per Function Point) for each new project. These productivity rates are often the basis of RFP management when outsourcing software realization projects.

Typical Function Point–based metrics questions that are encountered in RFPs are as follows:

Price
    Examples:
        • What is the price per Function Point that you offer for the realization (technical design, functional design, coding, unit testing, system testing) of this system in Java?

- What is the price per Function Point that you offer for the realization of change requests during the projects?
- What is the price per Function Point that you offer for the maintenance of the system after implementation?

Quality
Examples:
- What is the number of defects per Function Point that is expected to be detected during systems testing?
- What is the number of defects per Function Point that is expected to be detected during user acceptance testing?
- What is the number of defects per Function Point that is expected to be detected during the first three months in production?
- What is the number of defects per Function Point that are expected to be detected per year after the first three months in production?

Productivity
Example:
- What is your productivity in hours per Function Point for the realization (technical design, functional design, coding, unit testing, system testing) of Java projects?

These questions are impossible to answer if one is familiar with certain models from software metrics literature. Let's see now what suppliers have to do to answer questions like the above.

Supplier Issues

For suppliers it is very important that the information provided by the outsourcer is up-to-date and detailed. Especially in the case of fixed-price bids, the proposals offered by different suppliers usually also have a legal status. This means that when the client selects a specific proposal, the supplier is obligated to deliver the proposal against the price and conditions stated in the proposal. Needless to say that more details in the description of the functional and the non-functional requirements lead to better proposals (as the supplier can reduce its risk percentage due to unforeseen requirement and/or scope creep) and therefore to better prices.

Supplier organizations compete against each other to score the highest on the client's decision criteria in order to win the contract. As most of the typical questions asked in RFPs are related to metrics expressed in Function Points, it is important for supplier organizations to have an experience database with historical project data sized in IFPUG, NESMA, and/or COSMIC Function Points, which are compliant to the current ISO standard for functional size measurement models. Without this database, it is quite difficult to answer the questions above, and it is even impossible to defend the answers given objectively.

Depending on the decision criteria defined in the RFP submitted, the commercial people of the supplier will try to "bend" the bid in a way that they think suits the decision criteria best. It is important, however, to understand that according to McConnell [6], there is a distinction between target, estimation, and commitment. The supplier should be very careful first to estimate the project very thoroughly, before handing over the results to the commercial organization that is going to translate the estimation into a quotation. The estimate of the project should not be influenced by any commercial reasons.

Usually proposals are evaluated and a specific number of points are granted to different questions. The proposal that gets the most points in total is selected as the winner of the bid. The suppliers send in a proposal knowing that the outsourcer is going to select the "best" proposal. Unfortunately, the most important selection criterion is usually the price (per Function Point). Sometimes the number of points that a proposal can get for price is up to 70% of the total number of points that can be won in the total RFP. Needless to say that offering a good price is a very important issue for the suppliers that send in a proposal.

Requirements and the Moment Requests for Proposals Are Sent Out

One of the main problems in IT nowadays is that the quality of the functional and technical documentation is becoming lower over the years, while in outsourcing contracts the presence of complete and detailed documentation is crucial. In the past decades, it was quite normal to deliver detailed functional designs, ERD diagrams, entity descriptions, attribute descriptions, and function descriptions referring to the entities and attributes used in that function. This is almost not seen in this era any more. Client organizations do not really work out the functional design before asking for a fixed price proposal. This is already the first difficulty that suppliers have to overcome: what exactly does the client require?

One of the most used models for expressing the uncertainty about project deliverables is the "Cone of Uncertainty" [7]. Figure 30.1 illustrates that after the requirements have been defined and even after the functional design has been completed, there is still a significant percentage of uncertainty regarding the deliverables that should be realized in the project. According to McConnell, however, the narrowing of the cone is not guaranteed. Many decisions have to be taken to reduce uncertainty. Changing the decisions made during the project (for instance changes) widen the cone again.

The question that immediately pops up is of course: "Is it fair to ask for a fixed price quotation, while it is not completely clear what should be delivered?" In software, it is customary to use analogies to the world of building construction. Would it be possible to get a fixed price quotation from a construction

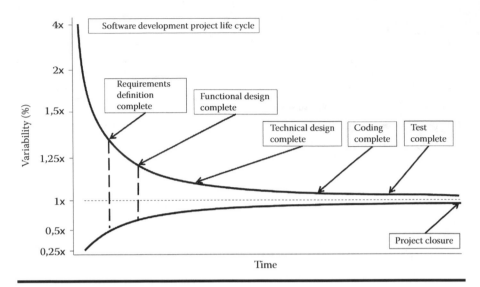

Figure 30.1 Cone of Uncertainity.

company on less than a very detailed description of the house you want them to build? Would they give you a "price per square meter house," if they know nothing about the exact sizes, the exact materials to be used, the duration required, etc.? Probably not. It is only in the IT industry that this is possible, even customary!

Expert Estimates versus Parametric Estimates

In more than 80% of the project estimates carried out in the world, only expert estimating techniques are used. Experts use their experience and some kind of informal analogy to estimate the number of hours needed to perform specific tasks that are required to deliver the system. The problem with expert estimates is that they tend to be optimistic. McConnell states that these expert estimates can be up to 30% optimistic. The main reasons are as follows:

- Experts usually come up with the first possible outcome as an estimate, even when the chance of success is very low.
- Experts often forget activities that are outside their usual working scope (e.g., experts in coding forget that the test people also have to write test cases).
- Experts are not always real experts (every project is unique).
- Experts are not going to do all the work themselves. Usually, there are less experienced people on the team that have to do a significant part of the work.

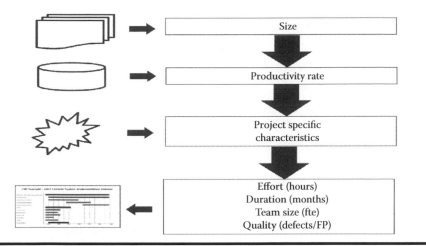

Figure 30.2   Parametric estimation.

Parametric estimation is done top-down. Based on the size to be delivered, the total number of hours is calculated using historic data or market data and taking into account project-specific characteristics.

In parametric estimates, the model illustrated in Figure 30.2 is used to come to an estimate.

Size

First, the size of the project is estimated. In most cases, a functional sizing method like IFPUG, NESMA, or COSMIC Function Points is used to measure the size of the functional user requirements. These methods are compliant to the ISO standard for functional size measurement methods, and therefore, the size can be determined in a standard and objective way. It is customary to express the functional size of the product to be delivered in a three point way: minimal size, likely size, and maximum size. The earlier in the aforementioned Cone of Uncertainty, the wider the range between minimum and maximum value. This range is a good indicator for the risks associated with the size measurement.

In practice, functional size measurements almost can never be carried out in a detailed way. Because of the incomplete or high-level specifications, a Function Point Analyst usually has to make a lot of assumptions in the mapping of the counting guidelines on the functional documentation. Although usually these assumptions are recorded and put in the size measurement report, after delivering the report only the likely size is probably used in the estimation model, while the assumptions made are discarded and forgotten.

Productivity

After the size measurement, the second step is to select the most probable productivity rate for the project. Since Albrecht [8] defined the Function Point Analysis method in the late 1970s, people have become interested in measuring productivity. When measuring productivity, one also becomes interested in the factors that influence productivity. During the years, many authors have researched and published lists of productivity factors. The methods COCOMO [9] and COCOMO 2 [10] are probably the most well-known and the most used methods worldwide, together with the IFPUG 14 General System Characteristics that compose the Value Adjustment Factor [11]. The International Software Benchmarking Standards Group (ISBSG) has published a new book recently [12], in which it is stated that the two factors that most influence productivity are programming language and team size. Factors that are generally considered to influence productivity are (non-limitative) as follows:

- Duration
- Project size
- Team size
- Development language
- Number of languages to be used
- Technical complexity
- Requirements volatility
- Influence of non-functional requirements

Preferably, the organization that has to carry out the project has a large database with historical data at its disposal. This means that parametric estimation can only be done in a proper way if an "Estimating and Performance Measurement" process is in place in the organization. In such a process, it is important to standardize work breakdown structures (WBS) and effort hours recording tools to be able to collect the data of completed projects and store them in a standardized way. Only then it is possible to use the historic data in parametric estimation.

When an organization does not have an Estimating and Performance Measurement process in place, which is quite common for organizations that operate on a CMMI level lower than 3 (i.e., most IT companies in the world), it is still possible to use parametric estimation. A public repository like the ISBSG "New Developments and Enhancements" is a good alternative and also the default settings of some estimation tools like Galorath SEER-SEM [13] or Quantitative Software Management (QSM) Software Lifecycle Management (SLIM) [14] can be used. Of course, the selection of the best reference projects to use in the estimate is an important activity, which influences the accuracy of the estimate significantly, and the best reference projects are the organization's own projects.

Project-Specific Characteristics

As every project is unique, there will always be a difference between the actual project characteristics and the characteristics of the historical data that is being used in the estimate. The influence of these project-specific characteristics should be taken into account in the estimate. Is there for instance a very experienced team in this particular project? Or are there perhaps more non-functional requirements than usual to be realized? Another project-specific characteristic is schedule compression, although in some organizations this is actually the same for all projects. An important activity in parametric estimation is to identify possible project-specific characteristics and the impact of these on the estimate. This is a difficult task and should be done by experienced estimators or cost engineers.

Estimate

When the functional size is known, the productivity rate is chosen and the effect of project-specific characteristics is taken into account, the total number of hours, the duration, the maximum team size, and the probable quality level can be calculated. Most organizations that are using parametric estimation use sophisticated tools for this. Some well-known and often used tools are SEER-SEM and QSM SLIM. One of the main features of these tools is the possibility to calculate multiple scenarios in a quick and easy way, like the impact of schedule compression or the maximum team size to be used. It is well known that project duration is actually a very important parameter in project estimation (one that is usually not taken into account in expert estimates!). The duration chosen for a project of a certain size in an organization with certain productivity impacts the necessary team size and therefore the number of hours needed to do the job.

The Impact of Duration on an Estimate

One of the main drivers that influence the effort hours needed for a project is the duration.

The influence of duration is shown in Figure 30.3 [15].

When we look at this figure, we see that for every software development project of a given size, it is possible to make a different estimate of cost and effort, depending on the duration chosen. There is an impossible area in which the project simply cannot be done. Also, there is a duration area in which the estimation is not very practical (as the project takes relatively too long, the benefits of the project will be less). The black line that indicates the duration versus effort/cost trade-off represents the productivity of a specific organization. This law is based on the fact that to be able to deliver a project in a shorter duration than with an optimal team

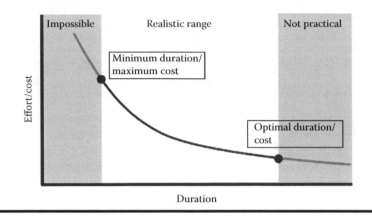

Figure 30.3   Impact of duration.

size, one has to increase the team size to be able to develop faster. However, as for instance ISBSG indicates, the optimal team size of a given project is about four persons. Any extra person on the team will reduce the overall productivity, as more communication paths arise, project management and planning will become more difficult, dependencies will increase, and the number of defects will also increase. This also means that large teams usually deliver worse software with regard to maintainability, which affects also the Total Cost of Ownership (TCO) in a negative way.

When we look at this figure, we can make the following observations:

- There is an impossible zone in which the project cannot be completed (the classic phrase of the nine women delivering one child in one month).
- The first possible duration indicates the minimal duration/maximum cost scenario.
- There are numerous estimations possible on the duration versus effort/cost trade-off, each resulting in a different effort/cost estimation and, therefore, also in different productivity (hours per Function Point) and cost per Function Point metrics.
- There is an optimal effort/cost estimation, although it is hard to calculate where.
- There is a duration zone in which it is impractical to realize the software (although still possible).

So let's consider one of the typical RFP questions that client organizations ask: What is the price per Function Point that you offer for the realization (technical design, functional design, coding, unit testing, system testing) of this system in Java?

Taking the figure above into consideration, what should be the answer? Let's see how the supplier's metrics desk would react to such a question.

A new RFP comes with the question above being the most important one to select the supplier. The metrics desk people have to come up with an estimate for this new project. First they measure the functional size of the application, and it turns out the size is exactly 1000 Function Points (minimum 900 FP, likely 1000 FP, maximum 1200 FP). After sizing, they select the most probable project delivery rate (PDR) from their historical database and they identify the project-specific characteristics and the possible influences of these on the project outcomes. Then they use a parametric estimating tool to derive Figure 30.4. Please note that there is no real data here, it is only for instructional purposes.

So, what would be the answer to this question? In fact, the question is unanswerable if they do not know the duration that the client has in mind. If the time-to-market is only 6 months, the answer is 1000 €/FP. If the duration is less important, the optimal duration/costs trade-off can be offered, which is 500 €/FP in this case. The people who are involved in estimating the project report this to the commercial people. The estimate involves a range of 1000 €/FP in 6 months to 500 €/FP in 12 months. The commercial people probably will decide to quote the 500 €/FP in their answer in order to score points against the decision criteria scheme of the client's RFP. They even may go for the 400 €/FP all the way in the impractical zone. However, one should be aware of the fact that after the project is won, the project has to be carried out against this price. Only then, the negotiations over the duration for the project may start. The result is shown in Figure 30.5.

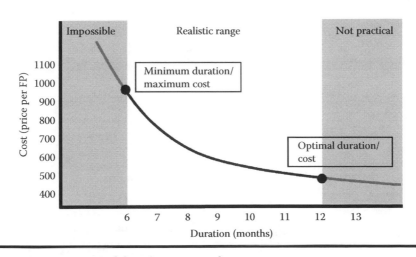

Figure 30.4 Impact of duration—example.

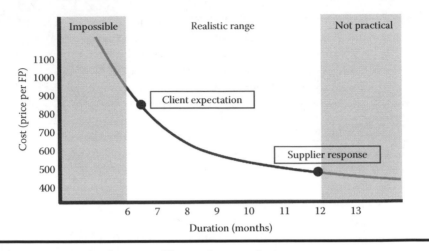

Figure 30.5 Result of not specific metrics questions.

Of course, this is not a very good way to start the project and probably there will already be problems in the relationship during these investigations. The reason for this: the RFP question was just not specific enough!

The Impact of Optimism and Pessimism in Requests for Proposals

The result of these types of non-specific RFP questions is that suppliers tend to quote an overly optimistic estimate (i.e., price per Function Point, total effort hours, or total costs). The effects of optimism are shown in Figure 30.6.

The figure points out that in the case of an optimistic estimation of the project (too few hours have been estimated regarding the duration and/or the other characteristics of the project), the realized extra costs of the project will be higher in a nonlinear way. Possible causes for this relationship are (not limitative) as follows:

■ Planning errors (team size, critical path, etc.)
■ Too little time spent on requirements and design and thus injecting more changes and defects
■ Ineffective strategies to win time (i.e., adding people to a late project makes it later and more expensive)
■ More status meetings, extra management attention, project stress (resulting in more defects)

Next to a failing project, the result may also be a product that is not satisfactory for the client. Because of the fact that the programmers did not have the time to think of good solutions for the problems they faced in the project, they probably

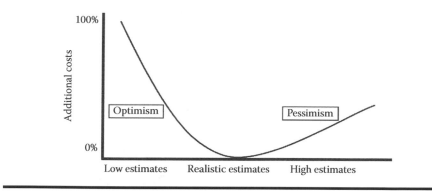

Figure 30.6   Optimism versus pessimism.

used techniques that allowed them to make quick progress, but in the end produced lower quality code (like duplicating pieces of code and not commenting in the code). The result is a system that is hard to maintain and the exploitation costs of the system will be much higher than necessary, resulting also in high TCO. All resulting from optimism in the project estimation phase! Optimism perhaps invoked by selecting the cheapest supplier that was not capable of producing a realistic estimate!

When the project is estimated in a pessimistic way, however, the extra costs of the realized project rise in a linear way. This is due to "Parkinson's law" [16] that states that work expands to fill the available time. A second reason is "student's syndrome," which states that when a project team gets too much time to do a task, they will wait until it is the last possible moment to start with the task and then work really hard to complete it in time. If a programmer says he can do a specific task in 40 hours, but he is ready in 36 hours, he will use the extra 4 hours to enhance the code (additional comments, extra unit tests, perhaps some nice-to-have's) until the 40 hours are spent. As the task is already finished, he will not exceed the 40 hours. A realistic estimation, however, would have been 36 hours, and so this pessimistic estimation in the end was evaluated like a good estimate. Pessimistic estimates are, therefore, very hard to spot. Some project managers report that all of their projects were successful, while, in fact, all their estimates were probably pessimistic, resulting in successful projects that were finished in time and on budget, but not in the most efficient manner. This can only be discovered by benchmarking the projects against similar projects (internal or external) to see whether the productivity that was realized in the project was any good.

Pessimistic estimation is, therefore, a much better option than optimistic estimation. However, the industry is focused on "the cheapest option." There is a constant pressure towards optimism.

The implications of these laws are evident. When a client organization submits an RFP and receives the different quotations of the different suppliers, it is crucial

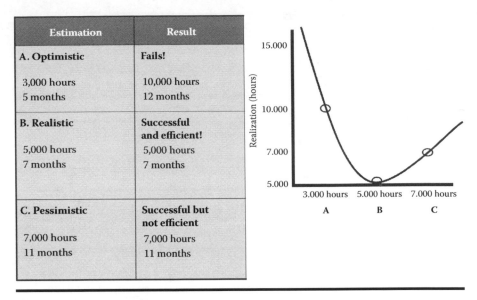

Estimation	Result
A. Optimistic	**Fails!**
3,000 hours	10,000 hours
5 months	12 months
B. Realistic	**Successful and efficient!**
5,000 hours	5,000 hours
7 months	7 months
C. Pessimistic	**Successful but not efficient**
7,000 hours	7,000 hours
11 months	11 months

Figure 30.7 RFP results.

to be able to judge whether the proposals are realistic! Let us look at an example of how things go in day-to-day practice.

An organization submits an RFP for a specific project and receives three quotations, A, B, and C. The quotations are shown in Figure 30.7.

An organization that is not able to recognize that the quotation submitted by Supplier A is unrealistic may (and probably will) go for this one because it is cheaper and it is faster. The result will be disastrous! The question now is of course: How can organizations identify which quotations are realistic and which are not?

Assessing Proposals

There are multiple ways to assess the reality of a proposal. In the remainder of this chapter, it is explained how this can be done using a few of the most widely used tools in parametric estimation: the QSM SLIM tool suite, Galorath SEER-SEM, and the ISBSG repository "New Developments and Enhancements" [17].

Quantitative Software Management Software Life Cycle Management Estimate

The QSM SLIM tool suite is a very powerful tool to estimate, control, analyze, and store projects.

When an organization possesses the QSM SLIM tool suite, it is possible to simulate the quotations in SLIM Estimate. To do this, the following information is needed per quotation:

- Start date and end date of the "Construction and Test" phase of the project
- Size to be delivered (functional size calculated to technical size in SLOCs)
- Effort hours of the "main build" activities

This results in a Productivity Index (PI) that is implied in the quotation. The PI in QSM shows the productivity, which is corrected with the duration. The black line in Figure 30.4 could for instance indicate the PI = 18.0 line. Although the number of hours per Function Point is different on every point on this line, the PI could easily be the same. When the PI that is implied in the estimate is known, it is possible to assess the reality of the quotation. In QSM, it is possible to compare the PI of an estimate with the average PI for similar projects that are present in the QSM database (over 8,000 projects) or with the PI of the projects that are stored in the organization's project history database. When an implied PI is much higher than the average PI for similar projects in the QSM database, the estimate is probably not very realistic and too optimistic. In that case, the organization should ask the supplier to present proof that they are able to produce software with a productivity that is that high. An example is as follows:

Three proposals have been administrated in the database of the tool (Figure 30.8). At first sight it seems that proposal Z is clearly the winning one, as it is cheaper and faster, resulting in a much higher PI than the other two proposals. The question is now if it is also a realistic quotation.

QSM calculates the PI implied in the estimations. Now we can compare the PI with, for instance, the PI that is reported by QSM based on their 2008 Dataset of Business Projects measured in Function Points. This analysis can be made in QSM SLIM Metrics. This is illustrated in Figure 30.9.

It seems that according to this tool, proposal X is the most realistic as it is closer to the PI that may be considered "market-average" (the black line). When the suppliers of proposal Y and Z do not have a good explanation and no proof of the fact that they can deliver software with a productivity that much higher than market average, it would be advisable to choose proposal X. This is of course a very difficult decision and it would require a lot of courage to make it. Therefore, it should be a

ID	Project Name	Effective FP	PI	Hours/FP	C&T Duration (Months)	C&T Effort (MHR)
1	Proposal X	400	13,8	57,5	6,00	23.000,00
2	Proposal Y	400	14,6	45,0	5,53	18.000,00
3	Proposal Z	400	17,3	37,5	3,53	15.000,00

Figure 30.8 Quantitative Software Management proposals.

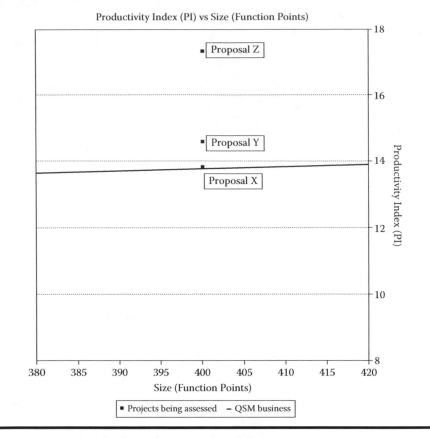

Figure 30.9 Quantitative Software Management assessment.

part of the RFP decision criteria that only realistic proposals are taken into consideration, unless the submitting organization can prove that they are able to deliver software against a much higher productivity than the market average.

Galorath SEER-SEM

The SEER-SEM tool is based on certain knowledge bases in which the knowledge of numerous historical projects are saved. In this tool, first a WBS should be constructed following the different parts of the software system to be developed. For each WBS item, a separate knowledge base can be used. If the project goal is to realize a basic management information system, the work breakdown items could possibly involve a graphical user interface (GUI) and a relational database. For these items, the GUI knowledge base and relational database knowledge base would be selected, while the rest of the software would be constructed under the general "Management Information System" knowledge base. After setting the right

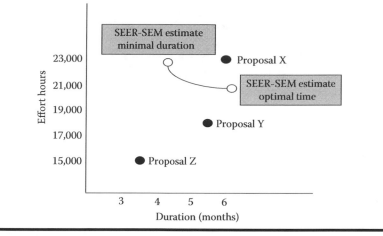

Figure 30.10   SEER-SEM assessment.

WBS, an estimate can be derived by putting in the expected size (in lines of code or Function Points). The tool then generates a valid estimate based on the knowledge base used, the size, and the other parameter settings. It's even better to use the tool to compute the 'minimal time' and the 'optimal effort' scenarios. These estimate could then be used as the base estimate to which the other estimates are compared. When a proposal deviates more than a certain predefined percentage from the base estimate, it would be wise not to choose that proposal. In Figure 30.10 we can see that there is a minimum time scenario. It's simply not possible to execute the project faster than the duration of this scenario. There is also an optimal effort scenario, which gives the optimal effort/duration scenario. In the figure, we can see that proposal Z is not realistic, as it is in the so-called 'impossible zone.' Proposal Y is in the right zone, but not very realistic when it comes to the effort hours needed. Proposal X is somewhat more expensive than the SEER estimate, but it is still the most realistic offer according to this analysis.

ISBSG "New Developments and Enhancements"

The third way to assess the proposals is to use the ISBSG "New projects and Enhancements repository." This is the only open repository with software realization project data available worldwide and it contains more than 5,000 projects in release 11. This assessment basically works the same as the previous two methods, but the main metric that can be compared here is the PDR in hours per Function Point. We have already seen that when this metric is used stand-alone, the usefulness is very low. However, when selecting the projects against which the supplier quotations are compared, the duration and size (and quality) of the projects are also taken into account, and the usefulness will be much higher. The ISBSG provides a tool for this analysis, which is called the comparative estimating tool. As the data is open, it is also possible to do project-specific analysis where the reference projects are selected by hand. After this, it is possible to do a statistical analysis. An example of such an analysis is illustrated in Table 30.1.

If one considers the realistic range for this project to be between the Percentile 25% value (which means that 25% of the 476 selected projects performed better than the value) and the Percentile 75% value, a realistic range can be determined (Table 30.2).

Table 30.1 Statistical Analysis of the Selected Reference Projects in the ISBSG Database

Characteristic	PDR (hours/FP)	Speed of Delivery (FP/month)	Duration of 400 FP Project (months)
Number of selected projects	476		
Average value	61.4	91	4.4
Percentile 10% value	23.4	84	4.8
Percentile 25% value	47.3	75	5.3
Percentile 50% value (median)	55.1	70	5.7
Percentile 75% value	78.8	62	6.5
Percentile 90% value	90.5	53	7.5

Table 30.2 Realistic Range Based on the Statistical Analysis of the Selected ISBSG Projects

Characteristic	PDR (hours/FP)	Speed of Delivery (FP/month)	Duration of 400 FP Project (months)
Percentile 25% value	47.3	75	5.3
Percentile 50% value (median)	55.1	70	5.7
Percentile 75% value	78.8	62	6.5

It is clear that only proposal X is realistic according to Table 30.2.

ISBSG also offers another specific tool called the ISBSG Reality Checker [18]. Although input options are at the moment quite restricted (size, platform, language type), ISBSG is in the process of updating the tool to accept more input criteria. The Reality Checker will find the realistic ranges of effort spent and project duration.

Proposals for More Effective Request for Proposal Management

Now that it is obvious which problems supplier organizations face when trying to answer an RFP and the implications this has on the ability of client organizations to choose the right supplier, a number of recommendations can be drawn up. The questions that are often asked are repeated and the recommendations are given. The first typical question is as follows:

> *What is your productivity rate for Java projects?*

The main recommendation is very evident. *Make the question as specific as possible.* A better question would already be the following:

> *What is your productivity rate (hours/FP) for a moderately complex Java project of 500 Function Points and a duration of 20 weeks?*

However, this question still lacks a lot of context. It is not clear which activities should be included for instance. Will the supplier be in charge of the full life cycle or perhaps only technical design, coding, and testing? It is crucial to supply this information!

A much better question would be the following:

> *What is your productivity rate (hours/FP) for a moderately complex Java project of 500 Function Points and a duration of 20 weeks? Phases to include are technical design, coding, unit testing, systems testing, and support of the user organization during the user acceptance test.*

This last question is easily answerable for suppliers who have a history database with project data. For the supplier, it is then quite easy to compare the different supplier quotations and to assess their reality to market averages or historical data.

Conclusions

Many outsourced projects are unsuccessful or even fail. Although there can be many reasons why individual projects fail, in this chapter the impact of RFP management was investigated. It is obvious that not only the suppliers who do the work are to blame for failing projects. Client organizations often increase the probability for project failure by the following:

- Not specifying the functional and non-functional requirements in sufficient detail
- Asking RFP questions that are not specific enough and that are therefore "unanswerable"
- Using an ineffective framework for decision making without assessing the reality of proposals (i.e., just picking the cheapest one)

Good RFP management, asking specific RFP questions, and selecting the best *realistic* proposal will increase the success rate significantly. This would mean, however, that both client organizations and supplier organizations have to become more mature in their estimation processes. Nowadays, most IT organizations worldwide are on maturity level zero or one in the estimation maturity model [19], using only "expert" estimation as the basis for project estimates. If we want the percentage of successful IT projects to increase, resulting in higher client satisfaction (actually the most important metric around!), the average maturity in the industry should at least go up to level two or three!

To conclude, good RFP questions should contain the following information:

- Metric to compare between competitors, for instance
  - Productivity (hours/FP, Function Points/hour, PI)
  - Costs (cost/FP)
  - Quality (defects per Function Point, mean-time-to-defect)
- Technology (for instance, Java, Oracle, or MS.NET)
- Size (in IFPUG, NESMA, or COSMIC Function Points)
- Technical/functional complexity (for instance, high/medium/low)
- Phases/activities to include (for instance, technical design, coding, unit testing, systems testing)
- Duration requested (days, weeks, months, years)

It is, therefore, recommendable to ask the questions in the format of (small) case studies.

References

1. The Standish Group. *Standish Chaos Report 2009.* http://www.standishgroup.com. Accessed June 11, 2011.
2. Wikipedia. http://www.wikipedia.org/. Accessed June 16, 2011.
3. IFPUG. 2004. *Function Point Counting Practices Manual, Version 4.2.* International Function Point Users Group. www.ifpug.org. Accessed June 16, 2011.
4. NESMA. 2004. *Definitions and Counting Guidelines for the Application of Function Point Analysis: A Practical Manual, Version 2.2.* Netherlands Software Measurement User Association. (in Dutch), http://www.nesma.org/. Accessed July 22, 2011.
5. Abran, A., and C. Symons, et al. 2003. *The COSMIC Functional Size Measurement Method Version 3.0, Measurement Manual* (The COSMIC Implementation Guide for ISO/IEC 19761: 2003). http://www.cosmicon.com.
6. McConnell, S. 2006. *Software Estimation—Demystifying the Black Art.* Redmond, WA: Microsoft Press.
7. Boehm, B. 1981. *Software Engineering Economics.* Upper Saddle River, NJ: Prentice-Hall.
8. Albrecht, A. J. 1979. Measuring application development productivity. In *Proceedings of the Joint SHARE, GUIDE, and IBM Application Development Symposium*, pp. 83–92. Monterey, California: IBM Corporation.

9. Boehm, B. 1981. *Software Engineering Economics*. Upper Saddle River, NJ: Prentice-Hall.
10. Boehm, B. et al. 2000. *Software Cost Estimation with COCOMO II*. Upper Saddle River, NJ: Prentice-Hall.
11. IFPUG website: http://www.ifpug.org. Accessed August 23, 2011.
12. ISBSG, Hill, P. (ed.). 2011. *Practical Software Project Estimation: A Toolkit for Estimating Software Development Effort & Duration*. New York: McGraw-Hill.
13. Galorath SEER-SEM website: http://www.galorath.com. Accessed September 21, 2011.
14. Quantitative Software Management (QSM) Software Lifecycle Management (SLIM) tool suite. http://www.qsm.com. Accessed June 18, 2011.
15. Putnam, L. H., and W. Myers. 2003. *Five Core Metrics: Intelligence Behind Successful Software Management*. New York: Dorset Publishing House.
16. C. Northcote Parkinson. 1955. *Parkinson's law. The Economist*, November 19, 1955.
17. International Software Benchmarking Standards Group (ISBSG). 2009. *New Development & Enhancements Repository R11*. http://www.isbsg.org. Accessed September 22, 2011.
18. International Software Benchmarking Standards Group (ISBSG) Reality Checker. http://www.isbsg.org/. Accessed September 10, 2011.
19. Estimation Maturity Model. http://www.galorath.com/wp/the-estimate-maturity-model-can-improve-project-success.php. Accessed July 11, 2011.

About the Author

Dr. Harold van Heeringen, CFPA, works for Sogeti Nederland as a senior consultant in software metrics. Harold graduated from the University of Groningen (the Netherlands) with a degree in business economics in 1997 and he has worked in information technology ever since.

Harold is an expert in the functional sizing methods IFPUG, NESMA, and COSMIC, and he is a certified practitioner in the two last methods. Furthermore, he is an expert on different software estimation models and benchmarking practices. In his role as metrics consultant, he advises clients on how to implement estimating and performance measurement processes into their organizations and he trains people in functional size measurement, project estimation, and benchmarking. Apart from his consulting work, he is also heavily involved in the Sogeti estimation process for fixed-price/fixed-date projects. Harold is an advanced expert in using estimation tools like QSM SLIM, Galorath SEER-SEM, and the ISBSG tooling.

Harold is also involved in a number of metrics-related communities:

- Netherlands Software Metrics Association (NESMA)—board member and chairman of the working groups for COSMIC and Benchmarking
- Common Software Measurement International Consortium (COSMIC)—Dutch representative in the International Advisory Council (AIC)
- International Software Benchmarking Standards Group (ISBSG)—president and member of the Product and Technical Advisory Group
- Dutch Association for Cost Engineers (DACE)—working group for parametric analysis

Harold is a frequent speaker at international conferences, like the Software Measurement European Forum (SMEF 2006–2011), the International Workshop on Software Measurement (IWSM 2007–2010), the International Software Measurement and Analysis Conference (ISMA 2007), and the Australian Conference on Software Measurement (ACOSM 2010). He has published a number of white papers and journal articles.

Harold can be reached through e-mail at harold.van.heeringen@sogeti.nl or through the website http://metrieken.sogeti.nl. He is present on LinkedIn and Plaxo. Harold shares his professional thoughts on twitter: @haroldveendam.

PROCESS IMPROVEMENT INTRODUCTION

Pierre Almén

Where there are no metrics, there can be no improvement

Taiichi Ohno
(father of the Toyota Production System)

To improve, change is necessary. But do all change initiatives improve the process? No, as you all know! But how do you know if the process improves? By facts, of course! Introducing software metrics in an IT organization has often met with resistance. Management commitment is crucial to succeed with process improvement. The management must show that they regard this as a strategic work by establishing a measurement program that will be a natural part of the application development and maintenance process.

Talmon Ben-Cnaan works for Amdocs in Israel, where he manages the quality operations in the Acceptance Testing division including more than 1500 testing experts in more than 30 sites worldwide. His chapter, "Effective Utilization of Software Testing Measurements," describes how software testing measurements can be used to improve the testing process. He has included actual examples of measurement analyses and how they helped the organization to identify how to improve software quality at a reduced cost.

Márcio Silveira, who works at HP in Brazil, reviews the basic concepts of Statistical Process Control (SPC) as another way to control the phenomenon of interest and properly forecast them moving from its own collection of historical data.

Sheila Dennis and Patricia Eglin are coauthors of the chapter "Human Performance Improvement: Measuring the Real Change of Process Improvement." Both Sheila and Patricia work for David Consulting Group in the United States. Sheila has worked with IT measurement for over 20 years and was one of the authors in the previous International Function Point Users Group (IFPUG) IT Measurement book and she is a recognized conference speaker. Patricia has approximately 12 years of experience in process improvement and has been working as a Capability Maturity Model Integration (CMMI) practitioner and coach. Sheila and Patricia show how to measure changed behavior, which is the change that is the most important ingredient in process improvement but has proven to be difficult to measure, at least until now.

David Herron from the United States is a Business Development Manager and Vice President of Knowledge Solution Services for David Consulting Group. He is an acknowledged authority in the areas of performance measurement and process improvement and has coauthored several books on topics relating to IT performance measurement. In his chapter "Understanding Your Organization's Best Software Practices," he shows with practical examples how an organization can identify, adopt, and deploy best practices of software development. One example from David is a performance measurement model that includes both quantitative and qualitative analyses.

Steve Neuendorf from the United States has over 40 years of experience within industrial engineering, measurement, and management and has been an independent management consultant for more than 20 years. Steve has published many books and articles on the subject of process measurement and improvement. In his chapter "Process Improvement," "building blocks" are presented that show the overall elements of software measurement and process improvement. Furthermore, he shows how the three process characteristics or metrics Efficiency, Cycle-time, and Quality, are influenced by the presence and level of the identified attributes on performance.

Joseph (Joe) Schofield is a former member of the Technical Staff at Sandia National Laboratories in United States, a Certified Software Quality Specialist, a Certified Software Measurement Specialist, a frequent Software Best Practice Webinar presenter, and the current President of the IFPUG. Joe shows in his chapter "Defects: Perspective on Prevalence and Prevention" how the capture-recapture method (CRM), introduced for estimating biological populations, can be used to estimate latent software defects. With CRM, thresholds can be established for latent defect acceptance.

Chapter 31

Software Measurements: Effective Utilization of Software Testing Measurements

Talmon Ben Cnaan

Contents

> *If you were to say to the grown-ups: "I saw a beautiful house made of rosy brick, with geraniums in the windows and doves on the roof," they would not be able to get any idea of that house at all. You would have to say to them: "I saw a house that cost $200,000." Then they would exclaim: "Oh, what a pretty house that is!"*
>
> **Antoine de Saint-Exupéry,**
> *"The Little Prince"*

Introduction

This chapter explains how software testing measurements can be used to identify ways to improve the testing process and the software development lifecycle. The chapter also provides actual examples of measurement analyses and describes how they help identify what needs to be done to improve software quality at a reduced cost.

Many articles and blogs on software testing present objections to measuring testing quality, efficiency, and productivity. Comparing different test cases and thereby counting them as "identical" is problematic and does not lead to accurate results. The same is true when comparing defects. One defect may have a catastrophic impact on the business, while another may cause significant but controllable damage to the business. What is the meaning, in this case, of combining and counting them as two?

The limitations on measuring complex processes must be considered when analyzing metrics. Understanding the inaccuracy of software measurements is important when analyzing the data. To identify a true trend, many data points need to be taken.

Basic Definitions

To understand the examples described in this chapter, let us agree on the following:

Measuring the Quality of the Software Projects

Several parameters affect the term "quality." Following the PMI (Project Management Institute) definition, a quality product "fits its purpose" [1]. Therefore, the quality of the software product includes customer satisfaction, functional quality (the software accomplishes the requirements of the business), and non-functional attributes such as performance, usability, security, ease of implementation, and so on. In many cases, counting defects relates to the functional aspect of software quality. (In our analyses, we count functional defects only. Other types of defects, such as those related to installation errors, documentation errors, performance, and so on are excluded.)

Moreover, we assume that the severity of a defect reflects the impact of this defect on the business and that there are no catastrophes, and so there is a correlation between number of defects (by severity) and the functional quality.

Measuring the Defect Removal Effectiveness of the Testing Team

Let us look at the following case study, in which High and Critical defects were tracked and analyzed. The project size was 450 Function Points (FPs); it lasted for 8 months, following 6 weeks of acceptance tests (AT). After design, code development, and unit test, there were three stages of testing:

- Subsystem test (SST; testing at application level)
- System test (ST; testing at suite level—several applications developed by the same vendor)
- AT (including all interfaces)

Two hundred eighty High and Critical defects were detected and removed in the SST; an additional 360 High and Critical defects were removed in the ST.

The AT was performed by a different vendor. They found 240 High and Critical defects.

Six weeks after deployment (which is the period used to count defects in production), there were 0 Critical and 100 High defects. Results are summarized in Table 31.1.

A graphical presentation of defect removal is shown Figure 31.1. Figure 31.1 shows the removal rate at each testing stage: The number of defects per FPs at each testing stage is marked with a different pattern. Actual results are shown on the left bar. The right bar presents a better defect removal (defects are detected earlier). The right bar shows the organizational target. This target is based on budget and time constraints and on historical data of similar projects. Different targets may require deeper organizational change.

Defect Density

Nine hundred eighty defects were injected by the Development Teams regardless of the stage at which these defects were detected. Therefore, the defect density is 980 defects/450 FP or 2.18 defects/FP. Defect density is presented by the total height of the bar in Figure 31.1.

Table 31.1 Example of Calculated Defect Removal Effectiveness and Defect Density

	Found	Escaped	Removal Effectiveness
Subsystem test	280		
System test	360		
Acceptance test	240		
Defects in production	100		
Total injected by development	980		
Defects that escaped from pre-delivery testing		240 + 100 = 340	(280 + 360)/980 = 65.3%
Defects that escaped from acceptance testing		100	240/(100 + 240) = 70.6%
Total removed	880		
Overall removal efficiency			880/980 = 89.8%

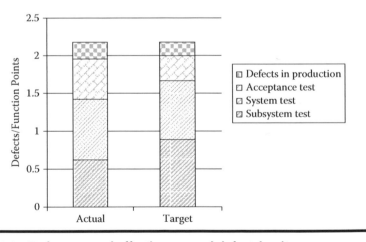

Figure 31.1 Defect removal effectiveness and defect density.

Better design reviews, unit test, and code inspection will reduce the total height of the bar. Improving the design and coding process is indicated as a better target in Figure 31.2. Figure 31.2 shows a new target, with fewer defects injected into the code, resulting in better quality in production.

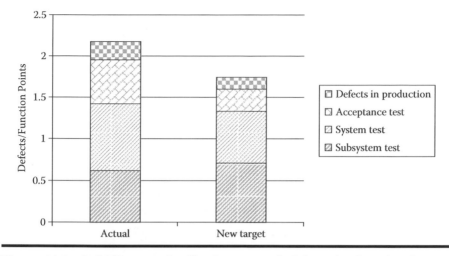

Figure 31.2 Defect removal effectiveness and defect density, showing an improved development process.

The defect removal effectiveness of the AT team is 70.6%. A higher removal rate is expected, obviously without increasing testing costs. In the following examples, we show how defect removal rate is tracked and analyzed.

Measuring the Productivity of the Testing Team

Productivity is a measure of output from a production process, per unit of input [2]. The main input of the testing "factory" is labor (assuming no need for additional hardware), measured in person-days or person-months. What is the output? Is it number of defects, number of test cases, or number of test points?

In this chapter, we assume that the role of testing is to verify that the solution meets its requirements (in other words, de-risking the delivery). To be on the safe side, we assume that code that was not tested will not work properly. Therefore, the output of testing is "verified functionality" or "tested functionality," measured by executed test cases. Defects are a by-product of the verification.

Note: The number of test cases by itself is a poor measurement for "verified functionality" as it does not indicate the coverage of the testing. Additional measurement is required to show coverage.

It is an interesting dilemma whether we should reduce testing after receiving clean code from the Development Team (let us complicate the catch … what if we receive three consecutive clean versions?). Can we trust the Development Team and go live without testing? Luckily enough, we have never faced this dilemma in real life.… .

Test cases may be big (long), small (short), simple, or complex. To overcome the diversity, some organizations "normalize" the test cases using the Composite

Weighting Factor (CWF). Some divide long test cases into short ones (this is done in my organization). When test cases are measurable, they can also be used to monitor progress! In this chapter, we assume that test cases have a similar size.

General Comment about the Scaling Used in the Figures

The figures that are presented in this chapter are real examples of measurement analyses, based on actual data from projects that were delivered to customers. For reasons of confidentiality and to avoid disclosing sensitive information, the scales of many figures were omitted. However, trends and the interpretations that result from the figures were kept as is.

Example 1: Good Testing Results Start with the Quality of the Code

Figure 31.3 shows post-production defects, normalized to the project's size (High and Critical defects). At the end of each version, we collect and count the Critical and High severity defects that were detected during the first 6 weeks after going live.

By looking at the results over time, we cannot identify a stable process or a clear trend. The quality of release V2 was poor, release V3 was the best, and in the following releases, more and more defects leaked to production.

Figure 31.4 shows the same information as in Figure 31.3, but another dimension was added to the figure. Since we also count the defects detected by our Testing Team (performing AT), we can calculate how many defects were in the code before acceptance testing. For example, if 240 defects were detected and removed during testing and 100 defects leaked to post-production, we assume that there were 340 defects in the software before acceptance testing.

We can now identify a high correlation between the height of the "brick" bars and the height of the "diagonal" bars!

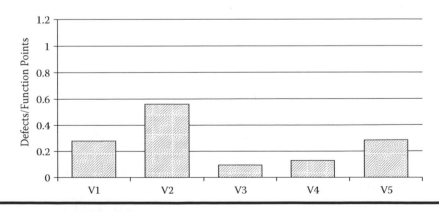

Figure 31.3 Defects leaked to production.

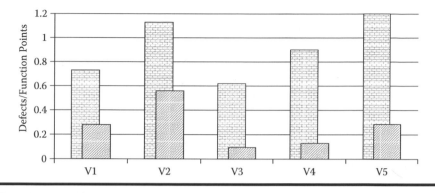

Figure 31.4 Defects delivered to acceptance tests and defects leaked to production.

The same pattern was identified in many other projects. The ability of the Acceptance Testing Team to deliver a high-quality product depends greatly on the number of defects they receive!

(Some readers may find this obvious: "Of course, the more defects there are, the more difficult testing will be, and the more defects there will be that manage to leak into production." Now try to sell that to management; they will always come back to us, the testers, blaming us for not having found more.)

Conclusion: If the Testing Team wants to improve its output, it should proactively push for better code! This was accomplished at our company in the following ways:

- The AT Team helps the ST Teams (that perform the previous testing stage) to test. Together, they analyze the root cause of defects, so that more defects can be detected by ST.
- The AT Team monitors Unit Test and Code Inspection. A small number of defects in these stages may indicate that Unit Test and Code Inspection were not exhaustive.
- The AT Team participates in design reviews to identify design defects. They also participate in ST design reviews to identify missed coverage, wrong interpretation of business requirements, and errors in selecting test data.

Example 2: When to Stop Testing

It is suggested that a basic criterion for stopping testing is when "the defect discovery rate has dropped below a previously defined threshold" [3].

Allow us to challenge this statement:

Figure 31.5 shows the defect discovery rate per week during AT. In week 10, the rate dropped by almost 60%, and the number of defects detected in week 11 and 12 was very low. So, could we have finished testing after 10 weeks?

Waiting and counting the defects after production showed us that 20% of the defects escaped testing. Only 80% were detected during acceptance testing. (It is shown by the line and the right vertical axis.)

Combining the measurement of the defect removal rate (bars) and defect removal effectiveness (line) in one figure has led us to a different conclusion:

- Testing was based on scripted testing. Test cases were designed before the code was delivered to Testing. It seems that these scripted tests were not effective enough to detect more than 80% of the defects, although there was sufficient testing time.
- We decided to perform exploratory testing, in addition to the scripted tests, to detect additional defects. Exploratory testing was added to the last 3 weeks of testing. Testers were instructed to test "everything that was missed."

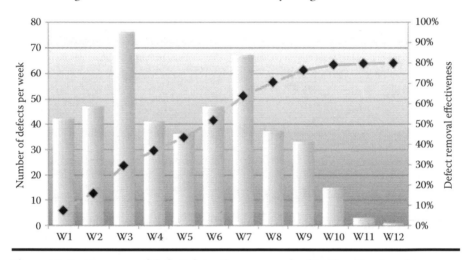

Figure 31.5 Progress of defect detection per week of testing (bars) and as a percentage of the total number of defects (line).

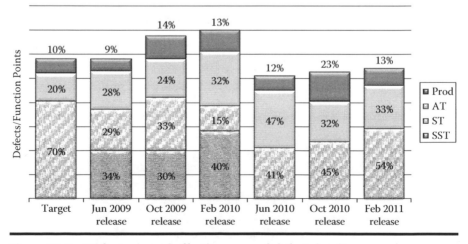

Figure 31.6 Defect removal effectiveness and defect density.

Example 3: Early Defect Detection or How Many Test Stages Are Needed?

Figure 31.6 shows six enhancement versions that were delivered to the customer from June 2009 to February 2011. Targets of defect removal per stage are presented in the leftmost bar. Testing stages are as follows:

- SST
- ST
- AT
- Prod (Production)

Until February 2010, there were two testing stages before delivery to AT. Then, the supplier of the software decided to cut testing costs and merge the two stages into one.

Let us analyze Figure 31.6:

1. Removal effectiveness before delivery to AT:
   Before combining the ST and SST into one stage, the removal rate was around 65%. However, in the first version using one combined testing stage, removal rate dropped to 41%!
   Problems were identified and fixed, and removal rate improved to 45% and then to 54%. However, the target removal rate of 70% was not met.
2. Defect density:
   The defect density in the first three versions was high (1.2–1.4). Because of extensive improvements in code inspection, we can see that, in the last three versions, defect density was reduced to a level of 1.0–1.1.
   Therefore, it was clear that the significant area to be improved is in ST rather than in Development.

Example 4: Effect of High Work-in-Process on Quality

To overcome the challenges of scope changes and late requirements, the Development Team divided its work into code drops using smaller waterfalls and not moving into Agile methodology.

The scope was divided into three code drops. When "Drop 0" development was completed, it was delivered to Testing, and the Development Teams started the detailed design and coding of the next drop. The Acceptance Testing Team tested each drop (including regression testing), and the entire release was then moved to Production.

Part of the root cause analysis of defects found in AT and Production involved identifying the source drop of the code. Results from two releases are shown in

Figures 31.7 and 31.8. In these figures, the defect density is presented by the bars and the left axis; the size of each drop is presented by the diamond shapes and the right axis.

In both versions, the first drop is cleaner than the others are and the last drop has a higher number of defects/FP.

The findings were presented to the Development Teams to try to identify the reason for the drop of quality from Drop 0 to Drop 2.

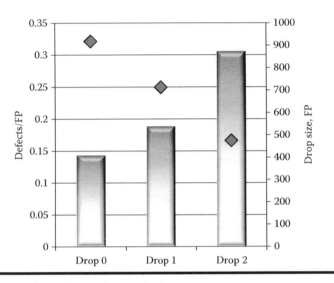

Figure 31.7   Defect allocated to code drops.

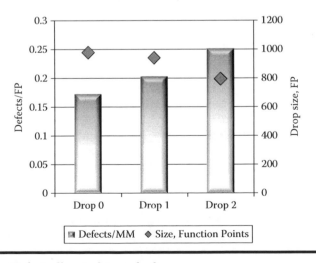

Figure 31.8   Defect allocated to code drops.

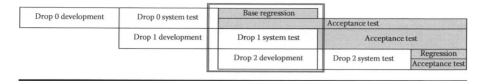

Figure 31.9   Project time line.

Surprisingly, the findings matched their assumptions. To explain the reason for this behavior, let us look at the development time line.

Figure 31.9 shows the time line of a typical version. Time is progressing from left to right; each line presents the activities of a software drop. All drops go live on the same day, represented by the right end of the time line.

During the development of Drop 0, developers can focus on the scope of this drop.

While developing Drop 1, the developers are also busy with fixing defects that are detected in the system test of Drop 3.

During the development of Drop 3, the developers are performing the following tasks:

1. Designing and coding of Drop 2
2. Analyzing and fixing defects that are detected in ST of Drop 1
3. Analyzing and fixing defects detected in AT "base regression"
4. Analyzing and fixing defects related to Drop 0 that were detected in acceptance testing
5. Merging the code fixes into the current code

The high Work-in-Process (WIP) affected the quality. Showing the correlation between high WIP and quality to the customer, it was decided that complicated scope items should only be signed off and delivered in the first drops.

Example 5: Defect Removal Effectiveness: Are We Improving?

Figure 31.10 shows the defect removal effectiveness of a Testing Team across eight versions. When this team started the testing (after taking it over from another team), the removal rate was 50%. Every second defect leaked to production! The result was not good enough, so steps were taken to improve testers' knowledge, and better reviews of the test design with the business and peer reviews were added to the test design process.

In time, defect removal rate improved up to 80%—a very nice achievement. A nice trend is shown on Figure 31.10: an average improvement of 4.55% for each version (see formula in Figure 31.10).

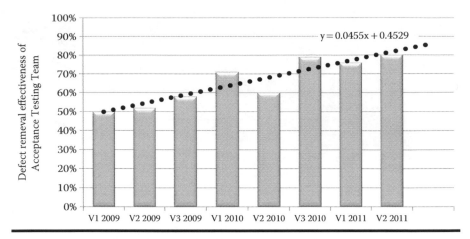

Figure 31.10 Defect removal effectiveness.

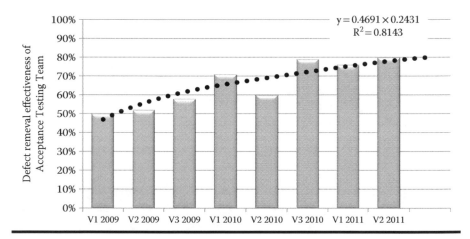

Figure 31.11 Defect removal effectiveness, nonlinear trend.

Is it?

Can we expect a removal rate of 86% in the next version?

We have decided to take a pessimistic approach. We also found it suspicious that, for the last three versions, the improvement shown has been very slow, if any at all.

Let us assume a learning curve attitude.

Figure 31.11 shows the same result, but the trend line is nonlinear. Using this trend line, we can project that the expected removal rate of the next release will not exceed 80%.

We have communicated to the customer and to our management that we expect 80%. Fortunately (or not), this was the outcome of the next release.

The previous actions taken to improve testing will not bring about further advances. Something new is required.

How Can We Evaluate a Testing Team?

A Testing Team is required to detect more defects and improve the quality of delivery. However, management often complains that testing cost is too high and should be reduced.

How can we compare the performance of the various Testing Teams? Many parameters affect the outcome of a Testing Team: the size of the development project, the amount of functionality already in production (that affects regression size), the nature of the products, the quality of work done by the development, and the tasks performed by the Testing Team in addition to functional testing. Can we "normalize" all these parameters into a measurable grade?

Let us try to define what a good Testing Team is:

1. Reasonable number of defects that escape to Production or to next testing stage
2. Lowest testing effort:
    a. High productivity: Fast design and execution of test cases
    b. High efficiency: Minimize the number of required test cases without impacting the testing coverage and the resultant quality

Figure 31.12 shows the expected improvement of a Testing Team as a three-dimensional vector:

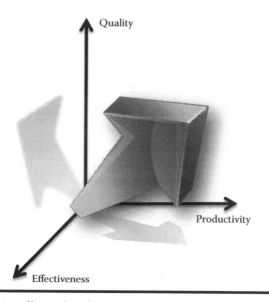

Figure 31.12   Three-dimensional improvement.

Quality

Quality is measured as the number of defects that escaped from the Testing Team, normalized to version size.

- Defect severity is important.
- Defects can be counted as all defects, High and Critical defects, or an equivalent defect count. Equation 31.1 is an example of a weighted count:

$$((1 \cdot \text{simple defects}) + (2 \cdot \text{medium defects}) + (4 \cdot \text{high defects}) + (9 \cdot \text{critical defects}))/4$$

$$(31.1)$$

- Equation 31.1—defect equivalence
  - The outcome is "number of defects equivalent to High."
  - The number of defects should be normalized to the version size. If FPs (or similar sizing method) are not in use, the total version effort or the net development effort can represent the size.

Productivity

As already suggested, testing productivity is measured by the number of test cases per testing effort.

- Productivity of regression testing and productivity of the testing of new functionality are independent. Averaging the two is meaningless.
- Automated test cases should be counted, as well as the effort to automate. Therefore, test automation may increase test productivity.
- Testing effort includes the effort to design and execute functional testing.
- High productivity does not indicate efficiency or quality. A Testing Team may perform many test cases that are not effective enough to detect all defects.

Effectiveness—Testing Depth

Effectiveness means doing the right thing. Being effective, a Testing Team should reduce its rework (redesign testware as a result of changes, testing errors, cancelled defects, and so on), as well as its idle time, such as waiting for code, reference data, or test data; environments that are not prepared on time; or show-stoppers (Critical defects) that impede testing progress.

An effective Testing Team prepares the testing environment on time, and extracting test data from the Production environment is a smooth and efficient process.

An effective Testing Team maintains high code coverage without increasing the number of test cases, for example, using pairwise or combinatorial testing techniques.

All of the above should be shown by measuring productivity. With less rework and less idle time, testers can design and execute more test cases with less effort.

So, what is effectiveness?

Suppose we have two testing teams. Both receive the same code with identical quality and both remove the exact number of defects. However, Group A has planned and executed 3000 test cases, while Group B met the same achievements with 6000 test cases. Assuming both teams have the same productivity, Group A will need half of the testing effort (or half of the time). Group A is more effective. Therefore, we can measure effectiveness as the number of test cases per FP.

Since FPs measure the size of the new (or changed) functionality, we can measure the effectiveness of new functionality testing. The number of regression test cases should not be proportional to the size of the version.

Summary

A good Testing Team should consider the following:

1. Deliver fewer defects (per FPs) to Production
2. Perform more test cases with less testing effort
3. Achieve a high level of quality with fewer test cases

Let us describe this graphically starting with two parameters: quality and productivity. The center point of Table 31.2 is the baseline. In the next version, we will be on one of the four quadrants.

Let us now add the third dimension, testing effectiveness. All dimensions are shown in Table 31.3.

The right side of Table 31.3 reflects the quality/productivity quadrants, where effectiveness is high (low number of test cases per FP); the left side reflects quality/productivity, where effectiveness is low.

Table 31.2 Quality and Productivity

	High Quality		
Low Productivity	High quality and low productivity: Good, but slow: Automate?	High quality and high productivity: We want to be here	High Productivity
	Low quality and low productivity: Skills? Management?	High productivity and low quality: Coverage issue: test cases not effective or not enough	
	Low Quality		

Table 31.3 Effectiveness, Quality, and Productivity

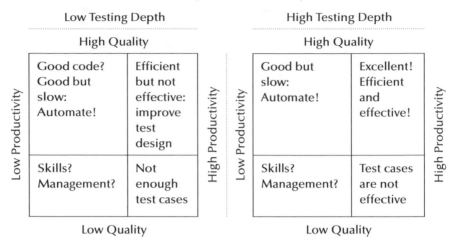

Summary

The examples shown above were used by the Measurements Team to drive organizational changes. When findings and conclusions are based on metrics, there cannot be any dispute about facts. Management and stakeholders see the results and trends and can accept the conclusions with more confidence that the right steps have been taken.

Moreover, when improvement is achieved, the Testing Manager can show this using same type of analysis, not by using stories or superlatives, but by showing pure facts: counting defects, test cases, FPs, and effort.

References

1. Project Management Institute, Inc. 2000. *A Guide to the Project Management Body of Knowledge*. 2000 ed. (ISBN 1-880410-23-0). Newton Square, PA: Project Management Institute, Inc.
2. Wikipedia, the free encyclopedia. *Definition for Productivity*. http://en.wikipedia.org/wiki/Productivity (accessed July 1, 2011).
3. Copeland, L. 2008. *A Practitioner's Guide to Software Test Design*. 8th printing (ISBN 1-58053-791-x). Norwood, MA: Artech House Publishers.

About the Author

Talmon Ben-Cnaan is a quality manager at Amdocs. He led the quality measurements effort in his company, was responsible for collecting and analyzing software measurements from software development projects, and provided quality reports to senior management, based on those measurements. The author was also responsible for implementing Function Points in his organization. He is an IFPUG member and a PMP.

Currently, the author manages quality operations in the Acceptance Testing division. The Acceptance Testing division includes more than 1,700 testing experts, located at more than 30 sites worldwide, and specializes in testing for telecommunications service providers.

Amdocs is the market leader in the telecommunications market, with over 19,000 employees, delivering the most advanced business support systems (BSS), operational support systems (OSS), and service delivery to communications service providers in more than 60 countries around the world.

Chapter 32

A Framework to Implement Statistical Process Control

Márcio Silveira

Contents

Introduction

With the market pressures for better quality, reduced cost, and increased productivity, companies are struggling to improve their processes to achieve enhanced levels of productivity and quality. One of the major reasons for this challenge is that companies are not addressing the activity to improve processes in a standardized way. Ad hoc initiatives, and actions that ignore the data and are based on guessing, are very common. Therefore, in many cases, the improvements are not sustainable and after time passes the process returns to chaos again. In order to improve processes, it is very important to address the problem with a process mind-set using a standard set of activities so that improvements will be permanent.

This chapter aims to introduce the basic concepts of Statistical Process Control (SPC), a set of processes and techniques to improve processes. The chapter will introduce SPC to the reader and identify the characteristics of processes that work well with SPC. A framework to apply SPC to processes is shown, and finally lessons learned are shared. A bibliography is provided at the end of the chapter for those that are interested in getting more details.

What Is Statistical Process Control?

To better define what SPC is about let us analyze Figure 32.1.

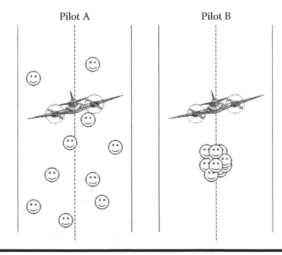

Figure 32.1 Which one do you prefer to fly with, A or B?

This picture represents places (happy faces) where the pilots A and B landed their airplanes. As you can see both pilots landed properly and safely in all flights, with neither missing the runway. So the question is: Which one do you prefer to fly with, A or B?

Maybe you can answer that it does not matter since both pilots landed properly and within the thresholds of the runway, but there is a fundamental difference between the two. Pilot B is more predictable than pilot A. Pilot B usually lands within the bounds. Pilot A tends to land in several different places.

The main difference between the pilots is that pilot A, when landing, accrues more variance in terms of where he is landing, whereas pilot B lands in the same place every time.

This example is relatively easy to understand, but sometimes understanding is only possible by doing statistical analysis on the data.

SPC is the process of applying statistical methods and techniques in order to analyze and then control the variation that a process may have.

Statistical Process Control Concepts

When analyzing process behavior using SPC, some concepts are important to understand. In order to define these concepts, we will use a type of chart that is a key technique/tool used to understand process variation. This tool is named a control chart. It is out of scope of this chapter to describe all different types of control charts, and we will use a simple one to help us to understand process variation.

In Figure 32.2, each diamond (observation) represents the number of defects that a product had. Therefore, axis *x* represents each product and axis *y* represents the number of defects.

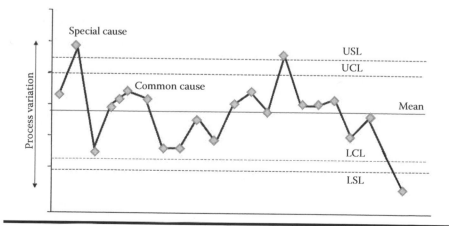

Figure 32.2   Control chart basics.

Let us then try to understand the elements of this chart. The first important element is *mean*. It represents, in this case, the average number of defects in each product. The mean is an important element for analyzing variation. If you have observations near the mean, it means that the process is more stable than another where the observations are dispersed from the mean.

Another important concept is the limits of specification and control. Upper Specification Limit (USL) and Lower Specification Limit (LSL) are the expected performance of the process by the user as it pertains to process (process capability). This range is what he/she expects the process performance to be. Therefore, in the example, we could say that at the maximum (USL) a product can have 15 defects and the minimum (LSL) of course should be zero. In other types of processes, LSL may be different from zero.

A similar concept is the limits of control. Upper Control Limit (UCL) and Lower Control Limit (LCL) are based on the real performance of the process. Normally UCL and LCL are calculated using ±3 standard deviation from the mean.

Finally, the two main concepts that allow us to understand process variation are special and common causes.

Special causes are observations that are above or below UCL or LCL. They are normally associated with something unexpected in the process. When a process displays special causes, we say that the process is unstable.

Common causes on the other hand are expected, they normally represent how the process should perform. If a process has only common causes, observations between UCL and LCL, we say that the process is stable.

Using the definitions of limits of specification and control, Table 32.1 summarizes actions that can be taken concerning process stability and process capability.

The intent of SPC is to understand the process behavior and variation and take actions to remove special causes to make it stable. Next, common causes are addressed to reduce variations making the process more predictable. Figure 32.3 summarizes the process.

Good Candidates for SPC

SPC can be applied to any process that can be measured. There are situations that may fit better than others. Table 32.2 contains reasonable candidates for SPC.

The Implementation of SPC

The implementation of SPC requires the introduction of several techniques and tools. These techniques must be understood by people, so that they can apply them during the process.

Table 32.1　Process Characteristics

Process Characteristics	Comments
Capable and stable	The performance of the process conforms to the user's requirements and only presents common causes. This is a good candidate for improvements.
Capable and unstable	The user is probably happy with the process, but the process has special causes. These special causes must be removed before we can improve it.
Not capable and stable	The process is not pleasing the customer even if it does not have special causes present. There is a need to work on the common causes to improve the process and make the customer happy.
Not capable and not stable	This is the worst situation. At the same time that we need to remove the special causes, we need to improve the process. Lots of work to do.

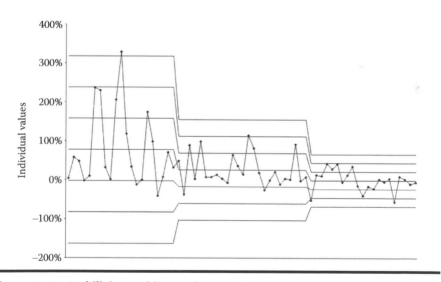

Figure 32.3　Stabilizing and improving a process.

Some examples of these techniques are shown in Figure 32.4.

In addition to tools and techniques training, the introduction of SPC activities must follow a set of steps/activities to be effective. Figure 32.5 presents the overall process that will be discussed in the section titled Establish Organizational Goals.

Table 32.2   Good Candidates for SPC

Process Characteristics	Comments
Process behavior out of specifications limits	It is very important to fulfill customer requirements. So the processes that are not performing as the customer expects are certainly good candidates for SPC.
Processes that will provide good ROI	To apply SPC concepts and techniques will cost effort and money; due to this it is important to select processes where the investment will be lower than the return.
Processes and subprocesses that most impact ROI	It is important to find processes and subprocesses that when optimized/improved will contribute to better savings with less investment. Stabilizing and improving several small processes may lead to big ROIs.
Processes and subprocesses that are:	• Simple and independent • Generate a reasonable amount of measurement data • Can be shared with other projects • Are primarily aligned with the improvement objectives of the organization

Scatter plot — Establish the relationship between two variables.

Run chart — Show the performance of a process across time.

Fishbone diagram — Indentify possible causes of a problem (can be used to understand special causes).

Pareto chart — Show the frequency of a variable.

Histogram — Show the frequency of variable classes.

Control chart — Show the performance of the process across time.

Figure 32.4   SPC tools and techniques.

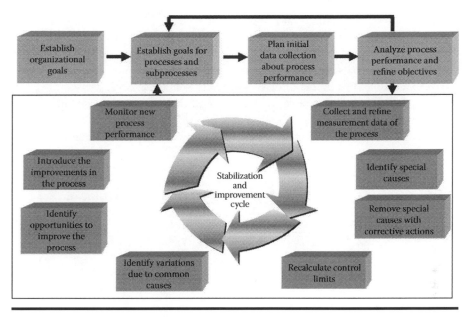

Figure 32.5 SPC utilization framework.

Establish Organizational Goals

It is very important that the organization establishes the objectives related to SPC. In defining these objectives, some questions must be answered:

- What do we want to achieve?
- What goals and objectives do we want to achieve?
- What are the pain points of the organization?
- Which quality and performance objectives do we want to achieve?
- Which objectives are common to all processes/projects and which are specific to a project?
- What measurement data we already have and can be used?
- What processes and procedures must be established in order to deploy SPC?

This list is certainly not complete. There are many other considerations that must be taken into account, but it serves as a starting point. An important aspect that must be understood is that these questions must be answered in light of organization business objectives; we stabilize and improve processes in order to improve the business and we do not improve just for the sake of improvement.

Establish Goals for Processes and Subprocesses

Once the organization has established the goals and objectives that they want to achieve with SPC, it is time to identify good processes and subprocess candidates for SPC. This analysis may take into consideration the process characteristics described earlier but also can select those that will bring the intended impact in the business.

Ideally, these goals should be written in quantitative manner, for example: "Reduce 10% the number of defects per part by March 2012."

Sometimes, it is not possible to create a quantitative goal because you do not have sufficient measurement data associated with that improvement. In this case, begin with goals that are more generic and then when you have enough data you can refine and make the goal more specific and quantitative.

Plan Initial Data Collection about Process Performance

It is very important to plan how you will collect initial measurement data about the process so that you can analyze it later. This initial collection will allow you to validate your objectives and see if they are reasonable.

This initial data collection can be done using several sources:

- Data obtained from past SPC projects
- Data from a benchmarking repository such as ISBSG (http://www.isbsg.org), Gartner Group (http://www.gartner.com/technology/home.jsp), SPR (http://www.spr.com/), etc.
- Data from organization baselines and models if available

Analyze Process Performance and Refine Objectives

Based on the initial measurement data, you can now take a look at the objective that was set up for the process and see if it needs adjustment or even make it more quantitative. Note that these objectives will be used in the further steps to see if they are being achieved by the corrective and improvement actions that are being taken.

In order to analyze process performance techniques such as control charts, run charts, and histograms can be used to help to understand process behavior.

Collect and Refine Measurement Data of the Process

At this point, the process is running and using the data collection plan that was created before, and you can begin to analyze process stability and capability.

This analysis will use the same set of techniques and tools discussed in the previous step Analyze Process Performance and Refine Objectives, but sometimes you need to use techniques that are not statistical in essence. The utilization of flow charts, SIPOC (Supplier, Input, Process, Output, and Customer), etc., can be used to better understand the process in terms of activities and identify reasons why it is not performing as expected.

Identify Special Causes

At this point, you need to identify the special causes that are part of the process. These special causes are causing instability in the process, and therefore, make it less predictable.

In order to eliminate the special causes, it is necessary to understand the root causes. The root causes can be identified using several techniques, and some of them are listed below:

■ Brainstorming
■ Fishbone diagram
■ Flowcharts
■ Statistical/quantitative methods (e.g., basic statistics, regression analysis)

Remove Special Causes with Corrective Actions

The special causes that you identified in the previous step, Identify Special Causes, must be removed in other to make the process stable. Figure 32.6 shows the identification and removal of special causes.

Special causes can be removed with several mechanisms, and some of them are described below:

■ Process automation
■ Implementation of checklists
■ Implementation of reviews and inspections
■ Training

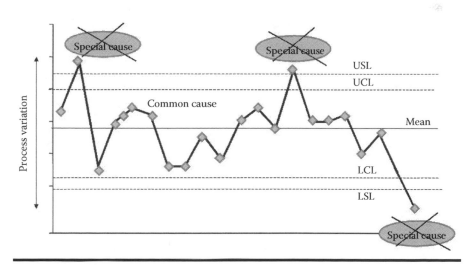

Figure 32.6   Removing special causes.

Recalculate Control Limits

Once you eliminate the special causes, the process now performs at a new level of performance and you may need to recalculate the control limits to see how the current process behavior performs, as illustrated in Figure 32.7.

Identify Variations Due to Common Causes

Once the process is stable with all the special causes removed, you can analyze the common causes and see whether you can remove some of them. This step allows

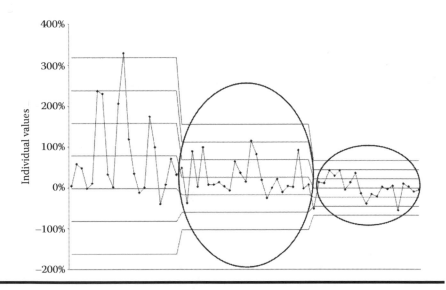

Figure 32.7   Recalculating control limits after improvements.

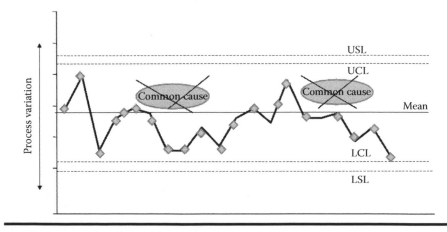

Figure 32.8   Removing common causes.

you to improve the process and make it more predictable. Figure 32.8 shows the identification and removal of common causes

Identify Opportunities to Improve the Process

During the analysis of common causes, you will frequently discover solutions that will revamp the whole process. Keep in mind that incremental changes are normally better and will result in a better return on investment (ROI). A good approach when trying new ways to execute the process is to use statistical tools like Minitab (http://www.minitab.com/) and/or simulation tools like Crystal Ball (http://www.oracle.com/us/products/applications/crystalball/).

Introduce the Improvements in the Process

Identified improvements need to be implemented. This implementation must be made in an organized manner. The best approach would be to deploy the improvement(s) using pilots so that the results can be validated. The following steps can be used:

- Select the pilot using predefined criteria
- Implement the improvement
- Collect measurement data
- Analyze the results
- Make adjustments if necessary
- Plan the final implementation
- Implement the improvement across the organization

Monitor New Process Performance

After the improvement is in place, you need to continuously monitor the process in order to make sure that it is achieving the objectives that were established and it continues to be stable and capable. If the desired results are not in evidence, a new cycle of stabilization and improvements should be started.

Lessons Learned

The implementation of SPC is not an easy task, and through the years we have accumulated several lessons learned that are being shared below:

- Senior leadership must be heavily involved in the process.
- Clear goals and objectives must be set up by senior leaders.
- People need to specialize in the methods and techniques (SPC, Lean Six Sigma, basic and advanced statistics, etc.).

- A new set of tools must be acquired (e.g., Minitab, Crystal Ball).
- Trying to make mistakes is part of the process.
- You need to develop a deep knowledge of the processes/subprocess that you are improving.
- A group should be available to mentor and coach people but make sure that the group is not doing the work for them.
- Frequently rethink the approach that you are using and consider better approaches that address the problem without invalidating the data already collected.
- Look outside your organization, benchmark, and gather information on how other companies are dealing with a specific process.
- Make the whole organization participate in the improvement process.

Summary

In this chapter, we introduced the basic concepts of SPC. The utilization of these concepts can benefit organizations that are interested in making their processes more stable, capable, and predictable.

Applying SPC using the framework that was shown in this chapter increases significantly the probability that improvements will be made in an orchestrated way and will be sustained over a long period of time.

Through improvements, companies can increase productivity, reduce costs, and provide products with better quality. In some cases if companies do not pay attention and constantly improve their processes, there is a great chance that they will cease to exist.

Bibliography

Deming, W. E. 1975. On probability as a basis for action. *The American Statistician* 29(4): 146–52.
Deming, W. E. 1982. *Out of the Crisis: Quality, Productivity and Competitive Position.* ISBN 0-521-30553-5.
Oakland, J. 2002. *Statistical Process Control.* ISBN 0-7506-5766-9.
Shewhart, W. A. 1931. *Economic Control of Quality of Manufactured Product.* ISBN 0-87389-076-0.
Shewhart, W. A. 1939. *Statistical Method from the Viewpoint of Quality Control.* ISBN 0-486-65232-7.
Wheeler, D. J. 2000. *Normality and the Process-Behaviour Chart.* ISBN 0-945320-56-6.
Wheeler, D. J., and D. S. Chambers. 1992. *Understanding Statistical Process Control.* ISBN 0-945320-13-2.
Wheeler, D. J. 1999. *Understanding Variation: The Key to Managing Chaos.* 2nd ed. SPC Press, Inc. ISBN 0-945320-53-1.
Wise, S. A., and D. C. Fair. 1998. *Innovative Control Charting: Practical SPC Solutions for Today's Manufacturing Environment.* ASQ Quality Press. ISBN 0-87389-385-9.

Acknowledgment

I extend my thanks to Joe Schofield for his suggestions to enhance the chapter's content and the readability of this text.

About the Author

Márcio Silveira has over 30 years of experience in the IT industry in positions related to database administration and system development and maintenance. He is currently a program manager with HP, supporting several HP development centers in Brazil. He is based in Rio de Janeiro, Brazil. During his career, he has worked in several technical and managerial roles.

He led and provided mentoring and coaching to an organization that raised its CMMI maturity level from 1 to 5 in 7 years. During this period, techniques such as SPC were used.

In the metrics and estimating area Márcio works with estimating models based on Function Points and other size measurements. He is the director of IFPUG International and Organizational Affairs, an international organization dedicated to promote Function Points and measurement. In Brazil, he helps to promote and increase the number of people certified in the Function Point technique.

Márcio has extensive experience as a project manager and has been certified as a Project Management Professional (PMP) by the Project Management Institute (PMI).

Márcio speaks frequently in congresses and events addressing several aspects of applications development and maintenance such as requirements determination, project estimation, project sizing, and process improvement. He has published articles in the proceedings of several events.

For 25 years, Márcio was an university professor at Pontificia Universidade Catolica do Rio de Janeiro.

HP

HP is a technology company that operates in more than 170 countries around the world. HP explores how technology and services can help people and companies address their problems and challenges and realize their possibilities, aspirations, and dreams. HP applies new thinking and ideas to create more simple, valuable, and trusted experiences with technology, continuously improving the way our customers live and work.

No other company offers as complete a technology product portfolio as HP. HP provides infrastructure and business offerings that span from handheld devices to some of the world's most powerful supercomputer installations. HP offers consumers a wide range of products and services from digital photography to digital entertainment and from computing to home printing. This comprehensive portfolio helps us match the right products, services, and solutions to the customers' specific needs.

Chapter 33

Human Performance Improvement: Measuring the Real Change of Process Improvement

Sheila P. Dennis and Patricia A. Eglin

Contents

Nationally and globally, we are all "enamored" with human performance and human performance statistics. How fast did the winner run the marathon? Which baseball team has won the most pennants? Who has lost the most weight and under what program? And rightly so, because after all, we are all human!

The business world is not any different however their drivers may well be. Organizational leaders want to see winners in their environment: to see teams successfully pass that Capability Maturity Model Integration (CMMI) assessment, to be International Organization for Standardization (ISO) certified, and to see projects consistently on time, within budget, and with acceptable levels of productivity. The underlying motivation to get to that winning position is bottom-line profitability.

Unless the organization is a fully automated environment, *humans* are interacting and performing the work. Humans are creatures of comfort and have a difficult time changing their behavior, even if it means fixing something that is broken. It is still easier to continue with the broken behavior than changing just because it is comfortable. And face it; typically, humans do not like to be measured. There is also the constant reminder that we should "dehumanize" our metrics—measure the process and not the individual or the people.

So how does an organization know when it is winning? When it has reached "success"? Most organizations continue to identify and measure the "success" of their process improvement initiatives by the results: number of processes developed versus outstanding, number of audits versus the number of noncompliance issues, estimates versus actual for budget and schedule, and maybe even a pass/fail for a certification of some kind. Common measures captured today may indicate *compliance* to a process that could be driven by rewards, fear, or organizational peer pressure. While these may be important operationally, is that really enough to know how successful a process improvement initiative is? Few organizations, if any, ever really think about or voice the true ingredient to a successful process improvement initiative: behavior change.

Although operational measures are important, we submit that equally important is sustainability, and sustained process improvement is gauged by *the measure of changed behavior*. Changing behavior is the most difficult and most important ingredient in the process improvement engagement and it can seem to be difficult to measure. However, there is a systematic and systemic approach to solve and measure performance issues in an organization—*Human Performance Improvement* (*HPI*). HPI is "the process of identifying and analyzing important organizational and individual performance gaps, planning for future performance improvement, designing and developing cost-effective and ethically justifiable interventions to close performance gaps, implementing the interventions, and evaluating the financial and nonfinancial results." It is an integration of standard process improvement with the human factor.

Value driven organizations are savvy enough to know that performance improvement is linked to process improvement. We are going to address successful process improvement and perspectives on measurement.

We ask you to think about your earlier experiences with process improvement. Has this ever happened to your organization? Countless hours and thousands of dollars are invested on process improvement initiatives. Just when you think you have them "right," you suddenly find it is a constant, uphill battle to get people to follow them? If you answered "yes," know that you are not alone.

Many organizations follow the same path. They ask, or task, the people responsible for performing the work to document their best work processes or perhaps use a process action team to determine how certain activities should be optimally executed. After much discussion and deliberation, eventually the process is documented, all stakeholders agree to the process, the process is rolled out, and then the inevitable happens...the processes are not being followed. But why? What went wrong between the time they were documented and agreed upon and the time in which people were expected to follow them?

One of the most typical reasons for this behavior is oversight: the processes under an improvement initiative may be so ingrained within the organization that the resources do not document all the steps needed to execute the process. Sometimes, it is quite difficult to document something that is commonplace. Some steps are actions that are performed "unconsciously" and therefore are overlooked (or not even considered) when documenting the process. These steps are almost so "obvious" to most people that the process owner assumes everyone will know to perform the action. Think about an everyday task you perform like brushing your teeth and see how many steps you would document if you had to tell someone how to do it. Did you think to document the step of removing the toothbrush from the holder, removing the cap from the toothpaste tube, or even turning the handle to turn on the water? If so, you may be a natural process writer. If not, you can see writing process is not as easy as it may seem.

The second major reason that processes are not followed is the "human" factor, a consideration that most organizations do not take into account. By nature, humans are creatures of comfort and habit and resist change. Why? Because performing actions that are familiar, even knowing something is not working and wishing it was different, is far easier than adopting change even if you know the change is for the better. So how do you measure the true success of process improvement, acceptance, and implementation?

It is commonly known that one cannot measure what is not clearly understood. Therefore, before we discuss measurement in the context of process improvement, we need to have a clear picture of what process improvement is. Let us review several different aspects and models from an organizational perspective—then we will explore the "human" factor.

What Is "Process Improvement"?

If you read Wikipedia, the term "process improvement" is defined as "A series of actions taken by a process owner to identify, analyze, and improve existing processes within an organization to meet new goals and objectives." Also, it "is a method to introduce process changes to improve quality, reduce costs, or accelerate schedules."

What do you think of when you hear the term? If you are like most people when you hear the term "process improvement," the words that pop into your head are models or methods, for example ISO, CMMI, Six Sigma, or Lean. Depending on your position in the company, other trigger words may be *money* (costs to implement), *savings* (return on investment—ROI), or *quality* (product improvement). Most organizations do understand that improving ones' processes will improve the quality of the product, reduce development and maintenance costs, reduce time to market, and in general, improve the satisfaction of their clients. The definition seems consistent with the usual thought. But where did it come from?

History of Process Improvement

Process improvement is not a new concept, it is sometimes used interchangeably with "quality management" or "performance management," and it has had a long history. Some of the most commonly known names related to quality management are W. Edwards Deming, Armand V. Feigenbaum, Dr. Kaoru Ishikawa, Philip B. Crosby, and Dr. Joseph M. Juran [1]. These men are known by many as leaders in the field; founders and forward thinkers when it comes to eliminating waste, reducing defects, and improving quality. Each developed their own philosophies concerning quality.

Deming was considered the "father" of process improvement. In his model, he created 14 principles surrounding quality (see Table 33.1) [2].

Table 33.1 Deming—Principles of Process Improvement

1. Constancy of purpose
2. The new philosophy
3. Cease dependence on mass inspection
4. End lowest tender contracts
5. Improve every process
6. Institute training on the service
7. Institute leadership
8. Drive out fear
9. Break down barriers
10. Eliminate exhortations
11. Eliminate arbitrary numerical targets
12. Permit pride of workmanship
14. Top management commitment and action

Feigenbaum devised the concept of *Total Quality Control*, which later became better known as *Total Quality Management* (TQM). The fundamental belief of TQM is that the quality of products and processes is the responsibility of everyone who is involved in the creation or consumption of the products or services created by the organization. This includes management, all resources, suppliers, and customers [3].

Ishikawa is linked to the use of *Quality Circles*. Quality Circles are typically supervised groups consisting of employees who identify and analyze organizational issues and present a solution to upper management for possible implementation [4].

Crosby created the *Principles of Zero Defects* [5]. The four principles are given in Table 33.2.

Juran encouraged training for managers and the focus of human relations problem in quality improvement. Juran believed the root cause of quality issues was cultural resistance aka, resistance to change [6].

Although the leaders in the field may have different principles or methodologies, the fundamental message is the same: improve quality through the improvement of processes. And although we are not here to challenge the concepts developed by the originators, we are here to challenge the ingredients of process improvement and make you question its success factors. Ask yourself, "What is the number one success factor behind process improvement? Does the success of process improvement really come from 'fixing' the process?" And how do you measure "success"?

Using a process improvement model is an efficient way to determine best practices to be implemented. Determining which model to base new or improved processes on and writing process may be the easy part for some although at times it seems the most difficult based on what we have learned about documenting the whole process. Alternatively, the most difficult and often frustrating part is the acceptance and adherence to the process. Months are spent determining how the organization performs; teams are assembled to document current processes; evaluations are done to determine compliance with the selected model; training is conducted; and overall, a great feeling of accomplishment by the team members is felt. Transitioning from the compliance model into sustainment then becomes the underlying problem.

When most organizations measure the "success" of their process improvement initiatives, they tend to measure the estimates versus actual for budget and schedule

Table 33.2 Principles of Zero Defects

1. Quality is conformance
2. Defect prevention is preferable to quality inspection
3. Zero defects is the quality standard
4. Quality is measured in monetary terms — the Price of Nonconformance (PONC)

and maybe even a pass/fail for a certification. Others measure the speed in which the organization got through the compliance to the model, the number of projects using it, and the number of noncompliance issues.

You can change processes: add steps, remove steps, or change steps. Some changes improve the process, whereas others miss the mark. We are not suggesting that you do not measure the impact a change makes on the cost, schedule, or quality. We are suggesting that you challenge yourself to go beyond the norm, beyond what you typically think of and measure when talking process improvement. We ask you to think beyond the definitions, philosophies, and methodologies to consider the true ingredient of process improvement—*people*. Because frankly, many leaders end up asking themselves, "I have done all I can do: I have support, I have the roles identified, and I have change agents with the right skills, so why then are people not following the new processes?" We answer once again: the human factor.

Real process improvement is driven by behavior change—by what is known as "human performance" factors. Look at the process development and implementation process through a different set of glasses and contemplate what measures can be collected to identify the level of success based on an employee's acceptance of the new process and its effect on the success of process improvement initiatives.

To truly improve process, you need to change the behavior of the organization's resources. It is typically senior level management who makes the decision to undertake a process improvement initiative. Many are of the mind-set that processes will be written, rolled out, and followed because "I said so" or because "we just need to." The issue with this mentality is that unless you work in a fully automated environment, you have humans interacting and performing the work. An organization cannot change on its own; *people* drive and need to change the organization. Humans are creatures of comfort and prefer to maintain the status quo, even if it is broken. It is just a psychological fact that most humans dislike change. So how often is this fact considered as process improvement is occurring?

Changing behavior is the most difficult and most important ingredient in the process improvement engagement. When measuring cost, implementation, and compliance, many organizations focus on the basic measures such as the actual cost of the project based on effort, number of processes developed versus outstanding, and number of audits versus the number of noncompliance issues. Organizations use these measures because they are most common and give a sense of how successful the organization was against its plan.

So you may be asking yourself, "If changing behavior is so difficult, why are so many organizations attempting process improvement? The answer goes back to where we started—the definition. The benefits received from improving the way an organization functions by changing the way it does business can be quantitatively measured in the reduction of costs, improvement of schedules, and improvement in the quality of products and traditionally outweigh the issues with implementing changes to existing processes.

Common measures captured today may indicate compliance to a process that could be driven by rewards, fear, or organizational peer pressure—but what is the sustainability?

When measuring the cost of a process improvement initiative, you are most likely collecting dollars spent by internal resources through labor hours and externally, if using a consultant, through the cost of time and material. It is difficult to determine how much of the total cost of improving processes came from the fact that resources resisted the change, and therefore, extended the schedule of the project, in turn increasing the cost.

Let us not forget that organizations also interact with resources outside their own walls. There is an interaction between the customer and possibly suppliers. You have to take into account the time spent changing the communication and interaction with both if your processes affect them.

Why Resist?

Some may ask themselves, if you know something is not working or there is an easier way to complete a task, why would not people jump at the chance to change? The answers are simple.

- It is comfortable remaining the same. Doing things the way you have always done them seems get the job done at least.
- They do not understand why they are being asked to change. They do not understand the benefits: What is in it for me? How is this going to make my life better?
- Priorities within organizations are always changing. Lack of clear vision can often cause confusion among resources as to what their focus should be. Add this to the fact that they are now being asked to change what they know and they are often left with feelings of chaos.
- The history of change within the organization's culture. Previous attempts may have tried and failed or just had mediocre success or were simply abandoned for what was perceived to be "something better." This constant reinvention or "jumping on the latest trend" without clear purpose fosters an environment in which the resources typically feel that any process improvement initiative is simply another "fad" that will go away if they wait long enough.

Understanding Change

What is change if not learning something new, even if that something new is a new behavior? Dictonary.com defines the word change as—verb (used without object)

- To become different
- To become altered or modified
- To become transformed or converted (usually followed by into)

Some of these definitions make change sound like a bad thing or at the least a scary prospect. Maybe that is why we are so resistant to it. As adults, we still have the capacity to learn, so it is not an inability to change; maybe it is a choice. Or is it human nature that as we get older we are less inclined to change?

According to the article, "Set in Our Ways: Why Change Is So Hard" published in *Scientific American*, "after a person's early 20s, the fascination with novelty declines and resistance to change increases. This pattern holds true regardless of cultural background" [7]. This can be a looming thought as an organization's resources can range from their 20s to their 60s, and many IT resources are now facing retirement age. It does however answer the question of why implementing process changes is so difficult within an organization. What can we do to mitigate the effects of the human factor? How can we address process improvement to make it truly successful? Understanding the people issues and selecting the right people to "lead the charge" can certainly aid in the success of changing the organization and reduce the discomfort of resources.

Key Process Improvement Roles

- Sponsor
- The sponsor does more than fund the project. The sponsor is the leader within the organization, usually at a senior management level, who communicates the need and desire to change whether it is the implementation of new processes through a process improvement initiative or the direction to improve current processes. The sponsor provides adequate resources to carry out the initiative and supplies the capability for needed infrastructure and training.
- Champion
- The champion has the vision and influence and helps promote, possibly even conceive, the process improvement effort. The champion monitors the initiative's activities and progress and removes obstacles to success.
- Change Agent
- The change agent has relevant skills and a willingness to change. The change agent supports senior management in bringing about purposeful transformation of the organization and defines the change implementation approach and schedule. The change agent is also a key in defining specific procedures, tools, and methods for change implementation. The most important characteristics of a change agent are to be experts of the changes and communicate to others. The communication has to go beyond the introduction of the process changes themselves and include the question everyone is asking, "Why am I being asked to change?"

Communicating the impact to the organization's resources can sometimes be a challenging task and therefore requires a change agent who:

- Believes in the approach
- Is patient and persistent
- Is honest, trustworthy, reliable, and demonstrates integrity
- Is positive and enthusiastic
- Is confident but not arrogant (able to admit ignorance and ask for help)
- Is a good listener, observant of others' feelings and behavior
- Is flexible and resourceful; seeks out alternative ways to achieve goals
- Is not easily intimidated
- Is able to maintain perspective (a good sense of humor)
- Is willing to take personal risks and to take on a challenge
- Is able to recognize and deal with office politics without becoming involved in politics
- Is inclined to adopt a cooperative, inclusive style

Rules to Implementation Success

The 9-Vector View of Human Performance identifies the top nine components to *the success of implementing change* [8].

1. *Stakeholder relationship management*
   Identifying stakeholders goes beyond the determination of those performing the work, it entails identifying those who are affected by the change also. The importance here for managers is to determine the skills being affected and more importantly any gaps in skills. Determining this information up front will help the manager prepare for training and plan the actions that need to take place.

2. *Leading changes*
   Part of planning for the impending changes is to know who the change agents will be. We discussed earlier the characteristics and traits of a good change agent and it may take some time to determine the appropriate resources.

3. *Change strategy*
   As with any project, planning is a key element to success and planning for organizational change is no different. Organizations need to determine the implementation "how." The actual changes may not be identified but the approach needs to be determined early on.

4. *Communication*
   As we identified earlier, change can be scary for some. The unknown can cause much anxiety among resources, which can derail the initiative before it gets off the ground.

It is imperative stakeholders at all levels understand the changes to come, why they are changing and what is expected from them. Communicating future expectations may help alleviate some of the concerns.

5. *Human capital management*

As organizations identify resources and skills gaps, it is essential to discuss resource capacity. Does the organization have enough resources to perform after the changes or are additional resources required?

6. *Learning and training*

We identified earlier that change really is learning a new way of performing. Skill gaps between the current state of performance and the future expectations need to be identified and addressed. A training strategic plan should be developed to assist the organization in moving forward to close the skill gaps.

7. *Process and infrastructure*

No organization should implement process just for the sake of having process. Identifying process needs or improvements to process should occur prior to making any changes. Planning process changes helps identify and maintain focus and reduce the amount of rework or rewrite that is done. Most organizations do not get all processes right the first time. It is not until resources execute the process that organizations can determine if they work as expected. Based on this, and the reluctance to change, it is crucial that the impact to the organization is reduced. Additional "fixes" to the process reduces the confidence level of those using the process and adds to the anxiety.

8. *Project management*

Process improvement initiatives are projects like any other within the organization; they are just internal. Project plans, budgets, schedules, resources, and status reporting are needed to keep stakeholders involved and aware. A project manager should be assigned and run the project the same as if an external client was paying.

9. *Performance management*

Despite all that has been written here, there is no one right way to implement change. Some ways are better than others are. But just as people are different, so are organizations. Each organization needs to determine, based on the individual culture, what is the best approach or methodology to implement. Performance management is more than determining methodologies; it is also identifying how the organization will measure the changes.

Measuring Change

Effective change management requires measures. The value of measures does not come from the sheer collection of data though, it comes from the decisions and the actions taken as a result of the data collection and analysis. Senior management needs to determine the goals and values that are important to determine information needs. Goals need to be clear as to how the data collected will be used. What is to be measured needs to be planned and the current level of performance needs to be baselined. If you do not know where you are at the start, how will you know if the changes being made are improving the organizational performance or making them worse? Some of the standard measures such as schedule, costs, and process compliance measures, if used together, will help you determine the present state of the organization. Figure 33.1 provides a visual road map to defining measures.

It is important to understand that while you are measuring behavior change, the information should not be used against those struggling to change. When measures are used to reprimand the participants, it often has an opposite effect than expected. Data can be manipulated to present the desired picture without actually changing the behavior. Resources often join together to help each other mask the fact that processes are not being followed. It is better to use the results to determine training and coaching needs than to use threats or immediate disciplinary actions. First, make sure you have the personnel and the skill set needed to effectively collect, analyze, and report the measures identified. Without the right skills, the data

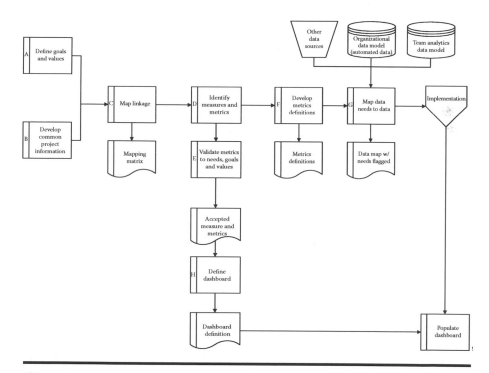

Figure 33.1   Measurement road map. © 2008 (From David Consulting Group, Philadelphia, PA.)

will not be collected consistently and may not be valid. Either of these will diminish the value of the process improvement and it will be seen as just another fruitless exercise by management that will soon be forgotten thus promoting the perception that "I do not really need to change."

How Am I Measuring This Change in Behavior?

Two of the key measures to be added to your measurement operational portfolio for changed behavior are *change sensitivity* and *percentage of positive change*.

1. To measure change sensitivity, you need to have the baseline data in place for comparison. A simple way to collect this measure is to run a simple *t*-test. A *t*-test is a statistical test used to determine whether a significant difference exists between two samples. The *t*-test will tell you if there are changes in the measure over time. The *t*-test calculates the mean difference between the sample and the known value of the population mean; the average value of the process conformity as a whole. Using the baseline measure as the population, you are able to make the decision whether the sample mean is showing improvement.
   a. Calculate the standard deviation

   $$S = \sqrt{\frac{\Sigma(X - \bar{X})^2}{n-1}} \qquad (33.1)$$

   b. Calculate the *t*-test sample

   $$t = \frac{\bar{X} - \mu}{S}\sqrt{n} \qquad (33.2)$$

   c. Calculate the degree of freedom (number of values in the final calculation that may vary)

   $$t = \frac{\bar{X} - \mu}{S}\sqrt{n} \qquad (33.3)$$

   d. Analyze the data
   If the calculated value is greater than the table value, there is a significant difference between the population and sample means.

2. Percentage of Positive Change Measure
   Measuring the percentage of positive change may be used to determine resistence on an individual basis. To measure the percentage of positive change, you need to identify the resources who are not following processes as they are

developed or changed. This measure works well when collecting noncompliance measures.

a. Collect noncompliance measures by resource
   Process reviews conducted $= X$
   Noncompliance issues $= Y$

$$\frac{Y}{X} \times 100 = n\% \tag{33.4}$$

b. Train or counsel resources with the highest percentage of noncompliance
c. Collect noncompliance measures by resource
d. Analyze the data
   A reduction in the percentage of noncompliance by resources indicates a modification of behavior.

In summary, there are methods that can be used to optimize success factors for process improvement and measures to gauge sustainment of organizational processes. These methods and measures should go beyond the standard quantitative, operational model and include the human factor.

References

1. Humphrey, Watts S. 1989. *Managing the Software Process*. Boston: Addison-Wesley Publishing Company.
2. Wikipedia. 2011. http://en.wikipedia.org/ (accessed May 26, 2011).
3. Wikipedia. 2011. http://en.wikipedia.org/ (accessed May 26, 2011).
4. Wikipedia. 2011. http://en.wikipedia.org/ (accessed May 27, 2011).
5. Wikipedia. 2011. http://en.wikipedia.org/ (accessed May 27, 2011).
6. Wikipedia. 2011. http://en.wikipedia.org/ (accessed May 27, 2011).
7. Westerhoff, N. 2008. Set in our ways: Why change is so hard. *Sci Am*, December 17.
8. Darby, M. 2011. 9-Vector View of Human Performance. *The Training & Development*. FindArticles.com. July 08, 2011.

About the Authors

Sheila P. Dennis has worked in the IT environment for 30 years and in measurement for over 20 years. She is a recognized Function Point and measurement expert, having held Certified Function Point Specialist credentials for over 15 years. After an outstanding career at the Department of Defense, she went into private industry serving as the vice president of Sizing Practices and director of the PMO for the David Consulting Group. She has built and supported a variety of measurement models, training programs, and process improvement initiatives for the government and in commercial practice for large organizations in the banking, insurance, telecommunications, and IT supplier communities. Her specialties include performance measurement, benchmarking, statistical calibration, quality control, and quality assurance. She is a published author (*IFPUG IT Measurement: Advice from the Experts*) and conference speaker. Sheila has a B.A. in General Studies—Mathematics from Columbia College and a Certificate in Management Studies from Golden Gate University.

Patricia A. Eglin has been working in process improvement for approximately 12 years. She is a seasoned process improvement engineer, having worked as a CMMI practitioner and coach, and currently holds the position of a process improvement/measurement specialist, Certified Intro to CMMI Instructor, and Six Sigma Green Belt. Ms. Eglin is responsible for the development, implementation, and training of processes related to quality management initiatives, governance, and improvement opportunities.

Ms. Eglin has extensive knowledge and experience in the implementation of measurement programs in that she has delivered training on the objectives and ingredients of a successful measurement program, and assisted organizations ranging from 30 to 3000 employees to determine their measurement needs and identify the correct measures to include in their measurements programs to meet their business objectives. Ms. Eglin works with organizations to collect reports and improve process based on the analysis of data using her experience with both CMMI's measurement process area and the principles of Six Sigma.

Chapter 34

Understanding Your Organization's Best Software Development Practices

David Herron

Contents

Understanding or identifying your organization's best practices is not a diffi-cult thing to do. The challenge for most organizations is that they have to work within the context of preconceived notions as to what a best practice really means and the misconception of how it should be effectively deployed. A best practice, as we will soon learn, can have a significant impact on an organization's ability to improve performance within the software development life cycle and to deliver quality products on time and within budget. Unfortunately, it can also become that ill-fated silver bullet that fails to produce the anticipated or desired results. The way forward is for an organization to understand clearly how to recognize a best practice, what makes for successful execution, and ultimately how to identify its own best practices.

We have all read articles about software development best practices of one kind or another. Sometimes, these articles entertain us with first-person stories about how a particular development method, technique, or development tool has had a positive impact on the development and delivery of software.

Over time, as we continue to hear more about a particular technique or software process that has provided positive results, we come to label these occurrences as best software practices. And I think that for the most part, the label is deserved. The relevant question at this point is to ask ourselves, what is the nature or what are the characteristics of a software development best practice?

Characteristics of a Best Practice

If we are to identify software best practices within our own organization, we first need a common definition upon which we can all agree. And as part of that definition, identify the core characteristics that help us to distinguish something as a best practice.

Currently, I am not aware of any industry standard or certification process that is used to qualify something as a best practice, nor are there any rules or guidelines that help us to classify something as a best practice. We talk about frameworks like Capability Maturity Model Integration (CMMI) as being a best practice or the Project Management Institute's Body of Knowledge as being a set of best practices, but why do we? How do we know if something is a best practice? What gives a practice or a process that special distinction of being the "best"?

In this day and age, it only makes sense to make good use of the Internet and do a Google search on the term "software best practices." Here are a few of the "hits" that came up.

> "Best practices are generally-accepted, informally-standardized techniques, methods or processes that have proven themselves over time to accomplish given tasks. Often based upon common sense, these practices are commonly used where no specific formal methodology is in place or the existing methodology does not sufficiently address the issue" [1].

> *"A best practice is a method or technique that has consistently shown results superior to those achieved with other means, and that is used as a benchmark."*

And best in class was defined as:

"The highest current performance level in an industry, used as a standard or benchmark to be equaled or exceeded. Also called best of breed" [2].

It would be difficult to find much of anything to really disagree with in the above definitions. They all sound about the same and the vast majority of people would agree that they could be accepted as a general definition of a best practice. If we examine these definitions a little closer we can find some key phrases that underscore some of the core characteristics of a best practice. Things like generally accepted, proven over time, shows superior results, and a well-defined method. These key words and phrases tell us that a best practice is quantifiable (shows superior results), relatively easy to understand (well-defined) and has a history of success (proven over time).

Let us look at two fairly standard quality-related practices that are typically referred to as a best practice. In addition, let us see if we can apply the key words to these two practices.

The first one that comes to mind is the practice of conducting a formal review and/or inspection. We all know that reviews and inspections involve the reviewing of artifacts such as requirements documents and design specifications for the purpose of identifying and correcting defects. The benefit of a formal review is to create a deliverable that is accurate and free of errors and omissions. I doubt there will be much debate among the readership that formal reviews could be classified as a best practice. The processes for conducting formal reviews and inspections are very well defined (e.g., Fagan). There are specific measures (defect analysis) that quantitatively can tell us that it is effective. And formal reviews and inspections have been around ... well, forever.

The second practice that is often mentioned in a discussion of best practices is requirements management. Requirements management as a best practice is a rigorous, definable, and repeatable process that enables analysts to extract requirements effectively from a customer or end user. There are numerous methods for defining requirements, and so this best practice is not labeling a specific process, but it is addressing the practice or methods associated with good requirements management.

Once again, we can certainly fit requirements management to the general definitions noted above. It is generally accepted. Good requirements practices have been proven over time. And the techniques associated with these practices have been well documented.

A brief look at some of the measures that are associated with the above best practices include process compliance, defect density, effective removal rates, and functional sizing.

Process compliance is the basic practice of creating a formal mechanism to monitor and report compliance to a particular process. It does not provide insight as to the effectiveness or efficiency of the process, but it does provide management with a view into the behaviors of the software development teams.

Defect density is often used to quantify and evaluate the number of defects attributed to a particular piece of software, systems application, or software product. It is calculated by dividing the total number of defects found by the functionality delivered (measured in Function Points). The measure can be used to assess the overall quality of the software and also to predict the potential need for ongoing support.

The effective defect removal rate is used to measure the rate of defect removal throughout that life cycle. The calculation involves calculating the number of defects removed at each phase of a life cycle divided by the total number of defects discovered. This activity occurs at various phases of a life cycle. So for a waterfall life cycle, you may have defect rates attributable to your requirements phase, your design phase, your coding phase, etc. This proves to be a very powerful quality measurement tool that provides insight as to the effectiveness of your quality practices.

Therefore, these two examples present us with our first clue as to why something may be called or labeled a best practice: it works; it can be quantified; and it can be proven to be successful. Case in point—have you ever worked in a software development shop that has initiated a process improvement strategy to include reviews and inspections (an agreed upon best practice) only to see that program not well defined and therefore not properly executed, then sooner or later the practice falls by the wayside for one reason or another? I am sure you have. So was it a best practice or not? And if it does not work in your organization is it no longer a best practice? Of course not. It simply was not executed effectively and therefore it did not provide the "best" results for that particular organization.

The point here is that a best practice such as design reviews or requirements definition is only as good as its execution. And the success of that execution is somewhat dependent upon measuring the process and the results. Measures do not make the process work better, but they will provide information about compliance to the process, measure the output of the process, and evaluate the impact; thereby ensuring the effectiveness and long-term use of the best practice. Measures will also ensure a return on the investment relative to the expense incurred to implement the particular best practices strategy.

Therefore, we have learned that in order for a best practice to be truly a best practice for any given organization, it has to have some measure of success. Simply "doing" the best practice is not enough. So when deciding to use one of these common and familiar best practices, it is important to understand not only the techniques and methods but also the governance and measures of performance that will be used to ensure the best use of a selected best practice.

Effectively Implementing a Best Practice

It is hard to explain why more organizations are not following well-known and well-documented best software practices. The software industry is mature enough to have the basis of experience to understand that there are in fact better ways of developing and deploying software. Why wouldn't an IT organization invest in the techniques that have been proven to have a significant impact on improving quality, delivering on time, and satisfying the end user? Unfortunately, I think the answer is simply that most organizations do not fully understand what it takes to implement successfully a best software practice. They buy into the concept, they want the results, but their expectations are not aligned with the reality of achieving a positive outcome.

To underscore the point, in an article describing "Nine Best Practices," the authors from Niwot Ridge Consulting, Niwot, Colorado, state that "In order for the Best Practices to be effective management must be engaged in specific ways" [3, pp. 9–10].

In summary, they suggest that management engagement involves the following:

Commitment—to the practices and the consequences of the practices. This commitment usually comes in the form of a formal endorsement of the process and the deliverables from the process. By officially sanctioning the Best Practices approach, both top management and all the participants agree in public that they are committed to make this work.

Action—to implement the best practices. Have a commitment is easy, making good on the commitment is the hard part. The action needed to deploy the Best Practices will be managed just like any other project, with a detailed project plan, well-defined outcomes, and measurable deliverables.

Funding—for the changes that will result from the practices. In order to accrue the benefits of the Best Practices, money must be spent. The actual funding details are not currently known. The total amount will be small compared to the total investment for the project. The return on this investment will be very large—a major contribution to the successful completion of the product.

Follow-up—for the behaviors that result from the practices. Using the Best Practice of Project-Wide Visibility of Progress Versus Plan the deployment of the Best Practices will become a visible project.

Measurement—of the outcomes of the practices. With measurement, management cannot take place. This is a Best Practice item that will be used for deploying the Best Practices.

Okay, so we have learned another lesson about best practices. Implementing a best practice is hard. It takes work and commitment. Oftentimes, it requires changes in organizational behaviors and perhaps even changes in the culture. But if an organization truly wants to improve, it must adopt known best practices or find some other way to position them to be executing at a performance level that will yield positive results.

We have been talking about known software development best practices as recognized methods and techniques that can be adopted by organizations and when properly executed can lead to success.

And we have also learned that just because something is labeled as a best practice there is no guarantee that it will be properly implemented and yield positive results.

So a best practice is only a best practice if it is applied effectively within a given organization. If we look at that from a different perspective why wouldn't we consider that there could be any number of development practices, techniques, and methods within an organization that are yielding positive results. Therefore, wouldn't those constitute best practices for that organization? After all, isn't that what is really most important—to discover our own best practices.

We have learned that two characteristics of a best practice are that it is well understood and that it provides positive measureable results. We need to have the means to be able to understand and to assess our current development practices. The assessment should have measures of performance as well as providing clear insight as to what specific practices are providing positive results. In other words, what are our current best practices? If we can isolate those instances in which we are effectively designing, developing, and deploying software, then we can learn from our own internal experiences and provide that knowledge across the organization.

Measuring Performance

An effective way to measure performance within an IT organization is to adopt a performance measurement model that includes both quantitative and qualitative analyses. The model can be applied to a selection of representative projects with the results yielding information about the effectiveness of the current development practices. This model will serve to identify both process weaknesses and process strengths that we would consider best practices within the organization.

The model shown in Figure 34.1 has all of the proper elements necessary to perform an effective performance assessment. There are a series of quantitative data points that can be collected and analyzed on a project-by-project basis, resulting in measures of performance. There is also a series of qualitative data points that can be collected and analyzed on a project-by-project basis, resulting in a series of capability profiles. Together they form an organization's performance baseline. From that baseline, further analysis will reveal opportunities for improvement and current best practices.

The simplest way to understand the model is to see it in action; therefore, we will walk through an example of how this model would be used in an organization.

We begin by identifying a sampling of recently completed projects. This sampling of projects should vary in size, complexity, and technology. They should also

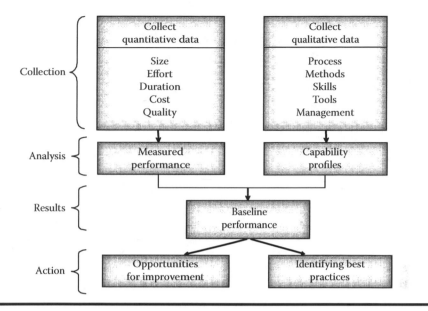

Figure 34.1 Performance measurement model.

be representative of the types of development work commonly performed in the organization. Once identified, data will be collected and analyzed to create a measured performance indicator and a capability score for each project.

The quantitative data elements include at a minimum four basic measures: the size of the deliverable, the effort required to produce the deliverable (cost), the overall duration required to define, design, and develop the deliverable and the quality, and the number of defects that were removed prior to delivery and that were discovered after delivery.

The basic measure used for size is Function Points. Function Point Analysis is a measure of the functionality delivered to the end user. The Function Point methodology is an industry standard and serves as the basis for numerous performance calculations. Source lines of code (SLOC) has been used in the past as a measure of size; however, it does not lend itself to a consistent source of comparative analysis. There is no industry standard definition for SLOC making it difficult to compare the effectiveness of one development effort over another. An effective size measure must be well defined, meaningful to both IT and the user, easy to learn and apply, and statistically sound. Function Point Analysis meets that criterion. Function Point Analysis is a well-defined standard supported by the International Function Point Users Group [4].

The level of effort required to produce the deliverable is basically a measure of IT labor. Measured at the project level, level of effort accounts for all labor expended on a project. Although there is no industry standard for measuring level of effort, the common practice is to measure effort in person hours. This includes the effort of all members of the project team including the project manager. It does not typically include end-user effort or effort recorded to the project by remote support functions such as a database support group.

Duration is the measure of calendar time beginning with the start of a project through delivery. There are several considerations when measuring duration. When does a project start? What happens when a project starts and is then put on hold? Typically, the start of a project begins when IT resources start recording time attributed to a project. The end of a project is when the software is fully tested and is "fit for use." If a product or a piece of software is being rolled out to the organization, then the end time of the project is measured when the first roll out occurs. In those organizations in which there are occurrences of projects starting then stopping then starting again, it is reasonable to suggest that the entire duration be measured and include the entire time period from the project's first inception until its final delivery. Under this scenario, a lag-time measure may be derived to show the nonproductive time as a percent to the total duration.

The measuring of defects includes the measurement of pre- and post-release defects. There are varying degrees of complexity in how defects may be measured. At the simplest level, defects are often recorded as problem tickets or problem reports that have resulted from user-discovered errors. At a more comprehensive level, post-release defects can be classified based on their point of discovery, severity, and origin. In addition to post-release defects, pre-release defect tracking and analysis can begin at the requirements phase and carry through each phase of the life cycle. When defects are discovered as a result of a design review or code inspection, the defect is recorded with information relating to where the defect was found and the origin of the defect thus providing the opportunity to analyze pre-release defect removal efficiency.

Numerous organizations are already collecting many of the above mentioned data points. For example, level of effort and start and stop times for a project are typically gathered and reported as part of the project management activities. However, collecting measurement data such as Function Points and defect data, particularly pre-release defect data, is not performed as frequently.

The collection of Function Point data is thought to be complex and time consuming. Clearly, if an organization is not currently involved in collecting size data, then any new activity designed to collect size information will be considered an additional effort (and burden) and therefore more time consuming. However, the collection of Function Point data is no more time consuming than the effort required to collect the level of effort data on a weekly basis from all the project teams in a department.

There have been advances made in the Function Point sizing arena making it easier to collect Function Point data and therefore less time consuming. By having highly experienced and dedicated individuals responsible for functional sizing, the effort to collect the size data can be significantly reduced. In addition, the advent of counting practices such as FP Lite can further aid in the timely and accurate counting of functional size [5].

Defect data collection is another area that organizations struggle with primarily because it can add effort and cost to the project. This perspective is shortsighted for several reasons. By collecting and analyzing defect data during the project life cycle, defects can be found earlier thereby reducing overall project costs. And the final deliverable results in a higher quality product being delivered to the end user. An easy point of entry for an organization to begin collecting defect information is to incorporate the practice of conducting document reviews and code inspections. Part of this practice should include the collection and analysis of defects. Once again, there is an initial investment required, but the return on that investment is significant.

Collecting quantitative data is usually done as part of a project management activity. Since many of the measures are used to manage the project, it only stands to reason that the project manager would be the individual responsible for collecting the data. An example of what the collected quantitative data may look like is shown in Table 34.1.

The qualitative elements in the measurement model include a variety of data points that are used to evaluate levels of competency regarding process, methods,

Table 34.1   Project Data

	Project	Start Date	Completion Date	Duration	Effort Hrs	Function Points	Hours/ Function Point
A	Project A1	4/1/2007	7/8/2007	3.3	1873	590.0	3.1
B	Project B2	3/1/2007	1/31/2008	11.2	3810.24	439.0	8.6
C	Project C3	5/7/2007	7/9/2007	2.1	92.61	28.0	3.3
D	Project D4	2/1/2007	9/17/2007	7.6	2041.2	200.0	10.2
E	Project E5	3/5/2007	11/1/2007	8.0	2041.2	188.0	10.9
F	Project F6	2/12/2007	9/26/2007	7.5	630	92.0	6.8
G	Project G7	2/1/2007	6/13/2007	7.5	773.76	276.0	2.5
H	Project H8	2/15/2007	7/26/2007	5.4	2402.4	815.0	2.8
I	Project I9	1/1/2007	3/30/2007	2.9	273	58.0	4.7
J	Project J10	7/2/2007	9/27/2007	2.9	235.2	70.0	3.4
K	Project K11	7/1/2007	9/1/2008	14.1	5913.6	1202.0	4.9
L	Project L12	9/3/2007	12/20/2007	3.6	1890	81.0	23.3

skills, automation, technology, management practices, etc. Although there are many ways in which this data can be organized and collected, many organizations develop their own proprietary process to collect and organize this data. For example, we first collect information relating to the technical aspects of a project. This includes general category information about the business/industry (telecom, manufacturing, finance), application type (new development, enhancement, maintenance), technical platform (mainframe, PC, client-server, web based), and language (language generation). These general categories are used to analyze the data based on selected groupings of like projects. For instance, selection of projects may include enhancement projects developed on a client server platform.

In addition to this general category, we collect detail data in six major categories. Those categories include information relating to project management, definition, design, build, test, and environment. There are approximately 80 different variables that make up these six categories. An abbreviated listing of selected variables is shown in Figure 34.2.

The management characteristics deal with issues relating to how the project is managed, how experienced the project managers are, and what management tools are deployed. The definition, design, build, and test categories are organized to collect information regarding the skill levels of individuals working on each phase of development, the processes and techniques used, as well as the level of automation. Environment data relates to general issues about training, the organizational environment, and the culture.

The goal is to collect data points for those characteristics that have a measurable impact on productivity and quality levels of performance. Furthermore, since the

Management
➤ Team dynamics
➤ High morale
➤ Project tracking
➤ Project planning
➤ Automation
➤ Management skills

Definition
➤ Clearly stated requirements
➤ Formal process
➤ Customer involvement
➤ Experience levels
➤ Business impact

Design
➤ Formal process
➤ Rigorous reviews
➤ Design reuse
➤ Customer involvement
➤ Experienced development staff
➤ Automation

Build
➤ Code reviews
➤ Source code tracking
➤ Code reuse
➤ Data administration
➤ Computer availability
➤ Experience staff
➤ Automation

Test
➤ Formal testing methods
➤ Test plans
➤ Development staff experience
➤ Effective test tools
➤ Customer involvement

Environment
➤ New technology
➤ Automated process
➤ Adequate training
➤ Organizational dynamics
➤ Certification

Figure 34.2   Qualitative data elements.

data needs to be analyzed, a historical baseline of data needs to be collected in order to determine which factors have the most significant impact.

The qualitative data is usually collected as a series of questions that can be answered by the project team. The format of these questions varies depending upon the collection vehicle. Questions may be segmented into relevant categories. Often a weighted value is applied to each question and then the values are totaled by category and by project total.

An example of what the collected qualitative data may look like after it is evaluated is shown in Table 34.2. Each project is listed in the first column. An overall score on a scale of 1–100 is noted. The higher the score the greater the likelihood is that the project is yielding positive levels of performance. The shaded areas along with the numeric values represent the scoring for each project in each subcategory. The lightly shaded areas are showing more positive results than the dark shaded areas.

Anytime an organization is collecting and analyzing data, the issue of data integrity is always present. The accuracy and integrity of these data points are critical. There is a great deal of effort that goes into the collection of performance data. If that data is suspect or lacks integrity, then the entire database of information may become suspect and the data labeled as useless.

There are several approaches that may be considered when developing a baseline of performance. If an organization already has a practice in place of collecting,

Table 34.2 Qualitative Project Data

Project	Score	Management	Req	Des	Build	Test	Environment
Project A1	56.2	68	62	68	58	41	35
Project B2	44.3	68	49	57	35	28	35
Project C3	60.2	73	74	68	65	41	27
Project D4	36.4	57	44	32	46	22	27
Project E5	37.5	50	51	25	46	28	27
Project F6	46.6	68	62	57	38	25	27
Project G7	53.6	77	64	50	46	50	31
Project H8	53.2	61	72	48	58	41	31
Project I9	52.7	61	64	43	58	44	31
Project J10	57.3	61	68	53	58	41	31
Project K11	59.8	77	69	55	58	53	31
Project L12	44.2	61	54	20	65	41	31

analyzing, reporting, and auditing certain data elements, then it may not be all that burdensome to add one or two additional data points that we have mentioned here. For the organization that has little or no data collection activity, a specific baseline initiative may be the best approach for collecting the data necessary to establish levels of performance.

Analyzing the Data

After all the data is collected, the process of sorting and analyzing the data begins. Each project has a measured performance and can be ranked according to their performance levels. Associated with each project there is also a capability profile. These data points provide indicators as to how well the project performed and the data can also be analyzed to determine what specific attributes may have contributed to high or low yields of productivity and quality.

In analyzing the data, we can see that the project's performance measures are in line with the profile scores. The performance measure used here is hours per Function Point. The profile scores are on a scale of 1–100 and the higher the score the more effective the processes, tools, and methods that were used in defining, designing, and developing the software.

For example, in Table 34.3, we can see that there is a group of projects (G7, H8, I9, J10, and K11) that had both high profile scores and high yields of productivity. Profiles in the 50 to 60+ range are positive.

As we look at the quantitative data, we find that these same projects have a high productivity rating expressed in hours per Function Point in the column on the far right of Table 34.4.

When considering best practices in an organization, it is better to look at the overall results of the performance data. In our examples in Table 34.2, we can see from the qualitative data that several categories performed consistently well. Practices related to project management activities and those practices relating to

Table 34.3 Analysis of the Results

Project	Score	Management	Req	Des	Build	Test	Environment
Project G7	53.6	77	64	50	46	50	31
Project H8	53.2	61	72	48	58	41	31
Project I9	52.7	61	64	43	58	44	31
Project J10	57.3	61	68	53	58	41	31
Project K11	59.8	77	69	55	58	53	31

Table 34.4   Analysis of the Quantitative Data

	Project	Start Date	Completion Date	Duration	Effort Hrs	Function Points	Hours/ Function Point
G	Project G7	2/1/2007	9/13/2007	7.5	773.76	276.0	2.5
H	Project H8	2/15/2007	7/26/2007	5.4	2402.4	815.0	2.8
I	Project I9	1/1/2007	3/30/2007	2.9	273	58.0	4.7
J	Project J10	7/2/2007	9/27/2007	2.9	235.2	70.0	3.4
k	Project K11	7/1/2007	9/1/2008	14.1	5913.6	1202.0	4.9

requirements management activities both scored very well. We can therefore conclude that these two practices are among the best practices in the organization.

Similarly, we see that there are several categories that did not perform as well. These include testing processes and some design processes. There were also some environmental issues that seem to have been problematic. These would need to be examined in greater detail to determine what the contributing factors may have been to cause these outcomes.

Once these organization specific best practices have been identified, the knowledge can be shared across the organization. Here we have an organization that has demonstrated that when they following rigorous requirements definition and management techniques along with some strong project management activities good results are soon to follow. These particular practices are truly best practices for this organization.

Conclusion

It is important for an organization to adopt and deploy best practices of software development. Best practices can be introduced to the organization based on proven techniques such as formal reviews and inspections or they may be identified and already exist internally as a result of a performance measurement activity as we noted above in Measuring Performance. Regardless, to be sure best practices are being properly executed and results are being realized it is necessary to apply a consistent use of metrics. The software industry is mature enough to have learned and evolved software development practices that are known to have a positive impact on software development. The question is whether or not senior management has matured and evolved enough to understand the level of commitment necessary to properly deploy those best practices.

References

1. Wikipedia. *The Free Encyclopedia, 1.* http://en.wikipedia.org/wiki/Best_practice (accessed June 1, 2011).
2. Business Dictionary, 1. http://www.businessdictionary.com/definition/best-in-class .html (accessed June 1, 2011).
3. Niwot Ridge Consulting, 9–10. http://www.niwotridge.com/PDFs/NineBestPractices .pdf (accessed June 1, 2011).
4. International Function Point Users Group. http://www.ifpug.org (accessed June 12, 2011).
5. Herron, D. 2006. *FP Lite – Is It a Statistically Valid Method of Counting?* Boston, MA: IFPUG Conference.

About the Author

David Herron is a business development manager and VP of Knowledge Solution Services for David Consulting Group. Over the course of his professional career, David has provided consulting and coaching services for a variety of IT organizations throughout the United States and Canada. He is an acknowledged authority in the areas of performance measurement, process improvement, and organizational change management. He is a noted author and lecturer and is a coauthor of several books on topics relating to IT performance measurement. He can be contacted at dherron@davidconsultinggroup.com.

Chapter 35

Process Improvement

Steve Neuendorf

Contents

Process improvement: The name belies its nature. Many people see it as the way to build products better, faster, and/or cheaper. In truth, there are many ways to be better, faster, and cheaper at whatever you are doing, and process improvement is only one of them. In addition, there are more aspects to process improvement besides just producing higher quality, quickly and efficiently. It is also important that we improve processes to make them more resilient. We will want to repeat and be able to build upon our success. Since software engineering is a labor-intensive process, we want to insure team stability when considering the changes that go along with improvement. We also need to include learning as a key element of process improvement to assure that we can reliably repeat our successes and not repeat our mistakes. We also must consider what I will call "externalities" in improving our processes. We want to be better, faster, and cheaper in ways that do not just pass quality problems or time considerations or costs on to others, either downstream along with our products or among others in our organization or in our business or community.

So we will look at process improvement as the most reliable because first it works on people and only then does it work on things like processes, procedures, and products. First, you must understand how good, fast, and cheap a process is and why it is that way. You also need to develop an understanding of why alterations of a process or adoption of changes and altogether different processes may be better, faster, or cheaper. With this understanding, you can then implement the changes that will result in improved performance.

To paraphrase Dr. Deming, process improvement is not something you talk about, it is something you do. For process improvement in software engineering, it is very much talked about, but in the end a lot less is actually done. The inertia lies in "do not mess with success" and "we are way too busy to make any changes now." As an industry, there has been much formalization of process improvement ranging from abstractions like process maturity to standardization of tools and methods, like Business Process Management (BPM), and to actual prescriptive processes, like Agile or ITIL (Information Technology Infrastructure Library). Of course, with most practitioners, success is generally defined as "not failing" (or at least not too much), and no real measures exist that give a real indication of results or the opportunity to improve results. The other generalization is that with improvement, you will accomplish more with less, and so you could be less busy to do the same thing or be just as busy but accomplishing more. What is worse though, is that far too much of what is done for process improvement is just plain wrong—the process is not better, and process improvement itself is besmirched. Let us look at process improvement and see if there is a way to effectively and consistently improve software engineering processes.

Process improvement is part of the much bigger discipline of change management. This chapter will focus on the process issues and change issues associated with process improvement. Your success in effectively improving processes will depend much more on the resolution of people and commitment issues. People tend to naturally resist change. Change poses organizational risk, but it is perceived by many or most people as personal risk, where they may not like their changed job or be able to perform it as well as what they currently do, or maybe they fear losing their position. On the whole, people issues are the greatest risk to achieving effective process improvement. It is even common for people issues to be represented as commitment, process, or measurement issues as a way to slow or stop the changes and their inherent risks and threats. After people issues, any organization undertaking process improvement must address commitment issues. There seems to be an irony that arises when asking for time and resources to end up saving time and resources, or when trying to get commitment for an improvement that ultimately will end up costing more or increasing time in one area while the benefit is realized elsewhere. And of course, one of the biggest commitment challenges is to obtain the commitment to abandon what has been done in the past. Resolving and managing people and commitment issues are beyond the scope of this chapter, but they must be resolved for the process of process improvement and measurement to work.

Two things need to be understood: the process or process improvement, and improvement, or the recognizable change in conditions and results. It may sound trite, but the number of different definitions and their imprecision lead to a great deal of confusion and misunderstanding about doing and achieving process improvement.

Process Improvement Defined

The operating definition of process I will use is "the definition of the way in which something is intended to be done." Any process has an accomplishment objective: what is to be done. A process must describe how to go about achieving (procedure) its objective (product), as well as identify means (attributes) for execution of the process. For convenience, I will use product to mean a tangible object or a service or a mix of both. Since this definition could apply to anything, for software engineering, our process is assumed to have a sufficiently formal definition such that it can be nearly repeated. A prerequisite for process improvement is to have a comprehensive process definition. But that is not quite as simple as it may sound. There are many variations of process depending on what is done and how it is done, and even by whom it is done. Table 35.1 shows several variations of process based on the products produced, the process used, and the attributes.

For products, the distinction is made as to how much influence the producer has on the product. There are two aspects for products that are of interest to our analysis: form and function. The consumer of the product generally controls the function of the product, either by specification before production or by the decision to consume an available product after it has been produced. The producer has control over

Table 35.1   Characteristics of a Process

Product	Procedure	Attributes	Example
Fixed	Fixed	Fixed	Repetitive manufacturing
Fixed	Fixed	Variable	Construction
Fixed	Variable	Fixed	Manufacturing/rework
Fixed	Variable	Variable	Craft
Variable	Fixed	Fixed	Art
Variable	Fixed	Variable	Large projects
Variable	Variable	Fixed	Software/systems engineering
Variable	Variable	Variable	Agile methods/computer programming

the form of the product, at least to the extent which form affects the final product function. The next aspect of process is the procedure, which is generally the collection of events involved in the production of the product and the sequence in which they are performed. To a large extent, these are controlled by the producer, though the consumer may exert some influence over what those events are and when they are performed. For example, a software product customer may require 100% testing (and whatever that may mean) of a product before delivery. The product itself may also inherently prescribe some of the events and their sequence (precedence), but the producer has a large influence over what the events are and when they are performed. The procedure may be fixed, such as in having a machine or set of machines that do the same task using the same sequence each time, or it may be variable in that the problem implies or defines the exact steps and sequence, and the process offers only guidelines and checkpoints. The final dimension of a process is what is defined as attributes. Our operating definition of attributes is any element of the process that (1) influences the result of a measure or metric and (2) which can be controlled or significantly influenced. Therefore, that introduces the need for an operating definition of measure and metric. We will define a metric as the product of one or more measures that provides useful information. We will establish an operating definition of measure as being some information about something, usually quantitative, but not always. For example, the measure of the functional size of a software product may be its Function Point (FP) count. Another example of a measure may be the number of hours recorded to develop that software product. In addition, we may also have a measure of how much the effort to develop that same software product cost. Given those three measures, we can identify the useful metrics of FP per hour, or per dollar, or total cost, etc.

It is obvious the family of attributes includes hundreds of items, and so it is useful to have a classification approach. There are several well recognized and adopted approaches and I will just pick one because it is illustrative and it happens to fall into the order that I think matches the importance of the significance of each category in software engineering. People, Environment, Tools, and Techniques is my chosen schema. A generalization of attributes is they are the assignable causes of variation in metrics. As such, it is also important to make the distinction between the common causes of variation and the special causes of variation. Common causes of variation are those conditions that affect performance consistently across several instances of the process. For example, the skill level of a team will influence each project where that team is assigned. Later, we will examine the distinction between process and project, but for how, we can note that a project is an instance of process. Any improvement in process will be realized across any instance of project where that improved process is used. However, there may be any number of attributes by our definition that influence the metrics of a single project, peculiar to that project, or perhaps randomly distributed across the total projects. For example, a hardware problem would only affect those projects where that hardware was involved. Or perhaps a labor problem would only affect those projects in process when that labor problem occurred. Contrast that with a common cause of variation example where a particular class improved the proficiency of all of the attendees, and that improvement was realized in every project where those attendees were a part of the team.

In addition, there is the question of how to classify those items meeting our first part of the attribute definition (influences a measure or metric) but not the second part (can be controlled or significantly influenced). Those elements fall into the category of special causes of variation or more generally risks. Those fall more into the role of project management than they fit into process improvement.

Contrast process with project. A process is the intended way, while a project is the application of resources to that process. Since projects are tangible, the only way we can "measure" a process is to measure projects and use the information to make inferences about the process. As a measurement tool, process is the category to which we assign the common causes of variation, while projects are affected by both common and special causes of variation. Working on special causes is (or should be) risk management, problem identification, and correction (firefighting), while working on common causes is process improvement. To go one step further, using special cause tools and methods on common causes and vice versa is called meddling. Meddling invariably causes "fires," and firefighting does not improve processes.

Three characteristics or metrics describe any process: Efficiency (E), Cycle-time (T), and Quality (Q).

Efficiency (E) is the relationship of use of resources to accomplished results. Sometimes people will use "productivity" interchangeably with efficiency, and they are half right. Later we will look at another definition of productivity and see its importance in overall process improvement.

Cycle-time (T) is the "design speed" of the process. Obviously, schedule is a very important aspect of projects as is duration and wait time. All are measures of how long. All are answers to "how long" questions, but all but cycle-time include elements of variations in pace (the rate of doing work) and delay and idle time. Cycle-time applies to processes and makes assumptions about pace, delay, or wait and is generally constant for a process and may be adjusted for size or other considerations when applied to a particular instance of the process. The other time measures generally refer to a project and can be significantly influenced by factors that are not directly associated with the process being applied.

Finally, every process has a Quality (Q) characteristic. There are many aspects of quality associated with the product, the procedure, and the attributes, and all play significant roles in succeeding in software engineering, but for process improvement, we will tend to focus on product defects and defect density. Definition of what is a defect may vary from organization to organization, but if it is consistent across measured instances of a process, it can be used to quantify the quality aspect of a given process. It seems counterintuitive, but the same process will always produce nearly the same number of defects in its outputs.

We always knowingly laugh when someone says, "good, fast, cheap—pick two." Actually, this is more insight than humor. For any process, there is a function $f(E,T,Q) = $ Constant K. For better, faster, and cheaper, you need a different process (change K).

In looking at process, we must also consider sequence. Sequence is the order in which things are done. There are two types of sequence: required (precedence) and discretionary. Required sequence is an order that must be followed. For example, putting on a second coat of paint requires that the first coat already be applied and cured. In software development, it is best to start coding after the requirements are gathered. Discretionary sequence is the order in which it is decided that something will be done. The required sequence must be observed. In practice, precedence and means availability control the process execution sequence decision. Later, we will discuss continuous improvement and innovation. Note here that some of the greatest opportunity for process improvement comes from innovation regarding the sequence of a project. For example, agile methods probably make the greatest changes over traditional development in the area of sequence than in any other aspect and with usually great results.

After sequence comes the attributes, as mentioned before, which will carry out the steps or tasks. We talk about a project being "the application of resources to a process to produce a result." We usually think of resources as labor, time, and money, but for understanding the process, we must consider other resources, such as tools, techniques, technology, and factors particular to "resources" such as the skill and experience of the team members. Therefore, we define the attributes to include all aspects we need to consider to understand and improve processes. It is helpful to consider the means in categories such as management, technology, teams (or people), tools, techniques, and environment.

Practically, an organization must consider all of its processes collectively. As defined so far, a process is a sequence and a set of attributes. By this definition, each organization would have an infinite number of processes (possible combinations of E, T, and Q). This introduces two more dimensions of process we must address: capability and capacity. Each combination of E, Q, and T possible defines a capability. The current ability of the organization to execute a capability defines capacity. This is not as complicated as it may sound. For example, one of the attributes defined as "Red Team" is comprised of members with certain experience and knowledge. Red Team projects are done faster, better, and cheaper than "Blue" or "Green" team projects. Red Team performance levels are a "capability." However, within the organization there are only enough members qualified to form Red Teams, so there is a capacity associated with the Red Team capability.

There are two categories of improvement: continuous improvement and innovation. Continuous improvement of processes is the systematic upgrading of lower capability attributes to give higher capacity at a higher capability. To use the prior example, continuous improvement of team capability would be providing training to Blue and Green Team members, so more Red Teams can be formed at a time.

Innovation is the introduction of new capability. Again, using the prior example, innovation would be training everyone in a new technique. Everyone, even the Red Team would have a greater capability to execute the new technique. The distinction between the two types of improvement is not so clear, but the important point for organizations is that innovation usually introduces learning curve dynamics and a risk of failure to a greater extent than continuous improvement.

Let us make another distinction between strategy and process improvement. Again using our example, if we were to just adopt a strategy to "let go" Green and Blue team members and replace them with Red Team qualified candidates (at similar cost), we would rightly expect better values of performance (E and Q and T). The reality is that Red Team caliber candidates are expensive and much harder to find and keep. On the other hand, effective process improvement requires understanding the process. That is we need to know what it is that will actually improve a process and by how much. That is, using our team example, we must first figure out the cost of making our Blue and Green team members perform like the Red Team and then figure out the benefit of improving team performance.

As in anything complex, what is "obvious" is not always true and what is true is not always obvious. Only by improving our understanding of the process can we manage the risk that changes will not result in the desired improvement.

Tools for Process Improvement

For all of the categorization we have done so far, there are still two categories of process that need to be considered in applying the process improvement tools available. There are repetitive processes, like most manufacturing, and there are non-repetitive processes, like software engineering.

Repetitive Processes

Virtually all of the common process and Statistical Process Control (SPC) literature focuses on repetitive process principles and examples. Characteristics of these processes are a mostly fixed precedence, sequence, and means. Generally, the process flowchart tool is used to understand and improve these processes, with care to use the decision element of this tool to divide flow into segments that are distributed in such a manner that SPC tools can be used to analyze data (see Table 35.2). Modern technology introduces some remarkable tools to make robust and even interactive flowcharts. They are discussed here not because they are the right tool for understanding the software engineering process but because they are useful for understanding those parts of the process, typically at the higher conceptual levels and some of the individual tasks, that are repeatable across instances of the process. Again, most modern tools not only allow you to make the flow chart pictures, but also can allow the capture of the element properties and a powerful tool for some of the process understanding and improvement.

Table 35.2 Basic Repetitive Process Flowcharting

Repetitive Process Flowcharting	
Process Flowcharting Symbol	*Symbol Properties*
Arrow ⟶	Flow volume
	Flow timing
Input/output ▱	Naming/responsibility notation
Storage/queue ▽	Volume
	Capacity
	Timing
Operation ▭	Resource use
	Timing
	Capacity
Decision ◇	Criteria
	Flow percentage

Non-Repetitive Processes

For non-repetitive processes, attempts to understand and improve using repetitive process tools and techniques yields the same results noted for trying to teach pigs to sing: you get no singing and it upsets the pig.

The key to understanding non-repetitive processes is that while the steps and sequence are never the same from project to project, the means generally are. That is, in most cases, the same teams (individuals and skills) with the same management (individuals and styles and leadership) using the same tools and techniques in the same environment will work on a different project. In any case, there are myriad things about the attributes that can be measured in some way, and so the variation in these measures can be related to variations in performance (E, T, and Q) for any project. BINGO!

Well, maybe not yet. If you look at the process flowchart tool description from Figure 35.1, notice that the volume property of the arrows along with the "normalization" use of decisions allows an analyst to "normalize out" variation due to throughput and size. For non-repetitive processes, project cost, defects, and duration will vary not just from differences in the means of accomplishing completion, but also due to the (deliberately) heretofore not elaborated upon size. The reason

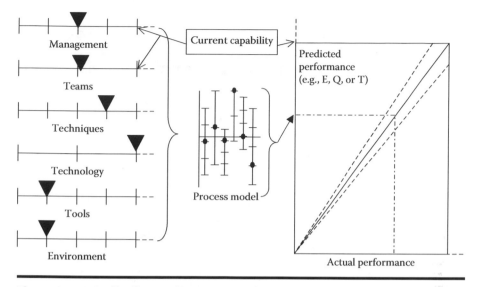

Figure 35.1   Attributive performance prediction.

I have not mentioned size measurement is that it seems to work like a light switch. Flip the switch, and about half the people turn on like a light, and the rest turn off like a light. The goal of a size measure is to get variation due to size out of the way of the analysis, without introducing another source of variation and without removing a process-related source of performance variation. If your size measure does this, and some straightforward statistical analysis will tell then you are on the right track.

Reviewing where we are, we now have recognized we are improving non-repetitive processes. Our understanding of these processes comes from analysis of the effects of variation in the means of production on performance.

To illustrate how this translates into reality, let us use an example with which I will assume that readers are familiar: the Software Engineering Institute (SEI) maturity modeling tools and techniques. (Several models have been published by SEI. At this writing, the Capability Maturity Model Integration (CMMI) is the most recent and most extensively documented version.) On its face, these techniques measure "capability maturity" on a scale of 1 to 5 with 5 being more mature. (The actual SEI definitions are 1, Initial; 2, Repeatable; 3, Defined; 4, Managed; and 5, Optimizing.) Several practitioners and analysts have also developed relationships between these maturity levels and performance in each dimension of process measurement (E, T, and Q). Notably, the higher the maturity level, the better the performance. From the analyses I have seen, the differences are substantial and I assume they are (statistically) significant. The non-repetitive process improvement model is analogous to this view of the SEI methods. That is, for each of the attributes, a scale of possible conditions is developed and the criteria for evaluating that attribute according to that scale are prepared. For example, say that project management is the attribute being evaluated. The low end of the scale would be no project management, maybe a lead and no formal tracking. The top of the scale would be a full-time project manager reporting to the Project Management Office and using a full set of project management tools (e.g., Project Management Institute (PMI)'s Product Management Body of Knowledge (PMBOK)). With all attributes identified and a scale created for each of the attributes, the values of the attributes for any given project constitute a process. Improvement of the process is really the improvement of the attributes, either by increasing the scale or by identifying alternatives. Figure 35.1 shows how a process is managed to obtain a performance result.

For the organization measured, the scale in each attribute (e.g., Management) represents the range of influence the measured capability has on performance. For any project, the actual value of the attribute (the triangle symbol) predicts the contribution of that aspect to the overall performance of the project. The process model shows the collective effect of the measured attribute values on project performance and gives the project predicted performance. The goal of performance measurement then becomes measuring actual performance against predicted performance to detect problems. Process improvement is working on the attributes, both for capability (higher levels on the scale) and for capacity (how much is available for use).

Project management is (1) identifying the process used (and predicted performance) and (2) assuring that the actual performance equals predicted performance.

Process improvement is (1) improving your capacity at each higher level of capability and (2) increasing your capability in each of the process areas.

Employing the right knowledge and skills, calibrating the model is straightforward. That is, for any given set of attributes, values for E, Q, and T (exclusive of special causes) can be predicted. It follows that if the model is calibrated, the effect of changes in the attributes (benefits) can also be quantified. Finally, understanding the attributes makes the actions and investments to move up the scale evident and their cost (time and money) easily determined. You now have the action, cost, and benefit of process improvement objectively in front of you. Now more can be done than said.

Another important thing to note is that even in a calibrated model, it is likely that the variation in performance effect for the lower levels of an attribute is much greater than for higher levels. That translates into the risk that the prediction at low levels will be off. In analysis, these are prediction anomalies called outliers and are ignored. In reality, these must be accommodated. Compare this with SEI Maturity Level 1 stellar performers—at Level 1, the model is not predictive. (However, the overwhelming odds are that Level 1 performance will be worse than the performance at higher levels.)

I glossed over the real key to process improvement in the first phrase of the second preceding paragraph: "employing the right knowledge and skills." There is nothing intuitive in doing something that makes its improvement obvious ("*perfect practice makes perfect*"). At risk of confusing a heretofore perfectly clear discussion of process improvement, the process you need to implement is one for "process improvement"; the result is an improved (software engineering) process. For process improvement to succeed, the skill level of the project team in "process improvement" must be high, not the skill level in software engineering. Most organizations do not have the requisite skills among their management or staff. No matter how motivated, facilitated, well led, etc., a team without the right skills is likely to fail in implementing process improvement. If you are in a typical organization, process improvement has failed at least once. If you blamed the team, you were wrong— you should never have expected them to succeed. If you blamed "process improvement" (i.e., will not work for an art), you were wrong too—it is alive and well and works great in the right hands. If you brought together the right resources in the right place at the right time with the right management and right leadership, you probably did not read this far.

Summary

Sometimes it is helpful to view everything in an overall context. A "building blocks" diagram (Figure 35.2) shows the overall elements of software engineering measurement and process improvement.

The first course of blocks represents the organization as a collection of activities and results. From the projects and production of activities and the products and services represented as results, we get measures about timings, costs, size, and the associated attributes. From the measures, we get several metrics, including indicators of our process efficiency, our quality performance, and our time performance. Here is where far too many organizations stop measuring. A robust set of metrics can be produced and control charts can be made and used to help identify problems and to implement continuous improvement.

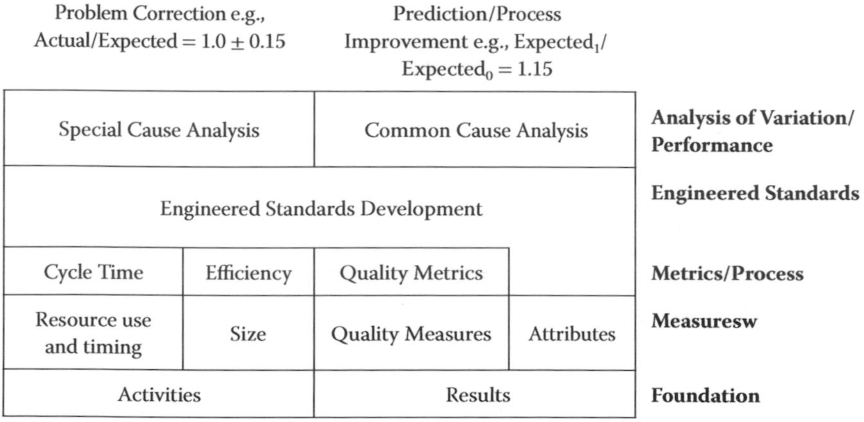

Problem Correction e.g., Actual/Expected $= 1.0 \pm 0.15$			Prediction/Process Improvement e.g., Expected$_1$/ Expected$_0 = 1.15$	
Special Cause Analysis		Common Cause Analysis		**Analysis of Variation/ Performance**
Engineered Standards Development				**Engineered Standards**
Cycle Time	Efficiency	Quality Metrics		**Metrics/Process**
Resource use and timing	Size	Quality Measures	Attributes	**Measuresw**
Activities		Results		**Foundation**

Figure 35.2   Measurement/improvement "building blocks."

The next opportunity is to analyze what I am calling the engineered standards or the quantitative effect of attributes on performance. Using the attribute and metric data collected for the organization, tools and techniques are available to accurately and consistently quantify how each of the process characteristics (E, T, and Q) are influenced by the presence and level of the identified attributes. This information can be used to accurately predict performance for the early and reliable identification of problems and also for engineering project performance by informing the selection of the attributes to assign to and apply on each project. With these methods, you can quickly understand that those who have good luck are those who can best make it for themselves. Good Luck!

About the Author

Mr. Neuendorf is an independent consultant. He has over 40 years experience in industrial engineering, measurement, management, education development and teaching, and process improvement with the most recent 30-plus years directly related to software engineering. Mr. Neuendorf has over 20 years as an independent consultant, working with a wide variety of clients representing many different types of organizations and opportunities. He has worked extensively with and is currently working with the David Consulting Group as an independent contractor.

Mr. Neuendorf worked 14 years as an industrial engineer specializing in "white collar" process measurement and improvement, particularly in software engineering. He has also worked for various consulting companies, focusing on Function Point and process improvement activities. He also has recently been a principal in a global project management benchmarking organization, doing analysis, research, and training, significantly for NASA.

Mr. Neuendorf has published many books and articles on the subject of process measurement and improvement, including *Six Sigma for Project Managers* (Vienna, VA: Management Concepts, Inc., 2004 [ISBN 1-56726-146-9]) and *Project Measurement* (Vienna, VA: Management Concepts, Inc., 2002 [ISBN 1-56726-140-X]).

Mr. Neuendorf has a Juris Doctorate from Seattle University School of Law (1989) and an MBA (1984) and BA (1983) degree from University of Puget Sound.

Chapter 36

Defects: Perspective on Prevalence and Prevention

Joseph R. Schofield, Jr.

Contents

[20]And God said, Let the waters bring forth abundantly the moving creature that hath life, and fowl that may fly above the earth in the open firmament of heaven.[21]And God created great whales, and every living creature that moveth, which the waters brought forth abundantly, after their kind, and every winged fowl after his kind: and God saw that it was good. Genesis 1:20—21, KJV

Software defects continue to plague our lives. Defects are often the culpable cause though sometimes insidiously disguised by schedule slippages, cost overruns, and credibility crashes. The prevalence of software in almost every aspect of our lives suggests that defects cost us much more, personally and institutionally. An ability to predict latent defects in software would enhance the credibility of the supplier and our lives as well.

Creation, defects, and predictive statistics have a common thread. Since the advent of creation, man has sought to identify and number the species. Even now new species are found constantly: the new 5-inch spider in the Middle East [1] and undiscovered species found every 3 days in the shrinking Amazon [2], as examples. Time magazine estimated the cost of identifying the remaining 5.4 million species (less than 20% currently identified) at $263 billion dollars [3]. Since we have found it improbable to account for the exact population of species that have been identified, we have devised methods for estimating population size. Enter *capture–recapture method* (CRM) [4], another name for *mark and recapture* found in the literature. A small minority of software engineers have adopted the use of CRM in software code peer reviews to predict the estimated number of latent defects in a software product. A reasonable challenge might be "why would anyone release a product known to be defective?" Another question might be "why would someone release a product when they do not know the gravity of the defects remaining in the product?" Both questions are reasonable. However, neither of these questions will be answered in the following pages; they only assume to address a motive. Rather, the target is the serious nature of defects and what to do about them. The two posed questions will continue to be the subject of litigation debated before judges by legal representation. Perhaps the context that follows will minimize the likelihood that you are a defendant in future software litigation.

Software Defects—It Is Getting Personal! (and More Frequent)

Most of us live day-to-day unaware of and unaffected by the prevalence of software defects. For instance, the world's (then) most advanced fighter aircraft—the F22 Raptor—lost many system flight programs when crossing the International Date Line; the cause, a few lines in the millions of lines of code that provided avionic support [5]. The F16 Fighting Falcon was plagued with a number of software defects—some that caused extensive damage to planes in flight and on the ground [6,7]. The Mars Polar Lander traveled 35 million miles to Mars before crashing on landing; a software defect was suspected but no one has retrieved the probe to confirm the cause. Wired [8] ranked what it considered the 10 worst software defects of all time. One-half of those defects listed occurred with computer operating systems and network applications, two occurred within aerospace, two occurred with medical equipment, and one with an intentional espionage plant. Most of us do not take those types of defects personally since they do not affect most of us directly—though some did. Intel's floating point divide and network outages are such examples.

While sometimes less visible, software defects are penetrating many aspects of our daily lives. In my household, shopping is exploited full time. In April of 2007, T. J. Maxx [9] was the victim of a suspected compromise of 45 million credit cards. By September, over $3M in losses had been identified [10]. By October, the number of compromised credit cards had risen to a potential 94 million [11]. In 2009, the Home Depot web page was availing malicious code to devices visiting its site. As of 2011, the defective software was "disabled" but was still present at the site [12].

Perhaps you are not a customer of the businesses above. Do you drive a car? In 2010, Toyota prepared to recall hundreds of thousands of its Prius cars due to suspected faulty brake software [13]. BMW, DaimlerChrysler, Mitsubishi, and Volvo experienced product malfunctions such as engine stalls, non-illuminating gauges, incorrect wiping intervals, and wrong transmission gears each due to software defects [14].

Perhaps you do not own a car. Do you take medications? Medical staff report that 770,000 medication mistakes occur each year in the US; these errors are more than handwriting issues, transcription, data entry, and other more preventable errors [15]. Over 1.5 million people are harmed every year from medication errors; the cost of these is estimated at $3.5 billion [16]. While most of these are not directly related to software, enhancements to medical systems could help to reduce or increase these effects.

Perhaps you do not shop, own a car, or depend on a health care system. It is still possible that defective software and data practices surrender your data through organizations like Marriott, Ford Motor Co., Sam's Club, and the US Justice Department [17]. Still not feeling the pain? Most of us pay taxes. Perhaps that strikes a chord. Early in 2006, a property in Indiana valued at $121,900 had its value assessed for tax purposes at $400 million. A "computer glitch" was the prime suspect [18]. The same characterization (computer glitch) was blamed for the shutdown of the check-in lines at seven MGM hotels in Las Vegas, five of those on the "Las Vegas Strip" [19].

As early as 2004, software defects were estimated to cost $60 billion dollars a year in the U.S. alone [20]. The cost of defects is not confined to the U.S.—the challenge of defects and costs are an international phenomena. The United Kingdom's National Health Care System development program spent $26B (billion is correct) over budget [21]. It may not be apparent that a large percent of this overrun is related to software defect discovery and removal until one realizes that as much as 40–60% of a software development project's costs are directly the result of rework from testing and intended defect removal. The word "intended" is key to this discussion, given that the correction of one defect frequently leads to the introduction of another.

The message here should be apparent. Historically, it has been easier to discount the impact of software defects because they are often attributed to large government applications, defense systems, and special use software. The ubiquity of software and the unabated proliferation of devices executing software, such as home computers, laptops, and millions of mobile devices raise doubt as to how each and every one of us can avoid defects in software. It is getting invasively pervasive!

The Hidden Cost of Software Defects

Forty-nine percent of all software projects are afflicted with budget overruns [22]. Software project managers and software developers would seem to be motivated to find the cause of these overruns and correcting them. Such steps would position proffered services favorably in a globally competitive market. Consumers of software products and services would seem to have similar interests stimulated by the hope of potentially lower costs or greater value for software investment.

Fortunately, the National Institute for Standards and Technology (NIST) has a potential answer as to why software overruns are so common. NIST reports that 80% of software development costs are traceable to *defect corrections* [23]. If this number were anywhere close to correct, it would seem that major initiatives would be undertaken to reduce the cost of defects. One approach for eliminating rework might seem to be early and frequent testing. However, testing only identifies the existence of defects; it does nothing to reduce the flow of defects into the product. The problem is more systemic than eliminating the defect. (Testing has been found to be ineffective when used as the sole process for defect reduction.) Gartner disclosed testing composed 25–50% of the software life cycle, and it is perceived of adding no business value [24]. And since testing necessarily is performed *after*, or in a minority of cases *during* software development, it is too late in the development life cycle. Most costly defects are introduced (injected) as a result of misunderstanding requirements or a faulty design. Jones notes that delivered defects that originate in requirements and design far outnumber those from coding [25].

Advancements in tools and improvements in removal methods are two possible solutions to the defect dilemma; but software developers are inexplicably creative and imaginative when it comes to injecting defects.

Alternatives such as peer reviews and formal software inspections are additional techniques for identifying defects. Both of these can be used early in the life cycle to reduce the longevity of a defect's existence. In this respect, the *detection* of a defect is closer to the point of its *injection*. The closer the *detection* to the *injection*, the less rework of subsequent work products is necessary. Boehm has historically demonstrated that these costs can increase as much as 100% and more for defects that originate in requirements. Keep in mind, however, that the original research on these escalating costs is now 30 years old [26]. It follows that less rework would lead to lower cost; the lower the cost, the less likely the product would be classified—as are nearly one-half of software projects—with cost overruns. The cost of rework offsets and is an economic drag on profits.

The Impact of Defects on Software Maintenance Costs

Historically, the cost of software support exceeds the cost of the initial development of the product. Because many of the same practices used to develop the original software are sustained during the production (also referred to as maintenance, operations, and support) "phase," production practices are subject to the same challenges as during development. In addition, defects from development cascade into production; these residual defects, discovered by the customer, are referred to as *latent* defects. This definition differs from the notion of a latent defect in the sale of a property for instance, "a fault in the property that could not have been discovered by a reasonably thorough inspection before the sale." One difference is that software defects "could reasonably have been discovered" given adequate test criteria. Further, while the word "inspection" may have a slightly different implementation, inspections (in this case of the code variety), while highly effective for defect removal, are seldom used on most software products.

The software community should not be startled to find that 47% of companies surveyed reported "higher than expected" maintenance costs associated with their software [27]. Despite the unexpected (and unnecessary) level of costs associated with software defects, for both development and production activities, the use of structured, disciplined, and rigorous processes are often shunned by software engineers. When I asked one such software engineer what his team was doing to eliminate defects and rework, he responded, "We shoot from the hip."

One last warning related to the cost of defects in production systems. Humphreys has found that small code changes (often introduced during production "fixes") are 40 times more likely to introduce new defects than original development work [28]. This value is so shocking that it should trigger reticence if not fear in the hearts of anyone submitting a change request to critical software. This predicament provides a new spin on an old saying: "If it's broke, don't fix it."

The Impact of Defects on Schedule

What role might defects play in the late delivery of software products? Recognizing that over one-half of organizations with software projects miss delivery schedules [29], how likely is it that defects might be a significant contributor to those delays?

Numerous studies identify the reasons why software projects are late: requirements volatility, lack of support, poor project management practices, customer and developer turnover, infrastructure changes, or delivery delays. No doubt, each of these causes plays some role in some floundering projects—often more than one of the above causes afflicts the same project. While some of these causes contribute to delays, they mask the more common cause; defects are the primary suspect again.

Thirty percent of project effort can be traced to rework [30]. The cause of rework, by definition, must have some link to the prevalence of defects. These defects can be masked as "requirements volatility" when in essence requirements were perhaps not validated, insufficiently elicited, elicited from other than relevant stakeholders, not managed in such a way as to reveal inconsistencies, or not requirements at all.

Defects can be injected in design: allocated to the wrong component, misunderstood by the designer, not integrated by the design team, prioritized in such a way as to overlook key features, etc. These requirements and design-injected defects are seldom discovered while testing code because the code typically performs according to the design specification (assuming one even exists). One way to mitigate many of these defects is to write the acceptance criteria in conjunction with the recording of the requirement rather than later in the development cycle. Rigorous peer reviews and inspections further reduce the chance that these defects will *escape* into a subsequent activity. We have no reason to doubt Jones' finding that even at delivery, defects injected during requirements and design tend to far outnumber coding defects [25].

A schedule slippage and cost overrun avoidance strategy that is used more often than acknowledged is the "hiding of overtime" by not charging "recovery" hours worked to the customer. The schedule often remains intact, and costs that might set off other "alerts" about the status of the project are hidden. This approach is a self-destructive behavior. Future estimates fail to account for the true cost of work (and time), thus ensuring that future "bids" will contain unknown variances putting future teams at risk when developing estimates. Often management may think that the work level (and results) is typical without the needed insight into the true performance of teams; thus, expectations become increasingly difficult to manage. Lastly, team members "burn out" and move to other work areas, giving the offending project a tarnished reputation and new incoming replacements an unarticulated disadvantage.

Defects are prevalent throughout the development cycle, beginning with requirements. The advent of these defects, upon discovery, triggers rework. Rework is time that is not typically highlighted on most work breakdown schedules. The addition of rework time to original delivery estimates often leads to a failure to meet schedule. Admittedly, some project teams will attempt to "make up" this difference by working heroic hours but, in lieu of credible defect removal strategies, they may also be accelerating the rate of defect injection.

The impact of defects on software delivery schedules is worthy of our attention. Sometimes the impact of latent defects on operational schedules gets overshadowed. Consider the grounding of United's 757 aircraft in early 2011 due to insufficient "checking" for measurements such as air speed and air pressure that interface with autopilot functions. In an era with small profit margins, constant profit threats from fluctuating fuel costs, and attempts to stay competitive in stressful economic times, United was forced to cancel flights for one-fourth of their fleet until the work was completed [31].

Dr. Dobb's article [32] described a client who spent an average of $4,200 to "deal with" every customer-reported defect. The first reaction of many of us might be to discount the veracity of that figure with some belief that the cost was unusually high. The resolving of United's "glitch" clearly cost United many times Dr. Dobb's amount.

In this document, the notion of taking personally the impact of latent defects on all of us is posited. What was the personal cost of each of United's passengers whose flight were postponed, delayed, or cancelled? Too often this "personal" cost is hidden and unaccounted for, while the schedule cost to the provider, in this case United Airlines, is more easily derived. And who assumes the cost again when United Airlines attempts to recover those lost profits with other fees and ticket increases? Is it feeling personal yet?

The Impact of Defects on Defects

Another reference identifies defect detecting and repair and associated rework as consuming almost 50% of resources for lower quality large software projects [33]. Gartner reports, "Testing consumes 25–50% of the average application life cycle and often is viewed as adding no business value" [24].

While the removal of defects would seem to be a noble endeavor to be fully appreciated if not valued and greatly endeared by the "client," an unexpected warning is warranted. The likelihood of injecting defects into a product while removing defects is significant when compared to developing new software. Why the increased likelihood? A number of candidate reasons exist:

- Lack of current familiarity by the developer (if being fixed by the same person)
- Lack of familiarity by the developer (if being fixed by a different person)
- Difficulty in finding all references to a changed variable
- Difficulty in finding all variables in a calculation
- Reliance on outdated comments in the code
- Reliance on outdated documentation about the code
- Failure to configuration manage all the products related to a defect repair
- Failure to update test cases related to defect removals
- (Let's not forget) failure of management to foster a culture of quality
- Failure to incent teams and individuals to perform
- The clustering tendency of defects
- Lack of training in formal test techniques
- Failure to test software against customer requirements (as opposed to the developer's interpretation of requirements)

■ Inability to elicit testable requirements
■ Reliance on software development approaches not intended for software of high consequence
■ A reliance primarily on testing to discover defects

Many techniques have been found to contribute to defect removal efficiency using more rigorous requirements elicitation processes. Since many of the defects that linger in software later in the development cycle are injected in analysis and design and are therefore much more difficult to detect—they have propagated their way into test cases that are now consistent with the code.

Both peer reviews and formal inspections can be used during analysis, design, and coding activities to identify defects. As powerful a technique that either of these may be for defect detection, another significant benefit often goes without notice. The use of peer reviews evidences the level of interest in defect removal and keeps quality goals visible during team activities. A raised "awareness" factor redirects energy and importance to product quality. However, these benefits are ancillary to the knowledge created and absorbed during peer review activities. Teams that practice peer reviews *learn* from each other and prevent future defects from being injected. They also become far more experienced in identifying product characteristics that are a breeding ground for defects. Ultimately, the knowledge gained from participation in peer reviews leads to the prevention of defects by elevating the ability of the primary (only) source of defects in software—the developer!

> Teams that practice peer reviews learn from each other and prevent future defects from being injected.

Great. Still Another Problem. Now What?

Why the earlier quote from Genesis regarding the creation of fish and fowl on the fifth day? (The land animals came on the sixth day.) Sometime after the population of the earth with animal species, man began to number those animals. In the case of Noah's collection of the living animals by two or by seven, an estimate of remaining animals was not necessary. In his case, the capture–recapture was more of a collect, store, and release [34].

Much more recently, over the past 120 years, man began to formalize the sampling techniques associated with biological species [35]. These techniques provided a reasonably consistent and reliable predictive model that did not require that mankind tag and release each instance in a population. Rather, an estimated total population could be derived by taking multiple samples. These techniques are known today as the "CRM" or "mark and recapture."

These same sampling techniques can be used in software inspections or peer reviews to estimate latent defects (or those that remain in a product). Equipped with this easily derived value, teams are provided with statistically valid measures by which they can decide to continue with either the work product "as is" or repeat a verification process. The intent of a repeated inspection or peer review would be to bring the predicted latent defect value within an acceptable threshold for product acceptance. In lieu of such a premeditated decision, products and their associated defects continue to persist in products. In more serendipitous outcomes, other (less effective) verification techniques like testing uncover the defect.

An Abridged Review of Capture–Recapture Method

While the use of CRM was introduced above for estimating biological populations, these same methods have also been used to estimate the prevalence of infections and diseases, primarily in human populations. The application of CRM has been traced to the late nineteenth century. Approximately 100 years later in the 1990s, more extensive quantitative use of CRM emerged as well as tools for more sophisticated statistical analysis [36,37]. More recently, CRM has been applied to estimate the spread of severe acute respiratory syndrome (SARS) and human immunodeficiency virus (HIV).

Interestingly, an estimate can be derived from as few as two samples as will be illustrated shortly with the fourth example. The two-sample approach, known as the Lincoln–Petersen method in Table 36.1 below [38], has some underlying assumptions that have parallels in peer reviews.

Table 36.1   Lincoln–Petersen and Peer Reviews

Lincoln–Petersen Assumption	*Peer Review Parallel*
The sampled population is static.	The work product is not undergoing change.
Each participant in the population being sampled has an equal chance of being sampled.	Each defect has an equal chance of being detected.
Being captured does not change the chance of being captured again.	Once a defect is detected by a participant, other participants can still detect the defect.
Samples are random.	Defects have an equal chance of being detected.
Captured items retain their "mark."	Defects are recorded and not lost across samples.
Accurate recording	All defects and detected occurrences are recovered.

Applications of Capture–Recapture Method for Estimating Latent Defects

It has been said that the best way to learn about something is to teach it; a corollary might be that the best way to learn how to do something is "to do it." This section contains examples of how to perform CRM using different sample sizes (number of participants) and slightly different outcomes. CRM is used in the last row in Table 36.2 below using the *summary of defects*.

The following examples in Tables 36.3 through 36.6 use *summary of defects* data. The "happy faces" in columns 2–5 indicate that the engineer detected a given defect in the review of the work product *before* the peer review session.

Example 1: Four Reviewers

The total number of defects estimated in this work product is eight. The total number of defects found in the review is eight. The total number of estimated latent defects in this work product is zero. Each of these three values is derived and any resemblance to above total numbers in columns X, Y, and Z in particular are coincidental (as we will see in the next example). The following breadcrumbs will help to clarify how those values were calculated. We will build this elucidation column-by-column.

- The first column is merely a unique identifier for each defect reported in the review. In this review a total of eight defects were detected.
- The second through fifth columns contain the defects detected by four different participants (Bob, Billy Bob, Joe Bob, and Jane Bob). For instance, Bob found defects 1, 3, 4, 5, 7, and 8 in his personal review before the plenary session.

Table 36.2 High-Level Peer Review Activities

Activity	Output/Exit State
A work product is distributed to some number of peers.	Peers have the work product in sufficient time to examine the work product before the "review."
The peers review the work product using guidance regarding the purpose and conduct of the review and document predefined defects.	Knowledge of product and suspected defects
Prepared peers meet and use a structured process for reviewing the product.	A list *summary of defects* detected by each participant and other tracking information such as preparation time, review time, and action items regarding detected defects

Table 36.3   Peer Review Results with Four Participants

Defect ID	Engineer "Bob"	Engineer "Billy Bob"	Engineer "Joe Bob"	Engineer "Jane Bob"	Column "X"	Column "Y"	Column "Z"
1	☺	☺	☺		✗	✗	✗
2		☺	☺			✗	
3	☺	☺		☺	✗	✗	✗
4	☺	☺		☺	✗	✗	✗
5	☺		☺		✗	✗	✗
6			☺	☺		✗	
7	☺			☺	✗	✗	✗
8	☺	☺			✗	✗	✗
Totals	6	5	4	4	6	8	6

Table 36.4 Peer Review Results with Three Participants

Defect ID	Engineer "Billy Bob"	Engineer "Joe Bob"	Engineer "Jane Bob"	Column "X"	Column "Y"	Column "Z"
1	☺	☺		✗	✗	✗
2	☺	☺		✗	✗	✗
3	☺		☺	✗	✗	✗
4	☺		☺	✗	✗	✗
5		☺			✗	
6		☺	☺		✗	
7			☺		✗	
8	☺			✗		
Totals	5	4	4	5	7	4

Table 36.5 Peer Review Results with Three Participants and a Tie

Defect ID	Engineer "Billy Bob"	Engineer "Joe Bob"	Engineer "Jane Bob"	Column "X"	Column "Y"	Column "Z"
1	☺	☺	☺	✗	✗	✗
2	☺	☺			✗	
3	☺		☺	✗	✗	✗
4	☺		☺	✗	✗	✗
5		☺			✗	
6	☺	☺			✗	
7			☺	✗		
8			☺	✗		
Totals	5	4	5	5	6	3

Table 36.6 Peer Review Results with Two Participants

Defect ID	Engineer "Joe Bob"	Engineer "Jane Bob"	Column "X"	Column "Y"	Column "Z"
1	☺	☺	✗	✗	✗
2	☺			✗	
3		☺	✗		
4		☺	✗		
5	☺			✗	
Totals	3	3	3	3	1

- Column X contains a mark for each defect found by the participant who found the most defects—in this case Bob; thus two columns will look similarly marked on the summary.
- Column Y contains a mark for each defect found by each participant other than the participant who found the most defects. In this example, Billy Bob, Joe Bob, and Jane Bob each found less than Bob.
- Column Z contains a mark for the "intersect" of columns X and Y. In this example, six defects were found by Bob and by at least one of the other participants.
- The last row provides a total that we will use to derive the values of interest.

The total number of defects *estimated* in the product is equal to the total of column X multiplied by the total of column Y, divided by the total of column Z.

$$X \cdot Y/Z \text{ or in our example } 6 \cdot 8/6 \text{ or } 8$$

The total number of defects *found* in the product is equal to the total of column X plus the total of column Y minus the total of column Z.

$$X + Y - Z \text{ or in our example } 6 + 8 - 6 \text{ or } 8$$

The total number of estimated defects latent in the product is the difference between these two derivations: $(X \cdot Y/Z) - (X + Y - Z)$ or $(6 \cdot 8/8) - (6 + 8 - 8)$ or 0. The derived CRM latent defect value is zero, suggesting that all the defects in the product have been detected. A product team should have confidence in moving forward with this work product.

Example 2: Three Reviewers

The total number of defects estimated in this work product is nine (rounding up). The total number of defects found in the review is eight. The total number of estimated latent defects in this work product is one. Notice that in this example, no resemblance of the derived values to above total numbers in columns X, Y, and Z occurs.

$$X \cdot Y/Z \text{ or in our example } 5 \cdot 7/4 \text{ or } 9$$

$$X + Y - Z \text{ or in our example } 5 + 7 - 4 \text{ or } 8$$

The obvious difference between our derivations in this example is one, suggesting that the team did not find all the estimated defects in the product. (Maybe they should include Bob next time.) The number one is not a large number but it does represent 11% of the defects in the product. Most product managers today would be elated with jubilation if they had statistical assurance that their product had 89% defect removal efficiency.

Two more curious examples follow. In the first, two of the participants (Billy and Jane) have found "the most" defects, raising a question as to which or how to "mark" column X. The answer to this apparent dilemma is to pick either and then to count the remaining participant's detections like any of the other participants. In Example 3, Jane is selected as the participant whose detections are noted in column X.

Example 3: Three Reviewers with a Tie between Two Participants for Most Defects Detected

The total number of defects estimated in this work product is ten. The total number of defects found in the review is eight. The total number of estimated latent defects in this work product is two. A similar decision persists on the part of the product owner regarding accepting the defect removal efficiency or using other defect removal techniques. No other comparisons or assumptions are intended or warranted between the previous examples, their participants, or the work product—that is, whether they are the same. The derivations for Table 36.5 include

$$X \cdot Y/Z \text{ or in our example } 5 \cdot 6/3 \text{ or } 10$$

$$X + Y - Z \text{ or in our example } 5 + 6 - 3 \text{ or } 8$$

Example 4: Two Reviewers with a Tie between Two Participants for Most Defects Detected

The total number of defects estimated in this work product is nine. The total number of defects found in the review is five. The total number of estimated latent defects in this work product is four. The defect removal efficiency is a paltry 55%. A product owner would be positioning himself or herself for a huge liability exposure if they allowed this product to proceed without a corrective action. Perhaps what is more troubling is the number of product managers who do not have quantitative data for making informed decisions regarding product quality. Jones and Bonsignour make this very point by proffering in expert witness testimonies for breach of contract litigations that management problems far outnumber software engineering problems [26]. The derivations for Example 4 follow:

$$X \cdot Y/Z \text{ or in our example } 3 \cdot 3/1 \text{ or } 9$$

$$X + Y - Z \text{ or in our example } 3 + 3 - 1 \text{ or } 5$$

Another significant point is suggested for this review; that is, the potential effectiveness and confidence associated with a peer review of just two participants. Logic posits that a third participant would have likely uncovered at least some of the "latent" defects with a fourth participant raising that likelihood even further. The argument must be made that additional participants provide an additional sample (thus the enhanced confidence in the results) and, more importantly, an additional opportunity for learning. This second benefit creates a reinforcing cycle (in a systems thinking context), wherein additional learning leads to reducing the injection rate of defects in future products, and the decline of injected defects in turn leads to increased relevant learning and improved practices.

Closing Thoughts

The prevalence of defects and the ever-increasing presence of software in almost every aspect of our daily lives will result in loss of personal time and value and, for businesses, an increased risk of catastrophic loss and litigation. All of these defects are not preventable with the current capability of people and technology; however, many of these defects can be identified, *captured*, and repaired before being released.

Unfortunately, most software organizations today rely on testing, testing, and more testing in attempts to address defect detection and removal. The reality is that testing improvements cannot sustain a pace to neutralize the rapid release of development tools and environments. More importantly, testing cannot offset the innovative nature of software engineers to introduce and inject defects.

Earlier, we noted that most latent defects originate in requirements and design activities. Some newer development approaches discount (discard would be a more accurate portrayal) software design, relying on iterations and sprint backlogs to prioritize customer needs. While the product owner rightfully plays a central role in the prioritization of requirements, they are not usually adept at understanding the consequence of fixing and re-fixing product features on a project deadline. In essence, the project development team expends its time on repairs. In exchange, the development team reduces efforts towards completing the product backlog, setting aside the use of formal quality techniques with proven time and cost performance long-term benefits.

The reality is that many project teams are quality-challenged. Teams attempt to test their way out, relying more heavily on extensive test scripts, acceptance testing, independent verification, and validation, without detecting remaining non-code-based defects. Project teams that are schedule-challenged often "cut corners" on testing and, unfortunately, do little else to detect and remove defects. Capers Jones and Bill Curtis remind us that as the number of users increases for a product, so too does the number of defects discovered [26]. However, when "crunched for time," teams may minimize the diversity and size of acceptance test groups that could closely resemble the eventual user population. Project teams that are cost-challenged likely have a hidden cause related to quality as evidenced by spending up to 80% of their budgets on identifying and correcting defects [39]. Up to 40% of all spending on projects is wasted as a result of rework [40].

The words of the late Watts Humphrey seem appropriate here: Through design and code reviews you will see more improvement in the quality and productivity of your work than you will see from any other single change you make in your personal software process [28]. Watts pinpoints one of the proposed benefits of peer reviews stated above: team learning that reduces defect injection. The extension of this wisdom to requirements reviews helps to address another source of the majority of defects that are latent after testing. According to the Meta Group, 60–80% of project failures can be attributed directly to poor requirements gathering, analysis, and management.

As dismal as the above findings may be, we have many reasons not to accept the current state of software engineering. CRM enables the software engineering community to understand and predict latent defects. More importantly, we can establish thresholds for latent defect acceptance (not less than 80% of defects identified in a work product). Our excuses can no longer be attributed to a lack of insight into product quality; it is an unwillingness to practice a century-old scientific approach for quantifying that quality. We can earn back the trust of our stakeholders as we emphasize the *engineering* in *software engineering*.

Acknowledgment

Thank you to Regina Trujillo, technical staff member at Sandia National Laboratories, for her suggestions that enhanced the readability of this text.

References

1. Ghose, T. *Giant Spider Species Discovered in Middle Eastern Sand Dunes*. http://www .wired.com/wiredscience/2010/01/giant-middle-eastern-spider-discovered. (accessed January 11, 2010).
2. Hance, J. *Life Shocker: New Species Discovered Every Three Days in the Amazon*. http:// news. mongabay.com/2010/1025-hance_newspecies_amazon.html (accessed October 26, 2010).
3. Time Magazine. April 4, 2011, p. 13.
4. Schofield. *Beyond Defect Removal: Latent Defect Estimation with Capture–Recapture Method*. CrossTalk, August, 2007.
5. Daily Tech. February 26, 2007.
6. "*Yes, Software Still has Bugs in it*". Yourdon Report, February 25, 2007.
7. Janssen, B. *F-16 Problems* (from Usenet net.aviation). August 27, 1986.
8. http://www.wired.com/software/coolapps/news/2005/11/69355 (accessed February, 2011).
9. InformationWeek. April 2, 2007.
10. InformationWeek. September 17, 2007.
11. *USA Today*. October 25, 2007.
12. Foxnews.com website (accessed January 11, 2011).
13. green.autoblog.com. February 9, 2010.
14. *Software Quality*. InformationWeek, March 15, 2004.
15. *Medication Systems*. CIO, June, 2005, p. 28.
16. InformationWeek. January 05, 2006, p. 18.
17. *December Data Exposures*. InformationWeek, January 02, 2006. p. 19.
18. *The High Cost of Flawed Testing*. CIO, November 15, 2005, p. 66.
19. Las Vegas Review-Journal. October 24, 2007.
20. *Behind the Numbers*. InformationWeek, March 29, 2004, p. 94.
21. News from the National Academies. July 20, 2006, nationalacademies.org.
22. Dynamic Markets Limited. August 2007.
23. National Institute of Standards & Technology. 2002. *The Economic Impacts of Inadequate Infrastructure for Software Testing*. US Department of Commerce.
24. *Two Reasons Why IT Projects Continue To Fail*. Gartner. March 20, 2008.
25. Jones, C. 1997. *Software Quality—Analysis and Guidelines for Success*. International Thomson Computer Press.
26. Jones, C. 2011. *The Economics of Software Quality*. Addison-Wesley Professional.
27. Dynamic Markets Limited. August 2007.
28. Humphrey, W. 1995. *A Discipline for Software Engineering*. Addison-Wesley.
29. Dynamic Markets Limited. August 2007.
30. *Dr. Dobb's Report*. InformationWeek, July 12, 2010, study by Dean Lefingwell, 1997.
31. *Computer Glitch Grounds United's 757 Fleet*. The Wall Street Journal, February 15, 2011.
32. Wiegers, K. *The Requirements Payoff*. InformationWeek, July 12, 2010, p. 39.
33. *Software Project Failure Costs Billions, Better Estimation & Planning Can Help*. Dan Galorath on Estimating, June 7, 2008.
34. Moses. 1982. NKJV bible. *Genesis* 7:2–3.
35. Petersen, C. G. J. 1895. *The Yearly Immigration of Young Plaice into the Limfjord from the German Sea*. Report of the Danish Biological Station, 6:5–84.

36. Suess, E. A., B. E. Trumbo, and C. Cosenza. *Tutorial on "R" Programming Language.* CSU East Bay, Department of Statistics and Biostatistics.
37. Pollock, K. H. 1991. Modeling capture, recapture, and removal statistics for estimation of demographic parameters for fish and wildlife population: Past, present, and future. *J Am Stat Assoc.*
38. Seber, G.A.F. *The Estimation of Animal Abundance and Related Parameters.* Blackburn Press.
39. National Institute of Standards & Technology. 2002. US Department of Commerce.
40. Bob Lawhorn presentation on software failures, March 2010.

Supporting Presentations and Readings

Repeatable and Relevant Functional Software Measurement Using Function Point Analysis. Lockheed Martin Measurement Workshop, Colorado Springs, CO, October 13, 2010.
Using Function Point Analysis for Software Measurement and Estimating. International Software Measurement & Analysis Conference, Sao Paulo, Brazil, September 14, 2010.
Problems with Using Lines of Code for Software Measurement. SPamCast Interview with Mr. Tom Cagley, April 20, 2009.
Documentation—How Much Is Enough. SPIN Panel discussion, February 18, 2009.
Lines of Code—Statistically Unreliable for Software Sizing? Computer Aid, Inc., Webinar, October 14, 2008.
Estimating Latent Defects Using Capture–Recapture: Lessons from Biology. Arlington, VA., International Software Measurement and Analysis (ISMA) Conference, September 18, 2008.
The Statistical Case Against the Case for Using Lines of Code in Software Estimation, 4th World Congress on Software Quality, Bethesda, MD., September 17, 2008.
Latent Defect Estimation—Maturing Beyond Defect Removal Using Capture–Recapture Method, QAI QAAM Conference, September 10, 2008.
Function Points: Sizing, Estimating, and More. Computer Aid, Inc., Webinar, May 13, 2008.
Life Cycle-Based Defect Removal with Capture Recapture Method. Computer Aid, Inc., Webinar, April 22, 2008
Garmus, D., J. Russac, and R. Edwards. 2010. *Certified Function Point Specialist Examination Guide.*
Beyond Defect Removal: Latent Defect Estimation with Capture Recapture Method. CrossTalk, 2007.
The Statistically Unreliable Nature of Lines of Code. CrossTalk, 2003.
Defect Management through the Personal Software Process(SM). CrossTalk, 2003.
Information Systems Management. 2003. *Lessons from the Ant Hill—What Ants and Software Engineers Have in Common.* Winter.
International Function Point Users Group. 2002. *IT Measurement: Practical Advice from the Experts.* Addison-Wesley. ISBN 0-201-74158-X

About the Author

Joe Schofield is a husband, father, and a former distinguished member of the Technical Staff at Sandia National Laboratories. He served as the SEPG chair for an organization of about 400 personnel that was awarded a SW-CMM® Level 3 in 2005. Joe has facilitated over 140 teams in the areas of software specification, team building, and organizational planning, using Lean Six Sigma and business process reengineering. Beyond Sandia, Joe taught graduate courses for 18 years and is a licensed girl's middle-school basketball coach. He has over four dozen published papers, conference presentations, and keynotes, including contributions to the books *IT Measurement, Certified Function Point Specialist Examination Guide, The Economics of Software Quality,* as well as this publication. He is an SEI-authorized Instructor for the Introduction to the CMMI® and two other SEI courses, a Certified Software Quality Analyst, a Certified Function Point Specialist, a Certified Software Measurement Specialist, and a Lean Six Sigma Black Belt. Joe is the current president of the International Function Point Users Group (IFPUG). He is a frequent presenter in the Software Best Practices Webinar Series sponsored by Computer Aid, Inc. Joe completed his master's degree in MIS at the University of Arizona in 1980.

PRODUCTIVITY
INTRODUCTION

XI

Dawn Coley

Productivity in the information technology arena is, and continues to be, a major area of struggle in many organizations. Significant inroads have been made in the determination of project productivity in completed projects. There is now a compendium of benchmarking data available to organizations who wish to compare their completed projects' productivity with others of like characteristics in the industry. Given these advancements, there are still huge gaps in measuring the productivity of software projects. Organizations are continually seeking ways to determine, track, and improve the productivity of their projects as they are executing. This capability remains one of the most elusive within the discipline of software measurement. Both of the authors in this section propose ways to deal with this tricky problem. Both proposed methods rely on robust historical project data being available to the organization that can be applied to assist in measuring productivity of "in-flight" projects.

Eduardo Alves de Oliveira has bachelor and postgraduate degrees in computer science and has applied this expertise for more than 11 years in the information technology discipline. He has served as a systems analyst, an instructor, and a consultant on software metrics and quality. He has taught and presented at ISMA conferences. His chapter "How to Improve Your Development Process using the Indicator of Productivity" presents the results of a case study he has been part of, which involves utilizing a method that is being proposed as a possible way to deal with the issue of measuring productivity in-flight on projects. Not only does his chapter discuss how to perform the appropriate measurements to determine productivity while the project is executing, he also presents the possible reasons for productivity issues and possible ways to address them.

Radhika Srinivas has a Master's degree in the computer science discipline. She has extensive experience spanning more than 10 years in the software industry. Her experience encompasses software development, software quality assurance, and software estimation. In her chapter "Monitoring Productivity Using Function Points in Various Phases," Radhika puts forth a rigorous use of Function Point Analysis as a basis for determining productivity measures during project execution. She discusses getting agreement early on in the project regarding the portions where Function Point based productivity measures will be taken and used to ensure project success. Radhika also explores how projects can make course corrections during various phases when discrepancies arise between contracted productivity levels and actual values.

Chapter 37

How to Improve Your Development Process Using the Indicator of Productivity

Eduardo Alves de Oliveira

Contents

Introduction

How can one tell if a team is being productive during the development of software? While the productivity of the development process should be monitored during project development, it is best to calculate productivity at the end of the project. The projects discussed in this chapter performed iterations, with each iteration being monitored. The purpose of this monitoring was to identify the productivity of the teams during the phases of developing the project. The following activity groups were monitored: requirements, analysis, design, implementation, and test. In the development process, actions, roles, and artifacts are grouped into defined groups of activities that meet a certain goal in the development cycle of a project. For example, activities related to requirements are grouped into a set called "requirements." Other sets are analysis, design, construction, and test. By measuring the productivity of these activity groups, it was possible to identify weaknesses in the implementation process and determine which ones needed to be modified to realize continuous improvement. To accomplish this, we developed a tracking spreadsheet that showed all the data functions and transactional sizes per use case. For each activity group of development, the process of development stipulated what percentage of the project's total effort would be expended. With this percentage, you can set the slices of Function Points (FPs) for each activity group for each use case. This spreadsheet was deployed to members of the team who developed the activities of each activity group, requiring them to record the amount of hours that they used. Knowing the size and effort allowed for the determination of the productivity of each activity group of the cycle, by use case. This same sheet was used to determine the consolidated values of average productivity per activity group of the development cycle. This work is based on an actual experiment in a real project of high complexity. It is an excellent opportunity to show how we can during the life of a software project improve its development process based on metrics. The project used the indicator of productivity, because it is easy to apply and understand. This chapter is divided into the following sections: Introduction; Scenario and Motivation; Analyzing the Indicator of Productivity during the Development Process; Improving the Development Process; Summary; About the Author.

Scenario and Motivation

Scenario

There are software projects that have a large scope and complexity. There are always deviations in the planned deliverables, and the consequences often impede the completion of them because there are deadlines and budget overruns. These projects are usually distributed among several development teams, much of the time spread to many regions of the country, in different departments and areas. It is understood that all teams involved in these projects follow the same process of software development. This complex scenario requires a more rigorous control of scope, effort, cost, and time of the projects. To evaluate this information at the end of the projects is important, but has not proven effective for the monitoring of ongoing projects.

Motivation

Making adjustments in the development process to improve the performance of the teams was the motivation. On the basis of this need, we started to develop a solution to the problem. Our development process already has indicators that are generated based on attributes of projects already completed. The purpose of these indicators is to enable a historical evaluation of various attributes of projects at corporate, department, and area levels. One of these indicators is the productivity of projects.

Before this study was performed, this indicator was calculated only for projects already completed, but there is a great need to evaluate the productivity of teams while the project is in development. This included the ability to make adjustments in development time and attempting to minimize risks that affect the duration and costs initially agreed upon with the client, and with other development teams located in other departments and business areas across the country.

Analyzing the Indicator of Productivity during the Development Process

Completed Projects

The productivity of projects completed uses two basic measures, which are collected from a control tool for projects. The first basic measure is the final size of the project in FPs, the second basic measure is the effort the team expended on the activities undertaken in the projects. The formula is as follows:

$$\text{Productivity (H/FP)} = \text{Hours Expended in Project (H)}/ \text{Final Size of the Project (FP)} \qquad (37.1)$$

Any project activity should be recorded in the project control tool. This recording is done daily by project resources. Each resource records the amount of hours spent to accomplish a given activity.

The project manager also records the final size of the project in FPs in the tool.

So, at the end of the project, you can see the final productivity of the project. The tool uses the formula shown above. What the tool does not calculate is the productivity of a project during its development cycle or productivity during the project or project activity.

Projects Running

The whole life cycle corresponds to 100% of project effort and size in FPs. To define the productivity of a particular activity group within the development cycle, we need to know the percentage of effort corresponding to it within the development process as a whole. Knowing this, we can calculate the percentage share of FPs and hours of effort corresponding to activity groups.

Setting the Estimated Percentage of the Project Activity Group

Every project manager has to keep in mind what the percentage of effort for each activity group is within the project. While the project is in development, this percentage will be estimated.

The development process has a table of estimated distribution, in percentage, by activity group (Table 37.1) for reference. This table was created and is adjusted based on historical data. The project manager may accept this suggestion or adjust it to the reality of the project. This adjustment should be based on experiences from previous projects managed by him and executed by his team. Upon completion of projects, it is possible to measure the actual distribution of this effort. It can be determined using the corporate tool for project control. Use the record of

Table 37.1   Suggested Distribution of the Estimated Effort Percentage by Project Activity Group

Activity Group	Percent (%)
Requirement	20
Analysis	10
Design	10
Construction	40
Test	20

hours spent in activities performed by project teams and then calculate the total percentage corresponding to the appropriate activities of the same project. Having defined these estimated percentages, we can have an estimated division of effort by activity group within the project development cycle. These percentages are critical information. With them, you can determine the size in FP, for each use case design, and the project activity groups.

Calculating the Size of a Use Case in Function Points

To calculate the size in FP for an activity group in a use case, simply use the percentage of estimated effort for each of the activity groups. Now you can work with an approximate FP size for each activity group. It is noteworthy that these sizes for activity groups are approximate and not exact.

Unfortunately, there is no precise and feasible way to do this calculation. For this reason, having a historical reference of projects is extremely important. Therefore, we can have a historical average of these percentages. Working with the historical average is more accurate than working with a reference value, as defined in Table 37.1.

For example, imagine a use case that has features that correspond to 200 FP. Using Table 37.1 as reference, we have the distribution of FPs per activity group process, as shown in Table 37.2. It shows that the features that the requirements analysts are responsible for is 40 FP.

Estimating Data Functions per Use Case

It is not difficult to determine the size of transactional functions that belong to a use case. This can be done by examining the features requested by the user that are grouped in the use case that is being counted. We define a premise to count the FP logical file (ILF or IEF). The use case that has the greatest influence on the

Table 37.2 Example of the Distribution of Estimated FPs by Project Activity Group

Activity Group	Percent (%)	Size (FP)
Requirement	20	40
Analysis	10	20
Design	10	20
Construction	40	80
Test	20	40

Table 37.3 Example of FP Count by Use Case

Use Case	Data Functions (FP)	Transaction Functions (FP)	Function Size (FP)
Create entity	7	6	13
Update entity	0	6	6
Delete entity	0	3	3
Read entity	10	6	16
Print entity report	0	7	7
Calculate entity data	7	6	13
Show calculating entity	0	4	4
Extract entity data	0	7	7
Total (FP)	24	45	69

maintenance of a file or reference should be the one in which the FPs are counted. Table 37.3 is an example of counting use cases in FPs. This example deals with the situation of using an iteration of the project and will be used to demonstrate how to calculate development cycle productivity of the project.

Distributing Function Point Estimated by Activity Group and Use Case

Assuming that the project has already gone through the project-planning phase, the use cases have already been defined and their sizes estimated. Distribute the FPs across all the use cases for the activity group. This distribution is shown in an example in Table 37.4.

Table 37.4 Example of Estimated and Final FP Distribution, for Project Activity Group and Use Case

Use Case	Function Size (FP)	Requirement (20%) (FP)	Analysis (10%) (FP)	Design (10%) (FP)	Construction (40%) (FP)	Test (20%) (FP)
Create entity	13	2.6	1.3	1.3	5.2	2.6
Update entity	6	1.2	0.6	0.6	2.4	1.2
Delete entity	3	0.6	0.3	0.3	1.2	0.6
Read entity	16	3.2	1.6	1.6	6.4	3.2
Print entity report	7	1.4	0.7	0.7	2.8	1.4
Calculate entity data	13	2.6	1.3	1.3	5.2	2.6
Show calculating entity	4	0.8	0.4	0.4	1.6	0.8
Extract entity data	7	1.4	0.7	0.7	2.8	1.4
Total (FP)	69	13.8	6.9	6.9	27.6	13.8

Table 37.5 Example of Allocation of Project Resources for Project Activity Groups and Use Cases

Use Case	Requirement (Resource)	Analysis (Resource)	Design (Resource)	Construction (Resource)	Test (Resource)
Create entity	A	D	F	H	J
Update entity	A	D	F	H	J
Delete entity	B	D	F	H	J
Read entity	B	D	F	H	J
Print entity report	B	D	F	I	J
Calculate entity data	C	E	F	I	K
Show calculating entity	C	E	G	I	K
Extract entity data	C	E	G	I	K
Total (FP)					

Defining Resources for Activity Group and Use Case

During project planning, the project manager distributes resources for activity groups and use cases. Table 37.5 shows the distribution that was determined for our example.

Distributing Function Point Estimated by Project Resources

Table 37.6 gives the distribution of FP by project resource, activity group, and use case of our example.

Collecting Effort by Resource, Activity Group, and Use Case

Throughout the iteration, the project manager must gather, in the project control tool, the total hours that each resource expended in the activities under their responsibility. In Table 37.7, we can see the amount of hours that each resource expended by activity group in the iteration.

Table 37.6   Example of the Distribution of Estimated FPs by Project Resource and Use Case

Resource/ Use Case	Create Entity (FP)	Update Entity (FP)	Delete Entity (FP)	Read Entity (FP)	Print Entity Report (FP)	Calculate Entity Data (FP)	Show Calculating Entity (FP)	Extract Entity Data (FP)
A	2.6	1.2	–	–	–	–	–	–
B	–	–	0.6	3.2	1.4	–	–	–
C	–	–	–	–	–	2.6	0.8	1.4
D	1.3	0.6	0.3	1.6	0.7	–	–	–
E	–	–	–	–	–	1.3	0.4	0.7
F	1.3	0.6	0.3	1.6	0.7	1.3	–	–
G	–	–	–	–	–	–	0.4	0.7
H	5.2	2.4	1.2	6.4	–	–	–	–
I	–	–	–	–	2.8	5.2	1.6	2.8
J	2.6	1.2	0.6	3.2	1.4	–	–	–
K	–	–	–	–	–	2.6	0.8	1.4

Table 37.7 Example Distribution of the Expended Effort by Project Resource and Use Case

Resource/ Use Case	Create Entity (H)	Update Entity (H)	Delete Entity (H)	Read Entity (H)	Print Entity Report (H)	Calculate Entity Data (H)	Show Calculating Entity (H)	Extract Entity Data (H)
A	40	18	–	–	–	–	–	–
B	–	–	16	60	24	–	–	–
C	–	–	–	–	–	66	20	34
D	10	6	3	6	7	–	–	–
E	–	–	–	–	–	12	6	25
F	13	6	3	6	7	13	–	–
G	–	–	–	–	–	–	4	7
H	8	5	2	2	–	–	–	–
I	–	–	–	–	2	5	2	8
J	24	12	6	8	2	–	–	–
K	–	–	–	–	–	32	16	32

Calculating the Productivity by Resource and Use Case

The project manager, after collecting the expended hours for each resource by activity group and use case, can calculate the productivity indicator by resource for the first iteration. Let us consider that the size of the use cases of our sample did not change during the development cycle of the iteration. Therefore, the FP size at the end of the iteration is equal to the estimated FP size, as shown in Table 37.6. In Table 37.8, we can see the yield calculated.

Calculating the Average Productivity by Resource and Activity Group

In Table 37.9, we have the average yield by resource and activity group. The last row in this table represents the average productivity per activity group. Thus, the project manager can analyze which activity group is above or below the expected productivity for the iteration of the project.

Calculating Average Productivity Iteration and Conclusions

By adding all the FPs and all expended effort of resources, we arrive at an average yield of the iteration of 8.4 H/FP. When the project manager performed the planning at the beginning of the project, the yield was determined to be 5 H/FP. We have a deviation of 3.4 H/FP. This deviation may have caused delays in product delivery, resource allocation, overtime (higher cost for the project), or loss of quality (skipping quality activities).

In the next section, we will analyze what actions should be taken during the next iteration to avoid continuing drifts in following iterations. Given the evolving development process, it is crucial to maintain productivity at the estimated target for the duration of the project. If we are not careful to monitor productivity, we run a high risk of not attaining the expected productivity of the project. If the estimated productivity for each iteration is not reached, the productivity target of the project as a whole is compromised.

Improving the Development Process

Evaluating Productivity Averages of Activity Groups

Except for the construction activity group, all other activity groups were below the expected productivity for the iteration.

Performance of Resources in the Requirements Activity Group and Possible Improvements

All resource requirements had a yield well below the estimated yield. The project manager must seek the reasons for their low productivity and take actions so it does not occur in the next iterations. Some of the reasons for low productivity include

Table 37.8 Example of Calculation of Productivity by Project Resource and Use Case

Resource/ Use Case	Create Entity (H/FP)	Update Entity (H/FP)	Delete Entity (H/FP)	Read Entity (H/FP)	Print Entity Report (H/FP)	Calculate Entity Data (H/FP)	Show Calculating Entity (H/FP)	Extract Entity Data (H/FP)
A	15.4	15.0	–	–	–	–	–	–
B	–	–	26.7	18.75	17.1	–	–	–
C	–	–	–	–	–	25.4	25.0	24.3
D	7.7	10.0	10.0	3.8	10.0	–	–	–
E	–	–	–	–	–	9.2	15.0	35.7
F	10.0	10.0	10.0	3.8	10.0	10.0	–	–
G	–	–	–	–	–	–	10.0	10.0
H	1.5	2.1	1.7	0.3	–	–	–	–
I	–	–	–	–	0.7	1.0	1.3	2.9
J	9.2	10.0	10.0	2.5	1.4	–	–	–
K	–	–	–	–	–	12.3	20.0	22.9

Table 37.9   Example of Calculation of Productivity by Project and Resource Activity Group

Resource/ Activity Group	Requirement (H/FP)	Analysis (H/FP)	Design (H/FP)	Construction (H/FP)	Test (H/FP)
A	15.3	–	–	–	–
B	19.2	–	–	–	–
C	25.0	–	–	–	–
D	–	7.1	–	–	–
E	–	17.9	–	–	–
F	–	–	8.3	–	–
G	–	–	10.0	–	–
H	–	–	–	1.1	–
I	–	–	–	1.4	–
J	–	–	–	–	5.8
K	–	–	–	–	16.7
Average	20.1	10.9	8.5	1.2	9.6

the following: (1) need for training or retraining of the requirements analysts to carry out the activities, (2) communication problems between the requirements analysts and users, (3) instability of the requirements specification for the user, causing rework, and (4) technical problems with the requirements elicitation.

Performance Resource Activity Group Analysis and Possible Improvements

The results of this activity group showed the second worst average productivity among all activity groups. It fell behind the requirements activity group, and the reasons for this low productivity must be investigated. Some of the reasons include the following: (1) need for training or retraining of analysts to carry out the activities, (2) problems in specifying the artifacts generated by the requirements group, (3) instability of the user requirements specification that causes rework.

Performance of Resources in the Design Activity Group and Possible Improvements

The resources involved in the design activity group were those that had kept the average yield closer (8.3 and 10.0). Despite not having achieved the productivity goal for the iteration, we can identify a consistency between resources. The main reason for this consistency could be the use of design patterns in the construction of design models. Still, the project manager should analyze what activities planned for this group can be tweaked or improved, leading to increased productivity. You may need to use another project-modeling tool, which may render the activities more automatable.

Performance of Resources in the Construction Activity Group and Possible Improvements

This was the only activity group in which the resources had better productivity than what was estimated for the iteration. This performance was achieved through the use of a framework for building source code in the language used on the project. Here, the productivity measurement showed that the framework is achieving its objectives and the resources involved are able to use it.

A point needs to be made here with respect to the quality of the source code. Often, when the construction of source code has good productivity, the quality may be poor or irregular. For this reason, we do a cross analysis with the measure of the defect rate per FP. This indicator shows the number of errors found by FP in the group test activities. We will not dive into this indicator in this chapter.

Performance of Resources in the Test Activity Group and Possible Improvements

The average productivity of this group was not too bad, but it contributed to reducing the average productivity of the entire iteration. Of the two resources participating in this group (J and K), K was the most unproductive. Some of the reasons for low productivity of K are as follows:

1. Need for training or retraining of resource K
2. Problems in specifying the artifacts generated by the requirements group and assigned to K
3. Rework generated by changes in the requirements specification of use cases reviewed by K
4. A high rate of defects in the source code reviewed by K

If the reasons for three and four can be identified, actions may be taken to involve the resources of the requirements and construction activity groups, respectively.

Summary

It was evident that this type of productivity evaluation brought significant results in controlling very complex projects. During later iterations, the measurement results indicated that resource productivity for activity groups had improved. For a future study, we would recommend that the following be considered. Replace the spreadsheets with an application that can be easily evolved and which has a real database and provide for comparative evaluation with other indicators that will allow for a validation of the productivity indicator, such as the rate of defects per FP and percentage of days of delay in delivery of an iteration.

About the Author

Eduardo Alves de Oliveira has a Bachelor's degree in computer science from UFRJ (Federal University of Rio de Janeiro) and a postgraduate degree from NCE-UFRJ (Electronic Computer Center—UFRJ). He has more than 11 years of professional experience in information technology. He is a systems analyst at SERPRO (Federal Data Processing of the Ministry of Finance) and has been a CFPS since 2004. He has performed as a consultant on software metrics and quality, an instructor and estimate coordinator for software projects, and an instructor at CCE PUC Rio's postgraduate courses (Project Management Metrics and Software Quality disciplines). He also teaches Function Point Analysis with Applications: Theory and Practice and Workshop Counts Software Analysis by using Function Points. He was selected to be ISMA Cinco's trainer for the Workshop "Using Function Points to Create Measurement & Analysis Indicators" and a speaker at ISMA presenting "Applying FPA in the Definition of Indicators from the BIT Perspective."

Chapter 38

Monitoring Productivity Using Function Points in Various Phases

Radhika Srinivas

Contents

The usage of computer-based systems has become paramount in today's modern world and one cannot think of this planet without computer applications even in their wildest dreams. Computer systems encompassing a variety of applications in leading cutting edge technologies in domains such as defense, banks, telecom, aerospace, insurance, healthcare, manufacturing, oil, and energy is the present-day norm. The marketplace is becoming very tough with aggressive competitors on one end and multifarious and extremely sophisticated requirements from the customers on the other side. These complex requirements combined with time-to-market pressures, cost-cutting measures, and issues such as customer data confidentiality create rigorous timelines. Current software outsourcing contracts dictate a variety of stringent specifications and adherence to all the quantitative attributes of the software. Any breach on the agreed contractual obligations might lead to cancellation of the contract, and organizations may end up paying a hefty price as defined in the penalty clause of the contract. In worst-case scenarios, this might either end up in bankruptcy or bring disgrace to the organization's history. A sample outsourcing contract should include service level agreement targets for software quality in terms of the number of defects, software size in terms of productivity of the organization, and cost in terms of effort and schedule. However, the above-mentioned targets may vary for different contracts based on the domain areas and customers' expectations. In the case of contractual validity stretching over multiple years, the rigor on the contractual targets set for software productivity, number of defects, and effort consistently increases year on year. Vendor organizations are exploring various avenues, processes, tools, and best practices to make sure they comply with the contract conditions, as none is ready to welcome software failures, effort overruns, and huge delays. To ensure that software development is progressing as per the contractual obligations, the current rate of software development needs to be measured with specific tools, processes, and methodologies. A positive outcome of this analysis results in gaining the confidence of the customer. It also helps in boosting team morale. Early warning of the project lagging behind signals a sense of caution and identifies an urgent need to implement some corrective measures to steer the development work in the right direction to achieve the required goals. This also helps in eliminating major shocks at the end of the development life cycle.

The topic of software productivity is highly subjective in nature. Software productivity is being influenced by several different factors that can be broadly classified into the following:

- People attributes
- Organizational process–related attributes
- Development environment–related attributes [1]

The people-related attributes include the following:

- The experience of the software developer
- The technical expertise of the developer
- Level of domain knowledge of the developer
- Interpersonal skills of the developer
- Team performance

The organizational processes–related attributes include the following:

- Project management–related processes like
  - Estimation
  - Project planning
- Quantitative project measurement
- Software life cycle–related processes such as
  - Requirements gathering
  - Technical design
  - Inspection
  - Reviews
  - Testing
- People–related processes such as
  - The internal training process

The development environment–related attributes include the following:

- Domain area
- Nature of the software project such as custom development, enhancement and package implementation, etc.
- Operating platform of the software such as mainframe, middleware, client/ server, etc.
- Software development life cycle that is being adopted like waterfall model, agile methodology, etc.

Function Points in Software Development

Function Points (FP) are a unit of measure designed to quantify the software functionality based on the end users' view. It also measures the software independent of the underlying technology. They can be used in the estimation of cost and resource requirements of a software development project. They also serve as a normalization factor for comparing various types of software. FPs can also be used in projecting the expected software productivity of a software development project. Measuring FPs during different phases of a project life cycle not only measures the size of the software being developed but can also help in monitoring and tracking the productivity in each of the phases as well.

Monitoring productivity through FPs in a corporate portfolio involves the following steps:

- Step 1—Define FP measurement applicable projects
- Step 2—Define life cycle tasks included in FP measurement
- Step 3—Define productivity categories for mixed type of projects

Define Function Point Measurement Applicable Projects

In a corporate portfolio, there can be different types of software projects. The projects may be defined as follows:

- Development projects which may involve developing a new application or software from scratch
- Major enhancement projects which may involve adding new business functions and/or deleting existing functions and/or changing existing functions on existing software
- Data migration projects
- Pure technical projects which may involve tuning the performance of an existing software system
- Perfective maintenance projects
- Corrective maintenance projects
- Infrastructure projects related to the installation of new releases or patches for software or hardware
- Platform migration projects
- Commercial off-the-shelf (COTS) software installation projects
- COTS-based customization projects
- COTS-based development projects
- Mixed projects which may involve different types of requirements including business functionality, maintenance-related requirements, and COTS software–related requirements

The organization needs to possess clearly documented guidelines on the definition and categorization of these different types of software projects. The applicability of FPs on each of the projects needs to be meticulously determined. This may require the approval from various stakeholders as well.

Define Life Cycle Tasks Included in Function Point Measurement

The waterfall software development model is a sequential model where the software development progresses in various phases—Requirements, Design, Implementation, Verification, Deployment, and Maintenance. Each of these phases encompasses various tasks as described in Table 38.1. Apart from the life cycle tasks, there are some other tasks which are essential for the success of the project and which are carried out in parallel with the software development. Such types of tasks are mentioned in Table 38.2. The life cycle tasks and other tasks that are included in FP measurement need to be explicitly agreed upon and documented. The productivity

Table 38.1   Software Development Life Cycle Phases

S. No	Life Cycle Phase	Life Cycle Tasks
1	Requirements	Requirements elicitation
		Requirements analysis
		Requirements specification
		Preparation of prototypes
2	Design	Architecture definition
		Preparation of high-level design
		Preparation of low-level design
		Design review by peers
3	Implementation	Coding
		Code reviews
		Unit test case preparation
		Unit test execution
		Rework
4	Verification	System test case preparation
		System test execution
		Integration testing
		Load testing
		Stress testing
		Regression testing
		Customer acceptance testing
		Reworks
5	Deployment	Release
		Installation
		Activation
		User manual
		Training
6	Maintenance	Condition-based maintenance
		Corrective maintenance
		Planned maintenance
		Predictive maintenance
		Preventive maintenance
		Proactive maintenance
		Value driven maintenance

Table 38.2 Other Software Processes Stretching over the Entire Life Cycle

S.No	Activity	Task
1	Project management	Estimation
		Pricing
		Project planning
		Project management
		Project tracking
		Project measurement and analysis
		Risk management
2	Supplier management	Supplier evaluation
		Supplier selection
		Supplier monitoring
		Supplier risk assessment
		Measuring supplier performance
3	Documentation	Repository setup
		Baseline documents
		Baseline approvals
4	Software quality assurance	Software audits
		Milestone reviews
5	Change management process	Analysis of change requests
		Update of baselined documents
		Re-baseline of documents
		Rework

of any other tasks apart from this set of agreed-upon tasks need to be measured and monitored with some other alternative metrics.

Define Productivity Categories for Mixed Type of Projects

As described earlier, a mixed type of project may involve different types of requirements with a varying nature. It is essential to define various productivity categories to separate out the subset of FP measurable requirements from the set of all requirements. An alternative measurement of productivity needs to be determined to address the software productivity of the requirements that are not measurable by

FPs. The productivity categories typically can include the following list. However, this may vary depending on the organization.

- FPs—This category includes the requirements that have business functionality impact and can be quantified by FPs.
- Technical Changes: Non-FPs—This category includes the requirements that are not measurable by FPs due to the very nature of the technical requirements or maybe due to the fact that they are changes that do not have an impact on the functional size of the project. Examples of this type may include the following:
  - Layout changes
  - Navigational changes
  - Updating code data
  - Cosmetic changes
  - Format changes

(Hopefully, these types of requirements can be sized in the future with the much-expected release of the IFPUG Software Non-functional Assessment Process.)

- Package Configuration: Non-FPs—This category includes the package-related configuration or customization in which changes are made to the values of the attributes and that cannot be sized by applying FP analysis.
- Infrastructure: Non-FPs—This category includes hardware or software upgrades, new patch installations, etc.
- Other: Non-FPs—Any miscellaneous requirement which cannot be sized by FPs and which does not fall in any of the other categories mentioned.

Feasibility Phase Function Point Analysis

During the feasibility phase, the requirements are still very abstract and are at a very high level. The requirements statements are more generic. The success of performing this feasibility phase FP analysis is dependent on the requirements gathering process of the organization. The requirements elicitation process needs to be meticulously carried out to gather the requirements of all the stakeholders involved. It also needs to ensure that the stated requirements are clear, unambiguous, and complete. Any confusing, unclear, or contradictory requirements need to be analyzed and proper resolutions need to be identified. Any missed, ambiguous, or contradictory requirements may lead to huge costs and enormous rework effort. The usage of prototypes or use cases becomes essential to ensure that the requirements are interpreted by the developer in the same way as intended by the customer. The gathered requirements then get documented in vehicles such as a Software Requirements Specification (SRS) or Business Requirement Document (BRD). Each of the requirements should get documented in as simple of a vocabulary as possible. Each requirement should have a unique requirement identifier to map its implementation in subsequent phases. In some scenarios, the requirements may be captured for more than a single release. So, the requirements scope for each independent release needs to be documented as well. The requirements document needs to be reviewed by a peer developer and should be approved by all the stakeholders. This approved version of the BRD or SRS then needs to be baselined. Any changes to this set of baselined requirements need to be treated as change requests to the project.

The FP analysis provided with the above baselined documents starts the feasibility phase's analysis. Once the FP analyst understands the requirements at a high level with a clear understanding of the scope of the requirements, the analyst may have discussions with the developer (and preferably with the user as well) to sort out the requirements as functional user requirements that can be sized by FPs and other requirements that belong to other productivity categories. At the end of this activity, the sorted requirement list is presented as in Table 38.3. It is important, as stated in Table 38.3, to also provide the estimated effort to implement each of the requirements. The interactions between the developer (and user) with the FP analyst needs to be documented for future reference. The FP results should clearly mention the scope of the requirements analyzed, the detailed FP counting logic, and the assumptions made by the analyst. Once the FP measurable requirements are sized and the corresponding estimated effort is sorted out, the estimated productivity of the software development effort can be obtained by using the following approach:

$$\text{Estimated Function Point based productivity during feasibility phase} =$$
$$(\text{Estimated size during feasibility/estimated effort}) + \text{Normalization factor}$$

(38.1)

Table 38.3 Sorted Requirements List

Req. Id	Req. Description	Logical Application	Estimated Effort (hours)	Productivity Category
BR1	Order description should be with new parameters	Order processing	8	Package—non-FP
BR2	New order screen should be used by the customer	User interface	25	Function Point
BR3	Format amount column by 2 places	Billing	2	Technical—non-FP
BR4	Develop user manual	–	10	Other—non-FP
BR5	Test server setup	–	2	Infrastructure—non-FP

The estimated productivity at this phase is a highly approximated value considering the following characteristics:

- The identified data files may not be accurate.
- The identified transactions may not be accurate.
- The complexities of data files and transactions are generally assumed to be average complexity.
- The identified impacted logical application boundaries may not be perfect.
- The productivity categories of the sorted requirements list may not be perfect.

If historical data for a feasibility phase FP analysis is available, then the normalization factor could be used to calibrate the estimated productivity.

Estimating productivity at the feasibility phase is dependent on both the soft and technical skills of the FP analyst.

- An analyst who possesses the domain knowledge of the software being developed would be able to relate to the business requirements in a sensible way.
- The language and articulation skills of the function analyst help in a thorough understanding of the abstract high-level requirements.
- The availability of logical application boundary baselines make the FP analysis in the feasibility phase much easier to ensure that the identified data files, transactions, and their attributes are in sync with those of FP analysis reports.

Design Phase Function Point Analysis

During the design phase, the requirements would have been translated into major architectural decisions and the level of detailing of the end system would be at a much more granular level. In the beginning of this phase, the high-level design of the system is available and, toward the end of this design phase, the low-level design of the system is prepared. The design document should account for the design considerations and include justification for the various design patterns. Generally, the design document contains a significant amount of technical jargon, acronyms, abbreviations, and design intricacies. These types of design documents are suitable for the project team or for a peer developer to conduct design inspections. The design document gets baselined after the review and any further design changes should be well justified.

When a FP analyst receives these documents for analysis, it may be hard to understand with all the technical information in it. So, the design document for FP counting should contain the description of the following:

- Various actors within the system, for example, manual user, and upstream and downstream systems
- A use case diagram depicting the entire flow from the source system to the various downstream systems

- The triggers and various events that take part in all the systems
- The entity-relationship diagram containing all the entities, their attributes, and the relationships
- Data models being used in the system
- Flowcharts depicting the visual representation of the flow of the system
- Block diagrams depicting the interaction between different modules
- Interface specifications between different modules
- Expansions of the acronyms and abbreviations used

The availability of this sort of design document helps the FP analyst to understand the design more fully and to segregate the business function–related requirements from other requirements. This would also help to determine the estimated productivity during the design phase more accurately with minimal variation from the actual productivity measured at the end of the project. The characteristics of a completed design FP analysis are as follows:

- A sorted requirement list which may or may not be updated based on the detailed understanding of the requirements
- Proper identification of physically and logically impacted applications
- Visibility provided to any new logical applications that are being created by this project
- Identification of all data files
- Classification of the data files into Internal Logical Files (ILFs) and External Interface Files (EIFs)
- Identification of accurate complexity for ILFs and EIFs based on the number of Data Element Types (DETs) and Record Element Types
- Identification of all transactions
- Classification of the transactions into External Inputs (EIs), External Outputs (EOs), and External Inquiries (EQs)
- Identification of accurate complexity for EIs, EOs, and EQs based on the number of DETs and File Types Referenced
- Identification of code data or substitution data

Thus, the design phase of the project provides the necessary insights into the system and is capable of predicting the actual productivity at the end of the project.

$$\text{Estimated Function Point based productivity during design phase} =$$
$$(\text{Estimated size during design phase/estimated effort}) + \qquad (38.2)$$
$$\text{Normalization factor}$$

A high variation between the design phase–estimated productivity and the agreed productivity target, as per the contract, signals the need to implement corrective measures to steer the development efforts to meet the productivity targets. The corrective measures may include deploying additional resources, changes in the schedules, extension of work hours, and skipping unessential tasks in the project. The FP analyst–related attributes do not pose a constraint for design phase FP analysis due to the level of detail available at this phase. So, this FP analysis can be performed by any FP analyst even one with relatively less FP analysis experience. However, a thorough review needs to be performed by an experienced analyst or by the analyst who had performed the feasibility phase analysis. Additionally, the count may need to be reviewed by the developer and/or the user of the system to ensure that all business functionality in the project's scope has been considered for FP analysis. At the end of this phase, the sorted requirements list and the documented FP analysis needs to be baselined. The interactions between the developer and the user with the FP analyst need to be recorded for any future reference. Comparative analysis may be conducted at this juncture to understand the influence of various factors contributing toward the difference between estimated productivity at the feasibility and design stages.

Closure Phase Function Point Analysis

The closure phase FP analysis is conducted just before the deployment of the software in the customer's environment. The scope of the closure count includes all the requirements provided by the customer irrespective of the phase in which the requirements were identified. Though most of the requirements would have been identified in the earlier phases of the life cycle, there may be some requirements that would have been requested during the design or testing phases in the form of change requests. The FP analysis at this phase is very critical as the actual software productivity of the project team is being measured. This would determine whether the contractual obligations toward productivity are being satisfied. During this phase, there is no scope for implementing any corrective or preventive measure as the project is already in its final stages toward completion. The analysis conducted in this phase validates the design FP analysis done earlier, allows for any needed updates to any of the minor details that were overlooked before, and ensures all the approved change requests are included in the scope for FP analysis. The sorted requirements list is finally validated to determine the final actual FP count–based size of the project. Assigning the same FP analyst who had performed earlier phase counts makes sure that the FP analysis is consistent across different phases. To ascertain that no requirements are missed out from the scope can be illustrated by mapping each of the entries made in the FP analysis results documents to the business requirement ids mentioned as per the SRS or BRD. A thorough peer review performed by comparing the final analysis results with the earlier phase analysis results provides any necessary justification for the scope changes or increase or decrease of the FP size. Finally, an inspection from the developer and user confirms the acceptance of the FP analysis at this phase.

> Actual Function Point-based productivity =
>
> (Actual size determined by the Function Points during closure   (38.3)
>
> phase/actual effort spent in the project)

It is quite common to observe uneven patterns of changes in estimated productivity in different phases. An inherent variation in the expected productivity is understandable, given the level of detail available in the life cycle phases. The normalization factors introduced in the above formulas for calculating the estimated productivity take care of this inherent variance imposed by the processes. These normalization factors for both the feasibility and the design phase productivity can be derived using the historical data of the organization.

Two other major factors may also contribute to a significant variance between the estimated and actual productivity:

■ Change requests
■ Design changes

Effects of Design Changes

In any development life cycle, the time spent on ensuring the correctness of the design is considered valuable. The time spent on design justification and design verification is inversely proportional to rework and the schedule slippages caused by the rework effort. This is directly proportional to the cost savings as well. Compromising on the design decisions and design reviews results in rework and additional cost and expense in the form of design changes in the subsequent phases. Changing the design in the implementation or testing phases triggers huge amounts of rework. The new design changes need to be incorporated in the baselined design document. All the subsequent phases again get repeated for this new design.

The baselined design document is the major building block of the estimated productivity during the design phase FP analysis. This analysis becomes crucial, as this is the perfect indicator of meeting the set productivity targets. Whenever any major design change happens, the FP analysis for the design phase needs to get repeated to determine the new size and the new expected productivity.

Effects of Change Requests

The change management process should start in the earlier stages of the development life cycle. Baselining of the requirements during the feasibility phase marks the beginning of the change management process. This would stretch through the other phases of the life cycle and would end during the deployment phase of the project. There can be any number of change requests of varying scope and magnitude in between these two phases. Any change requests in the life cycle would bring in additional effort as time and resources are spent in evaluation and analysis of them. The changes requested could be to address business functional changes, technical changes, or configuration changes related to a COTS package.

Change Requests on Business Functions

Change requests may increase the scope of software development by adding new functionality that was not proposed as a part of the initial solution. As a result, there is an expected increase in both the size and effort of the software project. Change requests may even decrease the scope of software development by cancelling some of the business function requirements or interfacing requirements that were agreed upon initially. This reduces the size of the software project and requires additional effort in updating the design documents and changing the implemented code. Some change requests neither increase nor decrease the existing functional size but can add additional project effort that is spent in analyzing the impact of them.

Change Requests on Technical and Commercial Off-the-Shelf Package

These types of change requests may increase the effort of the software development activity. These sorts of requirements are generally non-FP based. So, the effect of these new changes needs to be analyzed with the non-FP-based productivity metric. One way to control the effect of change requests on estimated productivity is to perform an efficient change control process on them where each change request is analyzed for its magnitude on the following:

- The cost involved
- The schedule impact
- The impact on the functional size of the software being developed
- The impact on the estimated productivity and productivity targets

Based on the above, judgments can be made on whether to include the changes in the current software project or if the requested changes can be treated as a separate independent software project.

Derivation of Normalization Factor

An organization measurement repository is the right place to store the historical data of various software projects and their productivity measures. Measures related to the software productivity at the project level need to be identified. The raw data from each software project needs to be split into its taxonomic attributes like the following:

- Nature of the project
- Type of the project
- Domain area of the project
- Technology platform of the project
- Programming language used in the project
- Resource headcount
- Team composition
- Experience of FP analysts
- Size determined during feasibility, design, and closure phases
- List of applications impacted in the portfolio
- Estimated productivity during feasibility and design phases
- Volatility of the requirements
- Nature of change requests
- Impact on FP size due to change requests
- Impact on FP size due to design changes

Applying various statistical analyses to the above raw data gives a meaningful measure of normalization factors both for the feasibility phase and for the design phase.

References

1. Jones, C. 2008. *Applied Software Measurement: Global Analysis of Productivity and Quality.* 3rd ed. New York: McGraw-Hill Osborne Media.

About the Author

Radhika Srinivas has earned her Master's degree in Computer Science. She has over 10 years of experience in the software industry encompassing software development, software quality assurance, and software estimation. Her expertise includes CMMI, ISO Standards, and Six Sigma. She is a Certified Function Point Specialist (CFPS) and a Certified Software Quality Analyst (CSQA). She is currently leading the India Function Point competency in IBM India.

PROJECT MANAGEMENT INTRODUCTION

XII

Dawn Coley

Performing effective project management has been a relevant topic since the need for the discipline in the information technology arena was first identified. Poor project management continues to be one of the most prevalent reasons why IT projects fail. Headlines can still be found touting the latest and greatest colossal project failure in terms of cost and schedule overruns. This section contains five chapters addressing various aspects of project management ranging from scope management to maintaining a rigorous requirements management discipline in order to ensure effective project and scope management.

Luigi Buglione is a Process Improvement and Measurement Specialist and an Associate Professor at the École de Technologie Supérieure (ETS)—Université du Québec in Canada. He is a regular speaker at international conferences on software measurement, process improvement, and quality. In his chapter "Project Management and Measurement: What Relationship?" Luigi presents a study of project management elements, models, frameworks, standards, and benchmarking data representing the state of the art about project management and measurement practices. He then presents a road map on steps to take to comprehend the appropriate amount of resource needed to perform effective measurement within a project.

Carol A. Dekkers is a recognized international expert in the software metrics and IT project management industries as well as serving as the president of Quality Plus Technologies, Inc. She is a many-times-over published author as well as the mentor and trainer of thousands of technical professionals. In her chapter, "Project Scope Management with Function Points: Achieving Olympic Success on Software Intensive Projects with Scope Management," Carol discusses two methods of scope management—northernSCOPE and southernSCOPE, which emphasize solid training and planning to solve some of the top reasons for project failure. She uses the analogy of comparing managing project scope to Olympic-style training and coaching for a triathlon to illustrate her point.

Christine Green has a Master's degree in Mathematics and Computer Science from a Danish university and has been an IFPUG Certified Function Point Specialist for the last 9 years as well as holding a PMI Project Manager Professional Certification. She is a well-recognized contributor to international conferences such as SEI ESEPG, PMI, and ISMA/IFPUG as well as holding the position the vice chair of IFPUG's IT Performance Committee. In her chapter, "Scope Management Technique Using Sizing process," Christine discusses the fact that while most projects have mechanisms in place to monitor and control scope, there is essentially no ability to quantify what is happening to scope. She presents a way to use Function Point Analysis along with scope management, requirements traceability, and a project specific sizing process called Unit of Size to trace the scope in an objective and quantifiable manner.

Robyn Lawrie has almost 40 years of IT industry experience in software development across a wide range of applications and technologies. She currently serves as a director and principal consultant for CHARISMATEK Software Metrics, an Australian-based company. Robyn cofounded the Australian Software Metrics Association (ASMA) and has been a regular presenter at IFPUG. In her chapter, "Quantitative Project Management—Measurement-Based Techniques for Managing Scope," she discusses measurement-based techniques to deal with the issues of scope management that arose out of experience with real-life software delivery projects. Her chapter includes conclusions and lessons drawn from a case study of a software delivery project that presented the classic symptoms of scope management problems.

Janet Russac has over 30 years of experience as a programmer, analyst, and measurement specialist in software application development and maintenance and is the founder of Software Measurement Expertise (SME). Janet is a published author, trainer, conference presenter, and has a long record of service in IFPUG including chairing and being a member on committees, and participating as a member of the Board of Directors. Her chapter, "Requirements: Building a Solid Foundation for a Successful Project," provides specific guidance on how to improve requirements authoring which, in turn, supports more accurate estimation of project size, effort, and schedule. Janet presents the various project life-cycle stages where requirements management is crucial, and the fundamentals of writing detailed requirements and managing change in requirements.

Chapter 39

Project Management and Measurement: What Relationship?

Luigi Buglione

Contents

Introduction

When looking at project management (PM) best practices and its practical daily application, *measurement* is implicitly recognized as a fundamental process within the management of a project. However, it is often not accounted for and evidenced in a separate way in the organizational historical data. The typical goals for the measurement process are as follows:

- To determine which are (and how many should be) the measures driven by the goals of an organization
- To monitor them during the project lifetime
- To gather data, and verify and validate those measures before their usage for estimating and for the decision-making process

However, too often, it is thought to be part of the PM process itself. This unclear view of measurement leads to a significant difficulty in quantifying the proper amount of resources that should be devoted to the measurement processes.

Another possible viewpoint about why measurement needs to be considered its own process arises from the observation of the well-known CHAOS reports about the status of information technology projects [1]. The three major causes of failure seem to be the (low) amount of monitoring and control resources, the lack of historical data, and the limited ability of internal staff to estimate effort and cost, as depicted in Figure 39.1.

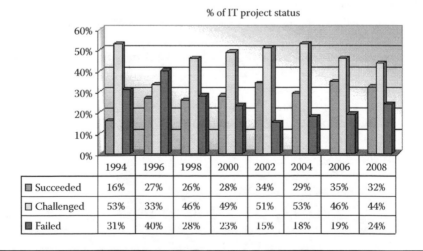

% of IT project status

	1994	1996	1998	2000	2002	2004	2006	2008
■ Succeeded	16%	27%	26%	28%	34%	29%	35%	32%
☐ Challenged	53%	33%	46%	49%	51%	53%	46%	44%
■ Failed	31%	40%	28%	23%	15%	18%	19%	24%

Figure 39.1 Information technology project status. (Adapted from Standish Group's CHAOS Reports (1994–2008).)

Going into more detail, cost and time overruns (Figures 39.2 and 39.3) are the two typical perspectives analyzed for determining the eventual success of a project. This does not take into account other possible (more technical) viewpoints contributing to the final overall success of a project. Thus, even if improved, the overrun percentages presented by The Standish Group are still significantly over an acceptable threshold.

An additional thought comes from Figure 39.4, which presents the relationship between cost of non-quality (CONQ) and cost of quality (COQ) [2]. Some feasible solutions to improve the trend depicted by the CHAOS reports could be improving the estimation abilities in the organization, as well as choosing and managing

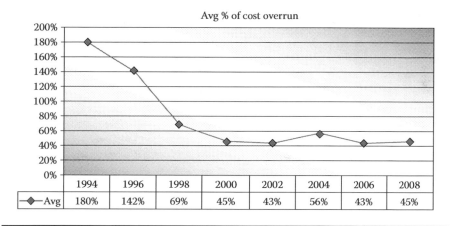

Avg % of cost overrun

	1994	1996	1998	2000	2002	2004	2006	2008
Avg	180%	142%	69%	45%	43%	56%	43%	45%

Figure 39.2 Average percentage of cost overrun. (Adapted from Standish Group (1994–2008).)

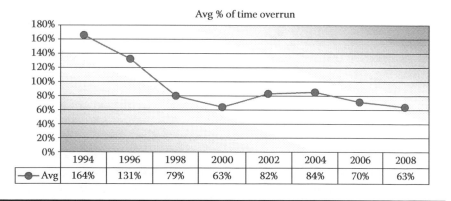

Avg % of time overrun

	1994	1996	1998	2000	2002	2004	2006	2008
Avg	164%	131%	79%	63%	82%	84%	70%	63%

Figure 39.3 Average percentage of time overrun. (Adapted from Standish Group (1994–2008).)

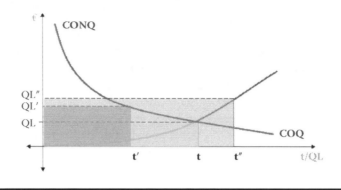

Figure 39.4 Cost of non-quality versus cost of quality.

the proper amount of information from the measurement process. Consider the following in detail:

- *Gather and use historical data at a minimum by using external repositories for benchmarking purposes*: Estimates by experience and analogy often lack reference values for evaluating the success rate and the level of acceptability for a certain estimation error by the project mean relative error (MRE). To progressively reduce the "Cone of Uncertainty" phenomenon [2] to an acceptable stage in an organization, the more data points that are stored into the internal Project Historical Database (PHD), the more the possibility of using specific and targeted clusters helping to lower MREs. External public repositories such as the International Software Benchmarking Standards Group (ISBSG) one* could be a way to provide support while starting or improving your own data collection program.
- *Do not use parametrical cost models in a non-critical manner*: Parametric models such as the Constructive Cost Model (sunset.usc.edu/csse/research/COCOMOII/cocomo_main.html) [3,4] or SLIM (Software Lifecycle Management) [5] apply values for their cost/scale drivers derived from a statistical analysis performed on a certain project sample. The details of the project samples are not often publicly available for further comparative analysis and they may not be a proper technical fit with the business of the using organization. Furthermore, the cost for modifying such parameters on a periodic basis is quite high, which makes them economically unfeasible as opposed to a project gathering data for creating its own estimation models and benchmarking data.
- *Learn and apply statistics* (at least a basic level): This would greatly help in reducing and controlling variability and allow the project to explore more concepts than using only the "arithmetical mean" as the most relevant indicator. At a minimum, the median should be examined, because it represents the frequency

---

* International Software Benchmarking Standards Group (www.isbsg.org).

in the distribution of data points in a sample.* When using only the arithmetical mean, the risk is to make decisions on over-or underestimates, detected a posteriori when determining the project MRE for the measured phenomenon.

■ *Choose and apply a proper number of measures to be tracked by the monitoring and control process*: Measuring more does not necessarily mean measuring better. The informative value arising from two related measures could be higher than from three separate ones, and it would be at a lower cost [6]. Thus, some basic questions could be as follows:

- How many measures should we use?
- Are they the right ones?
- Are they properly linked through the strategic plan?
- How much do they cost (in terms of percentage of the project budget)?

To improve project results and optimize the usage of resources, we need to know how to distribute the project budget by process(es) and how much should be assigned to measurement. The aim of this chapter is to analyze the relationships among PM and measurement in most known PM frameworks and models and propose possible solutions for the adoption of measurement best practices that can be leveraged in an organization.

Measurement in Project Management Frameworks, Models, and Standards

Let us start our discussion by analyzing the most well known PM frameworks, models, and general standards and determine the current and the future expected role and positioning of the measurement process and its related activities within them.

Project Management Domain

■ Project Management Body of Knowledge (PMBOK) version 2008 [7]: As in previous versions, measurement is not a process in the PMBOK schema, but is an activity split across the whole project life cycle. It stresses the need for measures to be gathered as project documents (outputs/work products). Furthermore, Chapters 6.3 and 6.4 are about "duration" and not "effort." However, to derive the duration, we need to first estimate the needed effort. Only recently, Project Management Institute (www.pmi.org) has published a complementary guide providing more detail surrounding the estimation issue [8].

■ Prince2 v2009 [9]: there is no specific measurement process in this methodology. In the Planning (PL) group, there is an Estimation process. As in PMBOK, measurement activities are split across several processes (e.g., IP1, Planning Quality; IP4, Setting Up Project Controls).

---

* See, for example, en.wikipedia.org/wiki/Median

- P3M3 [10]: This is the Office of Government Commerce (OGC; www.ogc .gov.uk) maturity model. First released in 2006, it represents an enhancement of the OGC's PM maturity model [11] and the current version 2.1 is dated February 2010. It contains seven process groups, but there is no formal measurement process in it. The two processes about measurement and metrics are both at Level 4 (4.1 Management Metrics; 4.2 Quality Management), with something included in the 2.5 process (Project Planning, Monitoring, and Control).
- P2MM [12]: This is the maturity model based on Prince2, covering only PM practices, which includes three levels on a staged representation. Measurement is an activity spread across some of the 16 processes defined (e.g., 2.5 Business Case; 3.5 Quality Assurance).
- International Project Management Association (IPMA)* Project Excellence Model [13]: This model represents a tailoring of the European Foundation for Quality Management (EFQM)† Excellence Model for the PM world and has an associated yearly award. As in the basic EFQM, measurement is included in the "process" part but with no evidence about its weight in terms of effort and costs.

Information and Communication Technology— Software/System Engineering Domain

- Capability Maturity Model Integration (CMMI [www.sei.cmu.edu/cmmi]) constellations (v1.3): In all the three current CMMI constellations (DEV, Development [14]; ACQ, Acquisition [15]; SVC, service [16]), at Maturity Level (ML) 2 there is the "Measurement and Analysis" (MA) process, whose purpose is "*to develop and sustain a measurement capability that is used to support management.*" A "measurement repository" is required at ML3 in Organizational Process Definition (OPD; CMMI ML3 process area) from the specific practice (SP)1.4. CMMI provides also a classification of processes by homogeneous groups and MA is classified as a "Support" process, while Project Planning (PP) and Project Monitoring and Control (CMMI ML2 process area) are in the "PM" group.
- International Organization for Standardization/International Electrotechnical Commission (ISO/IEC)‡ 12207:2008 [17]: The "measurement" process is described in clause 6.3.7 in the "Project processes" with two notes pointing to ISO/IEC 15939:2007 [18] for the specific list of activities and tasks to be performed and to ISO 9001:2008 clause 8 about the early requirements to be satisfied regarding the measurement of processes and products within the context of a Quality Management System (QMS) [19].

---

* International Project Management Association (www.ipma.ch)
† European Foundation for Quality Management (www.efqm.org)
‡ ISO (www.iso.org)/IEC (www.iec.ch)

- ISO/IEC 15504-2:2004 [20]: This is the Process Reference Model (PRM) of the SPICE (ISO/IEC 15504) model.* It introduces the measurement process in the MAN.6† process, under the "Management" process group.
- ISO 15939:2007 [18]: This is the "expansion" of the ISO/IEC 12207 original process on Measurement, with a more detailed view on each one of its elements. There is a central element from the first edition that is the "Measurement Experience Base," defined as a *data store that contains the evaluation of the information products and the measurement process as well as any lessons learned during the measurement process.*" This concept represents a middle ground between the CMMI concepts of Process Asset Library and Measurement Repository, as expressed in the OPD process.

Other "De Jure" Standards

- ISO 9000:2005 [21]: The "Factual approach to decision making" is one of the eight quality management principles identified as the core ones for organizations seeking to make decisions that are more effective.
- ISO 9001:2008 [19]: The ISO 9001 standard contains a list of requirements (and not processes) to be accomplished for a QMS. Clause 8 is about "Measurement, analysis and improvement." In particular, subclauses 8.2 (Monitoring and measurement) and 8.4 (Analysis of data) are the two most specific clauses for the topic under discussion.
- ISO 20000 Series: This standard presents the issue from the Service Management viewpoint in ISO/IEC 20000-1:2011 [22] about the requirements for a Service Management System (SMS). Clause 4.5.4 (Monitoring and review the SMS) asks to apply "suitable methods for monitoring and measuring the SMS and the services." Measurement actions are spread across several clauses and subclauses. From a process viewpoint, ISO/IEC TR 20000-4:2010 groups Part 1 requirements into processes and provides a related process (MAN.7‡) [23] in the "SPICE" style.
- ISO/IEC TR 19759:2005 (Software Engineering Body Of Knowledge [SWEBOK; www.computer.org/swebok]) [24]: In the current edition of the Institute of Electrical and Electronics Engineers (IEEE; www.ieee.org) Software Engineering Body of Knowledge, measurement is a "common theme" but not a process (in this case, a "KA, knowledge area"). There is a proposal for a new KA on measurement, further elaborating on the current content with extensions and updates [25]. It was submitted to IEEE for inclusion in the next SWEBOK edition.§

---

* SPICE is the acronym for "Software Process Improvement Capability and Determination" (ISO/IEC 15504-x standard).
† Management #6 (ISO/IEC 15504-2 process on Measurement)
‡ Management #7 (ISO/IEC TR 20000-4:2010 process on Service Measurement)
§ See the two current supplemental KAs downloadable at www.computer.org/portal/web/swebok.

Project Repositories and Historical Data

The key element for finding an answer to our initial question (How much does it cost to perform measurement in a project?) is to look for effort and cost historical data in internal or external benchmarks. One of the few and largest and complete repositories for information and communication technology (ICT) project data is the one managed by ISBSG. It provides two main types of data assets: development and enhancement (D&E) and maintenance and support (M&S) repositories.

International Software Benchmarking Standards Group Development and Enhancement Repository

The latest release of the D&E repository (r11) [26] contains 5052 projects mostly sized using functional size measurement (FSM) methods such as International Function Point Users Group (IFPUG; www.ifpug.org) Function Point Analysis (FPA) or the Common Software Measurement International Consortium (COSMIC; www .cosmicon.com) and contains more than 100 attributes derived from data gathered with detailed questionnaires, structured into seven sections and 141 questions [27]. Measurement process–related data are derivable only from two sections. They are the "Project Management and Monitoring" section (an extension from release 10, providing more evidence than only the PM process; however, there are only four qualitative questions to be answered) and the "People and Work Effort" section, which gathers project effort data. Also in the current release, a few macro-phases are defined: Plan, Specify, Design, Build, Test, Implement, and a residual "Effort Unphased" basket. The latest version of the ISBSG glossary introduced two tables mapping project phases to the possible components and projects steps from ISO/IEC 12207. It mostly addresses primary processes, with no direct reference to measurement, which are intended to be typically included within the "Plan" effort and partly as activity during all the other phases (Figure 39.5).

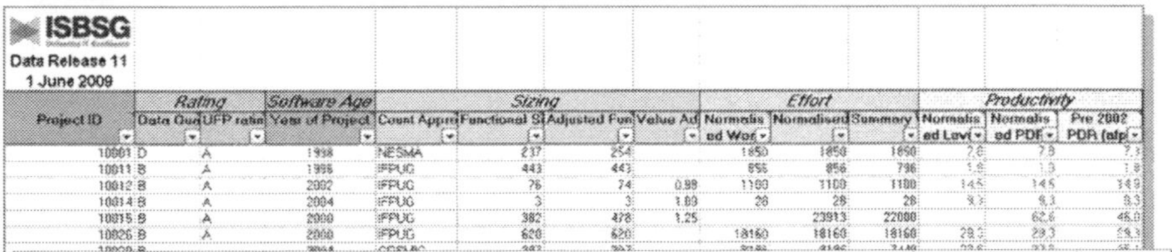

Figure 39.5 International Software Benchmarking Standards Group Development and Enhancement repository (r11) (excerpt).

Effort Profiles

In 2005, Dery and Abran proposed an elaboration of the ISBSG D&E r9 repository, which focused on 2562 out the 3024 total project data from IFPUG-sized projects, and they derived 32 possible "effort profiles" [28]. Using the above presented ISBSG macro-phases, it is possible from this approach to derive statistically some high-level proportions for distributing the effort by project phase. A quick method based on ISBSG D&E r11 uses an easy four-step process:

1. Choose your own software life cycle phase/process taxonomy.
2. Map your own processes to such schema.
3. Reclassify your effort data on such schema.
4. Count!

Selecting only projects with effort assigned to all of the basic ISBSG project phases, 53 projects sized with IFPUG FPA v4.x were obtained, as shown in Figure 39.6.

After filtering the data, the maximum/average/median/minimum values are computed on the list of projects, depicting the variability for all the quantitative variables, as shown in Figure 39.7.

Regarding effort, it is possible to calculate both the average and the median, looking at the distance between them. Of course, such values are not "the values"

	UFP	Eff.Tot (hrs)	Prod	Plan	Specify	Design	Build	Test	Implemen	Unphase
1	19	50	0,38	5	0	6	30	12	2	
2	32	714	0,04	98	65	40	349	256	4	0
3	41	503	0,08	155	41	23	281	153	5	0
4	46	140	0,33	10	4	22	72	40	2	
5	57	1546	0,04	264	109	80	556	697	104	0
6	71	2101	0,03	60	236	450	700	670	45	0
7	71	190	0,37	16	8	34	97	47	4	
8	88	2457	0,04	113	146	996	479	218	202	416
9	98	1082	0,09	109	229	132	316	392	13	0
10	99	1038	0,10	27	96	78	523	313	28	0
11	118	1495	0,08	21	90	436	606	339	24	0
12	120	3637	0,03	171	93	198	1164	1320	318	544
13	129	2175	0,06	284	307	371	882	398	199	18

Figure 39.6 Selecting International Software Benchmarking Standards Group Development and Enhancement r11 projects.

	UFP	Eff.Tot (hrs)	Prod	Plan	Specify	Design	Build	Test	Implemen	Unphase
Max	4104	16093	1,70	1807	5192	3423	7764	5280	2648	5490
Avg	567,25	4071,96	0,21	388,74	446,45	627,09	1795,70	752,57	199,08	391,38
Median	339,00	2520,00	0,14	224,00	223,00	219,00	1164,00	508,00	48,00	0,00
Min	19	50	0,02	0	0	0	30	6	0	-38
% Avg		100%		10%	11%	15%	44%	18%	5%	10%
% Median		100%		9%	9%	9%	46%	20%	2%	0%

Figure 39.7 Determining acceptable ranges of values.

Table 39.1   ISBSG R11 D&E Repository: Plan Percent Effort Data

Size	Size Range (UFP)	N	% Plan Phase (c.a.)
Small	1–449	30	9–10%
Medium	450–900	14	7% (both average and median)
Large	901+	9	9–10%

Table 39.2   ISBSG R11 D&E Repository: Unphased Percent Effort

Size	Size Range (UFP)	N	% Average Unphased Phase
Small	1–449	30	4%
Medium	450–900	14	19%
Large	901+	9	31% (1 outlier)

to be chosen at all, but can help during the estimation and plan steps for producing a more affordable plan based on past experience (which would be better if derived from your own organization's historical data). Looking at the example data, for the subset of 53 projects, the answer to our question would be approximately 9–10%. It is possible that the value could be influenced by the functional size, since those projects are in a range from 19 to 4104 Unadjusted Function Points (UFP). Thus, we split them into three UFP size ranges as given in Table 39.1.

Thus, the overall percentage effort value for the Plan phase seems to be quite constant, with a small reduction for the "medium"-sized projects. From the analysis of the dataset, another phenomenon should be observed that the "unphased" effort is not assigned in all projects (Table 39.2), using the same size ranges as in Table 39.1.

Looking at both tables, it is reasonable to deduce that there is a loss of accuracy in effort data gathering when the project is growing because of more attention and energy devoted to primary processes than to support/project management ones. Remember, this is benchmarking data. Thus, the main suggestion is that you start as soon as possible in your own data gathering for the measures that support your strategic goals.

How Much Does It Cost to Measure in a Project?

It is possible to approximate how much should be invested in measurement activities for the next project by answering a few questions about the overall project costs (estimated vs. actual) and looking at proportions from the effort data for the planning phase (considering an x% for the measurement process and activities). However, the cost of labor cannot represent the whole project cost, because projects also include fixed costs and other non-labor-related costs. Thus, a more refined activity-based costing taxonomy should be in place for properly deriving such information [29].

Currently, there are no available statistics with public, verifiable data about the cost of measurement (including the specific cost for applying and using a FSM method) in ICT projects.

An Improvement Proposal

Taking all these elements, models, frameworks, standards, and benchmarking data representing the state-of-the-art about PM and measurement practices, we run a quantitative root-cause analysis (Q-RCA; www.semq.eu/leng/modtechqrca.htm) to derive a starting point for possible improvements [30,31]. Figure 39.8 provides the overall picture while Figure 39.9 provides a detailed view on some of the leaves.

The analysis cannot be complete because it represents a personal viewpoint and not an absolute truth; however, anyone can replicate the process and verify the partial conclusions and evaluate how much their organization matches the situation.

The main suggestions arising from our analysis are as follows:

■ Establish more detailed data gathering [32]: As seen in previous sections, when too generic, high-level project phases in PHD are established, and they do not allow for useful reporting and information for estimation that is more precise and planning. For instance, a generic PM phase hides how much work was devoted to the real planning phase and how much to the "monitoring and control" phase. Alternatively, inside such a folder there could also be included the time for measuring and doing analysis of gathered data. However, the higher the reporting level, the lower the information for taking your decisions. Since there is not one absolute best way, choose your own preferred process schema. You should create, where needed, mappings that allow for the proper matching of detailed tasks with their related processes in your own taxonomy. Again, primary (or engineering) processes have a twofold facet: they can express effort from both functional user requirements (FUR) and non-functional requirements (NFR). For instance, a performance test is about the deployment of a NFR, while a typical black-box test is referable to a FUR. On the opposite side, management/support/process management processes are NFRs (e.g., also the effort needed for counting and/or auditing Function Points). Paradoxically, counting Function Points or doing any other kind of measurement is a process derived from a NFR. Therefore, the more we count, the lower the "nominal" productivity value (as currently defined and applied) would appear [29], while we would only run a further activity

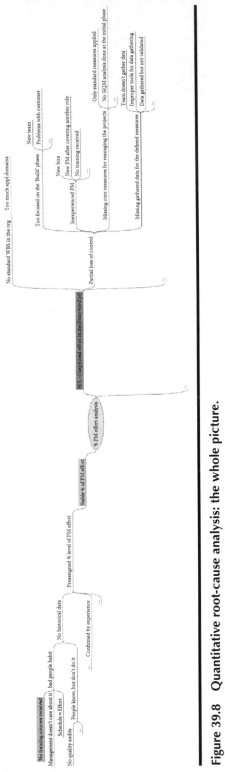

Figure 39.8 Quantitative root-cause analysis: the whole picture.

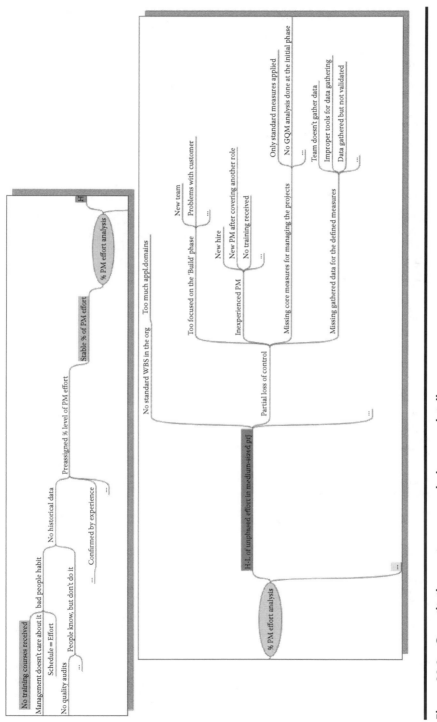

Figure 39.9 Quantitative root-cause analysis: some details.

within the project scope. This split of project effort into FUR-NFR-related effort can greatly help in creating more homogeneous clusters of projects from a PHD as well as return information about the amount of people by project role to involve in various kinds of projects.*

■ Set up a strategic map of your processes, establishing the causal relationships among processes as in a balanced scorecard (BSC) [33]. All ISO 9001 certified companies should be doing this (it is a mandatory requirement, see Section 4.1 lett. b), but it is possible that some of them do not properly use this information for lowering the cost for corrective/improvement actions. The eventual reduced capability of analysts to find the real, deepest cause for a certain problem could cost a lot, resulting in removing a partial cause, but not the deepest one. Furthermore, if properly read, understood, and daily applied, SPI models and frameworks represent a library of solutions for any detected problem. For instance, if an organization experiences error rates higher than expected in estimates, by referring to most known process models, it could be easily identified that the absence of historical data, the low experience of the estimator(s), or the lack of information available for deriving an estimate by experience or analogy could be one of the possible root causes. However, at the same time, looking at those processes on the "positive side," suggestions for corrective/improvement actions can be easily identified.

■ Establish a "balanced" measurement plan [34] that allows for the maximizing of return on investment as well as the return on information from the selected and implemented measures. The Balancing Multiple Perspectives (BMP) technique [6], jointly with a proper Q-RCA [31], can help an organization in determining the deepest root causes to be addressed along with prioritizing the actions on a quantitative basis and determining the right measures to use. Referring back to Figure 39.4, the solution lies in choosing the few, right measures for the core processes of an organization, which will allow for the anticipation of the break-even point (BEP) between COQ and CONQ.

The return is twofold: (1) From the social and technical viewpoint, the more data and information available within the organization, the higher the maturity and capability levels the organization can achieve. Consequently, the higher the social and technical performance values, the better the economic results obtained from the project. In addition, (2) the flow of a BSC strategic map can quickly make visible what has been said. However, before we achieve these benefits, we need to ask a series of "how much" questions along the project life cycle, as in life. That is measurement.

---

* See [28] for more information about this issue.

Conclusions and Prospects

One of the key processes in managing a project is to estimate properly how much effort it will need and cost. Therefore, the more information available, the lower the risk of estimation error and the overall performance levels achieved. Thus, a very important issue is to define properly processes across the project life cycle at the right level of granularity. Too often, measurement has been (and is currently) seen as a "part-of" the overall PM process. However, when dealing with the direct question, *How much should we spend for measurement for the next project?*, the answer tends to be difficult because most companies do not gather data at the level of detail that is needed.

The analysis of some of the most well-known models and frameworks in several application domains, as well as the ICT one, can help in determining the needed level of granularity as well as the needed differences between the measurement process and PM. Because of the causal relationship between PM and the organizational processes, it is fundamental to consistently gather historical data also on measurement to determine the trade-off and the right budget distribution according to the project's characteristics, both from the technical and environmental sides.

Even if this practice is recommended for most of the management system standards such as ISO 9001, 20000-1, 27001 etc., measurement is not consistently run in organizations. It faces a strong resistance to change [35]. Moreover, unfortunately, it seems not to be a question of organizational size. Rather, it is a common malpractice, but—if properly planned and run—it would return better estimates and savings, reducing the overall COQ.

The next challenge will be, therefore, to deeply face such resistance to measurement and find—through root-cause analysis to be run on local basis—the best tactics and strategies for removing that "original sin." It is not possible to improve if we do not have the proper level of control on our activities as well as an understanding of how far we are from established targets and thresholds. The turning point activity to achieve this is measurement.

"Analyze facts and talk through data" (Kaoru Ishikawa).

References

1. The Standish Group. 2009. CHAOS Report. www1.standishgroup.com/newsroom/chaos_2009.php (accessed December 1, 2011).
2. Jagannathan, S. R., S. Bhattacharya, and K. Matawie. 2005. Value based quality engineering. TickIT Int 1Q05:3–9.
3. Boehm, B. 1981. *Software Engineering Economics*. Englewood Cliffs, NJ: Prentice-Hall Inc., ISBN 0138221227.
4. Boehm, B. W., E. Horowitz, R. Madachy, D. Reifer, B. K. Clark, B. Steece, A. W. Brown, S. Chulani and C. Abts. 2000. *Software Cost Estimation with COCOMOII*. Englewood Cliffs, NJ: Prentice Hall, ISBN 0130266922.
5. Putnam, L. H. 1978. A general empirical solution to the macro software sizing and estimating problem. *IEEE Trans Softw Eng (TSE)* SE-4(4):345–61.

6. Buglione, L. and A. Abran. 2005. Multidimensional project management tracking & control—Related measurement issues. In *Proceedings of SMEF 2005, Software Measurement European Forum*, 205–214. Rome (Italy), www.dpo.it/smef2005/filez/proceedings.pdf (accessed December 1, 2011).
7. PMI. 2008. *Project Management Body of Knowledge (PMBOK), 4th version*. Newtown Square, PA: Project Management Institute, www.pmi.org (accessed December 1, 2011).
8. PMI. 2010. *Practice Standard for Project Estimating*. Project Management Institute, ISBN 9781935589129, www.pmi.org (accessed December 1, 2011).
9. OGC. 2005. *Prince2 Manual (Managing Successful Projects with Prince2)*. Office of Government Commerce, ISBN 0113309465.
10. OGC. 2008. *Portfolio, Programme & Project Management Maturity Model (P3M3), Public Consultation Draft version 2.0*. Office of Government Commerce, www.ogc.gov.uk/documents/P3M3 (1).pdf (accessed December 1, 2011).
11. OGC. 2002. *Project Management Maturity Model (PMMM), version 5.0*. Office of Government Commerce, www.ogc.gov.uk (accessed December 1, 2011).
12. OGC. 2006. *Prince2 Maturity Model (P2MM), version 1.0*. Office of Government Commerce, www.ogc.gov.uk/methods_prince_2.asp (accessed December 1, 2011).
13. IPMA. 2011. *IPMA Project Excellence Model*. www.ipma.ch/awards/projexcellence/Pages/ProjectExcellenceModel.aspx (accessed December 1, 2011).
14. CMMI Product Team. 2010. *CMMI for Development, Version 1.3, CMMI-DEV v1.3, CMU/SEI-2010-TR-033*. Technical Report, Software Engineering Institute. www.sei.cmu.edu/library/abstracts/reports/10tr033.cfm (accessed December 1, 2011).
15. CMMI Product Team. 2010. *CMMI for Acquisition, Version 1.3, CMMI-ACQ v1.3, CMU/SEI-2010-TR-032*. Technical Report, Software Engineering Institute. www.sei.cmu.edu/library/abstracts/reports/10tr032.cfm (accessed December 1, 2011).
16. CMMI Product Team. 2010. *CMMI for Services, Version 1.3, CMMI-SVC v1.3, CMU/SEI-2010-TR-034*. Technical Report, Software Engineering Institute, www.sei.cmu.edu/library/abstracts/reports/10tr034.cfm (accessed December 1, 2011).
17. ISO/IEC, IS 12207. 2008. *Systems and software engineering—Software life cycle processes*. Genève: ISO/IEC.
18. ISO/IEC, IS 15939. 2007. *Systems and software enginering—Measurement process*. Genève: International Organization for Standardization.
19. ISO. IS 9001:2008—*Quality management systems: Requirements*. Genève: International Organization for Standardization.
20. ISO/IEC. IS 15504-2:2004. *Information technology—Process assessment—Part 2: Performing an assessment—Measurement process*. Genève: International Organization for Standardization.
21. ISO. IS 9000:2005. *Quality management systems: Fundamentals and vocabulary*. Genève: International Organization for Standardization.
22. ISO/IEC. IS 20000-1:2011. *Information technology—Service management—Part 1: Service management system requirements*. Genève: International Organization for Standardization.
23. ISO/IEC. TR 20000-4:2010. *Information technology—Service management—Part 4: Process reference model*. Genève: International Organization for Standardization.
24. ISO/IEC. TR 19759:2005. *Software Engineering—Guide to the Software Engineering Body of Knowledge (SWEBOK)*. Genève: International Organization for Standardization.

25. Buglione, L. and A. Abran. 2005. Software Measurement Body of Knowledge—Overview of Empirical Support, in "Innovations in Software Measurement". In *Proceedings of the 15th International Workshop on Software Measurement (IWSM 2005)*, 353–68. Montréal (Canada), Shaker Verlag, ISBN 3-8322-4405-0, www.swebok.org; www.semq.eu/leng/swebok.htm (accessed December 1, 2011).
26. ISBSG. 2010. ISBSG D&E (Development & Enhancement) Dataset 11. www.isbsg.org
27. ISBSG. 2011. *Data Collection Questionnaire—New Development, Re-Development or Enhancement sized using IFPUG or NESMA Function Points, v5.14.* www.isbsg.org
28. Dery, D., and A. Abran. *Investigation of the Effort Data Consistency in the ISBSG Repository.* IWSM 2005, 123–36. Montréal (Canada), publicationslist.org/data/a.abran/ref-2040/909.pdf (accessed December 1, 2011).
29. Buglione, L. 2010. Some thoughts on Productivity in ICT projects, WP-2010-01. White Paper, version 1.3, www.semq.eu/pdf/fsm-prod.pdf (accessed December 1, 2011).
30. Buglione, L., and A. Abran. 2006. Introducing root-cause analysis and orthogonal defect classification at lower CMMI maturity levels. In *Proceedings of MENSURA 2006*, 29–40. Cadiz (Spain), ISBN 978-84-9828-101-9, citeseerx.ist.psu.edu/viewdoc/download?doi=10.1.1.90.3192&rep=rep1&type=pdf (accessed December 1, 2011).
31. Buglione, L. 2008. Strengthening CMMI maturity levels with a quantitative approach to root-cause analysis. In *Proceedings of the 5th Software Measurement European Forum (SMEF 2008)*, 67–82. Milan (Italy), ISBN 9-788870-909999, www.dpo.it/smef2008/papers/SMEF08_proc_107_Buglione.pdf (accessed December 1, 2011).
32. Buglione, L. 2008. Improving estimation by effort type proportions. *Softw Meas News* 13(1):55–64. www.gelog.etsmtl.ca/publications/pdf/1133.pdf. www.gelog.etsmtl.ca/publications/pdf/1133.pdf.
33. Kaplan, R. S., and D. P. Norton. 2004. *Strategy Maps: Converting Intangible Assets into Tangible Outcomes.* Boston, MA: Harvard Business School Press, ISBN 1-59139-134-2.
34. Pfleeger, S. L. 1993. Lessons learned in building a corporate metrics program. *IEEE Softw, IEEE Comput Society* 10(5):67–74.
35. Buglione, L., and C. Dekkers. 2006. A murphological view on software measurement: a serious joke or a funny serious thing? In *Proceedings of SMEF 2006, 3rd Software Measurement European Forum*, 315–29. Rome (Italy), www.dpo.it/smef2006/papers/c08.pdf (accessed December 1, 2011).

About the Author

Dr. Luigi Buglione is a process improvement and measurement specialist at Engineering.IT (formerly Atos Origin Italy and SchlumbergerSema) in Rome, Italy, and associate professor at the École de Technologie Supérieure (ETS)—Université du Québec, Canada. Previously, he worked as a software process engineer at the European Software Institute (ESI) in Bilbao, Spain. Dr. Buglione is a regular speaker at international conferences on software measurement, process improvement, and quality. He is also the vice president of the Italian Software Metrics Association (GUFPI-ISMA), member of the ISBSG Technical Advisory Group, and the ISO/IEC WG25 and WG10 Study Group, and among the reviewers of the SWEBOK project, coauthoring the proposal for a new knowledge area on software measurement for the new forthcoming v3 edition. He wrote the only Italian book on software measurement (*Misurare il Software*, FrancoAngeli, 3/ed., 2008). He received a PhD in Management Information Systems from LUISS Guido Carli University (Rome, Italy) and a degree cum laude in Economics from the University of Rome "La Sapienza," Italy. He is a certified software measurement specialist (IFPUG CSMS) Gold Level. Further info at www.semq.eu.

Chapter 40

Project Scope Management with Function Points: Achieving Olympic Success on Software Intensive Projects with Scope Management

Carol A. Dekkers

Contents

Why Does One Need Training to Compete in the Olympics?

Any athlete who wants to achieve success in a multidisciplinary sport such as the triathlon, knows that a good deal of preparation goes into both their favorite event, but also those that pose a challenge. To achieve Olympic-level success requires dedication, discipline, practice, and attention to minute detail. From the moment that one decides to compete, the initial preparations are already underway. Triathlon is one of the newest and most difficult of all Olympic sports, and the state of one's mental condition is as important as the physical conditioning required to become a serious competitor. Training to be a triathlon competitor presents a series of interdisciplinary challenges because of the diversity of the three different stages (swimming, biking, and running), each of which entails different but rigorous preparation and mental stamina.

Triathlon was first introduced in California in 1974 and became an official competition in 1978. According to the www.olympic.org website: "Triathlon made its Olympic debut at the 2000 Summer Olympic Games in Sydney after it was awarded full medal status 6 years earlier at the International Olympic Committee (IOC) congress in Paris. The international popularity of triathlon really started to grow after its inclusion on the Olympic program. By 2003, International Triathlon Union's (ITU) World Cup circuit expanded to 18 races in 14 different countries."

Triathlon Components

"The Olympic triathlon comprises a 1.5-km swim, a 40-km bike ride, and a 10-km run. After a mass start, the race remains continuous, with no stop between the three legs. Transitions are vital to race strategy" (www.olympic.org). Each component is as important as the next, and a serious athlete knows that mastery of all skills and the transitions between each component are critical to overall success. To win, one must excel as an athlete who masters the overall triathlon competition.

Event

Table 40.1 describes aspects of the events composing the triathlon along with transition stages.

Table 40.1 **Triathlon Components and Prerequisite Skills**

Event	Characteristics	Skills Needed	Hazards	Keys to Success
1.5 km swim	Slowest part. Results in this part set stage for remaining portions.	Excellent stroke mastery, endurance, patience, experience with various water conditions (wind, rain, darkness, salt water).	Wind, rain, darkness can all increase difficulty in maintaining direction and stamina to complete this event. Swimmers must be trained to stay on course and preserve energy by swimming according to pace rather than too quickly. Mental stamina must also be trained so as to overcome potential fear of natural hazards such as sharks.	Skills of individual competitors vary. However, it is critical to overall success to finish this event in the first third of competitors.
Transition	Remove wetsuit, goggles, and other equipment; do not dry clothes and shoes; obtain and mount own bicycle.	Speed, agility, and ability to remain calm during the transition phase are critical to overall finish time.	Confusion or disorientation; misplacement of equipment; impatience.	Speed and agility to perform and remain focused on tasks at hand.

(Continued)

Table 40.1 Triathlon Components and Prerequisite Skills (*Continued*)

Event	Characteristics	Skills Needed	Hazards	Keys to Success
40 km bike	Fastest and most technical part. Most potential for crashes with other articipants.	Excellent muscle strength and stamina for rugged and hilly terrain or high wind resistance.	Other bikers entering one's drafting zone (zone around individual riders); fallen riders or crashes in path ahead; inclement weather causing slickness of roadways; tightness of rider pack causing inability to break away. Hills and inclement weather may challenge inexperienced riders.	Overall endurance, speed, and skill; reliable knowledge about the progress of main competitors; ability to avoid crashes; prevail despite hills and inclement weather. Impact of skills of individual competitors will vary.
Transition	Dismount bicycle, change shoes. (potentially), hydrate, and begin run.	Speed, agility, and ability to remain calm during the transition phase are critical to overall finish time.	Confusion or disorientation; misplacement of equipment; impatience.	Speed and agility to perform and remain focused on tasks at hand.
10 km run	This final event is the hardest due to fatigue potential and mental attitude during this part of the competition.	Excellent running skills in fatigued condition; ability to pace oneself.	Fallen runners; crashes; debris on roadway; hills.	Overall endurance, speed, and skill; reliable knowledge about the progress of main competitors; ability to remain focused and pace oneself to the finish line.

Formalized Scope Management: Triathlon-Style Coaching for Information and Communication Technology Programs

Information and communication technology (ICT) programs are customer-driven initiatives that result in the delivery of one or more software intensive systems to meet a business objective. While the suppliers of such systems are typically well versed and skilled to deliver technology-based solutions when the user requirements are complete and well defined, the success rate is less than optimal when they are not. Published studies (such as the annual CHAOS report by the Standish Group—www.standishgroup.com) cite a one-third success rate on ICT projects (consistently for over 10 years of the study's publication)—a statistic that leads customer organizations to demand fixed price contracts up front—even before requirements are all known. Although it is easy to understand the folly of demanding a fixed price for a building before the floor plan is drawn, it is not so easy to understand the similar absurdity of so doing on ICT development. Wary customer groups want to curtail costs of their software intensive systems investment by demanding an upper fixed price estimate, while at the same time suppliers want to be paid for the work they perform on behalf of developing the customer-driven solution to requirements yet to be defined. This situation poses a multidisciplinary challenge to the success of ICT programs—how to coach and properly position the customer organization for the productive participation and trust necessary for success on ICT programs?

Customers as "Beginner Athletes" on Information and Communication Technology Programs

In the same way that a beginner triathlon athlete needs at least one or more coaches to fine-tune and train them for optimum performance for triathlon competition, today's customer organizations need similar fine-tuning and coaching to achieve success through the multi-phase complexities of ICT program development. The major "events" in ICT program development can be compartmentalized in a triathlon manner, each requiring specialized finely honed skills to achieve success in each event, then speed and agility to transition to the next phase or event. The ICT team "coach" for ICT program development is called a scope manager, who acts as a supportive, knowledgeable coach and trainer of the customer team members. A successful ICT development program is similar to a well-performed triathlon where the athlete comfortably completes all events in reasonable time.

Currently, there are two formalized triathlon-style scope management concepts (i.e., coaching) for ICT development programs: the first is called southern-SCOPE from the Victorian State Government in Australia, and the second is called northernSCOPE™ and was established by the Finnish Software Measurement Association (FiSMA 2007) and successfully applied in Finland. Both approaches focus on the concept of scope management as the core principle and employ various best-practice approaches. These include: early program and project estimating, unit pricing, baselining the software product size, formal change management, objective measurement, project management, communication, and the use of an experience repository for collecting lessons learned.

Definition of Success on Information and Communication Technology Programs

The successful completion of a triathlon is a function of rigorous training, motivational coaching, and well-planned support throughout the competition. Similarly, professional and systematic scope management support throughout the program is a necessary prerequisite to successful ICT development program completion. The support team for a triathlon athlete delivers targeted coaching and skills training, especially during the actual competition, and at its heart lays an enthusiastic, experienced, and analytical coach. Similarly, the customer of an ICT development program needs a support team who can deliver targeted coaching and skills training during the program development, and at its heart should lie an enthusiastic, experienced, and analytical "scope manager."

In addition to the support team, a successful triathlon depends on an eager and willing triathlon athlete to be trained and mentored, just as for a successful ICT program there must be an eager and willing customer.

A successful ICT program means that all of the component projects are finished to the satisfaction of the customer organization, thereby meeting or exceeding their specified requirements, incorporating mutually agreed upon scope changes, and finishing within the agreed upon schedule and budget.

The NorthernSCOPE™ Concept of Scope Management

The 2003–2010 publicly available research results of the CHAOS reports produced by the Standish Group (www.standishgroup.com) cites four major reasons for software-intensive project success including senior management support, scope management, user involvement, and formal basic requirements. Similar studies conducted in Australia support similar factors, of which 60% of the factors can be reliably overcome using formal scope management approaches (northernSCOPE and southernSCOPE). Table 40.2 shows the northernSCOPE™ ICT program phases and prequisite customer skills.

The Role of the Scope Manager in Information and Communication Technology Program Development

An experienced and knowledgeable scope manager is as critical and important to a customer engaging in a new ICT program as a trusted coach is to the athlete

Table 40.2 NorthernSCOPE™ ICT Program Phases and Prerequisite Customer Skills

Phase of ICT Development (per NorthernSCOPE™)	Characteristics	Skills Needed	Hazards	Keys to Success in Phase
Pre-contract award (several weeks to several years)	Feasibility study; preliminary requirements; request for proposal (RFP) preparation	Understanding the different types of development work; knowledge of best practices of requirements specification (functional and non-functional) and software sizing (functional size measurement) skills	Monolithic development programs with hybrid mixtures of unknown requirements; incomplete RFPs with ambiguous or missing requirements; overzealous suppliers; demand for fixed price based on imperfect and incomplete requirements	Early identification of need for and engagement of skilled scope manager; division of acquisition program into discrete projects; identification and early analysis of functional and non-functional requirements; early software size estimates; solid RFP preparation by project
Transition: Engage supplier (1–6 months)	Receive, open, evaluate, and compare RFP responses; supplier interview, negotiation, and selection	Analysis and negotiating skills; knowledge of contract and unit pricing models	Inconsistent proposals; selection of inappropriate pricing model; incomplete or unreasonable RPF responses	Trust and understanding established with chosen supplier(s)

(continued)

Table 40.2 NorthernSCOPE™ ICT Program Phases and Prerequisite Customer Skills (*Continued*)

Phase of ICT Development (per NorthernSCOPE™)	Characteristics	Skills Needed	Hazards	Keys to Success in Phase
Requirements specification (1–6 months)	Formalize and articulate complete set of functional and non-functional requirements for each project	Understanding requirements types and levels; excellent documentation, writing, and reviewing skills	Misunderstanding or impatience regarding the definition of requirements types and levels; scope creep and gold-plating based on supplier needs	Complete set of product requirements; baseline size for functional user requirements of each subsystem and project
Transition: Sign contract(s) and formally baseline project plans (days to months)	Contract(s) with suppliers signed for construction	Contract and legal experience; risk management skills	Overly complex or obscure legal agreements; incorrect pricing models; lack of legal advice; emphasis on sanctions instead of scope	Reality check validation for tendered prices (based on industry unit pricing in $/FP or Euros/FP whenever applicable)
Software intensive system construction (6 months to 3 years)	Systems and software design, construction, testing and pre-installation. Program closure occurs after delivery of all subsystems; results are evaluated and experience data collected and recorded.	Knowledge of customer business and objectives of program and subsystems; detailed eye to gauge progress and identify issues; project management skills; ability to formulate changes and identify errors; measurement skills	Uncontrolled scope creep; lack of senior management commitment; ad hoc or informal change management; lack of quality control; artificially imposed deadlines; risk ignorance	Measured and managed formal change control; earned value reporting and monitoring by subsystem (based on FP as applicable); progress monitoring; post-delivery payment based on delivered product size (unit pricing); data collection in an experience repository

training for his/her first triathlon competition. The scope manager is a professional who possesses a multidisciplinary set of skills that include the following:

- Business analysis
- Formal project management
- Knowledge of measurement industry productivity databases
- Software measurement (including functional size measurement and assessment of non-functional quality requirements)
- Understanding of northernSCOPE™ processes
- Senior advisory skills (negotiation, communication, progress reporting)

This set of competency areas is a prerequisite to the skills possessed by the experienced scope manager. The European Certification and Qualification Association (www.ECQA.org) formalized a new job role for a Certified Scope Manager (CSM) based on northernSCOPE™ and a body of knowledge (www.ECQA.org).

The scope manager acts as a customer advocate and is typically retained by (and paid by) the customer side of ICT program development. The corporate pain, expense, and overall frustration with earlier program failure are typically justification enough for seeking out and retaining an experience scope manager. In Finland (increasingly throughout the world), major national government departments have retained the skills of a certified scope manager since 2004. As additional organizations discover the value to cost ratio that is provided by a qualified scope manager, the demand for CSMs will increase.

Proven Results Using SouthernSCOPE and NorthernSCOPE™ Concepts

In 1995, the Victorian State Government in Australia introduced southernSCOPE on its custom software development projects. According to the originator of the method, "In 2000, a study of the extent and impact of its use was undertaken and resulted in the release of a revised approach. Although the number of projects that had used the approach was small, their nature was diverse. The results were outstanding:

- All projects completed within 10% of the initial project budget.
- They all had a high customer satisfaction in that the software met the intended business need.
- Their cost per unit was in the lowest 25% of comparative industry benchmarks" (Wright 2006).

Continuing in the same journal, "Why then is the southernSCOPE method so effective? The method successfully enabled the following problems inherent in the software engineering process to be addressed:

- Realistic cost estimates are provided at project inception.
- The functional requirements developed and agreed to are sound and unambiguous.

- The customer is able to make objective decisions in language he understands as to what functionality should be provided within the agreed budget.
- Scope creep is mitigated" (Wright 2006).

The Future for Creating More Olympic Finishes on Information and Communication Technology Programs

When we examine the similarities between a triathlon training program, the athletes involved, and the important of a dedicated coaching staff, one can easily see how northernSCOPE™ and other structured approaches to ICT program management give similar preclusions to a successful finish.

While athletes follow a strict regime that involves ultimate trust in the coach, the following aspects of preparation are seen to be of critical importance: proper physique for swimming, biking, and running; good health; stamina; and prior knowledge of and experience with all three major events: running, swimming, and biking.

Analogously, for customers involved in ICT program development, their success depends on ultimate trust in the scope manager and a focus on the following aspects of preparation: understanding of the core business and program objectives; subdivision of program components into discrete projects; ability to articulate and explore preliminary functional and non-functional requirements; clarity of purpose to prepare RFPs for supplier unit pricing responses; ability to objectively evaluate and select the most suitable supplier(s); stamina to remain committed to the program despite false starts; devotion to participate and review aspects of the ongoing program development; and commitment to scope management processes: functional size measurement, earned value/Function Point progress reporting, formal change management, program closure, and lessons learned review and identification. The jury is based on limited results already in Finland that reinforce the success of the northernSCOPE™ concepts: projects managed formally with northernSCOPE™ principles are remarkably on budget and on scope as attested to by the various national ministries employing a Certified Scope Manager.

In summary, the scope manager for an ICT program is similar to a triathlon coach in the following ways:

1. When requirements are vague or preliminary, this is similar to the difficulty triathlon swimmers experience in seeing the direction ahead. The scope manager provides guidance similar to a coach in a boat providing navigational advice about how to turn and whether to slow down and pace oneself in the event.
2. When a supplier has been chosen based on unit pricing and the RFP response, the requirements phase goes fast but can be laden with incomplete or incorrect requirements. The scope manager in this case is like the coach driving in a vehicle alongside a group of bicycle riders with extra tires and able to provide assistance should there be an accident en route.

3. During the main event (running for the triathlon, and the actual program development from design through to coding and final testing on ICT development), the scope manager provides regular roadside reporting concerning competitor progress, potential hazards, and challenges on the road ahead and provides an up-to-date report on expenditure of resources compared to the progress thus far (earned value management), reporting any upcoming changes to the course.

4. At the completion of the competition, the coach and the athlete review the race components and strategize on future training goals for continued success. At the completion of the ICT program, the scope manager collects data and reviews with the customer team the successful delivery plus what can be better done next time.

The triathlon was first introduced as a sporting event in the 1970s but it took almost 30 years for the competition to be become officially recognized as an Olympic event at the Summer Games in Sydney in 2000. The author is confident that northernSCOPE™ concepts along with the value proven on ICT program management by certified professional scope managers will soon become accepted principles in the mainstream of ICT program development. The time has come for predictable and managed Olympic performance on ICT programs worldwide.

References

Dekkers, C., and P. Forselius. 2008. Proceedings of the International Project Management Association (IPMA) global congress. Rome, Italy.

FiSMA. 2007. *The Finnish Software Measurement Association*. Finland: northernSCOPE™. www.fisma.fi

Standish Group. 2009. Press release for the 2009 Chaos Report (32% project success rate instead of 34%). www1.standishgroup.com/newsroom/chaos_2009.php (accessed January 4, 2012).

Wright, T. 2006. With or without a navigator?—It's your call. *Software Tech News* 9(3). www.softwaretechnews.com, published by the U.S. Department of Defense.

About the Author

Ms. Dekkers is a recognized international expert in the software metrics and IT project management industries and since 1994 has been the International Function Point Users Group (IFPUG) representative and project editor for ISO/IEC software and systems engineering standards in Function Points and benchmarking (ISO/IEC JTC1 SC7) as a United States delegate and ISO officer. She has also been the President of Quality Plus Technologies, Inc., a female-owned U.S. corporation, since 1994.

She is the author of *Function Points—Tools for Project Management Metrics* (Cutter, 2001) and the coauthor of an additional six ICT industry books including *The IT Measurement Compendium—Estimating and Benchmarking Success with Functional Size Measurement* (Springer, 2008); *The Program Management Toolkit for Software and Systems Development* (Talentum, 2008), *Practical Software Project Estimation*, 2nd and 3rd editions (ISBSG, 2008, 2010), and several others including the previous *IT Measurement: Practical Advice from the Experts* (Addison-Wesley, 2002), and *Fundamental Concepts for the Software Quality Engineer, Volume 2* (ASQ Press, 2007). She is widely known for her leadership abilities and her in-depth knowledge of project estimation and Function Point Analysis. She has taught workshops and delivered keynote presentations to professional audiences in over 27 countries.

Ms. Carol Dekkers is a Certified Function Point Specialist (CFPS), a project management professional (PMP), a certified scope manager (CSM), a certified management consultant (CMC), and a professional engineer (P.Eng. Canada).

In addition to teaching PMP preparation and leadership courses on behalf of registered education providers (REPs) for the Project Management Institute, she has established sustainable software measurement programs and supporting processes based on Function Point Analysis, including a global rollout of productivity-based metrics for several multinational corporations.

As the president of Quality Plus Technologies, she has mentored and trained thousands of technical professionals across a wide range of industries (including banking, healthcare, insurance, engineering, and government) to design and implement realistic frameworks for software measurement (consistent with IFPUG FP and ISO measurement standards such as the ISO/IEC 15939 Software Measurement Framework). She consistently receives high praise for both her instructional skills and consulting and facilitation leadership.

Carol was featured as one of the 21 new Voices of Quality for the 21st Century by the American Society for Quality's (ASQ) Quality Progress journal and also holds the distinction of being the number one webinar host (highest grossing attendance) for the webinar series by the IT Metrics and Productivity Institute (ITMPI) from 2006 through 2011 (featuring over 500 webinars).

For further writings by Ms. Dekkers, read her blog on software metrics and IT development at musingsaboutsoftwaredevelopment.wordpress.com. Ms. Dekkers is available for keynote speaking appearances and consulting engagements by contacting her by e-mail at dekkers@qualityplustech.com, Facebook (caroldekkers), Twitter @caroldekkers, or LinkedIn (Carol Dekkers).

Chapter 41

Scope Management Technique Using Sizing Process

Christine Green

Contents

Introduction

It seems that most projects find it challenging to control the scope from requirements to deliverables, regardless of how sophisticated their scope management is. Most projects that fail, fail due to lack of monitoring and controlling the scope.

As a result, the management and the traceability of the scope are important for the success of projects simply because scope changes, misunderstanding of requirements, clarification of the scope, and even sometimes lack of scope definition impact any project's ability to meet other project objectives such as cost, schedule, quality, ability to estimate and plan, and the ability to meet target deadlines—especially the end deadline.

Every project manager should ask himself/herself the following questions related to scope management:

- How accurate is the scope right now?
- How is the scope evolving over time?
- How is the project progressing in the delivery of the required deliverables?

While these questions seem simple enough, they have been shown to be complicated for most projects. Answering these questions require processes for assessment of the scope and traceability of the scope.

While many different approaches for good and solid scope management have been defined in the industry, they are often used without really having an objective and quantifiable control of the scope. Objective and quantifiable control of the scope must include sizing of the requirements. The sizing must be defined in a way where the project manager and team members can use it as a measure throughout the entire project and not just at specific milestones in the project.

This chapter will map scope management and requirement traceability to a sizing method using Function Point Analysis (FPA) and a project-specific sizing process called Unit of Size (UoS). The aim is to illustrate how sizing methods and the output from FPA can be used for tracking scope changes and will include a mapping between requirement traceability and the FPA process.

Introduction to the Scope and Sizing Management Process

Using a combination of sizing methods and the scope management process, it is possible to combine the benefits of the processes to trace the scope in an objective and quantifiable way. The aim is to have a process that will solve some of the issues that the project manager has in assessing scope for input to risk and estimates, as well as controlling scope for identification and measuring of changes to make sure that the project is on track or replanned as needed.

The scope and sizing management process requires the combination of three processes. The first two are already industry-recognized processes—scope management (in this case as defined by the Project Management Institute; PMI) and the functional size measurement method (in this case as defined by the International Function Point User Group [IFPUG]). In addition, there needs to be a size measure that is directly related to the project deliverables, and since this can vary from project to project or organization to organization, this would be a process defined specifically for each project. Let us call this size measure UoS.

During the life cycle of the project, the different processes will be used and the output of the processes will be used in the requirement traceability matrix to verify and control the scope.

Figure 41.1 shows the combination of the different elements:

- Scope management process to collect, define, verify, and control the scope
- Work breakdown structure (WBS) to define the life cycle of the project
- Sizing methods
  - FPA
  - A project-defined sizing approach called UoS
  - Calibration between the FPA result and the definition of a UoS

The model links the processes together by using the requirement traceability matrix throughout the project's life cycle for both collection and definition of scope

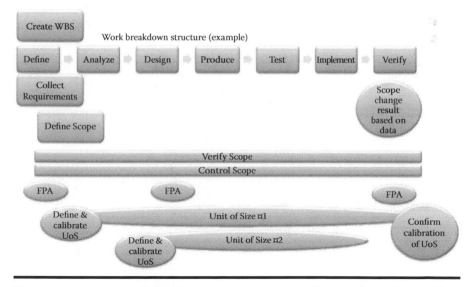

Figure 41.1 **Scope and sizing management process that consists of a combination of scope management and sizing methods.**

as well as verification and control of the scope. The result and output of the sizing processes as well as the list of requirements and assets produced during the life cycle of the project (such as designs) are stored in the requirement traceability matrix and are used to verify and control the scope.

Each time a project performs FPA, the requirements are verified. The FPA would be performed against the assets relevant at the time the analysis is performed.

Each time a UoS input is measured, it can provide to the project team a measure of the requirements change and the impact of changes and a measure of progress so that scope is monitored and controlled in an objective and quantifiable way. Using a UoS will enable the project manager to do this on an ongoing basis, not only at specific verification points during the life cycle of the project.

To fully understand this concept, it is necessary to define the scope management process, the sizing approach using FPA, and how a project-defined UoS can be defined and used in a bit more detail. This will be done in the next sections of the chapter.

Scope Management Process

Scope management is about constantly checking to make sure that all work is completed, the ability to monitor progress in the delivery, and the ability to control changes to the scope. For the purpose of using a commonly understood and documented approach for scope management, the PMI's Project Management Body of Knowledge (PMBOK) [1] definition of scope management is an excellent starting point. There are many other definitions of scope management processes, and in many cases, a mapping between the PMBOK definition and other process areas is fairly easy.

PMI PMBOK definition of scope management:

"All the processes required to ensure that project includes ALL the work required and ONLY the work required to complete the project successfully" [1].

Scope management is identified in the PMI PMBOK [1] as a separate knowledge area. It overlaps two process areas of project management. Figure 41.2 shows the five scope management knowledge areas linked to a WBS for a waterfall life cycle project.

The two process groups where scope management is used are as follows:

■ Planning
■ Monitoring and Control

The scope management process has knowledge areas defined as follows:

■ Collect Requirements
■ Define Scope

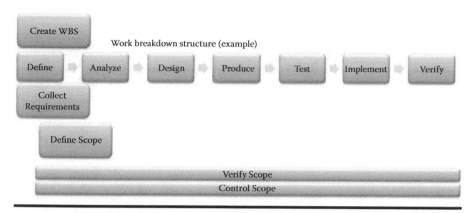

Figure 41.2 Sizing process and an example of a work breakdown structure defined for a waterfall process. (From PMI, A Guide to the Project Management Body of Knowledge (PMBOK Guide), 4th ed., Project Management Institute, 2008. With permission.)

- Create WBS
- Verify Scope
- Control Scope

Figure 41.3 shows the main purpose of each of the five knowledge areas and how the knowledge areas fits into the process groups—Planning and Monitoring and Control.

Collect Requirements has two important outputs relevant for the scope and sizing management process:

- Requirements documentation
- Requirements traceability matrix

The requirements documentation defines the individual requirements that are needed to meet the business needs. The requirements document should describe the requirements from a user perspective and should be seen as the main input for FPA performed early in the project. The requirements should be unambiguous, traceable, complete, and consistent.

For purposes of this chapter, the focus will strictly be on functional requirements.

Collect Requirements is usually about gathering the requirements from the user and as such is often referred to as high-level requirements. The sizing approach performed on requirements at this stage is often associated with a certain level of uncertainty. This uncertainty needs to be a part of the control scope approach to ensure that scope changes are clearly understood and controlled. Using the FPA method makes this uncertainty very clear. Depending on the level of granularity,

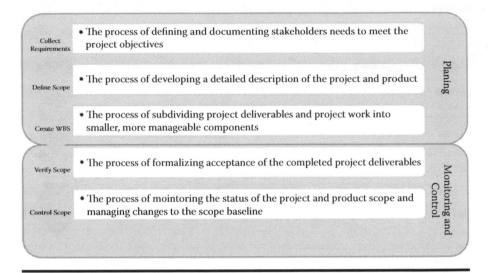

Figure 41.3 Definition of the five knowledge areas within scope management as defined by the Project Management Body of Knowledge. (From PMI., A Guide to the Project Management Body of Knowledge (PMBOK Guide), 4th ed., Project Management Institute, 2008. With permission.)

the FPA can be performed, and the accuracy can be measured in percentage of expected scope creep. See the section about the FPA process and the accuracy and reliability of the scope for more detail about this.

Define Scope is about clearly defining the detailed scope of the project. For software projects, this is related to having requirements that are clearly understood by both the users and the developers. The accuracy and completeness of the scope definition can be mapped to the level of detail at which an FPA is being performed.

Create WBS is about linking the project scope monitoring to the project life cycle. The WBS is closely related to the type of project that is being used. The WBS can be seen as a link between scope management and the Life cycle of a project. The WBS will be defined based on the methodology used to execute the project. This means that the WBS will vary depending on whether it is a waterfall, object-oriented, or agile project. This chapter will use the waterfall approach to ease the understanding of the utilization of functional sizing as a means of scope management. As a result, the WBS as defined in the scope and sizing process is a project life cycle from definition of requirements to verification of deliverables at the end of the project.

There is a strong link to risk in the association of correct scope. As complexity increases, the risk in defining scope also increases. The FPA process can be used as an important input to the risk associated with scope. How clearly the scope is defined can be translated into the level of detail at which the FPA can be performed.

As uncertainty increases, the risk also increases. Thus, as a requirement becomes better defined, the risk decreases by having less uncertainty on the defined scope.

As complexity on a project increases, the probability of missing something when defining the scope of the work is likely to increase. This can be measured by monitoring the changes to the scope and the type of changes to the scope. Using the traceability matrix and combining the traceability matrix with the output of FPA can support control of the complexity of the project as well as control of the amount of changes that are made during the life cycle of the project.

Verify Scope is the knowledge area that is used to ensure that the deliverables match the requirements. This knowledge area is important to ensure that there is a mapping between what is expected as defined in requirements and what is delivered as the end result. The requirement traceability matrix needs to map the connections between the requirements and the deliverables. The purpose of the requirement traceability matrix is to link requirements to their origin and track requirements throughout a project life cycle.

Control Scope is about controlling the changes and the requirements evolution. It is rare to have a project where there is no certain level of changes being made to the requirements regardless of these changes representing added functionality or just a matter of the requirements becoming more detailed during the life cycle of the project. Controlling the scope using a quantifiable method makes it possible to define thresholds that can be used as triggers for replanning actions. These thresholds can be defined during the life cycle of the project using the sizing input and the accuracy of the sizing as the thresholds. This ensures that both controlling and verifying of the scope is highly dependent on good requirement traceability during the life cycle of the project.

Functional Sizing

Functional sizing from the perspective of FPA is the measure of the functionality that an application provides to the user [2].

FPA provides a good size measure that depicts the software requirements by functionality. Source lines of code (SLOC) is also a frequently used size measure, but has the disadvantage of being heavily technology dependent. In addition, SLOC does absolutely nothing to control the scope changes, and it does not depict the relationship between the requirements and the solution being provided.

FPA is a well-known technique for sizing the scope and requirements as well as sizing the scope changes, but it is a method that can be used for more than just sizing. The output of an FPA is an excellent method of performing a peer review of requirements. Using an external resource for FPA would even create an independent review of requirements.

As an example, the FPA output with the documentation breakdown of the Function Point (FP) elements will be used as the requirement traceability matrix.

The project defined UoS for controlling the scope during the life cycle of the process will be directly related to the deliverables during the life cycle of a project. The UoS will be calibrated to a size measure defined as a number using the FPA. This way the FPA output will be used for several purposes:

■ Scope size and accuracy
■ List of elements identified during the FPA as traceability of the requirements
■ Verification of scope deliverables
■ Normalization of the project-specific size measure—UoS
■ Control of scope using a combination of FPA and UoS

Many projects or organizations that are using FPA for the purpose of improving estimates and normalizing the size within the organization are often just using FPA for the size measure—the number. The whole idea around combining the life cycle tracking (WBS), the scope management process, the FPA, and the project UoS is to utilize the power of the output from FPA and give the project manager the ability to control fully the scope during the whole life cycle of the project from start to finish.

The Function Point Analysis Process and the Accuracy and Reliability of the Scope

FP size quality usually depends on the detail and accuracy of the scope document. It is therefore important to assess the accuracy of the size estimate that is obtained.

An experienced FP analyst can provide an accuracy number to the size metrics provided.

The accuracy of an FPA depends on the method used. Accuracy is improved with better documentation and greater levels of detail documented by the analyst. Depending on the needs of the client and the project manager (PM), the different methods are all appropriate, but only the detailed approach is truly FPA.

Figure 41.4 shows the level of accuracy that can be expected when performing an FP count and the level of granularity that is used to identify the elements in an FP count.

Four stages are recognized here [3]:

1. The Ratio stage uses historical information such as 27 FPs per logical file or other rule of thumb techniques to calculate (i.e., estimate) the functional size.
2. The Robust stage identifies high-level physical transactions and tables, translates these into logical transactions and logical data, and determines complexity by utilizing assumptions.
3. The Limited stage identifies all logical transactions and logical data and determines complexity by utilizing assumptions.

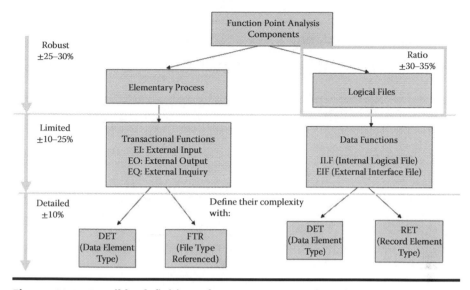

Figure 41.4 Possible definition of accuracy mapped to the level of detail at which the Function Point Analysis is being performed.

4. The Detailed stage is a full count using the defined approach in the IFPUG Counting Practices Manual all the way down to complexity rating. This is what is considered an FPA as defined by IFPUG.

The accuracy measure (the percentage measure) for each stage can be seen as a measure of the accuracy of the sizing output from the process, if we look at it from a functional sizing perspective, but what happens if we look at the same approach from the requirements reliability perspective?

If we size to a detailed level, then the requirements are fairly defined in detail at the stage where we perform the sizing. Therefore, where the accuracy of the size might be ±10%, we could state that we do not expect a larger amount of scope change than ±10%.

If we size to a detailed level but we sense that a part of the project is not yet described, then it might be that we have an accuracy of −10% but we are missing definitions in some of the areas of business covered, which means that the expected scope creep might be higher, ±20%.

FPA can be performed at different stages of the project:

■ At the beginning of a project to validate the requirements and their accuracy
■ As the project progresses, to control the changes incorporated into the project and to take corrective action
■ At the end of the project, when the application is already developed to verify deliverables and finalize the calculation of total scope changes

Functional Sizing—The Method and the Output

Remember that Function Points are just the size. However, FPA is the method that is used to produce the functional sizing. It is the method that should be used and be linked to the scope management process. The size should be considered one of the outputs of the FPA and not the only output of the process.

The method of performing an FPA is more than just aiming for the sizing output. The method is following all the steps in an FPA including documenting the findings (all the data elements and transactions, assumptions made during the count, the reference between the documentation used, and the elements found). This method results in a list of advantages by thinking about FPA as a method rather than just a size measure.

The method benefits a project by the following:

- Measuring software size, independently of underlying language and technology, from the user's logical perspective
- Decomposing functionality defined by the client
- Evaluating requirements during the software life cycle against work products produced
- Evaluating work products against requirements documentation
- Defining functionality scope and size
- Defining scope changes and size of changes
- As a requirement validation (peer review of requirements and work products)

The output is the resulting documents coming out of the FPA. The outputs benefit the project by producing the following assets and work products:

- A list of the functionality to be delivered
- The size of the requirements
- The size of the requirements after changes have been made

The documentation of the FPA being performed is an excellent input to the requirements traceability matrix. Many organizations using FPA are using tools to document their FPA. The output from these tools should be provided to the project team as a means of using it for traceability of the scope.

An example of the output from an FPA can be seen in Table 41.1. The reference for this is the definition of what goes into the maintenance of personnel information within an application. The requirements traceability can be seen as a table where during the life cycle the size might change—the scope might change due to additional requirements or change in the complexity. Therefore, the output of the FPA becomes the input to the requirements traceability matrix or looking at it the other way around, the requirements traceability matrix should be updated with the output of an FPA.

Table 41.1 Example of the Output of a Function Point Analysis

FPA No. 1				
Requirement Breakdown	Type	FTR/RET	DET	Detail Size
Use case definition xxx				19
Personnel file	ILF	1	11	7
Personnel—Show	EQ	1	13	3
Personnel—New	EI	1	13	3
Personnel—Cancel				0
Personnel—Update	EI	1	13	3
Personnel—Delete	EI	1	3	3

The Delivery Units and the Relationship to Function Point Size Metrics

Delivery units are usually valid only within a single project or within similar projects. A delivery unit is something that can be defined uniquely for the project, and it can be technology and project dependent. Delivery unit is a project definition and needs to be associated with some type of size or complexity. Usually delivery units do not provide data with historical use for future projects (Figure 41.5).

Delivery units and size are usually closely related, and the link between the delivery units and the FPA can be calibrated by analyzing the connection between the two. The most important aspect of the delivery units is that they can be tracked as a part of the delivery process. Requirement traceability is about tracking from requirements to delivery—and requirement tracking is an important aspect of scope control.

Unit of Size

UoS is a size measure that is defined with a direct link to the delivery units that are used within the project. Where the functional sizing is technology- and method-independent, the idea with introducing a UoS is to ensure that you track size that is relevant for the project. As such, the purpose of the UoS is to be a sizing approach that is project specific—not a new industry measure or a new organizational measure.

The UoS is about using the calibration between the functional sizing and the deliverables, and creating a size that can be measured by the project and be project-specific for monitoring and control of the scope throughout the project life cycle.

This does not mean that a UoS, if tested and proven to work on a project, could not be reused, but the idea is to reuse as a size—but still be project specific.

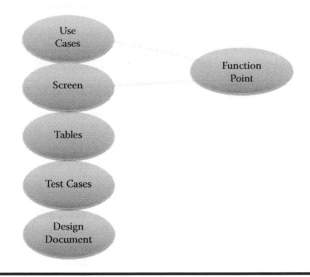

Figure 41.5 **Example of delivery units that are easy to map to the Function Point Analysis.**

The UoS should be used by projects for the daily, ongoing tracking of the requirements. The UoS is part of the internal project peer review approach, not the external independent peer review. The external independent peer review is performed using functional sizing and FPA resources.

The UoS should be defined as an easy-to-use measure, but it should be objective and repeatable for the project. A complexity matrix similar to the one used in FPA should be built for the UoS (Table 41.2).

For each complexity rating, a size measure should be aligned to the complexity (Table 41.3). The complexity rating is sized using a calibration between an FPA being performed on all deliverables or an FPA being performed on a sample of deliverables.

Using the average or median size in FP of all the delivery units that have been sized using FP, it is possible to identify the size measure. This means that delivery units need to have some type of FP count completed before the UoS is defined. If a UoS is defined based on a delivery unit that is not sized using FPA, a calibration using a sampling technique is needed—such as count a random number of delivery units and use the average for this count as the size measure.

You may argue that this sizing technique is not accurate—and you are quite right. The sizing technique for UoS is not an accurate technique down to a level of ±10%, but you need to remember that this sizing technique is only used to control scope and monitor progress, not for estimating. As a result, it is acceptable to have a high level of simplicity in the sizing approach and a low accuracy in the measure. In addition, it is important to remember that it is a more objective and accurate size measure than just counting things like number of pages, number of delivery units, etc., since it is directly related to the deliverables.

Table 41.2   Definition of a UoS

Delivery Unit	Condition 1		
	Threshold 1	*Threshold 2*	*Threshold 3*
Condition 2			
Threshold 1	Low	Low	Average
Threshold 2	Low	Average	High
Threshold 3	Average	High	High

Table 41.3   Definition of the Complexity Rating for a Unit of Size

Delivery Unit	Size
Low complexity	xx
Average complexity	yy
High complexity	zz

The Process Used during the Life Cycle

This section will illustrate an example of how the scope and sizing process is used in real life for a project. The example will focus on one requirement, "Maintain Personnel," and follows that requirement through the phases of Collect Requirements, Define Scope, Verify Scope, and Control Scope using the life cycle phases.

Be aware that the requirement traceability matrix illustrated in this section does not include references to work products created during the life cycle of a project. However, it is always important to use the requirement traceability matrix to trace the evolvement of the requirements into work products such as design documents, modules, tables, and other work products that are produced during the project to satisfy the requirements.

Define Phase

Collect Requirements gathers the following requirement specification from the user group of an application.

"We want to be able to maintain the personnel that we have within the company. The personnel information would include attributes such as employee name, address, employee number, etc."

Table 41.4 Example of the Requirement Traceability for the Define Phase

Requirement Traceability		Define		
Name	ID	Type	Complexity	Ratio Size
Maintain Personnel	1	Requirement statement	N/A	27

As a starting point, this is not much to go on from a sizing perspective. If the delivery organization were asked to create a cost estimate for building an application where the level of detail of the requirements is "two to three liners" for each group of data, I would expect the inaccuracy of the estimate to be pretty high due to uncertainty on the scope. Having said that, let us use the technique that the scope and sizing process gives us. In this case, the first step would be to map this to a high-level sizing estimate using our approach from the section, The Function Point Analysis Process and the Accuracy and the Reliability of the Scope.

For the requirement "Maintain Personnel," use a very simple rule of thumb stating that maintenance of a data group will provide an average size of 27 FP. If the organization has other data than this from past FPA such as a ratio between an ILF and the average number of Function Points, it is useful (Table 41.4).

Given the approach used for the sizing, the accuracy of the size at this stage of the project would be within the Ratio stage. As a result, it is expected that the scope will change somewhere between ±30%. This means that already at this stage of the project, we can use the size as an input to estimating based on the assumption that the "Maintain Personnel" functionality will be about 27 FP ±35%. As a result, an upper range and a lower range and an expected level can be calculated using any estimating technique.

The accuracy can be improved by using the FPA sizing approach and decomposing the requirements to an increasingly lower level of detail until the FPA is performed including complexity ratings. The complexity and size of the collect requirement and define scope work would guide the need for several iterations of the sizing approach from Ratio to Detailed.

Analysis Phase

During the analysis phase, a use case definition including a diagram is produced for each requirement. This use case definition includes details such as alternatives, attributes, etc. (Figure 41.6).

A use case is an excellent example of a really good delivery unit that can be used for the unit of sizing technique.

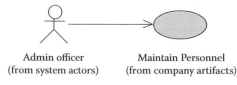

Admin officer   Maintain Personnel
(from system actors)   (from company artifacts)

Figure 41.6   Use case diagram for Maintain Personnel.

At this stage of the project—end of design or during analysis—the following activities should be performed:

- An FPA
- Definition of the UoS
  - UoS should be something that will be updated during the life cycle of the project, and as such, use case definition is excellent.
  - For other projects, design documentation might be suitable.
- Assessment of UoS on delivery units based on definition
- Calibration between the FPA performed and the UoS measure

A detailed FPA has now been performed. If we assume the resource performing this analysis is experienced and a Certified Function Point Specialist, the accuracy of the size measure is expected to be within ±10%. This means that the threshold that the project should set for scope changes is ±10%. If the UoS has been calibrated using the FPA and does not change more than ±10%, then a new FPA is not needed. If the UoS does change by more than ±10%, it is recommended that a FP sizing be performed and a project replanning be initiated (Tables 41.5 and 41.6).

The calibration used was the average size of all use cases counted at the end of Define phase.

The result of the assessment of size both for FPA and for UoS was added to the requirement traceability matrix.

Usually a UoS would be within the expected accuracy range for a Ratio stage estimate (i.e., ±30%), but since the calibration of the size measure was done using a detailed FPA, the size measure is most likely more accurately around ±20%. The accuracy can be improved and validated by recalibrating the UoS during the life cycle of the project.

Some of the information relevant for requirement traceability is stored in the requirement traceability matrix. The information stored should include both the breakdown of the FPA into elements and the UoS measure assessment. There will be a one-to-many relationship between these data, but using a spreadsheet or something similar would make it fairly easy for the project manager to store the data, so that it makes sense for the project (Table 41.7).

Table 41.5   Documentation of the UoS for Use Cases

Use Case	Alternatives		
	<3	3–6	>6
Attributes			
<15	Low	Low	Average
15–30	Low	Average	High
>30	Average	High	High

Table 41.6   The Documentation of the Size of the Complexity for the Use Case UoS

Use Cases	Size
Low complexity	23
Average complexity	33
High complexity	45

Table 41.7   How the Data Is Stored for Both the FPA Count and the UoS

FPA No. 1					Analyze		
Requirement Breakdown	Type	FTR/ RET	DET	Detail Size	Type	Complexity	UoS
Maintain Personnel	Use case def			19	UoS— Use case	Low	23
Personnel file	ILF	1	11	7			
Personnel— Show	EQ	1	13	3			
Personnel— New	EI	1	13	3			
Personnel— Cancel				0			
Personnel— Update	EI	1	13	3			
Personnel— Delete	EI	1	3	3			

We now have traceability between the original requirement definition in the Define phase and the detailed requirements as defined in the use case definition. We have two size measures that can be used during the life cycle of the project:

- FPA
- UoS for use cases

The assessment of the size for the requirement "Maintain Personnel" using the FPA shows that the use case definition has been completed, since it was possible to do a FPA on the requirements. This measure and the details stored in the requirement traceability matrix can be used for controlling deliverables.

If we had the define assessment for all the requirements with the Ratio size of in total 350 size units and we have only assessed the requirement "Maintain Personnel" in an FPA, we would have completed around 5% of the scope of the Analysis phase. This is calculated from the total size from the Define phase (as defined by our WBS) and the size of what has already been counted using FPA.

This is a quantifiable and objective measure of the verification of the scope during the Analysis phase. The same approach can be used for the rest of the phases in the life cycle.

Design and Produce Phases

During the Design phase, it was agreed that the UoS should continue as the use case definition since all agreed change requests (CRs) or future detailing of requirements would be updated in the use case diagram. A few changes were made during this phase, such as adding attributes to the use case definition.

The resulting changes were sized using UoS. At the end of the design phase, a second FPA was performed. The results were added to the requirement traceability matrix.

The FPA result stored in the requirements traceability matrix should at this point include the definition of what requirements have been changed, added, or deleted, along with a reference to the CR that has caused these changes (Table 41.8).

The UoS can be updated by the resource completing the deliverables associated with the changes being made. This will also make it visible if any major changes have been made to the deliverables (Table 41.9).

As shown, something happened with the scope when assessed during the Produce phase that impacted the complexity of the UoS measure for the requirement "Maintain Personnel." The earlier the impact is captured the better. Because of the nature of the UoS, each time something is changed in the use case, the resource performing the change should assess if the UoS measure is being changed. In this case, the developer received a CR impacting the complexity (Table 41.10).

To capture this specific CR and the impact to the scope, the FPA was updated to reflect specifically the changes to this requirement. This is not a recount, but rather an update to add or change the ratings on the FPA based on the CRs added

Table 41.8   Updated FPA Due to the Change Requests Received for the Project

FPA No. 2—End of Design					
Add/Delete/ Change	Requirement Breakdown	Type	FTR/ RET	DET	Detail Size
					23
	Personnel file	ILF	1	11	7
Change	Personnel—Show	EQ	2	15	4
Change	Personnel—New	EI	2	15	4
	Personnel—Cancel				0
Change	Personnel—Update	EI	2	15	4
	Personnel—Delete	EI	1	3	4

Table 41.9   Example of the UoS Input to the Requirement Traceability Matrix at This Point

Design				
Type	Attributes	Alternatives	Complexity	UoS
UoS—Use case	15	5	Average	33

Table 41.10   The Number of Attributes and Alternatives Changed during Produce, Which Impacted the Complexity of the UoS

Produce				
Type	Attributes	Alternatives	Complexity	UoS
Use case xxx	25	6	High	45

during the Design and Produce phases. The result of this CR was reflected in the requirement traceability matrix. In cases where it would be only minor changes, this update of the count might not have been needed (Table 41.11).

Test Phase

During the test phase, a test case was created for each use case diagram. Since the test case was a confirmation of the deliverables being produced, it was decided to

Table 41.11   Updated FP Count Due to the Changes in the Produce Phase

FPA No. 3 — Updated Due to Change Requests					
Add/Delete/ Change	*Requirement Breakdown*	*Type*	*FTR/ RET*	*DET*	*Detail Size*
	Use case definition xxx — CRYY				24
Change	Personnel file	ILF	1	16	7
Change	Personnel — Show	EQ	2	27	3
Change	Personnel — New	EI	2	27	3
	Personnel — Cancel				0
Change	Personnel — Update	EI	2	27	3
	Personnel — Delete	EI	1	3	3
Add	Personnel — List	EO	3	32	5

define and calibrate a test case UoS as defined below. Since there was one test case per use case, the calibration used for this was the same for both test cases and use cases. However, the definition of something being low, average, or high is different because the use case and test case are two different deliverables and different criteria are appropriate to determine their complexities.

The documentation of a UoS for test cases was to enable the tester that created the test cases and performed the test to size the deliverables before and after the completion of the test. If a UoS was not created specifically for the test cases, the tester would be unable to do this (Tables 41.12 and 41.13).

There were no changes made to the requirements during the test in this example. So the UoS can in this case be used for scope progress monitoring. If changes were made, it would make it possible for the project manager to identify potential scope creep that might impact the planning early in the process (Table 41.14).

Implementation Phase

During the implementation phase, the data stored in the requirement traceability matrix is used for validation of deliverables and calculation of the final scope

Table 41.12 Documentation of the Test Case UoS

Test Case	No. of Conditions		
	1–3	4–7	>7
Applications Impacted			
1	Low	Low	Average
2–3	Low	Average	High
>3	Average	High	High

Table 41.13 The Documentation of the Complexity Size for the Test Case UoS

Test Cases	Size
Low complexity	23
Average complexity	33
High complexity	45

Table 41.14 The Result in the Requirement Traceability Matrix

Test				
Type	No. of Apps	No. of Conditions	Complexity	UoS
Test case	2	7	High	45

changes during the life cycle. This also includes a final validation of scope of the application being delivered, by measuring the size of the scope delivered as well as calculating the final changes to the scope.

A recalibration of the UoS should be performed to determine if the size was accurately defined.

It could also be determined whether the UoS would be applicable or reusable for other projects within the organization using the same deliverable standard definition. In this case, the UoS could be reused by other projects using the same standard for documentation of requirements—use cases. Even though reuse is possible, it is still necessary to do a calibration between any project's first FPA and the UoS documentation to ensure that the UoS is applicable for the project for which it is reused.

It is important to recognize that the UoS is not meant as a replacement for FPA since the accuracy of the UoS is not as good as a detailed FPA and because a UoS is not recognized as an industry benchmark size. It is equally important to remember that the purpose of the UoS is to be project-specific, not to introduce a new organizational sizing method.

The Verification of the Process and End Reports

There are many ways to use the data that is stored in the requirement traceability matrix for quantifying the scope and the evolution of the scope. Using the process as defined and storing the result in a traceability matrix enables the user to monitor and control the process. The traceability matrix should be extended to refer also to CRs, defects found, and other measurements at a summary level. Using the data as it is stored in the traceability matrix is simple: If there are numbers then it is assessed and this can show progress.

An example of a visual summary view of the scope changes during the life cycle using the data in the requirement traceability matrix is shown in Figure 41.7.

This example can of course be used during the life cycle of the project as a visual trace of the requirements and the scope changes during the life cycle.

The sum of the size for the whole project can be shown in the same visual presentation.

Adding summarization in the requirement traceability matrix such as added size, changed size, deleted size would make it possible to do other types of analysis (Table 41.15). Based on the data in Table 41.15, percentage of scope changes can be calculated (Table 41.16).

A graphical presentation of this data can be viewed in Figure 41.8.

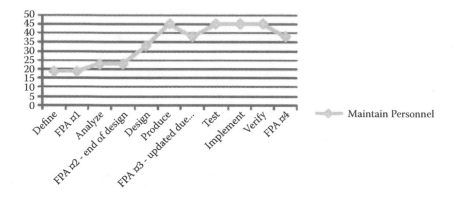

Figure 41.7 Graphical presentation of the scope changes for the requirement "Maintain Personnel."

Table 41.15 Example of Tracking the Summary of Sizing Data for UoS for a Project

Phase	Add UoS	Delete UoS	Change Old UoS	Change New UoS	Sum of UoS	Accuracy
Define	350				350	30%
Analyze	10	0	11	13	362	10%
Design	30	4	42	47	393	10%
Produce	33	0	14	14	426	10%
Test	21	4	20	25	448	10%

Table 41.16 Example of Percentage Changes to the Scope Using the Data in Table 41.15

Phase	Add %	Del %	Change %	Unchanged Scope %	Scope Creep %
Define	100%			0%	100%
Analyze	3%	0%	4%	94%	103%
Design	8%	1%	12%	80%	112%
Produce	8%	0%	3%	89%	122%
Test	5%	1%	6%	90%	128%

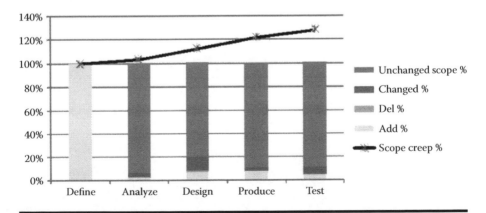

Figure 41.8 Example of a graphical presentation of the data being collected during the process of sizing. It requires that all size measures, both Function Point Analysis and Unit of Size, be recorded with a notation of additions, changes, and deletions of functionality.

The usability and presentation possibilities are endless and these are just a few examples to give some ideas about utilization in the future within a project. Again, this graph could be created during the life cycle of the project—not just during verification.

Summary

The aim of this chapter was to show how scope management and sizing approach could be used together to improve the scope management during the life cycle of the project using an objective and quantifiable approach.

FPA by itself has been shown to enable scope control only on fixed points during the life cycle. The introduction of a UoS combines the scope as defined, the deliverables during the life cycle, and the FPA using a UoS measure applicable for the project.

By combining the processes, we ensure planning, tracking, and analysis with the most accurate size by the following:

■ Using a sizing approach that can be understood by all parties and used as an input and tracking device by the project manager
■ Making it visual to PMs and management that size matters by making the data available as input for identification of scope creep thresholds, replanning triggers, etc.
■ Increasing maturity in sizing the scope by making it available for all phases within the project
■ Improving the PM's ability to manage the scope by linking the deliverables directly to the size and the FPA
■ Making it visual when a FPA is needed
■ Making FPA worth the investment (let's face it, doing an FPA is not cheap)
■ Making FPA a valid and needed process by linking it to other processes instead of just being a separate process

Using the additional tasks such as definition and calibration as well as reporting the end result as defined in the example, the process data can be used for verification and control of the scope. This means that the process can be seen as both an add-on to the scope management process and also as a better utilization of the requirement traceability matrix by using a combination of these approaches.

Using the requirement traceability matrix in this manner will promote areas required to be a mature organization as defined in Software Engineering Institute (SEI) Capability Maturity Model Integration (CMMI). The data can be used for the measurement and analysis process. It will be input for project planning and estimation. It can be used for project monitoring and control of deliverables. In addition, the FPA could be seen as an independent peer review of requirements.

It is the view that the benefits does not come from sizing processes by itself or Scope Management Processes by itself, but by combining the two processes into one process and utilizing the output in the requirement traceability matrix for the following:

- Better collection and verification of requirements
- Better definition and control of scope
- Objective and quantifiable measurement and control of scope

References

1. PMI. 2008. *A Guide to the Project Management Body of Knowledge (PMBOK Guide)*. 4th ed. Newtown Square, PA: Project Management Institute.
2. The International Function Point Users Group. 2010. *Function Point Counting Practices Manual*, Release 4.3. Princeton Junction, NJ: IFPUG Standards.
3. Houston, K. T. 2003. *Evolving Standards in Function Point/Lines of Code Ratios*. Presented to 18th International Forum on COCOMO and Software Cost Modeling.

About the Author

Christine Green has worked within the area of process improvement with special focus on measurement, estimating, and sizing processes for many years. She is a well-recognized contributor to international conferences such as SEI ESEPG, PMI, and ISMA/IFPUG, with a focus on getting the most usage out of a process and taking a practical approach to process improvement using processes within the areas of sizing, estimating, and measurement.

She is currently employed by Hewlett Packard (HP) as the EMEA Manager for the Estimating, Sizing, and Measurement team. She is also a consultant to major clients in the areas of estimating, benchmarking, measurement, and sizing for HP. Previously she was responsible for deploying metrics programs or CMMI implementations within various organizations and clients.

Ms. Green has a Masters in Mathematics and Computer Science from a Danish university. She has been an IFPUG Certified Function Point Specialist for the last 9 years and also has received PMI project manager professional certification. She is the vice chair of the IFPUG IT Performance Committee, working on researching standards for benchmarking within the software industry, and has been the project manager for the IFPUG Software Non-functional Assessment Process (SNAP) project.

Chapter 42

Chapter 42

Quantitative Project Management— Measurement-Based Techniques for Managing Scope

Robyn Lawrie

Contents

Introduction

The majority of large software delivery projects run late and/or exceed their budgets. Anecdotally, we hear as common explanations in defense of these outcomes:

- ◼ The project was much bigger than originally thought.
- ◼ The requirements were poor in the first place, and so it was really impossible to produce realistic estimates.
- ◼ The requirements kept changing.

These explanations have a common theme—there were issues with project scope. Given that standard project management attempts at controlling scope constantly fail, these same issues are likely to characterize future projects. Problems of this type can be expected to continue to impact projects negatively.

This chapter seeks to give project managers and other project stakeholders measurement-based techniques to deal with these issues in an effective way.

These techniques have been formed out of the practical experience of chasing change and churn to scope in real-life software delivery projects. In particular, this chapter presents conclusions and lessons drawn from a case study of a software delivery project that was:

- ◼ Much bigger than originally thought
- ◼ Had very poor initial requirements on which a fixed-price contract was based
- ◼ Overran schedule by some years

The project resulted in costly and drawn out litigation brought by the supplier against their client on the basis of change in scope. The supplier was successful in the litigation and obtained a substantial and satisfying payout.

During the project, the project dimensions were tracked, over a number of years. Measurement of size and scope was recorded in great detail at the completion of each project phase, as were other measures of cost and effort.

Two very important lessons in regard to scope were learned from the project.

1. Lesson 1—It is important that client and supplier stakeholders share a common view of scope.

   In the case study used in this chapter, the client and the software supplier each had a vastly different concept of what was meant by scope. From the supplier's viewpoint, the project scope grew alarmingly. The client, on the other hand, steadfastly maintained that there had been absolutely no change in the scope, from project outset to delivery.

   The client perceived "scope" as being delineated by the overall problem to be addressed by the software. The client saw their business requirements as being unchanged.

   The supplier understood "scope" as applying to the software solution to be delivered. The software solution on which their estimates were initially based was vastly different to the software solution that was eventually delivered.

   These two views of scope were obviously related, but they were not the same. In order to have any sort of meaningful discussion about scope, there must be a common view of scope and a common terminology, shared by the client and supplier as the principle project stakeholders.

2. Lesson 2—It is important to understand that project scope can increase for the supplier while client business requirements remain unchanged and to set realistic expectations for project progress based on this.

   Business understanding of scope generally assumes "whatever it takes" to achieve the overall business purpose for the application. The supplier scope relates directly to the amount of functionality required to satisfy the business requirements as the software solution that will facilitate and enable the business purpose. It is the definition of the actual software solution that drives supplier software scope—and it is when this definition changes or expands that growth occurs.

   When all project stakeholders understand where and why this growth happens, it is easier to set realistic expectations for growth, to monitor and negotiate scope, and to evaluate this growth against the business case for the project.

What Is Scope?

A web search will find a number of definitions of project scope. Definitions typically allude to ranges, extents, and boundaries. Some definitions are expressed in terms of project activities, whereas others talk about project outcomes.

Something Is In Scope or Out of Scope

The definition of scope used in this chapter focuses on project outcomes and specifically what the project delivers as a software solution or software product.

Note that many projects will deliver more than just the software product. Examples of other deliverables are implementation of hardware, data conversion, reference data population, and much more. These items are excluded from this discussion and control of these must be done in some other way.

Why Is It Important to Monitor Scope?

Each nontrivial project has a business case that is governed by cost and/or by delivery schedule. Late delivery may mean the business opportunity is reduced or even completely missed. Exceeding budget may mean the business case is invalidated or may even lead to project cancellation.

However, the decision to proceed with the project is made based on estimates of cost and schedule—and these in turn depend on an understanding of what is to be delivered.

Ideally, the agreed cost and time frame should not represent the actual business constraints. There should be some room to move, some contingency.

The vigilant monitoring of scope makes the business case easy to revisit. New values are fed into the estimation model. Should the business case start to look threatened at any stage, then stakeholders can be alerted and they can make a business decision on how to proceed.

Why Use Function Point Analysis as a Scope Monitoring Tool?

Function Point Analysis is ideally suited to a role as a scope definition and monitoring tool.

- Function Point Analysis is positioned in the "real-world" knowledge domain of the client. It uses the "real-world" terminology of that domain. All project stakeholders, whether clients or suppliers, can participate in a conversation about what is in scope or not in scope in terms that both groups readily understand. They can share a common view of what "scope" means. This is in contrast to describing scope in the technical terminology of the supplier's knowledge domain that is often not readily understood by the client.
- Function Point Analysis has a set of rules for identifying each and every software function that forms part of the software product to be delivered. These rules are well developed and have been well tried for over 25 years. The rules guide the decomposition of the whole of the software product into its

component functions, halting the decomposition at a level where the clients see the functions as being elementary but still meaningful to them. Functions identified during Function Point Analysis are in scope, and functions not identified are out of scope. When project scope increases, new functions are added. When a project is descoped, functions are removed from the software product.

▪ Function Point Analysis is designed to deliver, as an end product, a Function Point size that has a strong-recognized relationship with associated work effort. Thus, any change in scope can be readily extended to indicate impact on effort and further on cost and schedule.

In order to properly define and monitor scope, it is important that all functions that comprise the product to be delivered are identified and tracked. There is a small chink in the armor of Function Point Analysis in this regard. The current (IFPUG CPM 4.3 [1]) rules mean that from time to time, the analyst will encounter some functions that are identified but are not assigned Function Points and so are excluded from the Function Point size. These may include, for example, functions where no data or control information cross the application boundary and/or many automated functions. These functions must still be included and identified as within scope.

Establishing the Software Product Baseline

Capers Jones [2] has likened software development to hiking in a fog where the fog slowly lifts to reveal the landscape.

▪ At the beginning of a project, no one can "see" exactly what functionality the project will ultimately deliver.
▪ As the project progresses, the functional solution becomes clearer and plans must be adjusted to accommodate this new knowledge.
▪ At the end of the project, the scope will be perfectly seen and understood.

Early in the project, a baseline of all functionality to be delivered must be established and agreed between all stakeholders as being a representation of the scope as known at that time.

Function Point Analysis gives us the following rules for identifying functions:

▪ *Transactional Functions* represent the functionality provided to the user for the processing of data by an application. An elementary process is the smallest unit of activity that is meaningful to the user(s). The elementary process must be self-contained and leave the business of the application being counted in a consistent state.
▪ *Data Functions* represent the functionality provided to the user to meet internal and external data requirements. A data function is a user identifiable group of logically related data or control information.

These rules are used to identify the functions in the scope baseline. The baseline must list all Transactional and Data Functions that comprise the product as understood at the project milestone where the baseline is established.

Early in the project, some functions may not be precisely known but every attempt should be made to include at least a placeholder for them. For example, in the case study used here, the Management Reports were simply entered in the baseline as "Management Reports x60." Similarly, the Reference Tables were entered as "Reference Tables x40." These numbers were agreed with the client as being reasonable estimates of number of instances.

It is strongly recommended that each function be cross-referenced to at least one document appropriate to the project milestone at which the baseline is established. This means that the baseline is always open, auditable, and defensible. It also means that the task of monitoring change from baseline can be passed to someone else.

The baseline belongs to the project. It should be an agreed representation of the product scope and become part of the project documentation.

Tracking and Monitoring Change

The source of change to the software to be delivered can be thought of as being "external" or "internal" to the project.

An external source here means that the client is requesting change, usually via a formal change request. For this type of change, increased effort, schedule, and cost can easily be justified to the client. This type of change is understood by all parties and is usually handled through normal "change management" practices that typically result in separate costings. This type of change is NOT the main focus of this chapter. However, changes from formal changes requests can easily be included in the scope tracking.

An internal source means that new functionality comes from within the project as the project progresses through the life cycle. As the business requirements evolve into the detailed requirements for the software solution, it becomes apparent that the functions named in the scope baseline understate the functions actually required to be delivered. This type of scope creep is a real problem for the supplier. It is difficult to justify increased effort, schedule, and cost, as there is no change to the business requirements. This type of change is not handled—usually not even recognized—within normal "change management" practices.

However, a strong awareness of this source of change is absolutely essential for tracking change to project scope.

Changes to project scope must be continually monitored and all changes to scope must be recorded. At the very least, at each project milestone, as new documents become available, project scope must be revisited. In large projects, however, the time between milestones can be quite lengthy and during this period there may be significant events that seek to clarify requirements and will impact scope. These will include, for example, project workshops where software requirement details are developed. Be prepared to monitor scope on a regular basis.

Again, it is strongly recommended that each function be cross-referenced to at least one document appropriate to the project milestone so that the scope monitoring is fully defensible.

Case Study Description

Here is a very brief description of the project used to provide case study examples.

The project delivered a ticketing system for multimodal public transport. The transport modes covered were trains, trams, and buses, where each transport mode is governed by a different public authority. The system comprises three principal applications—Central Ticketing Management, Distributed Ticketing and other Machines, and Collection/Distribution that passes data between the other two applications. The case study examples are drawn from the software development project that delivered the Central Ticketing Management application.

The following were the key characteristics of this project:

- The supplier won the contract to deliver the Central Ticketing Management application through a tender process.
- At project outset, the Central Ticketing Management application was thought to be about 200 functions or just over 1000 Function Points. This understanding underpinned the fixed price costings provided in the tender response.
- At software delivery, there were 1369 functions or close to 7350 Function Points.
- The client steadfastly maintained that there was no change in project scope. They had requested an automated ticketing system and, from their point of view, anything and everything needed to make that implementation effective was included.

As you can see from the summary presented, this project experienced alarming scope creep. The substantial change emanated from internal sources.

Understanding Change in Scope

A Function Point Count was performed at a series of important project milestones. Analysis of how scope changed between these milestones suggested that the types of change observed could be categorized into the following groups:

- New Functions
- Split Functions
- Merged Functions

■ Dropped Functions
■ Adjusted Functions

Examples of each of these are provided below.

New Functions

A *new* function has no corresponding requirement at the preceding milestone. However, it is now present in the software requirements, system definition documents, or other project artifacts at this milestone.

In the project, two different types of scenarios led to blocks of new functions being added to the software product. Other projects will have different experiences.

Informal Agreement between Client and Supplier

This first scenario shows new functionality resulting from an informal agreement between the client and the supplier, specifically the end user as client and the analyst as supplier. In this type of scenario, the supplier agrees, without appropriate investigation, to enhance functionality at no charge. An informal agreement is reached—but with no understanding of the scope involved.

In the transport authority that manages bus travel, there is a central planning office that builds the bus schedules. Before this project, the schedules were printed and simply posted to the bus depots. This new project enabled distribution channels to pass data between the Central Ticketing Management application and the bus depots. The uploading of bus schedules into Central Ticketing Management and the distributed downloading of these to the bus depots probably seemed like simple and useful functionality that could be easily incorporated into the project. The distribution channels were already in place. This was just another file to be uploaded and then sent. How hard could it be? A meeting between users and developers informally agreed that this upload/download would be part of the new software.

In actuality, this additional functionality proved to be a challenge. The application used to develop the bus schedules had been built on a proprietary database and the skills and knowledge needed to extract an electronic upload were no longer available. The data would be delivered to the Central Ticketing Management application in a raw database format, requiring extensive development work to pull out the required data. The additional work resulted in 24 additional functions as 20 Transaction Functions and 4 Data Functions and 89 Unadjusted Function Points. Even at a conservative 10 hours per Function Point, this represents 20–25 additional weeks of work effort.

Of course, some informally agreed "new" functionality will be easy. Nevertheless, any new function represents an increase in scope and there will be a consequent increase in cost and schedule. This type of new functionality can obviously be avoided, but it is surprising how common it appears to be.

Operational Functionality

Requirements may completely overlook functionality required to support effective day-to-day operation of a system. In general, it is the client stakeholders who put the initial requirements together. Their focus will be on that part of the software with which they will interact. They may not consider the infrastructure that may also need to be analyzed, designed, constructed, and delivered—and indeed may not have the necessary knowledge to define it.

In this second example, the Central Ticketing Management application was required to distribute a large amount of infrastructure data to many distributed locations on a regular and ad hoc basis in such a way that all data updates were synchronized and data versions remained synchronized. There were close to 30 different groups of data to be distributed to many locations. This included, for example, new tables of fares and other equipment operating data to be sent to ticket and other machines.

The early requirements were quite clear that this type of data was to be distributed as equipment operating data. What was not understood was how complex the management and control of this distribution would prove to be. As it turned out, a change register subsystem was required to be built as part of the software to control and manage the preparation and distribution of this data. This new sub-system introduced 52 new Transactional Functions and 6 new Data Functions.

Split Functions

"The requirements were more complex than we originally thought."

How often do we hear this?

A *split* function has a corresponding requirement recognized at the preceding milestone that has resulted in a single entry in the scope baseline. With more detailed analysis, it is apparent that this same requirement leads to more than one function to be delivered as part of the software product.

This is the most common scenario leading to an increase in project scope. The supplier cannot argue that the requirement is new and may feel that they just "got it wrong." There is often an attempt to just absorb it into the project.

However, while each "split" on its own might not seem to have big impact, the total impact of all "splits" on the project can be substantial.

While it may be hard to claim additional functions as "new," one fact is certain. Where earlier the project was understood to have one function, there is now more than one. The project scope has expanded, and the business impact of this must be recognized and assessed.

Here are two examples to illustrate this type of "scope creep."

Example 1—Refund a Ticket

At an earlier milestone, a requirement to be able to "Refund a Ticket" was analyzed and a single function for this was included in the project scope. When the business rules were fully analyzed during the next development phase, it became clear that there were a number of independent, different sets of business rules and procedures governing refunds, for example, depending upon the circumstances of purchase and whether or not the ticket had been used.

At this milestone, the single function of "Refund a Ticket" expanded into three separate functions—Refund a Standard Unused Ticket, Refund a Standard but Partially Used Period Ticket and Refund a Non-Standard Ticket. This third function was agreed, only after extensive discussion between client and supplier, as the way to cater for the other many non-standard ways refunds are calculated. The amount of refund is determined offline and only the refund amount and refund reason are recorded in the system.

Example 2—Report Ticket Sales

Reporting is an area where broad-brush requirements are often found.

In this project, there was an early business requirement to be able to "Report Ticket Sales." The scope at this milestone recorded a single function providing this functionality.

Further analysis at detailed design revealed the full complexity of this requirement. For example, each of the different transport modes (trains, tram, and bus) had different organizational and reporting structures, each of which had their own business rules for defining the report. Furthermore, the reports could express sales in dollars or numbers of tickets sold. The single requirement traced forward to many independent detailed requirements for reports about ticket sales.

Many of the reports in this project experienced the same expansion of functionality.

Note: At the end of the project, in order to ensure that the project was not "overcounted" in this area, an analysis of the source lines of code (SLOC) of reporting was compared with the average for the whole project. This analysis showed similar SLOC per Function Point for reporting as for the project as a whole.

Merged Functions

A *merged* function results when a requirement is absorbed into or is identified as being the same as another requirement.

In a project with many stakeholders, it is common to have some duplicate or overlapping requirements that can be satisfied by a single function.

In this project, both of the government-run buses and private buses requested a report showing ticket sales. Early scope baselines recorded two entries—"Report Government Bus Ticket Sales" and "Report Private Bus Ticket Sales." Further analysis found that a single report would satisfy both requirements and the baseline was adjusted to show a single entry "Report Bus Ticket Sales."

Dropped Functions

A *dropped* function has a requirement at the preceding milestone but is no longer represented in the requirements or system definition documents for this milestone.

Requirements for some functionality may be dropped during the project. Typically, the number of functions that are dropped is quite small and does not balance out the growth.

In this project, there were a small number of functions that were represented in system definition documents at one milestone but which were not present at the next milestone. Their disappearance did not have any associated formal change request or other documentation. However, upon querying their disappearance, there was verbal assurance that they were no longer required.

In this project, early requirements were definite that data about hot-listed tickets would be kept in the central system and would be downloaded to ticket validation machines to catch offenders. The requirement for this data and its dependent functionality was dropped sometime after the functional specification—with no fanfare. It was simply no longer required.

Of course, lack of documentation may simply indicate a mistake and the functionality has simply been overlooked. Make sure you check.

Adjusted Functions

Functions included as placeholders in the baseline where the software solution was acknowledged to be vague are replaced by actual functions as requirements are further analyzed. Of course, original "best guesses" are often not entirely accurate. A placeholder for Management Reports x60 was included in the original baseline. As each report was defined, the number of instances for this placeholder would be reduced and the new report was included as its own entry.

Another scenario, in which adjusted functions are observed, is where a group of functions provided as the software solution is replaced by a different group of functions, providing a solution to the same requirements but in a different way. A generic solution is one example of this, where many functions can be reduced to a smaller group of functions.

Communicating Change in Scope to Stakeholders

Continual and regular reporting of scope to project stakeholders is imperative, even if it is to say that there has been no change.

Project stakeholders in the client domain readily understand the "presence versus absence" of functions. Even though, as a Function Point Analyst, you may be assigning Function Point scores, when communicating scope and change in scope, it is recommended that you communicate in terms of number of functions, wherever possible.

Table 42.1 shows one way of presenting a summary of growth in scope experienced in this case study, expressed in terms of number of functions.

A similar table can be used to express growth in terms of Function Points, for those stakeholders where this is meaningful.

Stakeholders always want summaries but often wish to "drill down" further to ensure a complete understanding.

Figure 42.1 provides an example of one way to show growth at the more detailed level of traceability of each function. This table shows Transactional Functions. A similar table can be used to illustrate growth in Data Functions.

This figure shows a mapping of functions through the project milestones. It is easy to see the life story of each function and how the scope changes.

For the case study, every function, whether Transactional or Data, was tracked through six formal project milestones. Response from project stakeholders for monitoring in this way was—"this says it all." So even though it represents a lot of hard work, it was recognized as a significant contribution to the project documentation and to the evidence for the litigation case.

Table 42.1   Growth in Number of Functions by Project Milestone

	Project Milestone				
Measure	*Tender Response*	*Requirements Specification*	*Functional Specification*	*As Clarified*	*As Built*
No. of Functions					
Transactional Functions	189	439	936	1016	1307
Data Functions	33	68	102	102	103
Total	222	507	1038	1118	1369

Project milestone		
Tender response	*Requirements specification*	*Functional specification*
Record ticket sale	Record ticket sale	Record ticket sale
		Record validated ticket sale
Record cancelled ticket sale	Record cancelled ticket sale	Record cancelled ticket sale
Record tickets issued to agent	Record tickets issued to agent	Record tickets issued to agent
		Record agent ticket returns
Record hot ticket usage	/////////	/////////
/////////	/////////	Record equipment cutoff time
/////////	Unreceived transactions report	Report unpolled locations
/////////		Report operators no transactions
/////////		Report equipment no transactions

Figure 42.1   Function traceability across project milestones.

Summary

The monitoring of scope is an important activity on any non-trivial project that delivers software, yet it remains extremely difficult to get proper recognition for this role. Over and over, we hear about out-of-control projects but really there is no excuse. The cost of including a scope management role on a large project is a very small percentage of overall project cost and the potential benefits are enormous.

Being able to readily adjust the estimation model and review the associated business case at any point in the project is surely just part of good project management.

Function Point Analysis is a ready-made tool for defining and monitoring scope, and there are many Function Point Analysts certified and ready for the role. The challenge now is to spread the word.

References

1. International Function Point Users Group (IFPUG). 2009. *Function Point Counting Practices Manual*, Release 4.3. Westerville, OH: IFPUG.
2. Jones, C. 2007. *Estimating Software Costs: Bringing Realism to Estimating*. 2nd ed., 374. New York: McGraw-Hill.

About the Author

Robyn Lawrie is a director and principal consultant for CHARISMATEK Software Metrics, an Australian-based company. Robyn has almost 40 years of IT industry experience in software development across a wide range of applications and technologies, the last 20 of these at CHARISMATEK. A major career focus has been the improvement of the software process, in particular, the application of the IFPUG Function Point Analysis and other measurement techniques to solving a range of practical business issues.

Robyn provides consultancy and training services in software measurement, both in Australia and internationally. She is a speaker at various educational institutions and conferences, such as the Australian Conference on Software Measurement (ACOSM) and International Function Point Users Group (IFPUG).

Robyn cofounded the Australian Software Metrics Association (ASMA) in 1990. She headed the southernSCOPE Special Interest Group and has presented a number of papers to both local and international conferences on this topic. southernSCOPE supports a fee schedule based on Cost per Function Point.

Robyn is the subject matter expert, analyst, and product manager for CHARISMATEK's Function Point WORKBENCH™. This software product for Function Point sizing and analysis makes a significant contribution to the IT industry.

Company Profile—CHARISMATEK Software Metrics

Created in 1991 and now well established as a significant contributor across the world and as the hub of an international network of metrics partners, CHARISMATEK Software Metrics provides the highest level of software metrics and measurement based consulting and training services and products and tools to our clients.

CHARISMATEK focuses on using software sizing, metrics, and quantitative analysis as a pragmatic and objective basis for addressing specific business issues. Real business and IT experience, in conjunction with unparalleled technical expertise, means that CHARISMATEK Software Metrics can provide practical and realistic assistance in a range of software and IT areas.

From project estimation to assess the validity of budgets and schedules within a proposed business case or to determine a project's risk profile—to scope management to clarify and negotiate software deliverables at project initiation and to track and control change throughout delivery—to value for money assessments to ensure value from your software delivery and support suppliers—to contract management to devise project budgets and undertake software portfolio assessments—and to Function Point Analysis to determine the size of your software projects and applications—CHARISMATEK Software Metrics has the expertise, experience, and business understanding required.

The Function Point WORKBENCH™, as a world leading software tool supporting the Function Point Analysis technique for sizing software, is designed and built by CHARISMATEK. It is specifically designed to be scalable for effective use by individual counters as well as for large scale, distributed IT environments and is an ideal counting tool for all software sizing needs.

Chapter 43

Requirements: Building a Solid Foundation for a Successful Project

---

Janet Harris Russac

Contents

Critical software issues in organizations include understanding the customer's requirements, effectively sizing the requirements, and accurately estimating the deliverable. Therefore, just as it is critical to have a solid foundation for the construction of a building, so it is for software development. Requirements are the blueprints for building software. They need to be complete, detailed, sizeable, and understood by both the customer and the development team. This chapter will assist the reader in improving their requirements writing to more accurately estimate size, effort, and schedule; to deliver a high quality product on time and within budget; and to deliver a product that meets the customer's needs.

The fundamentals in establishing effective requirements writing techniques include the following:

- The fundamentals of writing detailed requirements
- Writing requirements that are understandable by the customer and provider
- Writing requirements so that an accurate size estimate can be determined
- Managing change in requirements

This chapter will cover the following topics:

- Project life cycle stages and related requirements phases
- Risk assessment
- Creating quality requirements
- Fundamentals of writing detailed requirements
- Managing change in requirements

Project Life Cycle Stages and Related Requirements Phases

Before embarking on the task of writing requirements, it is necessary to understand the life cycle stages of a project and the requirements to be produced in each of those stages. A typical project consists of the following life cycle stages:

- Requirements stage
- Detail Design stage
- Construction stage (development and testing)

The characteristics of these stages as they relate to requirements are as follows:

Requirements Stage

The Initial User Requirements represent user requirements before the sessions between the users and the software developers and may have one or more of the following characteristics*:

- Incomplete
- Lack "utility" functionality
- Impossible to implement or very difficult to use
- Too general
- Do not address the needs of all users of the application
- Stated requirements without regard for application boundaries
- Expressed in a different context or a terminology incompatible with functional sizing

This is followed by the Initial Technical Requirements that represent the software developers' view of requirements created from the feasibility study. They include elements which are necessary for the implementation, but which are not considered in functional size measurement (FSM). They may have one or more of the following characteristics†:

- Technology dependence
- Terminology unfamiliar to the users
- Functionality may be determined by placing too much emphasis on technical constraints
- Boundaries may be determined according to the technical architecture rather than by business processes

Functional user requirements (FUR) are defined as a subset of the user requirements: requirements that describe what the software shall do, in terms of tasks and services (ISO 14143-1:2007).‡ FUR result from joint sessions between the user(s) and the software developer(s). The joint sessions are necessary to achieve consistent and complete FUR for the application. This provides the final version of the FUR before the development phase begins and has the following characteristics§:

- Terminology can be understood by both users and software developers.
- Integrated descriptions of all user requirements, including requirements from all groups of users, are provided.

---

* Refer to the International Function Point Users Group (IFPUG) Function Point Counting Practices Manual (CPM), Release 4.3, Part 2, pages 3–4.
† Refer to the IFPUG Function Point CPM, Release 4.3, Part 2, pages 3–5.
‡ Refer to the IFPUG Function Point CPM, Release 4.3, Part 5, page G–4.
§ Refer to the IFPUG Function Point CPM, Release 4.3, Part 2, pages 3–9.

- All business processes are fully defined, including all user actions, fields coming into and leaving the application boundary, sources of data are defined for each business process, and validations that occur as part of each business process.
- Each process and group of data is agreed upon by the user and developer.
- The feasibility and usability are approved by the software developers.

Once the FURs are finalized, an estimated functional size is calculated using them. This estimated functional size is then used to develop an initial project estimate of effort, duration, cost, and other measurements needed for the particular project. The estimate is based on the best available information. A poor requirements document will result in a poor estimate.

Detail Design Stage

After the initial requirements are agreed upon by both the user and developers, the project then moves into the design phase. A complete detailed design includes a prototype and programming specifications. During this time it will become evident that some requirements need to be changed, others added, and even others potentially deleted. That means that the initial project estimate will need to be revised. In doing so, all proposed added/changed/deleted functionality must be functionally sized and a revised estimate given. This must happen every time there is a change in requirements.

Scope creep (i.e., scope change) is probably the biggest reason a project does not come in on time, within budget, or even fails. Scope creep* is defined as additional functionality that was not specified in the original requirements, but is identified as the scope is clarified and the functions defined. Scope creep *must be controlled* by reviewing the requirements, estimating their functional size, and assessing the impact on the project. Budgets, schedules, and resources *must be revised* accordingly. When evaluating an organization's requirements writing, it is important to assess an organization's current/past process of handling scope changes and make the appropriate modifications in the procedure so that scope change is managed properly.

In summary, the following must be done throughout the design stage:

- Count proposed added/changed/deleted functionality using revised requirements
- Assess impact and determine "scope creep"
- Revise project estimates

Construction Stage (Development and Testing)

During this stage, requirement changes (new and/or changed functions) may, and probably will, surface due to various reasons such as programmers identifying

---

* Refer to the IFPUG Function Point CPM, Release 4.3, Part 5, page G–7.

changes, changes that become apparent during unit testing, and/or users finding an issue during integration testing. Just as in the Detail Design stage, requirements can be added, changed, or deleted; therefore, the same process must be followed throughout this stage as well:

■ Size proposed added/changed/deleted functionality using revised requirements
■ Assess impact and determine "scope creep"
■ Revise project estimates

Risk Assessment

To gauge the quality of your organization's current requirements and to assess the risk on your project deliverables, gather some requirements for a few of the latest projects and do a sample analysis. Assess requirements in terms of meeting needs for functional sizing. Highly refined requirements documents lead to the greatest project success. Ask the following questions as you assess your organization's requirements documents:

■ Who is responsible for writing the requirements?
■ Is there a procedure to follow?
■ Is there a standard for the written requirements?
■ Are the requirements reviewed by the project team, the business user, and all other stakeholders?
■ What requirements are produced at different stages of the project's life cycle?
■ What level are the requirements at to produce estimates?
■ What requirements are there already for a good estimate?
■ What requirements are missing?
■ What is lacking in the current requirements?
■ Is there a procedure for handling changes in requirements?

Most risk analysis tools and procedures for software projects have risk performance profiles that consider the strengths and weaknesses in categories such as Management, Definition, Design, Coding, Test, and Environment. Within the Definition category, clearly stated requirements are the strength. Requirements weaknesses include the following:

■ Requirements are not always clearly stated and tend to change frequently.
■ Customers are not very knowledgeable with regard to the business processes.
■ Customers are not familiar with the software processes.
■ Formal reviews are not consistently performed.
■ Requirements analysts are not very experienced.
■ Limited expertise among developers with regard to the business.

How does your organization rate in regards to these weaknesses? Turning weaknesses into strengths will help you create an environment in which to produce quality requirements.

Creating Quality Requirements

GET IT RIGHT UP FRONT! Getting it "right up front" will save a lot of time, money, and aggravation going forward and will result in better customer satisfaction. How do you go about doing that?

- Talk to the client! The requirements stage presents the best opportunity to do so.
- Properly set expectations early in the life cycle (the client's roles and responsibilities).
- Engage the user in the process; involve them in the process from the beginning.

Poor requirements *cannot* lead to excellent software. The quality of the product depends on the quality of the raw materials. This seems obvious but it is overlooked or ignored in many organizations. One of the problems is that few developers are educated on how to elicit, analyze, document, and verify requirement quality.

The key concept of creating quality requirements is to *reframe the requirements process as a goal-seeking dialogue, whose purpose is to manage the risk of building the wrong product*. The primary goal is to get the right requirements. The secondary goal is to have the ability to apply an effective sizing metric. This secondary goal is important because the sizing is important. Sizing is important to manage expectations in requirements; estimate accurately to manage resources; manage processes and process improvement; and manage the project and control change.

The term FUR was introduced earlier in this chapter. ISO/IEC 14143-1:2007, Definition 3.8, defines FUR as a subset of the user requirements specifying what the software shall do in terms of tasks and services. FUR includes, but is not limited to, the following:

- Data transfer (e.g., input customer data, send control signal)
- Data transformation (e.g., calculate bank interest, derive average temperature)
- Data storage (e.g., store customer order, record ambient temperature over time)
- Data retrieval (e.g., list current employees, retrieve aircraft position)

ISO does not provide a definition for non-functional user requirements, but gives some examples in a note. User requirements that are *not* FUR include, but are not limited to, the following:

- Quality constraints (e.g., usability, reliability, efficiency, and portability)
- Organizational constraints (e.g., locations for operation, target hardware, and compliance to standards)

- Environmental constraints (e.g., interoperability, security, privacy, and safety)
- Implementation constraints (e.g., development language, delivery schedule)*

ISO/IEC 14143-1:2007, Definition 3.1, defines base functional component (BFC) as an elementary unit of FUR defined by and used by an FSM method for measurement purposes. An example of FUR and BFC given in The International Function Points (IFPUG) Counting Practices Manual (CPM) is as follows:

- A FUR could be "Maintain Customers," which might consist of the following BFCs: "Add a New Customer," "Report Customer Purchases," and "Change Customer Details."[†]

The IFPUG CPM goes on to define data functionality as functionality that satisfies the FUR to store and/or reference data and transaction functionality as functionality that satisfies the FUR that process data.[‡]

Both FUR and non-FUR are needed for any software project; however, the remainder of this chapter focuses on writing FUR as in my experience, those are the requirements that are usually lacking in one or more ways.

Fundamentals of Writing Detailed Requirements

Requirements are the blueprints for building software. As such, they need to be the following:

- Complete
- Detailed
- Sizeable
- Understood by both the customer and the development team

To illustrate these points, the following hypothetical requirements scenarios are analyzed.

Examples of Inadequate Requirements

Using a hypothetical new application to track trains, what is wrong with the following?

- Consoles shall allow a dispatcher to perform the following functions:
  - Enter and retrieve data on train operations
  - Access the customer information signs and public address systems

---

* Refer to the IFPUG Function Point CPM, Release 4.3, Part 1, page 5.
[†] Refer to the IFPUG Function Point CPM, Release 4.3, Part 1, page 2.
[‡] Refer to the IFPUG Function Point CPM, Release 4.3, Part 1, pages 10 and 13.

- Perform automatic train supervision system functions such as computer-aided dispatching and routing
- Monitor train movements
- Access voice communications
- Generate and view reports
- Verify and modify train attributes

Do we know what data is to be entered and retrieved? Is it validated against other data stores? Can the data be updated and deleted? What are the different types of train operations that need to be considered? From where does the information on the customer information signs come? How many reports are to be generated? One? One hundred? What data is on the reports and from where does it come? How does a dispatcher know what reports are available? Is there to be a list of them from which to choose? How many train attributes are there? Can anyone modify them or is it limited to specific users? The questions go on and on.

Getting Better

Let us take just one item from that list of requirements, "monitor train movements," and break it down further as follows:

- Monitor train movements
  - The system shall accurately track and display the locations, identities, vehicle numbers, crew IDs, train schedule, and other pertinent data for all trains in a particular monitored area.
  - The system shall also track trains into and out of non-monitored areas.
  - The train tracking and identification function shall update train locations as new data is received from an existing train control system.

We get better here by supplying more detail on one of those requirements. Let us do some further analysis by asking some questions now about the first requirement of monitor train movements:

- The system shall accurately track and display the locations, train identities, vehicle numbers, crew IDs, train schedule, and other pertinent data for all trains in a particular monitored area.
  - Is this particular requirement complete with enough detail?
  - Can it be sized?
  - Can it be completely understood by the customer and the project team?

The answer is NO! Why?

- It is not complete.
  - For example, what other new and/or existing systems will need to interact with this new system in order for the requirement to be complete?
- There is still not enough detail.
  - For example, where does the data reside that will need to be displayed?
- There is no way to come close to sizing the functionality.
  - For example, we do not know how many data fields have to be displayed, how many logical data stores are involved, etc.
- There is too much ambiguity that will lead to misunderstandings between the user and project team.

Optimal Requirements

So what are we looking for? Let us take just one small piece of information from "The system shall accurately track and display the locations, train identities, vehicle numbers, crew IDs, train schedule, and other pertinent data for all trains in a particular monitored area." What questions might come to mind when you see the term "train identities"? Do you know what is meant by "train identity"? Do you know the make-up of a "train identity"? Do you know how a train identity is assigned? Can a train identity be modified? If so, what other applications or functionality within this application would be affected? Where and how is a train identity displayed? How is a train identity tracked? These questions are just a few of the many questions that a developer might have about train identities.

Remember that the final version of the FUR before the development phase begins has the following characteristics:

- Terminology can be understood by both users and software developers.
- Integrated descriptions of all user requirements including requirements from all groups of users are provided.
- All business processes are fully defined, including all user actions, fields coming into and leaving the application boundary, sources of data are defined for each business process, and validations that occur as part of each business process
- Each process and group of data is agreed upon by the user and developer.
- The feasibility and usability are approved by the software developers.

Keeping this in mind, let us write detailed requirements concerning train identities:

- Train IDs shall be composed of 13 alphanumeric characters as follows:
  - Train type (1 alphanumeric character)
  - Service ID (1 alphanumeric character)

- Departure time (4 digits, based on 24-hour clock, 1 character "+" for half minute indicator, e.g., "1024" is on the minute, "1024+" is half past the minute)
- Origin terminal ID (3 alphanumeric characters)
- Destination terminal ID (3 alphanumeric characters)

■ Authorized users shall have the capability to assign and modify train identifications.
  - The system shall ensure that a train ID is used only once in a service day.
    • Any attempt to assign a train ID that is already assigned to a train or has been assigned and terminated in the same service day shall be rejected and a message shall be issued to notify the responsible authorized users of the problem.
■ The system shall verify that the combination of train type, service ID, departure time, and origin terminal are unique in each train ID for a service day to ensure that the train type and destination can be changed without necessitating other fields to be changed to maintain unique train IDs.
■ The system shall generate an event message each time a train ID is assigned.

The actual requirements for train identities take multiple pages and cover such things as the following:

■ Train types and identification
■ Train identification presentation
■ Abandoned train identification
■ Work and other non-revenue train identifications
■ Unidentified trains
■ Reporting on train identifications
■ Etc.

Have we now achieved our goal?
Are our requirements as follows:

■ Complete? Yes.
■ Detailed? Yes.
■ Sizeable? Yes.
■ Understood by both the customer and the development team? Yes.

Managing Change in Requirements

Every time there is a change in requirements, it is imperative that they are treated the same as new requirements. Go through the steps outlined in the Fundamentals of Writing Detailed Requirements section.

Make sure the requirements are as follows:

■ Complete
■ Detailed
■ Able to be sized
■ Understood by both the customer and the development team

When the estimate has been done for the changed requirement, meet with the user and explain the impact on the project's budget and schedule. It is then up to the user to make an informed decision on whether to proceed or not with the change. If the user wants to, or has to proceed, they must then sign off on the change request that reflects the revised budget and schedule.

If your organization does not currently have a change control process and procedure, now is the time to implement one. Do not let scope creep kill your project. Manage it!

Conclusion

Follow these guidelines to effective requirements writing and start enjoying the delivering of a successful project that is on time, within budget, of high quality, and one that meets the customer's need!

Good requirements = happy customers and project teams!

Reference

The International Function Point Users Group. 2010. *Function Point Counting Practices Manual*, Release 4.3. Princeton Junction, NJ: IFPUG Standards.

About the Author

Janet Russac has over 30 years of experience as a programmer, analyst, and measurement specialist in software application development and maintenance. She is the founder of Software Measurement Expertise, Inc. (SME), leading a team of experienced consultants who offer expertise in Function Point counting, software measurement, estimation, benchmarking, auditing, training, and mentoring.

Russac is a member of the International Function Point Users Group (IFPUG) and served as the chair of the Management Reporting Committee (2002–2004) during which time she spearheaded the creation of an international industry certification for individuals in the field of software measurement (certified software measurement specialist [CSMS]). She served for several years on the Counting Practices Committee and on the Communications and Marketing Committee for IFPUG. In 2010, she was elected to serve a 3-year term on the Board of Directors for IFPUG, as Director of Applied Programs. She is a Certified Function Point Specialist and a certified software measurement specialist.

Russac is a published author and presents workshops at companies, professional organizations, and conferences, as well as being a featured speaker at conferences. Her books include the following:

IT Measurement: Practical Advice from the Experts, Addison-Wesley, April 2002, as a Contributor and Editor

The Certified Function Point Specialist Examination Guide, Auerbach Publications/CRC Press, 2011, with David Garmus and Royce Edwards

Please refer to the website of Software Measurement Expertise at www .softwaremeasurementexpertise.com to obtain other articles written by Janet Russac on software sizing, project management, and measurement.

About Software Measurement Expertise, Inc. (SME)

SME has expertise in the following:

Software sizing using Function Point Analysis
Developing software measurement programs
Estimation of software projects
Function Point training and mentoring
Function Point auditing
Software measurement training
Benchmarking

We assist companies in evaluating their needs, make recommendations, and set up the programs and procedures that they need such as estimation procedures and process improvement. We also help companies evaluate and improve upon processes that they already have in place and help them mature their software programs and procedures.

At Software Measurement Expertise, we have a staff of Certified Function Point Specialists who are tops in their field, including two past and/or present members of IFPUG's Counting Practices Committee. Combined, we have over 75 years experience in software development, software measurement, and Function Point Analysis.

Software Measurement Expertise, Inc. (SME) was founded by Janet Russac in 2008. For more information about the company, please visit us at www .softwaremeasurementexpertise.com. Additionally, inquiries may be sent to Ms. Russac at jrussac@softwaremeasurementexpertise.com or jrussac@gmail.com.

Index